P9-ASN-357

WITHDRAWN
L R. COLLEGE LIBRARY

791.4309
F62i

139663

DATE DUE			

IMAGES OF MADNESS

IMAGES OF MADNESS

The Portrayal of Insanity in the Feature Film

Michael Fleming and Roger Manvell

RUTHERFORD ● MADISON ● TEANECK
FAIRLEIGH DICKINSON UNIVERSITY PRESS
LONDON AND TORONTO: ASSOCIATED UNIVERSITY PRESSES

Associated University Presses
440 Forsgate Drive
Cranbury, NJ 08512

Associated University Presses
25 Sicilian Avenuè
London WC1A 2QH, England

Associated University Presses
2133 Royal Windsor Drive
Unit 1
Mississauga, Ontario
Canada L5J 1K5

791.4309
F62i
129663
aug. 1986

Library of Congress Cataloging in Publication Data

Fleming, Michael.
    Images of madness.

    Filmography: p.
    Bibliography: p.
    Includes index.
    1. Mental illness in motion pictures.   2. Mental
illness—Philosophy—History.   I. Manvell, Roger,
1909–   .   II. Title.
PN1995.9.M463F54   1985   791.43′09′09353   82-49022
ISBN 0-8386-3112-6

Printed in the United States of America

To Maureen and Françoise

Contents

Preface 9
Acknowledgments 11

**Part I Themes of Madness
Michael Fleming**

Introduction 17
  Madness in Movies 21
  Repetition of Past Images into the Present 21
  Summary 27
  Format 27
1 Society and Madness 30
  The Family and Madness 30
    Now, Voyager (1942) 34
    A Woman under the Influence (1974) 37
  Institutionalization of the Mad 44
    The Snake Pit (1948) 45
    One Flew over the Cuckoo's Nest (1975) 49
2 Possession as Madness 57
    Dr. Jekyll and Mr. Hyde (1931) 61
    The Exorcist (1973) 66
3 Eros and Madness 70
  The Struggle between Love and Aggression 71
    Secrets of a Soul (1926) 71
    Bad Timing: A Sensual Obsession (1980) 76
  The Love of Aggression 80
    M (1931) 80
    Straw Dogs (1971) 83
  Violence against Women 89
4 Murder and Madness 96
  Murder and Mothers 97
    White Heat (1949) 99
  From Motive to Motiveless Murder 101
    Badlands (1974) 106
5 War and Madness 112
  World War II 114
    Twelve O'Clock High (1949) 118
  The Vietnam War 121
    The Deer Hunter (1978) 126

6 Drugs and Madness   134
        The Lost Weekend (1945)   134
        The Rose (1979)   139
7 Paranoia and Madness   147
        Sexuality and Paranoia   148
        Paranoia as Reality   153
8 Sanity as Madness, Madness as Sanity   159
        You Can't Take It with You (1938)   161
        King of Hearts (1966)   164
9 Madness and the Psychiatrist   172

Part II Filmography: Synopses and Annotations
Roger Manvell

Introduction to Filmography   187

Filmography: Synopses   188
Notes to Filmography   323
Appendix: The Popular Portrayal of Insanity in the
        Elizabethan-Jacobean Theater   327

Part III

Bibliography   346
        General Psychological Works   346
        Works about Films and Allied Subjects   348
        Works about Individual Directors   349

General Index   354
Index of Film Titles   361
Index to Appendix   364

Preface

This book grew out of the authors' collaboration at Boston University, while teaching courses focused on the interaction between cinema and psychology. Ingmar Bergman has said that film "should communicate psychic states"; we came to believe that such depictions can be evaluated in the light of relevant psychiatric theory.

We chose to concentrate on major feature films that portray madness in all its many forms. This work is offered as an initial attempt to systematically approach the relationship between psychiatric and cinematic images of madness. As an introduction to the interaction of cinema and clinical psychology, the book assumes that the reader has no formal background in either discipline. At times the relationships between psychiatric and cinematic images of madness seem direct, as when a psychiatrist evaluated a film or when a screenwriter developed a case study. But more often, the relationships are very subtle and highly inferential. To bring order into this chaos, we identify nine major themes: Society and Madness; Possession as Madness; Eros and Madness; Murder and Madness; War and Madness; Drugs and Madness; Paranoia and Madness; Sanity as Madness, Madness as Sanity; and Madness and the Psychiatrist. For each theme we contrast an early film with a more contemporary one, in the hope of tracing the origins and underlying themes of different perspectives on insanity.

The first part, by Michael Fleming, explains the direct and contextual psychiatric and sociopolitical forces affecting the cinematic imagery of madness. The second part, by Roger Manvell, presents the films in terms of their plot evolution and their technical and historical components. Though many ideas were shared, each part represents the sole views of its author.

9

Acknowledgments

We would like to express our gratitude to the many people and organizations who have been helpful to us while preparing this work. First, we would like to thank Theo Gluck (graduate assistant at the time in the Department of Broadcasting and Film, School of Public Communication, Boston University) and Dr. Julie Levinson (now Assistant Professor of Film and Stage, Babson College), who researched important information on the numerous films mentioned in the text; Steven Moldin (undergraduate psychology major) whose dogged research and untiring efforts achieved significant connections between clinical and popular depictions of madness; and Barbara Spellerberg (undergraduate psychology major) who, from the start of this project, gave unfailingly of her time to explore and comment on the extensive psychological and social literature of each period.

We would like to thank our colleagues Professors T. J. Kline, Carl Ruck, James Hassett, and Sander Gilman, whose critical and insightful thinking has added greatly to our understanding, though they are, of course, in no way responsible for the conclusions we reach in the text. And we would like to express gratitude to the students in our various classes at Boston University who, through formal and informal discussions, helped us approach more critically the questions that arise constantly in any consideration of the elusive subject of insanity.

Then to Gloria Thompson of Media Services, Boston University, and to Jim Kent (Supervisor of Film Production, School of Broadcasting and Film, College of Public Communication, Boston University) and Justin Freed (Coolidge Corner Cinema, Brookline) we owe thanks for making our previewing of so many of the films cited possible.

We owe much to many painstaking and competent typists—particularly Leslie Minassian and Jeannette MacDonald, as well as Marcia Johnston, Jeanne M. Wallace, Michele Murray, Elaine Watson, David Desroches, Celia Tulman, Maria Morias—and to Marilyn Fartely (Administrative Assistant, Department of Psychology, Boston University).

Gratitude too should be expressed to the film companies and other organizations supplying stills illustrating this book, some of which come from the Roger Manvell collection, now deposited in the Photographic Archives at the University of Louisville, while others come from the skills department of the National Film Archive at the British Film Institute in London. We wish to thank the editor of the British Film Institute's *Monthly Film Bulletin* for permission to quote from certain reviews, and the editor of *New Humanist* (London) for permission to

11

reprint in revised form as an appendix to this book Roger Manvell's essay, "The Popular Portrayal of Insanity in the Elizabethan-Jacobean Theatre," which originally appeared in the *New Humanist* in the Spring 1981 issue.

Michael Fleming   Roger Manvell

IMAGES OF MADNESS

PART I
Themes of Madness

Michael Fleming

Introduction

We all have a need to believe that the world is a reasonable place which functions according to predictable, even immutable, rules of order. We therefore feel threatened by occurrences that contradict this notion. At the same time, we are fascinated by the irrational. When faced with people whose behavior fails to conform to our prescriptions for what is real and reasonable, we are forced to come up with some explanation that will ease our anxiety or doubt. Our most immediate response is to call the aberrant manifestation "madness," implying that it has no place in our world view.

Madness appears as a condition that stands in opposition to reason and sanity. It provokes fundamental questions about our place in, and understanding of, the world. It makes us look more closely at our definitions of the nature of things and at our expectation of what should follow. Madness therefore has profound implications for our interpretation of ourselves and of our environment and eventually leads us to question who we are and what we are.

The very occurrence of madness seems to generate questions about the nature of the human being. Or, perhaps the converse is the issue—that the manifestation of aspects of human nature that do not fit our suprahuman ideals is to be termed madness. As one reads the extensive literature on madness, it becomes clear that a more enlightened approach to the subject can be achieved by using an interdisciplinary perspective—optimally, through an integration of the natural sciences, social sciences, and humanities. The purpose of this book is to begin such an integration by investigating the interrelationship between clinical views of madness, espoused by the medical and social sciences, and the artistic depiction of madness, as presented in the feature film. Because of the disrupting and unnerving questions it raises the experience of madness has received a great deal of attention from both the science of psychology and the narrative art of film. For the psychologist madness is primarily something to be quantitatively understood and then cured. For the film artist madness is principally a subject whose depiction probes the darkest and most hidden side of our being. Our own personal experiences as artist and clinician reflect these viewpoints, and progressed beyond them to achieve the combined perspective presented in this book.

In exploring how madness has been viewed historically, we have discovered a gradual progression of interpretations and depictions, which interrelate closely with the development of civilization. Every age has produced, of course, those who were held to be mad, although the definition of madness has varied somewhat with the time and place. In fact the perception of madness has not been a single one but a combination of perceptions overlapping past and present and reflecting both popular and scientific views. One begins to question any definition of madness and the impact of labeling someone mad. Given this relativity of values, it has become clear to us that certain interpretations of madness have dominated each particular period and have often been repeated in later periods. An example is the medieval conception of the mad as "fools." Today, six centuries later, this portrayal is still being projected onto the mad, as seen in characterizations present in the films *You Can't Take It with You; Mr. Deeds Goes to Town; Harvey; It's a Mad, Mad, Mad, Mad World; Brewster McCloud,* and *King of Hearts.*

In investigating the numerous images of madness that have been created from prehistoric times to the present, one finds oneself returning continuously to certain visual depictions of the mad. This visual representation is especially powerful because it allows for a more immediate and concrete identification of what the artists of the period believed to be madness. Dürer's sixteenth-century woodcuts depicting madness as demonic possession, Goya's rendering of the furies of the unconscious escaping into waking life, Blake's drawings of hallucinatory experiences, or Munch's *The Scream* all convey the indescribable, unspeakable inner experiences we call madness. With this in mind one can maintain that it is perhaps the visual artist who has achieved the greatest impact in reaching the mass audience. With the passage of time, visual depictions have grown in strength, and in our present age visual imagery has often replaced the imagery projected by the spoken and written word. As the dominant visual art of the twentieth century, film has had the greatest potential for exercising a profound impact on the widest possible audience. Film thus has a special relevance to the investigation of the popular depiction of madness.

Originally attempts at mirroring the motion of the world, the "movies" in their earliest form were simply that—moving pictures of galloping horses, walking men, and smoke-belching trains. But they quickly went beyond the mere replication that had at first interested the Lumiére Brothers in France and Edison in America. Feature film has evolved over the years into a unique art form, which, in the words of Arthur Schlesinger, Jr., has "so much to disclose about the inner as well as outer life of America."[1] The possibilities that film offers not only for chronicling the evolving views of madness in American psychiatry but for impacting it has become the central focus of our work.

As we shall see throughout this study, film, even from its silent days (which ended with the technical development of sound-on-film in the late 1920s), has proven to be a medium peculiarly suitable for handling intimate psychological subjects. It is a medium of observation, the almost clinical recording of human behavior, with every nuance of expression and gesture enhanced in the close-up. Unlike theater, which expresses itself almost totally through the spoken word, the film provides the added and more essential aspect of facial expression. This is one element (albeit an element of the very highest significance) in the spectrum of human behavior that gives form, consciously or unconsciously, to the more real, inner feelings. As a medium involving the highly controlled flow of images, film is uniquely able to reflect the flux of mental-emotional experience with an impact similar to that undergone by a human being during a period of psychological deterioration. Through the subtleties of editing and the juxtaposition of sound and image, the film can dovetail the sensations and observations arising out of a character's relationship to illusions, hallucinations, dreams, and nightmares. Reality and fantasy as two forms of experience can be subtly, almost indistinguishably, interwoven, as can be seen preeminently in such films as Bergman's *Persona*, Fellini's *8½* or *Juliet of the Spirits*, Buñuel's *Belle de Jour*, or Altman's *Images*. On the level of purely exterior observation of behavior, without resort to depicting mental images, the cinema can also offer a sensitive interpretation of characters drawn downward toward destruction by psychological forces, as in Woody Allen's *Interiors*.

Given the importance of film in our culture and its unique capacity to depict madness, we have explored the history of this medium's portrayal of the vicissitudes of the human condition and its impact on the public.

What benefit can come from such an investigation of film? It is our assumption that by looking at the depiction of madness in the cinema, one can gain a better understanding of how the popular conception of madness changes over time. In this study we have restricted ourselves to certain major feature films, which have for the most part enjoyed wide distribution and general acceptance, and have assessed whether they represent the contemporary view of madness. A "popular" film is one that both reflects and to varying degrees affects audience attitudes toward madness. By tracing this depiction from the earlier days of feature film in the 1920s to the present age of Panavision and Dolby Sound, we hope to accomplish the following:

1. Chronicle the more prominent interpretations of madness presented in the feature film.
2. Analyze the particular thematic presentation of madness in terms of how it conveys the subjective experience of being mad and the popular as well as the clinical view of the theme at the time the film appeared.
3. Begin a critical investigation of the recurring nature of these themes and of what they tell us about our present view of madness.

When we set out to explore the cinematic depiction of madness we knew that there would be not one depiction but a vast array of complex images. We hope that we have created a more manageable format for understanding by taking multiple perspectives on the ways in which film reflects and affects psychiatric perceptions of madness. Through thematic analyses we have tried to show that the images of madness presented by a film have a unique relationship to the psychiatric theory and practice of the period immediately before and during the production and soon after the release of the film.

Our examination of the production background of films depicting madness has revealed that on occasion the psychiatric profession played an integral role in the creation and story line of a film, as in *Secrets of a Soul* (1926, chapter 3). More often, the direct input of the psychiatric community involved a more modified approach, in which psychiatrists were consulted on specific points, such as the disintegration of the mirror into delusional thought processes in *In Cold Blood* (1968, chapter 4). Beyond such instances were those in which the film production company sought out general comment from the psychiatric community, as did Fritz Lang in his attempts to understand the underlying thoughts of homicidal criminals for his film *M* (1931, chapter 3). On occasion the use of the psychiatric profession even included casting a real psychiatrist in the role of the film psychiatrist, as was the case in *One Flew over the Cuckoo's Nest* (1975, chapter 1) and *An Unmarried Woman* (1978, chapter 9).

Sometimes the way in which a film reflected psychiatric beliefs, however, could be explored only by investigating the relationships between the film's depiction and psychiatric interpretations. In this light we have presented an assessment of how and to what degree a popular film's particular depiction of madness mirrored psychiatric literature that preceeded the film's release. In particular we have sought to determine whether particular elements of the visual text, or the characterization, plot line, and cinematography reflected clinical phenomena as perceived in the psychiatric literature of the period. Characterizations such as Bette Midler's Rose in *The Rose* (1979, chapter 6), which so uniquely combined polydrug abuse with an insatiable and clearly self-destructive need for love and fusion, found their parallel in the prolific psychiatric literature on the narcissistic disorder of the borderline appearing shortly before the film's production. Similarly, the emphasis on oedipal love in *White Heat* (1949, chapter 4), mirrored the popularity of such psychoanalytic percepts in the clinical literature of that period.

A second perspective we have taken in investigating the relationship between psychiatric and cinematic images of madness involves the possible impact of the film on psychiatric opinion. We decided that the way to assess this impact was to look at clinicians' comments on the specific film. We discovered that a number of the films chosen were mentioned in the psychiatric literature that followed the film's release. Psychiatrists go to movies as do their patients, and it was not surprising to have found direct psychiatric comments on such films as *A Woman under the Influence* (1974, chapter 1), *The Lost Weekend* (1945, chapter 6), or *The Exorcist* (1973, chapter 2). *The Exorcist* in particular was pointed to as cinematic depiction of madness that in fact provoked madness in its audiences. This element of elicitation was central to the question of aggression, which we have explored in chapter 3, particularly as it relates to violence against women.

Throughout the book we have tried to deal not only with the relationship between psychiatry and cinema but with the broader sociocultural factors that have played a part in this relationship. For example, the sociopolitical factors of the 1970s influenced film producers to depict paranoia as a sane reaction to an insane world. Similarly, in the late 1940s social reform movements called attention to institutional miscare, as depicted in *The Snake Pit* (1948). In these and other cases we point to the zeitgeist that gave rise to a particular film's representation of madness.

Throughout most of the book we contrast a later film with an earlier film that depicted the same theme. The differences and, in some cases, similarities over a twenty- to forty-year range point to the subtle interaction between popular and clinical views. The very popularity of these films increase the likelihood that they were viewed by the public as having verisimilitude with clinical theory and practice. We have tried to show that they do in fact bear such a relationship, albeit in varying causal and conjunctive degrees.

Madness in Movies

Numerous studies have elaborated on the difficulty psychiatrists experience in establishing any common perception (or, as the social sciences term it, *inter-rater reliability*) in diagnosing or labeling a particular psychiatric disorder.[2] Some controversial studies have even questioned whether psychiatry is able to identify those who should be placed in mental hospitals.[3] If psychiatrists have such problems in agreement it is not surprising that the layman should also experience difficulty in determining what is or is not an example of madness. Is Michael (Robert DeNiro) mad when he forces Nick (Christopher Walken) to play Russian roulette in *The Deer Hunter* and laughs gleefully into the faces of his onlooking captors? Or is he doing the only sane thing that one could do in such an insane situation? Are Kurtz (Marlon Brando) in *Apocalypse Now*, Kane (Orson Welles) in *Citizen Kane*, the alcoholic writer (Ray Milland) in *Lost Weekend*, Juliet (Giulietta Masina) in *Juliet of the Spirits*, or Mabel (Gena Rowlands) in *A Woman under the Influence* mad? The accuracy or clarity of the depiction of madness can be understood in the last analysis only by the viewer. The authors hope in this book to make a modest contribution toward clearer thinking by both professional and lay observers who view films and thereby to bring about a better understanding of the experience of madness from various perspectives.

Contemporary explanations of madness and its treatment are derived from a long history of concepts and proposed solutions. An understanding of madness can perhaps only be reached by looking at this history, which, in cyclical-spiraling fashion, has continued to reiterate earlier concepts and to reintegrate them with later ones. One certainly finds this when viewing a film like *The Exorcist* and realizes the willingness of many people to believe in the possibility of "possession." Our study of the history of the interpretations of madness has revealed, to our surprise, much about what has been retained in popular beliefs about it.

Repetition of Past Images Into the Present

Before we discuss the portrayal of madness in film, it may be useful to review briefly the major trends in the perception of madness throughout history. The record of man's attempts to deal with madness comes to us from anthropological investigation and interpretation. Prehistoric man interpreted madness as the result of an invasion of the body—often specifically the head of the individual—by supernatural or magical forces. The proposed solution was to remove these forces in order to allow the individual to recover and become himself again. The person who claimed ability to remove, or *exorcise,* these forces was the *shaman,* or medicine man. His procedures often took the very literal form of drilling a hole in the patient's skull. The hole, approximately two centimeters in diameter, supposedly allowed the spirits to escape. Though we may tend to think that the shaman would have succeeded only in killing the patient, the evidence is to the contrary. These early neurosurgical probes, called *trephination,* may in fact have represented one of the first attempts to look for organic causes of madness, and some showed a high level of technological skill. From these stone-age beginnings have come many variations on the theme that madness is caused by something in the head.

Another source of early reference to madness is the Bible, which is filled with descriptions of trances, visions, convulsive seizures, self-inflicted flagellations, hallucinations, and unusual and unspeakable acts. There is some discrepancy in the way such behavior was interpreted. If the afflicted person was a person of stature—for example, a king or a religious leader—his hallucinations were interpreted to be "visions" or insights, and his mumblings or rantings were believed to be messages from God. Thus the statements were prophetic; the man has held to be a prophet. His otherworldly behavior and ideas were considered to be evidence of his association with the other, higher world of God. On the other hand, individuals of humbler social stature—those who did not speak and were unable to care for themselves—were simply considered to be deranged and were either left in the care of their families or left on the streets. Little attempt was made to explain their condition.

Systematical attempts to explain and classify such behavior arose in Greece and Rome of the classical period, where we can see the beginning of the so-called humors theory of illness. According to this theory,

> the body was composed of four humours, blood, phlegm, yellow bile and black bile, which were produced by physiologic processes in various organs of the body. Furthermore, each humour was endowed with a basic quality, such as heat, cold, dryness, and moistness. Disease developed when internal or external factors produced an excess of one of the humours. The resulting imbalance of these basic qualities acted on organs to produce deleterious effects. Madness, the disease of the mind, was produced in this fashion by excess of a humour. Black bile was a peculiarly potent cause, when present in abundance under certain conditions, of various forms of mental illness, particularly the conditions called melancholia.[4]

Along with this protoscientific view was the more popular conception which continued to link madness to possession. The possessors were understood to be dark forces of the underworld, whose victims were those who had transgressed against the gods. Once such individuals became so inflicted with the curse of the gods, they supposedly could contaminate anyone who associated with them. This was the beginning of the stigmatizing of the mad.

It is important to realize that classical Greek culture spanned a period of three centuries and that it established a series of perspectives on madness, which included, on the one hand, such diverse ideas as possession and, on the other, the concepts proposed by Hippocrates, who emphasized that the cause of epileptic seizures was a misfunctioning of the brain. Believing that the body would heal itself (homeopathic medicine), Hippocrates encouraged therapeutic treatment that called for rest, bathing, and dieting.

During the Renaissance the conception of madness became further complicated as a result, oddly enough, of what was thought to be an instance of social progress. In the mid-1600s the problem of poverty among the population of Paris and other large French cities became so great that institutions (usually old fortresses, jails, or crumbling estates) were given over to the housing of the poor and the incapacitated. An institution of this kind, termed a *hospital general,* supplied both housing and hospitality and was available to the general population.[5] Often within the institution itself were separate provisions and quarters for the mad; there were even some attempts at what would now be termed *therapeutic intervention.* That the hospital general was populated by all manner of individuals, however—from the simple poor to the criminal and degenerate—tended to cause confusion on the part of the general public and resulted in further stigmatization of the mad. This came at the time of the Protestant Reformation, which, spreading the gospel of work and economic gain, led to even greater problems for the mentally ill. The isolation of the mad to a central location advanced the position of the central administrator or warden to a new level of power. The practice of separating those who could work from those who could not led not only to a further segregation of the mad but also promoted the inclination to treat the mad as subjects for study. Madness became a discrete concept that not only could be studied but which became associated with particular forms of behavior and expectations, which the mad were forced to adopt. As a result the mad were no longer regarded as members of the normal community but were institutionalized and therefore excluded from open society. In the age of reason the asylum became an institution set aside for overcoming or conquering the unreasonable.

In the late 1600s rapid advancements in the sciences became the basis for an almost religious belief in the use of the scientific method. The mind-body relationship assumed major importance, particularly as a result of Spinoza's writings, which maintained that the two were inseparable. During this period most of the thinking on madness emphasized etiology. The anatomical perspective received a great deal of attention with the publication in 1621 of Burton's *Anatomy of Melancholy,* which brought the humors theory closer to scientific inquiry.[6] Increasingly, the older explanations of madness in terms of supernatural forces, were giving way to more "scientific" explanations. It must be remembered, however, that the scientific method did not, and still does not, guarantee that the interpretation or treatment of what is mad will be correct or enlightened. Even today clinicians can claim to be adhering rigorously to the scientific method while others reject their evidence as unscientific. The scientific method always depends on the available "facts," and these facts are always subject to human interpretation, which in turn is influenced by the times. The relativity of science can be seen in the seventeenth century's breakthroughs in chemistry, astronomy, and biology, which provided the model for exploring all things unknown. William Harvey, for instance, applied his findings regarding the circulatory system of the blood to the concept of madness. Too much blood, not enough blood, and hundreds of variations on the balance of bodily fluids, he held, were causes of psychic imbalances.

This theme of balance in the natural forces continued to be of profound interest and assumed its next notable scientific form in the work of Friedrich Anton Mesmer in the early part of the next century. Mesmer, an Austrian, believed that madness was due to an imbalance in magnetic fields that both surrounded and operated within the body. He felt that this imbalance could be corrected by bringing the patient in contact with strong magnetic fields. He had his patients hang on a large metal tub filled with magnetic filings. Later, he emphasized his role as a "magnetizer," implying that he possessed special magnetic properties that allowed him to "mesmerize" his patients back to a "proper state of mind"—a claim that gradually removed him from the more strictly scientific community. Mesmer's theories attracted great attention, particularly with regard to the impact of magnetic forces on the mind. His research interest in magnetism corresponded to the contemporary emphasis on naturalistic explorations of the world, which included studying the magnetic properties of the North and South poles. The concept of positive and negative charges in electricity generated great fascination. In fact one of the greatest popularizers of electricity, Benjamin Franklin, took particular interest in Mesmer's work.

Mesmer's activities were part of a long tradition in the use of hypnosis, and he sparked a renewed interest in its use in the treatment of madness. While the Austrian doctor was primarily concerned with curing madness, however, his contemporaries were more interested in classifying abnormal behavior and in etiology and prognosis. They considered his ideas to be a holdover from beliefs in witchcraft and discredited him and his treatment. Such scientists represented a perspective that is still dominant today.

Nevertheless, a group soon emerged who represented the opposite perspective. Beginning with Phillipe Pinel in France (1745–1826) and including such others as the Americans Dorothea Dix, Benjamin Rush, and Clifford Beers, these reformers believed that the mad should be treated, not simply rejected as pariahs of society. They introduced what can best be called a "moral" perspective, which emphasized a moral, humane treatment involving rest, recreation, and physical care in a healthy environment. This approach is represented today in psychiatric hospitals' use of milieu therapy.

In the nineteenth century, as in earlier periods, the scientific approach toward madness was strongly influenced by the contemporary understanding of man and nature in general. The eighteenth century's fascination with studying the forces of nature through science gave way to the nineteenth century's fascination with the seemingly inexplicable. This movement came to be called *Romanticism*. One of its principal concerns was the mysterious workings of the human mind, particularly with regard to the irrational. Man was no longer seen to be innately reasonable and rational but to be torn by forces of conflict similar to the powerful and destructive forces of nature. Freud (1856–1939), of course, was influenced by this tradition as he came to explore the madness that he maintained rested in everyone. Unlike theorists before him, Freud posited that madness was not a separate condition without referent in the lives of the sane but was an exaggeration of the vicissitudes of the *id,* or "animal nature" in us, which each individual attempted to control. Raising sex and aggression to major motivating forces of personality, Freud brought the subjective experience of the mad into the arena of scientific inquiry.

Freud remained uncertain, however, about his personal allegiance to the Romantic tradition. While fascinated by the exploration of an emotional basis for aberrant behavior, he maintained a scientific, or more explicitly physical, explanation for it. Freud's physical perspective came from the neurological training in which he had been well schooled and which remained the most popular model among physicians at the time.[7] Rejecting a *psychodynamic* orientaton, which emphasized the forces in the unconscious that were continuously in flux, the physicalistic school looked to an organic explanation for all forms of behavior, especially those that were abnormal. Germ theory had been introduced in the middle of the nineteenth century, and the physicalistic view maintained that the mad were suffering a disease for which there must be a cure, as there was for diseases such as small pox. One of the events that reinforced this view was the discovery of the syphilis bacillus. The continuous deterioration in the thought and emotional processes of the mad could now be explained as a result of a "mental disease." Such discoveries reinforced the view that personal distress and social deviance could be explained in the same terms as physical illness. In the late nineteenth century, the two opposing views, the dynamic and the organic, came to dominate psychiatry. Over time they became diffused into different combinations and permutations as the various theories, or schools, of psychiatry advanced.

These theories represent a complex matrix of explanations about the origins and treatment of madness and are efficiently summarized by adopting a paradigm based on models of madness elaborated by Siegler and Osmond.[8] All of these models grew out of the historical material we have presented. Taking a firm conceptual form in the nineteenth century, they have become increasingly distinct or discrete. Each offers a general explanation of madness, from its origins to its treatment. Each has developed a classification system, by which it hopes to make order out of the elusive problem of madness. They each represent a synthesis of ideas and, as a group, may offer the most coherent way of conceptualizing the numerous explanations that have evolved over time. The following is a short summary of each model. We will elaborate upon each one when we discuss how it applies to particular films.

The *medical model* rests on the notion of the doctor as the expert who defines what is and what is not madness. It is based on the assumption that madness is a mental sickness that corresponds to physical illness. This model calls for a careful diagnosis to determine the kind of treatment and the prognosis. The medical model traces its roots to Hippocrates (from whom the Hippocratic oath evolved), who is credited with initiating a tradition of careful investigation of bodily diseases that manifested themselves in aberrant behavior. From another Greek of the same period, Aesculapius, comes the role of doctor as ultimate authority, invested with the power to assign an individual to the role of patient. From this role follows the treatments of hospitalization, nursing care, physical treatments, and so forth. The hospital becomes the place for those who are mad, the place where they are treated, as opposed to where they live. They never "live" there or work for the hospital, and the only thing that is asked of them is that they try to get well. Throughout their hospitalization the doctor is in charge and is working on the assumption that from the etiology of the illness follows the type of treatment.

The *impaired model* is closely connected with the medical model; however, it views the mad as incurably insane. The doctor becomes the supervisor of custodians who take care of people who will always be mad. Patients lose their rights and are seen as wards of the state who are unable to take care of themselves.

The *moral model* rests on the assumption that madness is simply dysfunctional or immoral behavior. This behavior was learned somewhere, though it is not of great importance how or where it was learned. The objective is to alter that learning and replace the aberrant behavior with more socially acceptable actions. Treatment involves modifying the behavior through reinforcement and punishment. If the person's behavior is extremely dysfunctional, he may have to be put into an institution, but this does not necessarily have to be a hospital.

The *psychoanalytic model* emphasizes the belief that madness is simply an exaggeration of normal processes. Things become abnormal as a result of repression. Repression is a function of the kind of traumas experienced, and the degree of repression is partly determined by the way in which one was allowed to deal with these traumas. For Freud and most of his followers, madness results from too much or too little repression. While Freud was interested in the madness in each of us, he was not interested in treating people who were singularly mad—he never worked with institutionalized patients. His disciples (most of whom were physicians), however, adopted a different attitude when they moved to America and became more involved in the medical setting of the psychiatric hospital. As the American school of psychoanalysis developed, Freud's emphasis on the value of introspection, particularly in uncovering the psychic traumas caused by parents (especially mothers), came to be the goal of treatment with all patients. The "mad" were thus conceptualized as those whose traumas were greater than those of others and for whom introspection was both more necessary and more terrifying.

Several other models emerged during the 1960s and 1970s, and these are outlined as follows:

The *social model* emphasizes the relationship between the order of society and madness. The more chaotic and anomalous the social order, the more disorganized the behavior of its members. From this it follows that the mad are social victims and the product of a mad society.

The *psychedelic model* views madness as an altered state of mind that provides insight into another form of reality. Madness is a positive disintegration, which introduces patients to a new way of experiencing themselves, others, and the physical world. This model does not posit an etiology but, rather, sees madness as an exploration of other worlds.

The *conspiratorial model* emphasizes the impact of being "labeled" and implies that through a kind of self-fulfilling prophecy people become what they are called. Inherent in this view is the notion that madness does not really exist but is something fabricated or fantasized by those in power as a way of manipulating others.

The *family interaction model* merges the social and conspiratorial models in focusing on the collusion and the confusion involved in the communicational processes that lead an individual to madness. It investigates the ways in which members of the nuclear family come together in collusive unions to drive another member into madness. Such attempts are usually nonverbal and involve subtle processes of interaction.

Summary

Having outlined the history of perceptions of madness and having presented a tentative classification of general theoretical views, we would like to point out that in practice identifying views of madness is often not an easy task. While most theories of madness clearly find their roots in both traditional beliefs and current social and scientific influences, no one conception of madness is held by all members of a society at any given time.

Perhaps our own society is the best example. We believe that we have extraordinary powers of scientific investigation, combining impressive equipment, such as electron microscopes and CAT scanners, with highly sophisticated analytic techniques, made possible by computers. Yet there is no agreement in the medical or psychological community as to what is or what causes madness.

This confusion is counterpointed by what appears to be a fascination among the moviegoing population, at least, with what are normally labeled primitive conceptions of madness. Films dealing with ideas of possession, the occult, the supernatural, and the mystical have broken box-office records and have been the subject of much discussion in the press. Such films seem to reflect a basic distrust of scientific explanations alone. In their view science overemphasizes reason and is restrictingly concrete, particularly in its explanations of emotions that are not easily categorized. They see the scientific model as a belief system that lauds its latest tested finding as the truth while belittling the input of other disciplines. The criteria established by pure science for what is real is in continuous conflict with the natural human fascination with the nonscientific.[9] The concepts of madness as possession, as human nature gone awry, as enlightenment, or as a function of society, have been repeated, interwoven, and maintained throughout history and all held today even by various members of our so-called scientific society. The expression of these ideas in that medium of our times, the film, provides insight into our concepts and beliefs about madness, if not our understanding of it.

Format

Models of interpretation are helpful insofar as we do not adhere indiscriminately to any particular one. They enjoy popularity for a limited time and then fade into the background, only to reemerge later as if they were entirely new. As we have shown, they are inheritors of long-standing ideas, and we should appreciate them as such. Along with the models, there are particular themes that continue to reappear in the depiction of madness. These themes compose the focus of each of the chapters to follow. They are: Society and Madness; Possession as Madness; Eros and Madness; Murder and Madness; War and Madness; Drugs and Madness; Paranoia and Madness; Sanity As Madness, Madness As Sanity; and Madness and the Psychiatrist. Each chapter begins with a historical overview of the psychological literature on the theme. A particular time frame is then chosen, and the clinical literature of that period is presented. A feature film from the period is then summarized and is followed by a summary of the ways in which the film may have both reflected and affected clinical perceptions of the period. In order to show the changing or possibly repeating nature of clinical and artistic visions of madness, we have chosen time frames separated in most cases by at least twenty-five years. This helps us appreciate the relativity of our contemporary views and the importance of taking a historical perspective. We chose in most cases, with the exceptions being chapters 7 and 9, to concentrate on one early and one late film because we felt that the reader would need a complete summary of the film if he or she were to appreciate the subtle interrelationship between the film and the clinical literature of the period. Though we cite many other contempory major films that also depicted the theme, we felt that these would most efficiently be presented in the form of a filmography with synopses and annotations, found in the second part of the book.

The films we chose for each chapter were those whose imagery, we felt, best elaborated the given theme. This selection was clearly arbitrary on our part and therefore has some problems. The first is the emphasis we placed on what we regard as the manifestations of madness in a film when in fact it may have had less importance for the viewer. Possible examples are the mother-daughter relationship in *Now, Voyager,* the sudden paralysis of General Savage in *Twelve O'Clock High,* or Kit's composure after he commits murder in *Badlands.* The reader might claim that the film as a whole represents so much more than the one aspect we call madness, and we would have to agree to the extent that the significance of each film rests on what we come prepared to see in it. Nevertheless, we hope that this analysis will at least be provocative and enable the reader to better understand the complex images of madness.

Another problem involves the thematic categories we have identified. Because of their richness of motifs, many of the selected films could be categorized under a number of different themes. We have tried to meet this problem not only in our individual analyses but in our selected filmography, where we have indicated the major relevant themes that appear in each film.

There were also difficulties with reviewing the clinical literature at the time the film was being made and released. While we reviewed literature from two years before and two years after a film's release in order to assess the manner in which the particular theme was being treated, our selection could not be all-inclusive and was influenced by how well it complemented the film. An example from the theme of Madness and Murder (chapter 4) will help to clarify this point. For this theme the two major films selected for contrast were *White Heat* (1949) and *Badlands* (1974). The clinical literature on murder has not followed a clear linear progression between these time periods, and it is difficult to specify at any one point along this continuum the dominant school of thought. In 1949, when *White Heat* was released, there were multiple clinical interpretations of murder, and it would be erroneous to say that we have sampled them all and have presented the one that was at this point held to be the most accurate. There is no way of establishing the absolute dominance of a particular perspective on madness at any point in time, given the fact that many publications have a particular theoretical basis and reflect it in their articles. If one sought the current clinical view of murder in 1949 and turned only to psychoanalytic journals, there would be a particular emphasis that well might not be found in other journals or books of the period. While we therefore tried to survey as much of the literature as possible and to determine trends of consensus, there were always opposing views. The period literature that we have cited reflects a dominat interpretation, but how dominant is a moot point not only because of the extensive clinical literature available (books, professional journal articles, professionals' citations in lay publications) but because the views espoused in clinical writing did not always represent what was actually taking place in clinical practice.

In this book, then, we have presented each theme on madness with an analysis of a limited number of major films, which, collectively, span a period of approximately twenty-five years or more. We selected these films because they highlight some of the more interesting changes, as well as repetitions, in the depictions of madness that have occurred over a considerable period of time. The following chapters will, we hope, offer insight into the images that have changed, as well as those that seem ever-present, in the subtle interplay of clinical and cinematic interpretations of madness.

Notes

1. Arthur Schlesinger, Jr., in *American Film*, ed. J. W. Jackson (New York: Unger, 1979).

2. J. B. Kuriansky, E. Deming, and B. J. Gurland, "On Trends in the Diagnosis of Schizophrenia," *American Journal of Psychiatry* 131 (1974): 402–8. L. Blum, "On Changes in Psychiatric Diagnosis over Time," *American Psychologist*, vol. 33, No. 11 (1978), 1017–31. J. E. Helzer, and L. N. Robbins, "Reliability of Psychiatric Diagnosis, A Methodological Review," *Archives of General Psychiatry* 34 (1977): 129–33.

3. D. L. Rosenhan, "On Being Sane in Insane Places," *Science*, vol. 179, no. 4070 (1973), 365–69. See also R. L. Spitzer, "On Pseudoscience in Science, Logic in Remission, and Psychiatric Diagnosis: A Critique of Rosenhan's 'On Being Sane in Insane Places,'" *Journal of Abnormal Psychology* 84 (1975): 442–52.

4. G. Rose, *Madness and Society* (New York: Harper & Row, 1969).

5. M. Foucault, *Madness and Civilization* (New York: Vintage, 1973).

6. R. Burton, *The Anatomy of Melancholy* (London: G. Bell & Sons, 1926).

7. P. Rieff, *The Mind of the Moralist* (New York: Doubleday, 1961).

8. M. Siegler and H. Osmond, *Models of Madness, Models of Medicine* (New York: Harper & Row, 1976).

9. L. Hudson, *The Cult of the Fact: A Psychologist's Autobiographical Critique of his Discipline* (New York: Harper & Row, 1973).

1
Society and Madness

The history of madness is closely tied to the history of the institutions that have cared for the mad. At first it was the family or the village society that cared for the mad individual, who was believed to be suffering from spiritual or supernatural affliction. As societies grew in complexity, so did the organizations required to govern them and ensure their normative functioning. Eventually, psychiatric hospitals were established in order to contain the growing numbers of people who were considered mad and who needed to be excluded from society. The family and psychiatric institutions continue to function as the principal caretakers of the mad, and in fact the current emphasis on deinstitutionalization (reducing the number of institutions and the patients in them) has shifted a good deal of responsibility once again back to the family. As institutions, both the family and the psychiatric hospital share a number of similarities. At worst, psychiatric administrators evoke a patriarchal family analogue to describe the process by which the institution serves the needs of its regressed, "childlike," adult patients. The institutional staff plays the role of the controlling parent, while the patients are wards who must be continually tended if they are ever to assume adult responsibility.

For our purposes the important similarity between the institution of the family and the psychiatric hospital is the fact that they are the principal caretakers of the mad. However much both are currently being criticized for causing more harm than good, this has not always been the case. Like many of the themes to be presented the theme Society and Madness has undergone a complex evolution, which can be chronicled through cinematic depictions. The present chapter investigates the influence of the social institutions of the family and the psychiatric hospital. The two films to be contrasted under the depiction of the family are *Now, Voyager* (1942) and *A Woman under The Influence* (1974), while those dealing with institutionalization are *Snake Pit* (1948) and *One Flew over the Cuckoo's Nest* (1975).

The Family and Madness

Clinical psychology has come to be interested in the family as a whole unit only within the last few years. Considering the individual to be both influenced by and

30

influencing the family processes that lead to madness contrasts with earlier perspectives, which at best interpreted madness to be the result of a one-way process from parent to child.

The clinical literature on the family begins in early psychoanalytic case histories, where cursory comment is given to the actual relationship between the patient and his parents. The actual relationship, from Freud's perspective, came to be quite secondary; Freud emphasized not what had happened or what was happening in the family, but how the patient perceived what was happening. Freud believed that his patients' horrific stories about their parents—brutalization, seduction, etc.—did not represent real events but were fantasized wishes. He therefore spent little time investigating the actual family relationships since he felt that the problem lay in the patients' distortions, which were the result primarily of their unresolved oedipal conflicts. In time Freud's followers, interpreters, and critics modified and reshaped his interpretation of the family and introduced their own ideas. This chapter examines two films that reflect the evolution of these interpretations. We contrast the 1942 film *Now, Voyager* and the film *A Woman under the Influence,* made over thirty years later.

By the early 1920s Freud's theory of psychoanalysis had become popular in both medical and lay circles. Originally respected only in Europe, it was gaining increasing attention in America, though there was strong skepticism regarding Freud's radical ideas on sexuality. The theory was held in favor by artist expatriates who had emigrated to Europe after the First World War. Avant-garde figures such as Gertrude Stein and the Fitzgeralds helped to popularize the concepts of psychoanalysis through their semiautobiographical writings. It became increasingly fashionable to have been analyzed by Freud, and if one could not have the master, only one of his inner circle of followers would rank as an adequate substitute. Through both literature and art, psychoanalytic concepts began to emerge and, as we see in the film *Secrets of a Soul* (1926), the cinema began to reflect Freud's interpretations of the unconscious.

American psychiatry in the mid-1920s was receptive to attempts to educate both physicians and laymen through psychoanalysis. Freud sought to make his ideas available to a general readership, and he found much receptivity in America, where the interaction of scientific and popular culture was much in evidence. American psychiatry became therefore increasingly fascinated by psychoanalysis. Many psychiatrists went to Europe to be analyzed, and in 1930 the first psychoanalytic institute was established in America. American psychiatrists who had obtained psychoanalytic training increased the general proliferation of Freud's ideas, and for a time psychoanalysis assumed a major hold on American psychiatry.[1]

It must be remembered that the profession of psychiatry had been well established in both America and Europe before psychoanalysis emerged as a major force. Tied to neurology, psychiatry had as its basic orientation a medical model. During the 1920s psychiatry still emphasized a physicalistic approach, though some American psychiatrists, looking beyond mere chemistry, were beginning to stress the significance of human feeling in mental disease. In addition there was talk, particularly in its early days (c.1910 to 1918), about making psychoanalysis available to a wide range of patients through low-fee clinics.[2] Such ideas, coinciding, with the movement in the American medical community to offer greater services to the population as a whole, made psychoanalysis at first very popular.

By the late twenties and early thirties, certain psychiatrists had begun to question the intense fascination with Freud, though there had always been strong opposition to psychoanalytic thought both within and without the profession. One reason for this intense criticism was that Freud had become increasingly definite regarding his ideas about the life forces (Eros and Thanatos), which he felt ultimately dictate all human actions. Freud's pessimism—reflected in such statements as, "When things are going well, I know nature is not fulfilling her true prophecy" or "The purpose of psychoanalysis is to change neurotic misery into human unhappiness"—was at odds with the basic optimism of Americans. Another issue that lessened America's romance with Freud was his need to control the movement of psychoanalysis from one country to another. Psychoanalysis was his child, and he would not part with it except on his own terms. He often demanded absolute and literal acceptance of his ideas, and American defiance toward such patriarchal impositions grew quickly. Freud's dogmatism, real or distorted, became a sore point and resulted in movement away from his beliefs. Finally, there was the standing criticism that Freud's thinking was unscientific, which really meant that it focused on the psyche, not on the somatic determinants that lay in neurology and biochemistry.

The strictly biological and the classically psychoanalytic interpretation were not the only two schools of thought that explained madness. In the 1930s there was a proliferation of other theories, which both bridged these two schools and used them as springboards. Tired of domination by Continental theories, American psychiatry was quick to give attention to the work of Harry Stack Sullivan, who became one of the most famous American interpreters of madness.[3] Though he always gave credit to Freud's genius and to his substantial contributions to psychiatry, Sullivan felt that Freud's explanation for human behavior was too singular or delimited. Where Freud reductionistically emphasized the seething cauldron of instinctual processes in the id, as the central force of personality, Sullivan pointed to interpersonal relations as a crucial additional factor influencing the biological determinants. Espousing a more democratically based model of how people change, Sullivan disagreed with Freud's psychoanalytic premise that the therapist must always sit out of sight of the patient and encourage a transference neurosis. Sullivan felt that the therapist's relationship with the patient should involve more than just a projection of the patient's past onto the therapist. In Sullivan's words the therapist was a "participant-observer" and therefore had to assume a more active role in the therapeutic hour. Sullivan also differed with Freud on the treatment of schizophrenia and other forms of psychoses.

It must be remembered that Freud worked primarily with neurotics; according to him, psychoanalysis was not effective with psychotics. Though some of his followers did attempt to apply psychoanalytic methods to psychotics, they were cautious and tentative and still followed Freud's traditional concepts. Sullivan and others felt that while psychoanalysis clearly has merit, its view of psychotics as untreatable is unreasonable. Freud's pessimism was consonant with the general pessimism of psychiatry about the possibility of treating such patients. Both Freud's psychoanalysis and the organically based psychiatry of the period held that psychosis is organically determined and tended to emphasize the poor prognosis for those afflicted by it. The treatment of such patients was tied to a hospital setting and primarily involved a custodial approach. Basic treatment involved putting such patients into psychiatric hospitals, from which, it was felt, they would probably not reemerge. These hospitals were situated in rural areas, far away from cities. Their remote location was due to the popular feeling that the mad should be kept far away and out of sight, as well as to the belief in the curative effect of nature. The concept of nature's ability to heal, an idea that dates from the beginning of recorded medicine, gained much attention during the Romantic period. According to this view, moving away from the corrupt urban environment and living in direct union with nature results in freedom from all types of illness. (This will be discussed in more depth in the section on institutionalization.) Psychiatric hospitals were thus concentrated in rural areas from 1860 to 1950.

The state-run hospitals were generally overfilled and staffed by individuals with little, if any, training. Psychotics who were poor and who were placed in state institutions had little hope of receiving effective treatment, and recovery depended on spontaneous remission of their symptoms. Private sanitoriums which treated the rich, generally provided a higher level of custodial care.

Freud had never worked in such institutions, and his patients were generally healthy enough to remain outside these hospitals. The number of such patients, though kept hidden from both the public and the medical community, continued to concern psychiatry, and it was the plight of this clinical population that dominated the work of Sullivan. Though Sullivan accepted the necessity of hospitalization, he felt that the interpersonal origins of schizophrenia demand that the treatment include an interpersonal framework. He set up special wards where patients could enjoy a degree of privacy and trained his staff to be more than just custodians.[4]

Another dominant figure in American psychiatry was Adolph Meyer, whose "common-sense" theory of psychiatry has had a powerful impact on the treatment of the mad since the early 1900s. In Meyer's pragmatic approach "the main thing is that your point of reference always be life itself and not the imagined cesspool of the unconscious."[5] Meyer felt that Freud's ideas were too static—they did not allow for the changing nature of psychic life or pay enough attention to the broader situational framework that gives rise to a patient's problems. Meyer felt that Freud was building a highly specialized, denominational body of adherents, who used a selective vocabulary to further their speciality at the cost of general understanding. Meyer was concerned with making the public aware of the plight of the insane and involving them in the process of rehabilitation. He emphasized the importance of work as a way of restoring meaning to the individual's life. Hospitalized patients were encouraged to involve themselves in activities and exercises that would restore their psychic balance. Meyer stressed that on discharge they had to be involved in important and socially constructive tasks in order to prevent a relapse. Sullivan's and Meyer's formulations for treatment became increasingly popular and complemented the general American notion that work and social bonding are the best means to overcome a patient's problems.

By the early 1940s these three approaches—psychoanalysis, the interpersonal theory, and the somatic view—dominated the interpretation and treatment of the mad. Classical psychoanalysis had been modified to include some social determinants of behavior as well as to be applied to the treatment of psychosis. Psychoanalysis thus became more complementary to Sullivan's theories, though the classical interpreters of Freud strongly resisted such revisionary thinking. Three particularly distinguished dissidents from Freud's inner circle were Jung, Adler, and Karen Horney. By the late 1930s and early 1940s all three had established their own theories, which became well-known to the interested lay public.

On the eve of the Second World War psychiatry turned its focus on the forces of madness that were gaining world power. This interest was reinforced by the great number of well-known analysts and researchers of the psyche who beginning in the mid-1930s, were forced to leave central Europe. These European psychiatrists were, for the most part, greeted warmly by their American colleagues, and their ideas were quickly adopted as American.[6] This was the changing psychological climate in which *Now, Voyager* (1942) was made, and it is interesting to note the use of these theorists' formulations in the film.

Now, Voyager. Though to posit a causal relationship is difficult it is interesting to note that the changing psychological climate of the late 1930s and early 1940s was matched with changes in cinematic depictions, with regard not only to madness but, in the case of *Now, Voyager,* to women and madness. Indeed, *Now, Voyager* concentrates on women and madness. It is important to comment on how the depiction of women on the screen changed. During this period there were a genre of film that emphasized the theme of sacrifice. This sacrifice generally had the heroine rising above the everyday travail of life toward an almost beatific vision. Her existence did not depend on marrying and having children, though she always paid a great price for her deviation from the norm, as Molly Haskell pointed out in the book *From Reverence to Rape.*[7]

The heroine of the early 1940s could stand independent from the men with whom she was involved. Not simply a sex object, she was presented in diverse roles involving a range of situations. Bette Davis's role as Charlotte Vale in *Now, Voyager* makes sense in this context though, having had little experience with the topic of madness, Hollywood was reluctant to depict it.

In the opening scene of the meeting between Dr. Jackqueth and Charlotte's tyrannical mother, it quickly becomes clear that Dr. Jackqueth is not the classical passive psychoanalyst, who sits in the shadows waiting for the patient to disclose his innermost thoughts. That he has come to the Vale home indicates a more active approach, but of even greater significance is his exchange with Charlotte's mother. He makes it clear that he will not use the scientific diagnoses of Jung's personality types of introversion and extroversion. He presents himself to his patient in a manner very similar to that described by Sullivan in his work *The Psychiatric Interview*. Straightforward and clear, he presents himself as a friend and collaborator rather than as an all-knowing doctor. The opening exchanges between Jackqueth and his patient remind one of Meyer's common-sense psychiatry, as well as of the work of Freida Fromm-Reichmann (the real life analyst to Hannah Green, who wrote *I Never Promised You a Rose Garden*), who, as a student of Sullivan, went on to do some of the most effective pioneering work with psychotic patients. Fromm-Reichmann emphasized the importance of the "avoidance of scientific terms."[8]

Jackqueth takes Charlotte to his sanitorium in the woods of Vermont, where she can fully recuperate. Other members of the hospital staff are dressed informally like Jackqueth and present the same kind of collaborative manner. The warm presence of Jacqueth in the communal and relaxed bucolic atmosphere of the sanitorium is emphasized when Charlotte returns for a short visit after the death of her mother. As Jackqueth strolls the grounds with her, we observe that activities are going on everywhere, as in a summer camp. This is consonant with the contemporary emphasis on physical activities as part of the occupational therapy program. Meyer was a strong advocate of occupational therapy. The importance of activity as treatment is also evident during Charlotte's cruise, her undertaking the care of Jerry's institutionalized child, and her managing the fund drive for the new wing of the hospital. A clear relationship is drawn between these therapeutic activities and her recovery from madness.

Though the symptoms of Charlotte's madness supposedly indicate a severe depression, her behavior is more like that of a withdrawn, overly shy woman, rather than that of a regressed and primitive personality. Her depiction emphasizes timidity, in contrast to the overwhelming temerity of her mother. The mother is depicted as being the cause of her daughter's "illness"; as Dr. Jackqueth says, "Thanks to you, she is having a nervous breakdown." The role of mothers in causing madness in their children was just beginning to gain attention in the 1940s. The role of the mother as a tyrannical bitch fits nicely with the classical psychoanalytic literature of the period, which emphasized the castrating, phallic mother, who makes the child feel inadequate. Freud focused more on the little boy than on the little girl, and he openly admitted to not really understanding women. He did believe, however, that the little girl has a basic desire to regain the penis, which was taken away from her by her jealous mother. The little girl believes that the mother once had a penis (she was a phallic mother) and that when she was castrated, she also castrated her daughter.[9]

Freud's explanation is at best a very convoluted one, whose most important implication is that all women have penis envy. Freud believed that the woman who was likely to become psychiatrically ill was the one who had not resolved her conflicts about her desire to be a man. He and the first female analysts whom he trained, like Helene Deutsch and Ruth Mack Brunswick, believed that women who achieve success in their field do so at the expense of their "feminine fulfillment." This meant in essence that to be a woman involves acceptance and passivity. Women who do not conform to such an attitude were thought to be highly conflicted. Freud looked at such conflicts in the patients themselves and

Now, Voyager (USA, 1942). Director, Irving Rapper. With Bette Davis, Claude Rains, Paul Henreid. By permission of MGM–United Artists.

spoke little about the impact of the mother's behavior. When he did discuss the role of the parents in causing the patient's problems, he focused on the father in the oedipal conflict. The concept of the mother as an important element in the parent-child interaction first appeared in the late 1930s and early 1940s in the works of Sullivan.[10] Sullivan stressed that the mother's early interactions with the child were inextricably linked later in life to the diagnosis of schizophrenia. Though Sullivan did not go on to discuss in depth the nature of the mother-child relationship, he helped bring attention to the importance of the mothering process.

Karen Horney also brought a new perspective to the study of mother-daughter interaction. Disagreeing with Freud's instinctual theory, which saw women as basically passive, she maintained, "Women who nowadays obey the impulse to the independent development of their abilities are able to do so only at the cost of a struggle against both external opposition and such resistances within themselves as are created by an intensification of the traditional ideal of the exclusively sexual function of woman."[11] In the late 1930s and early 1940s Horney's controversial ideas slowly started to win over the psychiatric community, who, as a group, was beginning to be much more attentive to the social determinants of behavior. Ten years after her original work, her papers and the reaction to them were still frequently cited. It is interesting to realize how much of her work is relevant to *Now, Voyager.* She points out, "This defeat in relation to the father is of course the typical fate of the little girl in the family situation. But in these cases it produces specific and typical consequences because of the rivalry brought about by the presence of a mother or sister who absolutely dominates the situation erotically or by the awakening of specific illusions on the part of the father or brother."[12]

Certainly, this remark applies to the mother in the film. Furthermore, Horney points out that the reaction to such a mother is to either withdraw from any competition for men or to fall in love with those whom you can't have or whom you come to find you don't want—and this describes the girl's behavior in the film. Charlotte's relationship with men makes sense when we remember that her father died when she was a child and that she is the youngest child and only girl in a family of ten children. In one wonderful scene, she comes into a room crowded with all her brothers, who, with their wives, wait obediently for the entrance of the mother. As Charlotte moves with match in hand toward the fireplace, they all chant that there hasn't been a fire for as long as they can remember and that Charlotte should restrain herself. Of course, she refuses to listen and marches defiantly past them. It is this general defiance that comes to increase her sense of guilt. Horney points to the fact that however intrapsychically elicited this is, it is exacerbated by the cultural standard imposed on women. It is interesting to see the continuing relevance of these issues in *Frances* (1982).

Charlotte's final request to Jerry that he not ask for "the stars" can certainly be viewed in terms of her inability to ever marry because of her conflict as a result of the lost father and punishing mother, or it can be seen as the awakening consciousness of a woman to accept the imperfect world around her and give up idealized notions of love for a productive life of caring for and giving to others. The fact that the film does end with her not living happily ever after with the man of her desire is a major step towards the presentation of independence in women, which was increasingly to become a major theme in the films of the forties. The ending is also significant in that it allows her not to be simply cured and resolved of all her problems. She is still alone, involved in the recuperation of Jerry's daughter; she has adopted the hospital as her cause and, in this regard, her experience with madness is still very much a part of her life.

A Woman under the Influence. By the end of the 1950s one could sense that a new order of things was about to emerge. This was the age of Sputnik, the first satellite put in orbit, and the dawn of a technological explosion that would radically change the way in which human beings thought of themselves and their place in the world. Technology invaded the sciences, the arts, and the social sciences and spawned such new fields as general systems theory, cybernetics, information theory, chronetics, and media analysis. An important part of this technology was the communication of information. The "information explosion," which was first associated with the new science of space, quickly infiltrated every sector of American life. By the early 1960s Cape Canaveral became a major tourist attraction as Americans began to turn to the stars for a way out of the awesome social and economic problems of the day. They were beginning to question the belief that the earth can provide an endless source of raw materials to serve the ever-increasing demands of a species that set no limits to its exploding population growth. Along with this was a general restlessness that prompted the mass exodus of the middle class from the cities to suburbia and a growing willingness to resettle far from one's birthplace. The institution of the extended family was dying, and there was much talk about the radical social changes that would occur in the decades to come.

It was in this context that the theory and practice of family therapy began. Family therapy grew out of what we might call the *ecological approach,* in which events are viewed within the context of the social system, as opposed to a linear, unicausal interpretation. This perspective emphasized that human behavior is affected by multiple factors, both inside and outside the individual. Previous work, which had focused solely on the individual, came to be regarded as too limiting and myopic. The individual began to be studied no longer as a unit in and of himself but as part of a complex matrix of interacting forces.[13] One of the principal forces to be investigated was the family.

As we have pointed out in our analysis of *Now, Voyager,* the family up to this point had been primarily studied in terms of the mother-child interaction; little attention had been given to factors outside of this single dyadic unit. Developments in the late 1950s and early 1960s changed this perspective. First, there was a greater awareness of intergenerational conflict. Parents who had grown up in the period of the Depression and had struggled with severe economic fear suddenly saw their children taking for granted an opulence for which they had had to struggle only too hard. As a result there developed a schism between the generations and a breakdown of the extended family.[14] The younger generation had a different perception of time, centered on the notion that whatever was wanted could not only be had, but had now. With the general speedup in economic production, youth offered an important consumer market, representing a new way of life, the "good life." These overdemanding children, of course, posed a problem for their parents. The situation was cinematically portrayed in the classic *Rebel without A Cause* (1955). The film depicts a teenage world where parents are nonexistent or, if existent, are totally ineffectual and unable to understand their children. The family was in trouble, but the cause was depicted to be adolescent rebellion rather than a total crisis in the family process.

The advancements of technology, particularly the new media of television, brought new ways of selling the good life. In the late 1950s advertising became a billion-dollar industry, as mass production had brought former luxuries like television within everyone's reach. With the proliferation of goods and a matching consumerism, the possession of material objects no longer indicated the divisions and privileges of social class. Americans of all classes were encouraged to buy the material goods that had formerly belonged exclusively to the wealthy. The media ceaselessly presented images associated with wealth and encouraged everyone to believe that the products represented by these images were now obtainable by the ordinary man. This created problems for the lower middle class, who could not afford these products yet felt that they would be ostracized without them. There came to be a general diffusion of upper-middle-class values throughout America, and those who did not have the buying power to obtain its images were ostracized or felt certain they would soon be. Both parents and children were caught up in a frustrating game that, impossible to win, created a conflict between what they wanted and what they really needed.

Under such pressures the stability of the family deteriorated, and mental health experts, employing the tools of the new technology, began to investigate. Tape recorders, video tape, and one-way mirrors represented the new means available for looking at and listening to the problems of the family. Psychiatry lost its unique status as the only means of understanding human behavior and conflict. Cultural anthropology, social psychology, sociology, and communication theory, as discrete bodies of knowledge, became major disciplines for the study of the family. The psychoanalytic approach, which focused on internal manifestations of a problem, was replaced by one that saw problems in terms of the behavioral disorders of an interacting system. The individual was regarded no longer to be the only participant but, increasingly, to be a member of the nuclear and intergenerational family structure.[15] The psychoanalytic model, which had emphasized the therapist as "analyst," with external observer characteristics, was now challenged by that of the family therapist, who was more active and involved with the immediate processes presented by the family. The focus of treatment centered on the communication patterns between family members, and both language and nonverbal forms of communication received attention. Whereas Freud had maintained that it was dangerous for relatives to interfere with psychoanalytic therapy, the family theoreticians of the 1960s said that it was not only helpful but essential.[16] While the psychodynamic model emphasized that movement is always from the inside outward, the family model holds that movement takes place first from the outside.

There was then a general move toward seeing individuals as part of, rather than separate from, their environment. Psychiatrists came to accept the concept that individuals and their surroundings were interdependent and that the individual was part of a complex chain of interacting systems. The earlier emphasis on internal psychic functioning was replaced by attention to new areas, such as visual signaling, nonverbal messages, spatial relations, encounters, facial displays, communication channels, and the mutual regulation of behavior. Communication came to be seen as a continuous process involving a multiplicity of messages[17]—i.e., what an individual says has many different levels of meaning—and the social sciences developed a strong interest in deciphering them. It was almost as if there is a code, known by no one but understood by all, and it became the task of the psychiatrist, armed with the new knowledge of family therapy, to break this code in order to understand why people respond the way they do. Language became more than just the words we hear but the messages sent by touch, body motion, closeness, and even vocal sounds not regarded as language, like gasps and sighs. It was felt that all of these are elements of communication and that it is communication that influences the way we respond to one another.[18]

The family became a natural focus for the study of communication because it was clear that the family unit was breaking down. Messages communicated from one member to another became a principal area of study. For example, the withdrawal or aggression that, from an outsider's perspective, might seem totally unprovoked suddenly began to be interpretable through a microanalysis of the levels of communication.

The first investigation of such processes in the family focused, as we might expect, on the mother-child interaction. From the early 1940s up to the early 1960s the mother gained an even more ominous image. The "ice-box" mother, who was always to blame for the problems of the family, became the schizophrenogenic mother by the early 1960s.[19] At first vengeful and aggressive, she became over the years more passively vapid and devoid of emotion. The studies emphasized the difficulty she had with being a nurturing parent and showed how she communicated her withdrawal in a number of subtle but nonetheless direly effective ways. One of the most discussed means was the *double bind*.

First presented by Bateson (1956), the double bind became an accepted concept for explaining the type of communication that drives one to madness.[20] Though its original focus was the mother-child interaction, by the late 1960s and early 1970s it was applied to all family members. According to Bateson, three conditions are necessary for a double bind. First, an individual needs to be involved with another person in an intense emotional relationship in which the ability to discriminate what is being communicated is of the utmost importance. Second, the communication from the person loved contains two messages, each one contradicting and denying the other. Finally, the listener cannot discriminate which order or level of message to respond to and cannot resolve the contradictory nature of the communication.

Though the most reasonable reaction is to "unbind" the situation by metacommunicating (that is, communicating about the communication), this is not possible. The reason has changed since the concept of the double bind was introduced by Bateson. As pointed out earlier, the original focus of the double bind was on the mother-child interaction. By the 1960s the focus had shifted toward a conspiratorial model, which has certain members of the family joining forces to drive someone else into madness through the use of confusing communication.[21] Throughout this period the literature emphasized a one-way direction to the analysis, which explains the process in terms of victim and villain. As the analysis of the double bind and of the total communicational and ecological context of family relations has evolved, the notion of victims and villains has slowly been discarded. Where it has been replaced, a perspective emphasizing that there are no villains, only victims, has begun to enjoy some popularity in clinical literature and to a lesser degree in popular culture. There is, however, still a tendency to come back to the mother as the major provocation, if not the single cause, in the family's problems. This need to blame the mother and cast her in the role of the unloving and highly controlled bitch has certainly never left the mainstream consciousness of popular culture, as seen in the interpretation of the mother in the highly successful film *Ordinary People* (1980). No doubt this portrayal will continue to exist, along with more complex and clinically more accurate depictions of the mother-figure, as in such films as *A Woman under The Influence* (1974).

Cassavetes's film departs from the common depiction of the mother as a harpy or villain to a depiction of the mother as but one element in an arrangement of people caught in seemingly unchangeable and desperate ways of relating to others.

The choice of a lower middle class family for the central focus is a great departure from the usual Hollywood fare. Mabel (Gena Rowlands) and Nick (Peter Falk), her husband, represent the majority of Americans, whose unglamorous lives are seldom the topic of major feature films. Their home is quite typical of the ordered and indistinguishable homes that line the suburban sprawl of America, but their lives do not fit with the conventional notions of how families get along. Cassavetes shows us the subtle disappointments and binds that slowly begin to push Mabel into madness.

The film has been cited in clinical literature, with the emphasis that "the film's drama demonstrates that the complex interactions within the extended family victimizes all the participants.[22] Of principal interest are the multiple levels of communication, which, though occurring continuously, are never subject to metacommunicational analysis. The pernicious and destructive quality of this communication is emphasized as having no stopping and starting points but, like a self-feeding loop, perpetuates itself. This approach is consonant with the thinking of the system theorists who were writing in this period.[23] In this light the beginning and end of the film make perfect sense for they are just points along a continuing set of intersections. The fact that we are not given any background information but move directly into the couple's life at a random point in time would be seen as reasonable by proponents of the family approach. Bedrosian's commentary on the film in the *American Journal of Family Therapy* two years after its release, stated:

> The film does not provide information on the couple's past history, although we hypothesize that their previous interactions were similar. A more complete description of their relationship might encompass behaviors which occurred months, even years earlier, but even so, the attribution of causality would remain an arbitrary process.[24]

The films's emphasis comes to be a series of interactional sequences. Each of the characters triggers each other's next move, with the result that as Nick victimizes Mabel, Mabel victimizes Nick. The viewer is introduced to this process when Nick telephones Mabel from work to tell her that he will not be home because he and his crew have to fix a broken water main. We know that the crisis is real as we see the hip-high water and gushing break and are surprised at Mabel's reaction, which is to get drunk and barhop until she finds a man to bring home. Only on closer scrutiny do we begin to see the underlying communicational messages that make her nonsensical and aberrant behavior intelligible. Nick waited until the last moment to call Mabel though he had known that the break would require him to work most of the night. Though he is apologetic, there is an ambiguity about his sincerity. We are shown that Mabel has gone to great lengths to have the children taken care of and to put the house in order for the chance to be with her husband. The manner in which Nick presents his explanation for not coming home binds her into not being able to express her extreme disappointment. Her drunken sexual encounter may therefore be seen as a response to what Bedrosian called the "spiraling process of disengagement, provocation, and counterattack,"[25] which comprises the movement of the film from beginning to end. Throughout the film this process is aided by the continuous, abrupt movement of the camera from one figure to the other. This almost agitated motion parallels the anxiety of the characters, which continuously explodes, only to build again in an endless cycle of aggression directed toward both the self and others.

The film brings us into the subtly orchestrated dance of family relations, choreographed so that each spouse strikes and retreats with perfect timing. As with the husband-wife relationship in *Who's Afraid of Virginia Woolf?* (1966), the film goes on to add another dimension by including their children, parents, and friends. This intergenerational and network approach fits well with concerns that appeared in the clinical literature of the period. The children, parents, and friends form an interconnecting chain of action with Mabel and Nick and, from the viewpoint of family therapy, have to be included in any analysis.

The first appearance of Mabel's mother in the film, though brief, is telling. As she piles the kids into her car, she tells them—just loud enough for Mabel to hear—"Your mother's terribly nervous." We will see much of this kind of undermining of Mabel's competency. At one point, when Nick and Mabel are finally alone and about to have sex, her mother suddenly arrives with the kids. Mabel questions her bringing the children back with such calculated timing. Nick, however, symbolically supports the right of the mother to come between him and Mabel and deny them pleasure when he pulls the mother and the kids into bed with him and Mabel. Nick's mother is the most vocal in-law and the one most reflective of the "weak boundary around the spouse subsystem."[26] She is shown to be highly resentful of Mabel and is an important provocateur of Mabel's regression into madness. Like Mabel's mother, she is an important divisive figure in the marriage. She exerts an even more powerful destructive role in that she makes it continuously clear that her son should never have married Mabel. She does this by looking for every opportunity to make him aware of how poor a mother Mabel is. It becomes evident that Nick gives her information that feeds her derisions. For instance she says, ostensibly to the doctor who has come to institutionalize Mabel, but really to Mabel, "The stories my son tells me! Last night she brought a man into the house." The boundaries that usually separate a family system have clearly been corrupted, and the trust between Mabel and Nick has consequently been lost.

The parents clearly influence not only Nick and Mabel but their grandchildren. Nick's mother arrives at the perfect time to exacerbate the crisis between Nick and Mabel and the neighbor who has brought his little girl over to play. She finds Maria, the youngest child, running around naked and asks, "Who took your clothes off?" Maria answers falsely, but clearly with the answer her grandmother desires, "Mommy." As Bedrosian points out, "The inclusion of the children in triangular relationships with their elders undermines parenting and suggests that family problems will endure for at least another generation."[27]

The problems of the family are clearly connected to those around them as they too are drawn with seeming helplessness into the communicational morass. Cas-

savetes makes us see that, as people, they also find it difficult to metacommuni-
cate. This is shown at the dinner to which Nick invites his all-night coworkers. As
he tells them all to sit down, Mabel is clearly enraged with Nick for bringing all
these men home as a gambit for avoiding her and her disappointment. She once
again has difficulty in expressing her anger directly but does so symbolically
through gasps, facial grimaces, and seemingly unintelligible and half-completed
statements. Her difficulty, though much more exaggerated, is the same difficulty
that faces the multiracial group of her husband's coworkers, who cannot really
talk to one another about the tensions that run just below their strained convi-
viality.

The film emphasizes that whatever the individual problems of its central
characters, Mabel and Nick, it is their relationship that is the real key to understanding these problems. Such an understanding does not permit the viewer to
blame either of them individually but turns to a more ecological perspective.
This perspective is the result of a number of forces that came into dominance in
psychological research in the late 1960s and early 1970s in the form of family
therapy. Its reflection in the film is evident, as is the impact of the film on the
literature that followed it. As Bedrosian said:

> The description of a family system always requires the designation of artificial,
> somewhat arbitrary starting and stopping points. Although for convenience's
> sake, most family therapists seek to identify particular causal agents responsi-
> ble for psychopathology, human interactions are epigenetic phenomena as
> they entail a multiplicity of causes and developmental patterns. Similarly,
> when we view a family system, we see scapegoats, culprits, tyrants, and slaves,
> but we must bear in mind that the choice of who occupies these roles depends
> upon the available information, the temporal perspective, and the biases of the
> observers. In a dysfunctional family system all members are to some degree
> victim and victimizers. We have attempted to portray the members of the
> Longetti family in a manner consistent with such an ecological viewpoint.[28]

While the depiction of the family caught in such unending and desperate
isolation was the subject of many other films of the 1970s and 1980s, *A Woman
under the Influence* was one of the first American films to focus on process rather
than plot, as Cassavetes encouraged his actors to continuously improvise in order
to achieve the subtle interplay that binds a family into hopeless despair. Similar
comments could, of course, be made about Ingmar Bergman's *Scenes from a
Marriage* (1973). While this despair is certainly the major theme of subsequent
cinematic depictions of the family—two of the most notable of which are *Natural
Enemies* (1979) and *Interiors* (1979)—they do not seem to possess the spontaneity
and depth of *A Woman under the Influence.*

Each of these films clearly reflects period psychiatric views. Contrasting them
indicates how the social determinants have, over the years, come to occupy an
ever-increasing significance in popular and psychiatric explanations of madness.
While *Now, Voyager* seems romantic and guarded in its depiction of madness, it
must be remembered that there are some remarkable moments that anticipate
psychiatric thinking thirty years hence, e.g., Dr. Jackqueth's refusal to diagnose
his patient, a belief that was to receive great attention in R. D. Laing's work of the

1970s (see chapter 9). *A Woman under the Inflence,* however, shows much greater intensity and focus on what *Now, Voyager* only flirted with by innuendo. Cassavetes's creative use of the hand-held camera and close shot spirals the viewer up, through, and back into a network of family and social forces that trigger Mabel's psychotic break, a break far different from Charlotte Valle's genteel withdrawal. As we will find in so many contemporary films depicting mothers, there is no resolution or magical moment of cathartic cure. Existing in a shadow world of overwhelming and seemingly insolvable problems, and caught in a vicious circle of personal and social despair, Mabel and the antiheroes of other contemporary films depicting madness are seldom cured.

Institutionalization of the Mad

The concept of insanity is inextricably tied to the history of the institutions that care for the mad. Originally, it was the family unit, or the extended family of village society, that cared for the individual. In most cases, however, the mad were simply left to wander about the countryside seeking alms. When these individuals became a threat to themselves or others, they were put into jail. As societies have grown and become more complex, there has been a corresponding growth in the formal organizations required to govern them and ensure the social order of the community. With the formalization of such institutions the mad were increasingly seen as a threat to the normal functioning of society. Conceived in the Middle Ages, the mental hospital had become a fixed part of European society by the seventeenth century. This proliferation reflected the common belief that leprosy and madness should be treated in the same manner. Both were thought to be contagious illnesses which could be controlled only through confinement and isolation.[29]

Though set up to confine the mad, it is clear that these hospitals quickly became warehouses for a broad range of afflicted or unwanted individuals. Those who were social misfits, idlers, criminals, or simply unfortunates who had offended or had stood in the way of some influential person, were housed with the mad under terrible physical conditions. Herded together like animals, their stay was often brief, since death usually intervened to free them from their wretched existence. The dehumanization was exacerbated by visits from curiosity seekers, who paid to view them as they would view caged animals or attend other forms of spectator amusements.

Establishing the principle of egalitarianism, the French Revolution prophesied a new social order, in which all the oppressed would be freed. One believer in this doctrine was a young French physician by the name of Phillipe Pinel, who in 1792 freed the mad of Paris from their chains. In the same year William Tuke set up a retreat in the English countryside, where he and his fellow Quakers offered the afflicted humanitarian care. *Moral treatment,* as it was called, represented a sweeping reform, which by the nineteenth century had established a number of new treatment centers. Based on the principle of communal agrarian living, these centers had their patients work and play in natural settings and reintroduced them gradually to the world. In the United States Dorothea Dix introduced similar reforms. After spending some time in educational reform in Boston, she visited England. Here, she was influenced by Tuke's work, and when she returned to America, she devoted her life to psychiatric care. Rhode Island, where Dix took up her work, was like many other states in that it had no provision for the care of the mentally ill. Before Dix the fate of the mad was bleak: in Karl Menniger' words, "Justices of the Peace continued to commit to the county jails according to law, furiously mad persons dangerous to the peace and safety of the good people. Less violent people were confined at home, boarded out, or provided for in the local almshouse."[30] One center in the United States that adopted the reformist innovations was Worcester State Hospital. Between 1833 and 1846 this hospital reported a cure rate of sixty to seventy-five percent.[31]

For a number of reasons, not the least of which was economic, such centers began to be regarded as unscientific by the end of the nineteenth century. Large state hospitals were built, and influenced either by the use of moral treatment by contemporary farm communities or by the tradition of isolating the leprosariums during the Middle Ages—these state hospitals were all far from urban centers. Isolated from city medical services, these hillside fortresses were left to flounder, and little change was seen until the late 1940s and early 1950s, when renewed attention was given the inhuman conditions prevailing in such settings.

Within the psychiatric profession several factors brought about a major rethinking of the problems of institutionalization. First, psychoanalysis experienced a rehabilitation within the profession of psychiatry and began to be applied to hospitalized psychiatric patients.[32] Second, there was a renewed interest in the institutional environment. Maxwell Jones, a British psychiatrist versed in psychoanalytic theory, argued that the hospital should be established as a therapeutic community, where, similar to the principles of the early moral treatment, the whole staff—from the groundskeeper to the chief psychiatrist—serve as agent of therapy.[33] Finally, the discovery in the early 1950s of the so-called major tranquilizers, especially the phenothiazines, radically changed the care and management of hospitalized psychiatric patients. While these three factors dominated the psychiatric literature in the 1950s, the de-institutionalization of patients came to be the central focus of the 1960s. By the 1970s, however, the process of de-institutionalization was discussed in light of its political implications, and psychiatry came under attack not only from outsiders but from members of the profession. These people espoused a philosophy that became known as *antipsychiatry*.

The first film to be discussed, *The Snake Pit* (1948), was produced at a time when America first began to pay attention to the depravity of the state institutions. The second film, *One Flew over the Cuckoo's Nest* (1975), appeared when the political nature of institutionalization pervaded America's thinking about madness.

The Snake Pit. It is hard to believe that since the late 1800s the state of public psychiatric institutions had largely been ignored and that it was not until the late 1940s that they again became the subject of professional and public concern. The renewed attention was largely the result of the development of various neuropsychiatric disorders by veterans of World War II. A very real prospect existed that the already crowded institutions would have to admit record numbers. Though the care offered by such institutions was clearly limited, the general feeling was that the new age of scientific discovery would achieve a miraculous cure, as it had for so many other diseases. A quotation from a psychiatric article of this period conveyed this optimism:

> Tuberculosis, typhoid fever, small pox, pernicious anemia, and diabetes are only a few of the specific diseases that a few years ago were thought to be fatal, but which have been conquered by the application of intelligent scientific principles of prevention, intensive treatment, and follow-up care. Is it too much to expect in the light of the present trend, in reviewing results in the treatment of mental diseases, that they too may not capitulate to some extent at least to modern methods of attack upon the disease that have given favorable results in other types of illness?[34]

Psychiatry was regarded, as it still is, with a certain skepticism, and some people, while acknowledging the problems that had to be solved within the institution, felt that the public had too many false assumptions, based on erroneous reports of the press.[35]

Although in the 1940s the press did show some social concern, reporters who investigated social corruption and injustice were derided as muckrakers. One such writer was Albert Deutsch, the medicine and social welfare columnist of the *New York Star.* In 1948 Deutsch wrote a book entitled *Shame of the States,* which directed public attention to the neglect, overcrowding, and inadequate treatment that characterized state hospitals.[36] Deutsch observed state psychiatric facilities throughout the United States, and, though critical of all, he gave some of these facilities greater praise than others. One that he considered among the best was New York's Rockland State Hospital. Rockland in fact had received some earlier notoriety; it had been depicted in a popular novel of the late 1940s, *The Snake Pit,* by Mary Jane Ward.[37] The novel was a partly autobiographical account of a young woman's harrowing experiences in a state mental hospital.[38] (In both the novel and the movie version, released in December 1948, the hospital's name was changed to Juniper Hill.)

Up to the time of *Snake Pit,* Hollywood had taken some interest in madness but had done so primarily in terms of psychological thrillers. These often involved amnesia and presented a romanticized and schematic rendering of madness. As exotic versions of neurotic problems, most of these films gave little attention to the plight of those who were confined in psychiatric institutions. Hollywood became willing to shoot *Snake Pit* when Darryl Zanuck, the head of Tweuntieth-Century Fox, decided that the film should be made. He bought the film rights from an established director, Anatole Litvak, who in turn had bought them from Mary Jane Ward in 1945. Obviously greatly interested in the work, Litvak was made producer and director.

This was the period when successful movies were those that featured such stars as Grable or Gable and were shot in flamboyant Technicolor. Litvak and his associates, however, decided that their film would not follow such lines but would instead attempt an accurate rendering of the colorless world of the institutionalized. Litvak visited various state psychiatric institutions with his cast and technical staff.[39] Though he shot the film on a soundstage, not on location, he made a great effort to recreate the atmosphere found in the institutional ward. Even with these attempts at verisimilitude, it is interesting to note certain Hollywood style changes in the screenplay adaptation. In the novel Virginia Cunningham suffers from a psychiatric illness that is never defined and that never gets direct one-on-one treatment from a psychiatrist. The film changes this and in fact invokes the kind of Freudian detective work that film audiences expect. Through flashbacks we find that Virginia (Olivia de Havilland) has a strong oedipal attachment to her father, which has been further complicated by a distancing mother, whose pregnancy seemed to her a burden. Constantly reprimanded by her mother, Virginia moves closer and closer to her adoring father. The father is caught between the jealousy of his wife and the need of his daughter for his complete attention. The child, of course loses and, feeling rejected, symbolically throws to the floor the little soldier doll her father has given her and kicks its mangled body. Shortly thereafter the father dies, and, as we will come to understand, Virginia unconsciously associates her father's death with her angry wish for his destruction for favoring her mother over her. A later flashback in the film shows that the final cause of Virginia's nervous breakdown is the death of a suitor whom she has chosen because he resembles her father. While driving her to a dance, he asks her to marry him; panicking, she insists that he take her home immediately. As he turns for home, a passing truck suddenly loses control and rams the car, killing the young man. Virginia is unhurt physically but feels once again that she has been responsible for the "father's" death.

Virginia's recall of both these incidents is the result of the interventions of Dr. Kik, a psychoanalytically oriented psychiatrist who helps Virginia realize the origins of her fears, which in the film are labeled schizophrenia, a term never used in the book. Kik (played by the British actor, Leo Genn) is portrayed as a man who is married to the institutional care of the lost souls at Juniper Hill. Unlike the other staff psychiatrists, he believes in one-to-one treatment, and, though this treatment is never directly labeled psychoanalytic, he is constantly being shot in line with a small picture of Freud that hangs on the wall of his office. His treatment of Virginia, though highly humane, involves the use of electroconvulsive therapy, scopolamine, hydrotherapy, and restraints, all of which were very much in use in the late 1940s. In a psychiatric paper of 1949, J. E. Nicole pointed out

the modern tendency for placing a heavy emphasis on special treatments, especially such physical ones as drug convulsion, electro-shock, insulin coma, modified insulin therapy, prolonged narcosis and leucotomy.[40]

It should be remembered that the phenothiazines had not yet been developed, and the use of drugs was somewhat crude and experimental. One of the most graphic scenes involves Virginia's hydrotherapy. To contemporary viewers it might seem strange or even inhuman to place a person in a large tub, covered by a canvas blanket with only the head exposed, but even up to the early 1950s hydrotherapy was very much a preferred form of treatment for the regressed, "overactive" patient.[41] In the continuous tub bath the water was regulated to circulate at a temperature of ninety-three to ninety-six degrees Fahrenheit. As pointed out in an article written in 1948, "Continuous baths can aid the psychiatrist by providing all-important relaxation for the very tense neurotic patients, or patients on the borderline of a psychosis."[42] One finds constant mention of the sedative aspects of hydrotherapy, and the fact that it was not only more humane but much more effective than more active restraints like strait jackets.[43] The same was felt to be the case for the series of electroconvulsive shock treatments that Virginia endures.

Continuous use of such multiple forms of treatment during the 1940s reflected the belief that madness involves both a mind and body problem. As one commissioner of a state mental hygiene service said, "Not only general practitioners but the members of other specialties are becoming more and more aware of the very great importance of what has been called psychosomatic medicine."[44] This mind-body orientation is certainly evident in Kik's treatment, which involves multiple means to get Virginia to the point where she can look at the supposedly repressed and root causes of the illness.

The villains of the film are the institution and some of the power-hungry people who work in it. Because of the continuously increasing number of patients, the institution can barely function. In the words of one of the staff, "We don't have enough of anything, but patients." Overcrowding is stressed in the shots of patients sleeping in packed quarters or milling about in dayrooms with no activities. The implication is clearly made that because the patients have nothing to do, they turn to hallucinatory activities. This fits in with the call for therapeutic activities for the institutionalized in the psychiatric literature of the 1940s.[45] The only activity in the film is a dance, which brings together male and female hospitalized patients. Supervised by a stern and despotic male attendant, the inmates come together and dance joyfully. The bizarre and agitated forms of behavior that characterized earlier scenes are suddenly replaced by childlike sensitivity and helplessness. The feeling is intensified when one of the patients sings "Going Home." As the patients rock in time to the sad refrains of the song, there is a sense that they are homeless wayfarers who simply need a beacon to guide them. In the case of Virginia, this beacon has been the heroic Freudian knight, Dr. Kik.

While Kik is good, however, others are notably bad. Besides a number of seemingly indifferent nurses, the two most villainous members of the staff are Miss Davis and Dr. Curtis. Both enjoy exerting their power over others, and both subtly attack Virginia because of the special treatment she receives from Kik. Miss Davis is clearly jealous of Virginia, and when Virginia confronts her with this fact, the outcome is a muted rage, which triggers Virginia's regressing and results in her confinement to Ward 33, where the most primitive patients are housed. Here, she has the hallucination of being in a snake pit and says, "Long ago, people were put into snake pits so they would be shocked back into sanity as they had been shocked into madness." Dr. Curtis, a smug competitor to Dr. Kik, presses for Virginia's discharge from the hospital long before she is ready. He is unwilling to dedicate himself to his patients in the selfless way that Kik has done, and he is depicted as enjoying, in an almost sadistic manner, his control over others.

At the end of the film Kik explains to Virginia in a lecturelike fashion the reasons for the repressed fears that led her to schizophrenia. Taking the classical psychoanalytical position, he declares that from earliest infancy the child has oral feelings, which are tied to being helpless. At this point the film flashes back to a newborn child, squirming in swaddling. Kik then continues his explanation, which ends with the words, "You have learned that husbands and fathers can't be the same thing."

Though by adopting a simplified explanation it falls into the genre that it originally set out to surpass, *Snake Pit* was effective in presenting the forms of treatments and the institutional problems faced by state psychiatric hospitals in the 1940s. It revealed that problems come from overcrowding and the vicious attitudes of some staff and presented the treatments of electroconvulsive therapy and, particularly, psychotherapy as highly effective. The final message seems to be that the doctor knows best how to help the patient, and, despite overcrowding and an occasional sadist, the psychiatric hospital can provide a cure for the mentally ill.

One Flew over the Cuckoo's Nest. It is always difficult to determine the origins of any idea. As we mentioned in our introduction, the birth of an idea can never be traced to any one point in history or to any one person but appears to be the result of a process of accretion of previous ideas. What is falsely heralded as a new discovery is often an amalgam of older ideas.[46] The antipsychiatry and de-institutionalization movement likewise has its roots in countless thinkers who spoke and wrote about such concepts years before. Nevertheless, these ideas clearly enjoyed increasing popularity in the 1960s. For example, E. Goffman's 1961 essay "On the Characteristics of Total Institutions," which pointed out the roles that patients are induced to accept in institutional settings,[47] created an immediate stir in the psychiatric community. Thomas Szasz's *Myth of Mental Illness*, published in the same year, made him one of the best known psychiatrists in America.[48] Emphasizing the metaphorical nature of mental "disease," Szasz said:

> Starting with such things as syphilis, tuberculosis, typhoid fever, and carcinomas and fractures, we have created the class "illness." At first, this class was composed of only a few items, all of which shared the common feature of reference to a state of disordered structure or function of the human body as a physiochemical machine. As time went on, additional items were added to this class. They were not added, however, because they were newly discovered bodily disorders. The physician's attention had been deflected from this criterion and had become focused instead on disability and suffering as new criteria for selection. Thus, at first slowly, such things as hysteria, hypochondriasis, obsessive-compulsive neurosis, and depression were added to the category of illness. Then, with increasing zeal, physicians and especially psychiatrists be-

gan to call "illness" (that is, of course, "mental illness") anything and everything in which they could detect any sign of malfunctioning, based on no matter what norm. Hence, agoraphobia is illness because one should not be afraid of open space. Homosexuality is illness because heterosexuality is the social norm. Divorce is illness because it signals failure of marriage. Crime, art, undesired political leadership, participation in social affairs, or withdrawal from such participation—all these and many more have been said to be signs of mental illness.[49]

Psychiatry has always been attacked for its multiple and divergent theories and poor cure rate; the criticism of the 1960s provided a new twist. Psychiatry was said to be an institution that had become stagnant and disfunctional and a political force that determined the labels and treatment of those who were rule breakers. By the late 1960s this idea had found its best-known advocate in R. D. Laing, a Scottish psychiatrist who came to be heralded as the major proponent of anti-psychiatry. His writings were quickly adopted by the anti-establishment movement of the 1960s. This movement, dominated by youth, included Laing among a host of "gurus" (Timothy Leary, Baba Ram Dass, Maharaji) and authors (Norman O. Brown, Herbert Marcuse, Kurt Vonnegut, Ken Kesey), who became the evangelical seers of a new age.[50]

Throughout the 1960s Laing wrote and spoke, and many listened, particularly those who were confined in the institutions as patients. The definers and controllers of the mad were certainly not responsive to Laing's message, but the mounting pressures building up against established ways of running the institutions that held the mad were too great to be ignored. Though certain minimal changes began to take place within the institutions, the real impact of this movement lay in promoting alternative treatments and treatment centers, apart from the large, conventional psychiatric hospitals.

Laing's basic thesis was that madness is determined by its definition and that the definers are influenced by whatever norms contemporary society feels to be correct. From Laing's point of view, therefore, psychiatry is a political profession, used for the repression of individual differences. Laing presented psychiatry as a Kafkaesque system that treats the sane as insane and the insane as sane. Laing's admirers often quoted his story about a girl of seventeen who, while hospitalized, told him that she was terrified because she believed that an atom bomb was about to explode inside her. While admitting that she was experiencing a delusion, Laing emphasized that it is the heads of world government who in fact retain the bomb that can annihilate us all, and that they are the more dangerous and the more out of contact with reality. Laing's political concerns were interpreted in many different ways, and some associated his theories with the idea that madness is an enlightened state, a state next to godliness.[51]

In his controversial work *The Politics of Experience* (1967) Laing emphasized that the patient's experience of what is going on around him is the most important factor in establishing reality, and it is only a secondary importance for us to concern ourselves with the correspondence between the individual's ideas and whatever is commonly agreed to be the true order of things. Laing maintained that it is the beliefs of the schizophrenics that bring them into conflict with the social order in which they find themselves and that they are institutionalized as a result. "Madness need not be all breakdown," Laing pointed out, "it may also be breakthrough. It is potentially liberation and renewal as well as enslavement and existential death."[53] Laing therefore advised that instead of being institutionalized in prisonlike centers, the mad should be exposed to "an initiation ceremonial, through which the person will be guided with full social encouragement and sanction into inner space and time by people who have been there and back."[54]

Laing provided such an experience at Kingsley Hall, a treatment center he established in a suburb of London. Here, the distinctions between patient and therapist were discarded as a conspiratorial way of keeping people confused and in a helpless position. In Laing's democratic community patients were free to "journey" through the experience of madness, rather than be strapped in strait jackets and other restraints and injected with medications.[55]

Laing's writings emphasized that mental illness is often created by society through a process of conspiracy (a theme elaborated on in chapter 8.) Other writers of the 1960s believed that the very definition of the mentally ill as "patients" should be changed to that of "victims." This is seen in the book by Thomas Scheff, *Being Mentally Ill* (1966).[56] Scheff, a sociologist, believed that psychiatric symptoms are in fact "labeled violations of social norms" and popularized what came to be known as the labeling theory of madness.[57] In an excellent review of Scheff's work, Perruci pointed out:

> They are victims of situational contingencies such that in one case an act of rule breaking will be transformed into a psychiatric symptom, whereas in another case the very same act may be ignored or dealt with in other than a psychiatric framework. They are victims of their vulnerable status in society, which makes them less able to defend against more powerful family members or heavily credentialed experts whose job it is to pass judgement on the mental health of others. In addition, they are victims of their own humanness, which makes them responsive to the judgements of significant others whereby they take the views of others and internalize them as their own. In short, the social role of mental illness can be *created* by collective judgements imposed upon those who are socially vulnerable, and voluntarily adopted by persons as a defensive strategy. The end result is not a patient with a disease, but a victim of a socially constructed reality.[58]

The 1960s, when Laing's influence was at its height, saw the popularization of social psychiatry. Increasing emphasis was placed on environmental factors, and there was pressure to get institutionalized patients out of the state hospitals and back into the community. Up until 1975 the emphasis was on deinstitutionalization and the establishment of community-based treatment facilities, where the patients would not fall prey to the self-fulfilling prophecy that came with institutionalization. (The *self-fulfilling prophecy*, a major thesis of labeling theory, refers to the fact that people become what others expect them to be.) It was thought that individuals released from the hospital and brought back into the community from where they had originally come could be offered a range of services not possible in a large state institution. Community mental health centers were set up across America to provide the kind of care that would keep the patient from becoming a back ward "lifer." This "community" approach was in accordance with the political antipsychiatry movement to the extent that both reflected the feeling that the institutions for the mad are simply warehouses that offer little real help.

One major thesis of this group of thinkers is that psychiatric treatment should not be conducted without the agreement of those treated. This became a very controversial issue and is in fact still debated. By the mid-1970s the radical ideas of the antipsychiatry movement, which had threatened the establishment of psychiatry, were losing ground to more traditional views. Labeled the *abolitionist view*, antipsychiatry, while ostensibly defending the freedom of individuals, was criticised as being simplistic and detrimental to human needs. As Paul Chodoff pointed out:

> If efforts to enlist voluntary compliance with treatment failed, the abolitionist would not employ any means of coercion. Instead, they would step aside and allow social, legal, and community sanctions to take their course. If a human being should be jailed or a human life lost as a result of this attitude, they would accept it as a necessary evil to be tolerated in order to avoid the greater evil of unjustified loss of liberty for others.[59]

Antipsychiatry was considered to be an extreme position. As one psychiatrist put it, "Will we choose in the name of freedom to move from warehousing to abandonment?[60] Although de-institutionalization and the continuing sophistication of psychoactive drugs had dramatically decreased the patient population of large state hospitals, readmission rates were up, and the discharged patient was not receiving adequate care in the community. The great hopes of the 1960s for change were not being realized and by 1976 were widely considered to be irresponsible.

By the mid-1970s the strong critics of psychiatry from within the profession were receiving less attention, and an increasing number of studies pointed to the benefits of institutional care.[61]

Just as the swing back toward institutional care was gaining momentum, the film *One Flew over The Cuckoo's Nest* was released. The film was based on a book published in 1962 by the same title. Very popular during the 1960s and very reflective of the antipsychiatry movement, the book was followed by a highly popular theatrical production, which toured throughout the United States. Why did Hollywood take almost fifteen years to make a film version? Some have said that it was because of legal and financial difficulties, but one can't help but feel that some of this delay was linked to the studio executives' concern that the film's message was too controversial at the time.

Originally the rights to *Cuckoo's Nest* were owned by Kirk Douglas, who played in the Broadway theatrical production of 1963. In 1971, feeling "too old" for the lead role, he gave the work over to his son, Michael, who wanted to be the producer of the film version.[62] Though Kesey was called in to write the screenplay, his efforts were seen as "simply reinforcing problematic areas of his book."[63] After Kesey a number of other screenwriters came and went, until finally Lawrence Hauben, the senior writer, was superseded by Bo Goldman. One of the areas of greatest contention throughout all these changes was how much of Kesey's psychedelic motif was to be incorporated into the film. As Hauben said, "I created a warp and woof of time and space, like a trip in a nut house, using contrapuntal sound. Milos [Forman] didn't want any of that."[64]

To understand this, one need only go back to Kesey's original work, which has a psychedelic quality to its narrative. This, of course, was essential to Kesey, who had written parts of the book while on psychedelic "highs,"[65] and it certainly helped the novel become part of the drug-oriented counterculture of the 1960s. The novel is presented through the eyes of Chief Broom, a giant Indian who has received two hundred "treatments" of electroconvulsive therapy, or "electroshock." He pretends to be deaf and dumb but has a certain sensitivity, which emerges from his psychotic, metaphorical narration.[66] His account of the hospital in which he is placed revolves around the work of Nurse Ratched (Big Nurse), who runs the hospital for the Combine, the prime power center of society. Those who are in the hospital are sent there by the Combine because they are nonconformists. R. P. McMurphy comes into this hell and, through his actions, assumes a Christlike role, which ends with his dying so that his followers can be freed. At one point, when he is being strapped down to receive "shock therapy," he asks, "Do I get a crown of thorns?"[67]

The film version does not convey the Combine, psychedelic, or Christlike imagery, which so dominates the novel. Instead, it provides a subtle presentation of the problems of the ward, which is no longer just a symbol for the establishment. Said Pauline Kael, "As Jack Nicholson plays him, he [McMurphy] is no longer the Laingian Paul Bunyan of the ward, but he's still the charismatic misfit guerilla."[68] This is an excellent summary of the way in which the film accomodated the forces that were hostile to the Laingian thesis. The political nature of the Combine and McMurphy was substituted by what is in some way a simpler story of the great American hero, the Western gunfighter, who is always ready to take up a dare, even if it means giving up his life.[69] Whereas in the book McMurphy's actions allow his fellow patients to liberate themselves from their fear and to realize that they are sane, the film ducks these issues—the patients remain patients, except in the case of the Chief. The film version fits the view of psychiatry dominant in the mid-1970s, which, though it realized that institutions needed humanization, considered patients to be mad—they were no longer seen as individuals who were simply indulging in journeys of exploration toward self-realization and who were actually saner than the heads of state.

With regard to these "political" changes, it is interesting to note that the blatant misogynic position that dominated the novel was still evident in the film version. This was why a number of actresses (including Angela Lansbury and Anne Bancroft) turned down the offer of the female lead.

Only two references to the film are found in the psychiatric literature. One emphasized that both *Cuckoo's Nest* and *Snake Pit* have "convinced many laymen that state hospitals do no good and often harm patients".[70] The other, written from a very different perspective, said:

For those of us in the helping professions, whether therapists, ministers, teachers, counsellors, the film asks us to question seriously how we surrouond a nonfacilitating environment with our own expectations, demands, and "shoulds." The film asks us to question our particular school of thought, whether it be psychoanalysis, gestalt or what have you, and see if we are only communicating another set of expectations of our clients."[71]

Such differences in view point very much to the methodological problem to which we referred in the introductory chapter. As in any profession, there is no consensus of opinion in psychiatry. The fact that we rely solely on psychiatric literature further complicates our efforts, since the literature often makes very limited mention of the films that we have analyzed. Certainly, the first quotation, that of a director of residency training and clinical research in a large state hospital, would most likely appeal to other administrators of such hospitals, who are continuously having to deal with the patients and patients' families and induce them to see the institution as other than a snake pit or cuckoo's nest. The stigma fostered by these films is a real problem and can obviously lead to a reluctance to receive psychiatric care in people who might otherwise do so. This standpoint must be balanced with the position taken in the second quotation, which indicates the significance that a film like *Cuckoo's Nest* might have for the psychiatric profession. Clearly, it is a delicate balance, which will be seen as favorable or destructive for each individual according to his particular circumstances.

The contrast between these two films underscores the politicization of psychiatry over the last forty years. The paternal imagery of Dr. Kik and the waiflike quality of his charges singing "Going Home," has been replaced in *One Flew over the Cuckoo's Nest* by an inmate, McMurphy, whose incarceration has nothing to do with oedipal repressions. Far from it, he has an instinctual life that threatens the controllers of society, of which the psychiatric institution is now portrayed as being in the service. As already pointed out, however, by the time the film was released, the radical politicization of psychiatry had begun to weaken, and it has not since been, and probably will not be for some time, followed by a popular film that depicts psychiatric institutions as another of society's jails for rebels, dissidents, and all those who threaten the status quo.

Notes

1. G. N. Hale, *Freud and the Americans* (New York: Oxford University Press, 1971), p. 333.

2. Freud, *Lines of Advance in Psychoanalytic Therapy in Active Psychotherapy*, ed. H. Greenwald (New York: Jason Aronson, 1974), pp. 2–26.

3. Helen Swick Perry, "Preface and Introduction," in *Schizophrenia as a Human Process*, by Harry Stack Sullivan (New York: Norton Library, 1962).

4. Sullivan, *Schizophrenia as a Human Process*, pp. 246–309.

5. A Lief, *The Commonsense Psychiatry of Adolf Meyer* (New York: McGraw-Hill, 1948), p. vii.

6. G. N. Hale, "From Berggasse XIX to Central Park West: The Americanization of Psychoanalysis, 1919–1940," *Journal of the History of the Behavioral Sciences*, 14 (October 1978): 299–315.

7. M. Haskell, *From Reverence to Rape* (New York: Penguin Books, 1973).

8. Freida Fromm-Reichmann, *Principles of Intensive Psychotherapy* (Chicago: University of Chicago Press, 1950), p. 4.

9. S. Freud, "Femininity" in *New Introductory Lectures on Psychoanalysis,* trans. J. Strachey (New York: W. W. Norton, 1964), pp. 126–38.

10. Sullivan, *Schizophrenia as a Human Process.*

11. K. Horney, "The Overevaluation of Love, A Study of a Common Present Day Feminine Type," *Psychoanalytic Review* 28 (1941): 271.

12. Ibid.

13. E. Averswald, "Families, Change and Ecological Perspective," in *The Book of Family Therapy,* ed. Andrew Ferber (Boston: Houghton Mifflin, 1973).

14. R. Birdwhistell, "The American Family: Some Perspectives," *Psychiatry* 29 (1966): 203–12.

15. J. P. Geurin, ed., *Family Therapy: Theory and Practice* (New York: Wiley and Sons, 1976).

16. Nathan Ackerman, "Family Psychotherapy and Psychoanalysis: The Implications of Differences," in *Family Process,* ed. Nathan Ackerman (New York: Basic Books, 1970), p. 14.

17. A. Kendon, "How People Interact," in *The Book of Family Therapy,* ed. A. Ferber (Boston: Houghton Mifflin, 1973), pp. 354–58.

18. E. Goffman, *The Presentation of Self in Everyday Life* (New York: The Overlook Press, 1973).

19. Freida Fromm-Reichmann, "Notes on the Development of Treatment of Schizophrenics by Psychoanalytic Psychotherapy," *Psychiatry* 2 (1948): 263–73. See also Frances E. Cheek, "The 'Schizophrenogenic Mother' in Word and Deed," *Family Process* 3 (1964): 155–77.

20. G. Bateson, D. Jackson, J. Haley and J. Weakland, "Toward a Theory of Schizophrenia," *Behavioral Science* 1 (1956): 251–64.

21. David Olson, "Empirically Unbinding the Double Bind: Review of Research and Conception Reformations," *Family Process,* vol. 2, no. 1 (March 1972), 69.

22. Richard C. Bedrosian and Steven A. Kagel, *A Woman Under the Influence: An Example of Multiple Victimization Within a Family," The American Journal of Family Therapy,* vol. 7, no. 3 (1979), 51.

23. S. Minuchin, *Family and Family Therapy* (Cambridge: Harvard University Press, 1974). R. H. Rabkin, *Inner and Outer Spaces* (New York: Basic Books, 1973).

24. Bedrosian and Kagel, "A Woman Under the Influence," p. 52.

25. Ibid., p. 52.

26. Ibid., p. 57.

27. Ibid., p. 55.

28. Ibid., p. 58.

29. M. Foucault, *Madness and Civilization: A History of Insanity in the Age of Reason* (New York: Random House, 1965).

30. Karl Menninger, "The War Against Fear and Hate," *Rhode Island Medical School Journal* 27 (1944): 387, 391.

31. J. S. Bockoven, *Moral Treatment in American Psychiatry* (New York: Springer Publishing Company, 1963), pp. 55–68.

32. See Frieda Fromm-Reichmann, *Principles of Intensive Psychotherapy.*

33. *Maxwell Jones, The Therapeutic Community* (New York: Basic Books, 1953).

34. R. M. Fellows, "The Modern Mental Hospital and Its Place in the Life of the Community," *Diseases of the Nervous System* 5 (November 1944): 339.

35. J. W. Klapman, "Public Relations of the Mental Hospitals," *Mental Hygiene* 28 (1944): 381–86.

36. See Albert Deutsch, *Shame of the States* (New York: Harcourt Brace Javanovich, 1948).

37. Mary Jane Ward, *Snake Pit* (New York: Random House, 1946).

38. "Shocker," *Time* 52 (20 December 1948): 4.

39. Ibid.

40. J. E. Nicole, "Psychiatric Rehabilitation in Hospital [*sic*]," *Practitioner* 163 (1949): 533.

41. See, for example, "The Overactive Patient," *The Journal of Nursing* 47 (January–June 1947): 97–102.

42. P. A. Nelson and D. J. Erikson, "Hydrotherapy for Psychiatric Patients," *Medical Clinics of North America* 33 (1949): 1121.

43. See J. E. Davis, "Corrective Physical Rehabilitation for Neuropsychotic Patients," *Archives of Physical Medicine* 24 (June 1948). Veterans Administration, TB 10A–2, "Corrective Physical Rehabilitation in Neuropsychiatric Hospitals" (Washington, D.C.: September 1946). R. Wright, *Hydrotherapy in Psychiatric Hospitals* (Boston: The Tudor Press, 1940).

44. F. Tallman, "A state program of mental health," *Mental Hygiene,* vol. 32, no. 2 (1978), 271.

45. Nicole, "Psychiatric Rehabilitation in Hospital [*sic*]" *Practitioner* 163 (1949): 533.

46. See the arguments advanced by T. Kuhn, *Structure of Scientific Revolution* (Chicago: University of Chicago Press, 1970).

47. E. Goffman, "On the Characteristics of Total Institutions," *Asylums,* ed. E. Goffman (Garden City, N.Y.: Doubleday, 1961), pp. 1–24.

48. See Thomas Szasz, *The Myth of Mental Illness* (New York: Harper & Row, 1974).

49. Ibid., p. 44–45.

50. R. D. Laing and A. Esterson, *Sanity, Madness and the Family* (New York: Penguin Books, 1964); *The Divided Self* (New York: Penguin Books, 1965). Norman O. Brown, *Life Against Death: The Psychoanalytic Meaning of History* (Weslyan, Conn.: Wesleyan University Press, 1959); *Love's Body (New York: Random House, 1968). Herbert Marcuse, Essays on Liberation* (Boston: Beacon Press, 1969); *Counter-revolution and Revolt* (Boston: Beacon Press, 1972). Kurt Vonnegut, Jr., *Breakfast of Champions* (New York: Delacorte, 1973); *Cat's Cradle* (New York: Dell Publications, 1974); *God Bless You Mr. Rosewater* (New York: Dell Publications, 1974). Ken Kesey, *One Flew Over the Cuckoo's Nest* (New York: Viking Press, 1962).

51. R. D. Laing, in *R. D. Laing and Anti-Psychiatry*, ed. R. Boyers and R. Orrill (New York: Harper & Row, 1971), p. 211.

52. R. D. Laing, *The Politics of Experience* (New York: Ballatine Books, 1967).

53. Ibid., p. 93.

54. Ibid., p. 89.

55. M. Barnes and J. Berke, *Two Accounts of a Journey through Madness* (New York: Ballantine Books, 1973).

56. Thomas Scheff, *Being Mentally Ill* (Chicago: Aldine Publishing Co., 1966).

57. Ibid., p. 34

58. Robert Perruci, *Circle of Madness* (New Jersey: Spectrum, 1974), 17.

59. "The Case for Involuntary Hospitalization of the Mentally Ill," *American Journal of Psychiatry*, vol. 133, no. 5 (May 1976), 497.

60. A. A. Stone, "Overview: The Right to Treatment: Comments on the Law and Its Impact," *American Journal of Psychiatry*, vol. 132, no. 11 (November 1975), 1133.

61. J. E. Mayer and A. Rosenblatt, "Clash in Perspective Between Mental Patients and Staff," *American Journal of Orthopsychiatry*, vol. 44 (April 1974), pp. 432–41. R. D. Miller, "Beyond the Old State Hospital: New Opportunities Ahead," *Journal of Hospital and Community Psychiatry*, vol. 32, no. 1 (January 1981), 27–34.

62. Stanley Kauffmann, "'Arts and Lives' Jack High," *New Republic* 173 (13 December 1975): 22–23.

63. "'In the Picture' Cuckoo's Nest," *Sight and Sound*, vol. 44, no. 4 (Autumn 1975), 216.

64. Ibid.

65. Tom Wolfe, *The Electric Kool Aid Acid Test* (New York: Farrar, Straus and Giroux, 1968).

66. P. Kael, "The Bull Goose Loony," *New Yorker* (December 1975), 131.

67. G. Boyd, "Parables of Costly Grace, Flannery O'Connor and Ken Kesey," *Theology Today*, vol. 39, no. 2 (July 1972).

68. Kael, p. 132.

69. Stephen Farber, "Americana Sweet and Sour," *The Hudson Review*, vol. 29, no. 1 (Spring 1975), 95–102.

70. Miller, p. 64.

71. L. Myers and H. T. Kerr, "*One Flew Over the Cuckoo's Nest:* A Symbolic Review," *Theology Today*, vol. 23, no. 3 (October 1976), 287–88.

2
Possession as Madness

We have grown up with a belief that demons and demonic possession are nothing more than delusion. While considered folly by us, such ideas were accepted as reality by people before and during the Middle Ages. With the coming of the Renaissance and the scientific revolution (1500–1700) such "primitive" ideas were supposedly dispelled, never to be given any serious thought again. Science has advanced civilization to a new age of technology and rational understanding, yet however dominant our rational faculties seem to have become, we continue to be reminded that we are not so far from the notion of possession and the dark forces of the demonic as we would like to believe. In contemporary art, literature, clinical reports, and religious cults one finds the continued existence of such ideas. It is almost as if belief in the supernatural grows only with the growth of science. Films in particular have reflected our fascination with such issues, and the present chapter attempts to understand this phenomenon by looking at one theme that reappears over and over again with great box-office success—Possession as Madness.

While possession is often linked directly to the devil, it just as often involves takeover by a person who, while not the devil, is an evil, sinister force.[1] We will contrast two early films, *The Cabinet of Dr. Caligari* (1920) and *Dr. Jekyll and Mr. Hyde* (1931), with *The Exorcist* (1973). We will discuss them in terms of their depiction of a possessed individual, as well as with reference to the clinical literature of the period. The major focus will be the investigation of possession by psychiatry. We will at times go beyond the years surrounding the film to a general inquiry into the relationship between demonic possession, mesmerism, and Freud's work on hysteria. The continuity and exchange between these concepts throughout their evolution makes it clear that possession has been an underlying theme in both the popular and the clinical realms. Before studying the films, we would like to investigate this evolution.

Belief in possession is still very common in Western society—it certainly did not die with the Middle Ages. In fact demonology is more readily associated with a period long after the Middle Ages: the seventeenth century, with its massive witchhunts.[2] The church was, of course, heavily involved in establishing who was possessed and provided the treatment of such individuals through the ritual of exorcism.[3] Over time, exorcism steadily moved away from the punishment and

57

torture of the possessed individual to a more humanitarian treatment for ridding him of the demons thought to inhabit his body.

By the eighteenth century attempts were made to differentiate between real and imagined possessions, and various methods were developed for getting the devil to make himself known. Where demonic possession was found, two kinds were differentiated. The first was *somnambulistic possession,* in which the individual would suddenly lose consciousness and speak with the voice of the supposed intruder. In the second kind, *lucid possession,* the individual was constantly aware of a force trying to overtake him, and his struggles to prevent this from happening were destined to fail. According to Ellenberger, the basic tenets of exorcism may be seen as "a well-structured form of psychotherapy."[4] His description of the therapeutic aspects of exorcism has obvious parallels to current tenets of psychotherapy:

> The exorcist does not, ordinarily, speak in his own name, but in the name of a higher being. He must have absolute confidence in this higher being and in his own powers, as well as in the reality of the possession and of the possessing spirit. He addresses the intruder in a solemn way on behalf of the higher being whom he represents. He dispenses encouragement to the possessed individual and saves his threats and admonitions for the intruder. The exorcist's preparation for his task is long and difficult, often including prayer and fasting. The exorcism should, whenever possible, take place in a sacred spot, in a structured environment, and in the presence of witnesses, while at the same time avoiding crowds of the curious. The exorcist must induce the intruder to speak, and after lengthy discussions, a bargain may sometimes take place. Exorcism is a struggle between the exorcist and the intruding spirit—often a long, difficult, and desperate struggle that may continue for days, weeks, months, or even years before a complete victory can be achieved. Not infrequently does the exorcist meet with defeat; moreover, he is in danger himself of becoming infested with the very spirit he has just expelled from the patient.[5]

Treatment by means of exorcism became more complex over time and eventually began to be practiced by secular exorcists, who offered their services for a fee. With the proliferation of nonreligious exorcism, greater emphasis was placed on the power of the exorcist himself. One of the best known of the early treaters was Friedrich Anton Mesmer, who believed that a magnetic fluid permeated the whole universe, including the human body, and that it was an imbalance in this fluid that causes the symptoms that had once been singularly attributed to possession.

Playing upon the contemporary fascination with magnetic and electrical fields, Mesmer, calling himself a "magnetizer," claimed ability to bring these fields back to order in the "unbalanced" mind. In pointing to the similarity between exorcism and mesmerism, one modern scholar says, "The mesmeric relationship secularized the role relationship that existed between exorcist and demoniac (possessed person)."[6] In both instances the patient experienced convulsions, amnesia, demonstrations of increased intelligence, clairvoyance, and unusual feats, such as heightened sensory ability, all of which took place without the individual's conscious control. Mesmer eventually perfected his magnetizing to such a degree that he was able to treat a large number of people at a time. Wearing chiffon robes and blowing on a glass harmonica given to him by his friend Benjamin Franklin, he would move through the group of patients crowded around a tub of filings, called *baquet,* inducing in them states of hypnotic suggestibility. He would increase the intensity of both his music and movements while making exhortations on the curative effect of magnetism. Once he had brought the individuals to a state of extreme agitation, he would announce that their symptoms had vanished.[7]

Mesmer began to lose his power when the French Royal Commission, a group of scientists organized by the government, found his ideas on magnetism to be fraudulent.[8] The commission recognized that the influence of the mesmerist very much depended upon the impact of his suggestions on his subjects and encouraged further research. A student of Mesmer, the Marquis de Pusegur, observed that since the magnetized subjects would often enter a sleeplike state, mesmerism involved a process of "artificial somnambulism" (sleepwalking). The phenomenon of sleepwalking had long been associated with being taken over by a force that invaded one's body at night. Originally tied to spirits, witches, and devils, the term *somnambulist* came by the eighteenth century to stand for an individual who could be put into a sleeplike state and controlled by some other person. Somnambulism and mesmerism were therefore found to be one and the same and were eventually associated with the phenomenon of hypnotism. Either case involved the same two ideas. First, the subjects were able to move to a new level of consciousness. Second, they were reduced to powerless automatons, through which the other could act out his wishes—(This idea is more closely associated with somnambulism and mesmerism but is certainly evident even in the popular perception of hypnotism. By the mid-1800s hypnotism had become part of medical treatment of the mentally ill.[9]

Two of the best-known names from this period are Janet and Charcot, both of whom used hypnosis to cure hysteria. The symptoms of hysteria were found to be similar to those that the exorcist, mesmerist, and somnambulist treated, and "it became common among physicians of this period to interpret both the behavior of magnetized subjects and the historical occurrences of demonic possession as manifestations of hysteria."[10] Janet emphasized what he called *dissociation,* a term that reflected many of the earlier concepts of possession and mesmerism. Janet maintained that while thoughts and memories are normally coherent, integrated, and available to conscious awareness, they can sometimes be split off. In this abnormal state the individual does things for which he has no explanation. Though beyond conscious awareness, these separated thoughts still have power and can affect the actions and emotions of the person. Developing these and earlier ideas, Charcot said that the symptoms of magnetized subjects, as well as of those thought to be possessed, are simply manifestations of the disease of hysteria. As Spanos and Gottlieb point out:

> Many implicit conceptions of the hypnotic subject propagated by him and by most other 19th century investigators persisted as part of the general mythology of hypnosis well into the 20th century (e.g., the conception of the hypnotic subject as a helpless automaton). These notions, derived historically from

medieval and late medieval conceptions of the exorcist-demonic relationship, became an integral, often taken-for-granted part of 18th and 19th century conceptions of the mesmeric relationship and have persisted down to the present day as part of the popular public image of hypnosis.[11]

Charcot became the principal figure in reinterpreting the symptoms of possession in terms of the clinical model of hysteria. Both clinicians and lay people no longer spoke about possession but about hysteria, and in the late 1800s a great number of cases came to the attention of clinicians, most of whom were neurologists. One such neurologist was Sigmund Freud, who had just opened his own private practice in Vienna. Like most clinicians of his time, Freud was trained to look for organic causes for his patients' symptoms and was somewhat at a loss when he could not find any. Having encountered countless patients evidencing nonorganically derived symptoms of hysteria, Freud was pleased to hear about the work of Charcot in Paris, which was heralded as a major breakthrough in the treatment of such cases. In the late 1800s he went to study with Charcot and quickly adopted the Frenchman's use of hypnosis as a way of ridding the patient from the symptoms of hysteria. When he returned to Vienna, however, Freud found that this treatment was severely limited—the symptoms would return shortly after the hypnotic trance was removed—and he abandoned it.

What continued to fascinate Freud was the idea that there was another level of consciousness in which the individual said and did things that he was never able to remember in his waking, nonhypnotic state.[12] Freud called this the *unconscious* and felt that it held the key to explaining the true meaning of hysteria. Freud's use of hypnosis, though short-lived, allowed him a vehicle for initial exploration of the unconscious, and his findings paved the way for his theories of psychosexual development.[13]

Despite Freud's rejection of hypnosis, the technique has long held a place as an adjunct to psychoanalysis and other forms of psychodynamic therapy and behavioral interventions in the exploration and identification of the factors responsible for symptom formation.

With all of this in mind, let us turn to one of the earliest representations of the madness of possession, *The Cabinet of Dr. Caligari*. While we cover the political origins of the film in the appendix, we will discuss here the action of the film itself. Unlike the original story the film makes it seem as if all that had gone on was simply a dream. In the adding opening sequence, Francis, the protagonist, is telling another man a story. At the end of this story is a final scene that reveals that Francis; the somnambulist, Cesare; and Jane, the girl whom Francis has been trying to save from the somnambulist are inmates of an institution. As the three huddle together, a distinguished figure in the form of Dr. Caligari enters. He does not seem to be the malevolent figure who has guided Cesare but, rather, the benevolent head of the asylum in which Francis, Jane, and Cesare are patients.

While at first glance it might seem that Francis is simply a psychiatric inmate who has been having bizarre dreams, there is still a good deal of confusion about what is real or fantasy in the film. In his classic work *From Caligari to Hitler*

Siegfried Kracauer observed that the final scene involves the same kind of visual distortion that is evident in the first scene, where Francis begins to tell his story.[18] This raises the question of whether the final scene is also just a distortion and not reality. This confusion about whether people are who they appear to be is, of course, the central theme of the film and finds its most vivid expression in the control of the somnambulist Cesare by Dr. Caligari. The portrayal of Cesare as a robotlike somnambulist, who can easily be controlled (possessed) by the "doctor," corresponds to a popular belief still much in evidence today. Dominated at the time by the organic school of thought, psychiatry paid little attention to this relationship, dismissing it as a superstitious holdover from another age. Those who did take interest in it were linked to the French tradition of Charcot, Janet, and Bernheim, which evolved into the early psychoanalytic work of Breuer and Freud. The limits of the power of suggestion were, and still are, a controversial matter in psychiatry.

Cesare, when not carrying out the will of Caligari under the cover of night, remains in a coffinlike box. This image of an evil-possessed nightwalker is still popular, as is the idea that such a figure is inactive by day or even appears as someone else. These ideas are central in the next major film on possession, Mamoulian's version of *Dr. Jekyll and Mr. Hyde* (1931).[15] Appearing shortly after the introduction of sound-on-film, *Dr. Jekyll and Mr. Hyde* was recognized as a highly innovative work in that it introduced (1) voice over dialogue, which revealed the characters' thoughts, and (2) diagonally split screen in which characters in one shot indirectly interact with characters in another. Mamoulian used these to bring about a reinterpretation of Robert Louis Stevenson's classic. Unlike Stevenson, he emphasized that sexuality is a key factor in the motives for seeking transformation. A description of the opening scenes is helpful in establishing such motives.

Dr. Jekyll and Mr. Hyde. The horse-drawn carriage pulls up before the great hall and deposits its passenger, who is greeted warmly by the doorman. Not seeing the figure of Dr. Jekyll for the first several minutes of the film, but viewing the actions around him from his perspective, we are immediately drawn into an identification with him.[16] The huge auditorium door opens, and we find ourselves staring upward into the rows that line the medical amphitheater. The camera moves in on the older physicians in the front rows, and we overhear such comments as, "Jekyll is always sensational," and ". . . always indulging in spectacular theories." Suddenly, Jekyll is on the podium, reprimanding his peers for being "too parochial," afraid of moving toward the "unknown, the analysis of the soul, the human psyche."[17] In his early thirties Jekyll (Fredric March) is a very polished orator who preaches, rather than lectures, to his audience. When the camera looks up at him as he is discoursing on the soul-psyche from his pulpit, we feel a messianic intensity to his message:

My analysis of this soul, the human psyche, leads me to believe man is not truly one but truly two. One of him strives for the nobility. This we call the good self. The other self seeks an expression of impulses that bind him to some dim animal relation with the earth. This we may call bad. These two carry on an eternal struggle in the nature of man, yet they are chained together and that chain spells repression to the evil, remorse to the good. Now if these two selves could be separated from each other, how much freer the good in us would be. What heights it might scale, and the so-called evil, once liberated, would fulfill itself and trouble us no more. I believe the day is not far off when this separation will be possible.[18]

As Jekyll finishes, his face begins to fade into the crowd as students and senior physicians excitedly file out of the lecture hall. For a brief, almost subliminal, moment we see his receding face twist into a primitive aberration. The eyes darken and become sunken, the nose widens, the skin becomes darker, and the mouth twists into a hideous grin, revealing jagged, fang-like teeth. We quickly forget this as we join Jekyll with his older physician friend, Lanyon, who, though critical of the presentation ("You talk like a lunatic"), is underneath, quite fond of his younger colleague. He reminds Jekyll that he is expected for a consultation on the case of a wealthy duchess, and then for dinner with his fiancée. Jekyll says that he must tend a charity case rather than the duchess and that he will be late for the dinner engagement. He asks Lanyon to give his apologies to the hostess of the party, his fiancée, Muriel, and her father, General Carew.

Arriving late at the general's, Jekyll comes into the large baronial hall which is filled with elegant, dancing couples. Seeing Muriel, he rushes toward her, only to be interrupted by her father, to whom he must make apologies. Finally, the two lovers dance and sneak off to the garden, where Jekyll talks of his love for her and protests that he can wait no longer to marry her and will attempt to persuade her father to bring the date of their marriage forward. His efforts to persuade her father are of no avail—the stuffy general insists that this kind of thing "just isn't done." Jekyll answers impetuously that he cannot "regard that as a serious objection." Startled, the general turns to Lanyon and asks, "Is this another evidence of his eccentricity?" Realizing that he will get nowhere with General Carew, Dr. Jekyll bids everyone a goodnight and leaves with Lanyon. As they walk through London's befogged streets, Jekyll spurns his friend's recommendations to be more conciliatory toward General Carew, and, more important, to give up his "absurd experiments." Evoking his earlier speech to the medical society, Jekyll berates Lanyon for having no dreams, no curiosity. Lanyon says, prophetically, that there are bounds beyond which one should not go. Jekyll responds, "I tell you, there are no bounds." This conversation is interrupted by a street brawl, which, to Jekyll's dismay, involves the beating of a woman. Jekyll rushes forward and strikes the attacker, who flees. He bends over the victim, who by her appearance is a woman of the streets. She is the prostitute Ivy.

"Champagne!" she exclaims as Jekyll, after carrying her to her bedroom in a nearby house, revives her. The camera moves in on her legs as she seductively motions to her gentleman rescuer to inspect her injured knee. Her knee is perfectly alright, as are her ribs, about which she complains next. Both complaints allow her the excuse to take off her clothes, an action the camera discretely follows. She motions to Jekyll to bend down and kiss her, and as he does,

Dr. Jekyll and Mr. Hyde (USA, 1931). Director, Reuben Mamoulian. With *(left)* Fredric March. By permission of MGM–United Artists.

Lanyon abruptly comes into the room. Jekyll smilingly meets his friend's critical gaze as he moves toward the door. He looks around with a sensual, almost leering, smile after Ivy says for the second time: "You'll come back soon, won't you?" The image of her naked leg is superimposed on the two friends as they descend the stairs and only fades completely when Lanyon can hold his admonishment no longer and tells Jekyll angrily, "You ought to control those instincts." Jekyll responds, "We may control our actions, but not our impulses." Lanyon replies, "Why aren't you frank enough to admit that indecent self in you? No, you prefer to hide it. Pretend it isn't there. We have to accept certain things." At this point Jekyll emphatically says, "I don't want to accept them. I want to be clean, not only in my conduct but in my innermost thoughts and desires, and the only way to do it is to separate the two natures in us." Lanyon's only response is one of disgust, as he claims again that Jekyll is mad. "Mad, eh, Lanyon Oh, we'll see. We'll see," says Jekyll. His image fades and is replaced by his laboratory's test tubes and beakers, which herald the ominous transformation.

Frantically, Jekyll paces about the laboratory, mixing and adjusting, until he finally holds up a billowy, gaseous liquid. Looking into the mirror, he drinks the beaker's contents and suddenly clutches at his throat as his face starts to assume the grotesque appearance of which we had only a hint earlier. His face contracted with pain, he falls to the floor. The room starts to spin, and a series of dreamlike images appear: his plea to Muriel to marry him immediately as he can wait no longer, General Carew's caustic "positively indecent," Lanyon's "your conduct is disgusting," Ivy's "come back soon." We then return to the room and the mirror in which we had seen Jekyll's image. For a brief moment the mirror reflects only the contents of the room. Suddenly it is filled with a simian-like face, which shouts exaltingly, "Free!" His fanglike teeth, gloating, evil eyes, and apelike physiognomy overwhelm us as the bent figure runs with a loping movement around the laboratory. This is the birth of Hyde. Hyde leaves the laboratory by the back door and greets with glee the pouring rain, which beats down on him. Taking off his top hat, he sensuously lifts his face to receive the glistening drops. With his cape wrapped ghoulishly about him, he stalks off into the night.

What Mamoulian did was to bring to the screen a complex variation on the idea of possession—that of multiple personality. Where possession emphasizes takeover by a force outside the self, the concept of multiple personality presents the other force as a part of oneself. As Ellenberger pointed out, "The phenomenon of possession, so frequent for many centuries, could well be considered as one variety of multiple personality."[19] Up to 1910 a number of cases of multiple personality were reported in the psychiatric literature. From 1910 to the early 1930s there was a good deal of criticism of this phenomenon.[20] By the 1930s Freud's work on hysteria had begun to bring a broader acceptance in medical circles of the idea of dual personalities.[21] It is interesting that *Dr. Jekyll and Mr. Hyde* emphasizes the underlying sexual motives that came with Freud's work to dominate the dissociative explanation for multiple personality.

One of the first clinical studies of multiple personality was done by Morton Prince in 1904 on the celebrated Christine Beauchamp, who had four personalities. This case dominated clinical literature concerning multiple personality up until the case of Eve White, dramatized in the film *The Three Faces of Eve* (1957). Unlike the somnambulists, who do not remember what they do in their sleeplike state, Prince and subsequent researchers talked about coconscious personality dissociations as the basis for the ability to possess more than one personality. In coconscious dissociations one personality assumes a secondary role but nevertheless continues to function subconsciously and remains aware that another personality is functioning on the conscious, overt level. In the cases of both Christine Beauchamp and Eve White there were, along with the coconscious personality, alternating mutually amnesic personalities. This means that while one personality is aware of the others, the others are not aware of each other. Generally, these personalities are opposite from each other in actions, interests, desires, attitudes, wishes, and level of intelligence.

Prince's research was very important in that it described the functioning of multiple personality; it did not, however, attempt to explain it.[22] As we pointed out earlier, Freud's work on sexual repression as the basis for hysteria was gaining some popularity, though Freud never wrote on multiple personality as such, and multiple personality was by the early 1930s diagnosed as a form of hysteria. Freud, however, had written on the relationship between possession and hysteria.[23]

The dynamics of the repression in the dissociative hysterical processes of multiple personality involve isolating one's sexual ideas and emotions in a part of the self. Eventually, however, these ideas become totally separate and evolve into an independent personality of their own.[24] This sexual part of the psyche is what Jekyll is struggling with, and he tells us that this "so-called evil, once liberated, would fulfill itself and trouble us no more." He believes that the only way to deal with this "problem of sexuality" is to let it come out in a pure form. This, of course, involves a total transformation. It is interesting that the drastic physical transformation that Jekyll undergoes in the film was cited in a clinical description of a multiple personality patient experiencing the same process.[25] These physical changes were still given a great deal of attention in the literature of the early 1930s, when the film was made.

The psychoanalytic view, as elaborated by followers of Freud, emphasized the repression of infantile sexual wishes as the major cause for the sudden emergence of another self. This was most controversial as is evident in the work of Thigpen and Cleckley (1953–1957) where the authors vehemently attack such classical psychoanalytic concepts. Hollywood's interpretation of Thigpen and Cleckley's work, while also rejecting infantile sexual wishes, stressed early childhood trauma in the reductionistic manner that Thigpen and Cleckley had been critical of in their written work. The clinical treatment that was gaining the greatest attention emphasized hypnosis since it was felt that hypnosis was the only way to gain access to the various personalities. In the 1940s and 1950s increased attention was given to a method, based on learning theory, for inducing a hypnotic state. From the psychoanalytic emphasis on repressed sexuality as the basis for multiple personality, researchers turned to experimental learning theory for the answers.[27] A good example of this behavioral explanation was presented in the conditioning experiments that turned Laurence Harvey into a programmed killer in *The Manchurian Candidate* (1962).

Multiple personality, while not receiving much attention in clinical literature, has, of course, enjoyed great popularity in feature film. Corbett Thigpen and Harvey M. Cleckley's study on Eve White inspired the film *The Three Faces of Eve.* The introduction of the film by Alistair Cooke was an attempt to make the film a quasi-documentary of a clinical case study. Shortly after the film was produced, the theme of dissociation and multiple personality found a more dramatic representation in Hitchcock's *Psycho* (1960).[28] Anthony Perkins's transformation from a frightened, meek person into an aggressive knife-wielder brought a new twist to the depiction of the mad murderer. No longer would the movie screen's killers be simply depraved individuals. We were introduced to a new type of killer, a "psycho," who had multiple selves, one of which was pure evil.

It is interesting that the problem of multiple selves is not only a problem for Norman Bates. As we found in *The Cabinet of Dr. Caligari,* all the characters have a certain duplicity and mirroring of each other.[29] The resemblance of Vera Miles (Lila Crane) and Janet Leigh (Marion Crane) in *Psycho* can be explained by the fact that they are sisters, but that of Anthony Perkins (Norman Bates) and John Gavin (Sam Loomis) is not so easily dismissed. Hitchcock, from what is known about his painstaking attention to detail, was clearly making a point about the multiple selves with which we all struggle and the fact that at times they are violently separated, leaving us vulnerable to total possession by one. That each character has a double means that each could be considered to be part of the same self, half of which represents a darker, unacceptable aspect of the personality. This is certainly true of the two sisters, as Lila Crane has not committed adultery or stolen money and is presented as a virtuous person while her other half, her sister, is not. This is also the case with Norman Bates and Sam Loomis, who represent a clear separation between depraved murderous sexuality, on the one hand, and sexual control on the other. Hitchcock plays on this as he has Sam and Lila exchange looks and be mistaken as lovers, yet Sam is the perfect gentleman, in contrast to his double, Norman Bates. The link between the two darker selves of both characters is that they are sexual and evil and that they must be punished. For Marion Crane this means death; for Norman Bates, institutionalization in a padded cell.

From ideal citizen to mad killer, multiple personality transformation became a genre unto itself. Some of the most recent examples of this genre have occurred in a number of films. Examples are: *The Tenant, The Eyes of Laura Mars, Despair, Dressed to Kill,* and *Magic.*[30] After *Psycho* the next popular clinically treated case of multiple personality was *Sybil* (1973) and the subsequent television movie version (1976). In the seventies the theme of dissociation moved away from multiple personality back to its roots in possession. One of the foremost cinematic depictions of this is *The Exorcist* (1973).

The Exorcist. *The Exorcist* first appeared as a book by Peter Blatty. Following its release as a movie numerous reports of traumatic neuroses and psychoses similar to those portrayed in the film appeared.[31] Along with these reports were two full clinical case reports on the impact of the film as a trigger for emotional problems. The first reported on four patients who all sought psychiatric care after viewing *The Exorcist.*[32] They presented a range of symptoms, including insomnia, excitability, hyperactivity, irritability, and decreased appetite, and "moderate to severe disorganization."[32] The author views the film as a traumatic precipitant of the patients' problems and turns to a study on possession by Freud for an explanation of its dynamics.[34] Freud's clinical experiences led him to believe that trauma involves "an experience which within a short period of time presents the mind with an increase of stimulus too powerful to be dealt with or worked off in the usual way," and the result is disturbed personality functioning.[35] The conflicts experienced by all the patients were, in effect, triggered by the traumatic nature of the film, and, as Bozzuto said, "The common element in the movie that seemed threatening to all was the loss of impulse control to an ambivalently cathected person."[36] In other words all of us have ambivalent feelings towards people we love, and a film like *The Exorcist,* because of its "portrayal of uncontrollable forces within the person," can evoke in certain people an extreme fear that they, too, may experience and enact these feelings of hatred and destruction. The second major clinical case study focused on a person who, after seeing the film, suffered from "unremitting anxiety and a pervasive fear of being alone, especially at night, insisting that her husband be with her at all times and refusing to go to work."[37] In both cases the patient's symptoms disappeared after a short period of psychotherapy.

A more general study on the impact of the film was done by Heisler.[38] Heisler was interested in assessing the impact of the film on a general viewing audience and gathered together a heterogeneous group of fifty-nine subjects, thirty-five males and twenty-four female, ranging in age from fifteen to sixty-three and in education from grade eight to eighteen. Before and after viewing *The Exorcist,* the subjects took a battery of psychological tests, which assessed belief in mysticism, anxiety, guilt, hysteria, paranoia, and withdrawal behavior. Heisler found that some interesting changes did in fact take place. In general the subjects believed more in the possibility of mystical events and questioned more their power to change events in their own lives. Though they were more fearful of things they did not understand, the film did not increase their level of emotional disorder. This finding takes on an added dimension in light of the revelation that concern about bodily ailments and suspiciousness of the environment in fact decreased after seeing the film. Citing the work of Stampfl and Lewis,[39] Heisler tried to explain this paradoxical finding as follows:

In implosive therapy, the client is presented with immense anxiety in a situation he cannot avoid. Once subjects see the anxiety-laden stimuli do not produce aversive consequences, these stimuli become extinguished. The movie confronted its audiences with a child's body being tormented viciously by an ominous persecutor. Viewers were significantly more anxious immediately after the film, and this anxiety state was also experienced during it. The subjects may have been bombarded with immense anxiety-producing stimuli which may have imploded them and caused vicarious extinction.[40]

As if to remind us of the connection between possession and sexuality, Friedkin's devil is preoccupied with sex; this is made graphically evident in the scene where Regan masturbates with a crucifix.[41] But as we begin to adopt a psychological explanation, we are quickly presented with a number of scenes that contradict it.

Friedkin first encourages such an approach by presenting us with a psychiatrist who attempts to use hypnosis on Regan. This only results in disaster, as Regan bites this arrogant, omnipotent healer in the genitals. After this, Regan's mother turns to Father Karras, a priest, who is also a psychiatrist. Trained at Harvard, Bellevue, John's Hopkins, and "places like that," Karras is the ultimate figure to challenge the forces that have taken over Regan's body. He is also the perfect transitional figure for moving us out of a scientific approach to an acceptance of the supernatural. Psychiatry and medicine, of course, fail, and the only one who can help is the enigmatic and mystical Father Merrin. We are left with little belief in rationality, and any feeling that we might have had about how hard it must be to be both psychiatrist and priest is certainly exacerbated when Karras adopts a third identity by incorporating the devil into himself and jumping out the window to his death.

The popularity of the film does not perhaps so much affirm a sudden belief in the devil as it does a resurfacing of belief in possession, which was never, and most likely never will be, exorcised from consciousness. Possession involves not being ourselves, or, put another way, being other than the person we think we are, and as such becomes a major aspect of the phenomenon of madness.

From its early representation in a film like *Dr. Jekyll and Mr. Hyde* to the *Exorcist,* multiple personality has continued to fascinate the public. Though a number of clinical cases have been recently reported, the total number is still quite small. Those that have recently appeared usually find their way into the popular press and cinema. The public fascination with multiple personality is so strong that it is for many people the principal explanation for madness. The idea of possession—whether by another or by other selves within oneself—is a vivid representation of the fact that we all have a part or parts of ourselves that we find too objectionable to allow into consciousness. The erroneous common belief that multiple personality it a synonym for schizophrenia and madness itself points to the power of such feelings.

If we believe that film both reflects and molds popular ideologies, we can only deduce that a strong tendency exists to ascribe undesirable feelings to the supernatural. Multiple personality, or "split personality," becomes a way of dissociating from a part of the self that which is unacceptable, and all the films discussed present this self as sexually obsessed. Whether it be Dr. Jekyll's fascination with Ivy, Eve's trauma of the kiss, or a devilish pubescent child, sexuality rears its ugly head, and the only escape is through attributing responsibility for sexual thoughts to another.

Notes

1. See *The Innocents* (1963) for other worldly forces and *Whatever Happened to Baby Jane?* (1962) for a representation of a more worldly malevolence.

2. I. Kirsch, "Demonology and the Rise of Science," *Journal of the History of the Behavioral Sciences* 14 (1978): 149–57.

3. See Ken Russell's *The Devils* for a current portrayal of such issues and the influence of a post-Freudian view on its association with sexuality.

4. H. Ellenberger, *The Discovery of the Unconscious* (New York: Basic Books, 1970), p. 14.

5. Ibid.

6. See N. P. Spanos and T. Gottlieb, "Demonic Possession, Mesmerism, and Hysteria: A Social Psychological Perspective of Their Historical Interrelations," *Journal of Abnormal Psychology*, vol. 88, no. 5 (1979), 527.

7. Ellenberger, p. 64.

8. See A. Binet and C. Fere, *Animal Magnetism* (New York: Appleton, 1888).

9. James Braid, an English physician, witnessed a demonstration by the French magnetizer, LaFontaine, in 1841. Braid rejected the theory of magnetism, substituting one based on brain physiology. His use of the term *hypnotism* was more acceptable to the medical community.

10. Spanos and Gottlieb, p. 540.

11. Ibid.

12. See the movie, *Freud: The Secret Passion.*

13. J. F. Kihlstrom, "Hypnosis and Psychotherapy: Retrospect and Prospect," *Journal of Abnormal Psychology*, vol. 88, no. 5 (1979), 459–73.

14. See S. Kracauer, *From Caligari to Hitler: A Psychological History of the German Film* (Princeton, N.J.: Princeton University Press, 1947), pp. 60–70.

15. There have been many prominent versions of this story, including later adaptations with Spencer Tracy (1941) and Jack Palance (1968). Mamoulian's early sound film is by far the most impressive.

16. Unfortunately, with its marked use of the "subjective camera," the 16mm version in common circulation in America omits considerable footage from the opening sequence.

17. Rouben Mamoulian, *Dr. Jekyll and Mr. Hyde*, ed. R. Anobile (New York: Universe Books, 1975), p. 12.

18. Ibid.

19. Ellenberger, p. 127.

20. Ibid., p. 141.

21. Ibid., p. 145.

22. See M. Prince, *The Dissociation of a Personality* (London: Longmans Green and Company, 1930).

23. See S. Freud, "A 17th Century Demonological Neurosis," in *Collected Papers, 1923–1925*, ed. J. Strachey, vol. 19 (London: Hogarth Press, 1949), pp. 436–72.

24. These different selves are presented beautifully in Fellini's *Juliet of the Spirits* (1965) and in Altman's *Images* (1972).

25. See C. C. Wholey, "A Case of Multiple Personality," *American Journal of Psychiatry* 12 (January, 1933): 653–88. C. Thigpen and H. Cleckley, *The Three Faces of Eve* (New York: McGraw-Hill, 1957).

26. See C. Thigpen and H. Cleckley, "A Case of Multiple Personality," *Journal of Abnormal and Social Psychology* (1953), pp. 272–76.

27. See P. Harriman, "The Experimental Induction of Multiple Personality," *Psychiatry* (1942), pp. 179–186. T. X. Barber and S. C. Wilson, "Hypnosis, Suggestions and Altered States of Consciousness: Experimental Evaluation of the New Cognitive-Behavioral Theory and the Traditional Trance State Theory of Hypnosis," *Annuals of New York Academy of Science* (1977), pp. 34–47.

28. See P. Bogdonovich, *The Cinema of Alfred Hitchcock* (Garden City, N.Y.: Doubleday, 1963).

29. Three examples of such doubling appear in *Persona* (1960), *Images* (1972), and *Despair* (1976).

30. *Magic* is very similar in theme to *Dead of Night* (1945).

31. "Exorcist Fever," *Time*, vol. 103, no. 6 (1974), 53. "The Devil and Dr. Schlan," *Medical World News*, vol, 15, no. 7 (1974), 5. "*The Exorcist* Haunts M.D.'s at Georgetown," *American Medical News*, vol. 17, no. 9 (1974), 14.

32. See J. Bozzuto, "Cinematic Neurosis Following *The Exorcist*," *Journal of Nervous and Mental Disease*, vol. 161, no. 1 (1974), 43–48.

33. Ibid., p. 46.

34. S. Freud, "A 17th Century Demonological Neurosis," pp. 67–105.

35. S. Furst, *Psychic Trauma* (New York: Basic Books, 1967), p. 11.

36. Bozzuto, p. 47.

37. J. W. Hamilton, "Cinematic Neurosis: A Brief Case Report," *Journal of the Academy of Psychoanalysis*, vol. 6, no. 4 (1978), 569.

38. H. Heisler, "The Effect of Vicariously Experiencing Supernatural Violent Events: A case study of *The Exorcist*'s impact," *Journal of Individual Psychology* 31 (November 1975): 158–70.

39. L. T. Stampfl and D. Lewis, "Essentials of Implosive Therapy: A Learning Theory Based on Psychodynamic Behavioral Therapy," *Journal of Abnormal Psychology* 72 (1967): 496–503.

40. Heisler, p. 167.

41. Sex and possession were graphically portrayed in Ken Russell's *Devils* (1974).

3

Eros and Madness

The term *Eros* came to enjoy popularity in contemporary psychiatry through the work of Freud. Freud maintained that Eros was a life force, an instinct, to "preserve living substance," and that its key component was therefore sexuality.[1] As the ruling force of sexualty, Eros was the "pleasure principle," according to which individuals sought immediate gratification of their desires. For Freud sexuality involved more than just the genitals, it had to do with a wide range of behavioral and thought substitutes. In conflict with the life force of Eros was *Thanatos,* the "death instinct," which pushed toward destruction and an ultimate regression to a primeval, and eventually even to an inorganic, state. Thanatos expressed itself in three forms: (1) self-destructive, even suicidal, behavior, (2) aggression directed against others, and (3) a merging of aggression with sexuality—sadism or masochism.

Though Freud's early ideas on the mechanistic and biological roots of sadism and masochism have fallen into disfavor, his remarkable insights into the feelings and behavior that constitute these abnormal states are still highly valued. In the mid-1920s his ideas on sadism and masochism focused on the struggle between love and aggression. He commented, "Now, clinical observation shows not only that love is with unexpected regularity accompanied by hate (ambivalence), and not only that in human relationships hate is frequently a forerunner of love, but also that in a number of circumstances hate changes into love and love into hate."[2] It is this struggle and its various forms of resolution that occupies the central concern of this chapter.

The relationship between love and aggression is viewed along a continuum, and the present chapter focuses on the two extremes. The first section of the chapter investigates the struggle between love and aggression as depicted in two films, *Secrets of a Soul* (1926) and *Bad Timing: A Sensual Obsession* (1980). The emphasis is on the various forms of madness associated with the process of falling and being in love with another person. The second section of the chapter highlights that end of the continuum where the conflict between love and aggression has seemingly been given up for the love *of* aggression. At this point sexual pleasure is singularly derived from hurting or being hurt by another, and violence is thus the key component of the relationship. The two films discussed are *M* (1931) and *Straw Dogs* (1971). We conclude the second section by inves-

70

tigating the overwhelming number of films in the last three years that have focused on sex and violence against women.

The subject matter of the two sections is differentiated primarily by the focus of the conflict—the first emphasizes the struggle involved in the intimate relationships between men and women; the second, the displacement of this conflict onto virtually unknown victims. Another difference is the extent to which sexuality and aggression are in a state of tension. The first section centers on the struggle of these two forces, while the second involves the choice to move out of such a conflictual situation to a state where sexuality can only be expressed through violent aggression. The first section therefore presents a delicate balancing of primitive forces, which only rarely and momentarily erupt in overtly aberrant thoughts and acts, while the second section deals with the cessation of struggling with such tension in favor of a primitive immersion into sexual violence. In other words, the first section looks at the symbolic expression of aggression in sexuality, while the second deals with the symbolic expression of sexuality in aggression.

The Struggle between Love and Aggression

Hollywood has always found the portrayal of the male-female relationship to be a box-office success. The depiction of this relationship has gone through many evolutions; current depictions make it seem as if the image of Rogers and Astaire moving in perfect, synchronized step toward a happy ending existed only in antediluvian times. We want to remember the love affairs depicted on film from the 1920s to the 1940s as happy ones and tend to forget that at times the dancing stopped and the glamour gave way to the fears and pain that come with the vulnerability of intimacy. Portrayals of the struggle between love and aggression have obviously increased exponentially in the last twenty years, but by no means were they absent in the early days of films. This is perhaps best exemplified by the film *Secrets of a Soul* (1926).

Secrets of a Soul. *Secrets of a Soul* is fascinating for many reasons, but perhaps the most intriguing is that its portrayal of the relationship between love and aggression grew out of a direct collaboration between the film artists and psychoanalysts. It was the first film to deal explicitly with the "psychoanalytic conception of the mind, the causation of neurosis, and the psychoanalytic method of treatment."[3] These take form in the film's depiction of a seemingly happy marriage that slowly moves toward ruin when the husband is suddenly beset by an inexplicable fear that he will kill his beloved wife.

The film has an interesting history. After World War I, Germany underwent a period of intense intellectual and artistic productivity.[4] German cinema was a major force in introducing technological innovations to the studios, as well as daring story lines, which often focused on the social and psychological forces that shaped behavior. The director of *Secrets of a Soul,* G. W. Pabst, was part of the "new reality" *(Die Neue Sachlichkeit)*, promoted by the arts and was gaining a certain popularity within the broader cultural movement. In 1925 Pabst was asked by the largest German film company, Universum Film Aktiengesellschaft, to direct *Secrets of a Soul*. The script was the result of a collaboration between producer Hanns Neumann, writer Colin Ross, and two well-known members of Freud's inner circle, Karl Abraham and Hans Sachs. In his unpublished autobiography Pabst maintains that the film depicts one of Freud's cases though Freud's reaction to the film was negative from the very moment it was introduced to him by Abraham. Said Freud:

> I do not feel happy about your magnificent project. Your argument that if we do not do it, it will be done by others at first seemed irresistible. But then it struck me that what these people are willing to pay for is obviously the authorization. That they can get only from us. If they do something completely wild because we refuse, we cannot stop them and are not implicated. After all, we cannot stop anyone from making such a film without obtaining our consent.[5]

Freud's reluctance to get involved in the world of cinema began much earlier, when he had been approached by Samuel Goldwyn, the Hollywood producer, to collaborate on a film dealing with the epic love stories of history.[6] Freud was offered the staggering amount of a hundred thousand dollars, an amount equal on today's money market to approximately a million dollars. He unhesitatingly rejected the offer, as he felt that such a collaboration would only help to sensationalize the beliefs of psychoanalysis. Freud's objections to *Secrets of a Soul* were obviously complex, but chief among them was Hollywood's questionable ability to do justice to his ideas. "I do not believe" he said, "that satisfactory plastic representation of our abstractions is at all possible."[7] Nevertheless, Abraham and Sachs continued to work on the film. In time the project met with even more criticism from Freud and contributed to his falling out with Abraham. Though Abraham died a year before the film's completion, Sachs continued to collaborate. Upon the film's release he prepared a short descriptive guide, which provided the viewer with an explanation of relevant psychoanalytic concepts. The film depicted phobic and compulsive behavior which centered on the use of knives. This kind of behavior was seen as an attempt by the psyche to escape from an unacceptable thought. In the case of the protagonist, Dr. Fellman, this thought is to kill his wife by cutting her throat. Why Fellman has such murderous desires towards his wife is revealed to us by means of flashbacks and dream sequences.

It is important to remember that Freud viewed sadism and masochism in the context of a bisexual organization, according to which men are more likely to assume a sadistic posture and women a masochistic one. The basis for these aberrations was seen as biological—each of Freud's psychosexual stages (oral, anal, phallic), for example, has a component of sadism. The key element in all Freud's cases involved the oedipal conflict, which began in the phallic stage. We quickly learn that the couple sleep in separate rooms and have no children. The film makes this very clear, as well as the fact that Dr. Fellman is very much a mother's boy. Psychoanalytic thought emphasizes that "the patient's impotence, and the related absence of children, are necessary in view of the fact that a child would represent the fulfillment of a forbidden oedipal wish."[8]

The Freudian equation which has the wife acting as a substitute mother is therefore complete, and with it goes the sadistic phallic desires and consequent fears. All of these are repressed and find their symptomatic expression in Fellman's impotence. But the repression of these sadistic phallic forces is not so easily subverted into a single physical symptom like impotence. Because the defensive forces of repression are quite fragile, the inner instinctual forces of the id make themselves known through both physical and psychological symptoms. From Freud's perspective it is never a question of whether such symptoms are in evidence but, rather, how many and how virulent they were. Fellman's defenses are first put under attack in the opening shot of the film, in which he hears somebody screaming that there has been a murder. This happens at the same time that he is shaving the nape of his wife's neck for her, and his murderous wishes slowly rise to consciousness. They are given further impetus when his wife announces that her cousin Dick, who has always been Fellman's arch-rival, will be arriving shortly after a prolonged period abroad. Dick's impending visit becomes for Fellman the final precipitant for a fully developed obsessional compulsive neurosis concerning knives. Beneath this conscious fear of knives lies the unconscious wish to kill both his wife and her cousin. As Freud made clear in his classic work *The Interpretation of Dreams* (1900), such conflict quickly finds expression in dreams.[9] Fellman's dreams reveal the antagonism he feels towards Dick and his sense of powerlessness to prevent this rival from taking his wife from him. The roots of this problem are revealed in the final dream sequence, in which Fellman, his wife, and Dick are standing together as children to have their picture taken. His wife takes away a doll he is holding and gives it seductively to her cousin. Fellman is obviously heartbroken and enraged but can do nothing. This trauma, revealed by the dream, finally unlocks the underlying conflict of murderous feelings, which have driven Fellman to his current state of acute anxiety.

The filmmakers' choice to depict the conflict between love and hate seems more than just a random one when we realize the subject's importance in the psychoanalytic literature of the period (1923–25). Of course, much of this literature depended on earlier formulations, and it is important to reflect for a moment on those especially relevant to the relationship between love, hate, and aggression.

Freud published some of his thoughts on impotence in 1910. Impotence, he said, comes from a split between affectionate and sensual feelings.[10] The impotent man equates sex with primitive and bestial characteristics and therefore cannot give it expression with the woman he loves and to whom he attributes lofty qualities. This dichotomization has its origin in an infantile fixation of tender feelings toward the mother. The impotent man equates his beloved symbolically with his mother. By 1923 Freud was giving these ideas a great deal of attention. He emphasized its particular expressions in symptomatology. The oedipal feelings associated with impotence are, of course, totally unacceptable to the superego, that part of the psyche representing internalization of parental conscience and societal rules. The formation of symptoms represents a way around the superego's censoring functions. However painful, it protects the individual against conscious awareness of the taboo thoughts while allowing them symbolic expression.

In the period 1923–25 the superego and its censoring functions received increasing attention, particularly in terms of the role they play in obsessive-compulsive neurosis. (*Obsessions* refer to thoughts while *compulsions* refer to the accompanying behavior.) The obsession is the symbolic substitute for an unacceptable thought, while the compulsion is ritualized behavior through which the individual unconsciously attempts to undo the taboo thought. Dr. Fellman attempts to undo his murderous thoughts towards his wife by compulsive behavior that makes him avoid coming into contact with knives or sharp objects of any kind. Freud wrote, "In obsessional neurosis it has become possible, through a regression to the pregenital organization, for the love impulses to transform themselves into impulses of aggression against the object."[11]

Feelings of aggression and hate, which Freud believed are always components of love, are therefore given expression and emerge in the form of sadistic and masochistic thoughts and behavior. As these begin to gain more conscious expression, the individual increasingly resists them. Dreams are one area where such thoughts first break through. On the murderous and sadistic contents of dreams, Freud said, "The dreamer reacts to many of these dreams by waking up in a fright, in which case the situation is no longer obscure to us."[12] Certainly, this is the case in Fellman's first dream, in which he slashes with a large scimitar at the phantasmagoric form of his wife, who mockingly taunts his impotence. This is the last of a series of images dealing with his helplessness against the all-powerful cousin, and he awakens from his nightmare screaming. As his waking hours become increasingly like his nightmares, he is forced to run to the only haven he knows, his mother.

The move from his home is encouraged by a psychoanalyst from whom he has sought help. The contact with the analyst has come about as a result of Fellman's unconsciously leaving his key on a restaurant table. Having gone to the restaurant to escape the anxiety of being near the table knives at the welcoming dinner for Dick, he sits in an agitated and pensive state, dejectedly fingering his house key. At the next table an elderly, distinguished-looking man views his actions closely. Interpreting Fellman's forgetfulness concerning his key as a sign that he does not want to return home, the man follows him home and introduces himself as Dr. Orth. As Fellman's anxieties intensify, he seeks out the doctor, who has left his card with him. On the analytic couch Fellman begins to relate his concerns. After a number of sessions he relates a dream dealing with his childhood memories of rejection. Its disclosure of an early oedipal triangle between himself, Dick, and his wife brings with it an intense emotional reaction. He jumps off the couch and, grabbing a letter opener from Dr. Orth's desk, slashes out violently against the imagined forces that attacked him. When Orth comments on his action, the patient looks with utter disbelief at the heretofore untouchable knife in his hand. This is a moment of abreaction, a sudden emotional purgation that has come about through a sudden breakthrough of a deeply repressed

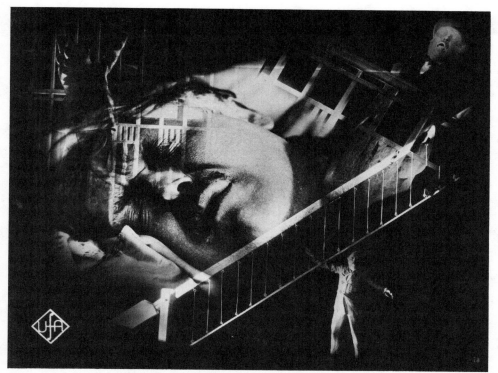

Secrets of a Soul (Germany, 1926). Director, G. W. Pabst. With Werner Krauss. Roger Manuell Collection, Photographic Archive, University of Louisville, Kentucky.

trauma. Fellman is now not only free from his obsessive-compulsive symptoms but is able to return to his wife as a fully potent man.

By current standards this quick cure through abreaction seems overly simplistic, though it was in the early days of psychoanalysis viewed as a necessary step for successful treatment. In one of his earliest works, *Studies on Hysteria* Freud, collaborating with Breuer, reported a number of cases in which the sudden breakthrough of the repressed emotional and ideational components of a sexual trauma brought sudden relief from the hated, but unconsciously protective, symptom.[13] For a brief period such a release was seen as the goal of treatment, and it was only over time that Freud became critical of such cures. Certainly, the depiction of the patient's sudden cessation of his problem through such a release would be viewed today as unlikely and simplistic. The purist of the psychoanalytic school sees no substitute for a complete analysis, which seldom brings a total relief from symptoms and the promise of a fulfilled and generative life. Today's classically oriented psychoanalytic school, invoking fitting passages from the master's work, presents a much more tempered, even fatalistic, perspective, which revolves around the trade of neurotic symptoms for the misery of everyday life.

At a recent screening *Secrets of a Soul* received a guarded positive reaction from the American Psychoanalytical Association. Summarizing the association's feeling, two reviewers wrote, "The results are far from successful when compared to real life, but far more accurate than the portrayal offered by most contemporary films."[14] They went on to say, "The film for the most part stands as a representative document of the psychoanalytic views of the day."[15] We know that the film enjoyed popular success upon its release in Berlin in 1926 and went on to have similar success in America. The reaction to the film by the European psychoanalytic community was also enthusiastic. In fact it was shown by Sachs at the psychoanalytic congress held to honor Freud's seventieth birthday and drew positive responses.

Bad Timing: A Sensual Obsession. When we follow depictions of the madness of love in film over a period of time, we witness an interesting evolution. Up until the early 1960s the madness emanating from a love relationship between a man and a woman tended to be portrayed as involving just one of the partners, as in such films as *The Blue Angel* (1930), *Pandora's Box* (1928), *Gaslight* (1940), *Sunset Boulevard* (1950), and *El* (1952). One of them was mentally imbalanced and inflicted his/her problems on his/her partner. The emphasis was on a one-way perspective, in which the conflict of loving and hating lay singularly within one partner. The usual scenario involved two forms. The first had the mad person helped either by his/her spouse or by an outsider, so that the imbalanced partner was brought back to his/her senses, and the relationship was reaffirmed. The second had the individual become increasingly confused and destructive to himself/herself or others until the partner's only alternative was to escape, and his/her mad pursuer met with the fate of death or institutionalization.

Though the older kind of portrayal continued to appear occasionally, as in *Juliet of the Spirits* or *Adèle H,*[16] a new trend emerged in the 1960s. The emphasis on insanity in only one of the partners was replaced by emphasis on a more interactional conception. Both partners came to be seen as contributing to the problem. They come together by more than just chance and chose each other not only for each other's strengths but sometimes in spite of them, as each is attracted primarily to the other's weaknesses.

The older notions of romantic love, which had relationships form from purely constructive factors, were replaced by those including destructive factors as well. Partners began to be depicted as slowly pushing each other toward the arenas of conflict in love and aggression. The ideal of perfect mutuality was drawn back to reveal the kind of aggression, fears, and deceits that drive relationships to an end. "No one is to blame" became a major theme as the agonies and anxieties of intimacy were revealed.

With this revelation came a change in the depiction of what really constitutes being "madly in love." The struggle between love and hate, which formed the nucleus in *Secrets of a Soul,* had formerly been presented as taking clear and exaggerated forms, such as obsessive thoughts and phobias. With the 1960s such clear distinctions were obscured by the muddled processes in which two people act out their conflicts with each other in symbolic and insidiously destructive behavior. The madness of love was no longer extreme and the exaggerated but, rather, the everyday—rageful parries and defenses of people's flailing embraces and panicky flights from each other. Those caught in such destructive unions were no longer presented as outsiders or the pariahs of society but as people of means and manners, whom others usually continue to see as totally functional.

Concerning such relationships another major theme was the interdependence between the partners. The theme of interdependence proved increasingly important in the depiction of the relationship between love and aggression. It focused on the extremes such conflicts can reach—the point of symbolic or literal destruction of each partner by the other. Examples are found in such films as *Women in Love* (1969), *Last Tango in Paris* (1972), *Who's Afraid of Virginia Woolf?* (1966), *Looking for Mr. Goodbar* (1977), *A Woman under the Influence* (1974), and most recently, Nicholas Roeg's *Bad Timing: A Sensual Obsession.*

Though perhaps not as notorious as other filmmakers, Roeg is considered a critical force in contemporary cinema. His most successful films—*Performance* (1970), *Walkabout* (1971), *Don't Look Now* (1973), and *The Man Who Fell to Earth* (1976) have received acclaim from major critics, and he has developed a devoted following, particularly among late adolescents and young adults, who are drawn to his cryptic and symbolic imagery. He delights in using cinema to present a Borgesian play on reality, with the intention of showing us that things are not as they appear to be. This is certainly the case in *Bad Timing,* which begins with its ending.

Roeg's story is, as Billie Holiday's song "The Same Old Story" puts it at the end of the film, "The same old story of a boy and girl in love, / The same old June night, / It's worth telling just once more." Roeg's retelling is not, however, what we might expect from such a lilting refrain, but involves, rather, the agony and despair of what has come to be, both cinematically and clinically, an integral component of the depiction of the madness of love. The love portrayed in his film is composed of the fantasied projections of two people, who, as they move further into intimacy, also become increasingly both dependent and destructive toward each other.

In contrast to earlier depictions, where lovers were, if not chronologically adults, certainly moving toward the world of adult commitments, the central characters of *Bad Timing* are immobilized and unwilling to move out of the middle space between childhood impulsiveness and adult responsibility. Dr. Alex Linden (Art Garfunkel) seems at first to be a responsibile person—as a research psychoanalyst with a university appointment in Vienna, he lectures students, has meetings with older colleagues, and even enjoys top secret clearance as a psychiatric evaluator for American Army Intelligence. Yet beyond his appearance of responsible commitment lies a subtly expressed, impulsive, manipulative, angry, and paranoid personality who cannot tolerate being alone. It is not surprising that he is attracted to a woman, Melina, who is just as needy and intolerant of being alone. She is exaggerated in her emotionality, masochistically manipulative—particularly through suicidal actions—and cannot seem to achieve any sense of competency, though she is clearly talented. They are made to torture each other, and in fact this is what the film is about. Not knowing how they present themselves in society, one could mistakenly infer from their clinical descriptions that Alex and Melina are two highly primitive and barely functioning individuals. The beauty of Roeg's presentation is that the true personalities of his characters come to be truly known only by us, the viewers, while the people of their world continue to know them as fully functional, competent, and attractive individuals.

Melina first encounters Dr. Linden at a party, where she seductively approaches him and bars his exit from the room by raising her leg and fixing it across his path. Seemingly helpless, he finally gets past her by kneeling and crawling under her outstretched leg. His passivity, however, is not as indicative of utter helplessness as we might first have thought. He subtly begins to draw Melina into needing him in the same masochistic manner that he initially demonstrated toward her. Melina, while seeming to be the bitch-enchantress at the beginning of the film, is slowly revealed to be a young woman who, having no real vocation or avocation, is totally dependent upon the sensual highs of drugs and sex. Her identity is at best a fragile one, which she seeks to protect by escaping from any commitment. Both she and Alex seem to function well at beginnings but cannot seem to sustain any intimacy beyond the opening night moves of pursuer and pursued. Both fear intimacy as a closeness in which one risks losing oneself and being absorbed by another, but each has a different defensive pattern for preventing such a terrifying occurrence. Alex's way of assuring his remaining in control is to move steadily towards and utterly dominate the other. Melina, on the other hand, calls attention to herself through sexual displays. She makes herself continually sought after—thereby maintaining her sense of worth—but never allows herself to be captured. Her greatest fear is that once she is in a permanent relationship, such as marriage, she will be suffocated by the boundaries that come with commitment.

This underlying fear of being absorbed and merging into the other is symbolically portrayed in *The Kiss,* a painting by Gustave Klimt, which dominates the opening shots of the film. Klimt's use of mosaic flecks of paint adds to the grotesquely haunting quality of the painting, which depicts two misshapen and emaciated lovers enveloping, almost devouring, each other. Melina comments that the figures seem to be very much in love, and Alex responds, "Wait until they get to know each other better." His prophecy will be realized in the relationship that he and Melina are just beginning. The struggle between them seemingly reaches its end with Alex's rape of Melina as she, having overdosed herself on barbiturates, lies in a semicomatose state. The story does not simply end with her recovery but with a fleeting chance encounter between the two sometime later in New York City. As Alex's cab races into the traffic, he presses his face against the rear window, straining to catch sight of his adored but hated Melina.

Such a depiction of the struggle between love and aggression is mirrored in the clinical literature on the *borderline personality.* The diagnosis of borderline has become very popular since the late 1970s. One of the key components of such a diagnosis is the patient's characteristic difficulties in intimate relationships. Some of these characteristics are very much like those underlying Melina's and Alex's symbiotic fusion. The literature on the borderline began to take concrete form in the 1960s, when the clinical community began to consider *object relations theory.* In contrast to the classical psychoanalytic theories, which focused on the individual's internal psychic struggles, object relations theory emphasizes the relationships between people and attempts to understand them by examining the internal image that each person has of the other.[17] The borderline personality is one who, having a rigidly fixed and stereotyped image of the other is not open to an appreciation of the other beyond an imposed projection of his own needs. The origin of such a distortion lies in the individual's earliest separation of the image of himself from that of his mother.

Mahler, one of the most seminal researchers and theoreticians of this process, proposed a developmental basis for understanding it. These can best be summarized in terms of the borderline personality's failure to complete three steps necessary for normal development. These are: (1) self and object differentiation, (2) the consolidation of loving and hating images and the ability to achieve object constancy, and (3) the integration of these images into "flexible psychic structure, for example, superego and ego ideal."[18] The first step involves the individual's separation from the original symbiotic fusion with the mother, and forms the basis for his ability to differentiate where he or she stops and others begin, particularly in intimate relationships. Failure to achieve such a separation would be reflected, in one's inability to love someone for what he or she is, as opposed to what one believes or wishes the other to be. The borderline individual seems to perceive the other as an extension of himself or herself, which has somehow been separated and which must be reconnected. As depicted in *Bad Timing*, the borderline's involvement with another is characterized by an intensity, which reaches life-and-death proportions as the sufferer is threatened with a loss of part of the self. The need to fuse and merge with the adored but elusive mother is depicted in the scene in which Alex has intercourse with the semicomatose Melina, who has chosen to kill herself because she cannot have Alex.

Both Alex and Melina cannot seem to exist with or without each other, a theme that relates to the second problem for the borderline personality—the difficulty with integrating both love and hate images of the same person. This is, of course, the basic thesis of this section of the chapter and was a basic issue in early psychoanalytic theory. Object relations theory discusses this conflict in terms of the individual's failure to consolidate the images of the mother as both gratifier and denier of pleasure and his adopting the defense of *splitting*. According to Kernberg, the borderline splits internally loving and aggressive feelings and fantasies in order to protect himself from being overwhelmed by the anxiety that would result if both feelings were allowed to come together in a relationship.[19] From the borderline's perspective a relationship is therefore either one that is completely gratifying or one that is completely frustrating and draining. As Shapiro pointed out, "When frustrated, the patient elaborates negative fantasies and loses all memory of the positive relationship."[20]

The inability to tolerate both loving and aggressive images of the same person leads to failure to attain *object constancy*, or the maintenance of the caring image of the mother and her symbolic representation in later life, even though she is physically absent. Difficulty with this is certainly evident in both Melina and Alex, who, unable to let go of their fantasized projections of each other, constantly need the other to give them the impulsive gratification they desire. Before proposing that they be married, Alex goes off into a reverie of how ephemeral and impermanent things are. He talks about an old and beautiful building that stood across a park through which he used to walk every day on his way home. The building served as a beacon, he says, and he goes on to ascribe human characteristics to it, such as warmth and dependability. He describes with despair how one day he looked up to find that it had suddenly disappeared, how it had been "taken away." The imagery of impermanence and loss is clear, and the ferociousness with which he holds onto and possesses things takes on new meaning. It is as if those things that he needs for survival can be arbitrarily removed; and their removal leaves him feeling lost.

This leads to the third development task that the borderline is unable to negotiate—the ongoing integration of both hating and loving images into a flexible psychic structure. The borderline cannot treat the other as anything but a projection of his own primitive fears and wishes. Unlike other instances of projection, there is a need to interact with the object of the projections. These often take the form of establishing intimate and binding relationships that will assure, in a self-fulfilling manner, the dreaded—but also unconsciously desired—fear. Both Alex and Melina respond to the other's needs in this way: each provides the pain and vulnerability from which the other runs, but to which the other is compulsively attracted. Each needs to make the other conform to the way in which each wants the other to be.

In summary, between 1926 and 1980 the psychiatric view of the struggle between love and aggression expanded from an emphasis on oedipal conflict to specific processes of early mother-child interaction. Fusion and separation became key foci, and the struggle was no longer that of just one partner but the complementary engaging of the distortions and destructive longing of two needy people.

The Love of Aggression

We now move from the dynamic tension existing between love and aggression to the cathartic release sought through frenetic immersion in the love of aggression. The tensions of loving and being loved were described in the previous section as always taking place within an ongoing relationship in which the individual exposes, to varying degrees, his vulnerability. This section discusses the move away from such a personal connection to a more anonymous relationship, in which the focus is aggressor and victim. The underlying basis for such aggression is still erotic, though often expressed in highly symbolic forms. The films to be contrasted are *M* (1931) and *Straw Dogs* (1971).

Because so many of the films that fall under this theme deal with the subject, we will also discuss the depiction of the brutilization of women.

M.   Coming at a time when the complex motives of murder were just beginning to gain some attention, Fritz Lang's *M* was a strategic film. Before Lang's work, murderers tended to be portrayed simplistically, as ghoulish figures of the night. Lacking a clear identity, such figures were mere automatons, pushed on by dark and unknown forces. Perhaps Lang himself was playing with such an image when he first introduces us to the huge shadowy reflection of the murderer, which is juxtaposed against a poster describing his crimes. The shadow comes with the terror of night to kill small, helpless children. Though never made explicit, there is in the killing of the little girls an unmistakable sexual element. Lang quite deliberately never shows an actual killing, nor in fact any of the violent aggression; about this he leaves the viewer to fantasize.

When the shadowy figure is finally revealed, we see, in contrast to our established fantasies, a fragile, pop-eyed little man, who nervously darts about frightened by the inner forces that haunt him. Lang wanted to depict these forces, though he clearly knew that they are highly complex and do not lend themselves to the reductionistic explanations so often used before. Coming from Vienna, Lang had had exposure to Freud's thoughts and had even gone into psychiatric hospitals to observe patients.[21] His interest in psychiatric problems focused on the psychopath, whose asocial character structure drives him to commit crimes. Lang studied such individuals, not only in the confinement of their institutional cells but through police records and even through personal underworld associations.[22] Some of the actors in M were actually from this underworld, which had come to fascinate Lang so greatly.

Lang authored the script for M with his second wife, Thea Von Harbou. It is interesting that his first wife had committed suicide after finding Von Harbou in her husband's arms and that Lang was for a brief period a primary suspect in the crime. Lang's fascination with crime thus had a very personal meaning, though his focus on child murder could have been influenced by the then-infamous case of mass murder, Peter Kurten, the "Vampire of Düsseldorf." The case involving the murder of ten children, dominated the more sensationalistic press at the time. Lang and his wife wrote the script for M before Kurten was actually caught and, though we can speculate on its influence on their perceptions, Lang maintained that M "derives from various sex crimes of the period, not just from the Kurten case."[23] Even with this caveat it is interesting that different underworld organizations in Düsseldorf actually volunteered to look for the Vampire and that Lang had read about this in the Berliner Tageblatt.

Earlier, we pointed out that Freud's psychoanalytic theory, focusing primarily on neurosis, gave comparatively little attention to psychotic states. Though he emphasized the sexual basis of behavior, Freud never dealt directly with clinical cases of child murder. While his theories gained increasing public and medical attention in the late 1920s and early 1930s, when the film was shot, they were not used to diagnose and treat the madness of murder. The psychiatric perception that was applied to murderers was based on an organic medical model. When psychiatrists were brought in to judge whether the defendant was criminally insane and therefore not responsible for his actions, they used as criteria such factors as memory and general organizational abilities, which the defendant revealed when defining himself in terms of place and time. These were all related to the McNaughten Rules, designed to determine whether or not the individual realized that what he did was wrong.[24] Psychiatry was therefore not concerned with the Freudian emphasis on the developmental traumas that might explain the complex motives behind the crime but focused on the criminal's conscious awareness at the time of the crime and his general state of functioning. When consulted for an opinion, psychiatry depended on a description of functioning rather than etiology.

In the late 1920s and early 1930s psychiatry, particularly German psychiatry, was in general tied to such a descriptive position. The emphasis was on careful observation and categorization of both external and, when possible, internal functioning. It was felt that such detailed and systematic observation would provide the kind of classification system necessary for understanding the biological factors thought at the time to cause madness. It is not surprising, then, to find that Lang took an almost clinically descriptive view of the murderer. He claimed that the film was a "documentary picture," in which the camera was consciously used to resemble newsreel shots to increase the sense of reality.[25] No attempt was made to chronicle the past, as all the action is in the present. Lang added that he "tried to make *M* an objective account," that his "intention was neither to excuse nor denounce such sick minds in our midst nor to create pity of them." Reviews of the period, however, emphasized that the film conveys tolerance, sympathy, and even pity for the "pathological helplessness of the man and the crippled, distorted qualities of mind and soul that have driven him to crime."[26]

Peter Lorre's portrayal was to make him famous and typecast him throughout his career as the homicidal murderer, a role from which he had a hard time escaping. He is the little man who kills, the pathological deviant whose constitutional frailties make him respond with explosive rage to others, particularly those who are helpless. Lang's careful and subtle characterization shows the compulsion to kill as a force that is all-consuming. When he is found guilty by the underworld's kangaroo court, Becker (Lorre) rises in his own defense and says: "I am always forced to move along the streets, and always someone is behind me. It is I. I sometimes feel I am myself behind me, and yet I cannot escape." This is followed by the cry of the defense attorney that Becker's urge to kill is uncontrollable and that he should therefore be relieved of any responsibility for his actions and should be turned over to a doctor.

This view of the murderer as driven by psychological forces was relatively new in film, and it certainly startled the audiences who flocked to see it in both Europe and America. Though admiring Lang's directorial genius, many reviewers were critical of such a portrayal. For example, the *New York Times* wrote:

> Why so much fervor and intelligent work was concentrated on such a revolting idea is surprising. It is regrettable that such a wealth of talent and imaginative direction was not put into some other story, for the actions of this murderer, even though they are left to the imagination, are too hideous to contemplate.[27]

Though we never find out the fate of Becker—the last scene is of police rushing in and taking him from the underground tribunal—we suspect that his fate will be the same as Peter Kurten's. After undergoing psychiatric evaluation,

Kurten was quickly found to be aware of his actions and therefore culpable. He stood trial and was executed in 1931.

Straw Dogs. Sam Peckinpah's name has come over the years to be associated with the depiction of violence, and the film that most firmly established this reputation was *Straw Dogs* (1971). For many this film personified America's increasing fascination with violence. The sixties were a period of massive revolt by youth and minorities against the established order. Violence, both by those in and out of power, was common. The Vietnam War presented a daily chronicle of such violence, as Americans were greeted every evening with a visual report from the war zone. The war came home and, with it, the atrocities that mirrored the violence America had previously been able to exclude from consciousness. There followed an increase in crime and a consequent reactionary movement toward stricter law-and-order edicts. Though many explained the increase in violence as a result of the current world state, others saw it as a natural historical evolution. Emphasis was placed on the emergence of the values of the American West, which emphasized a type of rugged individualism that had each man forging his own destiny through his own determination and the gun he packed at his side.

For many it was the assassination of young President Kennedy in 1963 that first made America aware of this past. In his eulogy Robert Kennedy, who was also to be killed five years later, maintained that America had to give up its historical fictions of Western expansionism and the gun morality that was tied to it. At this time psychiatry began to join with other disciplines in attempting to understand the historical roots of violence in America. *Social psychiatry* emerged to investigate the social-psychological factors that shape the interaction between people and their environments. One facet of this study, *psychohistory*, began to focus on the history of such interactions in order to understand their evolution into their present form. By looking at the social factors of the past, psychohistorians hoped to be able to explain the types of personalities that emerged to typify a period.[28]

Understanding the figures of the past as a way of understanding our heritage also became part of a general interest in understanding the real, as opposed to the fictionalized or idealized, personalities of history. Film, which had always played an important part in idealizing the violent history of America, now began slowly to reflect a more critical evaluation of the past. One obvious area to be reexamined was America's love relationship with the West. It was not surprising that the heroes of the frontier, upon closer scrutiny, were found to be violent men and began to be depicted as such. Wyatt Earp, General Custer, Pat Garrit, and others were shown to be figures who sought out violence and were different from the men they hunted only by virtue of the star or insignia they wore on their chest. The violent aggression with which they surrounded themselves was interpreted to be an important part of their identity, a way of establishing their manhood.

This new depiction coincided with, and was possibly related to, the increasing demands by minorities for an identity apart from that which they had inherited from class or caste oppression. The push for civil rights had to be fought for, and it came for many as no surprise when the nonviolent tactics of the earlier 1960s were replaced by violence. As major race riots swept through America in 1967, it seemed that the war in Vietnam was being fought in America's streets as cities underwent curfews and the divisions between the haves and have-nots were considered by many to be resolvable only through bloodshed. With the killing of Robert Kennedy and Martin Luther King, Jr. in 1968 violence seemed all-pervasive; any delusion that it was restricted to our leaders was quickly destroyed with the Kent State massacre in May 1970. At this small Ohio college the protest demonstration of college students suddenly unleashed a hail of bullets from national guard troops, who had been called in to maintain order. The dead and wounded were no longer just the vulnerable leaders of society, nor the disenfranchised militants of the cities, but middle class white college students as well. Violence had been brought further into the mainstream of American life.

The rebellion of young adults was certainly not a new cinematic subject—in fact at times its depiction even had psychiatric overtones, as in the 1955 film *Rebel without A Cause.* The theme of rebellion in terms of the love of aggression, however, had a unique and revolutionary depiction in Stanley Kubrick's adaptation of *A Clockwork Orange* (1971). The film's portrayal of the sadistic pleasure of Alex and his "droogs" in mutilating and maiming in a world that is corrupted and loveless, mirrored the hopelessness that many felt about the state of human affairs. The pervasiveness of such pessimism was indicated by the fact that *Straw Dogs* was released in America less than a year after *A Clockwork Orange.*

While America was undergoing these upheavals, the rest of the world turned its attention to the plight of the masses in the underdeveloped countries, which were beginning to throw off the shackles of economic and psychological oppression and take their place as a major force in world politics. The *third world,* as it came to be known, consisted of the peoples of Africa, Latin America, and parts of Asia, whose common bond was in their having once been colonized and not in their being white and moneyed. Their push to achieve freedom and independence had often been marked by violence, and continued violence seemed to many of them a legitimate and perhaps the only means for obtaining a sense of self.

Up to this point violence had been viewed as pathological and those who exhibited it, as a threat to society. Because violence often resulted in the death of others, violent persons, by virtue of the ancient code of an eye for an eye, had themselves to be killed. As civilization progressed, such punishment was replaced by sanctions involving institutionalization rather than immediate death. The violence of such persons came to be regarded as the result of many factors for which they were perhaps not totally responsible.

Until the 1960s violence was viewed as destructive, not only to society but to the persons who enacted it. The widespread violence of the late 1960s, however, caused a rethinking of the whole problem. One of the major reinterpreters was Franz Fanon, a black third-world psychiatrist, who discussed violence in terms of benefits. His thesis that violence is not simply pathological had immediate impact, and influential thinkers began to reflect his view, as evidenced in the following statement by J. P. Sartre about Fanon:

He shows clearly that this irrepressible violence is neither sound and fury, nor the resurrection of savage instincts nor even the effect of resentment: it is man recreating himself.[29]

Fanon talked about the colonial world as "a world divided into compartments," an artificial situation that allowed the colonist to treat the native as a nonhuman, an object to be used to gratify his needs.[30]

Fanon's writings were read by many Americans, both black and white, who were trying to make sense of the emerging violence, and his influence was manifested in works of the late 1960s, such as *Soul on Ice* (1968) by Eldridge Cleaver.[31] Espousing Fanon's theme of violence as a necessary step in obtaining a new identity and sense of purpose, Cleaver pointed to the impact of the erotic as an important component of such violence. He believed that the white man had made the black man his "body" as a result of the white man's need to deny himself his sensuality. Delving into the unconscious fusion between violence and the erotic, Cleaver presented a disturbing analysis of the forces that he predicted would lead to open conflict between the oppressed and the oppressors, the black and the white, the third world and its antagonists. The impact of such writings was to introduce a new perspective on violence. Violence became not something that had to be repressed but an integral component of human behavior. It was viewed as one of the mechanisms that man uses in his struggle to adapt to his environment.

In trying to understand violence psychiatry turned not only to the sociopolitical forces described by Fanon but to the work of *ethology*, the scientific study of animal behavior. Lorenz, one of the most popular and widely read ethologists in the 1960s, pointed out that aggression promotes adaptation. For example, it increases the distance between members of a group and outlines a dominant heirarchy, which maintains stability within the group and establishes a certain predictability.[32] The threat of violence brings order, and only when this order has been radically changed is there overt violence. One subject common in the literature of this period was the role of the erotic in interspecies aggression.[33] It was pointed out that "the males who are stronger and better fighters will cover more females and sire more offspring than will smaller, weaker, or sickly males.[34]

The issue of distance, as elaborated by Lorenz and others, led to seeing aggression as a response to the invasion of one's personal space, or territory. During the 1960s a very popular work on the influence of territoriality on aggression was that of Ardrey (1966).[35] He emphasized that human aggression, like the aggression of the primates from which we have evolved, comes from the instinct to conquer and maintain a fixed geographical territory. During the period of the late 1960s the question of the importance of personal space was receiving a good deal of attention in social psychiatry. Its sanctity was emphasized in numerous studies that showed how different cultures seem to have a built-in tolerance for how close another person should be. This can be seen in the distance quickly established between two people in conversation. As pointed out by Hall in *The Hidden Dimension* (1960), the distance established by two Frenchmen would be intolerable, if not provocative, for two Americans.[36]

Such, then, was the popular and clinical context in which *Straw Dogs* took form. Peckinpah was intrigued by a fictional work, *The Siege of Trencher's Farm*, which dealt with the hostility met by an American family upon their move to an isolated village in Cornwall. The head of the family, George Magruder, is an American professor of English literature, who is taking a sabbatical to write.[37] Arriving with his English-born wife and young daughter, he receives a cold reception from the inhabitants of the village. His efforts at moving toward the locals are met with rejection and hostility; this is made clear when his cat is killed outside his house. While coming home from a church social, he runs over the village idiot, Henry Niles, who, previous to his escape that same night, had been locked up for having killed several children. Not knowing this and concerned only that he has injured the wanderer, Magruder drives him quickly to his home, where he telephones for assistance.

Meanwhile, a local farmer, Tom Hedden, finds his young daughter missing and, hearing of Niles's escape and place of refuge, sets out after the man he believes has killed his daughter. Joined by some of his drinking companions, he arrives at Magruder's house and demands that Niles be given to them. Magruder, whose distrust has reached the point at which he is sure they will murder Niles, refuses. A neighbor suddenly comes upon the siege and tries to insert some reason into the situation, which is close to exploding. He is shot by Hedden, who then turns his gun upon the farmhouse. Magruder, though unarmed, is able to defend Niles and the story ends with his taking Niles back to town.

As pointed out by Hagenauer and Hamilton in their excellent analysis of the film *Straw Dogs,* the story line under the direction of Peckinpah underwent considerable changes.[38] One of the most important of these was the transformation of Magruder's wife into a nubile coquette, who seductively presents herself to the men her husband has hired to help repair the old farmhouse. She is a crucial, almost catalytic, factor to the fusion of sexuality and aggression that erupts into the horrific scene at the end of the film. Unlike the novel, where only the peacemaker dies, Peckinpah had all five of the intruders killed.

As in the novel, Magruder is an American, renamed David Sumner (Dustin Hoffman). The motive for his leave is tied to his need to escape the violence of America. He is not a professor of English but a theoretical mathematician interested in calculations of celestial bodies. Hoffman plays him as a figure who falteringly moves through the world, afraid of any kind of physical or emotional loss of control. This is in direct contrast to his young, Lolita-like wife, Amy, who impulsively exhibits herself and her emotions. She often goes about braless—and, on one occasion, topless—in front of her male admirers.

The Sumners settle in the remote Cornish village because of its proximity to Amy's family farm, which Amy had visited in her childhood and adolescence. On their arrival, she quickly receives admiring stares from the town toughs, with one of whom, we quickly learn, she had slept during one of her summer visits. Apparently unaware of their undressing stares, David invites the men to work on the old farm. They, of course, are only too willing. As they work, they look at Amy, who obligingly exhibits herself. Their comments, while focused on Amy, occasionally allude to David's impotence, which is evidenced by his difficulty in responding to his wife's sexual advances. In this context the fact that they are childless seems to be a purposeful change from the novel. The extent of David's sexual passivity and difficulty with self-assertiveness is made clear when he naively accepts the invitation of the four workers to go with them on a day's hunting trip. Having taken David far out into an isolated area, they abandon him, telling him to wait while they flush out the birds. The symbolism is not lost as the scene in which David sits, isolated and helpless, is juxtaposed with that of his wife's rape by two of the ruffians, Charles Venner and Norman Scutt. Scutt watches Venner have sex with Amy, who, though brutalized, seems only to partially resist him. Scutt then pushes Venner aside at the point of a gun and performs sodomy on Amy. When David returns, he is so absorbed by his own anger that he fails to notice his wife's despair.

It is against this backdrop that the story begins to progress toward the moment of ritualized catharsis. David becomes increasingly sullen. When, during a visit by the parish minister, he suddenly turns up to an almost deafening level the volume of a Scottish war march, we have the feeling that pagan primitive forces are close to erupting. The eruption finally comes after Niles, the village idiot, has unintentionally strangled the daughter of Hedden, the town drunk. Peckinpah portrayed Janice Hedden as a younger double for Amy, and it is her attempt to seduce the vulnerable Niles that brings about her death. Sexualized aggression is becoming more violent and diffused, and, as we will shortly see, infectious. His daughter's disappearance, after she was last seen with Niles, sparks Hedden to assume that some sexual crime has been committed, though Niles, unlike his parallel in the book, is not an affirmed child molester. It is important to remember that Hedden does not know that anything has really happened to his daughter, and we might surmise that the immediacy of his rage comes more from his own primitive projections than from any clear basis in reality. We have already been shown that this mammoth man is a vengeful drunk, subject to bursts of violence. These characteristics make him the unspoken leader of the four younger louts, whom he leads to the Sumner farmhouse. When they arrive, they are confronted by the magistrate of the village, Major Scott. That Major Scott is an old friend of Amy's father indicates that he, like Amy, is a member of the landed gentry, in contrast to the rowdies, whom he tries once again to control. Throughout the film he has been the one controlling force standing in the way of Hedden and his younger hedonists. As Hagenauer and Hamilton point out, Peckinpah's portrayal of him as a defective representative of law and order is suggested by the fact that he has only one good arm—the other lies helpless in a black sling.[39] While reaching for the gun that Hedden brandishes about, he is accidentally shot, and with his death the final control over the violent forces both outside and inside the farmhouse is obliterated.

In almost a paraphrase of the territoriality literature, David screams at Hedden, "This is where I live." This is the most obvious reason for the violence that follows: David is protecting his home and his possessions, which include his wife.

It is the elemental nature of this reasoning that dominates and replaces the abstract logic of the bumbling mathematician. His wife's taunt in the early part of the film—"You left America because you didn't want to take a stand"—are recalled as he begins to methodically prepare for the assault on his territory. If Hedden is coming to right the sexual wrong done to his daughter, the others are coming to destroy the impotent figure who stands in the way of their enjoying their bestial sexual pleasures. This is symbolically presented when Scutt, an exterminator by trade, throws a dead rat at Amy through one of the windows of the besieged house. David, once again turning on his records of Scottish war dance prepares his primitive armory. Boiling oil, knives, and the steel-toothed jaws of an animal trap are set in ready for the invaders. Their demise, one by one, leaves David with a smile of contentment. It is as if the violence has been cleansing, and, as one reviewer pointed out, "There is even the faint smile of satisfaction on the tarty wife's face that says she will have a new sexual respect for her husband."[40] It is, of course, this respect, achieved through violence, which dominated the work of Fanon, and we cannot help but feel that Peckinpah wants us to understand the change that comes from meeting violence with violence.

Commenting on the impact of the film on the clinical community, Hagenauer and Hamilton wrote: "This film with its compact story focusing with a high-powered lens on issues of violent behavior and directed by an acknowledged master of what could be called the 'esthetic of violence' on the screen, offers an opportunity to reexamine certain aspects of the complexities of aggression and violence."[41] Acknowledging that the strong contemporary interest in violence and aggression was influenced by many factors, they went on to note the importance of film for its ability "to slow down instantaneous events in such a way as to reveal new details and aspects of familiar occurrences never seen before."[42] Film provided a means to explore violence, which in both the popular and clinical press was enjoying great attention. One aspect of violence that was beginning to be discussed in clinical literature was its origin in narcissistic rage. Quoting Kohut one of the most prolific writers on narcissism, Hagenauer and Hamilton said:

> [Narcissistic rage] occurs in many forms: they all share a specific psychological flavor which gives them a distinct position with the wide realm of human aggression. The need for revenge, for righting a wrong, for undoing a hurt by whatever means, and a deeply anchored unrelenting compulsion in the pursuit of all these aims, which gives no rest to those who have suffered a narcissistic injury—these are features which are characteristic for the phenomenon of narcissistic rage in all its forms and which set it apart from other kinds of aggression. . . . In its typical forms there is utter disregard for reasonable limitations and a boundless wish to redress an injury and to obtain revenge. The irrationality of the vengeful attitude becomes even more frightening in view of the fact that—in narcissistic personalities as in the paranoiac—the reasoning capacity, while totally under the domination of and in the services of the overriding emotion, is often not only intact but even sharpened.[43]

The importance of narcissism in clinical literature was to grow steadily and, with it, the interest in primitive rage, particularly as evidenced in the borderline personality. It is interesting that Kohut's ideas eventually worked their way into the public domain with the publication of Christopher Lasch's *Culture of Narcissism.*[44] The impact of Peckinpah's film on clinical perceptions of violence was evident in Hagenauer and Hamilton, but it may have had more general impact in that it so beautifully represented Kohut's emphasis on the sharpening of the ability to reason while in the service of narcissistic rage," a rage which has come to be seen as the basis for much of contemporary psychopathology.

Violence against Women

As violent as the aggression is in *Straw Dogs,* it emerges from a studied character and plot development and represents an explosive and horrifying purgation. There is, however, a genre of film whose singular purpose from its opening frame is solely to portray sadistic violence against women, and the exponential increase in such films warrants some attention. The plot line of such films almost always involves a mad murderer who, as evil incarnate, stalks his helpless victims. The victims are almost always nubile females, and each consecutive film of this genre tries to outdo the previous one by making the sadistic attacks increasingly brutal. Both the killer and his victims have distinct characteristics, and the overwhelming box-office success of these films ensures them a categorization as a distinct genre.

The best-known expositor on such issues was the man after whom the term *sadism* was named, the Marquis de Sade. De Sade's exegetical writing in the last half of the eighteenth century anticipated the work of such philosophers as Max Stirner and Friedrich Nietzsche, as well as Freud's theories on sexual pathology. De Sade's central thesis was that true happiness involves sexual power over others through the infliction of pain. For De Sade imposing pain on others allows one greater gratification than giving pleasure in that it assures one of a greater sense of power and mastery. De Sade argued that the expression of sexual power over others is a human necessity, an instinct that, if blocked, only leads to greater evil in the form of sweeping economic and political oppression. De Sade therefore encouraged a series of minimally controlled external restraints that, while preventing murder, would provide the sexual perversions necessary for society to function.

De Sade's theory that sadism is a necessary part of life and that its repression only leads to problems is used today to justify the free expression of sadism in film. Makers of such films maintain that cinematic images of sexual brutality allow for a vicarious release of pent-up aggression, which otherwise would burst forth in overt destruction.

While sexual brutality has a long history in literature and cinema, it reached a new level in the shower killing of *Psycho* (1960). Audiences were certainly shown women being killed before this, but Hitchcock's images provided a unique perspective that seemed to play on the most primitive elements. Nude and in the shower, the star of the film is suddenly hacked to death for no apparent reason, and her fear and death spasms are the subject of careful study. We are encouraged to look, but it should be remembered that we never see the knife actually strike. Hitchcock has led us up to the act of murder, knowing that it is in our imagination that the fullest terror and sadistic fantasies lie. The film introduced a new twist to the connection between sexuality and death. Never before had the agony and helplessness of the victim been so fully emphasized. Not only were women not killed in such a dramatic fashion by an unknown assailant, but their murder came toward the end of the film, whereas in *Psycho* the protagonist is killed in the first half of the film.

Hitchcock's timing is made even more powerful by staging the killing in the bathroom. The use of the shower as a vehicle for Marion (Janet Leigh) to take off all her clothes is brilliant. The bathroom is the most sacred, as well as most profane, of places, and the camera has allowed us entrance. Seeking to rid herself of guilt, Marion has torn up evidence and flushed it down the toilet, and the shower is naturally the next place to wash off her sins. Artfully catching enough glimpses of her disrobing to encourage voyeuristic pleasures, the camera goes into the shower with her as we watch and feel the water beating down on her upturned face. It is as she lifts up her head and shuts her eyes to let the water enclose her face that the shower curtain slowly parts to reveal a knife hanging in mid-air. Hitchcock has seemingly shown us the unshowable. While not the pornographic fare of a low-budget movie, Hitchcock's *Psycho* shows us the most sexually sadistic act we can imagine, but it is, we must remember, all in our imagination. We never see the knife actually striking.

Since 1960 countless films have steadily replaced the imagined with increasingly explicit imagery of women's deaths. In so many of the deaths the killer is portrayed as a "psycho," a man who has become totally out of control. The fascinating thing to remember is that in many films of this period—for example, Hitchcock's *Psycho* and *Frenzy* (1972), and Michael Powell's *Peeping Tom* (1960)— the madman is a pleasant, highly solicitous young man whose outward appearance in no way belies the hideous, bestial rage that courses beneath his civilized exterior.[45] By 1974 this presentation had been largely replaced by an anonymous, overtly degenerate and crazed figure whose only purpose in life was to sadistically disembowel, dismember, and mutilate his victims in the most bizarre manner possible. The film that most dramatically broke with *Psycho*'s tradition was *The Texas Chain Saw Massacre* (1974). After making the rounds of New York's nameless Times Square movie houses, this low-budget film suddenly catapulted into prominence when the Metropolitan Museum of Art purchased a copy for its permanent collection. Quick to exploit this, the producers gave the work a highly publicized screening at Cannes, and the film became internationally known.

Unlike Hitchcock's victims, those murdered in *The Texas Chain Saw Massacre* have stolen no money, and even their sexual misbehavior is demure in contrast to Marion's affair with a married man. The victims, a group of middle-class kids (Sally, Jerry, Kirk, and Pam), are out for a ride. They are clean-cut and kind, as conveyed by their willingness to take Sally's invalid brother, Franklin, along with them. After wandering into a farmhouse, Kurt, Pam, and Jerry are killed by a huge male figure, whose face is covered by a leather mask. Franklin is the next to go, as his wheelchair and he are sawed up by Leather Face. Sally, though attacked, survives, and the rest of the film deals with her attempts to escape. In the meantime her friends and brother are turned into barbecued "beef" for sale at a roadside stand, run by the patriarch of the family, in which Leather Face is just one of the sadistically driven "boys." The point of such an atrocity is clear when we investigate more carefully the manner in which the victims are slain.

Kurt and Jerry are dispatched quickly and—as we come to realize—painlessly, as their heads are smashed by Leather Face. This is not the fate of Pam, who, coming to search for them, is grabbed by Leather Face and hung alive on a meat hook to squirm and dangle until dead. Franklin is sliced up alive by a chain saw. With the torturing of Sally it becomes even clearer that women—and those who are weak and symbolically castrated, like Franklin—are subject to a special kind of vengeance. They are, through the ministrations of their torturers, treated like hunks of beef. The film's sadistic violence toward women in particular seems to explain its public following and the use of its cinematic devices in countless films to follow.

Any clinical understanding of sadism begins with the work of Krafft-Ebing, Havelock Ellis, and Freud in the early 1900s. It is surprising how little has since actually been published on sadism, particularly in regard to its connection with murder.[46] What does seem clear is that the current cinematic imagery of mutilating, dismembering, and cannibalizing is not based on actual occurrences but, rather, on an otherwise unexpressed intrapsychic need. As Walter Bromberg said:

> Impulses toward dismemberment of the human body and cannibalism in part are more frequent in the fantasies and delusions of melancholic patients and the dreams of neurotic individuals, than in actuality.[47]

From this and other reports it becomes clear that such crimes are given disproportionate attention in the press.[48] Sexual homicide is not as frequent as one might believe from media coverage. The attention given to such crimes is likely a function of the threat and yet fascination that they hold for us. Concluded one recent study:

> The slaying of an individual who is either marginally known or unknown to the assailant, for reasons that are sexually motivated, so violates the predictability of human interaction as to require the kind of treatment that sets this behavior apart from all other behaviors.[49]

The sexually sadistic murderer is not a common figure in clinical studies, and where he does appear, he is far from the popular cinematic depictions. Within this context it is important to remember that while over 99 percent of rape victims are women, women constitute only 20 percent of homicide victims.[50]

The reporting on such crimes usually includes a developmental history that tends to search for a childhood trauma to explain the sadistic act. The emphasis on such a trauma is a bastardization of a traditional psychoanalytic belief that the origin of such acts lies in an arresting of psychosexual development: the murderer was acting out a problem that originated in the first six years of life, and the only hope for a cure lies in helping him discover these early conflicts. Freud, however, moved away from the idea that there is a single traumatic event whose uncovering can explain and cure the patient's problems.

Beginning with *Psycho*, which explained Norman Bates's act as a result of his being jilted by his mother, film accounts of sexual murders have increasingly been going back to simpler formulations. While sometimes involving revenge for the death of a loved one *(Prom Night, Friday the Thirteenth, Silent Scream, Scream for Revenge, An Eye for an Eye, Bloody Valentine)* or a social rejection *(Terror Train, Happy Birthday to Me)*, the more likely presentation involves a figure, almost always male, who simply is mad. He kills women, rarely speaks, and is animalistic in his primitive flailings *(Snuff, Maniac, Frozen Scream, Schizoid, Nightmares, Bloody Noses, Evil Speak, Macabra)*. These films follow *Texas Chain Saw Massacre* in including a sexual undercurrent, in which the victims are either thinking about or engaging in sexuality.

Halloween (1978), for example, begins with a tracking shot of two teenagers necking. Through the continued use of tracking shots, we watch the knife-slashing mutilation of the undressed girl, whose boyfriend is conveniently absent. This is all seen through the eyeholes of the Halloween mask of the killer, who, we find out, is the eight-year-old brother of the victim. Fifteen years later, this mad killer escapes from a psychiatric institution—on Halloween, of course—and comes back to murder again. After numerous murders of young adolescent girls who "fool around," he turns his full attention to the elusive Laurie. Appropriately enough, Laurie is played by Jamie Lee Curtis, the daughter of Tony Curtis and Janet Leigh, who played Marion in *Psycho*. The similarities are more than chance, and the equation between sex and punishment is again the key to understanding that sex kills. Both mother and daughter, and hundreds of women since, have played the parts of women who are destroyed with an ever-increasing brutality. *Halloween* delights in this brutality, and the mad killer is presented as unstoppable. The emphasis seems not so much on horror as a total immersion into sadism. The prettier and the more subtly or openly seductive the female victim, the more violent her death.

Halloween became a model for a multitude of films that focused on the mutilation of teenagers, particularly teenage girls. Such films have been particularly appealing to young audiences, who have crowded drive-in theaters or have stood in line for hours to see people their own age sexually attacked, impaled, and maimed. In many films of this genre the victim, after coming closer and closer to death as those around her are destroyed, finally manages to escape. The one thing that seems to explain why she is able to escape is that she still possesses, as Pauline Kael says, "the victim strength to do so."[51]

While *The Texas Chain Saw Massacre* was proclaimed to be based on an actual crime, appropriately enough in Texas, the state of the art had reached such extremes that by 1976 some films were claiming to show actual rapes and killings of women. Supposedly made in South America (where, as the ads maintained, "life is cheap"), these films enjoyed underground success in America and in late 1976 gave rise to the film *Snuff*. While it is difficult to imagine anything beyond the degradation and degeneration presented in *The Texas Chain Saw Massacre*, *Snuff* achieved, not so much in its imagery as in its clarion call to sadistic pleasure, the furthest extreme yet presented. Since then, the theme of sadistic violence against women has moved increasingly out of the porno districts of America to take its place as a major genre, enjoying staggering financial success. For example, *Halloween*, shot in twenty days, cost only $300,000 and grossed over a hundred times that amount. Now that the formula for assuring box-office success has been discovered, the production sharks have circled in for the kill, and the frenzy of thirty-day productions has become commonplace. Every month a new sadistic offering is presented to what seems to be an insatiable audience.[52]

The teenage victims depicted in *Halloween* have become a model for countless similar productions. The thematic emphasis on teenagers, sexuality, and death is certainly not new, and its popularity among teenagers can be attributed to the fact that adolescents, because of their confused sexuality and emotional excesses, find release and a strange kind of cathartic comfort in their screen counterparts' struggles. Regardless of their supposedly redeeming emotional, symbolic functions, however, the question remains why these films glorify sadistic violence, specifically against females.

While their focus is on teenage audiences, these films have their adult and young adult counterparts. An example is *Dressed to Kill* (1980). Updating *Psycho*, this film added the explicitness and overt mayhem that Hollywood believes audiences need. Norman Bates's transvestism becomes the transsexualism of a psychiatrist, Dr. Elliot (Michael Caine), and Marion becomes a middle-aged, sexually frustrated woman, Kate Miller (Angie Dickinson). The sexual "crime" is an anonymous tryst, which, unlike Marion's affair, has no possibility of a relationship but is simply an impulsive passion. The punishment for this crime is no longer delivered by a butcher knife but by a straight-edged razor, the sadistic slicing with which is more definite than what took place in *Psycho*. Though one can say *Dressed to Kill* and *Halloween* are very different films, they are joined by their focus on explicit sadism on female victims, and the impact of their imagery on audiences has come to be of major concern.

While some experts still agree with the 1981 Presidential Commission on Obscenity and Pornography, which maintained that there is no evidence of a relationship between viewing erotic material and erotic crimes, dissent has been increasing.[53] As films employing violence against women clearly attract large audiences, the idea that the mad killer's actions may serve to provoke similar behavior in real people is a frightening one. The basic findings of the research indicate that aggressive erotic stimuli lead to increased aggressive behavior toward women, especially in subjects previously angered.[54] Though these studies are done in the confines of laboratory settings, where subjects are experimentally exposed to highly controlled conditions, it is reasonable to believe that there is a carry-over to nonlaboratory conditions. It has also been found that the more deviant the behavior depicted, such as flagellantism and bestiality, the more likely it is to irritate rather than elate the viewer.[55] This irritation is thought to make an individual who is already frustrated and has experienced a lowering of aggressive inhibitions, more likely to demonstrate overt aggression against women. While there is still no hard data to show that the number of such crimes is really increasing, psychological research is pointing to the possibility that the occurrence of such crimes may well be connected with the continuous saturation distribution of the ever-increasing image of sadistic violence against women.

Notes

1. E. Fromm, *The Anatomy of Human Destructiveness* (New York: Holt, Reinhart and Winston, 1973), pp. 77–85.

2. S. Freud, "The Ego and the Id," vol. 19 of *The Collected Works of Sigmund Freud, 1923–1925,* ed. A. Strachey and J. Strachey (London: Hogarth Press, 1961), p. 43.

3. B. Chodorkoff and S. Baxter, "Secrets of a Soul: An Early Psychoanalytic film venture," *American Imago* 31 (1974): p. 319.

4. P. Gay, *Weimar Culture: The Outsider as Insider* (New York: Harper & Row, 1968).

5. H. C. Abraham and E. L. Freud, eds., *A Psychoanalytic Dialogue: The Letters of Sigmund Freud and Karl Abraham, 1907–1926* (New York: Basic Books, 1965), p. 384.

6. E. Jones, *The Life and Work of Sigmund Freud,* vol. 3 (New York: Basic Books, 1957), p. 114.

7. Chodorkoff and Baxter, p. 389.

8. Ibid., p. 330.

9. S. Freud, *The Interpretation of Dreams* (New York: Avon Books, 1967), pp. 277–310.

10. S. Freud, "On the Universal Tendency to Debasement in the Sphere of Love," in Contributions to the Psychology of Love, vol. 11 of *The Collected Works of Sigmund Freud,* ed. J. Strachey (London: Hogarth Press, 1961).

11. S. Freud, *The Ego and the Id* (New York: W. W. Norton, 1962), p. 53.

12. S. Freud, "Moral Responsibility for the Content of Dreams," vol. 19 of *The Collected Works of Sigmund Freud, 1923–1925,* p. 132.

13. J. Breuer and S. Freud, *Studies in Hysteria* (London: Hogarth Press, 1955).

14. Chodorkoff and Baxter, p. 328.

15. Ibid., p. 331.

16. Dr. Richard Gressitt, a colleague, remarked to me on the remarkable correspondence of *Adèle H.* to the psychiatric diagnosis of De Clermabaults Syndrome, which is elaborated in a work entitled *Uncommon Psychiatric Syndromes,* M. D. Enoch and W. H. Trethowan (Chicago: Year Book Medical Publishers, 1979).

17. E. R. Shapiro, "The Psychodynamics and Developmental Psychology of the Borderline Patient: A Review of the Literature," *American Journal of Psychiatry,* vol. 135, no. 11 (November 1978), 1305–15.

18. M. Mahler, "A Study of the Separation-Individuation Process and Its Possible Application to Borderline Phenomena in the Psychoanalytic Situation," *Psychoanalytic Study of the Child* 26 (1971): 403–24.

19. O. Kernberg, *Borderline Conditions and Pathological Narcissism* (New York: Jason Aronson, Inc., 1975).

20. Shapiro, p. 1307.

21. Lotte Eisner, letter to Michael Fleming, 28 June 1979.

22. L. Eisner, *The Haunted Screen: Expressionism in the German Cinema and the Influence of Max Reinhardt,* trans. (from the French) R. Greaves (Berkeley and Los Angeles: University of California Press, 1969).

23. Austin Riggs Cinema Study Group, Stockbridge, Mass. (29 March 1952).

24. F. A. Whitlock, *Criminal Responsibility and Mental Illness* (1963).

25. Program notes written for Princeton Group Arts–Film Workshop by Fritz Lang in 1936.

26. Richard Watts, "Film Review on *M*," *New York Herald Tribune* (16 April 1933).

27. M. Hall, "Film Review of the American Opening of *M*," *New York Times* (3 April 1933), p. 13.

28. R. Hofstadter, "Discussion of E. H. Erikson's Paper: Psychoanalysis and Ongoing History: Problems of Identity, Hatred and Non-violence," *American Journal of Psychology,* 122: 250–54. E. H. Erikson, *Childhood and Society* (New York: W. W. Norton, 1963).

29. J. P. Sartre, Preface to *The Wretched of the Earth* (New York: Grove Press, 1966), p. vi.

30. Franz Fanon, *The Wretched of the Earth* (New York: Grove Press, 1966), p. 31.

31. Eldridge Cleaver, *Soul on Ice* (New York: McGraw-Hill, 1968).

32. Konrad Lorenz, *On Aggression* (New York: Harcourt Brace Javanovich, 1966), pp. 23–48.

33. L. H. Matthews, "Overt Fighting in Mammals," in *The Natural History of Aggression*, ed. S. D. Carthy and F. S. Ebling (New York: Academic Press, 1964), pp. 23–32.

34. D. Daniels, M. Gilula and F. Ochberg, eds., *Violence and the Struggle for Existence* (Boston: Little, Brown and Company, 1970), p. 21.

35. R. Ardrey, *The Territorial Imperative: A Personal Inquiry into the Animal Origins of Property and Nations* (New York: Atheneum, 1966).

36. E. T. Hall, *The Hidden Dimension* (Garden City, N. Y.: Doubleday, 1969).

37. G. Williams, *The Seige of Trencher's Farm* (New York: William Morrow, 1969).

38. Fedor Hagenauer and James W. Hamilton, "*Straw Dogs:* Aggression and Violence," *American Imago* 30 (1973): 221–49.

39. Ibid., p. 229.

40. Pauline Kael, "The Current Cinema: Peckinpah's Obsession," *New Yorker* (29 January 1972), p. 83.

41. Hagenauer and Hamilton, p. 229.

42. Ibid., p. 230.

43. H. Kohut, "Thoughts on Narcissism and Narcissistic Rage," presented at the A. A. Brill Lecture to the New York Psychoanalytic Society, 30 November 1971.

44. C. Lasch, *The Culture of Narcissism* (New York: W. W. Norton, 1969).

45. While women were not as likely to be portrayed as the killers, there were notable exceptions, as in the sexually repressed Catherine in *Repulsion* (1968).

46. A. A. Williams, "The Psychopathology and Treatment of Several Murderers," in *The Pathology and Treatment of Sexual Deviation: A Methodological Approach*, ed. I. Rosen (New York: Oxford University Press, 1964). P. H. Gebhard, J. H. Garnon, W. B. Pomeroy et al., *Sex Offenders* (New York: Harper & Row, 1965).

47. W. Bromberg, *Crime and the Mind: An Outline of Psychiatric Criminology* (New York: Greenwood Publishing Co., 1948), p. 331.

48. B. Roshier, "The Selection of Crime News in the Press," in *The Manufacture of News*, ed. S. Cohen and J. Young (Beverly Hills, Calif.: Sage Publications, 1973).

49. V. L. Swigert, R. A. Farrell and W. Yoels, "Sexual Homicide: Social Psychological and Legal Aspects," *Archives of Sexual Behavior*, vol. 5, no. 3 (1976), 400.

50. S. K. Steinmetz, "Women and Violence: Victims and Perpetrators," *American Journal of Psychotherapy* 3 (1980): 337.

51. Pauline Kael, "*Halloween,*" *New Yorker* (19 February 1979), p. 128.

52. R. Watkins, "Demented Revenge Hits World," *Variety* (29 October 1980).

53. R. A. Berkowitz, "Sex and Violence: We Can't Have It Both Ways," *Psychology Today* (May 1971), 14–23. R. A. Dienstbier, "Sex and Violence: Can Research Have It Both Ways?" *Journal of Communication* 27 (1977): 176–78.

54. E. Donnerstein, "Aggressive Erotica and Violence Against Women," *Journal of Personality and Social Psychology*, vol. 39, no. 2 (1980), 269–77.

55. D. Zillman, J. Bryant, and R. A. Carveth, "The Effects of Erotica Featuring Sadomasochism and Bestiality on Motivated Intermale Aggression," *Psychology Bulletin*, vol. 7, no. 1 (March 1981), 153–59.

4
Murder and Madness

The theme Murder and Madness is considered to be distinct from the fusion of erotic and aggressive impulses treated in the previous chapter. In the erotic we have seen a continuum, which involves at one extreme the murder of passion as a result of a lost love, and, at the other, the sadistic mutilations of anonymous victims. The first of these is sparked by an avenging, jealous aggression, which leads to destroying the loved but also hated partner. In these crimes there is always a close relationship between the murderer and the victim. Such crimes of passion do not seem as perplexing as those involving no real relationship, only one fantasized by the murderer. In these cases the murderer is drawn to his victim or, more often, victims by a sadistic urge. Though often obvious, as in the case of the individual who sexually violates his victim during or after the murder, there are countless instances in which the erotic fusion with violence can be determined only after intensive, probing analysis of the murderer's motives, as in the case of the "Son of Sam." In these sadistic crimes the victims generally possess a uniform trait—for example, with respect to sex or age—though in some cases the variable that unites them is not obvious and can be determined only when the murderer is apprehended.

Some psychiatrists maintain that all forms of aggression, including murder, are the result of the fusion of aggression with the erotic. They use psychoanalytic theory to justify their position. This perspective, while historically enjoying great popularity, has in the last twenty years come under fire. Critics argue that murder is more than just symbolic reenactment of an oedipal or pregenital conflict, and psychoanalytic explanations have come to be challenged, transformed, and replaced by other theories. In both clinical literature and cinematic depictions murder is no longer linked just to the erotic. In film the principal focus is the confrontation between the murderer and the law. The murderer kills individuals whom he perceives to be directly trying to prevent him from achieving his objectives. The motive for such killings is never overtly sexual, as it is in the cases considered in the previous chapter. There is nothing "kinky" about these murderers; they are seemingly ordinary people who for unclear reasons have suddenly begun to kill. A brief historical review of the theories relating to the mad murderer will be enlightening and will prepare us for a better understanding of the two major films, *White Heat* (1949) and *Badlands* (1974), that are presented in this chapter.

Murder and Mothers

The question of insanity is very much tied to murder, since murder has always presented the gravest threat to the social order. The recognition that some murderers are culpable for their violent acts while others are not has its origins in early Judaic-Christian tradition.[1] Biblical injunctions emphasize that the determining issue in establishing culpability is whether or not there was malice and intent to kill. Common law, which over the centuries came to replace religious law, carried on the earlier biblical formulation. One of the earliest secular law rulings on madness and murder occurred in Britain in 1268. It maintained that "we must consider with what mind or with what intent a thing is done in order that it may be determined accordingly what action should follow and what punishment."[2]

Of all the various trials and rulings, one of the best known involved Daniel McNaughten (1843). The case drew considerable public attention because McNaughten had shot the private secretary to the prime minister of England, Robert Peel. The trial provided the basis for what has come to be called the McNaughten Rules. These concern the notion that a defense of insanity can be established only if, at the time of committing the act, the accused was experiencing "a defect of reason from a disease of the mind as to not know the nature and quality of the act he was doing, or if he did know it, that he did not know he was doing what was wrong."[3]

The McNaughten Rules served as the basis for insanity defenses in both England and the United States for over a century. In the early 1950s a new legal precedent came into being in the form of the Durham Rule. The Durham Rule questioned the ambiguity of the McNaughten Rules, particularly in its use of the words *know, nature and quality, reason,* and *wrong.* These remain a source of heated debate in any murder trial today. Both the defense and the state usually present an impressive array of psychiatric witnesses to argue the implications of these words, and it is clear that more than one psychiatric position can be taken, even in the case of individuals whom most people would judge to be crazy.

This can be seen in a recent case involving a California woman who, acting in response to "voices," strangled to death a two-year old black child, whom she had randomly kidnapped. The defense argued that "the former mental patient was an acute schizophrenic, who should be acquitted of the murder charge against her because she was insane."[4] To support this position five psychiatrists were called on to testify on the psychosis of the patient and her inability to control her depraved behavior. The prosecution also brought in psychiatric experts, the most famous of whom was Dr. Thomas Szasz. Szasz has over the last twenty years been the most visible figure in exposing the "myth" of mental illness.[5] He contended, as he often has at murder trials, that the defendant was "suffering from the consequences of having lived a life badly, stupidly, evilly, from the time of her teens."[6] Influenced by these arguments, the jurors found the defendant sane, and she was sentenced to life imprisonment. The trial is another example of the fact that there is no one recognized definition of madness, even among the experts, and that in the case of murder the defense of insanity is still controversial.

Medical psychiatry's role in the assessment of the mad murderer really began in the early 1800s, when it established criteria for assessing the complex motives for murder and the accountability of the murderer. It was realized that those who killed in what hitherto had been considered an insane fashion were, in fact, by virtue of their sense of right and wrong, sane and fully conscious of what they had done. This question received attention in the early nineteenth century in the research and writings of Phillipe Pinel, who was one of the first champions of the rights of the mad. He wrote about patients who have obvious emotional problems but who do not have perceptible difficulties with their ability to reason. He argued that there is a type of insanity not accompanied by delusions and hallucinations. His observations were retained by the nineteenth-century precursor to today's psychiatrist, then called an *alienist*.

By 1830 such ideas were enjoying greater attention. The famous British alienist, J. C. Pritchard, commented on those "whose passions were acted out involuntarily without any disease in their understanding".[7] This conception, which came to be called *moral insanity,* became a descriptive term in the diagnosis of murders. By the early 1900s the diagnosis of moral insanity gave way to that of *psychopathic inferiority.* This concept emerged from a strongly endorsed belief that all emotional problems have a biological basis, which clearly rests in one's visible constitutional differences. The murderer is different, and this difference is obvious just by looking at the shape of his head, the width of his chest, and so forth. The best-known endorser of such a view was Cesare Lambroso, whose theories on the "born criminal" gave rise to the view of psychopathy as a biogenetic condition.[8] Bromberg points out that in the late 1800s and early 1900s, when this view was popular, "widespread interest in anthropology, biology, and genetics had established for the generation, at least, the validity of the notion of hereditary transmission of morally, physically, and mentally defective individuals like the Jukes family study."[9] When the term *psychopath* was used by Kraepelin in the late 1800s in his famous psychiatric classification of mental disease, it was assured of a place in psychiatric and lay circles. The term quickly came to have many different meanings, as it was applied to the constitutional and the social, the instinctual and the behavioral.

In the 1930s the controversy around the causes of psychopathic insanity and the descriptive definition of the psychopath took on two new forms. Medical psychiatry, citing new discoveries, pointed to the organic as a cause of psychiatric problems, one of the most important examples of which was psychological aberrancy associated with encephalitis.[10] Psychoanalysis and dynamic psychiatry, on the other hand, maintained that the problems of the psychopath are more closely related to childhood maladjustment. These two viewpoints remain in conflict, though there have been attempts to integrate them. One such attempt was Cleckley's famous *Mask of Sanity,* which laid the groundwork for a description of the psychopath that was felt to constitute a clear set of characteristics.[11] Cleckley, Robert Lindner, and others who studied the psychology of the murderer in the early 1940s said that the psychopath is characterized by primitive drives and antisocial behavior. Many of the writers of this period were critical of Freud's sexual explanation for deviant behavior. "It is erroneous and biased," wrote one, "to assert that sex or pleasure can be regarded as the basis of all other drives."[12] They emphasized that the problem with the psychopath is a problem of control; when a person cannot control his behavior, he may be said to be psychopathic with respect to the behavior in question.[13] Discussion focused on the delicate balance between the strength of the primitive, antisocial tendency and the strength of the acquired control.

The theme of balance between two conflicting forces appears over and over again in the literature of the 1940s. The importance that psychoanalysis had given to social development was again recognized to be of major importance in effecting this balance. Anamnestic (history-taking) data increasingly became an important part of the psychiatric evaluation of the psychopath, and attempts were made to explain his behavior in terms of childhood circumstances that allowed him to feel "an exaggerated conception of his own intelligence, personal attractiveness, social charm, and general importance in the world."[14] This was often linked to the failure of the parents, especially the mother, to set proper limits. These various theories find representation in *White Heat*.

White Heat   *White Heat* is considered by many to be one of the earliest and most powerful depictions of the mad murderer. According to some film historians, it introduced "the psychotic hero to the gangster film."[15] It did so, however, in a manner that Americans at the time were very willing to receive because of the sense of disintegration that pervaded the country. Commented Eric Goldman:

> 1949 was proving the most nerve-wracking of all the disquieting periods the United States had known since V-J. Some years blur into a long continuing story. Some mark a fateful turn. . . . The year 1949 was such a turning point. August, the concession of China to the Communists; September, the announcement of the Soviet atom bomb; August and September and the months before and after, the explosive questions raised by the Hess case—1949 was a year of shock, shocks with enormous catalytic force.[16]

As J. Shadoian pointed out in an excellent book written in 1977, a great number of films produced that year dealt with "about every freakish calamity and human nastiness the mind can conjure up."[17] *White Heat* reflected the tensions of this period in its unique portrayal of the raw emotional life of the murderer. Unlike earlier films this one attempted to approach an understanding of the complex motives that drive the murderer.

The film begins with a train robbery by Cody Jarrett (James Cagney). As members of the gang blow out the door of the mail car, he and another gang member hold up the cabman and engineer. His accomplice is obviously new to the life of crime and twice calls Cody by name in front of the two men they hold at gunpoint. Cody says that there is only one way of correcting this mistake and unemotionally shoots both men. As one of them falls, he pushes over a lever, which releases a torrent of scalding steam on Cody's frightened accomplice.

Burnt over most of his body, he lies helplessly groaning as Cody goes back to check on the other gang members. Having successfully robbed the train, Cody is clearly in favor of leaving the injured man to die, but others show concern for their comrade and take him with them. Cody's indifference to human life and pain fits well with Cleckley's emphasis on the emotional shallowness of the psychopath, as does his explosively murderous aggression, which also came to characterize the psychopath.

The gang return to their hideout, where Cody's wife and mother await them. Cody's mother is clearly a dominant force in the gang, and the only person Cody seems to trust. While he responds with only reprimands and flashes of anger to gang members and his wife, he is attached to his mother in a childlike manner. This is graphically evidenced in a scene in which he threatens one of the gang members, Big Ed, for challenging his authority by trying to persuade the gang to leave the hiding place, as well as by making moves to take away his wife. As he pushes Big Ed to a showdown, he lets his gun fall to the floor, causing a shell to explode from its chamber. As everyone in the room leaps back, Cody, groaning in pain, clutches his head and staggers about the room. His mother rushes to his aid, pushing and half carrying him out of sight of the others. When alone with him, she pulls his flailing head to her breasts and massages his neck, assuring him that the pain will subside. He says that the pain is a splitting white light and feels like a buzz saw going through his head. As his mother clutches him, she sits him on her lap. Though the scene may well be considered overly contrived and emotional, it holds up well and indicates how fragile this killer really is. We quickly learn that Cody has experienced these migraine headaches for years. In his childhood he feigned them as an excuse to stay home with his mother, but in the course of time they became real, the ever-threatening trigger for a completely helpless condition.

It is interesting that Cody gets his headaches only twice more in the film. The first occurs when he is in prison and has just narrowly escaped death at the hand of one of Big Ed's boys. As he promises the would-be murderer that he will get his revenge, Cody suddenly begins to stagger and clutches his head. As he falls helplessly to the floor, one of the other inmates, Fallon (who is in fact an undercover G-man, or government agent), rushes to his aid. Fallon has been told about the power that Cody's mother has over her son, through whom she can express her rage at society. He seems to understand intuitively that he can win Cody's trust only by somehow associating himself with the maternal role. As Cody lies writhing on the ground, Fallon enacts this role. From some intuitive knowledge he paraphrases Cody's mother's words of encouragement and concern for not letting others see him in such a helpless state. As he removes him from the sight of others, he massages Cody's neck and cradles his head in a manner strikingly similar to the way Cody's mother had done. At the end of the film Fallon will, of course, not only reveal his true identity but will be the one who shoots him.

The final time that Cody is overwhelmed with a blinding headache is when he hears of his mother's murder by an assailant whom he incorrectly assumes is Big Ed. The news reaches him as he sits in the prison dining room. The buildup of tension in this scene is remarkable. Having entered the large hall, Cody sits down in unison with the hundreds of other inmates, and all silently begin to eat. Catching sight of a new con, who has just arrived, Cody whispers to the man next to him, "Ask him how's my mom." The word is passed from man to man until it reaches the intended con, who in turn whispers back, "She's dead." Again, the camera follows the whispered message, and as it makes its way back to Cody, it becomes like a burning fuse about to detonate a massive explosion. When Cody hears the words, he begins to rock and exhibit the general symptoms that antici- pate his incapacitating headaches. Unlike the previous collapses, Cody is not reduced to a simpering mass but externalizes the energy that has exploded in him. He jumps up from his seat and runs along the table, knocking over food and the men who try to stop him. He cuts an erratic pathway across the dining hall, careening off and over obstacles. It is not so much that he is trying to get out of the hall as to give vent to the explosion within him, which is stilled only by the repeated blows of the billy sticks of a number of guards.

The theme is a classical psychoanalytic one: the headaches are a symbolic enactment of Cody's rage, which he turns outward, and both are linked to the care and attention of his mother. His rage is not directed at his mother, quite the contrary; its only purpose is to serve as a way to get the approval and physical

White Heat (USA, 1949). **Director, Raoul Walsh. With James Cagney, Margaret Wycherly. By permission of MGM–United Artists.**

attention he so desperately craves. This is poignantly shown when his mother, cradling him on her knee after his first attack in the hideout, holds up a glass of water for him to drink and says, "Top of the world." The words imply a kind of omnipotence, which is very much associated with the regressive nurture that Cody receives from his mother. The early oral psychosexual basis for such nurture cannot be overlooked, as is made clear when Cody's mother leaves the hideout to get her boy's favorite food, strawberries. While somewhat heavy-handed, this scene agrees with the psychiatric explanation of the period, which emphasized that psychopathology is the result of an overly nurturant and over-demanding mother, whose conflicts are given expression in the behavior of the child. Cody's final gleeful scream of defiance to the G-men, "Made it, Ma—top of the world," before he explodes himself by firing into the breast-shaped oval on which he is perched, offers clear evidence that all of Cody's asocial, murderous actions were simply a function of his attachment to his mother.

From Motive to Motiveless Murder

Though psychoanalysis enjoyed a renewed popularity in the 1950s, there was at the same time a resurgence of behaviorism. While the two schools of thought struggled for dominance—the former emphasizing instincts; the latter, learning—some psychiatrists advocated a move toward synthesis. The publication of *Personality and Psychotherapy* by J. Dollard and N. Miller in 1950 was one of the first such attempts.[18] The book promoted the *aggression-frustration theory* of behavior, which emphasized that human problems, particularly those involving the expression of overt asocial aggression, are a function of frustrating experiences. While acknowledging the worth of psychoanalytic insights, Dollard and Miller maintained that aggression can be explained more effectively by adopting the frustration-aggression learning model. Throughout the 1950s experiments were conducted to test the validity of this model, and it was increasingly applied to clinical populations, particularly to murderers. These studies began to quantify the individual's internal controls against aggression and the degree to which he views a frustrating experience as arbitrary or unarbitrary.[19] By the mid-1960s interest shifted toward studying specific social forces that trigger aggression, as well as factors in the individual's history that might determine his response to these forces.[20] The notion of immediate environmental triggers of aggression shifted attention away from the clinical belief that the murderer is simply a highly impulsive psychopath.

The psychologist I. Megargee presented a more detailed analysis of the inadequate internal controls that characterized the murderer.[21] Megargee maintained that there are two types of murderer: the undercontrolled, who has had continuing problems with the law, and the overcontrolled, who, until he commits murder, was never assaultive, and in fact was rather passive. Research on the overcontrolled murderer typified him as a person who suddenly explodes, as the pent-up frustrations of a lifetime erupt in a single instance. The murderer's inhibitions against the expression of aggression are, up until the explosion of murderous rage, extremely rigid and absolute so that "his instigation to aggression builds over time."[22] It is interesting that Megargee affirms this buildup on the basis of the earlier work of Dollard and Miller on the frustration-aggression model.

Megargee used both intrapsychic and behavioral theories to explain the explosive and unprovoked murder. At about the same time, medical psychiatry was also investigating this problem, which it called the *sudden murder,* or the *murder without motive.*[23] Like Megargee's research, it focused on murders that appear to be "single, isolated, unexpected episodes of violent, impulsive . . . behavior, . . . which was never well thought out, . . . which had not obvious purpose, nor hope for personal advantage of profit in the forseeable future."[24] Though medical psychiatry did not directly confirm Megargee's theory of the overcontrolled and undercontrolled personality, it struggled with the same basic question of how a person who seems sane can suddenly commit murder without reason. Throughout all the research, attention was given to the extreme inability of the murderer to tolerate frustration and establish the controls that would have prevented the breaking point of murder.

Evident in both clinical studies and the popular press of the 1960s was increasing concern with understanding the steadily increasing number of such murders. The madness involved in the killing of John F. Kennedy and Martin Luther King, Jr. seemed to prepare the country for a rash of well-publicized murders, which were characterized by their senseless brutality and, more important, by the number of victims. One such murder occurred on a blistering hot day in the middle of August 1966. A twenty-five-year old part-time graduate student in architectural engineering, carrying three rifles, a shot gun, and other firearms, climbed to the top of an observation tower at the Austin campus of the University of Texas. From his vantage point, 307 feet above the sprawling campus, he carefully laid out his arsenal and then randomly shot forty-four persons, killing fourteen of them, before he himself was killed by police. While this was not the first time that a person suddenly went berserk and randomly killed those around him, it did set an American record for a one-man massacre. More important, it was but one of a number of multiple murders that came at a time when mass violence appeared to be erupting throughout America and was coming to be accepted as commonplace. It was this arbitrary and violent quality in murder that became the subject of two box-office successes of the period, *Bonnie and Clyde* (1967) and *In Cold Blood* (1968).

Arthur Penn's *Bonnie and Clyde* is not a film about the 1960s as such; the infamous criminal couple it so creatively depicts were active in 1931, during the worst period of the Great Depression. From a psychiatric perspective, however, their murders fit with the social violence of the 1960s. Wrote one contemporary reviewer, for example:

> It is a searing indictment of middle class America; of a country torn apart by race hatred, where the negro community in particular is producing many young people with the same problems as Bonnie and Clyde. It has been said that Bonnie and Clyde are not villains any more than those who turn to L.S.D. and marijuana today. The guilt is placed where it belongs.

I think, however, that the film's profound success with young people means that Arthur Penn's message has been partially misunderstood and that it will be taken as a sermon in praise of violence as the only possible protest against the conditions in which we find ourselves today. It would be unfortunate if sympathy for the heroes should lead the audience to come to the illogical conclusion that if one reacts violently against the community in which one lives, the violence can be justified, if the conditions of the society are bad enough.[25]

In Cold Blood, which came out three years after the book by Truman Capote, attracted an equal degree of attention. It is interesting that when the film was shot in Kansas, in the actual town where the four members of the Clutter family had been killed, the filmmakers consulted the prestigious, Topeka-based Menninger Psychiatric Clinic about the characterization of the two murderers, Perry and Dick. The psychiatrist selected to provide this help was Joseph Satten, who had done research on the murder without motive.[26] Perry's flashbacks were one area where Satten had direct input. He suggested that the first transition into Perry's childhood be done as Perry is looking at himself in a mirror.[27] In his work Satten had stressed that "in the historical background of all the cases was the occurrence of extreme parental violence during childhood,"[28] and this is certainly emphasized in the flashback in which Perry's father holds a gun to his son's head or in which he brutalizes Perry's mother for infidelity. Satten emphasized that all cases of such murders involve severe emotional deprivation and that "this deprivation may have involved prolonged or recurrent absence of one or both parents; a chaotic family life in which the parents were unknown with the child being raised by others."[29] The film very much emphasized the abandonment that Perry experienced at an early age and the fact that he was brought up in an orphanage run by an order of nuns. The film emphasized both his fear and hatred of the nuns: he panics when he sees two nuns in the bus station where he is to meet Dick; and he speaks about his dream in which a large yellow bird comes and destroys the nuns who had ill-treated him in the orphanage. This is reminiscent of Satten's comment that

> manifestations of a bizarre, violent and primitive fantasy life were seen in each of the men we examined. Repetitive dreams of violently killing, mutilating, burning, or destroying were seen; the brief T.A.T. stories of these men were filled with a quality of primitive, murderous hostility, in some cases glibly rationalized on the basis of the victim having 'provoked' their murderers, and others precipitated by rejection or rebuff, usually implying oral deprivation.[30]

The film, more than the book, emphasized that Perry's murderous rage is linked to his father. This is clear when we see the bound figure of Mr. Clutter fused with the image of Perry's father just before Perry stabs and shoots him. The connection is also clear when we see the hangman's face become that of Perry's father as Perry mounts the scaffold to his death. Again, all of this seems complementary to Satten's earlier research, in which he said:

> The murderous potential can become activated especially if some disequilibrium is already present when the victim-to-be is unconsciously perceived as a

key figure in some past traumatic configuration. The behavior, or even the mere presence, of this figure adds a stress to the unstable balance of forces that results in a sudden extreme discharge of violence, similar to the explosion that takes place when a percussion cap ignites a charge of dynamite.[31]

This imagery of an explosive ignition became central in the clinical literature of the sixties and seventies. Though it sustains Megargee's thesis of overcontrolled and undercontrolled murderers, there was still by the mid-1970s a great uncertainty about the determinants of murder.[32] We should not forget that there has never been any single explanation of murder. The existing explanations of the murder without motive was coming under intense criticism both from within and without clinical psychiatry. By 1974 murder was being discussed as a function of *behavioral discontrol.* Behavioral discontrol involves "short-circuiting events [that] rearrange the build-up state to the action state due to defect or alteration in the inhibitory capacities and failure of inherent restraint systems in the brain".[33] The clinical literature on murder in the early 1970s, the time before and during which *Badlands* was shot, interpreted murder as a sudden release of intrapsychic pressure. On the one hand we find in this literature a return to early neurological studies, which focused on the murderer's suddenly going into a seizurelike state, now described as a "short-circuiting."[34] This neurophysiological explanation had, of course, never left clinical literature since its early dominance in German psychiatry in the 1880s.[35] In the 1970s, however, it seemed to gain particular attention once more, as evident in the research of one of the most respected investigators of murder, Shervert Frazier.[36] Frazier pointed out that in the murderer there seems to be a triggering of the most primitive part of the brain, and for support he referred to the earlier work of MacLean on schizophysiology.[37] From this perspective the murderer is a person whose higher neocortex brain functions are precariously structured, so that they are quick to return to what MacLean felt was the reptilian, primitive brain.[38] Neurophysiological research allowed that there are, in addition to the biochemical anomalies, certain psychological defensive structures weakened by socialization processes.

This work gave rise, then, to the second thrust of the research in the early 1970s, which focused on the social factors that weaken the defenses and on the consequent expression of primitive rage. The literature increasingly focused on the sudden, impulsive homicide, in which a clear personal motive is absent and in which multiple murders are often involved. As such murders increased on both the national and international level and gained wider public attention, there was an increase in clinical attempts to explain them.[39] This became particularly evident as accounts of unprovoked murder by American soldiers in Vietnam began to be reported. Over and over again clinical research failed to produce real evidence of deliberate, systematic planning on the part of the murderer prior to his crime.[40] This is in contrast to earlier studies and cinematic depictions, in which the murderer's behavior was more structured and deliberate. The picture of the murderer that emerged in the 1970s emphasized the senseless and anonymous killing that erupted with no previous planning and resulted usually in the death of more than one person. This was not a crime of passion, but one that was committed entirely without emotion and involved killing almost without purpose. The killer was no longer a raging, primitive maniac who has always led a life of crime, as portrayed in *White Heat* and so many other gangster films of the forties and early fifties.

In the late 1960s and in the 1970s a new kind of murderer dominated the psychiatric and popular imagination, an outsider who killed neither for money nor out of passion but in motiveless death sprees. Unlike his precursor, he often did not have a history of murderous behavior but was marginally adjusted and, as so often stated in the clinical literature of the 1970s, "had not internalized the values of society."[41] With *Badlands* we are introduced to the question of what these values really are.

Badlands   More than anything else, Mallick's work was a statement on the banality of evil. Using as a model the 1958 killing of eleven people by Charles Starkweather,[42] Mallick wrote, directed, and produced a cinematic characterization of the possible motives of seemingly motiveless slaughter. His presentation is far from the classical psychoanalytic one that offered a sense of the ultimate causes of murder, as depicted in *White Heat*. Remarkably similar to a clinical study by Frazier published in 1974, the same year the film was released, Mallick transposed into vivid imagery Frazier's opening paragraph:

> Murder as a human action state does not allow simple reductionistic conclusions about the cause or causes. Action states require conceptual models, methods of definition, and definition or coexisting so-called etiologic forces—which are essentially descriptive.[43]

There was, then, no flashbacks or recollections of childhood traumas imposed by brutal, sadistic parents, but only the cataloging of a series of events that lead up to and follow the killing of eight people. This descriptive approach was difficult for many to accept, as evidenced in one criticism at the time of the film's release: "The film offers nothing in the way of explanation of these two pathetic misfits".[44] To emphasize the descriptive, rather than explanatory, interpretation of the film, Mallick had a good deal of the film narrated by Holly (Sissy Spacek), a fifteen-year-old living parody of teenage fan magazines and Nancy Drew aphorisms. Holly's voice opens the film, as the camera moves through a diffuse, unfocused color field to fix on a bedroom that reflects pubescent ambivalence in its contrast of childish dolls and stuffed animals with artifacts of adulthood. As if reading from a diary, Holly tells us in a singsong voice that her mother died when she was ten and that she and her father (Warren Oates), an artist, moved from Texas to Dupree, South Dakota. As if recounting a series of incidents in the past, she tells us about her father's strictness and her difficulty in making friends because she had nothing to say.

We have no sense that this is anything but a grade B adolescent love story when she says, "Little did I realize that all this would change when I met Kit." Kit (Martin Sheen), Holly tells us, is a look-alike for James Dean. He meets Holly as she walks alone down empty residential streets effortlessly twirling her baton, as if preparing to achieve glory as a majorette. Freckled and in shorts, she seems to resemble every fifteen-year-old girl in America—an impression complemented by her infatuation with Kit. Kit is very polite and solicitous and though they really only converse in platitudes, he tells her that she is very unique and that he would like to see her again. Reluctant, she says that her father is very critical of anyone who might ask her out, and Kit says this might be particularly so because he works for the city as a garbage collector. Their romance evolves, and though he is twenty-five, he seems more like Holly in age. He is filled with romantic extremism. After sleeping with Holly for the first time, for instance, he asks if she would like to commemorate the event with a suicide pact. Her vapid, emotionless state, which will again be evidenced in his killings, is reflected in her comment, "If that's all there is to it, then what's all the fuss about?" Their clandestine meetings are by a river, where Kit plans their future and talks of an idyllic life, based on childlike fantasies.

We learn almost nothing about Kit's childhood and his past. The only things we do learn depict him as a person who has led a rather marginal existence, which has included various low-level jobs and few relationships. He is an outsider and like his hero, James Dean, has little capacity for expressing emotion. Brooding and contemplative, he distances himself from others and reacts to frustration with a shrug and an internalizing of his rage. When Holly's father abuses and mocks Kit after Kit asks for his approval to marry Holly, the young man seems unaffected and simply walks away. Shortly thereafter, Kit goes to Holly's house and, finding that no one is home, enters. After packing some things for Holly, he waits for their return. When the father enters his home and finds Kit, he is enraged. As he goes to call the police, Kit shoots him several times.

Immediately after the killing, Kit calmly lights a cigarette and, as if the body lying near him does not exist, slowly draws on it. He tells Holly that they will wait until dark and then make their escape. Consistent with her emotional vapidness, Holly does not seem upset by her father's death, except to express some minimal concern about whether he is really dead. After disposing of the body in the basement, Kit returns upstairs with a toaster in hand. Shortly after dark, he sets the house ablaze, and they embark on their escape, but only after stopping at Holly's high school to collect her school books, for as she tells us, Kit does not want her to fall behind. While Holly gets her work together, Kit goes to a bus station. There, he records his explanation for killing Holly's father: "He was provokin' me, so I popped him." The term is accurately descriptive of the discontrol that suddenly erupts into murder. The hideout he selects is near their secret meeting spot by the river, and it is here that Kit's fantasy world materializes. He builds a crude tree house and sets up a series of traps for would-be pursuers.

Though Kit idealizes living off the land, it is but a short time before his explosive rage manifests itself. This is clear when he madly empties his gun at a river fish that has eluded his homemade net. Kit's beleaguered return to nature does not last long enough to be completely tarnished, for the law soon descends upon him in the form of three rifle-toting deputies. Hiding in one of the series of tunnels he has made, he surprises the lawmen from behind and kills them. Our sense of his remorselessness is only heightened by Holly's comment, "Kit felt badly shooting them in the back." These killings, and the four to follow, are all marked by the sudden explosion of murderous rage and an inability to register any concern for the victims, even when they lie dying in front of him.

As they escape into the North Dakota Badlands, Kit tells Holly that they will find safety in Canada. He will become a Mountie, he says. Kit's infatuation with the law is part of his need to attain hero stature, a need clearly evident in his statement, "I always wanted to be a criminal." He clearly wants to have an identity, particularly one that conveys a sense of mastery. He seems unable to differentiate between a criminal and a policeman; both seem to confer a sense of importance and mastery—and thus seems to be the only thing that matters. For Kit, life is little more than playing a role. This was also the case for the killer Charles Starkweather, after whom he is modeled. When finally caught, Starkweather said, "I wanted to be a criminal, but I didn't know it would be like this."[45]

As Frazier said:

> The acting out becomes a desperate attempt at mastery, an attempt that fails. The murderer has a learning defect that is reminiscent of the behavior of toddlers, for whom each act is a new event, an attempt to learn about the self. In early adolescence, the urgency is to learn who the self is.[46]

Kit urgently seeks an identity, a referent for establishing his existence. This is made clear in his throwing together a pile of rocks to commemorate the place where he was captured. This pathetic, superficial attempt at achieving an identity is, for Mallick, part of the American value system, which promotes self-inflated egocentrism, based on myths of heroism. The arresting officer is very much a personification of these values: he is dressed in a white hat, carries a six-gun low on his hip, and affects a James Dean persona.

Kit's difficulty in going beyond appearances is also evident in his explanation for his killings. He maintains that he is killing simply out of self-defense. He does not seem able to grasp the real reason that he is being pursued. This again fits Frazier's description:

> First murder may not be perceived as a violent action by the murderer himself. Often it fits so closely into a system of thinking that it becomes the only logical outcome because of the nature of the murderer's thinking and feeling. . . . The only way to escape the feeling of being systematically cornered is to murder, an action which is an end in itself.[47]

Badlands therefore reflected a perspective on murder that was evident in both the clinical and popular literature of the period. While it carried on the thematic tradition of the "outlaw couple"—so popularized by earlier films, such as *You Only Live Once* (1937), *They Live by Night* (1949), *Breathless* (1959), *Bonnie and Clyde* (1967), *The Honeymoon Killers* (1969), and by two concurrent films, *Sugarland Express* (1974) and *Thieves like Us* (1974)—it also presented a new type of murderer. This was the killer who murdered neither for money, nor out of a higher social consciousness, nor because his oppressors had forced him. The murders were seemingly without motive and took place almost reflexively. Unlike their

earlier cinematic role models, Kit and Holly were not really distinct per§
but rather one-dimensional figures who flatly imitated the daily occur
murder that Americans witnessed on evening television news programs. They
did not really have a relationship but reflected each other's inability to feel. They
were both loners, unattached figures, who simply floated until they suddenly
burst and spewed forth murderous rage. Kit's characterization in this regard was
to be perfectly imitated by Robert De Niro's portrayal of Travis Bickle in *Taxi
Driver*. Seeking similar heroic fantasies but lost in faceless anonymity, Bickle's
killings followed a scenario similar to Kit's. Their dreams of glory have become
our nightmares, from which we are still trying to awaken. It is interesting in this
light to realize the influence of a film like *Taxi Driver* on a figure like John
Hinckley, Jr., who attempted in 1981 to kill the president of the United States.[48]
The media described his acts as "unprovoked, random violence," and pictured
him as a murderous, drooling psychopath, who stalks his victims unrelentingly
and seems to be unstoppable: this is the star in *The Howling, Halloween, Prom
Night, Friday the Thirteenth, The Eyes of Laura Mars*, and at least a hundred more
titles of box-office successes of the last ten years. While these particular films
were distorted, sensationalized portrayals of sadistic murders, they have fused in
the public mind and have come to characterize all murders that are seemingly
inexplicable. Such murders have gained the greatest attention and have made it
seem that murder is the natural outcome of unprovoked, specious, and pervasive violence. The result is that we have jumped at any shadow or rustling heard
in the dark. The facts, however, have not supported the popular cinematic image
that most murders are indiscriminately perpetrated by faceless cretans of the
night who are, were, or should be psychiatric patients. The greatest percentage
of murders are committed by individuals who know their victims, and the
psychotic, schizoid, multiple personality killer is for the most part a construction
of the media. What has resulted from such sensationalizing is an association
between the murderer and the psychiatrically ill, as evidenced in an article in
Time about the killing of the rock star John Lennon.[49] The magazine linked the
process of deinstitutionalization of psychiatric patients to an increase in the type
of murderer represented by Mark Chapman, the killer of Lennon: "On the one
hand, having abolished civil commitment, we allow psychotics to wander the
streets. On the other hand, thanks to the free availability of guns, we allow them
to arm themselves."[50]
America has easily accepted this image, since it plays on some of the most basic
aspects of primitive thought, those which equate murder with the mad as a way
of distancing such an act from the world of the sane.[51]
It is important to realize that the literature on rage, aggression, violence,
assassination, terror, warfare, rebellion, and revolution has increased exponentially since the early 1960s. Writing in 1975, a year after *Badlands* appeared and,
more important, a year after murder in the United States attained a new record
(9.8 per 10,000)—one that was to last until 1980—Lawrence Freedman, a noted
researcher on violence, said:

In the past 12-month period, approximately 600 articles were written and
published in scientific journals on the subject of aggression. Conflict resolu-

tion, legal, exhortatory articles on war, terrorism, assassination, and personal violence increase this literature by the thousands. However, this explosion of rhetoric concerning this most violent of man's preoccupations attests to an extraordinarily rapid expansion of interest, not new information. When one quarter century ago I began my study of aggression and violence, all the literature available published within the previous decade was less than 1 percent of these figures, but they contained nearly as much information. Over 25 years, 25 million deaths, and 25 wars later, we are scarcely more informed concerning these matters than we were at the close of World War II.[52]

Though the number of murders seems to be increasing, there is still much controversy concerning how factual the data is on who murders, who is murdered, and why. What is clear is that the amount of media attention focused on murder is increasing and that this has an impact on the perception of both victim and murderer. One example of life's imitating of art in this regard is found in recent Senate testimony on Mafia activities by an undercover agent who pointed to the impact of the films *Godfather I* and *Godfather II* on the various Mafia families. The films, he said, were continuously discussed and the behavior of its characters were imitated.[53]

Notes

1. See J. Quen, Jr., *Anglo-American Criminal Insanity: A Historical Perspective* (The History of the Behavioral Sciences), vol. 10, no. 3 (July 1974), pp. 313–23.
2. Ibid., p. 314.
3. Ibid., p. 320.
4. A Press and P. Abramson, "A Law for Racist Killers," *Newsweek* (23 February 1981), p. 80.
5. Thomas Szasz, *The Myth of Mental Illness* (New York: Harper & Row, 1961).
6. Press and Abramson.
7. J. C. Pritchard, A *Treatise on Insanity and Other Disorders Affecting the Mind* (London: Gilbert, Sherwood, Gilbert, and Piper, 1835), p. 162.
8. C. Lambroso, *Crime: Its Causes and Remedies* (Boston: Little, Brown and Company, 1911).
9. W. Bromberg, *The Mold of Murder: A Psychiatric Study of Homicide* (New York: Grune and Stratton, 1961), p. 63.
10. D. Silverman, "Clinical and Electroencephalographic Studies on Criminal Psychopaths," *Archives of Neurological Psychiatry* 50 (1943): 18–33.
11. H. Cleckley, *The Mask of Sanity* (St. Louis, Mo.: CV Mosby Co., 1941).
12. H. Cason, "The Concept of the Psychopath," *American Journal of Orthopsychiatry* 18 (1948): 330.
13. Ibid., p. 302.
14. F. C. Thorne, "Etiological Studies of the Psychopathic Personality: The Ego Inflated Deflectively Conditioned Type," *Journal of Consulting and Clinical Psychiatry* 11 (1947): 307.
15. E. Rostow, *Born to Lose: The Gangster Film in America* (New York: Oxford University Press, 1978).
16. E. F. Goldman, *The Crucial Decade And After* (New York: Random House, 1965), p. 112.
17. J. Shadoian, *Dreams and Dead Ends: The American Gangster Crime Film* (Cambridge: Massachusetts Institute of Technology Press, 1977).
18. J. Dollard and N. Miller, *Personality and Psychotherapy* (New York: McGraw-Hill, 1950).
19. N. Pastore, "The Role of Arbitrariness in the Frustration-Aggression Hypothesis," *Journal of Abnormal and Social Psychology*, vol. 63, no. 1 (1961), 183–87.
20. L. Berkowitz, *Aggression: A Social Psychological Analysis* (New York: McGraw-Hill, 1962).
21. I. Magargee, "Undercontrolled and Overcontrolled Personality Types in Extreme Antisocial Aggression," *Psychological Monographs*, vol. 80, no. 3 (1966).
22. Ibid.
23. J. Weiss et al., "The Sudden Murderer," *Archives of General Psychiatry* 91 (1960): pp. 669–77.

J. Satten, K. Menninger and I. Rosen, "Murder Without Apparent Motive: A Study in Personality Disorganization," *American Journal of Psychiatry* 117 (1960): 48–53.

24. Blackburn et al., "The Sudden Murderer: Clues to Preventive Interaction," *Archives of General Psychology* 8 (1963): 289.

25. H. P. Hildbrand, "We Rob Banks," *Journal of the National Association for Mental Health,* vol. 21, no. 4 (1967), p. 17.

26. Satten, Menninger, Rosen et al., p. 48.

27. J. Satten, Conversation with Michael Fleming (1960).

28. Satten, Menninger, Rosen et al., p. 49.

29. Ibid., p. 50.

30. Ibid.

31. Ibid., p. 52.

32. D. Lester, "Murder: A Review," *Corrective and Social Psychiatry,* vol. 19, no. 4 (1973).

33. Shervert H. Frazier, "Murder—Single and Multiple," *The Aggression Proceedings of the Association for Research in Nervous and Mental Diseases* 52 (1974): 4.

34. Resnick, "Child Murder by Parents," *American Journal of Psychiatry* 126 (1969): 325–44.

35. E. Kretschmer, *Textbook of Medical Psychology,* trans. E. B. Strauss (London: Oxford University Press, 1934). D. Williams, "Neural Factors Related to Habitual Aggression," *Brain* 93 (1969): 503–20.

36. Shervert H. Frazier, *Violence and Social Impact, Research and the Psychiatric Patient,* ed. J. C. Schoolar and C. Gaitz (New York: Bruner Mazel, Inc., 1975).

37. P. D. Maclean, "Psychosomatic Disease and the Visceral Brain," *Psychosomatic Medicine* 11 (1949): 338.

38. Ibid.

39. J. Westmeyer, "Grenade-Amok in Laos," *International Journal of Social Psychiatry,* vol. 19, no. 3/4 (Fall 1973), 251–60.

40. M. W. Kahn, "Basic Characteristics of Murderers: Factors Analysis of Personality, Intelligence, and Background Variables," *Genetic Psychology Monographs* 84 (November 1971): 329–58.

41. Ibid., p. 344.

42. See "Crime: Eleven Lay Dead," *Newsweek,* (10 February 1958), 42–44.

43. Frazier, (1974), p. 1.

44. M. King, "Badlands: Shoot First." *Jump Cut,* no. 1 (May–June 1974), p. 7.

45. *Newsweek* (10 February 1958), p. 44.

46. Frazier (1975), p. 188.

47. Ibid., p. 188.

48. Kurt Andersen, "A Drifter Who Stalked Success," *Time* (13 April 1981), p. 41.

49. John Leo, "The Menace of Any Shadow," *Time* (22 December 1980), pp. 28–32.

50. Ibid., p. 32.

51. D. Lunde, *Murder and Madness* (Stanford, Calif.: Stanford Alumni Association, 1975).

52. L. Z. Freedman, "Violence," *Annals of the New York Academy of Sciences* vols. 259–61 (1975), p. 243.

53. "The Mob Takes Its Cues From Godfather Films," *Boston Globe* (2 March 1981), p. 1.

5
War and Madness

War has always been a subject of special fascination and fear and, as such, has been a favorite subject of filmmakers. The majority of films depicting war have done so in a highly stylized, romantic manner, but those that become classics usually represent explorations into the personal experience of war. Such films probe the inner, psychological responses of individuals in combat; frequently, they focus on madness, which is often depicted as both the cause and the effect of war. The first section of this chapter concentrates on the portrayal of forms of madness held to be the result of an individual's participation in the chaotic and debilitating experience of war.

Perhaps war is a topic of fascination because it represents such an overt contradiction of the principles that allow societies to exist. In war all codes, laws, and commandments are overturned—one is directed to kill at any cost. The soldier is drafted into a different reality, where he must kill on command and thus place himself in a position to be killed. The extreme mental stress incurred often results in aberrant behavioral and emotional reactions, which come to be called "madness." One might expect that the reactions of all human beings to extreme circumstances involving life and death would be the same, or at least similar. On closer appraisal one finds the contrary. There are great individual differences in human reaction to the horrors of war. It has been said that every individual has a breaking point, but to determine what that point is involves so many situational and intrapsychic variables as to be impossible to predict.[1] This does not mean, however, that military authorities and mental health experts have abandoned the task of defining the situations and personality factors that precipitate madness.

It is interesting that the films dealing with war and madness, like so many nonpropaganda war films, were released only after the particular war in question. It is almost as if the patriotic fervor needed to rally and maintain a nation's pursuit of war does not allow for a depiction of the cost of such combat to the human psyche. Perhaps we want to believe that because we are in the right and that God is on our side, the vicissitudes of human emotion should not and must not stand in the way. Such an attitude was graphically depicted by George C. Scott's Oscar-winning performance in *Patton* (1969). In one scene he hits a soldier who sits in an agitated state of fear in a field hospital away from the battle area. Patton expresses the anger common among those who value physical strength and disdain emotional needs. They reject the idea that a mental-

112

emotional—and therefore invisible and abstract—problem can be enough to incapacitate a soldier.

Every major military campaign in which the United States has been involved during the twentieth century has generated volumes of clinical literature on the madness associated with war. An examination of this literature reveals how dissimilar the interpretations of madness have been over time—it is as if each of America's major wars has generated a particular type of madness. Such variance can be explained from a number of perspectives. Critics of diagnostic labels argue that diagnoses are always changing and have more to do with the labelers' theoretical acrobatics than with the actual problems of patients. An example would be the change in the major psychiatric diagnoses for the three biggest wars—from *shell shock* (World War I); to *traumatic neurotic reactions* and *combat fatigue* (World War II); to *post-traumatic stress disorder,* or *Vietnam Syndrome* (Vietnam War). Though all may simply describe the same experience of breaking down under stress, it is also possible that they are in fact distinct. Each may represent a unique type of experience, which precipitated a different form of madness.

Of all the wars of this century in which the United States has played a major role, World War II and Vietnam have received the most coverage in terms both of cinematic interpretation and clinical literature. They have, and no doubt will for many years to come, continue to be the subject of interest for both filmmakers and clinicians. Though the other two wars, World War I and Korea, were probably equally costly in terms of human anguish, they did not become a popular subject of major filmmakers. Let us briefly discuss the possible reasons.

Regarding World War I, it might be claimed that the technology to produce such feature films scarcely existed during or immediately after this event. This is not the case. Lavish productions were made soon after the war. D. W. Griffith's *Hearts of the World* (1918) and *Isn't Life Wonderful?* (1924), for example, both were films made on location and involved fairly complex situations. They set the stage for an outpouring of films dealing with the costliness of war, though none focused on madness and all exuded a sense of patriotic self-righteousness. Emphasizing the theme War Is Hell, they included such films as the American productions *The Four Horsemen of the Apocalypse* (1921) and *The Big Parade* (1925) and the British films *Reveille* (1924) and *Dawn* (1927). Exceptions to the above pattern were Pabst's two German films *Westfront 1918* (1930) and *Kameradschaft* (1931) and Abel Gance's early French work *J'Accuse* (1919; remake 1937). Gance was the first to show the effects of shell shock, which affects the film's protagonist, a pacifist poet who is driven insane. Equivalent in the American cinema was the pacifist *All Quiet on the Western Front* (1930) and the British anti-war film on the Dardanelles campaign, *Tell England* (1930).

The theme that was always to dominate, however, was that of heroic action. It took until 1958, with Stanley Kubrick's *Paths of Glory,* for the full impact of madness through shell shock and trench warfare to be depicted. Though there were films in which some minor character succumbed to madness, no attempt was made to focus on the situational and intrapsychic pressures that lead to madness. A partial explanation for this could be that the medical model's primarily organic explanations of madness during the period of World War I left the general public, including the filmmakers in America and Europe, with a sense that little of the soldier's personal emotional needs had to, or could, be considered. The shell-shocked soldier had neither memory nor feeling, and one could do little but offer pity without understanding. The psychiatric literature of this period was given over to detailed analyses of neurological impairments and, in general, offered little by way of interpretation of the subjective, emotional trauma of the soldier.

An attempt to explain why so few films depicted the psychiatric problems associated with the Korean War presents even greater problems. An analysis of films made during this war shows that they also were primarily propagandistic. Those that followed the war treated the subject of madness, at best, in a highly schematic manner. John Frankenheimer's *The Manchurian Candidate* (1962), for example, made little or no attempt at bringing about clinical versimilitude. This was one of the first and most popular films to deal with brainwashing, a topic that came to hold particular interest for only limited sectors in both psychiatry and Hollywood. The clinical literature coming out of the Korean War was restricted, and a good deal of it focused on brainwashing—or, as it came to be psychiatrically labeled, "thought reform," or the psychology of totalism.[2] One explanation is certainly that fewer soldiers were involved in the Korean War and that fewer were therefore psychologically impaired, though one could also say that the forces of repression that insisted on labeling the war an "action" or "conflict" deflected the attention of both the general public and the psychiatric community away from the price paid in human lives and madness.

Because of the limited number of films depicting madness in both World War I and Korea, we have selected only films from World War II and the Vietnam War that focused on soldiers' deterioration into madness.

World War II

Since the First World War psychiatry, as a specialty, had gained a good deal of credibility with militarists. With the beginning of the Second World War it came to be viewed increasingly as an effective way of treating and preventing madness. In the early days of World War II the clinical term for describing madness was *traumatic war neuroses,* while in the later stage of the war the term *combat fatigue* was used.

As in all wars the new diagnoses, treatments, and views on prevention took time to develop. During the transition period, the interpretations and treatments of madness from the previous war slowly gave way to the new approaches. At the beginning of World War II, in particular, psychiatric interpretations from the previous war evidenced themselves in clinical explanations of madness. Any exploration of clinical views during World War II would have to include a summary of the interpretation of madness from World War II. During the earlier war psychiatry was tied to a neurological approach, which emphasized an organic interpretation of symptoms, including those that appeared to be the result of combat. These symptoms generally fell under the diagnoses of shell shock, which resulted from being too near an exploding shell. It was felt that the sustained shell barrages associated with trench warfare in World War I produced a type of acute paralysis and memory loss that afflicted a number of soldiers in very similar fashion. Soldiers would be found in semicatatonic states evidencing various levels of paralysis and amnesia. Psychiatry, which at the time was closely tied to neurology, first interpreted such symptoms to be a result of severe concussions and turned to an investigation of shell shock. Despite the absence of the kind of lesions expected, many psychiatrists continued to believe that there was an organic basis for the patients' disability. They tried such treatments as rest, hydrotherapy, and even experimented with electrotherapy.

One neurologist particularly interested in shell shock was Freud. Just beginning to explore the hidden reaches of the unconscious, Freud gradually noticed that the kind of paralytic symptoms he was seeing in the field hospital bore a remarkable similarity to those he treated in his private clinical practice in Vienna. Freud brought a new perspective to the study of shell shock. Up to this point there were two conflicting views, one that emphasized the neurological and one that viewed the sufferer as simply feigning a paralysis in order to escape the front lines. Freud's argument, which came to be expounded by others who followed his initial explorations (such as James McDougall, Sandor Ferenzci, Karl Abraham, and Ernest Jones), emphasized that these symptoms of withdrawal served to protect the individual from the fear of death.

By the time World War II began, Freud's thinking had become a core part of psychiatrists' thoughts on the treatment of madness associated with warfare. The shell shock of World War I had led to the discovery of the massive repression of a patient's fear of death, which in turn produced a total defensive withdrawal. The symptoms of paralysis, muteness, loss of sight, and so forth were attempts to remove the self from those senses that had registered the threat of death. A loss of hearing, for example, meant that the soldier was still protecting himself from the massive fear of death that had threatened to overwhelm him with the sound of an exploding shell. Each physical symptom was a barrier that prevented the emotion of fear from gaining entrance into consciousness.[3] The job of the psychiatrist was to move the patient gradually to verbally elaborate on this fear. Freud and his followers had begun to see that this fear of death took many different forms. One of the most common was the sudden onset of symptoms following the death of a comrade. Just beneath and complementing the symptoms of paralysis was a severe depression. By listening to the patient, psychiatrists found that he felt a great deal of guilt in relation to his friends. Early in his investigations of the unconscious Freud found that every fear was actually a repressed wish, and he applied this discovery to the fear in soldiers who were immobilized. Their grief and withdrawal were means for protecting themselves from consciously recognizing their preference for the death of their friends over their own. The voice of the unconscious spoke a horrible truth when it said, "If someone has to die, let it be another, not me."

These speculations on the impact of the unconscious had begun to gain some acceptance in military psychiatry by the Second World War, though the form of treatment encouraged by psychoanalytic theory was not considered to be feasible. Freud and his followers had argued that the repression of such fears could be recovered only through the patient's free associations in a therapeutic encounter that had the therapist as listener. Because of the massive medical needs presented by the soldiers of World War II, however, any treatment that took a long time and required passivity on the part of the therapist was not practical. Though Freud's theoretical ideas were given more attention than they had been in World War I, they were still not applied operationally to the soldier in the field evidencing madness. Freud's ideas, nevertheless, did help bring about a more tolerant, even informed, view toward the emotional needs of the serviceman.

Such ideas had even begun to work their way into the Pentagon, and there was an increasing interest in psychological research. Warfare had changed dramatically, and the type of psychiatric problem experienced by the soldier was different. Not only had warfare assumed technologically advanced forms (e.g., submarine and aerial), but there were multiple theaters of war. This is not to say that World War I did not have some of these components, but in World War II they had reached levels of specialization on an international scale that demanded a new way of understanding the needs of the soldier. The geographical ranges of airplanes and submarines and the fact that the war was spread throughout the world made it a conflict that would exact a far greater psychiatric cost than had the previous war.

The fact that warfare was no longer to be restricted to the soldier was quickly realized. Large segments of the civilian population could now come under attack. This attack would come primarily from the air, and it is not surprising to learn that a great deal of research was done on the result of air attack. This research was initially done by the British, since fear of shell shock on a massive scale was anticipated. Psychologists were asked how to best counteract the widespread shock reactions that would supposedly follow the type of aerial bombing that had been seen in Spain. The employment of psychologists by both the Allies and the Axis to empirically assess the effects of aerial bombing was consistent with the view, dominant until 1940, that psychology was primarily a science concerned with the measurement of human emotion, sensation, and perception. As the war continued, psychologists became increasingly involved in the clinical treatment of madness, in addition to predicting why it would be induced and whom it would effect.

One of the findings of the early studies of the London blitz was that the expected shock reaction in urban areas undergoing bombing did not materialize.[4] The assumptions derived from the diagnosis of shell shock during World War I were not applicable. It was found that people had an ability to adapt to the saturation bombing. The ability to tolerate such extreme conditions came to be of great interest. Analysis showed that those who were best able to deal with the bombing were those involved in essential services, such as civil defense, nursing, and, more generally, those who were not living alone. The clinical literature of the period emphasized that the more one felt part of a group and had a job to which one was totally committed, the more likely one would be free of symptoms.[5] Those who had jobs that involved taking care of others seemed to be even more immune from the symptoms of stress.

Now traumatic war neuroses, or combat fatigue, focused on excessive fatigue, recurrent bodily complaints, and persistent phobias. This is not to say that the concept of emotional shock was given up, but that there was greater sophistication regarding the range of symptoms. Neuroses were seen as originating from two contradictory motive forces, and this represented a major shift from the emphasis in World War I on the organic explanation. Another finding was that the longer the period between raids, the more traumatic the neuroses would become.

Psychologists adopted a more complex view of the range of war symptoms and their origin. They began looking at those cumulative factors of stress that induced traumatic war neuroses. The notion that one overpowering incident of explosive intensity caused a symptomatic withdrawal was given up when mental health workers realized that while there might have been an incident that finally triggered the madness, a series of previous incidents had lowered resistance.[6] The traumatic incident was the final blow that triggered a massive withdrawal. This cumulative effect of stress was one of the major issues portrayed in *Twelve O'Clock High* (1949), a film that depicted the psychiatric casualties of aerial warfare.

Aerial warfare in World War II received great attention. One reason for this was certainly its importance, particularly in the early days of British and American involvement, when Allied airmen faced incredible pressure because of the high mortality rate. According to a U.S. Army Air Force report, "In some theaters of the war, an airman's chance of completing a tour of operational duty were little better than 50 percent."[7] The high mortality rate of aerial warfare, particularly among the crews of heavy bombers, produced an excessively stressful situation, which resulted in a high incidence of combat exhaustion. Besides the knowledge that one's chances of returning from a mission were slim, slowly accumulating stress was inherent in being on a B-17 bomber mission. The missions, particularly in the early part of 1944, were exceedingly hazardous because of the heavy anti-aircraft fire and the Luftwaffe defense system. The B-17 flight plan was always over areas where these forces were bound to be encountered, so the airman knew that he was going to be exposed to heavy fire. His vulnerability was assured, and the fragile fuselage in which he was confined for hours before reaching the target did little to assuage such feelings. Pilots were seldom able to move out of formation, and the flack that exploded around these flying fortresses was inescapable.

It was this sense of being physically trapped in one space on an unchangeable trajectory that led to the helplessness and mounting anxiety that could result in combat fatigue. It is not surprising that the most vulnerable were the heavy bomber gun crews, who could do little other than watch the explosions around them. Though pilots could not often take evasive action, particularly on the final bomb run, they at least were in control of the plane, while the gunners were exposed to the level of helpless passivity.[8] Symptoms from such exposures were not long in coming, though it is interesting that they usually occurred after the mission, seldom during combat. Symptoms such as insomnia, loss of appetite, tremor, extreme startle reactions, irritability, jerky movements, and tension became increasingly manifest.[9] Eventually, they would become so pervasive as to be completely immobilizing.

All treatments involved removing the patient from the scene of action for a short period of time. Slight tremors or other symptoms demanded a day away from action, while a full presentation of symptoms required a hypodermic injection resulting in a forced sleep of from twelve to twenty-four hours. Such treatment generally proved effective in the short run—the symptoms disappeared and the airman returned to action. In many cases, however, symptoms continued even after the period of rest. Such a continuation of symptoms came to be labeled *anxiety reactions.* Treatment involved some of the same techniques involved in the treatment of combat fatigue, only on a much more intense level. Over the duration of the war emphasis in the treatment of anxiety reactions steadily shifted toward the use of psychoanalytic techniques. Emphasis was placed on the patient's discussing his unconscious conflictual feelings and on the role of the psychiatrist. The film *Captain Newman, M.D.* (1963) depicted both of these major aspects of treatment. There was, however, resistance to accepting this view, and the medical model, which emphasized the healing power of enforced rest and medication, was much more enthusiastically adopted, as can be seen in two earlier films, William Wyler's *Best Years of Our Lives* (1944) and William Dieterle's *I'll Be Seeing You* (1944). Both of these films dealt with the returning soldier who was still caught up in the madness of war, as manifested in general anxiety reactions. Both emphasized the notion that such a condition was possibly unchangeable.

As the Second World War progressed, more attention was given to the prevention of both combat fatigue and anxiety reactions. The psychiatric literature began to emphasize the importance of social bonding in helping to stop deterioration into madness. As Flanagan said, "The primary motivating force which more than anything else kept these men flying and fighting was that they were members of a group in which flying and fighting was the only accepted way of behaving."[10] The concern and commitment to one's buddies came to be a consolidating force protecting one against madness. Along with this went an emphasis on deliberate training in procedures that instilled confidence; "effective activity" was seen as the best antidote to fear. Air commanders who emphasized such practices became models for courageous behavior, who could bring about the kind of defensive controls that would depreciate the psychological stress leading to combat fatigue."[11]

Twelve O'Clock High   *Twelve O'Clock High* depicts many of the above issues. The image of the carefree and daring fighter pilot of World War I was transformed into that revealing the emotional cost of aerial combat, which slowly drove men into madness.

The film opens with a B-17 sliding uncontrollably across a landing field. When it finally settles to a stop, the captain crawls out of the bullet-riddled cockpit area, stands frozen for a moment, and then turns aside and vomits. Emergency field trucks and ambulances reach him and the rest of the crew, who are badly wounded. All are quickly taken to a field hospital. Sometime later, the captain is brought to a flight report room, where he is asked to specify the success of the bombing mission. As he gives his report, his copilot wanders aimlessly disoriented around the room. The flight surgeon is summoned and is told that the copilot saw the head of one of the crewman blown off and, though managing to hold himself together during the rest of the mission, was obviously reacting to the extreme trauma. The flight surgeon says that the copilot needs to be narcotized immediately and should be able to be back in action within twenty-four hours. From this initial action we begin to observe the everyday life of the 151st Bomber Squadron, one of the first United States aerial units to take part in the European theater.

The morale after months of intense combat is shakey. The squadron commander, Colonel Davenport, is too popular with his men and more concerned with their welfare as individuals than with the results they achieve. Discipline is lax, drinking is a problem, and even an officer, Lieutenant Colonel Gateley, is avoiding missions. General Savage, an officer renowned for his qualities as a leader, is sent by headquarters to replace Davenport, who is accused of overidentification with his men. Savage sets out to bring back order and morale to the squadron, factors that he believes are the cause of the poor strike record of the squadron.

Savage pushes his men relentlessly back through basic flight skills and demands a level of formality between himself and his men that leads to their becoming enraged with him. He refuses all requests to transfer from the squadron, and the men are caught in his tyrannical rules of service and order. At one point he tells them that they should all think of themselves as already dead so that they will have little fear or concern about their fates. What he asks of his men he also asks of himself, and slowly the men come to perform their perilous tasks more willingly. Winning over both noncommissioned and commissioned men, Savage comes to be a model of bravery, which becomes mirrored in the heroics of his men.

On one mission he is leading the squadron when they run into heavy anti-aircraft fire. After the bomb run he orders his wing commander, Lieutenant Colonel Gateley, to break out of formation. When Gateley does so, his plane gets a direct hit and bursts into flames. Savage screams over his radio for Gateley and his crew to bail out, but the other plane is already in a tailspin. As he watches the fall, Savage sinks back and asks his copilot to take command. Upon landing he denies completely that he has any feeling about the loss of his wing commander, whom he has come to respect. He discusses the event in the most dispassionate terms, ending the conversation with the remark that he is really tired and looking forward to a good night's sleep.

The next day an even more important mission is planned, and Savage once again leads his men out to their waiting planes. As he tries to hoist himself up through the cockpit entry hatch, he suddenly begins to have extreme tremors. His agonized attempts to overcome these are ineffective, and the flight surgeon, who is nearby, comes to his aid. Savage becomes more immobilized as the flight surgeon tries to move him away from the plane. He is carried back to the field command office, where he sits in a frozen position, incapable of responding to the remaining officers' questions. Reluctant to give him any narcoleptic drug, the flight surgeon says that this is probably a momentary exhaustive paralytic condition, triggered by the events of the previous day. He maintains that it will end with the successful completion of the mission, which the colonel was supposed to have led. With the flight radio on, the progress of the mission is followed, though Savage gives no apparent sign of being able to hear it. After the planes return to base, the mission a success, Savage suddenly stands up from his stupor and asks with a good deal of consternation what has been going on. The flight surgeon repeats that all the planes have returned and encourages him to rest. The film ends with Savage lowering himself to the cot as his officers, gravely concerned, look down at him.

The film, made in 1949, presents a rather sketchy approximation of the psychiatric view of madness in the early part of the war. It vacillates, as did the early psychiatric views, between a social and medical model. The use of narcoleptic treatment for paralysis was a holdover from the end of World War I, though there was increasing sophistication in its use. While the short beginning sequence emphasizes such an approach, the rest of the film focuses on social bonding and modeling and its effect on morale.

Savage is the quintessential portrayal of how a commander must act if he is to hold his troops together, and the state of paralyzing shock into which he is thrown represents the limit to which a Hollywood hero of the late 1940s was allowed to be stricken by the madness of war. His combat fatigue evidences none of the exaggerated emotional hyperactivity and total loss of control that we only briefly see displayed by others in the film. Madness for Savage is a momentary tremor and a period of sitting immobilized until his boys come home.

The film's attention to specific psychological formulations on aerial combat are at times well done; for example, the men's difficulty with irregular breaks in their mission schedule is stressed, as is their feeling of helplessness and anxiety as they maintain their flight coordinates all the way through the bomb run.

The film is important for several reasons. First, it was one of the few films to take as its central focus the issue of combat fatigue. Though one can be critical of the depiction, the film did, sometimes quite accurately, convey some of the concepts that clinical psychiatry used to understand and treat the casualties of aerial war. Second, unlike most previous films on World War II, this film treated madness as a major theme and had lead actors fall victim to it. *Twelve O'Clock High*, therefore, helped to establish a new precedent for war films. Finally, the date of the film's release, 1949, is significant. That Hollywood could not release such a film until four years after the Second World War tells us much about our society's resistance to dealing with the psychiatric casualties of war. While the late release of *Twelve O'Clock High* might seem to diminish its importance, the film met the needs of postwar America. The Korean War (and, later, the Vietnam War) only exacerbated the need to romanticize World War II, which increasingly came to be seen as a war that was clear in its divisions of good and evil, winners and losers.

The Vietnam War

It is important to note that with each successive war in the twentieth century, military psychology became increasingly sophisticated in its approach to keeping men operating through the horrors of combat. As long as a soldier was able to function, to kill, he was considered fit for war, and certainly not mad. Much had been learned during World War II and Korea, so that knowledge about how to prevent a soldier's decline into incapacitating madness had, by the time of Vietnam, reached a new stage of refinement. In particular three areas of such knowledge had become central to military psychology. The first dealt with the relation between combat and madness, and here the evidence pointed to a correlation between psychiatric casualties and the intensity of combat. The second area focused on noncombative variables that led to madness in situations where risk or hazard was ostensibly low. It was increasingly realized that such factors as time, boredom, inadequate diet, and chronic physical discomfort could insidiously undermine a soldier's hold on reality. The third area concerned psychological factors that would predispose individual soldiers to madness. In the face of this knowledge emphasis continued to be placed on the influence of group bonding in anchoring an individual to reality, regardless of what extreme pressures he was experiencing.

As the war slowly dragged on, these three areas of knowledge came to be united under one conceptual model, that of stress. By the end of the Second World War stress had begun to be seen as an important factor affecting mental health. It was not until the 1960s, however, that stress became a central focus in both psychological and physiological research. The concept of stress allowed scientists to approach the age-old mind-body controversy concerning the basis for behavior in a more holistic, interdisciplinary manner. Researchers discovered how particular types of stressful experience affect various somatic, psychological, and psychosomatic disorders. Psychological inquiries into the concepts of stress and madness have, of course, received government funding because they resulted in measuring the limits of individual tolerance to the pressures of war.[12] As the instruments of measuring psychological and physical states purportedly became more accurate, the concept of stress was lifted from its place in the science of engineering, where it had been an element in Hooke's law of elasticity, to a central place in psychology. This adoption of an inorganic explanation reflected and complemented the increased use of technology in Vietnam. "Body counts," the result of an intensity of "firepower" unparalleled in any previous war, were registered daily with the scientific dispassion that came from treating men as machines.

In his work on brainwashing in the Korean War, D. O. Hebb was one of the first to attempt to provide a connection between psychology and the physiological research of Hans Seyle.[13] Hebb and Seyle became part of an expanding number of researchers who were to begin not only to investigate stress in war but apply its tenets to everyday life. It is most telling to look at the application of this research to normal civilian life in the light of the war mentality of Vietnam. Such a relationship cannot help but spring to mind when one reads about the stress research of the late 1960s, a time when the Vietnam War was reaching the height of its intensity. Describing the importance of stress research, two noted researchers of this period pointed to the difficulty of maintaining physiologic and psychic equanimity in the contemporary world:

> There has been an appreciable increase in uncertainty of human relations as man has gone from the relatively primitive and more rural to the urban and industrial. Contemporary man in much of the world is faced every day with people and with situations about which there is uncertainty of outcome, wherein appropriate behavior is not proscribed and validated by tradition, where the possibility of bodily or psychological harm exists, where running or fighting is inappropriate and where mental vigilance is called for.[14]

Military psychology becomes the psychology of the everyday, and one cannot thus help but see the images of Vietnam coming home.

From the early prewar years, when only military advisors were involved, the overview of the Vietnam conflict was influenced by the psychiatric research of World War II and, to some extent, of Korea. Emphasis was placed on combat fatigue, and a great deal of attention was given to its prevention.[15] Advanced technology complemented the theoretical notions of how to eliminate combat fatigue, which was viewed as the type of madness most likely to affect the soldier. Soldiers were sent on search-and-destroy missions, which would take them into the jungle for short periods of time. Though the search, destroy, and return-to-base mode of operation was not compatible with increased U.S. intervention, belief in removing personnel from the combat area for short periods of $R \& R$ ("rest and relaxation") remained throughout the war. Unlike World War II and Korea, the determination of when and how to remove a soldier from combat operations became more sophisticated. Studies on combat effectiveness in the type of warfare experienced in the jungles of Vietnam moved toward exacting predictions that used time-stress ratios, which influenced the perception of how long men should remain in the field. Complementing this notion of removal was the ability to snatch an individual out of combat and remove him thousands of miles away by the end of the day. This was greatly facilitated by extensively sophisticated advances in air power, particularly with regard to long-range and booster-jet–accelerated helicopters.

Until 1968 such measures of intervention seemed effective, and the incidence of psychiatric problems requiring hospitalization was reported to be comparable to that for stateside forces. The military boasted that whereas twenty-three percent of all medical casualties from World War II were psychiatric, only six percent of medical casualties from Vietnam were psychiatric.[16] Self-congratulatory, war commanders claimed that their capacity to reduce such casualties was due to satisfactory training, equipment, and leadership. Attention to the total needs of the soldier, they maintained, was responsible for the spectacular diminution in the occurrence of madness in the ranks. They emphasized that men who are well cared for do not go mad and maintained that such things as providing hot meals by helicopter to men in the field proved this. It was also felt that the one-year tour of combat duty, with the exception of thirteen months for the Marines, was significant; it assured men that to get out they would not have to wait for the end of the war, death, or an incapacitating injury.[17] Early psychiatric statistics seemed to support the obvious conclusion that, through careful planning and appropriate intervention, madness in war had become a thing of the past, an aberrancy that had been brought under control through technology.

Closer inspection, however, revealed a statistic that did not lend itself to easy analysis and that had generally been ignored by the interpreters of statistics. This was the high number of disciplinary-administrative problems that did not seem to be related to emotional problems. From 1968 to 1969, for example, the number of dishonorable discharges increased by fifty-three percent.[18] Such cases eventually came under psychiatric scrutiny and were diagnosed as character disorders, in which the affected soldiers expressed their emotional difficulties by directly acting them out rather than internalizing or somatizing them, as they had done in earlier wars.[19] Directly acting out these problems manifested itself in antisocial behavior, one of the most frequent forms of which was drug abuse. Such findings began to diminish the self-satisfaction of the neuropsychiatrists. More overwhelming were reports that soldiers were actually turning their guns or grenades on their own officers. Explanations were sought, and a range of interpretations were offered.

The increasing number of disciplinary problems involving racial disturbances, drug abuse, and attacks on superiors was thought to be due to difficulties in morale, caused by the particular kind of war Vietnam had become. It was a war of wide-ranging contradictions. The war was increasingly becoming unpopular at home, and the soldier who was defending his country could easily feel that he was being attacked by both his enemy and his own country. The war was dragging on, though there were continued reports of considerable losses to the enemy and predictions of dates of surrender. The technology that could release a bomb at forty thousand feet and pinpoint its trajectory to within a few feet of its target did not seem able to stop the war effort of what was at best a pre-industrial society. Vietnamization only continued to create confusion concerning who the enemy really was, as time and again the American soldier felt betrayed by his Asian counterpart and disregarded by the native populace. The contradictions seemed forever to increase, wearing down the soldier's sense of purpose, identity, and hold on reality.[20]

Soldiers arrived in Vietnam with little understanding of such contradictions. Many enlisted out of a sense of adventure or patriotism, but the ceaseless wear and tear of the opposing pressures they encountered slowly began to tell on them, leading inevitably to confusion. In earlier wars there was a sense of purpose, of being on the side of right. This was not, and was never allowed to become, questionable. There was a closely defined enemy, who was seen as an aggressor against the United States, and Americans were simply defending their shores. The Vietnam War lacked this important motivation. The people of South Vietnam did little to support the soldier's sense that he was helping an oppressed people; on countless occasions they were even found to be subverting the war effort for their own profit.

Such factors not only diminished belief in the war but led the American soldier to question where he fitted into such a war. He found himself in a situation where he could be killed both in the front lines and in the back lines. The boundaries of the war and the actual identity of the enemy became increasingly vague, and the soldier seemed able to depend on fewer and fewer people. His emotional investment slowly moved inward from a belief in his country, in the war, in the army, the battalion, the unit, and his buddies, and finally rested only in himself and his individual survival.[21] For many Vietnam became a private war as they retreated further and further into themselves. Anyone who represented a potential threat—and that could mean almost everyone—had to be killed before he could kill you. Universal slaughter became acceptable for several reasons. First, because of the omnipresence of the enemy, the American soldier easily developed racial distancing from all the people of Vietnam. Second, the dilution of responsibility confused him about who was to do what, and as a result he often fired upon everything. Finally, advances in military technology allowed him to control devastating firepower, as evidenced by the aerial blanket of napalm that could result from a single ground soldier's request.

The personality type most adaptable to the wasteland of such a war was an amalgam of the character disorder, the psychopath, and the borderline. This was a person who had given up trust, an expert in avoidance and detachment, an isolate who never allowed himself to be subjected to vulnerable emotions. He was a person of impulsive violence who was mildly paranoid, who aggressively sought arousing stimuli, and who had developed a compulsive need to test the feeling that power and mastery determine what is right.[22] This was the type of madness that was described in the clinical literature and depicted by so many films on Vietnam: the drug abuser in *Who'll Stop the Rain?* (1978), the volatile personality of the protagonists in *The Deer Hunter* (1978) or *Taxi Driver* (1976), and finally the Kilgores and Kurtzes of *Apocalypse Now* (1979). All these characters isolated themselves in interior worlds, where reality and hallucination were undifferentiable. It was no surprise that as the troops came home, the madness that was, in some perverted way, acceptable in Vietnam became disfunctional stateside. The qualities that had led to survival in Vietnam needed to be redirected, controlled, and shaped to the expectations of a formal social order. It became problematic whether a man who had been exposed to sustained trauma, butchery, and depravity in a jungle war could make this transition. Unlike World War II, where the madness of war took the form of visible physical symptoms, such as tics, paralyses, and anaesthesias, the Vietnam veteran experiencing characterological symptomatology was not so easily distinguishable from any other soldier. As pointed out, the symptoms were to some degree adaptational, and not all who experienced the symptoms necessarily came under the scrutiny of legal or psychiatric services. As experts at avoidance and detachment, they were able to fade unnoticed into the mass of returning veterans, unnoticed until their explosive, impulsive rage and paranoia began to work free from the fragile moorings that held them tentatively in check. Cases of veterans involved in crimes began to surface and took representational form in such films as Scorsese's *Taxi Driver* (1976).

Before *Taxi Driver* a startling number of films depicted the Vietnam veteran as at best a loner and outsider in conflict with corrupt but powerful social forces (*The Losers* [1970], *Jud* [1973], *Slaughter* [1973], *Billy Jack* [1971]).[23] More often than not, however, the films of the 1970s depicted an emotionless figure, whose sudden, explosive violence was devastating (*The Old Man's Place, The Visitors, Welcome Home Soldier Boys, Open Season*). Emphasized especially in *Open Season* (1974) was the idea that the veteran who had been trained to kill needed to continue to kill; only seemingly reintegrated into American society, he eagerly sought to relive the violence that had become addictive. While asocial behavior was certainly an issue in clinical literature, such Hollywood characterizations often made it appear that the returning veteran was a sadistic, homicidal maniac who was particularly dangerous because he knew how to kill. While bearing some relation to reality, this view was primarily a way for civilians to hide from the personal despair that the Vietnam veteran experienced. It helped to turn him into someone to be feared, rather than cared for, and therefore allowed them to block awareness of America's defeat. The clinical evidence indicated that the personal psychic cost of combat often did not surface until after the second year of the soldier's return, when the deep grief of an encapsulated, never-ending past was clearly depriving the present of meaning.[24]

While Vietnam's effect in influencing veteran violence was given much attention in the press, little was given to the fact that many veterans openly identified with their victims in rebelling against the powers that had sent them there.[25] Vietnam veterans refused to disappear as part of America's desire to forget the war, and their efforts were supported by certain members of the psychiatric community, who called for action on their behalf and an end to the oppressive mentality that had enlisted them:

> Unless we professionals can respond with appropriate anguish to the outrages of social destructiveness, our scholarship is distorted, our science is counterfeit and our ability to eliminate human suffering will dry up and turn into mere technology.[26]

But while some in the psychiatric community called for social change, many more continued to apply their knowledge of human behavior toward perfecting military efforts.[27]

It is impossible to determine whether veterans were more likely to participate in violent crimes than a matching group who had not gone to war.[28] One can, however, study the overall data on veteran crimes and conclude, with Robert Lifton, that

> many will hold onto a related habituation to racism and the need to victimize others. Any of these patterns may appear very quickly in some, but in others lie dormant for a period of months or even years and then emerge in response to various internal and external pressures.[29]

This notion of delayed responses fits well with the ongoing interest in post-traumatic stress reactions.[30] Beginning with studies by Breuer and Freud, the repetition of trauma-related behavior continued to be researched. As the few who managed to survive the concentration camps of World War II had confirmed, the effects of such experiences were found to undergo massive repression into a fragile, crystallized form, which remain outside the individual's awareness. In time the walls of this structure are eroded by the effects of everyday reminders. The final trigger mechanism is then activated, and the individual begins to have sudden remembrances of the experience in the shrouded forms of fantasies and dreams.[31] Though often symbolic, their content becomes increasingly manifest, and the emotional pain begins to eat its way into conscious awareness (*Night Porter,* 1973). Such awareness is usually associated with the sudden onset of ideational denial, emotional numbing, and behavioral constriction.[32]

While the full impact of the Vietnam War on the veteran is unclear, the clinical literature on the violence they exhibited during the war agrees on certain key points. The exigencies of the war demanded constant vigilance and readiness to strike out at anyone. The continuing stories of children leading soldiers to sudden death caused men to fire in the direction of any unexpected movement, resulting in the killing of innocent people. Of the many depictions of such explosive loss of control, perhaps the most startling was in *Apocalypse Now,* in which an entire family of boat people are decimated merely because a little girl made a sudden movement to protect a pet. Reminding us of Lieutenant Calley and the My Lai massacre, this scene seemed to confirm that the normal affective significance of slaughter was readily circumvented in a war in which the enemy was everywhere.[33] The case of Lieutenant Calley only helped to further the confusion of the soldier. As one team of observers put it, "The soldier must obey orders and know that he is subject to court martial if he disobeys. . . . [in the Calley case] he is being told that if he obeys, he may be court martialed anyway."[34] This question about following orders received a good deal of attention in the psychiatric research of the 1960s.[35]

The constant infliction of brutal acts on others left the veteran in a fragile condition in relation to the expression of violence. This was well depicted in *Coming Home,* when Bob (Bruce Dern), with a fixed bayonet attached to his M-16 rifle, stands ready to blow apart his wife, Sally (Jane Fonda) and her lover, Luke (Jon Voight). He has come home from a world that made no sense to a world that he does not understand. When faced with his wife's infidelity, he resorts immediately to the kind of violence that became spontaneous during the war as the only way to survive. The reliving of such violence, directed now against his wife, leaves him in a state of emotional numbness and behavioral constriction similar to that of cases reported in the clinical literature.[36] The sense of retreat into such a state is made explicit when he methodically removes his clothes and walks into the winter sea, which so dispassionately engulfs him.

The Deer Hunter.   One film that stands out as consolidating the diverse clinical themes of Vietnam is *The Deer Hunter.* The relationship between the behavior of its protagonist and clinical reports of madness is clear.

The film opens with the looming image of the cab of a semi-tractor-trailer, belching sparks from its stacks and careening around corners in the indistinguishable light of either dusk or dawn. This in-between light dominates most of the film as if the sun has been permanently screened from memory. For a moment the ominous light is cut off by a brilliant shower of flame, which reaches out from a cavernous furnace hole, around which figures clad in white asbestos tend a giant ladle of lava. We are in the steel mill town of Clairton, Pennsylvania—a town caught between the old-fashioned view of second-generation Russian-Americans and the new morality of their children. This new morality has brought one of the principal characters, Stephen, to a forced wedding with a woman whom he, or someone else, has gotten pregnant, and it is the day of their marriage.

Among the figures that we just saw tending the fire furnace with Stephen are his best friends, Nick and Michael. The ominous beginnings of the film are seemingly forgotten as the group leaves the steel mill. They talk to each other of their upcoming departure for Vietnam and the more immediate pleasure of Stephen's wedding party that night and the deer-hunting trip that they will take the next day. Their jocularity is enhanced by the antics of three other friends, and we are led to believe that all have a close bond to each other. All six crowd into Michael's battered Cadillac and race off toward the smoke-covered town below the mill. They suddenly meet the truck that we saw at the beginning of the film, and Michael makes the challenge that he can pass the truck on the inside lane. With icy calm he accelerates and cushions the car between the truck cab, which towers above them, and a stone wall on their right. Gently touching both, he suddenly throttles the car past. We can take this as machismo, but there is a sense of detachment and an absence of fear that makes for a more complex interpretation.

Having arrived at a local tavern, the six friends drink themselves into a stupor to celebrate Stephen's imminent marriage. As the jukebox blares a pop song of the late 1960s by Frankie Valli with the pounding refrain, "You're too good to be true, can't take my eyes off of you," the six friends mimic the song by grabbing and embracing each other. While this is taking place, we flash to another side of life in this soot-covered mill town: the bride is pulling in her abdomen, trying to hide her pregnancy; her bridesmaid is being beaten by her drunken father; and the groom's mother is giving way to despair. The wedding, held at a VFW hall, is also a farewell party for the newly inducted soldiers. Beneath its surface of frivolity is a deep sense of tragedy, as shown symbolically by the spilling of the red wine, which, according to tradition, was to bring good luck if drunk without a drop falling from the lips of the couple. Gradually, we realize that things are not as they appear. The bride has not been made pregnant by her future husband, and the friendship of these men is troubled. Throughout the wedding party Michael is distant. His only emotional expressions are his combativeness with a green beret in the VFW bar and his manic explosion of energy as he refuses to let go of the newlyweds' car as it speeds away.

The next day the friends, except for Stephen, set off on their deer-hunting trip. Michael talks about killing deer in a distant, romanticized manner, emphasizing that it must be killed with one shot, cleanly. His unwillingness to lend

The Deer Hunter (USA, 1978). Director, Michael Cimino. With Robert De Niro *(left)*, John Savage. By permission of Universal Pictures.

his extra pair of boots to one of the friends, Stan, elicits from the latter squeals of vituperations, including the remark that Michael is a "control freak" and that he cannot "get it on with any woman." Michael is silent, yet we can sense the murderous rage that is just below the surface. It is clear that he is brooding and enigmatic.

From the hunt, conducted amid the mountain clouds, we are suddenly hurled into the midst of a burning village in the blood-covered fields of Vietnam. A Vietcong has just tossed a grenade into a bunker, which has served as a hiding place for women and children. Michael, lying wounded near a dead soldier, suddenly revives and with his flamethrower melts the offender in a bath of fire. Helicopters bring in reserves, including Nick and Stephen, who enlisted with Michael. Their joy at seeing one another is short-lived, as the Vietcong are streaming into the village.

The next scene is of a river encampment, where the Vietcong hold the three friends and a dozen others as prisoners. There are two holding pens. The Vietcong have devised a game of death involving two prisoners who, facing each other, must take turns pulling the trigger on a gun in which there is only one bullet. Bets are taken on the chances that each player has of surviving as he alternates with the other in the game. Michael and Stephen are forced to play against each other; Michael once again shows no fear and, indeed, encourages Stephen, who is having convulsive spasms. Stephen holds the gun to his head for the second time in the game and pulls the trigger. The crack of the bullet is heard, but Stephen has aimed the gun so that the bullet only grazes his scalp. He is quickly put into a submerged cage, which, filled with rats, has only a fraction of air space above the waterline. Here, the victims await their death.

The next two players are Michael and Nick. Michael tells Nick that their only way out is to play the game with three bullets, which will allow them a chance to kill their tormentors. They must eliminate the odds against their firing without a shell in the chamber, and this means playing the game at greatly increased risks. The agony that Nick shows is contrasted with the emotionless determination of Michael, who laughs in his captors' faces as he encourages them seemingly to raise the probability of their victims' deaths. They fire the three chambers, which come up blank, and then shoot their captors. Nick wants to stay to kick and maim the dead Vietcong, but Michael coolly pulls him away. Releasing Stephen, they manage to float downstream and are rescued by helicopter. Michael again shows an incredible lack of fear when he dives from the ascending helicopter to save Stephen, who has fallen back into the water. The helicopter is forced to leave the two, and Michael carries Stephen on his back until they reach the lines of the retreating South Vietnamese.

The next scene shows the recovery of Nick in a hospital in Saigon. We watch a doctor ask him the dates of his parents' birthdays, along with other absurd bureaucratic questions. He is unable to answer any of these and shows intense anguish. It is clear that he is making an extreme effort to block the memory of his recent experiences and that the interrogation undermines such efforts. We next cut to an embarcation area, where a group of soldiers are entering a room filled with telephones, from which they can call home to the States. Nick begins to dial the call but in the end cannot do it, and we next see him aimlessly walking the alleyways of Saigon. Coaxed hypnotically by a mysterious Frenchman, he is ushered into a gaming house, where Russian roulette is being played. Indeed, the horrors of the war have pervaded every aspect of life, and human life has become meaningless. The screams of the crowd's frenetic betting suddenly cease as the game begins. Nick stares blankly at the two participants. The game is short, and the blast of the .32 caliber pistol results in charred fragments of scalp and brain spewing out at the viewer. The camera moves slowly from Nick's frozen stare to a figure in the crowd who, unlike all the others, is not gleefully and frenetically betting. Nor is he Asian. The figure's face is suddenly revealed. It is Michael. Michael tries to reach Nick, but the latter is whisked off by the Frenchman.

After a chaotic chase through the back alleys of Saigon, the camera flashes back Michael's return to Clairton. His arrival is eagerly anticipated by all his old friends, including Linda, Nick's girlfriend. Seeing the cars in front of his trailer home, Michael has his cab pass it. The next day he goes to the house and finds Linda, who embraces him hungrily. They meet a number of times, but her efforts to elicit feelings from him are futile, as he is completely passionless. As we see him try ineffectually to relate to Linda, we are reminded of the earlier comments from Stan, after Michael rejected his plea to borrow the boots.

Shortly after, Michael and his buddies who did not go to war leave on another hunting trip. Michael once again is stalking a deer to achieve its death with one "clean shot." The clumsiness of his three companions contrasts with his own efficient stealth. Effortlessly, he tracks a big buck, which suddenly poses, still and majestic, barely a few yards in front of him. They look each other in the eye, and the hunter is somehow awed into a reverence that stops him from making the kill. Returning to the cabin, Michael finds Stan wielding a small gun and bragging about his sense of power. Michael's apparent spiritual union with nature suddenly bursts as he empties all but one of the bullets from Stan's gun and, spinning the barrel, holds the gun first to Stan's head and then to his own. But the chambers fired do not hold the remaining bullet.

Back to the scene in Vietnam, Michael finally finds Stephen, who has isolated himself in a Veterans Administration hospital. Stephen has had both his legs and an arm amputated as a result of his war injuries, but Michael's only reaction is to demand that he return to his wife and the people who care about him. Their conversation is superficial, but what most attracts Michael's attention is Stephen's statement that he has been receiving large sums of money from an unknown source in Vietnam. From the knowing look on Michael's face, we cut to the Walpurgisnacht of the last days of Saigon. Michael has returned to rescue Nick. Hunting through the burning chaos of Saigon, he finally finds the gambling house where Nick continues the game of death. Nick does not seem to recognize him, and Michael once again becomes his partner in the game. As both face each other, Michael pleads with Nick to leave with him. Just before pulling the trigger, which will send a bullet exploding through his brain, Nick says, "One should be able to do it with one clean shot."

The camera cuts to Nick's casket, carried by his friends, and the small attendance at the graveyard ceremony. Returning to a cafe owned by one of the six friends, the remaining five, with Stephen's wife and Linda, sit down for breakfast. The large, bullish owner, who has been portrayed as somewhat of an aesthete (after their first hunting trip, he played a Chopin nocturne to his drunken friends) prepares eggs while fighting back his tears. He begins to hum, "God Bless America," and when he enters, the others take up the hymn in a dirgelike fashion.

Though *The Deer Hunter* was well received in terms of box-office sales, the Russian roulette scene was often criticized. Critics emphasized that this game was never a proven occurrence, though some admitted that in the early days of the war, stories of such atrocities surfaced as rumor.[37] Most people seemed unwilling to believe that the film could have intended the game as a metaphor for both the fear of death and the fascination with it, which gains such a commanding control of consciousness in times of war, particularly a war filled with the moral contradictions of Vietnam.

Michael Cimino was trying to do more than make a war film; he was perhaps attempting to link the world of home and that of war in a way that had never been done before on the screen. Most previous war films had followed a linear sequence: the protagonist was either in the war exclusively or in the war and then at home. Cimino introduced a new order; half the film takes place in Clairton before the three friends go off to war. He moves us not into the confused postwar world of *Coming Home* but into the world from which these men came. The considerable time he devoted to exploring this world indicates a relationship between it and the jungle war of Vietnam.

This connection between Clairton and Vietnam might best be understood by looking at the character of Michael. The term *deer hunter* obviously applies to Michael, and it is perhaps also an allusion to James Fenimore Cooper's hero.[38] In its extreme form it is an American character type that incorporates elements described psychiatrically under the terms *sociopath, character disorder,* or *borderline.* Men who are heroes in war, are lost without it. Like Michael they are furtive searchers, who long for flights to mountains of isolation, where they can pit themselves alone against the powers of nature. It must be remembered that the powers of nature for Michael are no different from the power of a large diesel truck, for both are externalized projections of a need to overcome one's fear of impotency, a characteristic of which Stan accuses Michael. On this level Cimino was trying to connect the war to a basic flaw in American society.[39]

On another level there is an exploration of the type of survivor who emerges from the jungles of Vietnam. In all the four major movies depicting Vietnam— *Taxi Driver, Coming Home, The Deer Hunter,* and *Apocalypse Now*—these individuals share the characteristics described in the clinical literature of Vietnam. The three focuses of the literature—(1) the limits of stress tolerance, (2) the character disorder and asocial behavior, and (3) post-traumatic stress disorder—took form for Americans through these depictions. The impact of such depictions can be seen in a recent court case where the defense maintained that his client, a highly decorated Vietnam veteran, had been involved in drug trafficking as a result of post-traumatic stress disorder.[40] After showing sections of *The Deer Hunter,* the defense called upon psychiatric witnesses to argue that his client's actions resulted from the horrific traumas of war, which he needed to relive. One of these psychiatrists said: "He was compelled by the mental disease to participate. He had a need to release this pent-up rage and anger over the futility of the war and the horror of his experiences as a helicopter pilot. He was all bottled up in an explosive way."[41] While the defendant was eventually found guilty, the subtle but powerful relationship between screen depictions, psychiatric concepts, and the legal codes that reflect our social order was clearly evidenced.[42]

Notes

1. V. E. Frankl, *Man's Search for Meaning*, trans. Ilse Lasch (Boston: Beacon Press, 1962), pp. 149–215.

2. Robert Lifton, *Thought Reform and the Psychology of Totalism: A Study of Brainwashing in China*, 1st ed. (New York: Morton, 1961).

3. A. Kardiner, *The Traumatic Neuroses of War* (New York: P. B. Hoeber Inc., 1941).

4. P. Vernon, "Psychological Effects of Air Raids," *Journal of Abnormal and Social Psychology* 36 (1941): 457–76.

5. Ibid., p. 474.

6. R. Grinker and J. Spiegel, *Men Under Stress* (Philadelphia: Blakiston Press, 1945), pp. 729–39.

7. J. C. Flanagan, *USAAF Aviation Psychology Research Report, No. 1* (Washington, D.C.: U.S. Government Printing Office, 1948).

8. L. Schaffer, "Psychological Studies of Anxiety Reactions to Combat," *USAAI Aviation Psychology Research Report, No. 14* (Washington, D.C.: U.S. Government Printing Office, 1947), p. 143.

9. J. Dollard, "Fear in Battle," *Infantry Journal* (Washington, D.C.: U.S. Government Printing Office, 1944), pp. vii, 64. T. Lidz, "Nightmares and the Combat Neuroses," *Psychiatry* 9 (1946): 37–49.

10. Flanagan, p. 208.

11. Schaffer, p. 143.

12. E. K. Gunderson and R. H. Rahe, eds., *Life Stress and Illness*, "Based Upon Contributions to the Symposium on Life Stress and Illness. Sponsored by the Science Committee of the North Atlantic Treaty Organization in 1972" (Springfield, Ill., 1974). I. Spielberger and G. Sarason, eds., *Stress and Anxiety in Modern Life, Murnav, Ger., 1972. Sponsored by the Scientific Affairs Division of the North Atlantic Treaty Organization."*

13. *H. Seyle, The Stress of Life* (New York: McGraw-Hill, 1956).

14. A. M. Ostfeld and R. B. Shekelle, "Psychological Variables and Blood Pressure," in *The Epidemiology of Hypertension*, ed. J. Stamler, R. Stamler, and T. N. Pullman (New York: Grune and Stratton, 1967), pp. 321–31.

15. P. Bourne, *Men Stress and Vietnam* (Boston: Little, Brown and Company, 1970). W. Tiffany, "The Mental Health of Army Troops in Vietnam," *American Journal of Psychiatry*, vol. 123 (1967), 1585–86.

16. J. A. Renner, "The Changing Patterns of Psychiatric Problems in Vietnam," *Comprehensive Psychiatry*, vol. 14, no. 2 (March–April 1973), 169.

17. H. S. Bloch, "Army Clinical Psychiatry in the Combat Zone 1967–1968," *American Journal of Psychiatry*, vol. 126, no. 3 (1969), 289–97.

18. Renner, p. 171.

19. G. Bratz, G. K. Lumry, and S. Wright, "The Young Veteran as a Psychiatric Patient in Three Eras of Conflict," *Military Medicine*, vol. 136 (May, 1971), 455–57.

20. C. F. Shatan, "Through the Membrane of Reality: Impacted Grief and Perception Dissonance in Vietnam Combat Veterans," *Psychiatric Opinion*, vol. 7, no. 7 (November 1974).

21. M. J. Horowitz and G. F. Solomon, "A Prediction of Delayed Stress Response Syndrome in Vietnam Veterans," *Journal of Social Issues*, vol. 31, no. 4 (1975), pp. 69–72.

22. H. Langer, "The Making of a Murderer," *American Journal of Psychiatry*, vol. 127, no. 7 (January 1971).

23. J. Smith, "Between Vermont and Violence: Film Portraits of Vietnam Veterans," *Film Quarterly Studies* 26 (Summer 1973).

24. C. Shatan, "Special Report: The Grief of Soldiers: Vietnam Veterans Self-help Movement," *American Journal of Orthopsychiatry* 43 (1973): p. 640.

25. J. Nordheimer, "From Dakota to Detroit: Death of a Troubled Hero," *The New York Times* (26 May 1971), p. 1.

26. C. Shatan, "Membrane of Reality," p. 14.

27. P. Watson, *War on the Mind: The Military Uses and Abuses of Psychology* (New York: Basic Books, 1978).

28. D. Archer and R. Gartner, "The Myth of the Violent Veteran," *Psychology Today* (December 1976), 94–96.

29. R. J. Lifton, "The Scars of Vietnam," *Commonweal* (February 1970), 554–56.

30. R. J. Lifton, *Home from the War* (New York: Simon & Schuster, 1973).

31. H. Krystal, ed., *Massive Psychic Trauma* (New York: International Universities Press, 1968).

32. W. G. Niederland, "Clinical Observation on the 'Survivor Syndrome'," *International Journal of Psychoanalysis* 49 (1968): 313–15.

33. W. B. Gault, "Some Remarks on Slaughter," *American Journal of Psychiatry*, vol. 128, no. 4 (October 1971), 1851.

34. H. C. Kelman and L. H. Lawrence, "Assignment of Responsibility in the Case of Lt. Calley: Preliminary Report on a National Survey," *Journal of Social Issues*, vol. 28, no. 1 (1972), 209.

35. Milgram, "Behavioral Study of Obedience," *Journal of Abnormal and Social Psychology*, vol. 167 (1963), 371–78; "Some Conditions of Obedience and Disobedience to Authority," in *Current Studies in Social Psychology*, ed. I. D. Steiner and M. Fishbein (New York: Holt, Reinhart and Winston, 1965); "The Compulsion to Do Evil," *Patterns of Prejudice*, vol. 1, no. 6 (1967), 137.

36. V. P. Zarcone, R. Neil, and K. Kenneth, "Psychiatric Problems of Vietnam Veterans: Clinical Study of Hospital Patients, *Comprehensive Psychiatry*, vol. 18, no. 1 (Jan./Feb. 1977), 41–53. C. Shatan, "The Grief of Soldiers," *American Journal of Orthopsychiatry*, vol. 43 (1973), 640. G. Solomon, V. Zarcone, R. Yoerg, N. Scott, and R. Maurer, "Three Psychiatric Casualties from Vietnam," *Archives. General Psychiatry* vol. 25 (1971), 522–24.

37. W. Just, "Vietnam: The Camera Lies," Newspaper Days, *Atlantic Monthly*, vol. 244 (December 1979), 63–65.

38. A. Lubow, "Natty Bumppo Goes to War," *Atlantic Monthly*, vol. 243 (April 1979), 95–98.

39. Cimino presents some of the same characteristics in his screen plays for *Magnum Force* (1973) and *Thunderbolt and Lightfoot* (1974).

40. Pleading, "P.T.S.D. (Post Traumatic Stress Disorder)," *Time Magazine* (26 May 1980), 59.

41. W. I. Doherty, "Combat Made Them Insane, Court Told," *Boston Globe* (10 September 1980), p. 28.

42. It is surprising the scenes from *Who'll Stop the Rain* (1979) were not also shown.

6
Drugs and Madness

While many people may think that drug use is only a recent phenomenon, the history of civilization shows that such a view is erroneous.[1] One obvious example is wine, which has been known since prehistoric times. Hallucinogenic plants, particularly mushrooms, were used by the ancient civilizations of Indo-Asia and the Fertile Cresent.[2] Originally tied to religious ceremonies, these drugs in time came to have completely secular uses and became more likely to be abused.

Though a wide range of drugs has always been available to human beings, it is interesting that certain drugs have enjoyed popularity at one point, only to fall into apparent disuse. Whatever the specific explanation for these changes, it is clear that a drug's rise and fall in popularity is a function of changing social attitudes and forces. It is almost as if certain drugs suddenly enjoy a widespread marketing campaign that makes them highly desirable. This phenomenon is made evident in the clinical literature of the last fifty years. The purpose of this chapter is to investigate these changes in drug abuse and the cinematic depictions that coincided with them. The two major films that will occupy our attention are *The Lost Weekend* (1945) and *The Rose* (1979).

Drug abuse can be defined as the chronic and excessive use of a drug to the extent that it impairs social and vocational adjustment. From this definition it follows that any drug can be abused, though it is clear that the psychoactive, or "mind-altering," ones have enjoyed the greatest use. Drugs in this group include alcohol, barbiturates, tranquilizers, amphetamines, heroin, and marijuana. The problems caused by these drugs are of two kinds, *substance-use disorders* and *substance-induced disorders.* Substance-use disorders comprise the kinds of maladaptive behavior that surrounds the taking of the drug, while substance-induced disorders result from the ingestion of the drug itself.[3] Both kinds of disorders are graphically presented in *The Lost Weekend,* in which the lead character experiences both alcohol dependence and the substance-induced disorder of *delerium tremens.*

The Lost Weekend. The clinical literature of the 1940s gave alcoholism comparatively little attention. The one exception to this was the *Quarterly Journal of Studies on Alcohol,* a major vehicle for reporting the psychiatric and sociological findings on alcoholism. The founding of this journal in 1940 reflected a general desire in both the academic and lay community to understand alcoholism. Two

134

outstanding forces that fostered this interest were Alcoholics Anonymous, which was growing into a powerful national organization, and reformers within the academic medical establishment, who were developing a community outpatient approach to the treatment of alcoholism. The respectable alcoholic was brought out of hiding, and the image that all alcoholics were lower-class, bowery pariahs came to be challenged. Though the old stereotypes persisted to some extent, of course, a new interpretation of alcoholism was offered. In the early 1940s researchers, using an interdisciplinary model, began to investigate alcoholism from multiple perspectives. Leaders of this movement emphasized alcoholism as a disease.[4] This disease model has lasted to this day, but our image of alcoholism has greatly changed. The profile of the typical alcoholic is no longer that of the middle-aged male, and the abuse is no longer associated with a single form of drug.

The numerous studies on alcoholism that appeared during the early 1940s in the *Quarterly Journal of Studies on Alcoholism* tended to share a tone of optimism. Research funding was made available for alcoholism, and efforts were begun to consolidate disparate research findings already in existence. As one of those involved remarked:

> We were quite confident that we knew a lot about the immediate physical and psychological effects of the various amounts of alcohol. We were sure, as I am not sure today, that any amount of alcohol always acts as a depressant.[5]

Such optimism was aided by proclaiming alcoholism as a disease and thereby subsuming it under the medical model. Researchers of the 1940s struggled to get alcoholism labeled a disease because it would mean that the alcoholic would no longer be seen as morally degenerate. Alcoholism would then become something from which anyone could suffer. These ideas constituted the general medical and lay issues that formed the social context of the period between 1940 and 1944 and therefore are important in considering the film *The Lost Weekend*.

The Lost Weekend was based on a novel that enjoyed some popularity and gained attention in the psychiatric literature on alcoholism. Its description of an alcoholic binge was thought to be so accurate that the author was believed to have been an alcoholic himself. Unlike the book the film gave attention neither to the flashbacks experienced by the central character, Don Birnam, nor to his mother-dominated childhood.[6] Though it did mention the mother, as well as anger toward the brother, the film did not point directly to any early developmental, etiological factors that led to Birnam's alcoholism. This fitted the clinical thinking of the period:

> It is hoped to find some more or less specific traumatic experience of a peculiar personality makeup or character structure which is the source of the individual's alcohol addiction, or to reveal some pervasive emotional conflict (e.g., repressed homosexuality) which finds a release through alcohol. There is, however, no conclusive evidence for the several formulations that have been offered and apparently there is no way to resolving some of the conflicts among the several findings of different investigations.[7]

The film emphasized the compulsive craving for alcohol that drives the individual further and further into primitive, self-degrading behavior.[8] One of the great problems for Birnam, as for all alcoholics, is that because his tolerance level rises quickly, he had to continually increase his consumption in order to obtain inebriation. The film depicted the psychological and physical problems that eventually result from such a situation. It is appropriate that Birnam's descent into the underworld of the derelict drunk takes place during a weekend, for it is then that people are most often alone and experience the anxiety that comes from being face-to-face with themselves. Paradoxically, the weekend also becomes a time when they can be left alone to drink, and the alcoholic speaks of longing for such times in order to be alone.

The psychiatric literature of the 1940s investigated the drinking habits of alcoholics and moved toward a system of differentiating and classifying different types of drinkers. One article that dealt with this issue helps us to understand the interpretation of Birnam when it states:

> The daily inebriate is . . . characterized by a history of gradual habituation to alcohol, beginning early in life, until his drinking reaches proportions that signs of physical and mental deterioration may become manifest.[9]

Birnam is a daily drinker, and, as his tolerance increases, we follow his need for more alcohol. The physical and psychological result is a deterioration into delirium tremens. Delirium tremens is found in those who, like Birnam, have been drinking excessively over a considerable period. Symptoms include disorientation with respect to time and place and hallucinations involving small, fast animals like rats, bats, and beetles. The afflicted person frequently sees these animals to be going through terrifying transformations and to even be attacking him. Tremors of the hands and lips, high fever, and heavy perspiration are usually associated with these hallucinations. In the film these occur over a long weekend period (Thursday to Tuesday), when Birnam's brother is away in the countryside. This period of time corresponds to the course of the symptoms, which in fact lasts from three to six days. Afterward, the alcoholic generally recalls the panic associated with the hallucinations, and enters a period of abstinence. This period is generally short, however, as the individual tends quickly to return to excessive drinking.

Predictably, Birnam makes a resolve not to drink. We are led to believe that, unlike the typical alcoholic, he will not return to alcohol as a result of the support of his girlfriend, Susan. The intervention of Susan, who attains almost saintly heights of understanding and tolerance, might seem like part of the standard romantic fare of Hollywood, but there is another interpretation. Strauss said:

> Early in the 1940s the remarkable effectiveness of Alcoholics Anonymous was being attributed by some observers to the sympathy, understanding and positive attitude which alcoholics could find in their AA sponsor.[10]

This was certainly made clear in a psychiatric article, published in 1944, that emphasized that "sincere appreciation of the patient's capacities and poten-

The Lost Weekend (USA, 1945). Director Billy Wilder. With Ray Milland. By permission of Universal Pictures.

tialities, and friendliness toward him, are appreciated in proportion to the depth of his craving for them, no matter how well his desire for them is covered."[11] Persistent acceptance and an unconditional kind of love were stressed and might well account for the type of character Susan exemplifies.

The film enjoyed general praise from the critics. The *New York Times* acclaimed it as "shatteringly realistic" and the *Daily Sketch* and *New Statesman* of England praised it as "an uncompromising, unrelenting study of alcoholism" and as a portrayal "without gloss," respectively.[12] It was the first nonmelodramatic feature made by Hollywood on the issue of alcoholism. Because it attracted so much attention, an editorial review was written in one of the contemporary psychiatric journals.[13] The reviewer, begins with reserved approval. "As a serious portrayal of a particular alcoholic, as a case history of one Don Birnam, it is a competent job." He then pointed out certain inadequacies of the portrayal. The film, he said, obstructed recognition that the alcoholic is ill. Furthermore, the film implied that "anyone who drinks will become a Don Birnam," that "the situation of the alcoholic is absolutely hopeless," and, finally, that "hospitals and doctors are not only useless for this condition but are in addition heartless, inefficient, and horrendous." On the basis of these shortcomings, the reviewer maintained, "From the viewpoint of the professional student of the problems of alcohol and alcoholism, faulty, even potentially dangerous, implications are present in *The Lost Weekend.*"[14]

This was obviously a damning criticism, and, if it were all that a clinician could say about the film, one would have to conclude that the film was largely destructive. Another important reference to the film, however, appeared almost two years afterward. During this time interval the film enjoyed a good deal of popularity and obviously was considered to depict alcoholism with some accuracy. In order to understand the nature of the film's impact, Daniel Brower, a psychology professor at New York University, did a more specific analysis of audience reaction. Interested in testing the validity of Bacon's earlier assertions about the film's distortions Brower administered an opinion poll about the film in 1946.[15] He found that viewers thought neither that the film implied that alcoholism is hopelessly incurable nor that those who drink to excess would become like the hero. An overwhelming percentage felt, in contrast to what Bacon had presumed, that *The Lost Weekend* portrayed the alcoholic as an individual who is ill and who requires specialized treatment.

The one area in which Bacon and the general audience did concur was in the belief that the film created an impression that hospital treatment of alcoholics was brutal, inefficient, or at best apathetic. Brower linked this belief to a certain sensationalism in the film's depiction of delirium tremens. Such a depiction, Brower felt, could be harmful to the audience. He said:

> Scenes taken in operating rooms, autopsy rooms, disturbed wards of mental hospitals, and so forth, are essentially traumatic to movie audiences; the exhibition of an attack of delirium tremens with the necessary restraints, which give to the unsophisticated the impression of brutality, is certainly so.[16]

This was a very telling comment by a member of the mental health establishment of the period. It clearly implied that audiences should be protected from such displays on the screen and fit with a somewhat conservative conception, dominant at the time, of what films should and should not depict. Similar beliefs were implicit in Bacon's article. Both articles reflected the prevailing feeling, that medical and psychiatric problems should remain strictly under the aegis of the medical community and should not be presented to the public. Lay audiences were considered unable to face up to the mad aberrations of drug abusers. One can only ask whether this protection would really have been necessary or whether it would only have served to promote the general view of the alcoholic as a nonperson. Both psychiatric reviewers were ambivalent about how graphic the film should have been; both asserted that audiences should see the behavior and suffering of alcoholics, though how much they should see remained, it would seem, questionable.

The importance of *The Lost Weekend* was acknowledged by both clinicians, particularly by Brower, who stated that the faults "do not overshadow the good qualities of the film nor its educational merits."[17] Certainly, for the 1940s and the depiction of an alcoholic as a middle-class, middle-aged male, troubled but still resourceful, was important. This contrasted with the clinical literature of the period, which, based on studies of alcoholics from mental hospitals, jails, and skid rows, reinforced the existing stereotypes.[18] The impact of the film in changing such views was brought into question by the results of Brower's poll; only 12 percent thought that "all alcoholics are, in general, like the hero." This was certainly complementary to clinical perceptions of the film and spoke of an interesting correlation between lay and clinical perceptions of the period.

The full impact of *The Lost Weekend* is therefore difficult to assess, though it is clear in retrospect that the film was the first feature film to attempt seriously to depict the madness associated with alcoholism and that, at least to some degree, it was successful.

The Rose. At the beginning of the film, when Rose (Bette Midler) screams to her adoring, youthful audience, "There are only three things in the world: sex, drugs, and rock 'n' roll," we have the quintessential description of the contemporary drug culture. It was a problem very different from the portrayal of the single-drug abuse of the alcoholic, which dominated both clinical and popular literature in the 1940s and early 1950s. *The Rose,* loosely based on the life of Janis Joplin, brought the public up-to-date in characterizing the drug problem. It was no longer typified by the abuse of one substance, but involved multiple drug abuse. Of equal importance was the fact that the problem was no longer restricted to males but affects females as well. Finally, drug abuse was no longer the stigmatizing bane of helplessly distraught and isolated individuals but was part of the daily existence of an entire generation. *The Rose* captured this generation and was therefore an important film.

It might seem strange that a film like *The Rose* was made in 1979—first, because it derived from the life of a rock star who died almost ten years earlier, and second, because the drug scene that it presented seems to be dated. The explanation for its late appearance involves the way in which the drug problem evolved in America. The drug culture made its first, most visible home on the West Coast for many reasons. It thrived on the excesses that had become commonplace for the land of hot tubs, encounter groups, religious cults, and the Beach Boys. By the tens of thousands, people of all ages, but mostly adolescents, streamed to the West Coast for the "action."

It is interesting that so many of America's fads, especially those associated with the exaggerated, freak, or bizarre, began on the West Coast. It usually took about a year for the same phenomenon to appear on the East Coast and, anywhere from one to fifteen years for the rest of the country to catch up. This was certainly the case for the drug culture. The fact that *The Rose* made its successful appearance almost fifteen years after the drug scene had presumably reached its zenith in the enclaves of such well-known drug centers as Haight Ashbury, Venice, and Los Angeles, confirmed that America had totally absorbed the drug culture. People no longer talked of particular locales for attracting kids seeking highs, for every town and city in America has its suppliers, dealers, and users, and new, illicit drugs were, through marketing magic, quickly made available across America. *The Rose* became such a popular film because America caught up, and images that once symbolized the counterculture were absorbed into mainline America.

There is no question that the film is dominated by Midler and that her super-star persona helped the film enjoy wide popularity and become a box-office success. The story was so complementary to this persona, however, that it would be difficult to separate the two. Midler's portrayal of Joplin as the "ballsy," raucous, "no-shit," sexually diffuse, and constantly high idol of youth certainly complemented the image that Midler herself always projected and that always guaranteed her a following. Initially, this following was among the gay popula tion, which heralded her as another Judy Garland or Mae West, but her popular-ity quickly spread to older adolescents and youths who could easily identify with her espousal of rebellious sexuality. Her role in *The Rose* partially worked, then, because it corresponded to how she had come to be seen by millions.

Before we discuss the nature of this portrayal in the film, it might be helpful to give an overview of drug abuse from 1930 to 1980, the year the film made its way around the United States and into the homes of millions through home-box-office television. In the 1930s and 1940s drug abuse centered on alcohol; gener-ally no other drug was involved. By the 1960s there was a change to multiple drug use, or, as it came to be called, *polydrug abuse.* Different kinds of drugs, often including alcohol, were consumed together. The average age and the sex of the abuser was changing. In the 1960s adolescents were beginning to com-prise a significant number of the substance abusers who were being brought into the courts and clinic facilities. Teenage substance addiction was becoming so common that adolescent life came to be labeled the "drug culture." By 1975 one out of every six teenagers and one out of every eleven adults in America had a "severe addictive problem."[19]

Drug proliferation was greatly aided by the adoption of drugs as part of the rock star imagery of the 1960s. The rebellious and sexualized rock 'n' rollers of the 1950s came to be replaced by a new image, which centered around nihilism, raunchy sexualized violence, and self-destruction.[20] Rock 'n' roll became increas-ingly associated with the blues, and the carefree "boppers" of the 1950s were replaced by the cries of lament for lost loves and lost times of happiness. By the 1970s the intense but brief period of political concern and commitment was giving way increasingly to withdrawal from others and an emphasis on self-pleasure and staying stoned, the central focus of the drug culture.

Two of the most important factors underlying this change were the psycho-logical characteristics of youth and the socio-political view of youth in the 1960s and 1970s. With regard to psychological issues, there occurs in adolescence a retreat from parental directives and, frequently, rebellion against everything in which the parents believe and symbolically represent. The adolescent turns to his peers as the authority of what is, and is not, right. He has an intense impressiona-bility and need to be accepted. Adolescent group norms, becoming rigidly fixed, often focus on the issue of proving oneself as a way of obtaining an identity. In the sixties and seventies taking drugs affirmed that one was not conforming to the adult world. In this sense drugs gave one an identity, albeit a negative one. The use of drugs also allowed the adolescent to avoid the burden of entering upon the path of adulthood. Drugs removed the pressures of reality and offered an alternative in which there seemingly were no such concerns. Here, one could float and remain untroubled by the anxieties that came from being directionless.

Any discussion of the developmental vicissitudes of adolescence must also consider what adolescence means to American culture. This country has always romanticized the rebellion of youth, perhaps because of its own historical beginnings as a rebellious colony. The real heroes of America are not adult representations but the cowboys, who somehow never quite grew up but remained fixed in adolescence, the middle space between childhood and adulthood. It is a state to which older people often try to return, as evidenced by their adoption of the fads of youth. Images of youth dominate advertisements, and we are all encouraged to stay young and maintain the body and the libido of a sixteen-year-old. Notwithstanding this adoration of youth, there is an equally strong contradictory pressure that the adolescent grow up and accept, like everyone else, a place in society. He is expected to give up his excesses and fall into line, assuming the responsibility that comes with adulthood.

We have seen, however, that adolescence has over the years become continuously extended. Whereas by turning thirteen a boy used to be considered part of the adult community, one can now be thirty and still be living an adolescent lifestyle. Whereas well-established rites of passage once made growing up a clear process of fixed progressions, adolescence today is well extended. Terms like *youth* and *young adult* now pertain to individuals in their late twenties. Observers have commented on how many "young people" experience a "psychological moratorium," by which they have meant dropping out of all commitments and refusing the identity of an adult.[21] Since the Vietnam War the number of such individuals has increased.

The Vietnam War became a focal point for the nihilism of a generation that declared itself to be "burnt out."[2] This expression was aptly descriptive of a phenomenon associated with adolescence long before the 1960s. It involved a need to live life at such a frenetic pace that death would soon follow. The underlying motive was a fear that aging would bring a dissolution of self and individual freedom. The only real pleasure lay in getting all one could right now, with no concern about tomorrow. All that the morrow seemed to bring was a realization that one was even older and closer to the stultifying straitjacket of adulthood. Such intense self-absorption came to typify the 1960s, whose heroes have become and probably will always be, idolized. These include Joplin, Jimi Hendrix, Brian Jones, and Jim Morrison, whose heroic stature bore striking similarity to the stars of an earlier generation, such as James Dean. It is fitting that in one of the opening shots of *The Rose* Rose's parents show reporters, who have come to seek out the real story of her suicide, a wall full of photographs of her heroes. Two of the largest photographs are of James Dean and Jayne Mansfield. The uniting characteristic of these and other pictures of stars who cover the wall is their early death.

This is, of course, a central theme that the film will follow. The photographs show the stage personas of figures who, though outwardly strong and larger than life, were inwardly fragile and easily hurt. They therefore represent a mirror for the adolescent and young adult who himself is struggling to present a "cool" line to others while wracked by the pains that come with the internal and external pressures of adolescent development. This is not to say, of course, that all adolescents become suicidal but that many, because of their struggle for a new identity, are attracted to heroes who flirt with, and are sometimes absorbed by, self-destruction. This self-destruction, as earlier pointed out, is associated with a general level of emotionality and a need to be always on the edge of either total elation or total destruction. Such exaggerated emotional states are often present in adolescents but, with time, become more manageable and less pressing. For some, however, conflicts persist, and they remain ill at ease about who they are and what they are doing.

While in the early 1960s psychologists discussed this situation in terms of *ego and identity diffusion* the focus shifted in the 1970s to the concept of *failed ego identity*. This has come to be clinically characterized as the *borderline personality*. As pointed out earlier (chapter 3), the borderline has become one of the most common diagnostic categories. Its characteristics are pervasive feelings of loneliness and emptiness, a lack of stable ego identity, chaotic interpersonal relationships, and the existence of extremely aggressive feelings that are volatile and erupt in unpredictable mood swings.[23]

From a psychodynamic perspective, borderline is a diagnostic term often used in describing polydrug abusers. The term is used when describing their self-destructive quality, which for many clinicians is an important basis of explanation for their addiction. In reading the literature on the borderline personality it is intriguing to see how often the characteristics that Bette Middler presents are mentioned and how even Bette Middler herself becomes relevant in the context of the borderline. Reference to her in a clinical article entitled "Masochism and Ego Identity in Borderline States" is worth quoting:

> A few weeks later another patient described his fascination for Bette Middler. "I go to see her every chance I get and every single time I get depressed, but I love it. She represents something raw, primal, screaming, ranting, fuck-it-how-I-look. She magnifies her flaws. She's gut—I want to swallow her up and be her or at least part of her life. She has power and pain; I want to share some of that."[24]

The author maintained that such an identification is part of an "underlying thread of self-destructive, possibly masochistic, attitudes," which is a key component in borderline personalities. The intensification of self-inflicted painful emotions is an unconscious means through which borderline personalities try to express or experience their feelings.

In clinical literature borderlines are presented as existing in a state of identity diffusion, in which they are not sure where they end and others begin. Their problem originates in a difficulty with an absorbing parental superego, which makes them unable to deal with their love and hate feelings towards their parents. Many researchers hold that their relationship to the mother is the most crucial, for it is from the mother that the child first gains a sense of self. In their symbiotic relationship with the mother children in general fear that they will be absorbed, used up, or dominated and destroyed. In borderlines such a fear grows and becomes intensified to the point that throughout their later life they have profound problems in relating closely to others, particularly in intimate, binding physical relationships. It is posited that they have in fact been separated from their mother at some early age and that this causes a psychic wound that never heals. To be close, therefore, elicits an outpouring of primitive emotions, one of the most dominant of which is aggression.

The relationships of borderlines are marked by these fears, and in some cases they specifically seek out those who will respond in the familiar rejecting manner. It is as if they need to find this rejection and have it repeated again and again. As a result they develop a sense of emptiness and hopelessness that they will never be able to find someone who can give them what they really need.[25] This leaves borderlines continuously vulnerable to feelings of aloneness and abandonment.[26] With the disappointment of not getting what they need, the intense, child-based rage of their original deprivation and separation is activated, and they lash out at others or at themselves. When borderlines do allow themselves to be in a close, intimate relationship, it is generally only for a short time because "they fear the closeness they long for, partly because the merging they want brings the threat of mutual destruction, and partly because they fear their inevitable destructive fury."[27] Regression often occurs in response to the rage they feel, especially when there is "a real or fantasied loss of relationship."[28]

In their regression, borderlines often turn to drugs as a way of anaesthetizing themselves from the hurt. Drugs allow them to escape momentarily from a world that they perceive to be filled with nothing but pain. Seemingly, drugs offer them a level of control of the raw emotional vulnerability so close to the surface of their everyday interactions. Drugs also serve as a defensive attempt to fill up symbolically their sense of profound emptiness. As one clinician said:

> Likewise, emptiness may not be experienced and assume the central stage of treatment until sufficient regression has taken place and the defensive super-stratas have been lifted, e.g., manic-like flights into activity, promiscuity, drugs, etc., to temporarily fill the inner void via external supplies.[29]

The literature on the borderline abounds with images of the intense sense of loss of love, abandonment, and annihilation. The fragile self of the borderline continuously needs affirmation but never gets enough. More and more is needed, and the need arises to become part of others, as was the case for the above-quoted patient who spoke of fusing with Bette Middler. When not met, such intense emotional needs leave borderlines in acute fear of dissolving into nothingness, and they quickly turn to defensive maneuvers like promiscuity and drugs. Middler's characterization of this emptiness and fragile self is clear throughout the entire film. She needs the audiences to love her and in fact needs everyone to love her. This love is only possible, however, for brief periods of heightened intensity. She cannot sustain any ongoing intimate relationships because she fears being absorbed by the other person. It becomes clear that such a fear is a projection both of her own need to absorb that person and of the rage that originated from the mother's original rejection of such a dependent fusion.

All of this results in extreme ambivalence toward others and a diffuse sense of identity. Drugs become one way of artificially supplying the emotional states that she believes she really cannot feel.

Along with drugs goes sexuality, and Rose's diffusion in this area is clear. Near the beginning of the film she tells her manager that she really needs to "get laid," a statement that reflects not so much a genital adult need as a desperate cry to be held, fed, and joined with another person, any other person. The intensity of this need is reflected in her consequent lovemaking with first a man and then another woman, as well as in her sexual arousal by various people who float within her reach. The roots of her bisexuality emanate from a massive confusion about her own fragile self, almost as if it could be lost at any moment. As if to purposefully emphasize this, Rose, after being rejected by a well-known country western singer for being "foul-mouthed and dirty," goes to a club where female impersonators perform. Here, in a world of multiple identities she is well-known, and it is clear that she often frequents this place, where people are simply playing at being others and where the only thing that is clear is that they are not themselves. Completely at ease, she delights in the impersonations of the females, who, of course, bear a marked similarity to herself, and she even mounts the stage and performs with them. One of the boundaries that helps most people define who they are is sexuality, but it is apparent that this is not a clear referent for Rose, who diffusely races between male and female worlds. The ambiguity of this world becomes linked to hard drugs when one of the female impersonators, in drag as Phyllis Diller, offers her a score of heroin, which she hesitatingly refuses with the statement that she has been clean for a while.

Rose's acceptance of heroin, of which she will take an overdose, comes after she has been left for the last time by a man with whom she has throughout the film been 'in and out' of love. Standing alone outside a diner, where she has been reminded that she once sexually took on the entire football team in high school, she accepts a fix from one of her admirers. Alone and in a panic, she rushes to the high school football field, where she was "gang-banged" and, standing in a phone booth facing the field, invites her mother to attend her upcoming concert in her hometown. After her mother's expected rejection, she takes the heroin and sinks slowly to the floor of the booth. Though overly schematic, the mother's rejection certainly reflects the clinical literature's attention to the impact of the mother on the borderline. It is the failed relationship with the mother that edges Rose toward her death.

Throughout the film it is clear that Rose's mother has been symbolically substituted by her audiences, whom she at once adores and hates. The emotional primitivism filling her performances bonds her and her audience into a rhythmic rocking mass of bodies, which, through the camera's selected angles, seemingly meld into one unified mass. Throughout her performance the audience gives her the reaction that aids her regression. The major concert sequence in the film is heralded by her bursting onto the stage and screaming, "Hello, you motherfuckers." While not to be overplayed, the choice of such a term is significant to the central conflict of her life, the simultaneous rage and love she has felt toward her own mother. The expression of such contradictory feelings has marked her actions throughout the film as she moves rapidly towards self-destruction.

Drug abuse has clearly changed over the last forty years. More people, particularly younger people of both sexes, are using drugs associated with abuse and dependence. As made clear in both major films discussed in this chapter, the madness of drugs stems from two interconnected factors: (1) the hallucinatory experiences induced by drugs and, more generally, (2) the ability of drugs to bring about a loss of reality. The individual is not himself and enters a world where time and place, cause and effect, are distorted. But beyond the actual effect of the drug lie the kinds of behaviors that surround its use. For both Don Burnam and the Rose this involves a tragic progression toward self-destruction. As the drug culture has become a fixed part of American society, it is not surprising that a film like *The Rose* ends in death. Unlike *The Lost Weekend*, the people who care are portrayed as gone forever, and the answer to one's pain and disappointments lies only in the fierce flight from reality that drugs provide.

The idea of self-help and the belief that one must reach rock bottom before one can pull oneself up, emphasized in *The Lost Weekend*, no longer rings true. As the number and toxicity of drugs, particularly those abused by teenagers and young adults, increase, the more likely they are to lead to death. Though in both films the personality factors behind such a problem are sketchy, it is clear that in *The Rose* the escape is not just of one person but potentially of a whole generation who identifies with the lost and loveless figure to whom it pays homage.

Notes

1. E. M. Loeb, "Primitive Intoxicants," *Quarterly Journal of Studies on Alcoholism*, vol. 4 (1943), 387–98. C. Washburne, *Primitive Intoxicants: A Study of the Uses and Functions of Alcohol in Preliterate Societies* (New York: College and University Press, 1961).

2. T. Lidz and A. Rothenberg, "Psychedelism: Dionysus Reborn," *Journal of Psychiatry* 31 (1968): 116–18.

3. S. Cohen, *The Drug Dilemma* (New York: McGraw-Hill, 1969), p. 9.

4. R. Straus, "Problem Drinking in the Perspective of Social Change," in *Alcohol and Alcohol Problems*, ed. W. Filstead, J. Rossi, and M. Keller (Cambridge, Mass.: Ballinger, 1976), pp. 29–56.

5. Ibid., p. 23.

6. This was to soon change in films like: *I'll Cry Tomorrow* (1955), *Buster Keaton Story* (1957), *Too Much Too Soon* (1958), and *Rebel Without a Cause* (1955), where parental influence is portrayed as the cause of alcoholism.

7. L. Frank, "The Problem of the Alcoholic Personality," *Quarterly Journal of Studies on Alcoholism*, vol. 5, no. 2 (September 1944), 242–44.

8. The notion of needing to reach the very limits of social and personal degradation dominated later films, e.g., *Come Fill the Cup* (1950), *Come Back Little Sheba* (1952), *Days of Wine and Roses* (1962).

9. M. Miller, "Prognosis in Periodic and Daily Inebriates," *Quarterly Journal of Studies on Alcohol*, vol. 5, no. 3 (December 1944), 431.

10. Straus, p. 32.

11. Miller, p.

12. See J. Hillier, "Filmography," *Images of Alcoholism*, ed. S. Cook and M. Lewington (London: British Film Institute, 1979).

13. S. D. Bacon, "Current Notes: A Student of the Problems of Alcoholism Views *The Lost Weekend*," *Quarterly Journal of Studies on Alcoholism*, no. 3 (December 1948), 402–5.

14. Ibid., p. 405.

15. D. Brower, "An Opinion Poll on Reactions to *The Lost Weekend*," *Quarterly Journal of Studies on Alcohol* (March 1946), 596–98.

16. Ibid., p. 598.

17. Ibid., p. 598.

18. M. Gray, "A Study of 363 Cases of Institutionalized Behavior Problems in a Drug Addicted Population," *Journal of General Psychiatry*, vol. 31 (1944), 15–22.

19. N. Cummings, "Turning Bread into Stones: Our Modern Antimiracle," *American Psychologist*, vol. 34, no. 12 (December 1979), 1119.

20. These differences can be seen by contrasting the two versions of *A Star is Born* (1954; 1979).

21. E. Erikson, *Identity: Youth and Crisis* (New York: W. W. Norton, 1968).

22. See *Who'll Stop the Rain* (1979).

23. R. Grinker et al., *The Borderline Syndrome* (New York: Basic Books, 1968).

24. T. Saretsky, "Masochism and Ego Identity in Borderline States," *Contemporary Psychoanalysis*, vol. 12, no. 4 (1976), 433.

25. A. Miller, *Prisoners of Childhood* (New York: Basic Books, 1981).

26. J. Adler and D. Buie, "Aloneness and Borderline Psychopathology: The possible relevance to child development issues," Accepted for publication in the *International Journal of Psychoanalysis* (1979).

27. Ibid., p. 3.

28. Ibid., p. 13.

29. M. Singer, "The Experience of Emptiness in Narcissistic and Borderline States: Id Deficiency and Ego Defect versus Dynamic-Defensive Models," *International Review of Psychoanalysis* 4 (1977): 460.

7
Paranoia and Madness

Paranoia has often been a term found in historical descriptions of madness, and for many people remains today, as it was for the Greeks and Romans, a synonym for madness itself. Clinically it is not as pervasive a symptom of madness as one might think, and in fact there is a dearth of recent clinical literature on the subject.[1] The symptoms of paranoia fall into three major categories. The first involves the idea of being persecuted by others. The sufferer believes that others are spying on him or plotting to hurt or even kill him, and presents the reason for their treachery in a clear and cogent manner. The second category involves ideas of grandeur. The individual believes that because he possesses superior knowledge or status, others are pursuing him or plotting against him. Often he feels that he has a special mission and that others are out to stop him. Individuals in both of these categories are generally quite cogent and sensible and, except for their having paranoid or grandoise ideas, have established themselves as fully functional and normal members of society.

There is, however, a third aspect of paranoia, in which the personality shows evidence of deterioration and disorganization. Thoughts of persecution and illusions of grandeur are no longer logical and systematic but fragmented. Often called *paranoid schizophrenia*, this condition pulls the individual further and further away from others and causes him to lose his ability, or perhaps desire, to deal with others. His delusions become more changeable and often are joined by hallucinatory experiences, such as believing that he is being spoken to by God or by the devil. Most of the clinical literature describes individuals who fall into the first two categories, and it would in fact seem that paranoid thinking is not as bizarre a phenomenon as one might at first think.

The feeling that things are not going the way we would like and that the reason for this is that someone is working against us and arranging such frustrations is not uncommon. We all seek a reason for the major or minor sufferings we experience, and our explanations for our misfortunes tend to turn to concrete, causal interpretations in which someone else (either a specific person or a general unknown force) has directed his or her energies against our succeeding. We feel that our plans should be realized, for we have worked hard. The emphasis here is on the idea that because we wish for something, it should happen.[2] While this is certainly an egocentric and unrealistic way of thinking (which becomes modified to some degree as we get older), the failures that result even

147

after we have worked hard are not easily disregarded. The Protestant work ethic implies that by working hard, one achieves one's just reward. An individual who has made great efforts to succeed is therefore likely to attribute his bitter failure to a plot against him, rather than to the capriciousness of fate. The need to have an enemy, like the need for an imaginary friend, should pass with childhood, but for many people such an explanation for failure continues to hold power even to the point of becoming an obsession. The story of Xerxes, the ancient king of Persia, who had the straits of Hellespont flogged with whips and chained for destroying one of his floating barges strikes us at first as bizarre and even amusing. We must, however, recognize that on certain occasions we, too, have sought to anthropomorphize nature into a causal, humanlike force that directs powers for or against us. With, for instance, the personification Lady Luck, the uncontrollable becomes seemingly somewhat more approachable, and the gambler's ritualized attempt to appease the gods of chance bring to mind ancient and even modern religious practices.

As we have already pointed out, paranoia is often associated with grandiose ideas. As a matter of fact, the more obsessed an individual is with power, the more he becomes suspicious of others who would take his power from him. The cinematic portrayal of such figures has always met with great success, as in the case of *Emperor Jones* (1933), *Dr. Mabuse* (1922, 1932), *Citizen Kane* (1941), *The Caine Mutiny* (1954), *Patton* (1969), *Hitler* (1973), or *Aguirre, Wrath of God* (1972). Such individuals are often portrayed as having an insatiable need for power and greatness, and while this need might seem to be tied to serving the good of others, such an illusion quickly falls away to reveal the primitive impulses that fuel their actions.

The emphasis of the present chapter is on two major interpretations of the causes of paranoia as a general syndrome. The first etiological interpretation to be explored, dominant until the late 1950s, explained paranoia in terms of repressed homosexuality. The second view, which gained strength in the 1960s, maintained that the causes for paranoid thinking are not to be found in the individual but in the social environment in which he exists. Because of the subtle presentations of paranoia often found in film, we will consider a number of films, rather than follow the usual format and discuss two films from contrasting periods.

Sexuality and Paranoia

As one might suspect, the earliest clinical explanation for paranoia came from Sigmund Freud. From the autobiographical account of a well-known judge who had developed paranoid delusions, Freud was able to make a number of clinical inferences.[3] According to him, what the paranoid feels others will do to him is really what he wishes to do to others, but this fact is so intolerable that he must project it onto others. After investigating the different possible intolerable ideas that are projected, Freud found that the most basic and most frightening involves homosexual love. Conscious awareness of this proves so objectionable that

Dr. Mabuse, the Gambler (Germany, 1922). Director, Fritz Lang. With Rudolph Klein-Rogge. Roger Manvell Collection, Photographic Archive, University of Louisville, Kentucky.

the paranoid individual has to attribute such feelings to the person whom he admires. Even this, however, becomes too threatening, as it still raises the specter of homosexuality within the individual's life. The total repression of homosexuality can only be accomplished by completely denying any kind of loving or even admiration. This results in adopting feelings opposite to love: hate, anger, and hostile competitiveness. These violent feelings were still objectionable in that they are only once removed from the true feelings of love. To gain even further distance from the original feeling, the individual projects the hostility onto the other person. Freud's ideas on paranoia were, and to a lesser degree still are, accepted by clinicians. Certainly, in the 1940s and early 1950s the notion that paranoia can be linked to repressed homosexuality and that all homosexuals are therefore evidencing paranoia was dominant in psychoanalytic circles. As the famous psychiatrist A. A. Brill commented:

Having encountered hundreds of homosexuals, some of whom were prominent in artistic, philanthropic, and other fields, I have never found one who, on closer observation, did not show paranoid traits. They are all oversuspicious, "shadowy" and mistrustful. Most of them are unreliable, intriguing, picayune, and impetuous.[4]

Brill and others following the classical psychoanalytic interpretation believed that the roots of homosexuality emanate from anal-sadistic fixations and regressions.[5]

The image of paranoid individuals as repressed homosexuals was therefore a dominant one, and their portrayal in clinical literature often emphasized their being weak and of degenerate character. It is, therefore, not surprising to find that the implicitly homosexual cinematic characterizations of the 1930s, 1940s, and 1950s projected the paranoid male character as a diminutive, weak, effeminate, and unpredictable person, who exuded lurking sadistic malevolence. One of the clearest representations of this was in *The Maltese Falcon* (1941). Detective Sam Spade (Humphrey Bogart), is pitted against three male criminals, who personify the fusion of homosexual paranoia and degeneration, dominant in the literature of the time. First, we have Cairo (played by Peter Lorre, who with the success of *M* established himself in audiences' minds as an unseemly little figure whose sexual predilections encompassed all that was degenerate.) In contrast to Sam Spade, Cairo, is an unctuous, groveling, and effeminate character, who, while fearful of being attacked and plotted against, is at the same time plotting against others. In Dashiell Hammett's novel Sam Spade's secretary, after seeing Cairo, tells her boss that Cairo is a queer. The movie version, like all the films made about the subject in the 1940s and early 1950s, presented homosexuality in a very implicit, guarded manner. Besides Cairo's nonverbal characteristics, his homosexual identification is affirmed in the film by Spade's reaction to his perfumed handkerchief.[6] The other two criminals, Guttman, "the Fat Man" (Sydney Greenstreet) and Wilmer (Elisha Cook, Jr.), are particularly interesting. The Fat Man refers to Wilmer as his son, but the relationship is not based on a familial bond but on a homosexual bonding, in which Wilmer acts out his boss's sadistic cravings. Sam Spade reads the true nature of their relationship, and this makes Wilmer hate him. Throughout the film there is an undercurrent of distrust and double-cross, which rests on a paranoid vision. The film noir classic is filled with half-lit alleys and backrooms, which add to the general sense of foreboding and distrust.[7]

The paranoid and homosexual link is also presented in another film noir classic, Hitchcock's *Strangers on a Train* (1951). Guy (Farley Granger) wants to get rid of his wife and fortuitously meets another man, Bruno (Robert Walker), who says he can accomplish this if in turn Guy will get rid of his father, whom he hates with a passion equal to Guy's hatred of his wife. While Bruno kills Guy's wife, Guy has in fact never explicitly agreed to the homicidal contract that Bruno has so boldly proposed. Bruno, enraged, sets out to destroy Guy. Bruno's portrayal is again that of the sadistic degenerate, whose attitude and movements toward Guy have a decidedly sexual overtone. Their apparent collusion is more than just an excuse for displays of murderous aggression but also the suggestion of homosexual love. Such love must, of course, be guarded against, and thus Bruno pursues Guy as victim rather than as lover. Homosexuality is repressed and replaced by murderous pursuit, fulfilling a paranoid scenario.

Another Hitchcock work to play implicitly on the paranoid homosexual theme was *Rope* (1948). In this film, loosely based on the Leopold Loeb case of the

1920s, two cousins murder a young boy, whom they then put into a chest. Fusing paranoia and megalomania, they delight in eluding discovery and even invite their pursuers into the room where the chest is. Homosexuals are again presented as sadistic, effeminate types, whose warped paranoid vision of the world moves them away from others into degenerate crime.

In these various films Hollywood succeeded in furthering the association between paranoia and homosexuality. While playing on the element of repressed homosexuality and paranoia, the moviemakers clearly needed to add murder to the equation. One of the first explicit renderings of this was in *The Detective* (1968). A young homosexual has been killed, and a police officer (Frank Sinatra) has been called in to solve the crime. The criminal, of course, is not openly homosexual but a repressed homosexual, who has murdered his pickup lover out of fear that the latter will reveal the former's identity. The film emphasizes that it is the killer's repression that causes him to believe that he will be discovered and that he must kill to stop such discovery. While it is certainly true that paranoid ideations can contribute to murderous aggression, the pervasiveness of this theme in film would lead us to believe that all paranoids are homicidal maniacs. What clinical evidence does indicate is that paranoid delusions most often give way to murderous rage in marital or love relationships in which jealousy and loss of self-esteem are intensified.[8] As one clinician pointed out, "We would suggest that reactions involving only grandiosity and persecution provide an unlikely candidate as a murderer without the prominence of pathological eroticism and jealousy."[9]

With the 1950s the portrayal of the link between jealousy, paranoia, violence, and homosexuality began to be more overt. In *Rebel without a Cause* (1955) a full-lipped and effeminate teenage Plato (Sal Mineo) is a confused admirer of Jim (James Dean). Abandoned by his parents, he is the poor little rich boy who fears the world. Though never explicitly made clear, it is implied that what he fears is the revelation of his homosexual feelings for his attractive friend, Jim. The paranoid exaggeration of his fear is clearly evidenced when, having armed himself to fend off the forces of the night, he refuses to come out of the observatory to the police. His fears of persecution are presented as being, more than anything else, tied to his homosexual "weakness," and, like so many homosexual characters, he meets a violent death.

By the mid-1950s Freud's belief that paranoia is a response to unacceptable homosexual wishes began to be questioned. Psychiatrists recognized that the studies on paranoia had almost exclusively involved men and began to suspect the existence of important sex differences. Studies failed to produce evidence of homosexual concern in women diagnosed as paranoid schizophrenic.[10] There was increasing evidence that Freud's view of homosexuality was too limiting and that the emotional meaning of homosexuality should be given more attention. The literature of the period increasingly emphasized that men are put under great pressure to be tough, aggressive, and assertive.[11] Homosexuality became therefore, a metaphor for untraditional masculine feelings, which men find unacceptable as a result of socialization experiences. To have such feelings raises fears about being homosexual. Clinical literature of the 1950s introduced the concept that such beliefs form the basis for a good deal of what is considered homosexual and called such presentations *pseudohomosexuality*.[12] The paranoid individual was now viewed as fearing homosexuality because it is associated with a loss of power and assertiveness, traits that he feels he has never been able to master. The problem in paranoia was no longer perceived to be fear of homosexuality, but a fear of powerlessness, which took on an ambivalent quality. On the one hand, the individual with such feelings longs to derive strength from some other, more powerful person while at the same time fearing the vulnerability and destruction that he believes will result. Fear of losing power, as well as fear of needing power, were of central importance, and films gradually began to explore this theme.

For Hollywood the theme of power and paranoia was dominant in films like *The Caine Mutiny* (1954), in which the military trappings of supermasculinity were explored as a defense against feelings of failure, incompetence, and loss of power. While there was no overt homosexuality in *The Caine Mutiny*, the message of such doubts was subtly conveyed, and Bogart's handling of metal balls could only aid such imagery. By the late 1950s and early 1960s the subtleties of such depictions were replaced by a more open presentation of power, paranoia, and homosexuality, such as in *Reflections in a Golden Eye* (1967) and *The Sergeant* (1968). In both films the trappings of military machismo were exposed to hide grave conflicts over masculinity. The theme of power, homosexuality, and paranoia was usually linked to violence, and this was almost always directed by the homosexual against himself. It seemed that the only way out of the recognition of one's homosexuality was to kill oneself, as in *Advise and Consent* (1962).

While homosexuality's association with paranoia has undergone some major clinical revisions in the last twenty years, there is evidence that homosexuality is still viewed as tied to a paranoid world view. In *Cruising* (1980) homosexuals no longer kill themselves or get themselves killed by police but kill each other. Playing on some of the devices of *The Detective, Cruising* portrays the efforts of a seemingly straight detective, Steve Burns (Al Pacino), who enters the dark world of homosexual sadomasochism to find a killer. This was the underside of the depiction of homosexuality, which Hollywood in the previous fifteen years avoided in favor of portraying the gay life as a comedic event, as in *Boys in the Band* (1970). The message seemed to be that if not gay, frivolous, and fey, homosexuality is brutal, sadistic, and murderous. In *Cruising* Steve Burns comes to be part of the bondage-and discipline trade, in which everyone, even himself, becomes suspect. The film, as expected, met with much criticism, particularly from the homosexual community, who felt that it presented homosexuality as a murderous perversion. As such, it was a reactivation of earlier cinematic themes, though now innuendo and nuance had been discarded for explicitness.

In the 1960s power issues had become dominant in the explanations offered in the clinical literature concerned with homosexuality, and the guarded cinematic presentations of such themes was suddenly abandoned, exploding into imagery of raw brutality. Even with such power issues, however, the early psychoanalytic notion of repressed homosexuality as the basis for paranoia was still of key importance in the characterization of Steve Burns. Though the

American Psychiatric Association removed homosexuality from its list of psychiatric disorders in 1973, the view of homosexuality as illness has persisted. As evidenced by *Cruising*, homosexuality and paranoia are still very much tied to one another.

Paranoia as Reality

As America reeled from the assassination of its leaders and the eruption of street violence in the 1960s, there developed a certain uneasiness about whether the order of society was as well-structured as previously thought. The killing of President Kennedy brought a strong belief in a huge conspiracy, plotted perhaps inside the boardrooms of big business and government itself.[13] The posing of certain questions and the spreading of certain rumors promoted a belief in powerful and malevolent forces within the United States who were determined to destroy democracy. Beginning with *Dr. Strangelove* (1964), the thinking on

Dr. Strangelove (Britain, 1964). Director, Stanley Kubrick. With Peter Sellers *(center)*. By permission of Paramount Pictures.

paranoia began to move away from a sexual perspective to include not only the power motif but the idea that paranoia must be legitimate, given the political insanity that seemed to be gaining dominance. The clinical literature began to focus on views that a few years earlier would have been quickly dismissed. The work of Franz Fanon and other minority clinicians began to be read and taken seriously. Their view can be summarized by the 1969 statement of two black psychiatrists, W. H. Grier and P. M. Cobbs:

> We submit that it is necessary for a black man in America to develop a profound distrust of his white fellow citizens and the nation. He must be on guard to protect himself against physical hurt. He must cushion himself against cheating, slander, humiliation and outright mistreatment by the official representatives of society. If he does not so protect himself, he will live a life of such pain and shock as to find life itself unbearable. For his own survival, then, he must develop a cultural paranoia in which every man is a potential enemy unless proved otherwise and every social system is set against him unless he personally finds out differently.[14]

The belief that conspiracies and plots really were being formed by government leaders was vindicated as the Vietnam War continued and the Nixon years began. Paranoia came to be viewed as a legitimate and even adaptive perspective on the world as what appeared to be order and high morality were exposed as massive corruption and the basest needs for power. Through films like *Twilight's Last Gleaming* (1977), *Parallax View* (1974), *Three Days of the Condor* (1975), *Marathon Man* (1976), *All the President's Men* (1976), *The Domino Killings* (1977), *Blue Collar* (1978), and *The China Syndrome* (1979), the basis for paranoia came to be the external political reality rather than the repressed homosexual drives of a neurotic. The problem was a real one, which lay not in fantasies about persecution but in the actual megalomaniacal strivings of others. In numerous films the hero was accused of paranoia for his suspicions, which in the end were shown to be justified. As a matter of fact the more outlandish and bizarre the paranoid fear, the more likely its occurrence, as in *Network* (1977) and *Soylent Green* (1973). The science fiction incorporation of this paranoia can be seen in the 1978 remake of *Invasion of the Body Snatchers* (1956). Both films emerged from periods in which paranoia had some basis in sociopolitical realities. In the 1950s these realities included the meteoric rise and fall of Joseph McCarthy, the trial and execution of Julius and Ethel Rosenberg, and the Soviet explosion of an atom bomb. These events, like those of the 1960s and 1970s, led to feelings of alienation, dehumanization, and paranoia.[15]

One interesting change from the original in the 1978 version of *Invasion of the Body Snatchers* was the addition of a psychiatrist, David Kibner (Leonard Nimoy), who turns out to be a leader in the conspiracy of the pod takeover. Throughout most of the film Kibner's identity as a pod remains unknown to his friend Matthew (Donald Sutherland), and Matthew continuously encourages his friends to consult with him. Matthew tells his co-worker, Elizabeth Driscoll (Brooke Adam), that her fears that her husband is not acting like himself must have a logical explanation and takes her to Kibner's autograph-signing party.

Looking quite dapper in an ascot and tweed coat, Kibner relaxes everyone with his apparent mellowness until it is too late. As a psychiatrist, Kibner is portrayed as having power over other people's minds, and his intent is to turn them into emotionless automatons. Psychology is presented as the medium through which he can control others, and the effectiveness of his power is clear when we learn that one of his patients is the mayor. The mayor is but one of a number of high-ranking officials who, it is implied, have been taken over by the pods.

No longer set in a small town, as was the case of the 1956 version, the remake had the action taking place in San Francisco. As Matthew and his small group of potential pod victims—Elizabeth Driscoll, Nancy Bellicec (Veronica Cartwright), and Jack Bellicec (Jeff Goldblum), are on the run—the word *conspiracy* is raised over and over again. Matthew's warnings to government officials, which include the FBI, contains a clear statement that the pods have infiltrated everywhere. As in *Soylent Green,* no one can be trusted, especially those in positions of social power, who have become leaders in plots to turn human beings into nonthinking, emotionless automatons. Whereas the original *Invasion of the Body Snatchers* left open the possibility that the hero would be successful in alerting the world to the dangers of the pod takeover, the 1978 remake eliminates any such possibility and has the sole survivor, Nancy, betrayed by Matthew, who shrieks the alarm cry of a pod clone.

The exaggerations of science fiction were but a short step away from the unbelievable events occurring in the 1960s and 1970s. These reached their zenith with the Watergate conspiracy and the continuous revelations about the use of American intelligence services for spying on American citizens. While politicians as a group had always been viewed with some distrust, figures like the president and the remaining Kennedy brother seemed to transcend any such incriminations. They seemed to, that is, until a series of events revealed a president who was power-mad and a Kennedy who tried to cover up the death of a young woman, with whom he might have been sexually involved. The impact of such events are still very much with us, as seen in Brian de Palma's film *Blow Out* (1981).

Playing on some of the same premises raised by Antonioni in *Blow-Up* (1968), De Palma fuses the Kennedy event at Chappaquiddick with Nixonesque skulduggery. An operative who has been hired to reveal the philanderings of a presidential nominee, and therefore to ruin his chances for election, takes his job somewhat too seriously. The construction of an embarrassing situation for the nominee turns into murder. The problem is that there is a witness, a young sound-production engineer, who has been taping night noises at the bridge from which the nominee's car plunges. Our hero dives into the water but can only save the girl, who has accompanied the candidate for a sexual tryst. As it will turn out, she, like the overzealous operative, is part of a plot instigated by powerful political forces. The hero's audiotapes help him to find out that the apparent accident is no accident at all, but murder. Convincing others, however, presents a problem, for no one believes his tales of conspiracy. At one point the girl, who does not understand the conspiracy plot (of which she is a part), says that he must be paranoid and probably even believes that problems with his phone are the result of the same conspiratorial forces that have arranged the "accident." As she says this, the camera moves to his basement, where the operative is monitoring and redirecting his calls. The end result of the hero's failed efforts, similar to the central figure in *Blow-Up,* is his complete withdrawal from reality.

The difference between the two films is that *Blow Out* incorporated the political events and subsequent distrust that had come to make paranoia a reasonable reaction in a world of Machiavellian plots and counterplots. Forces that arrange wars *(Three Days of the Condor),* kill political candidates *(Parallax View),* undermine all privacy *(The Conversation),* deny the threat of nuclear catastrophe *(The China Syndrome),* and lobotomize us into vegetables *(One Flew over the Cuckoo's Nest),* were very much the subject of recent cinematic depictions, in which paranoia was no longer presented as pathological but a realistic perspective in a frightening world. The figures who exert the power were not given as much cinematic attention as those who are caught between them and a disbelieving public. An exception to this was Werner Herzog's *Aguirre* (1972), which clothed the seeker of political power in the garb of a sixteenth-century conquistador. His megalomania eventuates in a paranoid madness, which finds him brutally killing those around him. While Herzog showed us that the megalomaniacal leaders of the plots are themselves paranoid, the films of the last two decades did not focus on them as much as they did on their victims.

The cinematic attention to the individual thought falsely to be paranoid has its correlate in clinical literature. While it would support our thesis to claim that the idea that paranoia has a basis in reality is totally new, having its origins in the sociopolitical events of the last twenty years, this is not the case. Such an idea in clinical literature seems to have its origin in the writings of Freud.[16] Freud's editor, J. Strachey, pointed out that "the notion of there being a core of truth in paranoiac delusion has a long course of development in Freud's writings."[17] It is clear, however, that Freud was more interested in the individual's distortion than in reality.

It took until the 1960s for the reality core of paranoia to become a major focus in clinical literature. One of the seminal advocates of this position was Edwin Lemert, who maintained, "We make an explicit break with the conception of paranoia as a disease, a state, a condition, or a syndrome of symptoms."[18] Lemert's view of the paranoid emphasized that "others react differentially to him, and their reactions commonly if not typically involve covertly organized action and conspiratorial behavior in a very real sense."[19] Attention was now given to factors in the environment that would create a feeling of paranoia. Freud's case of the psychotic Dr. Schreber came to be reevaluated from a behavioristic perspective in terms of the brutal punishments that the subject received from his father.[20] Similarly, the whole movement of *family therapy* began to question the role of traumatic fantasy and placed emphasis on the actual behavior of the parents. The new *conspiratorial model of behavior* pointed to the ways in which people are driven into madness, not only by the family but by social forces as well.[21] Sociological thought came to have a great deal of impact in psychiatry's view of paranoia, as seen in the following:

We have far too long passively accepted paranoia as a purely psychic phenomenon, thereby restricting our thinking and our view of the individual. But, since a person cannot be seen apart from the society in which he lives, sociologic theory deserves as much a place in psychotherapy as is afforded psychologic theory.[22]

The works of sociological theorists like Erving Goffman and Thomas Scheff brought about revisions in traditional psychiatric thought, which up to this point emphasized the belief that the madness of paranoia is a creation of an individual and has little to do with the actual world in which he lives.[23] Their radical views found application in studies on the process of scapegoating and resulted in a greater willingness to view the paranoid individual as victim.[24] The ascendance of these theories in the last twenty years has certainly been encouraged by social and political events. A sign on the wall of the fourth floor nursing station at Massachusetts Mental Health Center conveys the theme with the words, "Even though you're not paranoid, it doesn't mean they're not after you." The staff people remember that it was put up a long time ago, sometime in the late 1960s, and the impact of the events that exacerbated such thinking is still very much with us. The sign seems in fact to be a variation on a line from Saul Bellow's *Mr. Sammler's Planet,* in which a character says, "I remember a famous anecdote about a demented man: someone said, 'You are paranoiac, my dear fellow,' and he answered, 'Perhaps, but that doesn't prevent people from plotting against me.' "[25] By the 1970s these feelings had become part of both popular culture and clinical literature and, if anything, had become more pervasive as a cinematic theme. The popularity of a film like *The Stunt Man* (1980) was certainly evidence of this. As Pauline Kael said, the film was about "the paranoia of snap judgements."[26] From the first words of Eli Cross (Peter O'Toole) "That's your point of view," the film flirted with a vision of paranoia which, by its popularity with American audiences, reflected the state of anxiety that seemed to have become accepted as part of daily living.

It seems, then, that the question of the paranoid's relation to the accepted world view remains open. In some cases it is the paranoid himself who distorts the image of the world around him. In others the chaos of the situation demands a protective paranoid shield as a means of survival.

Notes

1. J. C. Coleman, R. C. Carson, and J. N. Butcher, *Abnormal Psychology and Modern American Life* (New York: Scott Foresman, 1980), p. 429.

2. W. W. Meissner, *The Paranoid Process* (New York: Jason Aronson, 1978).

3. S. Freud, "Psychoanalytic Notes Upon an Autobiographical Account of a Case of Paranoia (dementia paranoides), in vol. 3 of *Collected Papers of Sigmund Freud,* ed. A. Strachey and J. Strachey (London: Hogarth Press, 1961).

4. A. A. Brill, "Sexual Manifestations in Neurotic and Psychotic Symptoms," *Psychiatric Quarterly* 14 (1941): 13.

5. F. Alexander and W. C. Menninger, "The Relation of Persecutory Delusions to the Functioning of the Gastrointestinal Tract," *Journal of Nervous and Mental Diseases* vol. 84 (1936). L. Bender, "The

Anal Component of Persecutory Delusions," *Psychiatric Review,* vol. 11 (1934), J. A. Arlow, "Anal Sensations and Feelings of Persecution," *Psychoanalytic Quarterly,* vol. 18 (1949), 79–84. O. Fenichel, *The Psychoanalytic Theory of Neurosis* (New York: Norton Publishing Co., 1945), pp. 421–31.

6. P. Tyler, *Screening the Sexes: Homosexuality in the Movies* (New York: Holt, Rinehart and Winston, 1977).

7. P. Schrader, "Notes on Film Noir," *Film Comment* 8 (Spring 1972).

8. D. W. Swanson, P. J. Bohnert, and J. A. Smith, *The Paranoid* (Boston: Little, Brown and Company, 1970).

9. W. E. Thornton and B. J. Pray, "The Portrait of a Murderer," *Diseases of the Nervous System,* vol. 36, no. 4 (April 1975), 178.

10. H. Klein and W. Horowitz, "Psychosexual factors in the paranoid phenomena," *American Journal of Psychiatry* 105 (1949): 697–701.

11. H. Barry, M. Bacon, and I. Child, "A Cross Cultural Survey of Some Sex Differences in Socialization," *Journal of Abnormal and Social Psychiatry* 55 (1957): 327–32.

12. L. Ovesey, "Pseudohomosexuality: The Paranoid Mechanism and Paranoia," *Psychiatry* 18 (1955): 163–73.

13. C. McCauley and S. Jacques, "The Popularity of Conspiracy Theories of Presidential Assassination: A Bayesian Analysis," Journal of Personality and Social Psychology, vol. 37, no. 5 (1979), 637–44.

14. W. H. Grier and P. M. Cobbs, *Black Rage* (New York: Basic Books, 1968), p. 149.

15. S. Higashi, *"Invasion of the Body Snatchers,* Pods Then and Now," *Jump Cut,* no. 24/25 (1978), 3.

16. S. Freud, "Determinism, Belief in Chance and Superstition: Some Points of View," from *Psychopathology of Everyday Life* in vol. 11 of *Complete Works of Sigmund Freud,* ed. J. Strachey (London: Hogarth Press, 1961), 236.

17. Ibid.

18. E. Lemert, "Paranoia and the Dynamics of Exclusion," *Sociometery,* vol. 25, no. 1 (1962), 3.

19. Ibid.

20. M. Schatzman, "Paranoia of Persecution: The Case of Schreber," *Family Process,* vol. 10, no. 2 (June 1971), 177–207.

21. M. Seigler and H. Osmond, *Models of Madness, Models of Medicine* (New York: Harper & Row, 1974).

22. L. Aaronson, "Paranoia as a Behavior of Alienation," *Perspectives in Psychiatric Care,* vol. 15, no. 1 (1977), 30.

23. E. Goffman, *Asylums* (New York: Anchor, 1961). T. Scheff, *Being Mentally Ill* (Chicago: Aldine Publishing Co., 1966).

24. G. Bateson, "Minimal Requirements of a Theory of Schizophrenia in California," in *Psychotherapy of Chronic Schizophrenic Patients* (Boston: Little, Brown and Company, 1960). T. Lidz, S. Fleck, and A. Cornelison, *Schizophrenia and the Family* (New York: International University Press, 1965).

25. S. Bellow, *Mr. Sammler's Planet* (New York: Viking Press, 1970), p. 226.

26. P. Kael, "The Current Cinema: As Swift as a Buzzard Flies," *New Yorker* (29 September 1980), 134–40.

8

Sanity As Madness, Madness As Sanity

The theme Sanity as Madness, Madness as Sanity, while of enduring interest, seems to have its most popular depictions in times of social crisis. At these points the world order seems to become, as it were, unglued, as all the traditional and established institutions go through radical change. This is a failing of our everyday expectations, and that which we have come to take for granted is suddenly unavailable. Things become out of place, and a sense of disorientation prevails. What was thought to be immutable is suddenly called into question, and the "natural" order is suddenly found to be more a human construction than an eternal truth.

In such a state it is not uncommon to find artistic representations of a world cut asunder. Artistic imagery is one of the most readily available vehicles for expressing human feelings during such times. One such period of reversals was the Great Depression, which brought about a sudden failing and plummeting of the American dream into a nightmare of social and political discontent. Another was the tumultous period of the 1960s, when war, assassination, and mass dissent became commonplace. The two major films discussed in this chapter, *You Can't Take It with You* (1938) and *King of Hearts* (1966), reflect the crises of each period. In the 1930s America, the land of plenty, suddenly found herself unable to provide for each citizen not only the resources and goods necessary to enjoy the accustomed luxuries but even those necessary to maintain a subsistence level. More and more people were losing their jobs, and as the possibility of work became nil, vast exoduses began from sections of the country like the Dust Bowl, where the land, like the American dream, had shriveled into barrenness (*The Grapes of Wrath*, 1940). Americans experienced a profound economic and social upheaval, which reactivated a vast ideological schism, previously submerged under a sea of optimism. This conflict centered mostly around the issue of class conflicts. The rich and powerful pitted against the little man became a dominant theme. Democratic values seemed to suddenly disappear as the hired muscle of big business broke heads in picket lines and farmers lost their land to banks. People who were independent were suddenly unable to find a means of living, and even the wealthy suffered such reversals that their only way out was the suicidal jump.

In such a world the concept of madness as sanity and sanity as madness seemed to apply to everyday living and easily found its way into the cinematic

159

imagery of the period, in the so-called screwball comedy. This was not the destructive, slapstick comedy of the Marx Brothers or of W. C. Fields, but a comedy of reversals, in which opposites were eventually unified. Of all the figures associated with this period genre of comedy, Frank Capra stood out as one of the most important. His films, which included *It Happened One Night, Mr. Deeds Goes to Town, Mr. Smith Goes to Washington, My Man Godfrey, Easy Living, Nothing Sacred, The Awful Truth,* and *You Can't Take It with You,* all presented whacky characters who experienced profound reversals, which, as Capra said, always resolved themselves into a comedy of unity and left the audience with "a glow of satisfaction."[1]

Capra's screwball comedies were made during and after the Great Depression. From 1929 to 1939 distinct themes, unique to the period, appeared and enjoyed great popularity. Andrew Bergman emphasized the relationship between films and this time period in this way:

> Why did people flock to gangster films in the early thirties and stop going to Westerns at the same time? What made *It Happened One Night,* released with little publicity by a second-rank studio, the most enormous success of 1934? And why was *Mr. Deeds Goes to Town* so beloved in 1936? Why was *Duck Soup,* now regarded as the ultimate Marx Brothers comedy, the least successful one they made from 1929 to 1937? How does one explain the huge success of the lush musicals in 1933—and their decline in the mid-thirties—or the resurgence of Westerns, along with the "G-Man" pictures, in 1935 and 1936?

The consistent scenario of the screwball comedy involved the sudden reversal of things and then a reconciliation of the seemingly irreconcilable. Opposite factions were shown to be, beyond their superficial appearance, similar, and a unification of differences occurred so that the conflicts were forgotten. Since one of the biggest differences in the depression was, of course, a financial one involving the haves and the have-nots, the screwball comedy brought these two factions together. This coming together took place through a comedy of errors involving mistaken identities; people were not who they appeared to be.

Mr. Deeds Goes to Town (1936) mirrored many of the same issues to which Capra was to turn in *You Can't Take It with You.* Longfellow Deeds (Gary Cooper) is seemingly a half-wit country bumpkin who suddenly receives an inheritance of $20 million. Upon being told of the inheritance, he says, "Twenty million! That's a lot, isn't it?" and then turns to play his tuba. Through a series of circumstances he is brought to New York, where he encounters a number of moneyed urban hustlers. Bankers, intellectuals, and heartless businessmen try to direct his money toward their selfish concerns, but Deeds, in an act that Capra labeled "Saturday evening post socialism,"[3] gives his money away to the poor, insisting that buying them small farms will do more to improve their lives than all the libraries and rarified intellectual charities, which only serve to flatter the pretentiousness of the city slickers who hound him. These forces react to Deeds's defiant act by trying to have him committed to an insane asylum.

The forces of good, which at first consist of the poor farmers and the prototypical honest newspapermen, are eventually joined by the urban hipsters. All unite to defeat the forces of evil, which come to be personified, interestingly enough, in the character of the prosecution's expert witness, a psychiatrist with a Germanic name, whom Deeds shows to be more insane than sane. All of this leads the judge to decide in Deeds's favor, proclaiming that he is "the sanest man in the courtroom."

You Can't Take It with You. Some of these same elements appeared in *You Can't Take It with You* (1938). Grandpa Vanderhoff and the rest of the social misfits that make up his communal home refuse to sell out to the munitions king, Kirby (Edward Arnold). Capra changed the characterization of Grandpa Vanderhoff from the one that Moss Hart and George S. Kaufmann had successfully brought to the stage version. Capra "changed Grandpa Vanderhoff from a whimsical old madcap to a serious denouncer of those who prefer gold to friends; and the minor, inoffensive Mr. Kirby, who had been a rich boy's father, to a sinister munitions man who causes at least one suicide."[4]

The forces of opposition became more insidious but true to form. Even the aloof Kirby is brought to accept the childlike sanctity of the Vanderhoff clan, as we find him playing a harmonica in the final scene of the film. The misanthropic clan led by Vanderhoff, who has not worked in years, has a varied assortment of "lovable cucks," who play out the kind of mad characterizations so popular in screwball comedies. Along with Grandpa Vanderhoff is his daughter (Spring Byington), who spends all her time typing plays that no one will ever read. The random nature of her activity is punctuated by the revelation that her writing emanates from her desire to make use of a typewriter mistakenly delivered to the house years before. One of her daughters, who has absolutely no talent, devotes all her time to becoming a great ballerina under the direction of a fake Russian impressario. Her husband, in the meantime, makes fireworks in the basement and appears upstairs only occasionally to play his xylophone. There are various others who inhabit this mad world, including an inventor of children's toys. The one to interact in a conventional manner with the outside world is Alice (Jean Arthur), the second Vanderhoff granddaughter, who gets a job and winds up in the Kirby conglomerate. There, she meets the younger Kirby (Jimmy Stewart) and between their immediate love for each other and the fact that she is soon revealed as part of the family that owns and refuses to sell the last parcel of land that will make Kirby's munition complex compete, the stage is set for the conflicts that will ensue.

The clash of poor and rich, a conflict so important to the thirties, complemented the screwball theme, which made itself clear by Grandpa Vanderhoff's indifference to the lure of wealth and his preference for the pleasure of his family and for his independence. He does not subscribe to the values of the social order and obviously promotes in those around him the same kind of beliefs. Foolishness, laughter, and the absurd win out over the rational, as reason is shown to be a hollow pursuit, second only in futility to mercantilism. Grandpa Vanderhoff points out the emptiness of such pursuits and, parallel to the theme Christ the Fool, asks Kirby to join him and the others in pursuing creative, childlike expressions, rather than the destructiveness of munitions.

Throughout the film, childlike fantasies and joyful delusions were shown to be of far greater merit than the ordinary thinking of so-called sensible, rational adults, who, caught in the world of commerce, forget the importance of the individual. While Kirby has given up such fantasy, his son (Jimmy Stewart) maintains it as he talks of harnessing the power of the sun, stored in every blade of grass. Capra seemed to say that fantasy must be nourished and is at times much more preferable to "realistic" pursuits.

While the reversals of the Great Depression influenced Capra's artistic play on the theme Madness as Sanity and Sanity as Madness, psychiatry evidenced cautious and more subtle expressions of such themes. Though we have considered psychology as a subset of psychiatry, it is important to point out the distinctions between them, which in the 1930s were quite clear. Psychology was at this point still very much tied to its experimental origins and the early work of Ebbinghaus, Fechner, Wundt, and others. The measurements of sensation, perception, and learning were emphasized, and the other fields of psychology were just beginning to be consolidated. The field in which we are, of course, most interested is clinical psychology, since it is the branch of psychology which deals with the definition and treatment of madness. While clinical psychologists had doubled in number since the previous decade, their primary interest was still in testing and measurement issues, related primarily to children. As Garfield pointed out, "In the late 1930s clinical psychology was a rather small and undistinguished speciality, and psychotherapy was not a major activity of clinical psychologists.[5] Beginning in 1938, however, clinical psychology's emphasis on testing was criticized, and a call was made for a change in view.[6] By 1939 clinical literature emphasized that the work of the clinical psychologist "must reflect biological, anthropological, historical, and cultural orientations, as well as a keen outlook on the world of men and affairs of today and the trend of human destiny."[7]

The choice of the term *human destiny* is more than just chance, for the specter of fascism was steadily gaining force, and Hitler's vision of a new world order was becoming a reality as his troops began to march. Humanist ideals and commitment to open intellectual inquiry, which characterized the Weimar Republic, were exchanged for a racist-based psychology, which had little time for understanding individual differences, let alone madness. In their desire to inform the world of "Aryan supremacy," Hitler and his ministers would not tolerate such an interest. Freud and his immediate followers had, by the end of 1938, left German territory, and many of those who remained were soon exterminated. Psychology was slow to deal with Nazi suppression, as evident in one psychologist's criticism that "the renunciation of unfounded theories of racial and national differences should have been the central theme of the 1937 meeting of the International Congress of Psychology."[8]

Though by no means was clinical psychology moving completely away from its roots in traditional experimental psychology, there were indications that new visions were being explored. Clinical psychology was clearly looking for an identity and, though pushed to choose between a measurement-testing perspective and a psychoanalytic one, found itself taking a more expansive, free-wheeling, interdisciplinary approach. This was a fairly radical change, and any attempt to understand its origins would have to take into account the writings of Henry Murray, who in 1938 published his brilliant but controversial work, *Explorations in Personality: A Clinical Experimental Study of 50 Men of College Age.*[9]

Murray received his medical degree from Columbia and, while having an interest in psychiatry, did not follow the conventional choice between an organic or psychoanalytic orientation. Like many of his American contemporaries, he soon found himself in Europe, where the study of the mind-body relationship was receiving more in-depth attention. Obtaining a Ph.D. in 1929 as a result of his work at the biochemical laboratories of Cambridge University, he soon took a 180-degree turn from traditional experimental methodology by studying at Jung's Institute of Analytical Psychology in Zurich. By this time Jung had begun to break with Freud, a thinker whom Murray admired. Murray came to believe that only a consolidation of the apparently divergent theories of the period could result in the advancement of psychiatry. The organic and psychological, he maintained, were not in opposition; they only needed to be integrated. He advocated adopting an expansionist perspective, which included disciplines outside the purview of psychiatry. His beliefs came to take material form through his work at Harvard University's Psychological Clinic.

Believing that psychiatry needed to study more than just abnormal behavior, Murray called for an investigation of the entire range of human behavior and emotion in what he called the *study of the person*. Interested in the determinants of personality, he began a cooperative research program to study individual lives through a totally unique perspective, the results of which came to public attention in his work in 1938. The originality of his research was evident in his opening pages, where he named the following kinds of individuals as contributors: "poets, physicists, sociologists, anthropologists, criminologists, physicians; democrats, fascists, communists, anarchists; Jews, Protestants, Agnostics, Atheists, Lewinians, and Allportians."[10] In those days such a view for a psychiatrist was considered extremely radical, but it was complementary to clinical psychology, which was also beginning to move toward an interdisciplinary position.[11] Murray was trying implicitly to move away from the traditional divisions within the social sciences and even suggested that the humanities had a distinct place in the study of *psychology* (a term Murray preferred over *psychiatry*). "A psychologist who believes that he can tell the truth without being 'literary,' he wrote, "has only to try writing a case history or biography, and then compare what he has done to a character sketch by any novelist of the first order."[12]

While it may have been mere coincidence that Murray's work was published in the same year that *You Can't Take It with You* appeared, it is nonetheless fascinating to consider the similarity of the motifs underlying each work. Capra's screwball madness was a vehicle for pulling opposites together, a way of extolling the benefits of democracy, in which differences complement and strengthen—people of divergent views and classes can, if brought together, find a common language and move closer toward the truth. Throughout his work he used humor as a way of undoing the rigidity and stuffiness of traditionalism. The old order is pointed to as reified and inflexible, taking itself too seriously in its pursuit of new acquisitions.

This same spirit is evident in Murray's work, in which, for instance, clinical subjects were playfully called by such pseudonyms as Mauve, Oriol, Bulge, and Zora. Murray emphasized the benefits of a democratic union in which apparently disparate and supposedly inconsequential views could be expressed in helping to move psychology toward a complete understanding of the determinants of personality. Murray seemed to reflect Capra's sentiments when he said:

> A man who has been trained in the exact sciences will find himself somewhat at a loss, if not at a disadvantage. He will find it difficult to fall in with the loose flow of psychologic thought. . . . And so, if he continues to hold rigidly to the scientific ideal, to cling to the hope that the results of his researches will approach in accuracy and elegance the formulations of the exact disciplines, he is doomed to failure. He will end his days in the congregation of futile men, of whom the greater number, contractedly withdrawn from critical issues, measures trifles with sanctimonious precision. . . . For the present the destiny of personology is best served by giving scope to speculation, perhaps not so much as psychoanalysts allow themselves, but plenty. Hence, in the present volume we have checked self-criticism, ignored various details, winked a little at statistics, and from first to last have never hesitated to offer interpretative hypotheses.[13]

While there might not have been a direct connection between *You Can't Take It with You* and period psychiatric literature, the general spirit of the time did seem to link the two. This was a spirit that delighted in playful reversals and paradoxes and asserted optimistically the unity of opposites. This optimism was, of course, not to last, and the depiction of the theme Sanity as Madness and Madness as Sanity was to undergo significant changes over the next thirty years, as evidenced in *King of Hearts* (1966).

King of Hearts.　　　　*King of Hearts,* though it did not enjoy mass attention, eventually established itself as an enduring classic among a limited number of what might be called *cult films.* Appealing primarily to college-aged adults, the film enjoyed sell-out status throughout the late sixties and early seventies and then continued to get star billing on campus film series lists. While it appealed to such audiences on many levels, its major attraction was derived from a political perspective that had become tied to the labeling and treatment of madness in the 1960s. The film's treatment of madness found its most avid audience following in youth, who have always questioned not only who they are but the very order of the social world around them. The film characteristically conveyed a sense that the adult world was corrupt and that the old order had to give way to a new, youthful vision of reality. While this conflict has been acted out microcosmically in every family's struggle with teenage rebellion against parental authority, there was a more global enactment in the political activism of youth.

One of the pressing questions with which youth has dealt is whether they are willing to fight the wars that their elders have created. While some have seen such wars as a heroic mission in which one may achieve glory not only for oneself but for one's country, there have always been others who see war simply as human destruction. In the most vocal dissenters from war, who have been primarily youth, there has been a tendency to characterize the makers of war as ineffectual human beings who deny their fears and sense of impotency by embracing rage against others. They are masters of deceit, who make it appear that their aims represent the moral concerns of others and that their call to war is a holy one. It was this imagery that made up the central structure of *King of Hearts,* a film set in the closing year of World War I.

A young soldier from the ranks (Alan Bates) is pushed into accepting a perilous mission to defuse a bomb that will blow up the town from which the Germans are retreating and which the Scottish troops are about to invade. The commanders of both the opposing German and Scottish troops are caricatures of the self-serving, conceited militarist, who longs for glory at any cost, and the journey of Pvt. Charles Plumpick (called "Pumpernickel" by his commander) from one mad world into another allows him to realize the folly of this kind of person. What Plumpick finds in the town is a group of citizens who treat the world not only with a delightful indifference but with beliefs that have no basis in reality. Their world is one of play, and pleasure and love are the only criteria for establishing what is real. What Plumpick does not know is that the ordinary townspeople have fled after being told that a bomb was to explode and that his new friends are really inmates of the local insane asylum, whose rooms were accidentally left unlocked and who, oblivious to the threat, have assumed the roles of the townspeople.

Plumpick's introduction to this world comes after he knocks himself unconscious from ensnaring himself in a fallen telephone wire. When he awakens, he finds the world stood on its head as people cavort and play and anomalies go unnoticed. The mad have taken over every position of social authority, and Plumpick's encounters with these carefree, blithe spirits leave him frustrated and confused. While Plumpick tries in vain to make them understand the peril they face, their major focus seems to be on persuading him, whom they crown the King of Hearts, to marry one of their number, a dainty acrobat called Coquelicot. Though resistant at first, Private Plumpick gives up his search for the bomb when he falls in love with his preselected bride, whose etherial nature is evidenced by her habit of walking on telephone wires. Just a moment before the bomb is to go off, Plumpick suddenly breaks the previously undecipherable code words that his commander received from an informant just before the latter's death. Racing to the church tower, he puts himself between the mechanized black knight and the clock bell that the knight strikes at midnight, thereby stopping the bomb from being detonated. The mad inhabitants of the town respond to his joy, rather than to the fact that he has just averted a catastrophe.

Soon afterwards comes the arrival of Plumpick's commander, whose own antics do not allow him to recognize the madness of the townsfolk around him. The main difference between his behavior and that of the mad lies, of course, in his aggression, and when he awakens from the celebration, he and his German counterpart and their respective troops, confront and destroy each other. When the French forces arrive, together with the original townsfolk, the old order of things is restored. Plumpick is quickly ordered back to the front for another perilous mission, and the inmates, having had enough of the sanity of the out-

King of Hearts (France and Italy, 1966). Director, Phillippe De Broca. With Alan Bates *(second from left)*. By permission of MGM–United Artists.

side world, gladly retreat back into their cells. As the soldier passes the asylum, however, he leaps from the truck and, appearing nude before the nuns in charge of the gate, seeks admission into the sane world of the insane. This last scene, involving the casting off of all worldly remnants, recalls the mythic and ritualistic themes of the comedy that we discussed earlier. The new king, the King of Hearts, or emotion, has finally arrived, and he has brought nothing of the old order but himself, reborn. In this childlike state he represents a rejuvenation of a dying kingdom, a new beginning, which allows the sacred marriage to be completed. The dark forces have been defeated (graphically depicted in his battle with the black knight), and a new reality can now prevail.

While the imagery in *King of Hearts* seems tied to early literary and historical interpretations of the comedy, it became associated with a psychological interpretation of madness popular in the late 1960s. The sixties were a period of acute upheaval, in which America and Western Europe was wracked by one social crisis after another. The crisis came from the failure of the Great Society and the sudden explosion of rage from the disenfranchised, who adopted revolution as a means for change. While the revolution came to be heralded by many different factions, it was the young who made the most energetic call for change, and, as we will show, *King of Hearts* was perfectly orchestrated to complement these beliefs. The sixties were very much a time of youth; they not only had become a potent political force but an untapped market for commercialism as well.

The revolt of the young was focused primarily on technological dehumanization, evidenced in all aspects of society but most poignantly in the horror of the Vietnam War. Centered around university campuses throughout the Western world, the youth movement established itself through intense calls for change. A note attached to the door of the Sorbonne in May 1968, was typical: "The revolution which is just beginning will call in question not only capitalist society but industrial society. The consumer society must perish of a violent death. The society of alienation must disappear from history. We are inventing a new and original world. Imagination is seizing power."[14] The college-aged population, which had doubled since the 1950s, intensely feared the very same technology that their parents, in contrast, revered as the answer to most of life's problems.[15] Though, as a rule, financially well-off, the young felt a sense of alienation and extreme insecurity about their place in a world dominated by the threat of atomic holocaust.

The young found their fears mirrored in many literary works of the period, some of the most popular of which were those of Freudian Marxist Herbert Marcuse, the gestalt-therapy anarchist Paul Goodman, the apocalyptic mystic Norman O. Brown, the Zen master Alan Watts, the psychedelic tripper Timothy Leary, and the interpreter of madness R. D. Laing.[16] Each of these authors, while offering different interpretations of the reality that the counterculture was experiencing, came to be adopted as a guru of a new vision of how things should be. The greatest obstacle to realizing this new vision was seen as the establishment's commitment to progressive technology over the needs of human beings. This was most evident in the conscription of the young to fight in a jungle war manufactured by the experts of technology. The fight against this technology of power, while focusing on the Vietnam War, took on many areas in which technology was seen as becoming tantamount to human feeling. Criticism of such social bastions as the stock market, education, and medicine often seemed to advocate chaos. As pointed out by Lewis Mumford, "Since ritual order has now largely passed into mechanical order, the present revolt of the younger generation against the machine has made a practice of promoting disorder and randomness."[17]

Mumford's observation was reflected in psychiatry in the works of the anti-psychiatry movement. Representing an amalgam of different disciplines and a range of formulations for how much of the traditional had to be eliminated, this movement gained some attention from professionals and laymen alike in the early 1960s and by the late 1960s enjoyed wide popularity. Of all those in the psychiatric profession who called for a radical revision of the view of madness, R. D. Laing was the most visible. Going against accepted definitions, Laing said that the goal of true sanity was "in one way or another, the dissolution of the normal ego, that false self competently adjusted to our alienated social reality: the emergence of the 'inner' archetypal mediators of divine power, and through this death a rebirth and the eventual re-establishment of a new kind of ego functioning, the ego now being the servant of the divine, no longer its betrayer."[18]

Laing argued first for giving up objective consciousness and turning to individual experience as the ultimate reality. As pointed out earlier, he held that madness is really a label given to those who experience a reality different from the norm. The mad merely see a different reality, and, as Laing was to point out in so many of his works, they are often more sane than those who proclaim themselves sane. Espousing ideas similar to such thinkers as Bertrand Russell (who said, "I would rather be mad with the truth than sane with lies,") Laing argued for the honesty of madness in a world that had lost reason. Laing emphasized the importance of individual experience and questioned the means adopted not only by psychiatry, but by the social sciences for understanding the individual.[19] He pointed out that such professions gave too much attention to theories and not enough to the experiences that formed the source of their theories. Laing's use of the term *inner archetypal mediators* pointed to what he meant by these individual experiences. He emphasized a Jungian and, more important, a humanistic perspective, which credits sources other than the sciences with an understanding of the human experience of madness. In so doing, he commented on the limits of objective truth and the importance of other levels of consciousness.

It was just this issue that the former Harvard psychology professor Timothy Leary popularized with his touring light-and-sound shows, which emphasized the benefits of psychedelic tripping. Extolling the advantages of "dropping out, turning on, and tuning in," Leary, along with another psychologist, Richard Alpert (soon to be known as Baba Ram Dass) started to do a great deal of research on the similarities between an LSD trip and madness.[20] Laing, Leary, and others achieved nominal cohesion through the term *antipsychiatry* and seemed to conclude that madness was not a bad thing but was in fact a special journey, a journey of potential enlightenment into the true nature of things, in contrast to the mass attachment to material technology, which many antipsychiatry proponents attributed to the propaganda of the military-industrial complex.

Throughout the psychiatric and social science literature there were works that reflected such new and radical thoughts. One example was the anthropological study *The Teachings of Don Juan: A Yaqui Way of Knowledge.* Another was the work of the West Coast psychiatrist John Weir Perry.[21] In his exploration into the mental imagery of the mad, Perry came to believe that there was a pattern that, when closely investigated, was recognizable as a cosmic view evident in ancient myths and rituals.[22] Perry described the psychotic's world in the following manner:

> For it is a world in which there is a center, a cosmic axis running through and connecting the human world with the Sky World and the Underworld. In this center powerful events take place. There, the psychotic individual has died and has found himself in an afterlife state. There, occurs a clash of opposite

powers, of light and dark halves of the world, either threatening disintegration or maintaining integration of the whole of the cosmic order. There, he is thrown back in time to the Creation and the first beginnings, and he repeats the evolution of the world step-by-step. There, he is raised up into a position of supremacy, of world rulership or spiritual leadership. There, a new birth or rebirth takes place in association with an extraordinary marriage to some divine personage. And, finally, around this center come resolutions of cosmic proportions in the form of a redeemed society and a *quadrated* world structure in harmonious equipoise of four continents, powers, races, creeds, or elements.[23]

While in his writings Perry had intimated such ideas as early as the 1950s,[24] it was not until the late 1960s and early 1970s, a period during which *King of Hearts* was enjoying highly successful runs in countercultural centers throughout America and Europe, that Perry's work began to enjoy popular as well as professional acclaim. Such an acceptance was evident in his being awarded a grant by the National Institute of Mental Health to develop the application of his ideas to the treatment of the mad.

The fact that Perry first presented the work just quoted at the Esalen Institute in Big Sur, California, is also most telling. Esalen became in America the center for anti-psychiatry's exploration of what came to be called the *human potential movement*. Esalen was where the ideas of Timothy Leary, Fritz Perls, Ida Rolf, Perry, and so many other leaders of the body-awareness, consciousness-raising, and group-sensitivity movement, met to preach and practice their beliefs on the affluent adults who were following their children's credos and dropping out. Esalen was not a treatment center for the mad but for those who were in fact thought to be too sane and in need of a touch of Dionysian madness to explore their true potential. As this new psychology sold itself, encounter groups sprang up throughout America, as graphically depicted in the film *Bob and Carol, Ted and Alice* (1969).

Underlying all of this was the idea that madness can be a positive experience and that sanity is an uptight, bourgeois state of mind. From such early intimations of this theme in such films as *Sundays and Cybelle* (1962) and *It's a Mad, Mad, Mad World* (1963) came its searing politicizations in such films as *Dr. Strangelove* (1964), *Marat-Sade* (1967), *King of Hearts* (1966), *Morgan: A Suitable Case for Treatment* (1966), *The Magic Christian* (1969), *The Ruling Class* (1971), *Harold and Maude* (1971), *Outrageous* (1977), and *Equus* (1978). The production of such films, which markedly increased in the late sixties and early seventies, clearly emerged from a particular social, political, and psychological zeitgeist.

A few further comments on the psychological context of this period seem appropriate, since it was a period of revolution. As we have said, the early sixties involved a movement away from a view that emphasized the individual alone, toward a *systems perspective,* which emphasized the individual's interaction with others. A good example was the work in 1968 by the psychologist Robert Rosenthal, which called attention to the idea that what you expect people (in this case, children) to become, they in fact become.[25] The numerous new studies advocating a systems perspective emphasized not only the family social system but the greater social system, with the implicit assumption that mental illness is a symptom of a sick or, at best, corrupted society.[26] Embedded in these ideas was the notion that madness is in the eyes of the beholder, and this was a very popular theme in the sixties, when the youth movement felt that it was time for Americans to know who was really running the country. It was not long before such unconventional interpretations of madness as a mind-expanding trip or journey to a new, more enlightened reality came to have popular representations in feature films, and *King of Hearts* became one of the most acclaimed films of this genre.

Notes

1. F. Capra, "Sacred Cows to Slaughter," *Stage* (July 1936), 41.
2. A. Bergman, *We're in the Money* (New York: Harper & Row, 1971), p. xv.
3. B. Thomas, *King Cohn: The Life and Times of Harry Cohn* (New York: Putnam, 1967), p. 121.
4. G. Hillman, "Profiles: Thinker in Hollywood," *The New Yorker* (24 February 1940), 29.
5. S. Garfield, "Psychotherapy: A Forty-Year Appraisal," *American Psychologist*, vol. 36, no. 2 (February 1981), 171.
6. N. Ridenour, "Notes on the State of Clinical Psychology," *Journal of Consulting Psychology*, vol. 11, no. 3 (May–June 1938), 142.
7. E. Doll, Jr., "Preparation for Clinical Psychology," *Journal of Consulting Psychology*, vol. 11, no. 5 (September–October 1938), 138.
8. J. B. Maller, "Impressions of the Eleventh International Congress of Psychology," *Journal of Consulting Psychology*, vol. 11, no. 3 (May–June 1938), 70.
9. H. Murray, *Explorations in Personality: A Clinical Experimental Study of Fifty Men of College Age* (New York: Wiley and Sons, 1938).
10. Murray, p. xi.
11. Doll, p. 138.
12. Murray, p. 608.
13. Murray, p. 21.
14. E. Mortimer, "Reports from Paris," *The* (London) *Times* (17 May 1968).
15. T. Roszak, *The Making of a Counterculture* (New York: Doubleday, 1968).
16. H. Marcuse, *Eros and Civilization* (New York: Vintage Books, 1962); *One-Dimensional Man* (Boston: Beacon Press, 1964); "Love Mystified: A Critique of N. O. Brown," *Commentary* (February 1967), 73. P. Goodman, in F. Perls, R. Hifferline, P. Goodman, eds., *Gestalt Therapy* (New York: Delta, 1951), Gestalt Therapy Verbatim. N. O. Brown, *Life Against Death: The Psychoanalytic Meaning of History* (Middletown, Conn.: Wesleyan University Press, 1959). A. Watts, *Psychotherapy East and West* (New York: Pantheon, 1961); *This Is It* (New York: Collier Books, 1967). T. Leary, *High Priest* (New York: World Publishing, 1968). R. D. Laing, *The Politics of Experience* (London: Penguin Books, 1967).
17. L. Mumford, *The Myth of the Machine* (New York: Harcourt, Brace and World, 1967), pp. 62–63.
18. R. D. Laing, *Politics of Experience* (New York: Random House, 1967), p. 119.
19. R. D. Laing, *Sanity, Madness and the Family* (New York: Penguin Books, 1964).
20. B. Ram Dass, *Remember, Now Be Here, Be Here Now* (San Cristobal, N.M.: Lama Foundation, 1971).
21. G. Castenada, *The Teachings of Don Juan: A Yaqui Way of Knowledge* (Berkeley and Los Angeles: University of California Press, 1968).
22. J. W. Perry, *Lord of the Four Quarters* (New York: Braziller, 1966).
23. J. W. Perry, "The Value of Psychotic Experience," in *Panel Poetry of Madness*, presented through the Esalen Institute (San Francisco, 1968).
24. J. W. Perry, *The Self in Psychotic Process* (Berkeley and Los Angeles: University of California Press, 1953).
25. R. Rosenthal and L. Jacobson, *Pygmalion in the Classroom* (New York: Holt, Rinehart and Winston, 1968).
26. J. Haley, *Strategies of Psychotherapy* (New York: Grune and Stratton, 1963); *The Power Tactics of Jesus Christ and Other Essays* (New York: Avon Books, 1971). T. R. Sarbin, "On the Futility of the

Proposition That Some People Be Labelled Mentally Ill," *Journal of Consulting Psychology*, vol. 31 (1967), 447–53. N. H. Krauss, "Schizophrenia: A Self-Fulfilling Labelling Process," *Journal of Psychotherapy, Research, Theory and Practice*, vol. 5 (1968), 20–45. T. J. Scheff, *Being Mentally Ill: A Sociological Theory* (Chicago: Aldine Publishing Co., 1966). T. Szasz, "Voluntary Mental hospitalization: An Unacknowledged Practice of Medical Fraud, *New England Journal of Medicine*, vol. 287, no. 6 (1972), 277–78.

9
Madness and the Psychiatrist

Depictions of the psychiatrist have been prominent since the earliest days of feature films. Because of the large number of major films of this genre (nearly eighty) and because of the extensive literature published about them during the last thirty years, this chapter will differ in format from most of the previous chapters. Instead of focusing on one early and one late film, we will cite every major film of this kind made between 1906 and 1981. While each work clearly differed in its characterization of the psychiatrist, close investigation will reveal the distinct influence of its precursor.

In this chapter the term *psychiatrist* will represent anyone who works in a psychiatric capacity, treating those defined as mad. It will include hypnotists, psychologists, psychiatric nurses, occupational therapists, marriage and family counselors, and social workers. Three clinical works will form the basis of our study. Each, in varying degrees, focused on the interaction between psychiatric and cinematic depictions of madness, our central topic. The first is the 1950 work by M. Wolfenstein and N. Leites, *Movies: A Psychological Study.*[1] While its central thesis was that feature films represent a culture's unconscious psychological underpinnings, the book offered an excellent review of films of the 1940s and 1950s that depicted psychiatrists. The two other articles, Leslie Rabkin's "Celluloid Couch: Psychiatrists in American Films (1977)" and Irving Schneider's "Images of the Mind: Psychiatry in the Commercial Film" (1977), dealt specifically with the portrayal of the psychiatrist from the earliest days of film up to the mid-seventies.[2]

The first American film to depict the psychiatrist was *Dr. Dippy's Sanatorium* (1906). While dominated by the usual chase scenes between attendant and patient, it showed Dr. Dippy, a popular comic-strip character of the period, calming his patients, albeit by the rather unorthodox method of giving them pies to eat. Like all films of this period, *Dr. Dippy's Sanatorium* was short, and the appearance of the star, typical of early portrayals of psychiatrists, was brief. The first European film to depict a psychiatrist was *The Lunatics; or, Dr. Goudron's System* (1914). An asylum is taken over by the inmates, and, after they kill the psychiatrist, his place is taken by one of the madmen, who develops his own gruesome form of therapy. These two themes—that of the ludicrous, ineffectual psychiatrist and that of the malevolent and villainous one—continued to reappear. The latter theme often took the form, as it did in *Lunatics,* of a madman's assuming the

172

identity of a psychiatrist. This was the case in one of Douglas Fairbanks's early films, *When the Clouds Roll By* (1919), in which the doctor, Ulrich Metz, is exposed at the end of the film as an escapee from a New York insane asylum.

The theme that the treaters of the mad are mad themselves was central to the well-known German film made the same year, *The Cabinet of Dr. Caligari.* Dr. Caligari, a somnambulizer, was originally presented as a sinister being who induces others to carry out his primitive, impulsive desires. In the later film version, which is narrated by one of his patients, he became the benevolent head of a psychiatric institution (see chapter 2). Regardless of the apparent distortion by the narrator, the image of the doctor as madman very much dominated the story line and obviously fits the perception of the psychiatrist that was, and still is, popular.

In the 1920s Freud's psychoanalysis began to enjoy world popularity. The Roaring Twenties was a period marked by fascination with romantic permissiveness. (Such an interest prompted Samuel Goldwyn to produce a film about the great love stories of history and to offer Freud, unsuccessfully, a hundred thousand dollars to serve as consultant.) In fact *psychoanalysis* had become a synonym for "psychiatry and sexuality." The American rendering of this association was evident in *The Boomerang* (1925). In this comedy the plot line and characterizations pointed to some of the associations prevalent at the time. A clientless doctor, deciding that what the public really wants is "hokum," becomes a psychoanalyst and opens a sanatorium. As a specialist in affairs of the heart, he treats romantic troubles by encouraging his patients to arouse the jealousy of their partners. As if to parody this absurdity, a clairvoyant uses the doctor's jealousy treatment on him to get him to fall in love and marry her.[3]

While European cinema dealt with the association between sexuality and psychiatry without reducing the psychiatrist to a buffoon or pervert (The German film *Secrets of a Soul* was one example), American film continued to treat the psychiatrist superficially and generally suggested his inadequacy. A film of the late twenties, *Plastered in Paris,* was representative of this. Two World War I veterans, Sammy Nosenblum and Bud Swenson, return to Paris in 1928 to attend an American Legion convention. Sammy suffers from kleptomania, which he attributes to trauma caused by a war wound, and his friend makes him go to a famous psychiatrist for treatment. The treatment, however, does more harm than good.[4]

The early 1930s were reintroduced to Fritz Lang's character, Dr. Mabuse. In *The Testament of Dr. Mabuse* (1932) the theme of the evil psychiatrist was again dominant.[5] In this case a power-mad fiend disguises himself by assuming different roles. The film was banned by Goebbels when the Nazis came to power—and Lang said that he in fact had had Hitler in mind when he made it.

A world caught up in massive economic depression, however, was more attracted to another kind of film. Americans, in particular, sought relief from the misery of their lives, and Hollywood gave them the romance and laughter they desired. The word *zany* became part of America's vocabulary, and the psychiatrist bore the brunt of some of the madcap, fun-filled antics of this period. *The Flame Within* (1935), and *Carefree* (1938) were films that portrayed the psychiatrist as a "ludicrous, obtuse, and vulnerable individual, at best no different from you and I."[6] Their role was often to comment on affairs of the heart. *The Flame Within*, the first film to depict a female psychiatrist, had the doctor helplessly drawn to an alcoholic ex-patient of hers.

The film that offered some form of light social commentary was also popular during this period. A leading director in this field was Frank Capra, who portrayed the problems of the depression in terms of the plight of the little man. *Mr. Deeds Goes to Town* (1936), *You Can't Take It with You* (1938), and *Mr. Smith Goes to Washington* (1939) were all films that portrayed the conquest of the weak over the business and political figures who exploited them. Done in a light, comedic style, these films mirrored the obvious sense of impotency that the average American felt when confronted by his oppressors (see chapter 8). In *Mr. Deeds Goes to Town* (1936) psychiatrists were depicted as being a part of these forces. The chief psychiatrist who attacks Mr. Deed's sanity speaks with a heavy European accent and is dressed in the professional style associated in America with continental formality and stodginess. The psychiatrist's inflated and arrogant sense of scientific right is contrasted with the simple, rustic wisdom that characterized so many of Gary Cooper's roles. Deeds of course, is, modest and diffident about his virtues; In the words of one contemporary reviewer: "He cannot understand why other people do not have the virtue too. To him his wisdom is not wisdom; it is a minimum of horse sense, it is merely the starting point for an inquiry. This is what throws the wisdom of the world into its proper relief, and what makes the film on the whole both so interesting and so plausible."[7] It is this very plausibility that could have left the audience feeling that all psychiatrists, like the one in the film, were self-serving egocentrics who felt that they understood reality while in fact they had never really lived it. The casting of the psychiatrist as European became very popular; and the more villainous he was, the more German his accent and manner became—a characteristic that became more prevalent as anti-German feeling grew.

As the power of Hitler increased and Germany and German-occupied territory became intellectual wastelands, many psychiatrists, Jews and non-Jews alike, fled to such havens as Great Britain and the United States. Most of them were quickly assimilated into the psychiatric community of the host country. Though relatively few were able to establish a private practice, many got positions in the large state psychiatric institutions, where their medical background, often more than their psychiatric experience, made them desired. This, of course, was particularly true of psychoanalytically trained psychiatrists, who had always been somewhat distrusted by their American colleagues.

One film that anticipated the exodus was *Private Worlds* (1935). Based on a novel of the same title by Phyllis Bottome (1934),[8] the film dealt with the professional and personal lives of psychiatrists in a psychiatric institution. A European psychiatrist (Charles Boyer) becomes the superintendant of an American hospital. Initially having only disdain for the abilities of his female coworker (Claudette Colbert), he eventually becomes sold on her, not only as a professional but as a person.[9] A real psychiatrist, Dr. Samuel Marcus, served as a technical advisor for this film. Paralleling the movie and the general movement in American psychiatry, Marcus had studied in Vienna and London, where he had specialized in what was termed by the period "borderline mental cases."

While the intellectuals of Europe were gathering in America's cities it should not be forgotten that the mass of Americans still lived in the countryside. They were naturally more interested in a film like *Laddie* (1935), which, released at the same time as *Private Worlds,* was solely concerned with whether a young man should give up farming.

Most Americans were antagonistic toward the power exercised by the psychiatrist (as in *Mr. Deeds Goes to Town*), but they also were awed by this power. Filmmakers therefore tended to exaggerate it. This was clearly the case in *Blind Alley* (1939), which analyzed the forces that underlie criminal behavior. One psychologist of the period, who wrote a good deal on psychiatric depictions in film, commented: "The worst boggle was an utterly unconvincing professor of abnormal psychology who behaved with that godlike detachment which professors practically never have, apparently for the purpose of assisting the audience in disentangling the gangster's complexes. I should add that the film was an exciting melodrama."[11] While the reviewer may have been critical of the depiction of the psychiatrist, one cannot help wondering what the general audience felt.

As we have already pointed out, one of the principal themes in Hollywood's depiction of madness in the 1940s involved amnesia, including that caused by shell-shock, and in fact Americans showed increasing awareness of the number of neuropsychiatric casualties of war. This theme was central to the 1949 Stanley Kramer film, *Home of the Brave.* A black soldier returns from combat paralyzed from the waist down. The drug sodium pentothal, which by this time had become part of the standard treatment intervention of Hollywood, is used to reveal the psychological guilt that caused the paralysis. The psychiatrist is a tough, straight-shooting army doctor, who knows how to handle the psychiatric casualties of war. The film gave the white-black issue little attention, in fact, as Rabkin pointed out, the film psychiatrist implies that "suffering from discrimination is mainly a matter of being too sensitive."[12]

Other films of the 1940s that featured the psychiatric treatment of amnesia included *The Snake Pit* (1948, see chapter 1) and Hitchcock's *Spellbound* (1945). *Spellbound* carried on the tradition of ambivalence felt toward the psychiatrist by presenting two kinds of psychiatrists, a good one—Dr. Constance Peterson (Ingrid Bergman)—and a bad one—Dr. Murchison (Leo G. Carroll)—who is, of course, European. Each is pitted against the other and in the end confront each other—he, armed with a gun; and she, with a slick and masterful series of psychological interpretations. Naturally, she wins with the same confidence that she showed in curing her amnesiac lover, John Ballentine (Gregory Peck). (Peck also portrayed amnesia as Colonel Savage in *Twelve O'Clock High.*) *Spellbound* also included the obligatory European psychiatrist, the confidant and former teacher of Dr. Peterson. While taking on a rather doddering, octogenarian appearance, he is revealed as being a shrewd, calculating, and highly competent clinician, as he would have had to be as the teacher of such a star pupil as Peterson. All the psychiatrists are presumably psychoanalysts, since the film begins with a caption that, addressed to the audience, extolls the virtues of psychoanalysis. Hitchcock wanted, in his words, "to turn out the first picture on psychoanalysis. . . . I worked with [screenwriter] Ben Hecht, who was in constant touch with prominent psychoanalysts."[13] Fearing was generally critical of the film's depictions, and especially of Dr. Peterson's falling in love with her amnesiac patient.[14]

Whirlpool (1949) presented a variation on the amnesia theme of *Spellbound*. An amnesiac heroine has been falsely accused of murder, and the murderer, a hypnotist, watches her struggle to defend herself from the circumstantial evidence that he constructed to entrap her. It is only through the efforts of her psychiatrist husband that she is able to find the truth. Here again, the ambivalence that has always been felt toward psychiatry was evident; in this case the antagonism was shifted to the long-standing fear of the powers of the hypnotist. Atavistically, hypnotism has always been associated with the dark forces of evil, and these dark forces became a central theme of the films of the mid-1940s, which came to be called *film noir,* a term reflecting the pessimism and cynicism that dominated post-war films. Filled with scenes involving muted lighting and nighttime action, they portrayed characters who moved in almost dreamlike terror against sinister forces only barely distinguishable. This was a period of unease and of psychological, more than economic, depression. Although the war had ended, the paranoia lingered on in the terror of the atomic bomb and the burgeoning menace of a cold war with Russia.

The word *dark* dominates the titles of a number of films of the 1940s that featured psychiatrists. In *Dark Waters* (1944), appropriately set amidst the bayous of a Louisiana plantation, a young woman (Merle Oberon) is on the verge of insanity. Through the intervention of her doctor (Franchot Tone) she eventually rids herself of the threatening shadows that seem to stalk her every movement. In another film, *The Dark Mirror* (1946), a psychologist (Lew Ayres), a specialist in twins, has to determine which of two twins is responsible for a murder.[15] Introducing the Rorschach Ink Blot Test, as well as word association tests, he manages to expose the villain. In *Nightmare Alley* (1947) the malevolent force is a woman psychologist who blackmails a patient. In perfect noir convention expected realities are turned upside down, and the hero unsuccessfully struggles against overwhelming forces.

The theme of the untrustworthiness of the trusted psychiatrist was portrayed in *The Locket* (1947), in which a psychiatrist (Brian Aherne) reveals some deep secrets to the bridegroom of his former wife. Filled with many of the twists and surprises of Hitchcock's *Spellbound,* the film dwelt on the inability of the psychiatrist to differentiate between what is real and what is not. Though other noir films did not go so far as *Nightmare Alley* in upsetting the patient-doctor relationship, they did reemphasize the vulnerability to which we are all exposed. Using the plot line of *Blind Alley* (1939), *Dark Past* (1949) involved a flashback to the sudden nocturnal intrusion of a killer (William Holden) into the home of a psychiatrist (Lee J. Cobb). The doctor's slick interpretations slowly wear down the defenses of the killer, and at the end of the night the latter is a changed man. The vulnerability of the psychiatrist to a night world filled with hidden terrors came to be a repeated theme in films like *Woman in the Window* (1944) and *The Upturned Glass* (1947). Even with such emphasis on human frailties there were still occasional depictions of the psychiatrist as a romantic figure, as in Kurt Weil's musical psychoanalysis in *Lady in the Dark* (1944).

Whatever the characterization, it was clear that the depiction of the psychiatrist was good box-office fare. This is not surprising when one realizes that by 1945 the number of psychiatrists in the regular Army Medical Corps had swelled to nearly seventy times what it was in 1941. The increased number of neuro-psychiatric cases and an enhanced confidence in psychiatry's ability to treat them were what prompted the military to make such a dramatic change. From the military, acceptance of psychiatry eventually diffused into the general population. This gave rise in the fifties to a genre of film labeled the *case study*. Films like *The Snake Pit* (1948), *Home of the Brave* (1949), *Shadow on the Wall* (1950), *The Cobweb* (1955), *Fear Strikes Out* (1957), and *The Three Faces of Eve* (1957) characterized the psychiatrist as an effective, generally humane individual whose job was to help the patient regain memory of a repressed traumatic experience. Such a depiction was also evident in three films of the early 1960s, *The Mark* (1961), *Pressure Point* (1962), and *David and Lisa* (1962). In all these works psychiatrists were presented as somewhat one-dimensional figures, whose life is their work, and they were never shown beyond the confines of their office or hospital.

The general interest in the case study and the psychiatrist peaked with John Huston's cinematic study of the early life and work of Freud (played by Montgomery Clift). Originally released as *Freud* (1962) and poorly received, the work was rereleased under the title *The Secret Passion*. The public's erotic associations with psychoanalysis were played on in ads that proclaimed, 'He dared to search beyond the flesh." Having seen psychoanalytic theory in action during his filming of a World War II documentary on neuropsychiatric casualties, *Let There Be Light* (1945), Huston was highly committed to the film. Freud and his struggles with the fears of his patients and his own tortured dreams, however, did not interest a society that was beginning to deal with social upheaval and revolution. The torment of the 1960s concerned the social order, an order that some feared would totally collapse. This fear was given impetus by a general belief that the killing of the Kennedys and Martin Luther King, Jr. was part of a conspiracy by powerful and tyrannical forces within the established order. The establishment came under fire, and psychiatrists, as holders of power, came to be associated with repressive and conformist forces in such films as *The Detective* (1968) and *Coogan's Bluff* (1968). While sometimes ineffectual, as in *Psycho* (1960), in which the psychiatrist offers a simplistic explanation of the murderer's motives, they began once again to take on the malevolence of a Dr. Caligari. In *Peeping Tom* (1962), for instance, a psychologist father subjects his son to horrible experimental procedures in order to measure fear threshholds, an experiment that leads the son to become a compulsive murderer.

As psychiatry came to be increasingly associated with an Orwellian Big Brother oppression, there was a trend to picture psychiatrists as Wizard of Oz buffoons. They were seen as professionals who influenced the lives of powerful people, as in *What's New, Pussycat* (1965) or *The President's Analyst* (1967), and at the same time as people who were helplessly incompetent, sexually crazed, and generally out of control in private life. A series of pornographic films in the 1960s played on this sexual loss of control, including *Coming Apart, Dr. I'm Coming, Dr. Shrink,* and *Dr. Sex.* Throughout the decade emphasis was given to the notion that psychiatrists could not be trusted and that not only were they unable to help but were often at least as sick as their patients. In *A Fine Madness* (1966) a bohemian and misanthropic poet sums up a popular attitude by telling his psychiatrist, "You promote what is; I envision what can be."

The 1970s introduced a new twist to the depiction of the psychiatrist—the casting of actual therapists to give the role greater verisimilitude. *Blume in Love* (1973), *Taking Off* (1971), *One Flew over the Cuckoo's Nest* (1975), and *An Unmarried Woman* (1978) are examples. In *An Unmarried Woman* the therapist appears to be a grown-up hippie. Hawklike in expression, she sits on the floor in a lotus position, barefoot and weighted down with Indian jewelry. She admits to being divorced and encourages her patient to feel guiltless. Beyond their status as actual therapists, these psychiatrists all seemed to share a kindred characterization, which emphasized a nondirective and rather impersonal distancing. While they reflected their clients' concerns, their characterizations were sketchy, and patients often got better solely as a result of their own efforts.

This was certainly the case in *Klute* (1972), in which Jane Fonda portrayed a high-class prostitute who is being tracked down by a sadomasochistic killer, whom she once serviced. He is a captain of industry who, perched in his glass office above the New York skyline, directs world commerce while intermittently listening to a tape recording of one of their sessions of bondage-and-discipline. A variation on the theme of the absolute corruption of power, the film dealt with his directing a private investigation of a murder that he in fact committed. Fonda struggles to make sense out of her internal and external fears by going to her therapist, a dignified gray-haired woman in her late fifties, who listens faintly smiling to her patient's trials. At the point where Fonda is about to confront her would-be killer, she calls her therapist to ask for help and, as if to underscore the limits of involvement that define their relationship, gets a protective, mildly arrogant answering service, which has little to say other than that the doctor is in Connecticut for the weekend.

The idea of the psychiatrist who was not there when needed and who remained uninvolved was part of the general disillusionment that the lay public and members of the psychiatric profession began to evidence in the 1960s, and by the 1970s this was a dominant theme. The antipsychiatry movement complemented a general attack on doctors who sat removed from the real heartaches of the world and let themselves feel little of their patients' pain. Their passivity received criticism not only from the political elements of the movement but from certain clinical factions, who argued that action and direct intervention were critical to treatment. Among those who gained attention in this regard was Arthur Janov, a West Coast psychologist, who maintained that patients needed to do more than just talk about their problems but to physically act them out.[16] Incorporating some of the work of the Gestaltists and the Esalen movement, Janov, and those who were to follow him, argued for a more action-oriented approach, which often did away with words.

In the seventies attention was also given to the role behavior of psychiatrists, that is, the ways in which they played out a professional image. Their insularity and one-upmanship were often criticized, and the image of the kind and helpful healer seldom appeared.[17] Not only psychiatry but science itself came to be seen as corrupted and sterile, as evident in the psychiatrist and other medicos who appeared in one of the biggest box-office successes of the 1970s, *The Exorcist* (1973). Brought in to hypnotize the possessed patient, the arrogant clinician succeeds only in having his genitals bitten. The other psychiatrist in the film is also a priest, Father Karras, who finds both science and religion unable to heal the squalor in which the world is steeped. He gives up both roles and, in an act of total commitment, sacrifices himself. This seemed to be the only alternative to a troubled society that believed that only action and total commitment could triumph over the forces of evil that hid behind benign and smiling faces. The psychiatric profession came to be linked to the oppressive forces of the establishment. Patient rights groups and other forces emphasized the great danger of psychiatrists who administered psychosurgery and electroconvulsive therapy in the name of "proper and humane treatment." Certainly, this fit the image of Dr. Brooks, the real-life superintendant of Oregon State Hospital, in *Cuckoo's Nest*.

In retrospect it is understandable why Ken Kesey's *Cuckoo's Nest* came to the screen in 1975, almost fifteen years after its publication as a book. The film complemented a rather pervasive antipsychiatric feeling in America, which was no longer associated just with a left-wing radical and youthful rebellion but with criticism from within the very heart of the established psychiatric community. One example was a work by E. Fuller Torrey, a research psychiatrist at the National Institute of Mental Health.[18] Going beyond the earlier work of psychiatric dissidents, Torrey's book was a stunning indictment of the obsolescence of psychiatry and the concept of mental illness. It reflected the increasingly common view that psychiatrists kept psychiatry alive as a medical specialty because they did not wish to give up the status and power derived from the medical model. Receiving endorsement from the law enforcers and codifiers who used psychiatric illness as a convenient label under which they could dump the rebels of society, psychiatry flourished on dogmatic faith, rather than on scientific credibility. In *Cuckoo's Nest* Dr. Brooks, of course, is the person who orders the prefrontal lobotomy that will turn McMurphy (Jack Nicholson) into a walking vegetable. While not evil, his portrayal is that of an ineffectual bureaucrat who tends his patients from an administrative desk and leaves them to the mercy of repressive heavies like Big Nurse Ratched, who know how to squeeze every last bit of individuality out of their charges in shaping them into emasculated automatons.

The film, as we pointed out earlier (chapter 1), was a great financial success and won three academy awards. Given its portrayal of psychiatrists, it is surprising that the American Psychiatric Association at its annual meeting in 1976 praised the film for its "timely relevance" and pointed to the "hope that it will break down some of the barriers that have made mental disease a hidden quality in American culture."[19]

These depictions in the 1970s left the psychiatrist and psychiatric institutions looking not only hopeless but totally unaware of how hopeless they in fact were. Ingmar Bergman's *Face to Face* appeared in 1976 to give a helping hand. The first film to intensely investigate the private lives of psychiatrists, *Face to Face* went beyond the villain-victim syndrome to reveal personal, human struggles, with which psychiatrists, like their patients had to contend. With such an approach it is not surprising that his psychiatrist was a woman, in contrast to the conventional depiction of male psychiatrists. Unlike both her precursors and successors, she was neither romanticized nor defamed, but made human.

Married and having a child and a status career as a psychiatrist, Jenny seems in outward appearance to be a total woman. Slowly, however, we see that all is not perfect as human frailties emerge and crack the exterior calm of an overcontrolled life. The terrors of her patients become hers as her perfect world becomes subject to the imperfection that comes with allowing oneself to feel pain and joy. It is interesting that at one point Bergman contrasted the heroine's vulnerability and pained immersion into self-doubt with that of a male psychiatric colleague. Discussing a highly regressed and autistic patient, Jenny tentatively argues for human touch and understanding while her friend self-assuredly emphasizes that psychiatrists don't know what they are doing and would be better off accepting a behavioral model, which at least lends a ray of scientific objectivity to an otherwise mired mass of confusion. Her doubts—or, more accurately, her fear of doubting—take her to the point of attempting to kill herself, and it is in the dreams of her death sleep that Bergman symbolically portrayed the fears that she has so resolutely denied. Discovered in time and brought back to life, she realizes that beyond human frailty is love, which is a source of strength and faith that life holds meaning. Though prosaic in plot, the film constituted a remarkable investigation into the private lives of those who helped others and who so often denied their own fears of being helpless.

This sense of helplessness also pervaded *Equus* (1977). The personal sterility of Dr. Martin Dysart (Richard Burton) was counterpointed with the emotional pathology of his patient, whose cure leaves the psychiatrist stranded once again in self-isolation. While attempting to capture the brilliance of the 1975 theatrical production, the film failed in choosing to present a sensationalized portrayal of Alan Strang's pathology, rather than the personal struggles and tortured self-doubts that invade the psychiatrist's ministrations to his patient.

The depiction of the psychiatrist as human slowly began to fade into the background as stereotypes were reactivated. After *Face to Face* and *Equus* came *I Never Promised You a Rose Garden*, (1977), in which the psychiatrist is a somewhat superior being whose life is totally devoted to her patients. Living in an almost archetypal little house in the woods, she is the prototype of the good psychiatrist who, like Dr. Kik in *Snake Pit* (1948), has given up the outside world to devote her life selflessly to her patients. This beatific vision could, as one might suspect, only be followed by a downward spiral. In *Willie and Phil* (1980) the psychiatrist was depicted as ineffectual and unconcerned, as he was in *Ten* (1980), *Starting Over* (1980), *Serial* (1980), and *Oh God, Book II* (1980). While psychiatrists were not always directly shown in action, a particularly inept image was conveyed by references to his being "some sort of witch doctor" (*Fame*, 1980), to his needs

Face to Face (Sweden, 1976). Director, Ingmar Bergman. With Liv Ullmann, Erland Josephson. By permission of Film Institute of Sweden, Stockholm.

being greater than those of his patients (*Private Benjamin*, 1981), or to his specializing in "contemporary suicide" (*Simon*, 1980). Psychiatrists came to be portrayed as existing in their own worlds, unable to deal with others and with the realities of everyday life, as in *It's My Turn* (1980) and *Stardust Memories* (1980). Eventually, this separation from the real world reached extremes, as in *Bad Timing* (1980) and *Dressed to Kill* (1980).

In the latter film, which played on one of the most basic fears of the patient, the psychiatrist was back to being totally out of control and a crazed sex maniac. He not only preys upon the patient's revealed secret fantasies but punishes her for them in a razor-blade attack that won the director, De Palma, an uncontested position as one of the top impressarios of violence. Though the theme of the psychiatrist as a mad, degenerate killer was not a new one, De Palma's rendition was unique in that he masterfully manipulated the interactions between patient and therapist by using the catch words and artifacts that had become part of the psychiatric encounter. The psychiatrist, Dr. Elliot (Michael Caine) has his office in an East-Side traditional Brownstone, where he meets his patients in a modern but subdued interior, whose tastefully selected earth colors convey a sense of calm and order. Dr. Elliot himself is a middle-aged man, whose kindly features and calm exterior instill immediate trust. Throughout all of this there is clearly a stylized slickness, but it is this facade that De Palma so carefully constructed as he presented this man of reason.

At one point, when his provocative patient (Angie Dickinson) tries to seduce him, he openly admits to his being attracted to her but asks her to think about the true meaning behind her desires and to reality test the ramifications. While extolling such adult virtues, he looks at a small picture frame on his desk, which we, though we cannot see it, are led to believe by his comments holds a picture of his wife. It is this picture frame that takes us into the Hyde-like world of our contemporary Dr. Jekyll, for the frame holds only a mirror, in which the good Dr. Elliot gazes at himself in a self-love that has degenerated into transsexualism. As we are finally to learn from his own psychiatrist (a characterization very similar to the sanctimonious, uncaring clinician in Hitchcock's *Psycho*), Dr. Elliot was denied a sex change operation and, as a result, his "problems of maladaptation" have manifested themselves in murderous rage towards women to whom he is sexually attracted.

De Palma, then, updated the sexually crazed doctor theme with the sen-

Dressed to Kill (USA, 1980). Director, Brian De Palma. With Michael Caine, Angie Dickinson. By permission of Orion Pictures.

sationalized transsexual phenomenon and did so in a manner that reduced both the psychiatrist and the transsexual to hideously depraved figures who could suddenly explode with primitive aggression at those around them. Here, De Palma played on the basic core of stereotypical thought that centered on fear of the different and the unknown. His work appealed to primitive fear of the psychiatrist's power to control people's minds and actions, as well as to the resulting desire to see the holder of such power defiled and even destroyed. A variation on this theme was expressed by Dr. Herman Pardes, director of the National Institute of Mental Health, who said, "Resentment against the psychiatrist as a paragon of mental health virtue creates the wish to decrease his normality by taking him down a peg or two."[20] The need to believe in the omnipotence of the doctor as a way of making ourselves feel that someone does have the answer to our problem contains within it the anger that is associated with our dependence on such figures and our jealousy at not having such power. We therefore need both to exalt and defame those in power, and De Palma's film was but the latest, and slickest, presentation of such an ambivalence.

Another important aspect of the film was its portrayal of transsexualism. De Palma played upon one of the most pervasive fears about psychiatric problems in portraying the patient—in this case, a transsexual—as a primitive ghoul with homicidal sexual impulses. In truth most murders are not committed by the mentally ill, and the willingness to believe in a *Halloween* vision of the murderer revealed the need to resort to simplistic and categorical thinking, which evaded the complexity of murder by transforming the murderer into an animal or nonperson. Portraying the transsexual as such a figure was consistent with such thinking, for it assumed that transsexuals cannot be other than totally mad for having a belief not based on the reality of their biological sex. The desire to change one's exterior body in order to conform to one's felt gender identity in fact has been shown not to be the act of a mad person.[21] What De Palma and others involved in film and television did was depict those considered mad as one-dimensional figures and to subject them to the worst type of stereotypical projections.[28]

Because the films of the 1970s and early 1980s depicted such a negative image of the psychiatrist, it is not surprising that the other side of the ambivalence eventually surfaced. In the vastly acclaimed film *Ordinary People* (1980), Dr. Tyrone C. Berger (Judd Hirsch), while invoking the case-history approach of the 1950s and the earlier theme of amnesia and success through a breakthrough of the repressed, also seems to convey a degree of humanity that makes him very appealing. This is not to say that his characterization is not filled with cliches and stereotypical imagery. Dr. Berger is, first of all, a Jew and, as such, fulfills one of the long-time stereotypes that all psychiatrists, like Freud, are Jews, who, as outsiders, cannot be trusted. As an outsider, Berger appropriately dresses in a casual manner and, throughout the therapy sessions with Conrad, his young patient, always seems to wear the same cardigan sweater. His office is, simply put, a mess,—and this fact confirms that he has little interest in the usual concern for appearances—and his language is filled with curses and emotional inflection. Further negative stereotypes are conveyed by Berger's attention to his fifty-minute hour even when his patient is close to the magical breakthrough of the repressed, feared-but-desired wish, and by his not answering Conrad's phone call at a critical point.

For all of this, however, Berger is a caring and human figure who is willing to give attention to Conrad at the time when he most needs it, while at other points demanding that his patient take full responsibility for his anguish and pain. When Conrad reaches a total panic in the middle of the night as a result of familial separation and the suicide of a close friend, whom he met when he was institutionalized, Berger answers his call by immediately coming to him and embracing him as a friend. This human action, in context with Berger's clear, professional acumen displayed in helping Conrad to grow, made the film's depiction highly instrumental in diminishing the negative attitute toward the psychiatrist, which was so pervasive. While displaying both sides of the ambivalence felt toward the psychiatrist, the film conveyed primarily a view of a skilled and humane treater of those who were overwhelmed by fear.

Notes

1. M. Wolfenstein and N. Leites, *Movies: A Psychological Study* (New York: Dover Publications, 1950).

2. L. Rabkin, "The Celluloid Couch: Psychiatrists in American Films," presented at the annual meeting of the American Psychological Association, Div. 10 (September 1977). I. Schneider, "Images of the Mind: Psychiatry in Commercial Film," *American Journal of Psychiatry*, vol. 134, no. 6 (1977), 613–19.

3. Rabkin, p. 10.

4. The American Film Institute Catalogue of Feature Films, 1921–1930 (New York and London: R. R Bowker Company, 1971).

5. Lang had already introduced the character in the celebrated early German thriller, *Dr. Mabuse the Gambler* (1922).

6. Rabkin, p. 13.

7. M. Van Doren, "Second Comings," *The Nation* 142 (13 May 1936), 623–24.

8. P. Bottome, *Private Worlds* (Boston: Houghton Mifflin, 1934).

9. Film Review, *Newsweek*, vol. 5, no. 14 (6 April 1935), 36.

10. Ibid.

11. F. Fearing, "The Screen Discovers Psychiatry," *Hollywood Quarterly*, vol. 2 (January 1946), 156.

12. Rabkin, p. 16.

13. F. Truffaut, *Hitchcock* (New York: Simon & Schuster, 1967).

14. Fearing, p. 157.

15. Film Review, *The Commonweal Magazine* 45 (1 November 1946).

16. A. Janov, *The Primal Scream* (New York: Putnam, 1970).

17. Haley, *The Power Tactics of Jesus Christ* (New York: Avon Books, 1971).

18. E. F. Torrey, *The Death of Psychiatry* (New York: Penguin Books, 1974).

19. Rabkin, p. 24.

20. L. Martin, "The Psychiatrist in Today's Movies: He's Everywhere and in Trouble," *New York Times* (25 January 1981), pp. 18–19.

21. H. Benjamin, *The Transsexuals Phenomenon* (New York: Julian Press, 1966). R. Green and J. Money, *Transexualism and Sex Reassignments* (Baltimore: John Hopkins University Press, 1969).

22. "Six TV Myths about Mental Illness," *TV Guide* (13 March 1976), 4–8.

PART II
Filmography
SYNOPSES AND ANNOTATIONS

Roger Manvell

Introduction to Filmography

The films discussed in this second part of the book were selected because of their outstanding importance for artistic or technical quality, or—however indifferent the films may be from the strictly artistic standpoint—because they nevertheless have significance for their handling of the subject.

The principal categories of insanity involved, and their treatment, are listed below, numbered according to chapter (part I). After the credits of each film the various catgories of insanity depicted are indicated numerically in the order of their importance for that particular film.

1. Society and Madness
   a. Family and Madness
   b. Institutionalization of the Mad
2. Possession and Madness
3. Eros and Madness
4. Murder and Madness
5. War and Madness
6. Drugs and Madness
7. Paranoia and Madness
8. Sanity as Madness, Madness as Sanity
9. Madness and the Psychiatrist

FILMOGRAPHY: SYNOPSES

AGUIRRE, WRATH OF GOD
(West Germany, 1972). Direction, script, and production: Werner Herzog. With Klaus Kinski (Aguirre), Cecilia Rivera (Flores de Aguirre), Ruy Guerra (Don Pedro de Ursua), Helena Rojo (Inez de Atienza), Del Negro (Brother Gaspar), Peter Berling (Don Guzman). 7.

Don Lope de Aguirre and his fifteen-year-old daughter, Flores, are members of a conquistador expedition led by Gonzalez Pizarro, who has just conquered Peru.Setting out on New Year's Day 1561, Pizarro is determined to search out the legendary golden city of El Dorado, thought to be hidden in the hinterland. Aguirre, along with the gluttonous and boorish nobleman, Don Guzman, and the cadaverous priest, Gaspar, are sent ahead by Pizarro on an exploratory mission upriver by raft to penetrate the jungle. They have a party of some forty men under the leadership of Don Pedro de Ursua, whose adoring wife, Inez, in her utterly unsuitable courtly dresses, keeps close beside him.

As the expedition is gradually depleted through loss of life, Aguirre emerges as a Machiavellian, power-obsessed figure, determined to take over the lead. His intrigues culminate in the overthrow of Ursua and Aguirre's proclamation of the deficient Guzman as puppet emperor of El Dorado. One by one, the members of the expedition meet tragic fates—Ursua is hanged; Guzman, the self-destroying glutton, is murdered; Inez, silent and crazed following the death of her husband, vanishes into the darkness of the undergrowth, her long dress trailing around her; and Flores, too, dies. The Indians concealed in the trees that flank each bank of the river are slaughtered the moment they emerge, whether they are friendly or hostile. Aguirre's remaining, disease-ridden crew, exposed on the huge open raft that drifts downstream in the swift and treacherous currents, are picked off, one by one, by the arrows of invisible assailants. Proclaiming himself in his madness the Wrath of God Aguirre is left alone on the raft, his only companions a pack of chattering monkeys. He stands in rigid posture, his body sloped, his neck twisted, surviving in the grip of his obsession with power.

The film is dominated by the bizarre presence of Klaus Kinski, whose stylized performance turns Aguirre more and more into the very image of a bird of prey. Like some monstrous, larger-than-life Shakespearean madman—an Iago or a Richard Crookback—Aguirre seeks domination first of the isolated, microcosmic world of the raft, and finally of the visionary land he has come to conquer and inherit and where he intended to found a new dynasty by marrying his daughter, who is now dead. Making this film on the waters of the Amazon in the Peruvian jungle imposed on the unit and cast many of the hazards that faced the expedition they were reconstructing.

APOCALYPSE NOW

(USA, 1979). Direction: Francis Coppola. Script: John Milius, Francis Coppola. Direction of photography: Vittorio Storaro. Commentary: Michael Herr. With Marlon Brando (Kurtz), Martin Sheen (Willard), Robert Duvall (Kilgore), Frederic Forrest (Hicks, "Chef"), Dennis Hopper (photojournalist). Shot in the Philippine Islands, with the Montagnard tribesmen impersonated by the Ifugao people of the Philippines. 5.

Apocalypse Now is a monumental attempt to create an expressionist epic about the war in Vietnam. It is epic because it endeavors to bring the actions it portrays to a level that makes them reveal the horrifying degradation to which the prolonged American campaign against the advance of communism in Southeast Asia was reduced. It is expressionist because every action that takes place and virtually every line of narration and dialogue contains an urgent message about the war. To enhance the moral implications of his film Coppola acknowledges his debt to Joseph Conrad, upon whose story *Heart of Darkness* the film was initially based.[1]

Like his friend Henry James, Conrad attempted to uncover the more profound moral issues with which his chosen characters were faced when in extremis—usually when isolated in some exotic wilderness with only the inner secrets of their souls to occupy them. In *Heart of Darkness* (1902) this self-searching character is Kurtz, a senior agent for a company dealing in ivory and stationed upriver in a region Conrad calls "the heart of darkness." This region possesses "the stillness of an implacable force brooding over an inscrutable intention." Marlow, Conrad's narrator, is sent to Africa from Europe to seek out Kurtz, and after a dire journey upriver he finds him to have become a mysterious presence surrounded by savage African adherents, who deify him. For Marlow his appearance seems almost abstract—a voice in the wilderness. In his service is a white spokesman, a motley enthusiast of Russian extraction, but in the end even he cannot hide the mental and physical collapse of the leader he so much admires. Marlow finds this strange personality—as much poet and prophet, it would seem, as tyrant—in the last throes of a mortal sickness. "I saw the inconceivable mystery of a soul that knew no restraint, no faith, and no fear, yet struggling blindly with itself. . . . His was an impenetrable darkness." Kurtz's final words are, "The Horror! The Horror!" and in Marlow's memory he remains "a shadow darker than the shadow of night and draped nobly in the folds of a gorgeous eloquence."

Taking his cue from Conrad, Coppola set out to create a study of men absorbed into an exotically beautiful but evil setting that gradually erodes their moral fiber. In one way or another they are drawn into the heart of darkness of the sinister jungle, where they are required to fight an intractable, and frequently invisible, enemy. They become a prey to everything evil and sinister in themselves, a sickness inspired by the very nature of the climate and location of their war. They are like locusts destroying the land they have been sent to liberate. Friend and foe alike become their prey as they exploit their all-powerful and sophisticated weapons in a wholly primitive and unsophisticated territory.

Coppola shot his film in the Philippine jungle—over a million feet exposed, at a cost of over $31 million. But the real cost appears to have been to the nervous systems of Coppola and his colleagues, one of whom (the actor Martin Sheen, who played Willard) suffered a heart attack during the filming. Filming lasted 238 shooting days. A million feet of film is some thousand hours of screentime, and two years went into editing this vast mass of material into a film of some 150 minutes. At the 1979 Cannes Film Festival, where his film was the joint winner of the Grand Prix, Coppola said: "We went into the jungle with too much money, too much expensive equipment, too little understanding of the conditions, and the jungle swallowed us up. What happened to the United States in Vietnam is what happened to us when we shot the movie in the Philippines."[2] About his debt to Conrad he added: "There are philosophical concepts that are in both works, but they don't belong exclusively to Conrad any more than they do to me. I was certainly influenced by Conrad, but there are many more influences in the film too. I was just as influenced by some current writers—John Milius, for instance, or Michael Herr, whose book, *Dispatches,* was a profound lesson. . . . But ultimately, this is my film."[3]

The basic action is as simple as Conrad's, though the central character, Willard, is a figure very different from Conrad's stolid narrator, Marlow. A beat, drunken, and demoralized American army captain, Benjamin Willard (who had a nervous breakdown as an underground killer for the military) is picked up by commanding officers and unceremoniously sent upriver into Cambodia on a hushed-up mission to find and "terminate" a Green Beret colonel, Walter Kurtz. Formerly an outstanding officer but now considered unsound, Kurtz has disappeared into the jungle to conduct his own war in his own crazed and sadistic fashion with a private army of hipped-up deserters and Montagnard tribesmen. Treated like a god, he rules his followers from a base in the jungle, a vast, ruined temple like Ankor Wat, overgrown with tropical foliage. After an incredible journey by patrol boat, crewed by men half-crazed with fear of the jungle, Willard confronts the mysterious Kurtz, a highly articulate man, who is barely visible in the shadows of his domain except for the great glistening dome of his bald head, which shines like ivory. Although half-captivated by his victim's semi-mystical ruminations, Willard finally succeeds in killing him and leaves the settlement in his boat (at least he does so in the version of the film most widely shown).

But Coppola enlarges this action until it reaches another, universalized dimension. *Apocalypse Now* is, in effect, two films: the first, a condemnation of the Vietnam War as a vast, prolonged technological assault on a peasant population, spectacularly staged in a succession of sequences; the second, an evocation of the moral issues involved when a military authority, using methods that belong to the jungle but lacking the sophisticated veneer of modern military technology, condemns one of their number to death when he deserts them to carry on the war on his own.

The film opens without title or credits, initiating the first apocalyptic sequence—in effect, the drunken Willard's nightmare of war as he lies, dreaming of a recall to action, in the bedroom of a hotel in Saigon. A peaceful vision involving a beautiful line of palm trees is suddenly interrupted by the roar of approaching choppers, the fearful, whirring images of their attack, and a fierce explosion of flame engulfing the long stretch of trees. Quiet romantic music gives way to a voice singing, "This is the end, I'll never look into your eyes again," and the whirling blades of a helicopter dissolve into the rotating arms of a fan suspended from Willard's bedroom ceiling. His face is seen upside down, staring upwards. He speaks as narrator. "I wanted a mission. For my sins they gave me one—a real choice mission. When it was over, I never wanted another." The commanding general who summons him back to duty quietly explains the background of this particular task: "In this war, things get confused—morality and military necessity. It becomes a temptation to become a god—temptation between the rational and the irrational, the good and the bad. Every man's got a breaking point. Kurtz has reached his and gone insane." He must, says the general, be stopped.

The mission begun, the film divides into three distinct sections, each with its cumulative impact of madness. The first section presents an attack by an air cavalry unit, commanded by the hysterical Colonel Bill Kilgore, on a Viet Cong village, its nearby beachhead specially chosen because of the excellent surfing Kilgore craves. Gliding up on the peaceful village scene with all the menacing slowness of a prolonged, foreshortened shot, the helicopters arrive through the red dawn like great predatory insects. "It scares the hell out of them," says Kilgore. "My boys love it." As the crews mete out death by bomb and firepower, he orders the tape they have of the ride of the Valkyrie to be played loud and clear. "Get the shit out of them," yells Kilgore. When he finally lands, Kilgore pirouettes around in high boots and a uniform adapted to make him look like some star player in a Western.

The second section involves Willard's sudden extraordinary encounter in what appears to be the wildest, most deserted upriver terrain with a huge army supply base, lit up at night like a surrealistic stage set. It is here that the half-demented crowd of GIs are entertained overnight by a team of half-naked playmates, flown in to provide a powerful dose of sexual hysteria for this mob of screaming youths, high on drugs and rock 'n' roll.

More and more as the mission proceeds, one is reminded of the terrorizing threat of the jungle in Herzog's film *Aguirre, the Wrath of God*. One by one, members of Willard's faint-hearted crew are picked off by unseen assassins lurking in the riverside jungle. The men in the patrol boat respond with the panic-inspired killing of innocents on the bank or in rivercraft; whether Viet Cong or not, no one seems to care. As they approach the area where Willard believes Kurtz to be, one of the crew remarks, "You're in the asshole of the world, Captain."

The third section begins with the nightmarelike reception given the patrolboat by Kurtz's tribesmen. They stand mute and statuesque in a fleet of sampams, while a distant drum is heard in the background and the bodies of men guilty of some misdemeanor are seen suspended from the branches of trees. "Everything

I saw," says Willard in narration, "made it clear Kurtz had gone insane. Everywhere—bodies." Conrad's weird Harlequin character, dressed in motley, a crazy spokesman for Conrad's Kurtz, is matched in the film by the mad photojournalist (Dennis Hopper), an aide to Coppola's Kurtz, who tries to put some kind of face on the mass slaughter Kurtz has so evidently perpetrated. Indeed, Willard himself is captured and subjected to torture before he is finally able to confront Kurtz, the man who has succumbed to the heart of darkness and assumed the godlike leadership of ferocious men, whose inhuman practices against an equally ruthless jungle enemy have reduced warfare to the ultimate savage cruelty. In his sickness and delirium Kurtz philosophizes, bringing Conrad's shadowy and exotic character virtually a century forward to project the torments of the men in Vietnam.

Coppola allows his Kurtz to echo precisely the same words as Conrad's—"The horror! The horror!"—just prior to his ritualistic slaughter by Willard, which is crosscut with the ritual slaying of a bullock by Kurtz's tribesmen. It is even implied that Kurtz's followers would accept Willard as their new god if he cared to assume the leadership. But Willard marches straight through them back to the patrol boat, though it is evident enough that Kurtz's words have fascinated him; indeed, he has agreed to carry back to Kurtz's son the father's "testament" about the war.

The final cataclysmic and highly stylized air raid destroying Kurtz's base, which ends with Willard's departure, shown in the 70mm version of the film at Cannes, was omitted from the 35mm version put into universal distribution. In the earlier version Willard remains undecided about taking Kurtz's place, which is then followed by the destruction of all that Kurtz has established in the jungle. According to his wife, Eleanor, Coppola remained for a long time undecided how to end the film.[4]

Coppola's intention was to create" a film experience that would give his audience a sense of the horror, the madness, the sensuousness, and the moral dilemma of the Vietnam war."[5] As many commentators have pointed out, he did not touch the political issues involved in the war, only the moral and human ones affecting the fighting men. But *Apocalypse Now* is by far the most impressive and devastating study of the Vietnam campaign on film, conceived surrealistically as a nightmare of lurid beauty, born out of the conscience of a participant who was forced to look into the heart of darkness itself. Coppola "We went insane," said Coppola, "the film was made the way the war was fought."[6]

BAD TIMING
(Britain, 1980). Direction: Nicolas Roeg. With Art Garfunkel (Dr. Alex Linden), Theresa Russell (Milena Flaherty), Harvey Keitel (Inspector Netusil), Denholm Elliott (Stefan Vognic). 3.

A young American psychoanalyst, Dr Alex Linden, a faculty member at the University in Vienna, meets Milena, an American girl who has recently parted from her Czech husband, Stefan. They enter into a sexually voracious, but also very disturbed, love affair—he, anxious for marriage and tormented by the knowledge that she has relationships with other men; she, claiming to be divorced while still legally married and increasingly resentful of his sexual obsessions. She prefers to live for the moment, without any hard ties with him or any man. After a holiday with Alex in Morocco, Milena decides to leave him when she discovers he is preparing a file about her for U.S. Army intelligence in order to discover for himself more and more about her background. Once they are separated, however, she begins to drink excessively. Aware that he is seeing a former girlfriend, Amy, Melina starts to persecute him with despairing telephone calls, culminating in a final, desperate appeal for help after taking an overdose of drugs. Alex decides he should go to her apartment. Finding her near to death, he succumbs to his overwhelming desire to possess her recumbent body; he calls for the ambulance only after having (in effect) raped her in a last, hopeless effort to secure the ultimate, possessive love that Melina has denied him.

The whole of this story of sexual obsession gradually emerges through the framing device of Police Inspector Netusil's grilling of the reluctant Alex while the medical team at the hospital fights (with very explicit medical treatment) to save Milena's life. Meanwhile, her husband, Stefan, arrives. Melina does indeed survive, but Alex finds he is freed from his obsession as a result of his forced confession to Netusil about the nature of his relationship with her.

The film is constructed in such a way as to emphasize the uncertainty, the ambivalence, as well as the sheer masochistic self-torture that results from the form of obsession Alex develops for Milena and from the particular demands she makes of her men. Finally, she too becomes trapped by the excesses of the passion she so deliberately provokes. Going far beyond the mere physicality of their relationship, Roeg penetrates into the unreasoning demands that love prompts when Alex insists on probing painfully into the mystery of the personality of his love partner. As one reviewer says of Alex:

> The problem in his affair with Milena is that he is trying to probe the mystery in order to achieve perfection; and this, as his story bleakly argues, is a contradiction in terms. Standing on one side of the mirror, Alex demonstrates how the passion aroused in him by the mystery of Milena falls short of love when it aspires to total understanding; while on the other side, his reflection, Stefan, shows how the love born of an understanding that mysteries must be accepted falls sadly short of passion. As a psychoanalyst . . . Alex is only too well aware of the human propensity to know more than it is necessarily good to know. Being human and therefore subject to the fallibility of the species, he is excusably unable to prevent himself from trying to ask too much of and about Milena; where his failure lies (especially as a psychoanalyst) is in his attempt to interpret what he thinks he has learned as though it were objective truth.[7]

The close relationship that exists between the interrogator and the interrogated in *Bad Timing* is in many ways similar to that in *Crime and Punishment*. Alex draws ever closer into his relationship with the mercilessly insistent, yet somehow sympathetic, Inspector Netusil, almost to the point where they merge into being dual aspects of the same person. Alex, it must be remembered, is a psychoanalyst, and throughout the film one is tempted to parody the Bible by saying, Psychoanalyst, perceive and heal thyself!

BADLANDS
(USA, 1974). Direction and script, Terrence Malick. With Martin Sheen (Kit), Sissy Spacek (Holly). 4, 3.

Holly, aged 15, kills her hostile father, a widower, without sign of emotion when he threatens her with the police after her declaration she is determined to abscond with her lover, a former garbage-collector aged 25, who, having recorded a fake suicide confession by Holly's father, coolly sets the house alight with the body in it. Kit and Holly then enjoy themselves living rough in the South Dakota countryside, killing off a group of bounty-hunters who come in search of them; Kit also just as casually shoots a former work-mate when it seems he might betray them, and leaves two other innocent victims for dead without bothering to check whether they are so or not after he has shot them. Sought now alike by police and vigilantes, Kit steals a Cadillac and the couple reach Montana together, though Holly, feeling estranged from her lover, deserts him and is arrested. Kit deliberately brings about his own arrest and, although treated like some kind of folk-hero, is finally tried and executed, while Holly marries her defence lawyer.

The story of this remarkable first feature by Malick is said to be based on the true activities in 1958 of Charles Starkweather and Caril Fugate in the Dakota badlands. It is narrated with a chilling directness by Holly, and Malick achieves a form of terse stylization designed to match the utter nonchalance with which these young people commit murder after murder, displaying no more feeling for their victims than if they were indulging in target practice. The mood is reminiscent of Godard's *Breathless* as well as *Bonnie and Clyde*. Their behaviour is made to seem like a romantic exercise in escape from any form of social or moral responsibility, characterized by a sociopathic lack of emotional involvement.

BELLE DE JOUR
(France, 1966). Direction and script: Luis Buñuel. Based on the novel by Joseph Kessel. With Catherine Deneuve (Séverine), Jean Sorel (Pierre), Michel Piccoli (Husson), Geneviève Page (Anais), Pierre Clementi (Marcel). 3.

Buñuel usually prefers not to comment on the potential significance of his ambivalent films, and when he does he takes delight in making this significance even more ambivalent. "They are secretive films, in which nothing is immediately obvious or apparent."[8] The essence of the surrealist approach is that the surrealistic film and its imagery have originated in the first place from the subconscious, with as little intrusion as possible by any form of rationalized reshaping in order to impose neatness and coherence on the story. *Belle de Jour*, a production in color with a more generous budget than Buñuel normally has at his disposal, is nevertheless a film of true surrealist appeal. Having made no concession to the box office, Buñuel claims surrealistic integrity for *Belle de Jour.* Of Joseph Kessel's novel, published in 1929, Buñuel said:

> I don't like Kessel's novel at all, but I found it interesting to try to turn something I didn't like into something I did. There are some scenes in the film which I'm very pleased with, others with which I'm not at all. I ought to say I enjoyed total freedom during the shooting and I therefore consider myself entirely responsible for the result.[9]

After completing the script, he declared:

> This novel of the twenties . . . done in a realist style, is about the masochistic impulses of a woman who, fearing that she is frigid, ends by working in brothels. I hope I can save such a stale subject by mixing indiscriminately and without warning in the montage the things that actually happen to the heroine, and the fantasies and morbid impulses which she imagines. As the film proceeds, I am going to increase the frequency of these interpolations, and at the end, in the final sequence, the audience will not be able to know if what is happening to her is actual or the heroine's subjective world—reality or nightmare.[10]

But as Francisco Aranda asserts in his book on Buñuel, "For surrealism, reality and dream are one."[11]

If Buñuel did not like Kessel's novel and said so, the novelist himself was generous enough to express his delight in the film:

> Buñuel's genius has surpassed all that I could have hoped. It is at one and the same time the book and not the book. We are in another dimension, that of the subconscious, of dreams and secret instincts suddenly laid bare.[12]

The storyline of the novel is abundantly clear. Séverine Sérizy, the beautiful young wife of a handsome and wealthy surgeon, Pierre, loves her husband deeply but is, nevertheless, always frigid when lying in his arms. He remains kind, considerate, and polite, but they cannot make love. Consumed by guilt, Séverine develops a masochistic urge to be sexually assaulted and decides to work part-time (during the afternoons) in a small, clandestine, and elitist brothel, catering (illegally) to wealthy patrons with rather specialized sexual tastes. One of the patrons, Marcel, is a young, self-indulgent hoodlum. Séverine finds herself falling in love with him in spite, or because, of his somewhat sadistic handling of her. When one of her husband's friends, Husson, happens to visit the brothel, Marcel sets out to kill him in order to prevent him from informing Pierre of his wife's afternoon activities. But Pierre intervenes and is wounded in such a way that he is confined in a wheelchair and rendered impotent. Séverine, her sense of guilt now redoubled, confesses what she has done and is immediately rejected by Pierre, who refuses ever to speak to her again.

Buñuel, naturally, disliked this ending ("because morality is saved") and reacted against the novel's sharply defined storyline. As he had done previously with *El* he made the psyche of the leading character the center of interest by interspersing moments of actuality with moments of fantasy, all portrayed with equal clarity and conviction. Everything that happens (whether external to Séverine or purely hallucinatory) appears equally real for her, and Catherine Deneuve's superbly glacial performance, stressing Séverine's imperturbable behavior, is exactly right, for the calm acceptance of every humiliation imposed on her is the very essence of her self-punishment. So a great part of what happens on the screen did not appear at all in the novel, and incidents that are clarified in the plot of the novel, become relatively ambiguous in the film. For example, in the novel Husson humiliates Séverine by copulating with her (she is the wife of his close friend) at the brothel, whereas in the film he refuses to do so, perhaps all the more to humiliate her since he has, after all, chosen her in the first place from the group of available girls. But, above all, the end of the film is rendered entirely ambivalent. We are not only left merely to assume Husson has revealed Séverine's secret to Pierre; but cannot even be sure whether or not Pierre has in fact been sexually incapacitated, since at one moment he is confined in his wheelchair and at the next, walking about normally.

But from the very beginning of the film—when Séverine is riding with Pierre through their elegant country estate in a landau accompanied by two coachmen, who, at Pierre's sudden command, stop, lead her into the woods, and strip and whip her—the ambiguity of all we are to see is established. As Buñuel himself said, "The ambiguity is established by the landau, which is the symbol of the irrational."[13] The landau recurs later, when Séverine is hired for an assignation with a wealthy patron who suffers from necrophilia.

Séverine's problems seem to have originated when she was sexually molested as a child by a passing workman in some isolated corridor. We see her as a child refusing to accept the host from the priest in church—either a memory of something that actually occurred or an illusory incident she invented. In her unfortunate married life she becomes obsessed with visions of humiliation, of being whipped and violated and covered by the servants with mud, her abasement associated with the fetishistic imagery that has always amused Buñuel (whips, cords, chains, boots, and shoes) and that he so often slips slyly into his films. (The gynecologist who is a regular patron of the brothel arrives carrying his official-looking medical attaché case, which is stuffed full of such equipment so that Séverine may ritualistically set about humiliating *him!*) Indeed, tongue in cheek, Buñuel has offered us another slant on *Belle de Jour;* it is, he said, "a pornographic film," adding, "by that I mean chaste eroticism."[14]

BLOODY MAMA
(USA, 1969). Direction: Roger Corman. With Shelley Winters (Ma Barker), Don Stroud (Herman), Bruce Dern (Kevin Dirkman). 4.

The action is set back in the Great Depression of the 1930s. The pathologically self-willed mother, Kate ("Ma") Barker has left the backwoods during the 1920s with her four overindulged and overviolent sons, at least one of whom, Herman, is a sociopath. Under Ma Barker's leadership they have become a notorious gang, joined by another young criminal, Kevin Dirkman. Herman, on Ma

Barker's instructions, murders a girl whom one of the brothers has tried to rape, but they refuse to carry out their mother's instructions to kill a wealthy kidnap victim in their charge, a man they have actually come to like. Herman forces his mother to capitulate and takes charge of the gang himself. They move to Florida, where their criminal exploits lead to a siege by the police on their hideout. They die as violently as they have lived. Ma Barker's creed has been freedom at any price, secured mainly through ill-gotten gains and the ruthless destruction of anyone (however innocent) who offers a threat to herself or her family. She emasculated her husband in the past and seeks to do the same to the kidnapped prisoner, and she even guns down Kevin when he tries to escape during the siege. Ma Barker is, in a sense, a study in despair and desperation in a desperate period in American history. The part is played by Shelley Winters with a ruthlessly sentimental panache, though the slightly comic brio of her screen personality seems to take the edge off the horrifying pathology of Ma Barker's character.

THE BLUE ANGEL
(Germany, 1930). Direction: Josef von Sternberg. Adapted from the novel, *Professor Unrath,* by Heinrich Mann. With Emil Jannings (Professor Rath), Marlene Dietrich (Lola). 3.

The film presents the self-destructive passion that an elderly schoolmaster conceives for a sensuous cabaret singer. Pompous and dictatorial in the classroom, the old man sneaks away to hear the cabaret artiste perform and falls so madly in love that he leaves his profession and marries her. The singer immediately starts to exploit him, turning him into a clown who has to cry like a cock while eggs are broken on his head. Eventually he goes mad with jealousy when she courts other men younger than he and attempts to strangle her. Cast out as insane, he returns secretly to his old school and dies at his desk in the empty classroom. Jannings gave his usual slow-motion performance, studied and melodramatic, in this early sound film, which is distinguished by Sternberg's highly stylized direction and use of sound and by the performance by Marlene Dietrich, which took her to Hollywood.

BOB AND CAROL AND TED AND ALICE
(USA 1969). Direction and script: Paul Mazursky. With Robert Culp (Bob), Natalie Wood (Carol), Elliott Gould (Ted), Dyan Cannon (Alice). 9.

Bob and his wife, Carol, are the self-conscious and self-satisfied products of group therapy and "confrontation psychology," which aims at resolving their conventional inhibitions. Returning home feeling triumphant about being sexually spontaneous, they burn to pass on their discoveries to their friends, Ted and Alice, his wife. The result is a network of extramarital activity, for which none of the partners proves adequately adjusted, though they are at least determined to keep what they call "civilized" about everything that happens and sidetrack all pangs of old-time jealousy. They end up in a formidable kind of foursome orgy, all in bed together.

BONNIE AND CLYDE

(USA, 1967). Direction: Arthur Penn. Screenplay, David Newman, Robert Benton. With Warren Beatty (Clyde Barrow), Faye Dunaway (Bonnie Parker), Gene Hackman (Buck Barrow), Michael J. Pollard (C. W. Moss), Estelle Parsons (Blanche), Denver Pyle (Frank Hamer), Gene Wilder (Eugene Grizzard), Evans Evans (Velma Davis), Dub Taylor (Moss).

Arthur Penn, a director who has specialized in serious studies of violence, comes close to romanticizing the relationship of this shabby young couple who during the 1930s secured an extreme notoriety for themselves through their petty bank robberies and heartless murders in small communities of Texas and nearby states. As interpreted by Faye Dunaway and Warren Beatty, their ruthless exploits become endowed with the poetic mystique of a fable. Clyde's impotence is emphasized as being in marked contrast to his potency with guns; when the runaway couple are joined by the semi-moronic motor mechanic, C. W. Moss, and by Clyde's elder brother, Buck, a small-time crook with a hysterical wife, the Barrow gang rove the countryside like half-crazed predators, while Bonnie composes semi-literate ballads in praise of their exploits. The press records their deeds with a mixture of admiration and fear. They are seen to be ruthlessly sought out by the law, and finally betrayed by Moss's father, a seemingly goodhearted but ultimately sinister character. The deaths of Bonnie and Clyde, performed in bloody slow-motion as they are gunned down by the Texas Rangers, have all the appearance of a martyrdom of romantic youth by malignant age. A brilliantly directed and acted film, the pride in and enjoyment of violence as experienced by sociopaths has seldom been better portrayed than it is by Faye Dunaway and Warren Beatty. The film grossed $22 million in the domestic market alone, and its popularization of the Bonnie and Clyde "legend" is important in screen crime history. Although the basic facts are relatively close to actuality, the interpretation of character has become the subject of considerable criticism. Sheriff Hamer filed a lawsuit against Warren Beatty, who had produced the film, claiming that his character had been traduced, and that the young gangsters had been given due warning before the final shootout.

THE BOSTON STRANGLER

(USA 1968). Direction: Richard Fleischer. With Tony Curtis (Albert De Salvo), Henry Fonda (John S. Bottomley). 4.

The notorious strangler's activities from 1962 to 1964 in Boston, Massachusetts, terrorized the whole area. A series of women, old and young alike, were found strangled—the work of a single sociopath. Eventually, an unassuming and seemingly happily married man who had two children and was employed in maintenance, was accused by the police but denied all involvement in the face of what was held to be irrefutable evidence. This put his mental condition into doubt. In the film he is interrogated by Assistant Attorney General John Bottomley and finally breaks down and admits to the murders, convinced now himself that he must have been the strangler. He then claims to have been responsible for some two thousand cases of rape. He is classified as a schizophrenic and considered incapable of standing trial.

The film shows, first of all, the prolonged and frustrating stages through which the official investigation went and, after this, concentrates on Bottomley's interrogation of a man who is made to seem quite pleasant and has total amnesia as far as his crimes are concerned. The initial investigation reveals a considerable deal about the strange sexual practices of men who appear otherwise quite normal. The film inevitably simplifies (for censorship and other reasons) a very complex psychological case, giving it something of a Jekyll-and-Hyde appearance.

LE BOUCHER

("The Butcher." France, 1970). Direction and script: Claude Chabrol. With Stéphane Audran (Hélène), Jean Yanne (Popaul Thomas). 4.

This study of repressed love leading to insane violence centers on Popaul Thomas. Having originally left the little Périgord town for service in the army in order to escape from his domineering father, who is the local butcher, Popaul is back now and courting the polite, reserve Hélène. Hélène is a lonely and somewhat alien schoolmistress, who suffered a breakdown when deserted by a past lover. She insists on keeping their relationship platonic. Popaul, who has now succeeded his father as the butcher, gives her choice cuts of meat, wrapped and presented like bouquets. Meantime, two successive murders of girls have occurred in the district, and Hélène gradually comes to realize that her would-be lover is the murderer.

The film ends with Hélène's being cornered by Popaul in her schoolhouse at night. He carries a knife and, deeply ashamed that she knows the truth about him, stabs himself in the stomach as if to castrate himself. Hélène, distracted, drives him to the hospital, but he dies after confessing his love for her. Possibly his finest film, Chabrol handles its violent subject with great subtlety, and both leading players give sensitive performances.

THE CABINET OF DR. CALIGARI

(Germany, 1919–20). Direction: Robert Wiene. With Werner Krauss (Caligari), Conrad Veidt (Cesare), Friedrich Feher (Francis), Lil Dagover (Jane). 2.

Sitting in the garden of the asylum where he is confined, Francis, the young hero of the film, tells the story of how he conceives that he came to be there to a fellow inmate. The story involves his friend Alan; Jane, the girl they both love; and certain other patients, and makes the director of the asylum the villain of the situation in the guise of an insane traveling showman, Dr. Caligari, who tours small-town fairgrounds in his caravan, in which he transports a somnambulist, Cesare, who is in his power. Caligari uses Cesare, when partially awakened, to tell fortunes in his showbooth by day, while at night he sends him out to murder his chosen victims. Among those whose murders he induces in this way is the quite innocent Alan, whose death Cesare has foretold. Later Jane, the equally inno-cent heroine of the film, is abducted by Cesare, but her life is spared. Investigat-ing his friend's death, Francis manages to expose Caligari, who manages to escape back to the refuge of the asylum. Here Francis tracks him down. That night Francis and the officials of the asylum discover the director's secret diary, in which he has recorded his aspirations to become successor to a famous medieval murderer named Caligari, who uses a somnambulist to carry out mur-ders on his behalf. At the close of the film, however, we find once again that the whole story is the invention of Francis's distraught mind and that the benign-looking director of the asylum is convinced that he will be able to restore his patient's reason since he now knows the nature of his obsessions.

The Cabinet of Dr. Caligari is an example of films that use the hallucinations of insane people for the purpose of creating fantasy-melodrama, as Fritz Lang's films about the insane criminal Dr. Mabuse were to do. The magnificently eccen-tric performance by Werner Krauss as Caligari and the obsessive impersonation of Cesare by Conrad Veidt create images of half-grotesque, half-macabre madness, which still remain unique after over sixty years. The sets, purporting to reflect the distortions of the young hero's mind (though, illogically, they continue to serve as background to the film after we have returned to the world of reason) are strikingly beautiful in spite of their extreme simplicity and austerity of struc-ture. The movement of the action has a compulsive, dreamlike quality, enhanced by the emphatically slow progress of the images, and the inspired mime of Krauss and Veidt, their movements in marked contrast—the former jerky and staccato, the latter slow and trancelike. The film is full of memorable fantasies that, once seen, cannot be forgotten: the fairground booth, where, amid slanted planes of black and white, Cesare slowly mouths the fortunes of his victims; the whorls and curves that fill the screen in the rooms and corridors of the asylum; the beautiful succession of sets in the sequence when Cesare abducts the heroine. In spite of its somewhat simplistic melodrama the film seems to possess the qualities of some haunting nightmare that stays like a residue in the memory.

The true creators of this celebrated expressionist film, made in postwar Berlin at very lost cost, are writers Carl Mayer and Hans Janowitz, the set designers, and the actors, not the director, who received the assignment late in the day, replacing the intended director, Fritz Lang, who was occupied with other work. Research by Siegfried Kracauer[15] uncovered the fact that the two young scriptwriters (one of whom, Carl Mayer, was to become Germany's most cele-brated screenwriter of the silent period) had intended their original story to be a satiric exposure of Prussian wartime authoritarianism, using hypnosis to turn young men into somnambulistic killers, as Caligari induced Cesare to commit murder. Erich Pommer, Germany's senior film producer, acquired the script, but changed the format of the story, totally altering its message by making the whole action quite clearly from the very start the hallucination of the youthful protagonist. This young man is portrayed as totally insane, believing the worst about the director of the asylum in which he is confined.

The film, made on a budget of some eighteen thousand dollars and produced in a very small studio, was experimental only in its use of the expressionist sets designed by the team of artists, Herman Warm, Walter Reiman, and Walter Röhrig, the former two of whom were to become well known as designers for the cinema). When completed, the film was thought uncommercial by Pommer and achieved initially only limited exhibition. Its fame was acquired outside Germany, while the expressionist style, in many various forms, became a distinct vein in German silent filmmaking during the 1920s, especially for films reflecting mental disturbance, eccentricity, or the supernatural.

THE CAINE MUTINY
(USA, 1954). Direction: Edward Dmytryk. With Humphrey Bogart (Captain Queeg), Fred MacMurray (Lieutenant Keefer), Van Johnson (Lieutenant Maryk), Tom Tully (Captain DeVriess), Jose Ferrer (defense officer). Adapted from the novel by Herman Wouk. 7.

This film is a study of an "unhappy ship," whose officers—including a frustrated intellectual, Lieutenant Keefer; a conscientious plodder, Lieutenant Maryk; and an idealistic young ensign—are ill-matched and whose beat and overly nervous commander, Captain DeVriess, has been replaced by the martinet Captain Queeg, who proves to be eccentric, paranoid, and cowardly. The ship strikes a typhoon and Maryk feels forced to take over the command on his own initiative. At the subsequent court martial, Maryk is deserted by his fellow officers, who (Keefer especially), should have supported him. The defence officer, however, manages in the end to break through Queeg's facade and drive him to reveal his neurotic condition. Although the film as a whole is mediocre, with too many concessions to conventional treatment, Bogart's performance is outstanding. The initial appearance of the firm and disciplined leader gives way gradually to shiftiness of manner and touches of hysteria, and then to the symptoms of persecution mania and, finally, panic.

CAPTAIN NEWMAN, MD.
(USA, 1963). Direction: David Miller. Based on a novel by Leo Rosten. With Gregory Peck (Captain Josiah Newman), James Gregory (Colonel Pyser), Eddie Albert (Colonel Bliss), Bobby Darin (Corporal Tompkins), Robert Duval (Captain Winston). 9.

This film pays tribute, somewhat sentimentally, to Captain Josiah Newman, who is in charge of the psychiatric ward in a U.S. Army air base hospital during World War II. Newman makes persistent efforts to make his commanding officer, Colonel Pyser, realize that men who are psychiatric cases are not all malingerers. His principal cases include Colonel Bliss, who has become schizophrenic because of guilt feelings about the men he has sent to their deaths;

Corporal Tompkins, now an alcoholic because he left his best friend to die in a burning plane; and Captain Winston, a catatonic case after remaining for eighteen months in a celler in occupied France. Tompkins is later returned to duty and is killed in action, while Bliss commits suicide. In fact, under pressure from Pyser, Newman's task is to get his men well enough as fast as possible and sent back to the battlefront. Winston, the most difficult case in the film, is with the aid of his wife finally edged out of his trance by Newman's care. The intention of the film is better than its actual achievement, but it remains the only fiction film wholly devoted to showing the place of psychiatry in the Second World War.

THE CARETAKER
(Britain, 1963). Direction: Clive Donner. Script: Harold Pinter. Adapted from the play by Harold Pinter (1960). With Alan Bates (Mick), Robert Shaw (Aston), Donald Pleasence (Davies). 1a, 1b.

The tenement attic in a near-derelict house in western London represents a microcosm of human mental imbalance and the portrayal of a mentally sick society. The inhabitants of this seemingly empty house are two brothers, Mick (in his late twenties) and Aston (in his early thirties). Aston has become permanently retarded after electric-shock treatment (administered against his will but with his mother's consent). All he now wants to achieve is the construction of a garden shed, which he somehow never gets around to doing. Mick, on the other hand, restless, overly excited, and sadistically inclined, is impelled by vague ambitions to turn the house into the fulfillment of his illusions of grandeur. The only furnished room is the attic, where beds and bric-a-brac have been dumped. Among this is a plaster figure of the Buddha, representing an imperturbable calm amid the tensions of this insane environment.

In his vain search for companionship and help in building his shed, Aston introduces into the house an old tramp he has rescued from a punch out in the street. The tramp turns out to be a drifter of the worst kind, laying off brother against brother while sponging on both. He has neither possessions nor a real identity and makes every excuse not to attempt to find them. His worst act is to betray the confidence Aston places in him when he tells him the tragic story of his maltreatment in the hospital. Davies merely mocks him as a looney while continuing to exploit him. Only too soon, Davies finds himself rejected by both brothers. Mick loses his temper and smashes the Buddha. Davies is condemned to leave the house forever because of his selfish ingratitude, and a sudden crisis of utter fear siezes him. Thus ends this traumatic and claustrophobic adaptation of Pinter's play, which was largely filmed within the constricted environment of a real attic in an empty house in London.

THE CARETAKERS

(USA, 1963). Direction: Hall Bartlett. With Robert Stack (Dr. Mcleod), Joan Crawford (Matron Lucretia Terry), Herbert Marshall (Dr. Herrington), Polly Bergen (Lorna Melford), Robert Vaughn (Mr. Melford, her husband), Constance Ford (Nurse), Janis Paige (Patient). 1b, 9.

Set in a West Coast mental hospital, this comparatively neglected film makes a serious attempt to advocate through its protagonist, Dr. Mcleod, a more enlightened form of care for seriously disturbed "borderline" patients in an experimental ward where he conducts group therapy designed to encourage patients to care mutually for each other. Of psychiatrists he says, "We are the caretakers of their hope." The main authorities in control of the hospital are a more traditionally-minded psychiatrist, Dr. Herrington, who is trying to keep an open mind about the more modern approach to treatment represented by the work of Mcleod, and the Matron, Lucretia Terry, who is openly hostile to Mcleod, regarding the patients as dangerous enemies who must be kept secure behind bars and under strict control. She requires her nurses to line up for drill and learn judo for self-protection. Principal among the many kinds of women patients whose cases are revealed in some detail is Lorna Melford, who has become increasingly unbalanced since the death of her only child, which she believes she caused through a car crash, and who experiences alienation from her husband. Her husband cares for her, but has felt forced to have her committed to the institution. *The Caretakers* should be compared to *The Snake Pit* (1948) among the pioneer efforts to bring more advanced aspects in the treatment of mental patients before the public. Like *The Snake Pit,* the film ends happily when the principal patient openly learns to care for her fellows and assist in bringing about various stages in their recovery.

CATCH-22

(USA, 1970). Direction: Mike Nichols. Script: Buck Henry. Adapted from the novel by Joseph Heller. With Alan Arkin (Captain Yossarian), Jack Gifford (Doc Daneeka), Martin Balsam (Colonel Cathcart). 5, 8.

Fifteen million dollars of production money went into lavish scenes of war violence depicting the lunatic experiences of the men attached to the US Army Air Force base in the Mediterranean during the Second World War. "Catch-22" is spelled out to the protagonist, Captain Yossarian, by Doc Daneeka—namely, that no sane man would choose to fly in combat and that therefore anyone who, like Yossarian, tries to be grounded because he is no longer mentally fit for it proves that he is only too sane. The unit is commanded by Colonel Cathcart, whose particular lunacy is to pile missions on his men until they are driven to various extremes of self-destruction—all, that is, but the terror-stricken Yossarian, who escapes the mass insanity that takes possession of his fellows and is rewarded by those in authority for dropping his bombs in the sea. *Catch-22* is black humor with a vengeance, its nightmare ironies soaked in blood and guts.

CITIZEN KANE

(USA, 1941). Direction: Orson Welles. Script: Orson Welles, Herman J. Mankiewicz. With Orson Welles (Citizen Kane). 7.

Citizen Kane is a much earlier study than, for example, *Patton* or *Aguirre, Wrath of God,* though made with equal psychological insight into the nature of a man obsessed with power. In Kane's case this power is activated through a newspaper, which he has made the mouthpiece of his personality and his idiosyncratic social and political views. He has been divorced by his first wife for his infidelity with Susan, a pretty but totally insignificant girl whom he is determined to make a great singer in grand opera. Kane, however, is frustrated—first, by her inability to fulfil his dreams of stardom (which is evident to all except himself) and second, by her whining refusal as his new wife to stay imprisoned with him in the extensive isolation of the great mausoleum called Xanadu, the cathedral-like monument he calls his home and which is the final manifestation of his megalomania. When without warning she leaves him and his egocentric will is frustrated, he makes an uncontrollable, insane outburst. He stumbles bemused along the corridors that lead to the small, intimate room that she made her bedroom and refuge from him, and with the lumbering, arthritic movements of some aged gorilla he proceeds to tear it apart furiously. Then, his paranoia emphasized by his multiple reflection in a chain of mirror images, he walks in a trance past a line of awestruck servants, returning to his solitude to brood over this act of desertion, a permanent affront to his ego.

THE COLLECTOR

(USA and Britain, 1965). Direction: William Wyler. Adapted from the novel by John Fowles. With Terence Stamp (Freddie), Samantha Eggar (Miranda). 3.

This rather slow-moving adaptation of John Fowles's novel features (as, for example, Chabrol's *Le Boucher*) a sociopath who, though dangerous, is somehow more likeable than his victims. Freddie, a lonely and repressed bank clerk who collects butterflies, wins substantial money on the football pools and, freed from daily work, buys a deserted mansion. He lures Miranda, the hitherto unobtainable girl he has admired from afar, to his house and makes her a prisoner in a comfortably furnished basement in the hopes that time will induce her to fall in love with him. As soon as she has become adjusted to the initial shock of her imprisonment, she begins to make such demands on him that she assumes increasing control over the situation until she actually assaults him with a spade—though he manages to lock her in before getting himself to a hospital. Left alone in the basement without heat, Miranda falls seriously ill and, shortly after his return, dies. The film ends with the implication that Freddie is already on the lookout for a substitute to abduct. Terence Stamp manages to give the character of Freddie humor as well as charm, though Wyler's direction is solidly professional rather than imaginative in a film which requires a more ambivalent touch.

COMING HOME
(USA, 1978). Direction: Hal Ashby. With Jane Fonda (Sally Hyde), Jon Voight (Luke Martin), Bruce Dern (Captain Bob Hyde). 5.

Coming Home involves the triangular relationship that develops when Sally Hyde, whose husband, Bob, is a Marine captain serving in Vietnam, falls in love with a paraplegic, Luke Martin. She helps Luke to overcome his embitterment caused by his condition and to look more outwardly to others. As a result he chains himself to the gates of a Marine Corps recruiting base in protest against the war after another, deeply disturbed friend of Sally, Billy Munson, commits suicide while in the hospital. Sally and Bob have meanwhile grown distant from each other, and the crisis comes when Bob himself returns home as an invalid. The FBI, investigating Luke on account of his passionate aversion to the war, reveals Sally's unfaithfulness to Bob, who in a fury threatens her with a rifle. Luke manages to disarm him and convince him of Sally's deep love for him. Nevertheless, Bob goes out and drowns himself. This strongly pacifist film emphasizes how human relationships suffer in time of war but does comparatively little to illuminate the real psychological issues resulting from the predicament of the injured men.

COMPULSION
(USA, 1959). Direction: Richard Fleischer. Based on the novel by Meyer Levin, which was in turn based on the Leopold-Loeb case. With Dean Stockwell (Judd Steiner), Bradford Dillman (Artie Straus), E. G. Marshall (State Attorney Horn), Orson Welles (Jonathan Wilk). 1a, 4.

In Chicago during the 1920s two wealthy law students, both homosexuals, kidnapped and murdered a young boy. They considered their motiveless crime a demonstration of their superiority as intellectuals to the common emotions of most people and to the common law. Similar to Hitchcock's *Rope*, the film attempts to cope with the fantasies of these two callous killers, with Artie ostensibly the more pathological. After their arrest, State Attorney Horn demands the death penalty, but the skillful defense put up by Wilk (who convinces the youths to plead guilty and thereby puts the responsibility for sentence solely on the judge himself, not on a jury's verdict) secures them a life sentence.

CRUISING
(USA, 1980). Direction and script: William Friedkin. Adapted from the novel by Gerald Walker. With Al Pacino (Steve Burns), Richard Cox (Stuart Richards), Don Scardino (Ted Bailey), Jay Acovone (Skip Lee), Karen Allen (Nancy). 3.

This controversial film combines extreme violence with a savage portrayal of the homosexual West Village "leather" bars in New York. After a series of stabbings police patrolman Steve Burns is assigned to work undercover in the gay district to find the sociopathic killer. Disguised as a gay, he gradually finds himself being drawn into their way of life. The principal suspect and eventually proven killer is Stuart Richards, a Columbia graduate student, though many potential murderers seem to be portrayed in the heavy leather bars. Burns, somewhat affected by his contact with the community, becomes to a degree alienated from his girlfriend, Nancy. Richards is the most overtly disturbed character in this disturbing film, with his cache of unmailed letters addressed to his long-dead father. The antihomosexual tone of Gerald Walker's novel, in which both the killer and the cop are "queer-haters," is not evident in the film. Friedkin suggests that the killer in the film is in fact straight, though in the novel he turns out to be secretly gay. The film, rather, is antipolice: it shows them committing violence against gay victims, and these victims, as in the novel, neither invite nor deserve trouble. Nor is Steve represented as antihomosexual. Nevertheless, the film was picketed by the gay community in such cities as Boston.

THE DARK PAST
(USA, 1948). Direction: Rudolf Maté. With William Holden (Al Walker), Lee J. Cobb (Dr. Collins). 4, 9.

Walker, a sociopathic killer fearful of incipient insanity and suffering from recurrent nightmares, escapes from prison and holds hostage in their home Dr. Collins, an eminent psychiatrist, and his family. Collins accepts that Walker is a "case," and the main action of the film consists of his efforts, finally successful, to resolve Walker's fears so that when the police arrive to take him back into custody he offers no resistance. Both Holden and Cobb give impressive performances, and the film makes an attempt, serious for its period, to come to terms with the psychology of the disturbed criminal.

DAVID AND LISA
(USA, 1962). Direction: Frank Perry. Based on a novel by Theodore Isaac Rubin. With Keir Dullea (David), Janet Margolin (Lisa), Howard Da Silva (Dr. Swinford). 1a, 9.

This film is set in a special school for disturbed adolescents. Though subject to nightmares and terror of being touched, David forms a relationship, based on childish rhymes, with Lisa, a schizophrenic girl. Both patients are under the care of an understanding psychiatrist, Dr. Swinford. David's evident improvement is frustrated by his mother's suddenly withdrawing him from care, with the immediate result that he defies his parents, particularly his dominating mother, and runs back to the hospital, where he cooperates with the doctor in an effort to overcome his touch-obsession. A moment of anger with Lisa, however, drives her in turn to run away. When she is found and brought back, she manages for the first time to speak to David without using rhymes, and he brings himself to take her by the hand.

This highly responsible, low-budget film, based on real case-histories, made a considerable reputation for itself at the time of its initial release. It tends, however, to put an emphasis throughout on reassurance, making the cure for deep disturbances seem too facile and comfortable. One French critic asked how David managed to achieve so neat a haircut if he cannot be touched. A more serious objection might be, Is the contribution of the love affair to the cure of these patients overstressed?

DAYS OF WINE AND ROSES
(USA 1962). Direction: Blake Edwards. With Jack Lemmon (Joe Clay), Lee Remick (Kirsten), Charles Bickford (Kirsten's father), Jack Klugman (Hungerford). 6.

Developing at first the eccentricities, and later the sheer tragedy, of alcoholism, this film tests very hard the skills of the leading players. Jack Lemmon plays Joe Clay, a fallen public relations man, and Lee Remick, his wife, Kirsten, who is the daughter of an up-tight Victorian father. In the alcoholic ward where Joe ends up with delirium tremens, he is introduced to Alcoholics Anonymous by a former addict, Hungerford. Joe faces up to, and overcomes, his addiction, but his marriage to Kirsten, in spite of the young daughter they have to look after, breaks up because Kirsten, also an alcoholic, is unable to undergo the rigors of cure. The action spans several years, and although the film starts lightly enough it changes mood, trying ruthlessly to face the problems of alcoholism, though not without melodrama and sentimentality.

DEAD OF NIGHT
(Britain, 1945). Section direction: Alberto Cavalcanti. With Michael Redgrave (ventriloquist). 2.

This composite film, dealing with macabre and supernatural subjects made by several different directors, includes one episode in which a ventriloquist is "possessed" by his dummy. Michael Redgrave gives an unforgettable performance of the man's gradually increasing subjection to the dominant and evil-minded doll, with which his art is so closely identified. This brief film was one of the best works by Cavalcanti and should be compared with the later film with a very similar theme of possession, Richard Attenborough's *Magic* (USA, 1978).

THE DEER HUNTER
(USA, 1978). Direction: Michael Cimino. Adapted from an original story. With Robert De Niro (Michael Vronsky), John Savage (Steven), Christopher Walken (Nick), Meryl Streep (Linda). 5.

The Deer Hunter should be regarded on any evaluation as a major film and as an extraordinary step forward as its maker's second feature film. His first, *Thunderbolt and Lightfoot,* was relatively small-scale, though he was scriptwriter for *Silent Running* and, more important perhaps, *Magnum Force.* Cimino seems to be aiming to signalize America's traumatic Vietnam experience through the instinctual, totally irrational reactions of a close knit, ethnic Russian community of steelworkers in Clairton, Pennsylvania. The scenes include striking steel-town vistas (marvelously photographed by Vilmos Zsigmond) set against snow-capped and forested mountain landscapes, in which the film's protagonists seek recreational deer hunting. These Americans of Russian immigrant stock are seen in the first part of the film to be closely bound together; the action begins on the wedding day of the youngest, Steven, on the eve of his departure for Vietnam along with his principal friends, Michael and Nick. Michael and Nick are unmarried.

The ethic of these men and of their close friends is comradeship through hard work, hard drinking, and the establishment of a rough, good-natured, masculine presence among their womenfolk. They are dominated by the self-contained, semireclusive personality of Michael (Robert De Niro), who is the eldest and most mature of the three and who stays apart from women, his recreative resource being the deer hunt. His ethic, like that of the rest of his group, seems to be intuitively "establishment," finding sufficient fulfillment in the industrialized society that gives him work and money and seems to take no exception to unruly masculinity when he and his friends are drunk. (It is remarkable in this American film of urban society that no cop ever makes his appearance.) Michael, however, possesses his own narrower, more demanding personal ethic, claiming that deer should never be killed except with a single, master shot. This disciplined, perhaps protofascistic, expression of willpower reflects the philosophy that man should control alike himself and his environment. It parallels the philosophy that underlies *Magnum Force.*

After the prolonged opening section of the film, with its highly ethnic emphasis—the marriage taking place in the Russian Orthodox Church; the drunken, brawling, good-natured wedding reception; the cooling off of the deer hunt after dawn—the action is projected suddenly into Vietnam (the locations used by Cimino being in Thailand). The three protagonists, Michael, Nick (now all but engaged to a Clairton girl, Linda), and Steven (the youthful husband) are all prisoners of the Vietcong, who torture them through imposing on them the death-defying game of Russian roulette, the captors betting on each shot whether the victim will blow his brains out or not. Here Michael's ethic of willpower is put to its severest test; after managing by sheer, desperate force of personality to induce his captors to put more than one bullet into the revolver and making Nick, whose nerve has by now completely collapsed, share in the new, considerably increased risk of the game, he eventually turns the more fully loaded weapon on his captors and kills them. Then he effects the rescue of the badly shocked Nick and the severely wounded Steven, getting them, in one way or another, out of the jungle and into the hands of the American medical authorities. His will has prevailed over all, captors and captives alike.

Michael returns to his community on leave, a veteran and a war hero, his nerve intact and his moral leadership reinforced. But Steven is left a legless war veteran, while Nick (in spite of Michael's attempts to salvage him) has disappeared into the lawless jungle of Saigon society, where in secret downtown hideouts is played the illegal practice of Russian roulette, using heavily paid professional "victims," on whose chances of survival hysterical gamblers place heavy wagers. Linda, alone and mourning the disappearance of the man she regards as her fiancé, takes refuge with Michael, who slowly acclimatizes himself to her need for love. But when he returns to Saigon, now in the throes of the American withdrawal, he discovers Nick to have declined into a near-catatonic condition, and he fails to stop him from blowing out his brains in his professional capacity as "victim" in the continuing game of Russian roulette. However, although his highly disciplined nature has been severely but successfully tested in war, Michael is withdrawn into himself and incapable of any warm sexual response to Linda when she tries to offer him her affection. Nevertheless, a certain potential degree of change in him is prefigured in his deliberate choice after his return from war not to shoot a deer perfectly placed to receive the single bullet from his rifle with which in the past it has always been his pride to kill his prey.

The last major sequence of the film is Nick's funeral at the Russian Orthodox Church back in Clairton and the ethnic ceremony in the church and at the graveside, which complements the wedding ceremony in the major opening sequence. The sad group of Nick's friends gather to drink coffee after the funeral and, with an instinctual need for close national identity after these grim external experiences, spontaneously and with a quiet emotional intensity, sing "God Bless America."

DESPAIR

(West Germany and France, 1978). Direction: Rainer Werner Fassbinder. Script: Tom Stoppard. Based on the novel by Vladimir Nabokov. With Dirk Bogarde (Hermann Hermann), Volker Spengler (Ardalion), Klaus Löwitsch (Felix Weber), Andrea Ferreol (Lydia Hermann). 2.

Despair is the first film to be made in English by Fassbinder, the maverick writer-director-actor who was born a year after the Second World War. The film was his first high-budget production and the first to feature an international star of the standing of Dirk Bogarde. It is, in fact, a fascinating amalgam of three highly individual talents—Nabokov, the Russian emigé novelist who wrote the novel from which the film is derived in 1934; the British dramatist Tom Stoppard, author of such precisely developed plays of the absurd as *Rosencrantz and Guildenstern are Dead, Jumpers,* and *Travesties;* and Fassbinder himself, whose specialty in the course of his comparatively brief but prolific career seems mostly to have been the portrayal of more intimate relationships, both heterosexual and homosexual, and of the sufferings resulting from exploitation, deception, and betrayal, as seen in such films as *The Bitter Tears of Petra von Kant, Fear Eats the Soul, Effi Briest,* and *The Marriage of Maria Braun.*

The film is set in Berlin in 1930, with the Nazis advancing their political power at a time of acute economic recession. It concerns the complex personality of a highly cultivated Russian emigré, Hermann Hermann, a refugee claiming aristocratic connections who has left Soviet Russia; and the latter's wife, Lydia, a sensual and somewhat stupid woman who exactly represents a communist propagandist's view of what a bourgeois lady should be like. They have lived in Germany for seven years. Hermann is a manufacturer of luxury chocolates for elite consumers, but when the film begins his prosperity is in decline, owing to Germany's political and economic uncertainty following the Wall Street crash. While contemplating his wife's persistent carnality with effetely erotic pleasure, Hermann has been undergoing increasingly frequent dissociation experiences, which give him the illusion that he is watching himself make love to her rather than actually doing so. She takes refuge in extravagant clothes and demonstrations of subservient affection for her husband, while openly indulging in childish lovemaking with her cousin Ardalion, a talentless Ukrainian painter who poses as a Bohemian artist while spending most of his time in bed with Lydia in Hermann's apartment. This small but lavish residence, full of mirrors, glazed walls, and other surfaces, is elaborately decorated in the stylish art-deco way of the 1920s. Hermann treats his wife and her lover with contemptuous patronage, almost as if relieved that their relationship absolves him of further responsibility for ministering to her pleasures. "She needs a patronizing husband," he says, "while I need a patronizable wife." Nevertheless, he has hallucinations of dominating her sexually when, sporting a black SS-like officer's cap, he sits in his bedside armchair watching her kiss the shiny black jackboots he imagines himself to be wearing as he towers over her.

Hermann is totally egocentric, a man with dubious artistic pretensions. Nabokov's novel makes no reference to politics, whereas the film stresses the overweening presence of the Nazis both in the streets (standing in the windows of a Jewish store, for example) and even among the senior staff at Hermann's chocolate factory. When he seeks a merger with another chocolate manufacturer in Düsseldorf, he is rejected tersely by the Nazi owner and told to keep his "fucking sheckels," which reveals that Hermann is identified as a Jew. The despair that gradually envelops Hermann is therefore, it would seem, in part due to his racial connections as well as the dubious nature of his domestic situation and the decline of his business.

These tensions persuade him to take an extraordinary step. By a Freudian slip of the tongue when telling his wife of his forthcoming trip to Düsseldorf to effect a *merger*, she thinks that he says *murder*, and perhaps indeed he does. In the maze of glazed walls, mirrors, corridors, and revolving doors which characterize the various environments through which Hermann seems to pass, he encounters an ill-shaven and near-destitute tramp, Felix Weber, in whom he claims to detect a remarkable resemblance to himself. It is an illusion, perhaps inspired by a silent film melodrama he saw with his wife and Ardalion, in which twin brothers feature, respectively, criminal and policeman, one killing the other in a final confrontation. Insuring his life for a considerable sum and posing as a film actor who needs a double for his work, he finally succeeds in bribing Felix to go along with an elaborate plan that he only partially explains. His scheme is to exchange identities, kill Felix, and then have Lydia collect the insurance money and join him in a new life in Switzerland. Lydia herself is easily deceived by a further fabrication by Hermann that he has an identical twin brother (hitherto quite unknown to her), who is set on self-destruction and whose convenient voluntary suicide in the guise of Hermann would enable them to live in comfort on the insurance money. Lydia is quite happy that this is merely an insurance swindle, and she is only too eager to play her part as the tragic widow. "'I want to give you the gift of my death,'" Hermann tells her his "brother" has offered. Hermann bribes Felix with a thousand marks to meet him in a lonely spot. After exchanging clothes with the victim, Hermann grooms Felix into some sort of likeness to himself. This done, he shoots him in the back and leaves at once for Switzerland, believing he has committed the perfect murder, namely, that in which the victim kills himself.

The deception, of course, entirely fails, for although the body is found to be carrying Hermann's papers, it has no real resemblance to Hermann; in addition, Hermann neglected to remove Felix's walking stick, which bears Felix's name. This the police discover near the body. The Swiss press cover this strange murder story in some detail, revealing that Hermann is identified as the murderer, and it seems to him in his Swiss retreat that he is being watched with gathering suspicion by residents in the succession of pensions where he stays in a lakeside village, still wearing the tattered clothes of the tramp and posing now as a cellist. Realizing his defeat, Hermann declines into total, insane despair; his superior manner, his contemptuous elitism, his cultured façade all disappear, and he finally takes on the unshaven appearance of the man he once believed to be his double. Hermann is Felix; Felix is Hermann. Perhaps there was even a hint of homosexuality in their final, destructive relationship, for Hermann had insisted on seeing Felix naked and in their last moments together had trimmed his hair, his fingernails, and even his toenails in the fervor of his attention to every detail of this merging of identity. When he is finally traced and arrested, he resumes his former role of film actor and descends to meet his captors with all the dignity of Norma Desmond in the closing scene in *Sunset Boulevard.* "Good people," he says, "We are making a film here." Fassbinder surely offers a Brechtian touch during the final moments in this film.

The theme of the double runs throughout this film, beginning with the substantial extracts from the silent film melodrama. There are, indeed, interesting parallels to Dostoevsky's story The Double.[17] The theme of betrayal and "double-crossing" is also recurrent in this film, including in the inventions of Hermann about his past, his family, and his wealthy connections. (His mother's dowry, he says, was her weight in gold coins, but the coins turn out to be gold-wrapped chocolates.) In a perceptive criticism of the film Tom Milne complains that Stoppard's and Fassbinder's elaborations on Nabokov's story turned it from a fascinating murder-mystery into a psychotic study, in which the victim with the double name (Hermann Hermann) declines from dissociation to ultimate schizophrenia.[18]

Fassbinder's first film in English is characterized by its complications, and a single viewing is inadequate to detect the symbolic elements involved, such as the significance of Ardalion's bad picture of two roses and a briar pipe, which is set in a landscape that so haunts Hermann's imagination and which has a swastika on its reverse side. Lighting and the use of constant close-ups and a roving, restless camera enhance the unnerving visual emphases of this film. Nobody keeps still for long, and the impressive performance by Dirk Bogarde—so often seen with but half of his face lit as he peers out of the frame—is one of the best he has given in a distinguished career.

THE DEVILS

(Britain, 1971). Direction and Script: Ken Russell. Adapted from the book *The Devils of Loudun* (1952), by Aldous Huxley, and from the play *The Devils* (1961), written by John Whiting. With Vanessa Redgrave (Sister Jeanne), Oliver Reed (Urbain Grandier). 2.

Set in seventeenth-century France during the reign of Louis XIII, Huxley's book was based on an authentic case of sexually induced group "possession" in a convent of youthful nuns, most of whom were the younger daughters of aristocratic families who had pressed them into entering nunneries whether they had a religious calling or not. Father Grandier, a priest by profession but a lecher by inclination, figures as the principal object of their desire, but the film also stresses his political activity—a struggle to preserve some measure of local self-government in opposition to Cardinal Richelieu's campaign to subject provincial towns to the rigors of his regime in the name of the weak and homosexually self-indulgent King. Sister Jeanne of the Angels, a deformed but violently sex-starved Mother Superior still in her twenties, sees Grandier in a vision in the guise of Christ on the Cross and licks the blood from his wounds. But she jealously denounces him, the man she wants as her confessor, when she discovers that he has contracted an illicit marriage.

Under Sister Jeanne's influence the nuns go collectively mad, possessed (it is thought) by devils, stripping themselves naked and cavorting about erotically in public and causing grave scandal. The exorcist, Father Barre, who is sent in to deal with the case, tortures them sexually and so goads them into ever-greater exhibitionism, while Grandier is arrested, tortured, and burned alive as a sorcerer in league with the Devil himself. The film develops its own innate hysteria, resulting in time in hideous overstatement and abandoning all the restraint of Whiting's play. The exhibitionism of the naked nuns is turned into an erotic charade in the effort to make the point that these young noblewomen, obsessed by desire for the attentions of the man they want to become their confessor, should never have seen the inside of a convent.

The associated phenomena of possession by demons and the practice of witchcraft, widely considered in the past to be deliberately undertaken by women who were agents of the devil, has been presented in certain films, for example, Carl Dreyer's *Day of Wrath* (Denmark, 1943) and Raymond Rouleau's *Sourcières de Salem* (France and East Germany, 1957), scripted by Jean-Paul Sartre as a loose adaptation of Arthur Miller's play *The Crucible*. Both films were set in the seventeenth century, and the latter was based on the notorious trial in Salem, Massachusetts, in 1692. Films concerned with the trial of Joan of Arc—most notably, Carl Dreyer's *Passion of Joan of Arc* (France, 1928) and Robert Bresson's *Trial of Joan of Arc* (France, 1962)—tend to accept that the voices and visions she experienced came to her from God because the church that had once condemned her finally canonized her in 1919. But it should be remembered that for Shakespeare, when writing *Henry VI, Part One* around 1591, she is represented as a courtesan and a witch possessed by the devil.

DIRTY HARRY
(USA, 1971). Direction: Don Siegel. With Clint Eastwood (Inspector Harry Callahan), Andy Robinson (killer). 4, 7.

This film contains one of Clint Eastwood's most impressive performances as Inspector Harry Callahan, the rogue cop who instinctively wages a personal vendetta against violent crime and is determined to violently avenge the innocent and destroy, in his turn, all those who practice violence against society. In *Dirty Harry* the criminal at large is a roof-top sniper, whose successive killings are causing the district attorney grave political embarrassment at city hall. The situation is aggravated by Callahan's unorthodox tactics in tracking down the sociopath. Callahan seems masochistically to accept the martyrdom his job thrusts upon him; the police department deliberately give him the most noxious cases to solve. But his utter disgust with the worst in human nature as he understands it, either in the criminal or in the timeserving values of those who try to exercise authority over him, drives him in the end to toss his badge into the river where the body of the killer floats after the final shoot-out. We are left to wonder, What will Callahan do, what will he be like, without his vendetta, without the obsessive confrontation with crime, which made up his entire existence?

DR. JEKYLL AND MR. HYDE
(USA, 1931). Direction and Script: Reuben Mamoulian. Based on the story by Robert Louis Stevenson. With Fredric March (Jekyll-Hyde), Miriam Hopkins (Ivy Pearson), Rose Hobart (Muriel Carew). 2.

This film would not normally find a place here because it would appear to be at first sight wholly a fantasy-fable, not a psychological study of insanity. However, stories of this kind (like *Frankenstein, Faust, Dracula, The Turn of the Screw,* Poe's *Henry Wilson,* or Wilde's *Portrait of Dorian Grey*) frequently involve themes of great psychological significance, and this is especially true of Stevenson's story. His "shilling shocker," as he called it, originated in a dream and was written in a white heat of creative energy within three days. Its immediate success when published in 1886 has been sustained ever since. Stevenson was concerned with the duality (good and evil) in humankind and created this extreme, nightmareish story as a projection of this theme.

Like Mary Shelley's obsessive scientist, Frankenstein, Stevenson's Jekyll is a brilliant and distinguished medical man who cannot leave natural man alone. As a result of his secret experiments. Jekyll transforms himself into the evil monster, Hyde, condemned to his overriding desires to murder and destroy. In Stevenson's story any indulgence in sexual lust and violence is only vaguely hinted at—

the now respectable Jekyll was once "wild" in his youth, and there is a later reference to Hyde's "vile life." What is remarkable about Mamoulian's striking film version is the total transformation of Stevenson's story in the direction of Jekyll-Hyde's sexual libido. The still youthful doctor, played by Fredric March with bounding energy, makes no secret that he can barely wait to possess his future bride and resents bitterly and openly her father's insistence on what seems to him to be a prolonged period of engagement. He also finds difficult his resistance to the physical attractions of the prostitute, Ivy Pearson (played so uninhibitedly by Miriam Hopkins in the days just before the clampdown of the American film censorship code), whom (as Jekyll) he rescues from assault in the dark depths of London's Soho. Hyde's sexual exploitation and eventual murder of this girl, as well as the tragedy of Jekyll's final, totally involuntary changeover to Hyde and his assault on the girl he (as Jekyll) so genuinely loves, transforms the nature of Hyde's violence as originally presented by Stevenson, who wrote during the period of Victorian restraint.

So popular was the Jekyll-Hyde theme, there were no fewer than eight silent film versions (mainly American and British) of the story from 1908 onwards, followed by five in the sound period, including those with Fredric March (1931), Spencer Tracy (1941), and Jack Palance (1968) as Jekyll-Hyde.

DR. MABUSE, THE GAMBLER

(Germany, 1922) and *The Last Testament of Dr. Mabuse* (Germany, 1932). Direction: Fritz Lang. With Rudolph Klein-Rogge (Mabuse). 7.

Both Dr. Mabuse films are among the most celebrated melodramas of power-madness to come from pre-Hitler Germany. In the first film (a two-part feature, which Lang claimed to be "a document about the current world")[19] he was represented as a criminal-genius who used multiple disguises (one as a psychiatrist) in his attempt to found an empire of crime in the anarchy of the postwar world. Adept at hypnotizing his victims in his thirst for power over men and women alike, he seeks to dominate a world without law. When he is finally exposed and defeated, he becomes, like Caligari before him, a raving lunatic confined in a secret cellar. As Siegfried Kracauer pointed out, the film "attempts to show how closely tyranny and chaos are interrelated."[20] The brochure accompanying the film says, "Mankind, swept about and trampled down in the wake of war and revolution, takes revenge for years of anguish by indulging in lusts . . . and by passively or actively surrendering to crime."[21] It should be kept in mind that the film was made during a period when Germany was undergoing galloping inflation, and when Berlin was becoming the great center in Europe for every kind of sexual indulgence.

When in 1932 Lang (who had Jewish blood) revived the character of Mabuse, he gave him certain traits which, he claimed when he subsequently came to America, were derived from Hitler. A noted psychiatrist, Dr. Baum, is kept in a state of permanent hypnosis by Mabuse, who is his patient and an inmate in the asylum of which Baum is the director. Mabuse occupies his time planning the destruction of civilization. As Mabuse's alter ego in the world outside the asylum, Baum heads the great underground organization dedicated to the achievement of Mabuse's will. When Mabuse dies, Baum regards himself as Mabuse reincarnated. When he in turn is exposed by the police, he becomes totally insane and is confined in Mabuse's former cell. In 1943, ten years after he made the film, Lang said: "This film was made as an allegory to show Hitler's processes of terrorism. Slogans and doctrines of the Third Reich have been put into the mouths of criminals in the film." The film was banned by Goebbels, and Lang escaped from Germany. An uncut print survived in France.[22]

DR. STRANGELOVE; OR, HOW I LEARNED TO STOP WORRYING AND LOVE THE BOMB.
(Britain, 1964). Direction and coscripting: Stanley Kubrick. With Peter Sellers (Group Captain Lionel Mandrake, President Muffley, Dr. Strangelove), George C. Scott (General ["Buck"] Turgidson), Sterling Heyden (General Jack D. Ripper), Keenan Wynn (Colonel ["Bat"] Guano), Slim Pickens (Major T. J. ["King"] Kong). 5, 7.

Kubrick's courageous satiric fantasy of the basic insanity of the cold war's weaponry inventors and controllers sprang directly from the hysteria of the 1960s and the paranoia about the nuclear bomb and the ultimate forces of destruction poised between the USA and the USSR. In what he called his "nightmare comedy," Kubrick posits a network of insane individuals who happen at one and the same time to be in a position to initiate the destruction of civilization and the human species without the desire or authority of either government. Ripper (convinced his "vital fluids" are being secretly contaminated through a communist conspiracy) goes insane, seals off his Air Force base, and launches an all-out B-52 attack on Russia. For complex technical reasons it proves impossible for the US president to recall them. Ripper kills himself, convinced of a communist takeover. The USA and USSR presidents, communicating over the "hot line," unite ineffectually in an endeavor to destroy the fatal aircraft before a nuclear bomb is dropped, and the Russian ambassador, summoned to the vast Pentagon War Room as a witness, reveals that the Russians have an ultimate weapon, the doomsday device which, impervious to human intervention, is programed to destroy the world in the event that a hostile nuclear bomb explodes on USSR territory.

Meanwhile, one lone plane, its radio contact destroyed, still flies at treetop height to one of its assigned targets. It is piloted by another crazed commandant, the Texan T. J. ("King") Kong, who relishes his suicide mission. Sitting astride the bomb while whooping like a cowboy in a rodeo show, he sails earthward to trigger off what will become the destruction of mankind. Back in Washington the USA president's scientific adviser reveals a plan to save a very select few. This is Dr. Strangelove, an ex-Nazi who is entirely insane in his love for weapons of total destruction. He claims that a few selected members of the "master race" (at the very thought of which, Strangelove's metal arm raises itself in automatic Nazi salute) can survive the radiation underground, where they and their descendants would remain a hundred years, breeding from what it is hoped will be sexually attractive women.

While Kubrick's film is itself preeminently sane, its characters are either unnervingly insane or, like the two presidents and their military staff, utterly incompetent. As the reductio ad absurdum of the nuclear arms race, the film is terrifyingly funny. Its realization in the 1960s warrants the highest tribute paid to Kubrick and his creative team. The final irony is the semiconcealed perverse sexuality of the names given the more insane of the characters, who collectively bring about world destruction.

DRESSED TO KILL

(USA, 1980). Direction and Script: Brian De Palma. With Michael Caine (Dr. Robert Elliott), Angie Dickinson (Kate Miller), Nancy Allen (Liz Blake), Keith Gordon (Peter Miller). 3.

This psychological melodrama, with its recurrent echoes of Hitchcock's *Psycho* (including an opening showerbath sequence of sensual indulgence) features a transsexual psychiatrist who, in his male form, detests women to a homicidal degree. Kate Miller, one of Elliott's patients who rouses his hatred by making advances to him, is razor-slashed to death by Elliott—disguised as a blonde woman—thus disposing of a key female star player early in the film (a similarity to *Psycho*). Elliott in female disguise adopts the name Bobbi and poses as one of his own patients, even recording messages to himself (as the male psychiatrist) demanding treatment to be freed from loathed confinement in a male body.

Meanwhile Peter, Kate's son (a precocious genius in media electronics), forms an unlikely but amusing alliance with a high-class prostitute, Liz Blake (who had happened to witness Kate's murder, and is by way of being a suspect) to discover the murderer. Peter contrives to rescue Liz when she is threatened with an attack by the blonde killer, and reveals to her that he has been making filmed records of all Elliott's patients as they have arrived for consultations, including film of the blonde herself. Liz and Peter break into Elliott's office to trace the identity of the blonde; but when Liz is forced to resort to assumed seduction to distract Elliott's attention, her actions only lead to a physical assault by Elliott made in his blonde disguise. Another psychiatrist, Dr. Levy, from whom Elliott as Bobbi has sought treatment, provides the concluding explanation (another parallel to *Psycho*) that Elliott, the transsexual, is driven to insane homicidal rage by any woman who excites the masculine element that he detests in his make-up. A gratuitous coda to the film is Liz's nightmare that Elliott has escaped from a mental institution in order to terrorize her. The film is layered with trick devices to confuse the viewer momentarily and set up red herrings, and technical devices such as roving camera movement and split-screen images give a superficial panache to what is in the end the exploitation of a case of psychological disturbance in order to produce a sensationalistic horror film.

EASY RIDER
(USA, 1969). Direction: Dennis Hopper. Script: Dennis Hopper, Peter Fonda, Terry Southern. With Dennis Hopper (Billy), Peter Fonda (Wyatt), Jack Nicolson (George Hanson). 6.

Their money made from selling cocaine near the Mexican border, Billy and Wyatt set out to motorcycle to New Orleans, encountering on their way various communes and eccentric individuals. One of these is an alcoholic civil defense lawyer, George Hanson, who secures their joint release from a Texas jail and becomes a fellow traveler with them to New Orleans. Their wild appearance leads a group of extremists to form a lynching party to attack them at night, and Hanson is clubbed to death. Billy and Wyatt reach New Orleans intact, but have a bad LSD trip with a couple of prostitutes in a cemetary. During their further journey in the direction of Florida they are summarily and without provocation shot to death on the road by a truck driver and his lynch-minded companion.

Described by Peter Fonda as "cinéma-vérité in allegory terms," the film is an exposure of what human habitation has done to ruin the magnificence of the American scenery down south and of how man's aspirations contain the seeds of his self-ruin. Urban civilization, it would seem, has betrayed the dreams of the pioneers. But Billy and Wyatt are themselves drug pushers and drug users, escapists searching for an illusory freedom from their dissatisfactions with life, only in their turn to be destroyed by man's inhumanity to man and his inability to accept the "outsider."

8½
(Italy, 1962). Direction: Federico Fellini. With Marcello Mastroianni (Guido), Anouk Aimée (Guido's wife), Sandra Milo (Guido's mistress), Claudia Cardinale (Guido's potential star), Edra Gale (Saraghina). 1a, 3.

JULIET OF THE SPIRITS
(Italy, 1965). Direction: Federico Fellini. With Giulietta Masina (Giulietta, Juliet), Sandra Milo (Suzy), Mario Pisu (Juliet's husband), Lou Gilbert (Juliet's grandfather), Caterina Boratto (Juliet's mother), Sylvia Koscina (Silva), Valentina Cortese (Valentina), Valeska Gert (Bhishma). 1a, 3.

Both of these films deal with mental and emotional stress; *8½*, with the actual nervous breakdown and partial hospitalization of a celebrated film director who cannot fulfil his obligations to start on a new subject; *Juliet of the Spirits*, with the hallucinatory experiences of a middle-aged woman who lives in a state of self-doubt and acute depression, whose husband is unfaithful, and whose relatives and friends take on a menacing aspect of superiority, which threatens her identity and self-confidence. In her case she cures herself, but only after a period of intense, menopausal suffering, which forces her to take stock of her whole life, past and present, in the wealthy, self-indulgent, sophisticated, and pretentious upper-class circle in which she moves.

Fellini has always denied that *8½* is entirely autobiographical, in spite of the closeness of the subject to his own profession. Since he has also said, however, that "making films is my psychoanalysis,"[23] there is good reason to accept that Fellini has put much of himself into Guido and his psychological dilemma, which brings him very near to, if not actually into, a state of breakdown.

Fellini gained his initial experience in films by working closely as an assistant in scriptwriting and direction to the Italian neo-realists, especially Rossellini and Lattuada. With Rossellini he learned something of the art of improvisation before the camera, and his scripts for Rossellini's *Il Miracolo* ("The Miracle") and *Francis, God's Jester* both dealt with what might be called insanity—in *Il Miracolo* the ignorant and simpleminded peasant woman, who believes that she has conceived Christ after being seduced, and the simpleminded little brothers associated with St. Francis, who behave like God's fools. In 1943, while only twenty-three years old and still assisting other directors, Fellini married the young actress, Giulietta Masina, one year his junior. This association was to prove invaluable to Fellini when he became fully established as a director in his own right and made films that became personal in subject to them both.

Guido, like Giulietta in *Juliet of the Spirits* becomes subject to pressures that prove unbearable—from his producer, his scriptwriter, the studio publicity representatives, and the journalists, who are all intent on making him reveal his intentions in his next, only too imminent film. He is equally subject to pressures from the women in his life, his sardonic wife, his mistress, of whose prettily sexual tricks he has long since tired, and the many actresses who are pestering him for parts in his new film. His one desire is to escape from them all—but they pursue him to the fashionable spa to which he retires for peace and prebreakdown treatment. His hallucinations turn largely on his childhood at a Catholic school in the care of priests who punish him for his childish escapades and sexual curiosity. His inadequacies with the women who are already in his life or who are trying to be so conjure up boyhood memories of being spoiled by his mother and the servants. Now he compensates by imagining himself the one, sole male in a harem peopled by the women who are trying in one way or another to master him. In his dreams it is he who commands them—with a long whip.

Dragged back to actuality by the insistent presence of his producer, he is physically hauled by the film company representatives to a press reception held on the open location, where a vast rocket-site set has been constructed. Here he imagines crawling under the table on the speakers' rostrum and shooting himself. But, like Juliet is to do, he recovers himself, orders the dismantling of the useless set, which represents for him the bondage of a misconceived and useless subject, and, with a positive gesture, takes up the director's loudspeaker to supervise a circuslike chain dance of all the "characters" in his life, including his dead parents and a group of marching clowns with musical instruments, with whom he himself, as a child dressed up in a fanciful uniform, parades as the lights go down and the film ends.

Fellini, like Bergman, has come to weave film subjects out of his own psychological preoccupations. They reflect a surreal world that moves in and out of the actualities of human experience, with its subconscious and irrational interests and memories, the objective merging with the subjective and the eccentric with the exotic. This is very much the case with *Juliet of the Spirits,* a film he said he made out of his deep affection for his wife.

Juliet lives mostly alone with her maidservants since her husband is always making excuses to be away from home and she has no children of her own. Her neat and beautiful house is set amid trees on a small estate by the sea. It is a dream house, both inside and out, a highly decorated and luxurious dollhouse. Her two maids are like acolytes—attentive and polite but nevertheless gliding around her like spies, at once familiar and remote, knowing too much about her, full of intimate curiosity. Her tall and handsome husband, Giorgio, is a shadowed, depersonalized figure, seldom more than a silhouette; he is kindly, polite, and mildly attentive when he is there. Juliet, however, unlike the rest of the people in this film, is a typically solid, well-dressed, and wholly bourgeois figure; even in the wildest, most flamboyant moments in this exotic film, she never seems to lose this quality of ordinariness. She remains rational, but bemused, never quite able to keep pace with what is going on around her. But her emotional insecurity makes her depressed and above all vulnerable. As Fellini put it, "Where there is a vacuum of the soul, the spirits may move in",[24]—evil spirits, mischievous spirits, tempters and betrayers.

Juliet's circle is made up of people far more self-assured than herself—her beautiful but overpowering mother, her pregnant sister, her butterfly stepsister, all of them extravagantly extroverted. They seem to Juliet always to be probing, criticizing, urging her to become, or at least to act, as sophisticated as themselves. They draw her into such eccentric and disturbing pastimes as improvised seances and table-tapping or attendance at sessions of fashionable gurus like the maestro Genius and the strange, sexless Oriental medium, Bhishma, who produce the mumbo-jumbo craved by the rich whom the Catholic religion can no longer keep entertained. Of Juliet they say, "She is very receptive," and certainly the spirits seem to be making a bid to possess her at a seance which becomes the major event of her wedding anniversary, which her husband appears almost to have forgotten. Other people who move in to shape her way of life—her cynical physician, her elderly lawyer, her female psychiatrist—all weigh her down with professional advice she seems unable to take in.

Juliet is half-fascinated, half-repelled by her nearby neighbour, the wealthy Suzy, whose exotic practices and presumed sexual orgies rouse Juliet's excited curiosity to the point of outright hallucination. As Juliet dozes under the sun by the sea, Suzy's beach caravan, a large mobile tent, arrives like some strange pagan procession. She dreams of an old man emerging from the sea, hauling on an endless rope, which he finally leaves her to pull. Then she sees a mysterious barge full of half-naked figures, images conjured up by Suzy's sensually beautiful presence. When she awakens, Juliet finds the real Suzy enticing her sister's two small twin children, dressed identically in frilly white dresses, with little gifts.

Valentina, her stepsister, takes her to an elaborately staged session with the medium, Bhishma, who, falling into a trance, advocates sensuality after the manner of the fashionable *Kama Sutra.* Bhishma's oriental aides pantomime a ceremonial accompaniment to her prophetic moans and utterances. Juliet is affected by it all; the vacuum is being filled by alien and unhealthy spirits. "I feel

I have lost everything," she confesses. Thunder and lightning accompany Bhishma's seance, and Juliet returns home to find that Giorgio has brought an equally depersonalized male friend as a houseguest. He is Don Rafaele, a middle-aged, well-behaved Spanish Valentino figure, towards whom Juliet feels some kind of sublimated attraction. As a romantic, idealized seducer, he sanguinely offers Juliet the liquor of oblivion. In actuality, spurred on by her mother, she employs an enquiry agent (another grotesque figure, who moves around disguised as a priest) to spy on her husband's encounters with his youthful mistress.

Juliet is constantly projected back into the past, into the period of her convent schooling and the disruption caused by her eccentric grandfather, an atheist and enthusiastic pioneer of flying, who is in love with a circus bareback rider (linked now in Juliet's disturbed mind with Suzy, and played by the same actress, Sandra Milo). As a small girl she was brought up to think of her grandfather as in league with the Devil, especially when he interrupted a convent stage play about a Christian martyrdom in which Juliet was playing a child-martyr who is grilled in the fiery furnace of a pyre. Grandfather had insisted on rescuing his "little beefsteak" from the flames of hell.

Juliet finally decides to explore Suzy's exotic establishment and Suzy's cat's arrival gives Juliet the excuse she needs. (We have heard earlier that cats are supposed to represent a bad influence.) Taking the cat with her, Juliet walks warily through the gates leading into Suzy's estate and enters the house of sensual delights, which, as she imagines it, is peopled by strange and haunted characters—a fetishist, a crazy girl addicted to suicide attempts, and exotic young men who appear to minister to Suzy's insatiable sexual demands in her vast bedroom, with its mirrors and a chute sloping down to a bathing pool below. Outside in the park she has a gondola-elevator leading up to a woodland love nest, constructed in the treetops. Juliet, a thoroughly alien presence among such decadence, tries her best to enter into the spirit of it all. She is even offered Suzy's Indian godson as a consort, but a sudden burst of guilt—a flash of childhood hellfire—sends her scurrying back home.

Here she experiences a climax of guilt-ridden images; lines of crouching, hooded nuns haunt her in the background. Her androgynous woman psychiatrist attempts to give her sound advice, such as "You identify too much with your problems" and talks to her about psychodramas. Juliet even attempts to visit her husband's mistress; this, however, fails, and she is forced to resort to the telephone, only to be rebuffed for her pains. Claiming he does not feel well, Giorgio departs on a private vacation. Apparently, things are not quite right between him and his mistress; he needs, he says, a rest in order to think out his position.

Juliet shuts herself away in the house; she orders the shutters of the windows to be closed. She decides to confront her phantoms boldly and to suffer no more advice from anyone. The phantoms crowd in on her with their manifold temptations, but she manages to oust them. "You no longer frighten me," she cries, encouraged by the positive memory of one single fantasy—her atheistic grandfather, the man who turned sin into fun. "I'm your invention, too," he warns her, and vanishes.

Juliet's sense of guilt disappears, and with it her depression. She no longer feels an absolute need to hold onto her husband. Savoring her independence, she goes out to walk in the sunshine amid the trees. She even allows her spirits to stay with her—she simply accepts them now because she is no longer in awe of them.

With its extravagant designs by Piero Gherardi, its color cinematography by Gianni De Venanzo, and its music by Nino Rota, this film is a masterpiece of the so-called baroque cinema. It is more extravagant than anything else Fellini did up to then and more imaginative in mingling the light with the serious, humor with sadness, gaiety with the macabre. It was more successful than *Satyricon* or *Casanova* because of its more personal nature. *Juliet of the Spirits,* however, had excited widely divergent reactions—condemnation for excessive, even vulgar, self-indulgence; and praise from those responsive to its flights of fancy, which are soundly rooted in their observation of the psychology of a certain kind of woman, whom Giulietta Masina embodies so well. The film proves to be a remarkable study of the obsessive images experienced by a woman approaching menopause and suffering from acute depression and a consequent sense of inferiority and inadequacy in the socially sophisticated circle of her husband, her relatives, and those who pass for her friends. It is also the study of a dependent woman's step towards liberation from that dependence—from her husband, from her friends, from the conventions of her society.

Said Fellini, "although the film lends itself to esoteric, psychoanalytical interpretations, I would like it to be seen in a simpler light: humane and imaginative."[25] And elsewhere: "The majority of people come to marriage completely unprepared because this event has been made into a myth, told in an inexact and treacherous manner. . . . I don't believe that marriage is what it is superficially thought to be, and I am certain that it is a matter of far deeper rapport. Thus in my films I have called attention to the degeneration, the caricature of this rapport. . . . The independence of women is the theme of the future."[26]

EL

(Mexico, 1952). Direction and coscripting; Luis Buñuel. With Arturo de Cordova (Francisco), Delia Garces (Gloria), Luis Beristain (Raoul). 3.

El belongs to the group of films Buñuel made in Mexico during his second, postwar career as a filmmaker, starting in 1946 and lasting until his increasing involvement in production in Europe, which began in 1955. He endeavored to give his own particular interpretative twist to the novelettish subjects he was initially forced to make in Mexico until he was reestablished with an international reputation. His budgets were low; his performers often indifferent. In spite of this, *El* is a markedly Buñuel subject—the story of the paranoiac jealousy of a wealthy man, Francisco, when he marries for the first time in middle life. Buñuel introduces every significant psychological implication that he can. The performance by Arturo de Cordova seems at first scarcely helpful, but his middle-aged, Spanish-style, matinée-idol appearance and manner add their own touch of irony to the fearful acts his mental condition causes him to perpetrate.

Buñuel's lifelong anticlericalism and distaste for bourgeois convention (used so often, he has emphasized, to give the cover of gentility for what is ugliest in human nature) are very evident in this film, for the wealthy Francisco is as much a pillar of the church as he is a pillar of local society in Mexico City.

The film in fact begins in Francisco's church. As a lay attendant, he is assisting at the priestly ceremony of the washing of the feet of the poor. He performs dedicatedly because he is a foot fetishist. While studying the feet of the adolescents to whom the priest is attending, his eye wanders and catches sight of the neatly shod and delicately enticing foot of a well-dressed girl in the congregation. The moment the ceremony is over, he attempts to follow her and suffers acute frustration when the parish priest detains him and she slips away.

Francisco is next seen following up another of his obsessions—the vain pursuit of possession of a large tract of land in the provinces, to which he feels entitled. His lawyer fails him and is dismissed. Francisco also dismisses, quite summarily, a maidservant who works in his mansion because he has caught her receiving (albeit unwillingly) the attentions of his favorite manservent, Pedro, on whom he relies for "mothering" when adversity sends him to bed with a headache.

His memories of the girl with the lovely feet draw him back to the church. He eventually rediscovers her there but at the same time finds out she is engaged to Raoul, a civil engineer whom he knows well. He exploits this acquaintance to invite Raoul and his fiancée, whose name is Gloria, to a dinner party, at which he speaks most eloquently about the instinctive nature of love. "Love must spring up by force," he declares. Afterwards, he manages to isolate Gloria and press his suit upon her. Meanwhile, Pedro has trouble in an anteroom, and dirty smoke belches out into the salon—a typically Buñuel touch of ironic symbolism.

There is a time lapse. Gloria meets Raoul, whom she has jilted in order to marry the wealthy, aristocratic Francisco. Raoul, however, seems to bear no resentment; he senses all is not well with her and offers her his help should she ever need it. This becomes the framework for the rest of the film—Gloria makes Raoul her confidant, telling him of her various experiences since her marriage, which are shown in the film as straightforward flashbacks.

Even on their honeymoon, Francisco has shown unnatural jealousy of Raoul and other men whom he claims have pursued her. The honeymoon is spent in the region where Francisco is vainly trying to claim rights of property. Here, another old friend of hers excites his abnormal and publicly expressed jealousy, especially when it is found that he occupies the room next door to theirs. It is now that Francisco shows the sadism latent in his nature. He gives a sudden thrust with a knitting needle through the keyhole of the connecting door between the two rooms (fortunately to no effect). He even stages a fight with the man in the corridor. Angered, Francisco shouts at his bride, "I'll never forgive you."

During a birthday party at their home, Francisco gives Gloria a gift while continuing to express jealousy over the way in which she dances with his new attorney, whom he has pressed her to entertain. The priest, a constant guest at Francisco's house, sides with him in criticizing the perfectly natural and correct way in which the couple are dancing—the priest and Francisco prefer that the bodies are seen not to touch. In jealous rage Francisco locks his wife out of his bedroom as well as his office and refuses to speak to her during meals; however, the sight of her feet when he bends down to pick up a dropped napkin momentarily softens him. He makes allies out of her mother as well as the priest, both of whom scold her when she turns to them for help and advice. Knowing of this, Francisco suddenly confronts her with a pistol, which he fires directly at her. Although it is loaded with blank shot, she falls out of sheer shock. Suddenly contrite, Francisco begs her forgiveness.

Persuasively, he offers to take her out, only to lead her to the top of a lofty bell tower. With a commanding echo in his voice, he proclaims; "I like it here. These people down there are mere worms. I could crush them. Mankind fills me with loathing. If I were God, I would destroy them." Then, turning suddenly on Gloria, he shouts, "I could punish you as well; I could hurl you down." He leaps at her, but she manages with a quick movement to elude his clumsy action and escapes down the steps of the bell tower. She rushes to Raoul for help and advice, but he sees fit to warn her, "It seems to me that you enjoy suffering, Gloria."

When Francisco accuses her of meeting Raoul, she in turn violently accuses him of abusing her. Francisco immediately collapses under her purely verbal attack—it is the first time she has confronted him with fierce and direct opposition. Breaking down totally, he rouses his manservant, Pedro, in the man's bedroom and weeps in his presence, sitting head in hands on the bed. Pedro is respectfully solicitous. "Would you kill her!" demands Francisco as if he were Othello addressing Iago. Pedro desires no such role. "And spend the rest of my life in jail," he says. "No." Leaving him, Francisco walks up the grand staircase of his mansion in a zig-zag fashion. He sits down on one of the steps, drumming noisily on the bannisters with a loose stair rod. The drumming wakes Gloria.

Francisco becomes desperate over the failing fortunes of his land claim. He is unable to compose the right letters, seeks Gloria's help, and then as forcefully rejects it. She continues stoically to put up with all this impossible behavior. Francisco then appeals to her sense of pity, tries to shoot himself, and then collapses. Late at night, he arises in his room in order to prepare the instruments of his final revenge upon her—rope, scissors, cottonwool, and needle and thread. He enters her room like Othello creeping up on Desdemona, but when he clumsily attempts to bind her she awakens and screams, rousing the household. He rushes back to the security of his room and collapses on the floor, weeping.

The next morning, Gloria is gone. His jealousy roused to fever point, Francisco sets out in pursuit of her, who he is certain has gone to Raoul. He is beset now by hallucinations that he is being mocked, first by a concierge he questions about Raoul's whereabouts. When he vainly pursues a young couple into his parish church, in belief that they are the guilty pair, he imagines he is being mocked once again by the whole congregation and even by the priest himself in the midst of conducting the service. Distraught, he sets upon the priest—the sign that he has finally collapsed into madness.

The epilogue to the film comes many years later, when Gloria and Raoul are married and go on a visit to the Catholic asylum where Francisco is confined. He appears calm and even cured, but as he leaves them after their brief visit he can be seen weaving his way from side to side, just as he had done years before on the grand staircase of his mansion.

THE EMPEROR JONES
(USA, 1933). Direction: Dudley Murphy. Script: Du Bose Hayward. Based on the play by Eugene O'Neill. With Paul Robeson (Brutus Jones). 7.

An early sound film of Paul Robeson's magnificent performance as Brutus Jones; the play was originally written by O'Neill in 1920, to some extent under the influence (like the film *Apocalpse Now*) of Joseph Conrad's story, *The Heart of Darkness*. Paul Robeson played the part on the stage in 1924 both in New York and London, though O'Neill himself had always preferred the original black actor, Charles Gilpin, the first creator of the part of the insane power figure. The play was to a certain extent sensationalized in the film, but even so it was not a box-office success.

Brutus Jones, a Southern black man jailed for murder, has managed to escape from a chain gang by killing a guard. Working his passage to the Caribbean as a ship's stoker, he jumps ship at an island. Here he usurps the throne of the king and makes himself dictator and emperor. The native islanders rise against him, but he manages to escape to the forests, where he ends up naked, bleeding, and demented, his fine uniform torn from his body. Throughout his flight he is tormented by the steady drumming of distant tom-toms and by hallucinations of "little, formless fears," which pursue him like the Furies. Reincarnations of the men he killed appear to haunt him. His visions become increasingly primitive, taking him back to the superstitions and fears of his race in the Congo. His pursuers eventually find him and shoot him down, using carefully forged silver bullets of the kind he has always reckoned were the only ones that could kill him.

EQUUS
(Britain, 1977). Direction: Sidney Lumet. Script: Peter Shaffer. Based on the play by Peter Shaffer. With Richard Burton (Dr. Martin Dysart), Peter Firth (Alan Strang), Colin Blakely (Frank Strang), Joan Plowright (Dora Strang), Harry Andrews (Henry Dalton), Eileen Atkins (Hester Solomon), Jenny Agutter (Jill Mason), Kate Reid (Margaret Dysart). 9, 8.

Alan Strang, a stableboy, has suddenly blinded six horses in his care. He is assigned to a middle-aged psychiatrist, Dr. Martin Dysart, for observation and treatment. At the time, however, Dysart is undergoing self-doubt, fearing that psychiatric treatment can so deaden a patient's responses to life as to deprive him of all the enriching possibilities for passionate feeling. A dilettante of Greek mythology, Bysart has developed a certain penchant for these ancient mysteries. Communication with Alan proves very difficult initially but eases when he is invited to use a tape-recorder in private to unburden himself about his divided upbringing—his mother being fervently religious and his father a repressed, but equally dedicated, antireligionist. Alan has found an outlet through horses, achieving a combined religious-sexual release by worshipping God in the form of Equus, in actuality a horse called Nuggett in his stable, which he rides naked at night. Alan manages to express on tape his obsessive emotions, his sexuality, his masochism, culminating in his admission of his impaired relations with a girl, Jill, who is in love with him and who was responsible initially for introducing him to the stable where he works.

Listening to the tapes, Dysart experiences humiliation on a personal level because his relations with his wife, Margaret, have become remote and indifferent. When given what he believes to be a truth drug, Alan finally confesses that when Jill induced him to try to make love to her one night in the stable, the physical presence of his horse-god rendered him impotent. First, he was driven to beg forgiveness of the horse, then in a frenzy of revulsion to blind Nuggett and the other horses in the stable. Alan may have experienced release from his painful disturbances by making this confession, but Dysart is left all the more in doubt about his role as healer and alleviator of the distraught.

The film and the play from which it is derived both seem to lean favorably towards Alan and his highly individualized obsessions, as if modern rationalism has somehow deprived us of needful superstitions and their emotional aura, which we, the rationally intelligent, can only now recollect in tranquility through academic interest. Yet surely Alan is as much the deluded slave of his pseudorituals and his horse-worship as any primitive religious masochist, and Dysart would surely be better off with his purely intellectual interest in the destructive mysteries of the past than in partially envying the patient he seeks to cure of his self-torture—the torture that finally leads him to inflict a hideous retribution on the innocent animals in his care.

The play—undoubtedly an effective theatrical event on the stage, with its beautifully stylized portrayal of the horses by human mimes with splendid masks, and with its removal of acts of violence from the stage in the Greek tragic tradition—concealed the arguable premise on which the story is based. Lumet's far more earthy and naturalistic presentation on the screen, with the blinding of the horses exhibited to the full and with Richard Burton, at the head of an exceptionally distinguished cast, analyzing his self-doubt at length direct to the camera, deprives the play of its theatrical panache and in so doing makes much more obvious the debatable nature of its theme.

THE EXORCIST
(USA, 1973). Direction: William Friedkin. Script: William Peter Blatty. Adapted from the novel by William Peter Blatty. With Ellen Burstyn (Chris MacNeil), Max von Sydow (Father Merrin), Jason Miller (Father Damien Karras), Linda Blair (Regan MacNeil), Lee J. Cobb (Lieutenant William Kinderman). 2.

THE EXORCIST II: THE HERETIC

(USA, 1977). Direction: John Boorman. Script: William Goodhart. Derived from, and acting as successor to, the original story by William Peter Blatty. With Richard Burton (Father Lamont), Linda Blair (Regan MacNeil). 2.

In his adaptation from his novel, William Peter Blatty manages to involve in what is essentially a horror movie of the supernatural a range of themes, both traditional and contemporary, that include "possession" and the interrelationship of modern psychiatry and religion. The film achieved outstanding success at the box office, leading to the completion in 1977 of a successor, *The Exorcist II: The Heretic.*

In a prologue episode Father Merrin, an elderly Jesuit priest who is also a recognized archeologist, experiences severe shock during excavations in Iraq after examining a newly discovered beast-headed figurine and an accompanying medallion. The shock is due to an overwhelming sense of evil emanating from these artifacts, and the priest, for all his profound religious belief and archeological knowledge, appears scarcely able to resist the force of this dire supernatural experience, which is also associated with a life-size, beast-headed statue at which he gazes on his way back to town.

The film then leaves Father Merrin in order to take up an entirely new story line, set in Georgetown, Washington, D. C., where a film actress, Chris MacNeil, while resident in the town and working on location in a Jesuit College, suddenly undergoes a succession of terrifying experiences in the old house she has rented for herself and her twelve-year-old daughter, Regan. Regan, a quiet-mannered and demure child, becomes possessed by evil forces that gradually transform her appearance, personality, and voice. Her bedroom is constantly subject to disturbances of increasing violence through poltergeistlike activity—her bed bucks up and down, and the child herself levitates up to the ceiling. At the same time, a statue of the Virgin in the Jesuit College chapel is hideously desecrated. But far worse, Regan becomes a creature of preternatural, evil-induced strength; her voice grows harsh and demonic, and her face converts to animal ferocity, while the house continues to be subject to various kinds of supernatural activity and phenomena. Her distracted mother seeks the aid of doctors and psychiatrists in vain.

Matters are brought to a head when the director of Chris's film is found dead, having been thrust through the window of Regan's upstairs bedroom. The police are forced to assume that he has been murdered, and it seems that no one but the child could have been responsible. Chris, in desperation at her daughter's inexplicable condition, implores the Jesuit College's psychiatric adviser, Father Karras, to help her. Father Karras, who is experiencing certain personal problems relating to loss of faith and guilt over his relationship with his mother, whose death has been very recent, is deeply troubled by his inability to cope with this case of Satanic possession. This has now become total, making Regan into a monster who can no longer be regarded as a child but, as he sees it, a body taken over by the Devil. It is now that the aged Father Merrin, who has returned to America, reenters the scene. As an official exorcist for the Catholic church, he is prevailed upon to undertake the case. He confronts and challenges the demon in Regan's body, a struggle that takes on such proportions that at its climax he suffers a heart attack and dies. Karras then attempts to take the matter into his own hands, calling upon the Devil to enter his own body and leave the child free. This evidently happens, for Karras, suddenly possessed, leaps from the girl's window to his death. But Regan is rid of the possession and immediately returns to normal with no recollection whatsoever of what has happened.

Possession and exorcism are still accepted in religious circles, and it would seem that this film has been taken seriously by some representatives of the church, and indeed no less than three priests are credited with acting as technical advisers. It would seem better, however, to regard the film as a traditional thriller rather than as a serious study of the psychological phenomenon of possession. The child's changed appearance—like that of a rabid animal, with gray skin, large green eyes, and bloodstained face—is a function of the makeup department, her revolving head a matter for special effects, the green bile she spews over the faces of her would-be saviors an unpleasant, artificial shock device, her hoarsely cavernous voice a feat achieved for the sound track by the actress Mercedes McCambridge. The film is therefore much less serious as a study of possession than its far more affecting predecessor, the Italian film, *Il Demonio*, made ten years earlier, in 1963, with a remarkable and courageous performance by the Israeli actress, Daliah Lavi, as the insane girl.

The prologue to *The Exorcist*, set in Iraq, seems a somewhat overcharged addition, barely related to the principal story, in which the statuette reappears without explanation as associated with the death of the film director, while Chris comes into possession of the medalion. The statuette is later made out to be a representation of the Devil himself. The subplot of the film, concerning the director of the production in which Chris is appearing, an unpleasant drunk, is also intrusive. The story of Karras's relationship to his neglected and dying mother acts as a further distraction, and his loss of faith seems an insufficient reason for him to sacrifice his life to save the girl, even though at one stage the child speaks to him in the voice of his mother. Why should the demon elect to leave an innocent child and take possession of a man whose soul is in any event in serious jeopardy? Presented with Dolby Stereo effects, the film was just as programmed to excite neurotic fright in its audience as the murder in the shower in *Psycho*. But Hitchcock never asked for *Psycho* to be taken seriously, as the makers of *The Exorcist* purport to do.

The Exorcist II: The Heretic (USA, 1977) was directed by John Boorman and starred Richard Burton as Father Lamont, the spiritual successor to Father Karras, while Linda Blair reappeared as Regan (now an adolescent) and Max von Sydow returned as Father Merrin in a flashback episode. The film was scripted by William Goodhart as derivative from, and a successor to, the original story by William Peter Blatty. In this new story the demon exorcised from Regan is named Pazazu, an ancient Assyrian devil of great power. Father Lamont rescues a woman psychiatrist when, during a monitoring session with Regan, the young girl is overcome by a recurrence of the former "possession." Later he is himself subject to possession by Pazuzu and taken back in time to Africa, where Father Merrin once exorcized a young African, Kokumo, who was gifted with a supernatural power to fight the swarms of locusts that plagued his people. Regan is now thought to possess similar powers. Following this experience, Lamont goes to Africa in actuality to search for the adult Kokumo. Increasingly subject to Pazuzu, Lamont, when back in America, is overcome by visions of locusts in the original haunted house in Georgetown used in the first film, and he dies when the house is split asunder by Pazuzu.[27]

FACE TO FACE
(Sweden, 1976). Direction and script: Ingmar Bergman. With Liv Ullmann (Jenny Isaksson), Erland Josephson (Tomas), Gunnar Björnstrand (grandfather), Aino Taube-Henrikson (grandmother), Kari Sylwan (Maria), Sven Lindberg (Erik Isaksson), Ulf Johanson (Wankel).

Face to Face is unique in our series of studies of madness. In it Jenny, a married woman with an adolescent daughter, Anna, is a professional psychiatrist who suffers a severe nervous breakdown. Her lack of human response to one of her more severely disturbed patients, Maria, who feels intense need for physical contact and attempts to touch Jenny's face, offers the first sign of Jenny's inhibitions. She withdraws herself immediately, reacting strongly against being touched. (In the published script Maria openly suggests they make love, but this is not the case in the film itself.) Maria, revealed as a highly intelligent woman in spite of her condition, accuses her analyst of being "unreal."

Jenny is equally out of touch with her preoccupied husband, who is away on professional business in America. Since her parents both died in a car accident when she was still a child, Jenny has only her grandparents to turn to in her loneliness while her husband is abroad and her daughter away from home. She goes to stay with them. Her grandfather was once a noted scientist, but he is now long retired, sick, and partially paralyzed. In fact, he is dying. Jenny wonders at her grandparents' "state of grace" after so prolonged a marriage—man and woman, they have grown together in married unity and a mutual understanding that has withstood any temporary differences.

Jenny, back in a grandmaternal environment where, as a child, she was deeply unhappy, begins to be haunted, both in noctural dreams and momentary waking hallucinations, by a grey-robed old woman, a death figure, one of whose eyes is missing, presenting only an empty socket, and whose dried-up lips seem always to be seeking urgently to communicate some unvoiced warning. Although Jenny is now a mature and successful woman on good terms with her grandmother (who sometimes treated her, as a child, with unfeeling cruelty), she still experiences acute depression and turns with relief to a new acquaintance, Tomas, a gynecologist who happens to be Maria's half-brother. Although their affectionate relationship remains platonic, Tomas provides her with a stable male confidant with whom she feels able to communicate. On one occasion when she is alone with him, Jenny lapses into unaccountable hysteria, her hypernervous condition exacerbated by an attempted rape by two men, acquaintances of

Maria, whom they have carried to Jenny's empty, furnitureless home. Maria and the two men are on drugs.

Jenny is then left entirely alone; even her grandparents, unaware anything is wrong, have left for a visit to the countryside. She is sleeping in the same room she had as a child, and her nights are disturbed by evil memories. She is haunted by nightmares—of her dead parents (whom she assaults violently for their neglect of her), of her grandparents, of her patients clamoring for attention, of her own death when nailed down alive in a coffin, which she proceeds then to set alight. Her rescuer in dream is the one-eyed woman, the death figure, the only being to show her kindness and consideration for her emotional needs.

Jenny's husband, embarrassed and anxious to get back to Chicago, pays her a visit in the hospital after she has attempted suicide. Her adolescent daughter, with whom she is equally at a loss as to how to communicate, also pays her a perfunctory visit. It is Tomas who offers her continuous understanding as both friend and healer. It is revealed that he is a homosexual, who has no sensual needs attached to his love for her. He tells her his greatest need is to be "real," as he puts it, echoing Maria, and "to hear a human voice and to be sure it comes from someone who is just like I am." Jenny gradually recovers, largely as a result of his care and returns renewed to her professional life. It is notable that the psychiatrist who is Jenny's superior at the hospital where she works, the cynical Dr. Wenkel, has been of no help to her.

Bergman wrote that his films are a form of dramatized therapy designed to alleviate his own anxieties. He is, Liv Ullmann said, his own psychiatrist. *Face to Face* is possibly the finest, most profoundly realistic, presentation of a nervous breakdown to have been created for the screen, and Liv Ullmann's sensitive and enduring performance is outstanding.[28]

FAMILY LIFE
(Britain, 1971). Direction: Ken Loach. Script: David Mercer. Based on a television play for the BBC, *In Two Minds*, by David Mercer. With Sandy Radcliff (Janice Baildon), Bill Dean (Mr. Baildon), Grace Cave (Mrs. Vera Baildon), Malcolm Tierney (Tim), Hilary Martyn (Barbara Baildon), Michael Riddall (Dr. Donaldson). 1a.

The film opens in the middle of a session in which a psychiatrist, Dr. Donaldson (back to camera), is asking his patient, Janice Baildon, about herself and her family—where she lives, what she does, what her father does, and so forth. Mr. Baildon is a storekeeper, and it is evident that Janice reacts a little more warmly at this stage towards her father than she does towards her mother, about whom she is unresponsive, bridling slightly at the questions. "Does it upset your mother that you've had so many jobs?" he asks.

The next several sequences are flashbacks showing how Janice came to her present condition. We see Janice briefly as a salesgirl behind the counter of a large store. Then there is a sharp cut-over to the London Underground, the subway—a harsh transition to the crashing sounds of trains, crowds, and the stress of rush hour. The camera whirls with the crowd. As people board the train, we see a station attendant helping a girl from a seat; it is Janice. Next, we are in a police station; a policewoman is trying to discover her identity. Janice, recovering slightly, is taken home in a police car. We see her home environment—a decent little two-story suburban house with garden.

The dialogue scenes that follow are conducted in terms of absolute naturalism—the subdued, seemingly improvised speech of ordinary, conventional people who are very worried and upset. Janice's father (a northcountryman with a pronounced north-country accent) has come home and is exercising a certain masculine, working-class, no-nonsense form of self-assertion in his effort to find out what's behind all that's happened. His wife, socially a little superior to her husband, tries to quiet him down. We next see them face to face with the psychiatrist, both parents embarrassed by the situation, and the mother bridled at a suggestion from the psychiatrist that parents are sometimes responsible for their child's misdemeanors. "How much respect should parents get?" asks Mrs. Baildon, who even registers shock that the psychiatrist and his secretary use first names. "Are we to be dictated to by the rising generation?" she asks. "They've got to show a little respect for their elders. We might as well go back to the jungle."

A brief scene is cut in here showing Janice as part of a group of young people listening to pop music. This is to prepare us for the next dialogue scene in Janice's home, in which the dominance of her mother emerges more fully. The dialogue is still muted, hesitant, embarrassed. Both parents are nonplussed—the father drawing somewhat apart, since the problem seems to him to be entirely female, though he tries now and then to resume his head-of-the-house attitude.

FATHER: What do we do? Get her an abortion?
MOTHER: Don't use that word in this house.
JANICE: I won't kill my child.
MOTHER: I say you don't want it. I know exactly what you want. You're my daughter.
JANICE: It's there, I mean.
MOTHER: You're confused. We're trying to help you.

Janice is then seen lying in bed, thinking. She is drawing a face on her enlarged belly with an eyebrow pencil. Her future baby is becoming a person to her.

In the next scene the father is alone with the psychiatrist, who manages to probe him about his relations with his wife and daughter.

FATHER: I don't think the wife likes me coming here.
PSYCHIATRIST: How did you get on with her [Janice]?
FATHER: I wasn't allowed to. She come between me and Janice. But she was a very happy child; Janice really kept us together.

The psychiatrist even manages to query his sex life with his wife. He hems and haws, head down. "Vera's not like that," he says. "Funny. Tells me to get covered up." Then he tries to extricate himself: "I don't know what this has to do with Janice. She's a good woman, Vera. She's done her duty."

We next see Janice with her boyfriend, Tim, who is an art student and a sympathetic young man, though with a background very different from that of the Baildons.

JANICE: Do you know my mother's trying to kill me. Kill my baby. She made me go to this hospital. [Tim holds her to him.] She thinks I'm bad. In trouble. [Her head is bent down; she mutters.]
TIM: You get yourself in a state, don't you.
JANICE: Do you think I'm mental?
TIM: Everyone's a bit peculiar. [He then suggests she leave home.]
JANICE: I can't. It would upset mother.
TIM: Get away from your family. There's nothing to keep you there.
JANICE: It's so much easier to do what she wants.

Tim takes her back on his motorcycle, which makes noise enough to rouse the neighborhood. It is very late, and snowing. Janice's mother, aroused from her bed and furious, refuses at first to let her daughter in. In a rage Janice makes Tim take her away, and they roar off just as Vera relents and comes down to open the door. It is too late. This event leads to further trouble. In a brief scene with the psychiatrist, Vera pleads, "I didn't *mean* to lock her out. . . ." Again she grumbles about the young: "The world's like that today."
But when Janice eventually does return home, dirty and bedraggled, there is a fearful scene, with Janice using gutter language, which shatters her parents' susceptibilities and finally drives her father to use language almost as bad.

JANICE: Fuck you. [Pointing to her mother.] She cut my baby out.
FATHER [seizing and shaking her]: It's not a bloody doctor she wants; it's the police.
MOTHER: You're so wicked, you are. No self-respecting person would behave like you do. [Her voice rises in hysteria.] There must be something the matter with you, child.

They take her to a mental hospital. There they are immediately surprised at the seeming informality of the place.

MOTHER: It's not like a usual ward.
FATHER: What about the discipline? The difference between right and wrong?
MOTHER: Look a bit more cheerful, Janice, for heaven's sake.

The scenes that follow close the gap between the opening sequence and the prolonged, explanatory flashback that followed. In a succession of scenes she is observed being worked into the routines of treatment and establishing relations with other patients, assessing herself. "I don't feel people hurt me like I've hurt my parents," she says. "What about when you lost your baby?" asks the psychiatrist. Janice does not answer this but gets up and moves away, her head in her hands. As she sees it, her baby was becoming another, new person, growing up inside her. The abortion on which her mother had insisted was wrong. Meanwhile, she begins to quarrel with some of the other patients over which television channel to view, but the psychiatrist intervenes, restores order, and once again gets them to talk about themselves.

JANICE: They say I'm crazy, but I think I'm being myself. They say I'm destroying myself. But I want to destroy them in me. I don't want them in me. My mother's a good woman, but I had a baby, and she killed it. If they say you're bad and you don't think you're bad, then you're really bad.

In immediate contrast to this, we get Vera Baildon's viewpoint.

MOTHER: Permissiveness. Drug-taking. Demonstrations. It all seems to be tied up. To what end? I feel we need control; we must have more control.
PSYCHIATRIST: Janice says she's had too much control.
MOTHER: It's very hard to take when you've done your best. We can never get back on an even keel.
PSYCHIATRIST: You've got to be capable of accepting her, just as much as she you.
MOTHER: She's doing diabolical things. She can't have it both ways.
PSYCHIATRIST: You want it both ways. You want her to be herself and at the same time do what you want.

Alone with Janice, the psychiatrist tells her: "Cutting yourself off from the world is the only way you *can* be yourself. All the same, you seem to need your parents' approval. You've got to be able to stand up to them, without hating them."

The film cuts at this point to a scene in which the administrative and medical committee of the hospital are debating whether or not to retain the services of the psychiatrist who has been looking after Janice. They decide that his methods, though favorably thought of, are not really in line with the general policy of the hospital, and his temporary appointment is not renewed. Janice then finds herself placed in a different ward in the charge of a woman psychiatrist with more traditional views. Against her will she is given an injection that puts her to sleep before she is given shock therapy.

In a succeeding scene her parents are told that the days of long stays in mental hospitals are over, that their daughter is schizoid, and that the hospital "will eliminate the symptoms and provide drugs." Janice is next seen leaving the hospital with her parents. She is being led by her father, while her mother follows unhappily behind, her shoes making a hard, clattering sound on the hospital floor. Then the film cuts to a factory, where, amid the din of broadcasted pop music, Janice is seen to be doing piecework.

Janice takes up again with her original boyfriend, Tim. She visits the studio in his college and sees some of his experimental work. She confesses she dare not take him home to meet her disapproving parents. Together, they look out over the city rooftops seen from the high-level studio window. "*That*'s your mother and dad," says Tim, "You can't change it." But she does take him to her home during her parents' absence, and they have fun spraying paint all over the garden, coloring the leaves blue. Then she paints Tim's hair blue, and for the first time in the film we see Janice laugh.

When the Baildons return, Mr. Baildon (whose pride centers on his small garden) loses all self-control. "You stupid, bloody bitch." he shouts. "You're raving mad." The scene then moves ahead to a family meal at which Janice's elder sister, Barbara, and her two small daughters are present. The table is soon seething with resentment because Barbara has always seemed too independent for her parents' liking. When Janice joins them, they quarrel openly about Janice in her presence. "She's been a very sick child. . . . Look at the state of her." Barbara bluntly puts the blame on her parents. "You've done this to her," she says. As the dispute grows, the small children can be seen flinching—glance-shots of them show their reactions to this display of family life. "You cheeky, bloody bitch," shouts Mr. Baildon. "I've brought the family up the normal way," asserts Mrs. Baildon. The climax comes in the form of a prolonged scream from Janice. Barbara (who offered earlier to take her younger sister into her home) holds on to Janice in a possessive embrace. The storm ends with the abrupt departure of Barbara with her two children.

The screen goes dark for a while. Then, to light, gentle music we see Janice alone at night in the dark. She is digging into the dining room table with a screwdriver. Suddenly she starts smashing up the room, including her father's presentation clock, a recognition of his services from a grateful employer. Both parents descend upon her. "I'm killing time," Janice says. "You should be *doing* bloody time," shouts her father. In the next scene, after her parents accuse her of looking like a loose girl and she cheeks them about reading the sexier Sunday papers (a tradition in working-class British life), her father beats her.

Janice inevitably has to go back into the mental hospital. Here she takes up with Paul, a young male patient working in the grounds. She knows that his interest in her is sexual and accepts his hint that "she has had more pricks in her than a second-hand dartboard." The nursing sister is aware of Janice's interest and discreetly warns her about Paul, who is soon to leave the hospital. "We don't want you to be taken advantage of," she says. Janice becomes violent and has to be given sedatives.

Janice's parents visit her, evidently more out of duty and a gesture of self-esteem than because they love her. "Who's been right? Us!" declares her father. "Try and behave yourself, for God's sake." Tim also visits her, out of love. Since she is a voluntary patient, he persuades her to run off with him. In a scene alone together, they discuss her feelings. "I don't feel I'm real," she says. "I don't feel anything." But a doctor visits them in Tim's room and puts pressure on them to let him take her back into care. He says that she must either go back voluntarily or be forced to do so by compulsory order. She is eventually carried out to a waiting ambulance.

In the closing sequence we see her being used as a demonstration patient in a medical lecture theater by an academic doctor, who treats her like a dummy. She has become, he says, an extreme case of mutism. And with that the film ends.

It is clear in this film (written by the dramatist who was also responsible for *Morgan: A Suitable Case for Treatment*) that the whole family—Janice's parents and even her elder sister—are part of a collective family case study and that Janice, the weakest link in the family chain, is also its victim. In her love for Tim, and in his for her, and in her desire to have Tim's baby, she is the person who exhibits the healthiest, most positive human values, but conventional dominance by her parents make them imbalanced enough in their treatment of her to destroy her. Surrounded by overly possessive feelings on all sides, she can escape only into insanity.

FISTS IN THE POCKET
(Italy, 1965). Direction and script: Marco Bellocchio. With Lou Castel (Sandro). 1a

This is a portrait of a doomed family living on the outskirts of a small Italian village. The widowed mother is blind and helpless. Of her four children, Augusto alone is normal—employed and engaged to be married. Of the others, two, Sandro and Leone, are subject to epileptic fits, while the single daughter, Giulia, is neurotic. Leone exists in a partially catatonic condition, while Sandro and Giulia have a near incestuous relationship, though they quarrel incessantly. Sandro, determined to help, murders his mother and Leone, but his sister, terrified by these acts, becomes bedridden and semi-paralyzed. Sandro begins to consider eliminating her too but suffers a violent epileptic fit. Knowing he wants to kill her, Giulia makes no attempt to help her brother.

Sandro's violent movements convey his disordered mind and uncontrollable energies, and his impulses to kill his family are totally sociopathic. The part is brilliantly played and directed in Bellocchio's first film, made when he was still in his twenties. Of it Bellocchio said:

> Film sometimes needs symbols, and to me the epilepsy meant all the frustration, all the troubles and weaknesses, often found in the young. . . . I believe that audiences will feel not simply that my main character is ill, but that he expresses a certain period in the life of any young man. . . . I was raised in a bourgeois family in the same sort of provincial milieu as that described in the film. This is all part of my own experience, and my life has been a strong reaction to my bourgeois and Catholic adolescence. . . . It is autobiographical in its description of a milieu which I had to get away from in order to survive.[29]

FRANCES
(USA, 1982). Direction: Graeme Clifford. Script: Eric Bergren, Christopher Devore, and Nicholas Kazan. With Jessica Lange (Frances Farmer), Kim Stanley (Lillian Farmer), Jeffrey DeMunn (Clifford Odets), Sam Shepard (Harry York). 1b, 9, 8.

This film attempts to encapsulate in scrapbook form the more presentable of the appalling experiences of Frances Farmer, the American film star of the later 1930s; she is heroically impersonated here by Jessica Lange, who has a most remarkable physical likeness to Frances Farmer. The girl from Seattle achieved her initial notoriety around 1930 at the age of sixteen by gravely offending the local community when she read in public her essay, "God Dies." She went further to challenge the neighbors by accepting a communist journal's invitation to visit

Moscow. She returned to become a kind of instant film star contracted by Paramount; this seemingly good fortune she sacrificed to leave Hollywood, become the mistress of Clifford Odets, and star in the Group Theater's production of his play, *Golden Boy*. Deserted by Odets, she went back to Hollywood only to become committed, through a series of bizarre accidents, to a mental sanatorium in Los Angeles, where she received insulin shock-therapy. Her mother, represented in the film as being as demented as she was vicious in her attitude to the girl now wholly in her power, institutionalized Frances time and time again until her daughter was regarded as incurably insane. While under the most dubious forms of care she appears to have been raped, assaulted, subjected to electro-shock treatment, cold-water therapy and finally lobotomy. She was eventually released and she managed to return to her profession of film actress. The film closes with a recreation of the notorious *This is Your Life* television show in which she was featured in a zombie-like condition.

Frances is a latter-day *Snake Pit*, exposing not only the savage heartlessness of what passed for therapy in a punitive mental institution, but also the wickedness of a mad parent who hungers for the publicity that can be obtained through her daughter's stardom while at the same time punishing her for her wilfulness by repeatedly institutionalizing her. The film tends to be formless without being informative, and though packed with incident, lacking in any sensitive analysis of this sad girl's mental condition. The virtue of Jessica Lange's performance lies in its strength, endurance and versatility in a role that constantly calls for rage, hysteria, and the portrayal of an increasingly tortured, uncompromising resentment against the demands of show-business and the demands of her insatiably exploitive mother. It was no doubt for reasons of dramatic license that the screenwriters introduced a wholly fictional, if only occasional lover into Frances's life, Harry York (played by Sam Shepard); this serves to confuse the issue, and lessen her tragedy. Verisimilitude demands that he can do nothing effective to help her since, unhappily, she had no such ally in real life. Seldom has anyone in the public eye been so absolutely alone and unprotected by any form of civil rights.

FRENZY

(Britain, 1972). Director: Alfred Hitchcock. With Jon Finch (Richard Blaney), Barry Foster (Bob Rusk), Alec McCowan (Inspector Oxford), Barbara Leigh-Hunt (Brenda Blaney), Anna Massey (Barbara Milligan). 4.

Mystery surrounds a succession of so-called necktie strangulations of women in London. These are in fact the work of Bob Rusk, a wholesale fruiterer in Covent Garden, which, at the time the film was made, was still London's main center for the distribution of soft fruits and vegetables in the area. Rusk's friend, the seeming ne'er-do-well Richard Blaney, divorced from his wife, Brenda, who is manager of a marriage bureau in Covent Garden, becomes the initial suspect after Rusk rapes and strangles Brenda in her office. Blamey had, unfortunately, visited Brenda in her office just prior to Rusk's fatal intrusion. Hitchcock, as usual, allows us to know the truth while the rest of the characters—including Inspector Oxford, who is in charge of police investigations into the murders—do not. We are cunningly enticed into direct complicity with the sociopathic murderer and led into making our principal interest his smooth ability to fool everybody, since we alone have witnessed his orgasmic pleasure in squeezing the life out of his victims. "Lovely, lovely," he breathes in rhythmic delight as he does away with Brenda, his fingers pressing down on the gasping woman's throat. The camera's positioning forces us to experience (perhaps even vicariously enjoy) the act of murder, since we occupy Rusk's physical position at the time.

Rusk's next victim puts Blamey under even greater suspicion. Blamey's new girlfriend, a barmaid called Barbara, is raped and strangled by Rusk in his apartment. That same night he stows her body in a sack of potatoes lying near the rear edge of a delivery truck bound for the provinces. But it is an unexpected flaw in Rusk's moves that finally undoes him—in her death struggle, Barbara tore away his monogrammed tiepin. He does not discover this until the truck is on the verge of departure. Rusk dashes back and climbs aboard. There follows a macabre, desperate struggle with the corpse, Rusk finally being forced to break the dead woman's fingers, which are set in rigor mortis around the fatal tiepin. Rusk then jumps clear of the truck, but mobile police discover the crime almost immediately when the girl's grey leg is seen protruding from the sack, which is about to fall off the back of the speeding truck.

Blamey is convicted of both crimes and is only finally exonerated when, after absconding from a prison hospital, he manages to penetrate Rusk's apartment, where a third victim lies strangled. The police pursuit of Blamey coincides with their discovery of Rusk's guilt.

Hitchcock manages to involve us throughout far more with Rusk than with Blamey, the shiftless but nonetheless wholly innocent character, and so to imply—as so often is the case in his films—that we all belong together to the same species that breeds the murderers and criminals we condemn. Although, of course, no actual sympathy is ever shown for Rusk—far less, in fact, than is the case with the murderer in *M*, who is allowed to plead his total inability to resist his murderous impulses—the psychosexual nature of his assaults on women is very plainly revealed.

FREUD: THE SECRET PASSION
(USA, 1962). Direction; John Huston. Script: Jean-Paul Sartre, Charles Kaufman, Wolfgang Reinhardt. Medical consultation: David Stafford-Clark. With Montgomery Clift (Freud), Susannah York (Cecily Koertner), Larry Parks (Breur), Fernand Ledoux (Charcot), David McCallum (Carl von Schlosser), Rosalie Crutchley (Freud's mother), David Kossoff (Freud's Father), Eric Portman (Dr. Meynert). 9.

LET THERE BE LIGHT

(USA, 1945). Direction: John Huston. Made for the war department at the Mason General Hospital on Long Island, N.Y. Film remained unavailable for screening until 1980.

John Huston (born 1906), son of the actor Walter Huston, led a peripatetic life, developing a certain flamboyance and independence of style. He was a boxer, a cavalryman serving in Mexico, a painter, an actor, and a writer. He established himself in Hollywood in the late 1930s, working as a scriptwriter before directing his first film, *The Maltese Falcon* (1941). During the war he directed several official documentaries, including *The Battle of San Pietro* (1944) and *Let There Be Light* (1945), a closely restricted study of the mental and physical condition and psychiatric treatment of men suffering from various forms of breakdown under fire. Although the film itself did not become available for screening until 1980 (primarily to protect the patients involved), a transcript of it was given in *Film—Book Two: Films of Peace and War* (1962), edited by Robert Hughes.[30] The film ran forty-five minutes. Huston's experiences while making this documentary record (during which he first learned about psychiatry at first hand and himself practiced hypnosis) are described in his autobiography, *An Open Book*.[31] He claims that his work at the Mason General Hospital affected him "almost like a religious experience."[32] It excited his permanent interest in psychiatry and inspired him and a co-worker on *Let There Be Light*, Charles Kaufman, to discuss the possibility of making of a biographical film study of Freud, concentrating on the earlier part of Freud's career, the successive phases through which he passed while making his initial discoveries and the relationship of these discoveries to his own private disturbances. Huston originally worked with Kaufman on the script for *Dr. Ehrlich's Magic Bullet* (1940), the Warners film about the discovery of a cure for syphilis.

Huston said he decided to commission Jean-Paul Sartre (who, as an avowed communist, was technically an anti-Freudian, at least on the social plane) to prepare an initial script.[33] This finally emerged in the form of a script of over three hundred pages, which, if realized, would have exceeded five hours of playing time. After much discussion over cuts, Sartre's revised script proved even longer than the first! The final script, was written by Reinhardt (who was something of an expert on Freud) and Huston (with Kaufman's initial assistance), and Sartre requested that his name be withdrawn from the credits. Nevertheless, Huston acknowledged that Sartre's influence on the final script was considerable.

The film can be described as "impressionist" biography, compressing into a single dramatic continuity events and investigations that in fact covered many years in Freud's career. It starts in Vienna in 1885, when Freud (born 1856) is already approaching thirty. He is a young neurologist profoundly dissatisfied with the approach of his senior colleagues to the treatment of hysteria. In the same year, he goes to Paris to study under Charcot, who is using hypnosis to prove that certain hysterical symptoms of a physical nature are brought on by mental stress.

The following year, 1886, he returns to Vienna, marries Martha Bernays, and goes to work with a senior colleague, Dr. Joseph Breuer, who is sympathetic to his investigations. In particular he has two hysteric patients, Cecily Koertner and Carl von Schlosser. Cecily suffers from blindness and paralysis of the legs; Carl has made a homicidal attack on his father. The latter case reawakens in Freud certain fears that strangely reflect difficulties he has experienced with his own father. As a consequence, he abandons the case. When he learns later that the boy killed himself, he is shocked into realizing he deserted this troubled patient because of subconscious influences in himself. He concentrates therefore on Cecily. It is the resolution of her case—a combination in a single person of many patients in Freud's experience—that comes to reveal the emergence of sexuality in infancy. This, together with his own efforts at self-analysis, combines to make up the main themes of the rest of the film. Freud is still only thirty-three at the end of the film, when he reads his paper on infant sexuality to a convention of doctors. The subject is so utterly repellent to the taste and ethical susceptibilities of the period that he meets with the strongest opposition and is even rejected by his staunchest supporter, Dr. Breur.

The film, originally 140 minutes long, was drastically cut for exhibition and, unhappily, proved a failure at the box office. The cuts, totalling some 20 minutes, disturbed some points of continuity in the film. It was shot on location in Munich and Bavaria at the high cost, for the period, of some $3 million. The two patients demonstrated by Charcot in the scene set in Paris are claimed to have been real patients undergoing actual hypnosis for the film in the presence of their normal doctors, who remained with them on the studio set.[34] Not only did Huston have considerable difficulties with the script but had further problems with Montgomery Clift, who was far gone in both alcohol and drugs and barely aware in any rational sense of what he was doing. Nevertheless, Clift's performance, extracted moment by moment by Huston, has a remarkable quality, which somehow seems to relate to the problems that make up the subject of the film. Since this film is central to one of the major themes of this book, a detailed analysis is warranted.

In the opening sequence Freud, a young neurologist, openly challenges a senior physician, Dr. Meynert, when the latter declares in a hospital autocratically that a woman patient in a catatonic condition is merely "putting on an act." To prove his point, Freud punctures her leg with a sterilized pin, revealing through her lack of any reaction the extreme nature of her withdrawal. Freud, anxious to get away from the hidebound medical atmosphere in which he has to work in Vienna, manages to leave for a while to study under Charcot in Paris. Charcot is a pioneer in the use of hypnosis to cure cases of hysteria. At the railway terminal in Vienna, Freud's father gives him the present of a watch, but Freud immediately drops and smashes the watch after boarding the train. (This incident, with its psychological implications concerning the relationship of Freud and his father, is never clearly explained in the film.)

In Paris Freud watches Charcot demonstrate to his students two patients, one afflicted with trembling and the other with paralysis of the legs. Under hypnosis Charcot manages to make them exchange their physical symptoms. "Gentlemen," says Charcot, "we have witnessed the birth of an hysterical symptom.

However, we understand, but we cannot cure." Back in Vienna, Freud lectures on the subject of hypnosis and the physical symptoms induced by hysteria and is derided for his pains by everyone except Breuer, who subsequently invites him to become his associate, since like Charcot he is using hypnosis to assist in the analysis, if not the cure, of patients suffering from hysteria. Meanwhile, Freud marries Martha, who also supports him in what he is doing.

The initial case on which Breuer consults Freud is that of Cecily Koertner, with whom Breuer has only had very limited success. Huston (as narrator) speaks aloud Freud's thoughts at this period—Could there be a psychic mechanism that blocks the entry of undesirable thoughts to the conscious mind? Breuer also introduces Freud to another troubling case—that of Carl, a young man who has made a homicidal attack on his father yet insists on keeping his father's youthful officer's uniform on a dummy by his bedside. Under hypnosis Carl recalls the memory of his father's carving of meat and his childhood belief that his father was seeking to kill him. Carl has consequently harbored the desire to kill his father before he was himself killed, and behind this obsession lies the traumatic thought that his father "raped a young girl, my mother, every night." With this, Carl strips the uniform off the dummy and clasps the dummy to himself. It is of female shape. "Mother!" he cries. Freud, deeply upset himself by this, gives up the case. This leads to his first dream:

> Freud stands at the mouth of a deep cavern, linked by a rope to Carl. Inside the cavern he sees Carl embracing his [Freud's] mother. Freud attacks and destroys him, cuts the tethering rope, and is himself drawn to destruction. Crying out, "Mother! Mother!" he wakes.

After a gap in time, Freud in some distress approaches the gates of the great mansion that is Carl's family home, only to learn from a servant that Carl has died in a mental institution.

Freud is next seen with Breuer, with whom he has resumed his association. Breuer says, "You divorce yourself from psychology for a whole year and then come back with a new theory." His colleague declares he does not believe that sex is the only cause of neurosis. Freud returns to the case of Cecily, whose symptoms he now believes to be caused largely by childhood sexual pressures. She is still blind and paralysed. She dreams frequently about her father's death, but her account to Breuer of its circumstances elicits Freud's distrust:

> Cecily is staying in a hotel in a foreign country with her father. She is sleeping at night in her room; her father has gone out. Suddenly she is awakened; two doctors are knocking loudly on her door with news of her father's death in a hospital. She gets up, dresses, and goes with them to the hospital. The nurses are sitting around in casual attitudes. She is led to a back room, where her father lies dead.

Freud immediately interrogates her afresh, and the dream emerges differently:

> It is the police, she screams, who knock on her door and take her, not to a hospital but to a brothel [she screams again], where her father has died. The

women are not nurses but whores, sitting half dressed, waiting for clients. Her father lies in the bed where he had died in the arms of a whore. She is forced by the police to identify him.

Freud commands her, "When you wake, you will remember everything." She wakes and finds that she can see; nevertheless, she curses Freud for raising to her consciousness the bitter shame of her father's death. Freud, however, takes complete charge of her case because she has become infatuated with Breuer, and in consequence the latter feels that he can no longer act for her. Breuer's departure with his wife on a long vacation causes a recurrence of Cecily's hysteria—this time in the form of a phantom pregnancy.

Freud now has complications in his own life. His wife, Martha, reading the notes he has made on his various cases, reacts against the intimate, and (to her) offensively sexual, nature of the information he has probed out of them. Freud insists these are precisely the questions that must be posed, however distressing they may seem. The work, he admits to her, is dangerous. "Tomorrow," he says, "they may stone me in the streets." These troubles concide with his father's death. After the funeral he has a nightmare in which he finds he is barred from entering the cemetery where his father's grave is situated. Over the cemetery gate he sees a mysterious sign, The Eyes Shall Be Closed. He awakens in fear, unable to probe the problem of his love-hate relationship with his father. He consults Breuer: "'The eyes shall be closed.' Could that mean that dreams are ideas escaping into expression?" Did he, in fact, love his father? In the dream he saw everyone moving into the cemetery with eyes closed; his remained open, and so his entrance had been barred. Sons, it would seem, must close their eyes to the sins of their fathers. Breuer accompanies Freud back to the cemetery, but still Freud finds himself unable to enter and visit his father's grave. A hysteric symptom prevents him because (he thinks) his father once refused to contest an insult given his Jewish origins.

Freud once again takes over Cecily's complex case. She has remained paralyzed since the age of fourteen, when she collapsed on Red Tower Street. She tells Freud, "My mother was brought up as a prostitute." Correcting her Freudian slip, she says, "Protestant." Cecily cannot be hypnotized because of her infatuation for Breuer, which has now been exchanged for an infatuation for Freud. Freud says to Breuer. "We are images that represent something deep in her." He finds out that her mother once attacked her after, as a child, she had used cosmetics to make up her face like that of a dancer (actress, prostitute). She also witnessed at the age of nine a servant dismissed by her mother, who called her a prostitute because Cecily's father had molested the girl. In her next dream Cecily sees

> a painted woman beside a tall tower; an unrecognizable man turns and runs while her mother looks down out of a window in the tower. She dreams of a further association of words—the name Pettifer (Potiphar, putain, prostitute); Joseph (Joseph Breuer), and Potiphar's wife. "I'm the painted girl whom Joseph rejected."

None of us can bear to realize all our wishes, Freud tells her. He also realizes by now that he can penetrate into the unconscious mind *without* hypnosis, making use of dreams. The narration once again reflects Freud's rumination, Is Cecily's father the man she is unable to recognize? Freud persists in using memory analysis in place of hypnosis. In another dream

Cecily recalls she was running through dark streets, following her father, who is not going where he had told her. He is visiting a prostitute in Red Tower Street, preferring the prostitute's company to that of his daughter. "He lied to me," screams Cecily. "I hated him! I hate men!"

Believing that she may now be cured of her long-term hysterical paralysis, Freud commands her to get up and walk. But she falls. Why? In further discussion with Breuer, Freud considers there is still something hidden in the father-daughter relationship. In his own case some intimacy he witnessed between his own father and his sister led to a similar distress in himself. Further investigation with Cecily reveals that her father once rescued her as a child from a beating by her mother. He then took her to his bed, undressed her, and then promised her a doll if she told nothing of this sexual encounter. It is now that Cecily's legs come back to life. "My father was a criminal," she cries. The doll she has always clung onto since childhood she should rightfully hate. Freud then recognizes still further the parallel with his own case; at the age of four he slept in his mother's room, after being frightened on a train. She called him "my little Arab," and gave him her expanding bracelet to play with.

Freud goes out to search for Cecily, who has disappeared "on the town." Heavily made up, she is playing the part of a prostitute in Red Tower Street. Freud finds her on the point of attempting suicide. He is forced to draw on her affection for him to induce her to abandon the attempt. Back again with his mother, he examines the bracelet, which she still has. He then has another dream:

The image recurs of the painted lady deep in a cavern. Again Freud finds himself at the end of a long tether and stands at the mouth of the cavern, looking in. He is being dragged down towards the woman, who holds out to him a live snake. The woman clings to a child.

Awake again, Freud recollects that when he slept in his mother's room as a young child, he saw her strip to the waist and experienced acute jealousy when his father came in from his bedroom and led her away. Meanwhile, in the present, Freud's difficulties with his wife continue. She confesses her jealousy and even hatred of her husband's women patients, with whom he maintains, as she sees it, such intimate associations. Freud pacifies her, talking about the nature of his analyses. "The false," he says, "is often the truth standing on its head." He has by now become convinced of the hard fact of the manifestations of sexuality in childhood.

Cecily now has to face the truth about her mother. She was a dancer in a cheap cabaret and above everything wants to forget her past life with Cecily's father. After she became pregnant, he never touched her again. All he wanted was a domesticated harlot. Cecily's father was in fact a neurotic, obsessed with having sex with prostitutes. Her father caressed her in place of her mother; she became her father's substitute wife, so deeply jealous of her mother.

Freud admits to himself that he too once planned in a dream to kill his father. He says to Cecily, "Your symptoms are all gone now, except your love for me." This is what must now be cured. Their work, he tells her, is only just beginning. One day she will be able to face life on her own terms.

The film enters its final phase with Freud's lecture on childhood sexuality to a professional medical audience, who for the most part reject such wholly unacceptable concepts. Even Breuer admits that he cannot accept the idea. Freud now finds that he can visit his father's grave. Huston, as narrator, ends the film by declaring, "Know thyself." This is the keynote to Freud's work and discoveries.

GUN CRAZY

(USA, 1950). Direction: Joseph H. Lewis. With John Dall (Burt Tare), Peggie Cummins (Annie Laurie Starr). 4.

Another pair of youthful hoodlums—in this case, the boy egged on by the girl—commit armed robberies, which end in murder. A well-made film, acted with energy and style, and anticipating *Bonnie and Clyde* (1967) and *Badlands* (1973).

HALLOWEEN

(USA, 1978). Direction: John Carpenter. Script: John Carpenter, Debra Hill. With Donald Pleasence (Dr. Sam Loomis), Jamie Lee Curtis (Laurie Strode), Tony Moran (Michael Myers). 3, 4.

This melodrama about a compulsive killer in Haddonfield, a small town in Illinois, features Michael Myers, an asylum patient who has been under the care of Dr. Sam Loomis since the age of six, when he brutally killed his sister. Now twenty-one, he has remained utterly speechless since the murder. When he escapes from the asylum, Loomis remains certain he will return. The story then centers on Halloween night, involving the actions of three young schoolgirls, Laurie Strode and her friends, Annie and Lynda. Michael does return. He strangles Annie and also murders Lynda and her boyfriend. He then proceeds to attack Laurie, who manages to wound him with a knitting needle and with the knife he produced to frighten her. Loomis, who has been following Michael, then arrives and shoots Michael down; his body, however, mysteriously disappears. John Carpenter, it would seem from statements he has made,[35] has no interest in making films with any marked social or psychological implications. Like Hitchcock, he merely wants to entertain through the skilful scaring of his audience, using elaborate tracking shots to identify the viewer with the stalking actions of the killer. Loomis, the psychiatrist, who has the same name as his predecessor in *Psycho*, does little to elucidate Michael's condition in psychological terms; he prefers to resort to traditional, irrational explanations by claiming that Michael is an incarnation of evil.

HAROLD AND MAUDE
(USA, 1971). Direction: Hal Ashby. With Ruth Gordon (Maude), and Bud Cort (Harold). 8.

Harold and Maude was something of a cult film with young American audiences of the 1970s because of its anarchic humor and good-natured eccentricity. Harold, dominated by his wealthy mother, is fascinated by death. He attends funerals in a hearse and stages suicide attempts to shock his mother into a sincere reaction and to shake up the psychiatrist she employs to cover her embarrassment at her son's behavior. She even tries to get him married through a computer dating service, but he manages to frighten off the girls who arrive to see what he is like. His reaction is to take off with a kind of fairy godmother and eccentric old lady of seventy-nine, called Maude, who in spite of her advanced years enjoys participating in every wild experience that comes her way. They end by sleeping together, and Harold says he wants to marry her. This is frustrated when, at the age of eighty, Maude decides to take her own life.

HARVEY
(USA, 1950). Direction: Harry Koster. Adapted from the play by Mary Chase. With James Stewart (Elwood P. Dowd), Cecil Kellaway (Chumley). 9, 8.

Elwood Dowd is an amiable alcoholic who believes himself to be accompanied everywhere by Harvey, a rabbit six feet tall. In spite of his sister's endeavors to have him committed to a lunatic asylum, he manages to convert the asylum doctor, Chumley, to accepting Harvey's benign existence. His sister decides to accept the fact that Elwood is obviously better off mentally with Harvey as his boon companion than he would be without him. Elwood and Harvey set off happily to the nearest bar. The essence of the situation is that the audience, like the doctor, has to be induced to accept the presence of the (to them) invisible Harvey—a fantasy perhaps better suited to the stage, where make-believe is more naturally ready-made than in the photographically realistic medium of the film.

HERZ AUS GLAS
("Heart of Glass." West Germany, 1976). Direction and coscripting: Werner Herzog. With Josef Bierbichler (Hias); Stefan Guttler (factory owner). 4, 9, 8.

Herzog is quoted as saying: "People should look straight at a film. Film is not the art of scholars but of illiterates. And film culture is not analysis; it is agitation of the mind."[36] This applies directly to *Heart of Glass,* which involves a visionary herdsman, Hias, who is summoned, fruitlessly, to use his powers to help rediscover the lost formula for the making of glass, which was formerly in use at the local factory. The factory owner, who is insane, claims that he knows the formula, an essential ingredient of which is human blood. To obtain this, he kills a serving girl. Communal madness seizes the village. One man, Wudy, dances with the corpse of a man with whom he was locked in silent conflict. Hias himself succumbs to a vision of ceaseless war. The factory owner sets fire to his factory before facing imprisonment. Hias's ultimate vision is of an island inhabited by forgotten men who believe the earth is flat, though there is a touch of hope when four of them set out in a boat to discover whether or not this is true.

From the start the film suggests cosmic destruction with an image of clouds pouring like a cataract across the firmament above the trees of a forest, while the anguished human beings of the village are like ghosts haunting an inhospitable space. Herzog is credited with having subjected his whole cast to hypnosis while at work with them, with the single exception of the actor who plays Hias.

HITLER: THE LAST TEN DAYS
(Britain, 1973). Direction: Ennio De Concini. With Alec Guinness (Hitler). 7.

Hitler never permitted an actor to impersonate him in any German feature film during the twelve-year span of the Third Reich. Stalin, on the other hand, frequently allowed himself to be represented in fiction films conceived on an epic scale. Employing actors who were his "doubles," such as Mikhail Gelovani (a fellow Georgian) and Alexei Diki, they portrayed the monolithic Stalin as the all-wise, paternalistic—indeed, godlike—leader of his people. The single feature film in which Hitler was the protagonist, Leni Riefenstahl's *Triumph of the Will*, remains an outstanding example of romantic self-projection, but since this is a documentary it lies outside the range of our survey. The real-life Hitler could otherwise only be seen in newsreels and documentaries.

Hitler was, however, represented by numerous actors in British, American, and postwar German and Austrian feature films, usually as a frenzied caricature portrayed psychologically in the tradition of melodramatic insanity.[37] The following is a selection of these films over and above the British film featuring Alec Guinness:

> *The Great Dictator* (USA, 1940). Direction and script, Charles Chaplin. With Charles Chaplin (Adenoid Hynkel).
> *The Strange Death of Adolf Hitler* (USA, 1943). Direction, James Hogan. With Ludwig Donath.
> *The Hitler Gang* (USA, 1944). Direction, John Farrow. With Robert Watson.
> *The Magic Face* (USA, 1951). Direction, Frank Tuttle. With Luther Adler.
> *Ten Days to Die* (Austria, 1954). Direction, G. W. Pabst. With Albin Skoda.
> *Hitler* (USA, 1962). Direction, Stuart Heisler. With Richard Basehart.
> *Our Hitler* (West Germany, 1977). Direction, Hans-Jürgen Syberberg. With Heinz Schubert.
> *The Bunker* (USA, 1981). Direction, George Schaefer. With Anthony Hopkins.

At the time of the initial release of *Hitler: The Last Ten Days*, I wrote: "[the film offers] a portrait of Hitler in decline played almost to the point of sympathy by Alec Guinness, a performance conceived with great restraint. Hitler passes to his final extinction through suicide after attempting to browbeat the remnants of his General Staff in the seclusion of the Bunker, and defend Berlin with nonexistent forces. Much is made of his relationship with Eva Braun, for whom at this stage he appears to have more contempt than sympathy."[38]

THE HONEYMOON KILLERS
(USA, 1969). Direction and script: Leonard Kastle. With Shirley Stoler (Martha Beck). Tony La Bianco (Ray Fernandez). 3, 4.

Based on a real-life partnership—the original murderers were executed in 1951—this unusually convincing film deals very coolly and realistically with the sociopathic murders so casually committed by an unlikely pair of lovers—Martha Beck, a two-hundred-pound spinster nurse; and Ray Fernandez, a middle-aged Spanish immigrant, who have met through a "friendship club." They con and kill mostly aging women (she posing as his sister). After it appears that one of the more attractive, younger victims is pregnant by Ray, Martha shoots her and drowns her little daughter by using a bucket of water. She then telephones the police. When in prison awaiting execution, Martha treasures the love letter Ray sends her.

I NEVER PROMISED YOU A ROSE GARDEN
(USA, 1977). Direction: Anthony Page. With Bibi Andersson (Dr. Fried), Kathleen Quinlan (Deborah Blake). 9.

This film concerns the successful struggle by a woman psychiatrist, Dr. Fried, to rescue Deborah Blake, a sixteen-year-old schizophrenic girl, from the fantasy figures, notably a tyrant called Anterrabae, who hold her back from recovery and whose brutal terrain is made manifest in hallucinatory sequences. Only through Dr. Fried's care and after a number of setbacks due to less sympathetic treatment from other attendants and doctors, does Deborah finally win. The film is rather obvious in its presentation of Deborah's case, and the girl herself is very well played by Kathleen Quinlan.

THE ICEMAN COMETH
(USA, 1973). Director, John Frankenheimer. Adapted from the play by Eugene O'Neill. With Fredric March (Harry Hope), Robert Ryan (Larry Slade), Lee Marvin (Hickey). 6.

This is one of O'Neill's plays that was inspired by direct experience—of the bars he once habituated in New York. The principal characters, all alcoholic failures, are drawn from life, except for the truth-seeking visitor, Hickey, who tries to restore them all to the sense of reality from which they are so desperately trying to escape. The film is notable for the sensitive and moving performances by the late Robert Ryan and the late Fredric March (the last before his death).

I'LL BE SEEING YOU
(USA, 1944). Direction: William Dieterle. With Joseph Cotten (shell-shocked soldier). 5, 9.

Joseph Cotten is outstanding in his performance of a shell-shocked patient undergoing psychiatric treatment. The romantic element in the film supervenes at the end, when he is cured through a love affair, but the clinical sequences of the film give it validity.

IMAGES
(USA, 1972). Direction and script: Robert Altman. Music: John Williams. With Susannah York (Cathryn), René Auberjonois (Hugh), Marcel Bozzuffi (René), Hugh Millais (Marcel), Cathryn Harris (Susannah). Filmed on location in Ireland. 2.

Images, like *Psycho,* uses the actions of a deranged person for the purpose of producing sensationalistic entertainment. Hitchcock's *Psycho* does this by allowing us to see the effects of this derangement only in the violent behavior of the affected person, who succeeds in killing two of the protagonists and is about to kill the third and last when prevented from doing so at the climax of the film. Altman's *Images* does it by drawing us into the mind of the deranged person so that we share her hallucinations and gather what facts we can about her past and current relationships as we strive to find our way through the maze of actuality and hallucination presented in the film with equal verisimilitude. We end up uncertain about what is fact and what fantasy.

Images is like *Repulsion* in that we share the fears and illusions of the woman protagonist, but in *Repulsion* there is no mystery—indeed there is little doubt about what is actuality and what hallucination. Both Polanski and Altman use their special effects liberally and with striking, often horrifying, effect. Both films become very violent, but in *Images* one is never certain whether or not the violence is real—whether it is the vivid precipitation of wish-fulfilment; the recollection of violence done in the past; or, indeed, violence being performed right now, in the present. There is also deliberate mystification on the simplest level— the telephones look Anglo-Irish but sound American; the locations (actually Irish) are never identified, but cars are driven on the left-hand side of the road; and the railway station in the countryside is resolutely Anglo-Irish. Two important members of the cast are continental Europeans, while René Auberjonois is American and Susannah York is English.

The film opens in a lavish town apartment, where the protagonist, Cathryn, is alone, her husband absent at a business dinner. She is writing a fabulous story in the Tolkien style, *In Search of the Unicorn,* which involves a race of little people she calls the Ums. A friend telephones her, but over her prolonged slew of gossip the voice of another, unidentified woman keeps intruding, insistently telling her that her husband is with another woman. Cathryn replaces the receiver, but the caller persists until finally Cathryn leaves the receiver off the hook and goes to bed. Her husband, Hugh, returning very late, manages to reassure her when she challenges him, and he promises to take her to their country home, since she is so unnerved. When he finally kisses her, she bursts into a sudden fit of screaming because momentarily he turns into her dead lover, René. The camera meanwhile has explored all the paraphernalia of the apartment—pictures, books, paints, cameras, and wind chimes (the latter to become a motif of the film).

Their country house, called Green Grove, is remotely situated in a beautiful, wooded valley near a lake. When Hugh halts the car on the top of a hill to admire the view, he spots some quail and, leaving Cathryn, stalks them with his gun. Cathryn then has her second hallucination. From the top of the hill she watches herself drive to the entrance to the house below. Cathryn II glances up and sees Cathryn I looking down at her, a minute figure in silhouette on the distant hilltop. This duality is to recur frequently, as if Cathryn I is left permanently on the hilltop.

Once inside the house, Cathryn's hallucinations increase. They involve her directly with two men, René and Marcel, as well as with her husband, Hugh. One of them, René, appears to be solely a figment of the mind since he inhabits the house like some solid kind of ghost, taunting Cathryn sardonically. Her husband is unaware of this presence. Cathryn may even have killed René, to judge from implications in their dialogue. "You have been dead for three years," she says. Enraged, she flings an object at him, drawing blood. He then says, "You might have killed me." She responds, "Again?" Later, indeed, she does shoot him, as if reenacting some past incident. (Alternatively, Cathryn may have put René on a plane that crashed. It also appears that she may have miscarried his child.) The second man, Marcel, a neighbor, is introduced into the house by Hugh. Marcel treats Cathryn with the insolent familiarity of a macho lover. In his case too there is a mystery. He has no wife but a small daughter who appears suddenly in a closet-cupboard in the house, having presumably hidden herself there to surprise Cathryn, to whom she bears a remarkable likeness.

That night Cathryn appears to make composite love with all three of the men at once—Hugh, René, and Marcel. The next day she has a further encounter in her house with her seeming lover of the present, Marcel, and their disputation leads him to challenge her to shoot him—and she does, with horrific realism. It is unclear, in fact, whether she has actually killed both lovers or has merely imagined killing them out of some obscure desire to destroy them. She acts throughout as if she wants the attention of these men, including her somewhat brusque and unpleasant husband (very ably and convincingly played by René Auberjonois), while at the same time wanting some independence from them—a life of her own, symbolized by her literary imaginings. She retires to the hillside, with its steep waterfall, and there meets her alter ego. One Cathryn wears a brown coat, the other white. The two Cathryns appear to reflect the direct experience of schizophrenia; which of the two is the actual one is deliberately left ambiguous.

Hugh departs by train from the nearby village in order to fulfil an engagement back in town, leaving Cathryn alone for three days with her fantasies. When she returns home from the station, she discovers Marcel waiting for her. This proves more than she can stand. Taking a knife to him, she stabs him to death and then slices up his body. Blood streams in quantity over the carpet. Marcel's child then arrives but completely disregards her seemingly dead father. Cathryn then drives the girl back to her home, where Marcel is discovered to be present, alive and well.

On the drive back over the moorlands, Cathryn encounters on the open road, first her original lover—the dead René—and then her other self, of whom she is both afraid and resentful. She deliberately rams the car into Cathryn II, and the body plunges down a precipice into the waterfall. Immediately afterwards, Cathryn leaves for town. As she drives through rain and stares at the lights of oncoming cars through the moving blades of her windshield wiper, a fantasia of color images builds up in her mind.

Back in her town house, Cathryn takes a shower (the images here are reminiscent of *Psycho*). The other Cathryn continues to haunt her. The film ends when she retires back to her writing about the unicorn. The body of her husband is seen lying at the foot of the waterfall. Cathryn, it would seem, has subconsciously disposed of him, though his death could be conceived of as actual.

IN COLD BLOOD

(USA, 1967). Production, direction, and script: Richard Brooks. Based on the book by Truman Capote. Camera: Conrad Hall. Music: Quincy Jones. Filmed with the cooperation of the people and law enforcement agencies of Kansas, Missouri, Colorado, Nevada, Texas, and Mexico. With Robert Blake, (Perry Smith), Scott Wilson (Dick Hickock), John Forsythe (Alvin Dewey), Paul Stewart (reporter), Gerald S. O'Loughlin (Harold Nye). 4.

Both the novel (originally published as a four-part serial in the *New Yorker*) and the film created considerable controversy at the time of their appearance. Capote's aim appears to have been to recreate as nearly as possible in a piece of documentary fiction the detailed events leading to the murder on 15 November 1959 of the Clutter family in Holcomb, a remote rural community in Kansas. He traces the subsequent action of the killers, of the police handling the case, and of the people in the area where it had happened; the events leading to the arrests of the murderers in Las Vegas, the police interrogations, the trial in Garden City, Kansas, and the execution of the murderers after unsuccessful appeals. The backgrounds of the two murderers are revealed through their own comments, which in the film lead to numerous brief flashbacks and police visits to their parental homes.

In the novel the reader is left to interpret the evidence and draw his own conclusions about the validity of the motives and psychological explanations. He is also left to either accept or reject the final issue of the justice of capital punishment. In contrast, as a result of Brook's very dramatic screen treatment, Conrad Hall's spectacular cinematography, and the suggestive appearance and manner of Robert Blake and Scott Wilson (who played the killers), the film cannot avoid seeming to take sides. Further bias, often to the point of excess, is given by Quincy Jones's melodramatic music.[39]

Capote's detailed, four-hundred-page narrative, is crosscut like a film from the Clutters and their community to the complex movements of the killers-to-be (their meeting, once Perry is out on parole; their long journey to Kansas; right up to the moment they park their car and douse their lights outside the Clutters' isolated residence). Tension mounts from the sheer accumulation of dry and detailed fact before the bloody event, already known by the reader as the inevitable follow-up. In the film these events are treated somewhat differently, as the gathering drama of a conventional crime thriller, shot with all the highlights and shadows of black-and-white cinematography. Given that difference, the film is excellently done, with all the added gruesomeness that results from knowing we are seeing this reconstruction take place in the actual Clutter home, indeed in the actual rooms where the original crimes were committed, while many of the people who were present at the time and knew the Clutters as friends and neighbors take part in the movie.

Capote said that he wanted Brooks above all other directors to make the film because he alone accepted without question that it should be shot in black and white, played by actors relatively unknown (that is, without "public faces"), and made on the exact Kansas locations involved.[40]

Whether one uses in describing the killers the newer term *sociopath* or the older *psychopath* (still in common use in accounts of this film, as well as of more recent films such as *Taxidriver* and *Dirty Harry*), the film raises the issue that it may well have created too much curiosity or even sympathy for such unusual personalities, leaving the victims, who are duller people, to stew in their own blood. This becomes evident in the film's treatment of Dick and particularly Perry during their childhood (which might seem to imply that *they* are the real victims, not the colorlessly conventional, church-going Clutters), culminating in the trembling bemusement of Perry as he faces the gallows and becomes a bound and hooded figure dropping in slow motion, suspended by the hangman's noose. The film certainly ends with capital punishment fully exposed as society's taking a life for a life, "in cold blood."

Capote researched his macabre subject in a spirit, some might say, close to voyeurism. Indeed, the very literary excellence of the book in all its detailed and delicately spun irony enhances this voyeuristic effect. Capote's shadow in the film is the grim-faced and sardonic reporter, played by Paul Stewart (the caretaker in charge of Xanadu in *Citizen Kane*). He is permitted, like Capote, to interview the incarcerated murderers, who in real life waited five years before facing execution (an event which in the film seems, rather inevitably, to come soon after the trial).

Before assessing whether or not these men should be considered criminally insane, it has to be noted that both were judged fit to stand trial, of which we hear nothing in the film but the final, damning rhetoric of the prosecuting attorney when he addresses the jury, slamming on the open Bible, from which he quotes the vengeful words from *Genesis*, "Whoso sheddeth man's blood, by man shall his blood be shed." In the film we only have the overt behavior of the two men, the constant expression of their morose attitude towards life, and the flashbacks to their youth to guide us as to the nature of their personalities. Of the two, Dick is the more normal; although a man of twenty-eight or so, his motivations are those of a vengeful adolescent whom life in prison has retarded. He has no conscience about ripping off small goods in stores, and he glories in stealing cars and passing off dud checks on unwary salesmen. He boasts that when they rob Clutter—about whom he has heard so much gossip from a fellow prisoner in jail and who, with a safe full of money in his house, Dick assumes to be rich—they will have to be ruthless and "leave no witnesses." He openly displays his gun on the back seat of his car as if he were going out shooting game. It is he who organizes the journey to Kansas in his old car, he who plans the robbery, he who voices all the challenging threats against a society he wants to punish. He has no conscience about what he does and no feeling for his potential victims. But he is certainly not insane; he is completely, rationally responsible for everything he does, though he never seems conscious of this responsibility or able to act in a responsible fashion.

Not so with Perry Smith, who was thirty-one at the time of the murders. While Dick comes from what Capote described as a "wholesome lower middle-class Kansas family,"[41] Perry is the son of a wandering gold prospector and a beautiful Cherokee Indian woman, a rodeo rider, who finally left her husband because of his cruelty. Living alone with his father, Perry was eventually turned out of their cabin in the wilds at the point of a gun—the father seriously pretending to shoot his son with a gun that was not in fact loaded. Capote said that he had great difficulty penetrating Perry's protective facade, only breaking through initially because he could genuinely claim to have known Humphrey Bogart, Perry's screen idol. It is Perry who actually claims to have taken to the family during the brief time he knew them and indeed intervened to stop Dick from raping the young daughter. The murders are finally committed with astonishing untidiness—a kind of nonchalance mixed with acute anxiety. The killings come after attempts at casual conversation with the bound victims, who are kept separated from each other in different parts of the house. It would seem that neither Dick nor even Perry could have committed so appalling a crime had they operated singly, but together they formed a team capable of any act of violence. Each had a deep need for the support of the other. As the Capote-like character says at the end of the film: "Neither would have done it alone. But together they made a third person." Though virtually no hint is given in the film of any homosexual link between them, this certainly could have existed in a latent form.

Perry has obsessive adolescent dreams of fame as a guitar player and pop star, and of success gold-prospecting in Mexico. In the film he also tends to undergo flashbacks (if not hallucinations) to bad moments in his childhood—his father thrashing his Indian wife with a belt when she was unfaithful; or leveling his gun at him, threatening him with death. Punctuating the film, these flashbacks serve to build up a certain sympathy (or empathy) for Perry, who reached only the third grade at school. He also retained his childhood belief in the protection afforded him by a great yellow bird—a creature of vengeance that descends to attack the nuns who used to beat him for wetting his bed. He asserts that his previous sentence in jail was for homicide—he beat a man to death with a chain. "Why did you kill him?" Dick asks. "Don't know," says Perry. "For no reason at all." "That's the best reason of all," says Dick, with cynical bravado. Perry carts around with him not only his guitar but a large and heavy cardboard carton full of scripts, books, and letters. At any confrontation, however casual, he appears nervous, and he constantly retires to the men's room to swallow quantities of aspirin. It is with his execution that the film concludes. His final, heavy heartbeats dominate the sound track, after his last, bemused words, "I think maybe I'd like to apologize—but who to?"

In the film the attitude of the police is one of disillusionment, even cynicism: "Murder's no mystery, only the motive. . . . Who could do such a thing as the Clutter murders? These days, take your pick on any street . . . if you allow them life imprisonment, in seven years they'll be eligible for parole." The reporter, present at the executions, acts like a kind of dramatic chorus. About the hangman he is asked, "How much does he get to hang him?" and replies, "Three hundred dollars." He is then asked rhetorically, "Has he got a name?" and replies, "We, the people."

No film has done as much as this one to stress the "banality of evil," to quote Hannah Arendt's celebrated phrase in connection with Eichmann. It is arguable that the film actually elicits any real sympathy for Perry—rather, perhaps, some measure of understanding how he instinctively came to do what he did as the deeper, more mysterious part of the combined Dick-Perry psyche. But understanding is not the same as sympathy. He had no motive for killing the Clutters, yet he did so, brutally, deliberately, "in cold blood." It is this inescapable fact that both the novel and the film cannot fail to establish.

THE INNOCENTS
(Britain, 1961). Direction: Jack Clayton. Adapted from *The Turn of the Screw,* by Henry James. With Deborah Kerr (Miss Giddens), Martin Stephen (Miles), Pamela Franklin (Flora). 2.

In this very well-made version of Henry James's ambivalent story, Deborah Kerr plays the distressed spinster governess confronted by the possession of two overly sweet-mannered, parentless children by the spirits of two family employees, both of whom have recently died. In their lifetime they gained an evil, corrupting hold on the children and now haunt the mansion and the estate where the children, their governess, and the housekeeper live together, totally isolated from the outside world. In her performance Deborah Kerr hints at this well-raised young woman's sexual repression and the approaching obsessive love she feels for the boy, Miles. Though no character in this film is certifiably insane, the children are as much "possessed" by the vicious controlling spirits as the child is in *The Exorcist.*

INTERIORS
(USA, 1978). Direction and script: Woody Allen. With Kristin Griffith (Flyn), Marybeth Hurt (Joey), Richard Jordan (Frederick), Diane Keaton (Renata), E. G. Marshall (Arthur), Geraldine Page (Eve), Maureen Stapleton (Pearl), Sam Waterston (Michael). The script of the film was published in *Four Films of Woody Allen* (New York: Random House, 1983). 1a.

As if made to lay the ghost of what he has come to regard as an overly-successful career in the comedy of contemporary maladjustment, *Interiors* is Woody Allen's first wholly serious work. It has been (I think improperly) compared disparagingly to Bergman's work, as if it were some sort of inferior imitation. Bergman is admittedly a director Allen admires, but there is a great difference between his rootedly American film—full of social-cultural preoccupations and desire for success or recognition in a monied world—and Bergman's agonized and very Swedish later films, with their groupings of characters essentially isolated from outward social commitment.

Interiors concerns the self-indulgent family of Arthur, a rich New York lawyer and an essentially decent man who is in the process of a divorce and remarriage. His first wife, Eve, is a neurotic, overly-complicated, and emotionally demanding wife. The new woman in his life, Pearl, is a disarmingly cheerful and affectionate widow with no cultural ties or hang-ups whatsoever. Eve, a totally dominating, even sinister, woman (played with a heavy emphasis by Geraldine Page) is an interior decorator prepared to impose her cool and formalized tastes on her wealthy clients and family alike. Of her three daughters, only the youngest, Flyn, an actress, has achieved complete independence. Having failed to hold Arthur any longer through emotional blackmail, Eve is prepared to go to the lengths of attempted suicide to retain her familial hold on her other unhappy daughters. These are Joey, who works for a publisher and lives with Michael, a filmmaker trying unsuccessfully to make films with a political message; and Renata, an established poet, who is obsessed with death and married to an unsuccessful novelist.

The film is primarily concerned with the emotional ties and struggles of these three women—Eve, Joey, and Renata—and to a minor extent of the daughters' two dependent men. Toward Pearl, the girls adopt a culturally snobbish attitude. Eve "celebrates" Arthur's wedding, attended by the girls and their menfolk in the family beach house on Long Island, by arriving after the ceremony and solemnly marching into the sea to meet her death.

The film is admirably directed and acted, and impeccably decorated and photographed. In a sense the troubles of this family, and of the daughters' menfolk, are all self-imposed, emerging from what they think they ought to be in the eyes of society rather than what they innately are. In this they are quite unlike Bergman's principal characters, whose sufferings are innate and unavoidable. Both the elder girls resent their mother's hold on them yet feel guilty when they neglect her, however impossible she may seem. And it is Joey's final outburst that Eve has ruined her children's lives that drives Eve to suicide, just as much as her former husband's remarriage. In this family, dog eats dog, and Eve's totally unbalanced nature leads not only to her own fatal undoing but to the unease and unhappiness of her two elder daughters.

IT'S A MAD, MAD, MAD, MAD WORLD
(USA, 1963). Direction: Stanley Kramer. With an all-star cast of comedians, including Milton Berle, Sid Caesar, Ethel Merman, Mickey Rooney, Phil Silvers, Terry Thomas, Jim Backus, Jimmy Durante, Buster Keaton, Edward Everett Horton, Joe E. Brown, Zasu Pitts, Jerry Lewis, Jack Benny, and the Three Stooges. 8.

The action of this three-hour slapstick comedy of multiple chasing after buried treasure invites laughter at ceaseless burlesque violence, repetitive destruction and pratfalls, and comic beating-up. The protagonists are a frenetic and vicious lot, looking out for themselves at everyone else's expense. It would seem that some allegory about the insanity of modern society is intended.

J'ACCUSE
(France, 1919). Direction: Abel Gance. With Marise Dauvray (Edith), Severin-Mars (François), Jean Diaz (Remould). 5.

Remould, a poet, is in love with Edith, the wife of François Laurin. The men, both in the French army during the First World War, become reconciled. Edith is taken prisoner by the Germans but returns from captivity with a baby, which rekindles François's jealousy. After both men return to the front, François is killed and Remould driven insane through shell shock. Back home he invites the villagers to witness the march of the dead and wounded through the countryside. The vision leaves those who witness it horrified and conscience-striken. Remould tears up his prewar poems with their pacifist message. His new message is, "J'accuse"; he accuses the sun for giving its light to so evil a world. And with this he too dies.

The period of 1914 to 1918 came too early in the development of the silent cinema—its third decade of short filmmaking but only virtually its first in films of feature length—for the complex subject of shell shock and other forms of psychological disturbance caused by the strain of service on the battlefronts to appear as a likely issue in films. Neither the filmmakers nor the public understood these matters and preferred to limit themselves to such issues as heroism and endurance in the trenches and outright villainy and sadism of the enemy. The only negative factor in men's behavior under battle conditions was cowardice and fear, which had, naturally enough, to be overcome by all soldiers who called themselves men. As melodramas of patriotism, the war films of 1914 to 1918 and of the more immediate postwar period pictured Allied soldiers as heroes and the Germans as sadistic villains, and left it at that.

Perhaps the most sensitive of First World War films (many of which have not survived) were made by D. W. Griffith. These included *Hearts of the World* (1918), largely shot on location in France during the last phases of the war, and *Isn't Life Wonderful?* (1924), his postwar film, made on location in Germany and showing the impact on a Polish immigrant family of the runaway inflation of 1922–23. Other notable American story films were *Four Horsemen of the Apocalypse* (1921), *The Big Parade* (1925), and *What Price Glory?* (1925), all exposing the horrors of war and the sufferings endured by soldiers and civilians alike—a theme directly taken up a few years later in the British films *Reveille* (1924) and *Dawn* (1927) (the story of the martyrdom at the hands of the Germans of the heroic nurse, Edith Cavell) and in the German film *War Is Hell* (1931).

The only exception to this during the immediate postwar period was Abel Gance's pioneer film, *J'accuse,* a symbolistic work with a strong antiwar message. It was first released in 1919 and remade with sound in 1937. Produced with the help of the French army, who supplied Gance with footage of the war front, the first version aimed to expose the horrors of war and the martyrdom of France at the hands of German militarism. The high point, the allegorical sequence he called the March of the Dead, was later contrasted markedly in the somewhat re-edited version of 1922 with the Victory Parade, staged by Joffe, Foch, and Clemenceau. It involved, however, the only attempt of the period to fully show the effects of shell shock on the protagonist. The sound-film remake of 1937, unfortunately, does not equal the original version in power.

Only in later First World War films, made during the period when pacifist sentiments became predominant, do we find the destructive effects of war shown on the *minds* of the protagonists. One example is the German film *Maedchen in Uniform* (1931), which shows the militaristic dictatorship imposed by a Prussian-minded head teacher in a girls' school and the effects of her strictness on an overly sensitive girl, who in the end commits suicide. Other examples are Pabst's two German films *Westfront 1918* (1930), in which a young lieutenant goes mad under stress, and *Kameradschaft* (1931), during which a French miner, while being rescued after a pit disaster by a German rescue worker in a gas mask, is suddenly projected back into memories of hand-to-hand fighting with gas masks in the trenches. *All Quiet on the Western Front* (1930) and the British film of the Dardanelles campaign, *Tell England* (1930), both exposed war as endured by the fighting man. But the greater output of First World War films, even during the later 1930s, involved the heroic-action image of their predecessors.

JULIET OF THE SPIRITS
(see 8½)

KING OF HEARTS
(France and Italy, 1966). Direction: Philippe De Broca. With Alan Bates (Plumpick), Geneviève Bujold (Coquelicot), Jean-Claude Brialy (duke of Clubs), Pierre Brasseur (General Geranium), Micheline Presle (Madame Eglantine). 8.

It is 1918, and the Germans are evacuating occupied territory in France. Hearing rumors that the retreating Germans have mined a small rural town north of Paris, where they have been based, and that the buildings will go up at midnight, the citizens evacuate. Only the lunatic asylum, though deserted by its staff, is left inhabited. The Resistance gets word about the mines to a Scottish unit poised to liberate the town. The pompous Scottish colonel is intrigued by the mysterious German code messages, in particular, the "mackerel that are frying" and the actions at midnight of the Black Knight. He details Plumpick, a young misfit in the unit, to enter the town alone, decode the messages, and defuse the mines, even though he has no technical knowledge of such matters, his only occupation being to look after the carrier pigeons.

Plumpick enters the seemingly deserted town with his bird cage just as the last of the German personnel are leaving. Hiding from them in the lunatic asylum, he assumes the white garb of the other lunatics. The mad folk greet him with delight as their long-lost King of Hearts, their much-loved monarch returning to them at last. The Germans gone, the lunatics take over the town, assuming what identities they choose—generals, bishops, dukes, brothel-keepers, whores, and the like. They even liberate the encaged animals of a traveling circus, deserted by its owners.

Plumpick's coronation is arranged immediately, and his engagement to Coquelicot, the most virginal of the inmates of the newly established brothel, announced. Now wearing civilian clothes, Plumpick is entranced by it all and almost forgets his mission—defusing the mines. While dispatching despairing messages to his colonel by carrier pigeon, he finds his attention completely divided between living up to the romantic fantasies of his coronation and engagement and stopping the town from being blown up at midnight. He even tries to persuade his new friends to leave the town as normal citizens have done, but they refuse. To survive in this world, they assure him, you have absolutely got to keep away from it. "It's too dangerous outside," they affirm. "Life is really quite simple. It's a game of generals and whores." Plumpick, on the point of leaving on his own to report the failure of his mission to save the town, finally opts to stay. The lunatics receive him back with delight.

Only at the eleventh hour does Plumpick realize that one of the codes refers to the rotating figure of a black knight that strikes the church bell at midnight. It is this figure that will set off the fuse controlling the mines. With heroic effort he manages to stop the figure from striking the church bell—in fact, he receives the blow himself instead and so saves the town. A midnight fireworks display, set off by the delighted lunatics, convinces the retreating Germans that their mining operations have been successful.

The following day, opposing units of Scots and Germans meet in the town, confront each other, and with the lunatics as observers of the folly of others, wipe each other out to a man. "I think they're overacting," says one of the lunatics. The sole survivor, Plumpick is decorated and congratulated by the commanding officer of the French unit that arrives to liberate the town. The original inhabitants return, and the lunatics sadly retreat back into their asylum, the only place they now feel to be safe. Fantasy, after all, begins at home.

Plumpick is left on his own to decide what to do. He opts out of the "real" world, in which he now feels out of place. The final shot reveals him standing naked with his bird cage, facing the nuns who have resumed their care of the asylum inmates, whom he seeks to rejoin.

KLUTE
(USA, 1971). Direction: Alan J. Pakula. With Jane Fonda (Bree Daniels), Donald Sutherland (John Klute). 3.

This celebrated psychological thriller concerns the strange relationship that grows up between Klute, a small-town detective from Pennsylvania, and Bree Daniels—a New York call girl whom Klute consults persistently for certain information. Klute has come to New York to search for a missing friend, Tom, a research scientist who has been missing for six months. Though a seemingly highly respectable man, Tom is known to have written Bree an obscene letter. Her occupation notwithstanding, Bree is a very middle-class would-be actress and model, who is at once nervous, vulnerable, independent-minded, and very articulate. She is extremely resistant for a while to Klute, in spite of his gathering affection for her and desire to protect her. Bree is totally explicit about herself to her clients and to her psychiatrist—an extraordinary performance that won Jane Fonda an Academy Award.

Klute worms his way gradually into Bree's confidence with promises to help her with a menacing client, who has caused the death of two other call girls. The missing scientist turns out to have been murdered by the same man, who is his former employer in Pennsylvania, a psychopathic killer with a penchant for tape-recording his victims and, as he confesses in his final confrontation with Bree, turned on to killing "girls like you." It is, of course, Klute who manages to rescue her at the last moment.

James Monaco said of the film: "Jane Fonda dominates this filmed portrait of a woman who as prostitute is both classic victim and psychological master of her situation. Screenwriters Andy and Dave Lewis . . . couch . . . their . . . portrait of this archetypal woman in a mystery . . . a character who reflects with specific verisimilitude the ultimate dilemma of womankind."[42] Penelope Houston wrote: "Brilliantly, Pakula and his cameraman Gordon Willis keep splitting the screen almost in two, focussing the attention on areas of light but also leaving a half-conscious awareness of the shadowy other side: a great technique for voyeur's cinema. . . . *Klute* taps specifically urban apprehensions: the vulnerabilities and the corrupted defences of a decaying city."[43]

LADY SINGS THE BLUES
(USA, 1972). Direction, Sidney J. Furie. With Diana Ross (Eleanora Fagan), Billie Dee Williams (Louis McKay). 6.

Based on the autobiography by Billie Holiday, the action is set in New York in the early 1930s. Eleanora Fagan, a black prostitute, aspires to show business and manages to become a Harlem club singer under the name of Billie Holiday. When on tour with a white band, she finds herself subjected to persecution. After her arrest on a drug charge, she loses her licence to perform in New York, and her lover, a gambler called Louis McKay, tries unsuccessfully to help her. Her final success in a concert in Carnegie Hall fails to secure the restoration of her licence, and, remaining hooked, she dies at the early age of forty-four. The film milks every possible sensation associated with the life of this celebrated, highly individual singer, including rape, violent sexuality, murder, drugs, and hysteria.[44]

LAST TANGO IN PARIS

(Italy and France, 1972). Direction and co-script, Bernardo Bertolucci. With Marlon Brando (Paul), Maria Schneider (Jeanne), Jean-Pierre Léaud (Tom), Maria Michi (Rosa's Mother), Massimo Girotti (Marcel). 3, 7.

This film centers around Paul—a middle-aged American, who, depressed and self-obsessed, has a worn-out, hunched-up, down-at-heel appearance—and a young Frenchwoman, Jeanne, who has the look of a sensual girl-about-town. While viewing an empty apartment in Paris, Paul and Jeanne meet acidently and, virtually on sight, have instinctual intercourse. They then go their separate ways—she to meet Tom, her fiancé—a boringly intense young filmmaker who believes he can capture all he needs to know about her by making her the subject of a cinéma-vérité movie; Paul, to a shabby hotel run by his adulterous wife, Rosa, who has just committed suicide. Without introduction or explanation, Jeanne and Paul continue to meet and lovemake—their only rule is that they must remain completely anonymous, drawn together solely by their primitive and at times savagely sadistic sexual desire. Meanwhile, the film fills in the background to the lives of both protagonists—Paul's relationships with his wife, his sentimental mother-in-law, and his wife's former lover, Marcel (with whom he feels a certain sympathy) and Jeanne's relationship with her widowed mother—who is fixated by the memory of her dead husband—and with her fiancé, Tom.

After the third day of intimacy with Paul Jeanne wants to abandon her imminent marriage because she has fallen in love with Paul. At first Paul receives her admission of love (and its consequence of getting to know him as an individual) with a depressive cynicism, but soon he too capitulates, proposing marriage himself. Breaking his self-imposed rule of anonymity, he tells her the sordid details of his life and reveals the misogyny that has sprung from his love-hate relationship with his now-dead wife. He drags Jeanne to a low-class dance hall, where a tango contest is in progress, but by now she is both disillusioned and frightened and breaks away to run back home. Paul, drunk, follows her to her mother's apartment, where she shoots him with her dead father's pistol. She then proceeds hurriedly to fabricate a story about assault by a stranger to explain her impulsive act to the police.

Last Tango in Paris is, as it were, an image for the dance of death of contemporary mores in mating and loving—egotistic, fraught with an urgent need to escape loneliness, which seems no longer possible to overcome, through the illusory attachments of romantic love, which attracted former generations. The emphasis is on the separation of the sexes—Paul and Rosa, Marcel and Rosa, Jeanne and Tom, Paul and Jeanne—as well on as the anxious loneliness of the women of the older generation—Paul's mother-in-law and Jeanne's widowed mother. The credits to the film are backed by portraits by Bacon of vulnerable, exposed, distorted humans, male and female, recumbent or, like Rosa, laid out in the stubborn tranquility of death. As Jan Dawson pointed out in an exceptionally perceptive review of the film:

> The screen is literally divided in two; and despite the magnificent baroque arcs of Vittorio Storar's camerawork, Bertolucci keeps it almost as literally divided thereafter, underlining his characters' emotional conflicts and essential separateness with some masterly chiaroscuro effects. Paul, filling the left half of the frame, hears the details of his wife's suicide from a maid busy mopping up the blood behind a shower curtain on the right; a doorframe separates him and his mother-in-law for much of their initial altercation; after their first, brutal copulation, he and Jeanne lie exhausted on opposite corners of the floor; while the amber light of the Passy apartment in which he seeks to exorcise, or perhaps merely affirm, an oppressive reality is diagonally cut through by the dark reflection of the slatted blinds.[45]

In fact, the whole aesthetic of the film is a visual reflection of the theme of living and partly living in the half-light and shadow of unavoidable semi-isolation. Only Paul, musing angrily and tearfully over his wife's beautifully robed and decorated corpse, realizes this truth: "Even if a husband spends two hundred fuckin' years, he's never going to comprehend his wife's true nature." Jan Dawson continued:

> It is no mean irony that the foul-mouthed and anally-fixated Paul should emerge as the true Romantic hero, the dispossessed heir not just of Hemingway and Scott Fitzgerald but also of an older tradition which acknowledges the inseparability of pain and passion, Eros and Thanatos, and glorifies the elements of solitude, mystery and mortality.[46]

This could be claimed to be Marlon Brando's finest single performance, a summation, verification, and fulfillment of all that he has stood for in the most revealing of his screen performances since the 1950s, when Bertolucci was in his early teens. Poet and filmmaker, Marxist but also individualist, Bertolucci was thirty-two when he made *Last Tango in Paris,* which was banned from showing in Italy.

LET THERE BE LIGHT
(see: FREUD, THE SECRET PASSION)

LILITH
(USA, 1964). Direction and script: Robert Rossen. With Warren Beatty (Vincent Bruce), Jean Seberg (Lilith Arthur), Peter Fonda (Stephen). 3.

Vincent Bruce, who has a history of madness in his family, joins the staff of an asylum for wealthy schizophrenics as a trainee therapist. He comes under the spell of the patient Lilith and, in spite of his position, they become passionate lovers, although she has lesbian tendencies and other mysterious preoccupations. His jealousy of another patient, Stephen, who is also in love with Lilith, leads to Stephen's suicide, with the result that Vincent commits himself as a patient. Lilith's love has been as much a torment to him as a paradise; she is both a predator and a bestower of love, and she has a powerful narcissistic trait. In a review Tom Milne spoke of "the film's central argument, that madness is a two-way mirror, depending on whether you are talking about what it *looks* like, or what it *feels* like", and added "*Lilith* is a remarkable attempt, completely success-ful for three-quarters of the way, to dig a little deeper in an almost untilled field, and to throw some light on that mystery of mysteries—the relationship between madness and the creative imagination."[47]

LONG DAY'S JOURNEY INTO NIGHT
(USA, 1962). Direction: Sidney Lumet. Adapted from the play by Eugene O'Neill. With Katharine Hepburn (Mary), Ralph Richardson (James), Jason Robards, Jr. (Jamie), Dean Stockwell (Edmund), Jeanne Barr (Cathleen). 1a, 6.

Another of O'Neill's plays that drew on his own personal experience (see also; *The Iceman Cometh*), this lengthy study of the Tyrone family (the menfolk al-coholic, the mother addicted to drugs) was O'Neill's portrait of his own family and a way, as he put it, "to face my dead at last." Although the individual characters are brilliantly acted as near-solo performances, the family itself, bound together by their Irish blood and heritage in a perpetual state of love-hatred, scarcely come across as closely bound or entirely Irish.

LOOKING FOR MR. GOODBAR
(USA, 1977). Direction and script: Richard Brooks. Based on the novel by Judith Rossner. With Diane Keaton (Theresa Dunn), Tuesday Weld (Katherine), Wil-liam Atherton (James), Richard Kiley (Theresa's father), Richard Gere (Tony Lapato), Alan Feinstein (Martin Engle). 3.

Looking for Mr. Goodbar recounts with a somewhat heavy hand the mental and physical collapse of a strictly raised girl, Theresa Dunn, second of three daugh-ters in a Roman Catholic family dominated by a tyrannical father. After graduat-ing, Theresa becomes a teacher of deaf children, but the film concentrates on the tragic outcome for her of a series of sexual encounters with a self-centered teacher, Martin Engle (another uncaring father figure) which began at college and continues after she leaves home to neighbor her older married sister, Katherine, in Manhattan. Among the men with whom Theresa becomes in-volved is the restrained, solicitous social worker, James, who falls obsessively in love with her, though their relationship remains platonic. After having herself sterilized and taking to drugs, Theresa's final decline sets in. She begins an affair. She meets many men in a singles' bar. The first of these is the irresponsible Tony Lapato, who has sex with her and who eventually beats her up. At the very time she is hoping to amend her way of life she is raped and murdered by a drug-addicted homosexual, Gary, whom she picked up at the bar.

In spite of the melodramatic violence of the end, the film manages, largely through the seriousness and intensity of Diane Keaton's understanding of this highly disturbed girl, to convey how the roots of her trouble stem from her family's collective neurosis and her unconscious struggle to free herself from the rigors of her upbringing through indulgence in sex. She is also haunted by the fear of congenital spinal trouble, originating from a sickness in her childhood, which put her for a period in a plaster cast. In an effective review John Pym wrote:

> Beneath the fractured surface of *Looking for Mr. Goodbar*—the broken-backed episodes, the staccato aphorisms and strident tones in which the characters communicate, the multitude of self-conscious mirrored images, the frequently over-obvious camera set-ups—there exists a movie which, for all its lack of subtlety, attempts with a certain bludgeoning success to communicate a black vision of one human being's self-willed destruction. Viewed as a parable of the fate awaiting modern, oversexed American womanhood . . . the film is palpably flawed and overstated; seen, however, as Theresa's version of her own self-destruction—in which respect it is significant that nothing happens in the film unless in some way she engineers it—the best-selling, pulp story assumes a greater unity and conviction.[48]

THE LOST WEEKEND
(USA, 1945). Direction: Billy Wilder. Scenario: Billy Wilder, Charles Brackett. Based on the novel by Charles R. Jackson. With Ray Milland (Don Birnam), Phillip Terry (his brother), Jane Wyman (Helen), Howard da Silva (barman). 6.

This film, an early work in Wilder's career, is unusual because he was to specialize increasingly in sardonically entertaining comedies about the pretentiousness and hypocrisy of the affluent, materialistic, and unscrupulous in American society (*Sunset Boulevard, Kiss Me, Stupid, The Apartment, The Fortune Cookie*, etc.) Taking alcoholism very seriously *The Lost Weekend* would seem an unacceptable subject for the box office. It is, however, a balanced and well-developed film, taking every advantage it can to dramatize the dire situation of the hero, Don Birnam, a thirty-three-year old failed writer, who has for six years been living off his long-suffering brother.

The film begins at the point where Don's brother can no longer tolerate the situation, and where a young woman, Helen, moves almost simultaneously into the scene to take over the seemingly impossible task of the alcoholic's redemption and rehabilitation. The film has a hopeful, upbeat ending, as the alcoholic becomes genuinely frightened by his condition after temporary confinement in the common alcoholic ward in a tough state hospital.

The first part of the film shows realistically Don's obsessive behavior as the alcoholic who is trying to conceal his obsession, in particular from his brother. His supplies of whiskey are resourcefully concealed around the apartment for any possible indulgence. He seeks moments of isolation; he deceives his brother; he boasts about his future achievements as a writer. Stealing the home help's wages, he goes out for booze, spilling his hopes and fears into the sardonic ears of a neighborhood barman, who knows him only too well. He eats nothing, only drinks, and once drunk loses all sense of time.

He first meets Helen at a performance of *Rigoletto*. Not realizing his trouble she takes to him, and they become friends. She even tries to introduce him to her parents—a meeting he nervously avoids by getting drunk once again. The lost weekend itself is the result of his brother's going away for a few days out of sheer despair (they were due to go away together), while he himself dodges meeting Helen, whose concern for him redoubles once she discovers that the man she loves is an alcoholic. She learns of this from his own lips.

Now entirely on his own for the weekend, Don drinks himself into such a condition that he wrecks his brother's apartment in the hopeless search for hidden bottles and then goes out on the town to pawn his typewriter in order to have money for more liquor. In the course of his desperate and fruitless odyssey (the local pawnshops are all closed because of Yom Kippur), he ends up in the alcoholic ward of a state hospital. Here he observes firsthand the horrors of delirium tremens, which, once he is released, he experiences himself when he finds a forgotten supply of whiskey in the apartment. Delirium, a "disease of the night," afflicts him; he screams as he hallucinates the vision of a mouse working its way through a large hole in the living-room wall and of a bat flying around the apartment and finally devouring the mouse. It is from this state of absolute fear and despair that Helen determinedly rescues him, dedicating herself to his rehabilitation and future career as a writer.

The film realistically reflects the primary symptoms of alcoholism: the withdrawal from the world of actuality, fruitless attempts at abstinence, deceit and lying to secure further indulgence in alcohol, the need ceaselessly to boast about achievements to come, disorientation in time and space after drinking, lapses into violence against objects or persons, and gradual collapse into a condition that induces delirium tremens. The delirium causes nervous tremors, hallucinations of noises, illusions of being attacked by other people, and scarifying images of small animals (such as insects, mice, and bats), which either merge into each other or devour each other.

The Lost Weekend was a courageously realistic film, especially for its date and period, and gained Oscars for Wilder and Milland.

LUDWIG
(Italy, France, and West Germany, 1972). Direction: Luchino Visconti. With Helmut Berger (Ludwig). 7.
LUDWIG, REQUIEM FOR A VIRGIN KING
(Germany, 1972). Direction: Hans-Juergen Syberberg. With Harry Baer (Ludwig). 7.

Ludwig II, the notoriously mad king of Bavaria, withdrew from all political responsibilities to indulge his fantasies. He succeeded to the throne at the age of nineteen, and his career (or noncareer) was an extreme example of the search (or nonsearch) for an identity. Like his brother Otto, he was declared insane when he was forty and died mysteriously soon after, in 1886. (Visconti posited that he was murdered—shot—though the official verdict was that he murdered his doctor and then committed suicide.[49]) He was noted as the builder of romantic, fairy-tale castles and also had a mania for the music of Wagner, who exploited the young king shamelessly. Ludwig's fantasies helped him create a personal vision of himself as a creature of both ecstasy and despondency. He had an inclination towards homosexuality, and he became a recluse.

Visconti's film is an aesthetically inspired re-creation of the period, slow-moving, or as the British critic Derek Malcolm put it, "preserved in aspic."[50] Says the king, "I want to remain an enigma to others, and also to myself." He does so, meanwhile totally neglecting Bavaria and draining its resources, especially in his patronage of Wagner. He exists in a condition of ultimate romantic decadence. In an interview with Gaia Servadio, Visconti said at the time the film was in production, "I am fascinated by the man as a clinical case: the story of a person who lives at the extreme limits of the exceptional, outside the rule."[51] Visconti stresses Ludwig's homosexuality—or failed heterosexuality—and his inability to face marriage as the real problem in his life. He emerges in the film as a tragic figure.

Syberberg's film lands at a totally opposite point in the spectrum of technique adopted for the projection of the past for audiences of the present, more especially the German present in Munich. It was conceived in twenty-eight episodes, which fragment time and coherence of narrative—a metaphor for history rather than any attempt to assemble its so-called facts, what the American critic, David Thomson, called "history as a psychic projection." Past and present mingle kaleidoscopically, and become the occasion for a kind of romantic insanity (or nonreason) in portraying Ludwig as a cultural symbol for Germany itself. Although long (139 minutes), it was filmed in eleven days at the incredibly low budget of some one hundred twenty thousand dollars. The "sets" are photographic backings; there is no acting as such, only appearances (or poses) in costume. The music is by Wagner.

Both films were made in the same year. Syberberg was to go on to make a composite projection of Hitler, another mad king living in a state of fantasy.[53]

M
(Germany, 1931). Direction: Fritz Lang. With Peter Lorre (M), Otto Wernicke (Inspector Lohman), Gustaf Gründgens (leader of the underworld). 4.

M, the story of the hunt for a compulsive child-murderer,[54] was based on a recent notorious series of murders that had taken place in Düsseldorf. The film attempts to bring some understanding to bear on the murderer's psychological condition when the climax is reached. Fritz Lang, born in Vienna in 1890, had some Jewish blood in his veins. After war service (in which he lost the sight of an eye), he entered films in 1919. In the 1920s he rose to be one of Germany's most noted directors, making such films as *The Nibelung Saga, Spies, Metropolis,* and the two *Mabuse* subjects. *M* was his first sound film, written, like most of his previous films, by Thea von Harbou, his wife at the time. *M* revealed a new trend towards the powerful dramatization of social and psychological subjects in Lang's work, which he was to develop after leaving Nazi Germany to settle eventually in Hollywood.

In *M* the police in Düsseldorf, led by Inspector Lohman, are baffled by the series of murders of small girls that have taken place in the city, all of them identified by the letter *M* as the work of one psychotic. From the beginning Lang makes the audience aware of the presence of this man, for whose capture a large award is offered. He appears first as a shadowy, unidentified menace looming over his next victim, and finally as a sympathetically portrayed, mild-mannered, almost effeminate, figure wandering the streets in isolation until the next compulsive fit overtakes him. Until the end, he is virtually speechless. The action, brilliantly developed, becomes threefold: the fruitless investigations by the police to unearth the murderer in every corner of the city's underworld; the more fruitful, but much less orthodox, search by the criminal community, who resent the prolonged presence of the police in their midst; and the actions of the murderer himself, a lone figure in the great city, discovered and put to flight when about to assault yet another child through the intervention of the agents of the underworld (one of them a blind beggar).

The murderer is finally cornered in a large office block, empty at night. A posse from the underworld invades the building, taking it apart. The wanted man is captured in a state of terror and subjected to a kangeroo court. He is goaded into pleading in his own defense, crying out that he is unable to control what he is doing during his periodic fits of blackout and revealing his horror afterwards when he discovers in the press what he has done. The assembled underworld (men and women alike) demand that he be lynched, while he and the man the criminals have nominated to conduct his "defense" plead that he be handed over to the police for medical treatment. At the height of this hysterical scene, the police arrive, and official justice takes over.

The sympathetic performance given by Peter Lorre as the murderer dominates the film. Lorre (1904–64), born in Hungary, was a stage actor, trained by Bertolt Brecht, before entering films. Though the treatment of the court scene, in which he voices his despair, is fundamentally melodramatic, Lorre's performance has a terrible sincerity about it, giving the film an almost documentary value, which raises it above the level of the thriller. Lang's fine direction makes *M* a remarkable debut into the era of sound. The city itself—filmed at night as a place of dark streets, covered alleyways, and sinister buildings obscured by shadows—becomes a perpetual image of menace. There are many notable scenes—the washerwoman, mother of a child victim, crying out for her daughter down the empty well of a tenement staircase; the murderer's shadow cast over the poster offering the reward for his capture while beneath him the child pursues her rolling ball, and her balloon floats up to catch in the telegraph wires above; the murderer's nervous whistling of a theme from Grieg's *Peer Gynt* before he acts; the police raids on the city's underworld; the constant use of mirrors and reflecting surfaces like shop windows to show the murderer's wanderings and lonely self-contemplation; and the murderer's final horror when pursued and trapped in the office block.[55]

MAGIC
(USA, 1978). Direction: Richard Attenborough. Script: William Goldman. Based on the novel by William Goldman. With Anthony Hopkins (Corky Withers), Ann-Margret (Peggy Ann Snow), Burgess Meredith (Ben Greene). 4.

This melodramatic story is reminiscent in some respects of the episode in the British film *Dead of Night* (1946), in which Michael Redgrave played superbly the inhibited ventriloquist whose personality becomes totally subject to the brash identity of his dummy. Anthony Hopkins, as Corky Withers, in *Magic* is in exactly the same position. His need to fulfill himself as an entertainer and overcome his basic shyness find an outlet over the years through the dummy, Fats. Fats is a foul-mouthed alter ego, who not only dominates his performer but injects him with homicidal tendencies. In a moment of confrontation with his agent, Ben Greene, Corky is driven to kill him. He throws the body in a lake near the solitary cabin where he has been making love to Peggy, a former school friend. When Peggy's estranged husband, Duke, returns, he finds Greene's body washed up on the lake shore. Duke is then himself killed by Corky. Jealous of his relationship with Peggy, Fats tries to induce Corky to kill the girl, but instead Corky kills himself and in so doing destroys Fats as well.

THE MALTESE FALCON
(USA, 1941). Direction and script: John Huston. Adapted from the novel by Dashiell Hammett. With Humphrey Bogart (Sam Spade), Mary Astor (Brigid O'Shaughnessy), Sydney Greenstreet (Kasper Gutman), Elisha Cook, Jr. (Wilmer), Peter Lorre (Joel Cairo). 7, 3.

The Maltese Falcon was twice adapted for the screen, unsuccessfully, before Huston's own adaptation was made. As his first directorial assignment, it was a marked success both for himself and Bogart. It also involved the first film appearance of English stage actor Sydney Greenstreet. The entertainment value of this thriller turns on a story continuity so involved that throughout the action no one knows where he or she is in relation to the rest. Sam Spade, a relatively innocent and good-natured private eye, depending entirely on instinct and hunch rather than on logic or reason, becomes attracted by his engaging, but utterly untrustworthy, client, Brigid O'Shaughnessy, and as a result finds himself in conflict with a highly eccentric male gang (Kasper Gutman—the leader—Joel Cairo, and Wilmer) in the hunt for a jeweled statuette, only to find in the end that it is a fake.

Of Peter Lorre's performance, with its marked homosexual undertones, John Huston wrote: "Peter Lorre was one of the finest and most subtle actors I have ever worked with. Beneath that air of innocence he used to such effect, one sensed a Faustian worldliness."[56] The homosexual strain in fact runs through the entire film in the characters played by Lorre, Greenstreet, and Elisha Cook, Jr. The film, too, turns on the paranoia of mutual distrust. The complex relationship between Sam Spade and Brigid O'Shaughnessy—"the enchanting murderess," as Huston called her—as well as the tensions behind Spade's relations with the three men, lie entirely in the total mutual distrust represented by this network of malefactors.

THE MAN WITH THE GOLDEN ARM

(USA, 1955). Production and direction: Otto Preminger. Script: Walter Newman, Lewis Meltzer. Adapted from the novel by Nelson Algren. With Frank Sinatra (Frankie), Eleanor Parker (Zosch), Kim Novak (Molly), Darren McGavin (Louie). 6.

This very violent picture is notable for its pioneer handling of drug addiction as the subject for a Hollywood film. Otto Preminger deliberately operated outside conventional censorship patterns in America when he undertook this production in the mid-1950s. At the beginning of the film, Frankie, a drug addict who has been cured while in jail, returns to the slums of Chicago to renew his life, hoping to exploit his newfound talent as a drummer. Due to the combined pressures of his neurotic and crippled wife, Zosch; his former employer, Schwiefka; and Louie, a dope peddler, he is, however, driven back to his former occupation, poker dealing and, soon afterwards, to drug-taking. Only his girlfriend Molly stands by him. The climax of the film—which involves Zosch's murder of Louie, with Frankie as suspect—becomes Frankie's violent cure, undertaken with withdrawal symptoms emphasized, when he is hidden away by himself in Mollie's room. The film has a positive end. Frankie, freed from his marriage by Zosch's suicide, is able to contemplate a happy future with Molly.

The film was refused a seal of approval under the MPAA censorship code. In a CBC broadcast in 1956 Preminger stated, "This picture is a warning against the consequences of taking narcotics",[57] and the MPAA disapproval was, he considered, "a pedantic interpretation of a code which was written thirty years ago."[58] About Frankie's drug addiction, Preminger went on to say: "The physical cure is comparatively easy today, if you take it in the hospital with the help of drugs and doctors. But the psychological cure is very hard. Statistics show that people fall back into the habit in alarmingly high numbers because of mental unhappiness. Maybe it starts with the pace of the life we live, with mature people taking sleeping pills and benzedrine. Then they go on to more harmful poison."[59] Guy Phelps pointed out that the film was operative in getting the MPAA to change the regulations concerning the subject of drugs.[60]

THE MANCHURIAN CANDIDATE

(USA, 1962). Direction: John Frankenheimer. With Frank Sinatra (Bennet Marco), Laurence Harvey (Raymond Shaw), Angela Lansbury (Raymond's mother). 5.

Having been a POW brainwashed by the communists, Sergeant Raymond Shaw returns from the campaign in Korea. He is conditioned to kill when triggered to do so, with no knowledge or memory of what he will have done. One of the other former prisoners, Major Marco, has been less successfully brainwashed, and his partial recovery occasions an official enquiry into what really happened to the platoon. Shaw has meanwhile been successful in killing a leading journalist. Then, coming under the control of his mother, who proves to be acting as a Russian agent, he kills his own wife and her father, a liberal senator. It is Marco who finally penetrates Raymond's enclosed mind and prevents him from assassinating the presidential nominee at a rally in Madison Square Garden. Instead, Raymond shoots his mother, his stepfather (her tool) and, finally, himself. A brilliantly made melodrama, the film scarcely conforms to the clinical view of the limits to brainwashing.

THE MARAT-SADE

(Britain, 1966). Direction: Peter Brook. Developed from the stage production for the Royal Shakespeare Company of the play by Peter Weiss. With Ian Richardson (Marat), Patrick Magee (Marquis de Sade), Glenda Jackson (Charlotte Corday), Michael Williams (Herald), Robert Lloyd (Jacques Roux), Clifford Rose (Coulmier). 1b, 8.

Comte de Sade's final detention without trial began in 1801 in the form of an "administrative punishment" for what the police authorities were to term his "incessant licentious insanity" and for the semi-underground publication of such infamous works as *Justine* and *Juliette,* written during the 1790s. The detention was to last until the end of his life in 1814. On the pleas of his family and his devoted mistress, Mme Marie Constance Quesnet, he was removed from prison in 1803 to the celebrated asylum at Charenton. Charenton, a *hospice* in which Sade had been previously confined in 1789, had been reestablished by the Ministry of the Interior in 1797 and placed under the direction of M. de Coulmier, who believed in an enlightened treatment of the insane. In spite of some initial difficulties with Sade, Coulmier took to him and treated him with considerable favor, acting to some degree as his protector and even permitting Mme Quesnet to lodge with him at Charenton from 1806.

Part of the therapy for the inmates was the frequent production of plays, some of which Sade wrote as well as directed—after the revolution he had had certain of his plays produced at the Comédie Française. Sade's biographer, Gilbert Lély, quoted a contemporary witness to Sade's activities at Charenton: "Sade became an important figure at Charenton: parties, festivities, balls, shows, all were in his hands. He chose the plays, some of which were of his own composition; he did the casting; he presided over it all and rehearsed the players. . . . large numbers of outsiders were invited, a number of men of letters and many theatre celebrities."[61] By 1810, however, all this stopped, and Coulmier was forced to place his patient in close confinement, his only companion the faithful Mme Quesnet.

This forms the background for the play by Peter Weiss.[62] A theatrical experimentalist—who was also novelist, dramatist, painter, and filmmaker—Weiss called his original work, *The Persecution and Assassination of Jean-Paul Marat As Performed by the Inmates of the Asylum of Charenton under the Direction of the Marquis de Sade.* In *Marat-Sade* Weiss uses the device of a play within a play to project the history of the French Revolution up to the murder of Marat by Charlotte Corday in 1793, satirizing the whole political process by having it acted out by lunatics to a controversial script written by Sade. History is thereby shown to have its roots in the insanity of the people and their rulers alike. Every so often the performance stops, either because an ideological argument has broken out between a near-sane Sade (representing the extreme individualist) and the near-sane lunatic playing Marat (who represents the radical organization man controlling the revolution), or because of the intervention of the suave director of Charenton, Coulmier, who attempts to calm them all down and make diplomatic remarks to the supposed audience of visitors, who are in fact the actual audience for the play or film. The Charenton lunatics as a whole (most of whom seem to be confined against their will in the madhouse) readily identify the revolution with personal liberty and anarchy and present their view of events in the form of a charade, a mock pageant of history presented in mime and song and led by a quartet of players made up as clowns. Another near-sane actor plays the Herald, who acts as narrator, linking episode to episode with sardonic irony. The mad, in fact, act out the great events of recent history in their own insane image. This is the theater of the absurd with a political vengeance.

When redirecting the same cast for the film, Brook retained the same striking theatrical technique he had adopted on the stage. The setting is the bathhouse at Charenton, converted into an improvised stage, and a sinister wall of strong iron bars separates the performers from their supposed audience. Brook was able to use in the film even more radical imagery than was possible on the stage in order to induce the audience to see these events in human history through the eyes of the insane. In his introduction to the published play, Brook speaks of the importance of the Brechtian device of so-called alienation as "the art of placing an action at a distance so that it can be judged objectively and so that it can be seen in relation to the world—or rather, worlds—around it."[63]

The film is one of the most powerful, as well as the most startling, representations of insanity that exists on film, all the more impressive for its intense stylization. As I wrote about this technique in a previous work:

> The unreal atmosphere of the occasion is emphasized by frequent halation in the lighting, the picture (in color) almost bleached out by the strong sunlight from the big windows of the bathhouse. The camera is very mobile (sometimes moving to the rhythm of speech and song), shifting either into large close-ups of the players or recording them in close-shot (profile; full-face) as they move in and out of the frame. . . . The fullest impact of mental disturbance among the leading players comes from Glenda Jackson's portrayal of the melancholic girl who plays Corday. She is never more than fractionally with the part of Corday, and this dual performance by Glenda Jackson (as the mad girl and as the mad girl approaching the task of playing Corday) achieves the highest point of "alienation" in the production. Her involvement seems to be only in the act of stabbing, and she gets ready for this too soon and has to be drawn back by de Sade, as author-producer. . . . Every so often, the camera glances away to observe the strained, withdrawn or overexcited faces of the mad—the chorus of patients, sitting, lying, standing around, watched over by the nuns and the tough male nurses of Charenton, who are like wardens in a primitive kind of prison. Most of the patients seem to be turned in upon themselves until suddenly roused by some common emotion at given moments in the

action. To emphasize this visually, shots are frequently foreshortened or otherwise distorted, the perspective curving in. . . .

In Peter Brook's production, the chaos at the end reaches extreme proportions. The assault on Coulmier and his family is total. His wife is in danger of being raped, and the wardens have to set upon the prisoners with their clubs. The film ends with a fade on this scene of revolt, at which de Sade merely laughs. This, after all, is what his play has been about.[64]

THE MARK
(Britain, 1961). Direction: Guy Green. With Stuart Whitman (Jim Fuller), Rod Steiger (Dr. McNally), Maria Schell (Ruth, Jim's friend). 1b, 3, 9.

The Mark concerns the difficult period of rehabilitation facing Jim Fuller, whose crime (abduction and attempted sexual assault of a small girl) brings a prison sentence upon him. But the prison psychiatrist, Dr. McNally, has faith in him. After his release and return to employment, Fuller experiences the beginning of a normal relationship with a young widow and her ten-year-old daughter. His rehabilitation is set back, however, by the vicious actions of a journalist, who makes a sensational revelation of Fuller's past. Fuller returns to the care of Dr. McNally and eventually regains with his help the trust of his woman friend. This is a comparatively early film to portray a psychiatrist in any depth, and Rod Steiger is outstanding as the sympathetic doctor.

MARNIE
(USA, 1964). Direction: Alfred Hitchcock. Script: Jay Presson Allen. Based on the novel by Winston Graham. With Tippi Hedren (Marnie Edgar), Sean Connery (Mark Rutland), Diane Baker (Lil Mainwearing), Martin Gabel (Sidney Strutt), Louis Latham (Bernice Edgar), Bob Sweeney (Cousin Bob), Alan Napier (Mr. Rutland). 3.

Marnie is another of Hitchcock's films seriously involved with a protagonist whose mind is severely disturbed. Marnie is a professional thief who uses a variety of expert disguises. Her relationship with her mother, who loathes men, has led her to become sexually frigid, and she has an unaccountable, traumatic fear of anything colored red—an obsession sustained in childhood when her neurotic mother worked unwillingly as a prostitute. Mark Rutland, a rich widower, falls in love with her—a love that in turn becomes obsessive once he finds out the truth about her activities, curiously associating her compulsion to steal with his own sadistic desire to possess her through rape. He marries her, becoming at once her protector and analyst.

In his biography of Hitchcock John Russell Taylor describes the severe tension that arose during production between director and star. Tippi Hedren (Marnie) was under contract to Hitchcock, who tended to act like a Svengali figure in his command over her. Taylor claims, however, that these tensions were in fact to the film's advantage, increasing the effect of inexplicable disturbance that lies at its root.[65]

Hitchcock admitted to Truffaut that, although his initial attraction to the story was the fetishistic aspect of Mark's love for Marnie, this sadistic aspect almost disappears in the film.[66] Hitchcock adds, "I was forced to simplify the whole psychoanalysis aspect of it. In the novel, you know, Marnie agrees to see the psychiatrist every week, as a concession to her husband. In the book her attempts to conceal her past and her real life added up to some very good passages both funny and tragic. But in the picture we had to telescope all of that into a single scene, with the husband doing the analysis himself."[67]

The film received a highly mixed critical reception. Robin Wood, who held it to be a masterpiece, answered typical objections to the film in his book on Hitchcock, where he also gave a detailed analysis of it.[68] For instance he defended the artificial-looking back-projections to the street where Marnie's mother lives and also in the horseback sequences, as quite deliberate. They give these scenes a necessary unreality, he said. The recurrent red suffusions of the frame and the injection of storms are introduced, said Wood, to bring the audience into as close an identification as possible with Marnie in moments of mental crisis.[69] He also defended the film from attack on the grounds that its psychology is simplistic:

> Scarcely more here than in *Psycho* is Hitchcock offering us the detailed analysis of a clinical case; the essentials of Marnie's mental disorder and of the preliminaries to its cure are given us with great force and clarity, but we are not given a *detailed* study of her behaviour, her symptoms or the minor components of her neurosis. To demand this is to demand at entirely different film: Hitchcock uses, as usual, all he needs and no more, and the film would be in no way improved if it went into Marnie's case in more detail. . . . Marnie's reactions to red, to the thunderstorms, to tapping, her recurring nightmares, constitute an artistically valid shorthand.[70]

METROPOLIS
(Germany, 1926). Direction: Fritz Lang. With Brigitte Helm (Mary), Rudolph Klein-Rogge (Rotwang), Alfred Abel (John Masterman), Gustav Fröhlich (Erik, his son). 7.

This spectacular and melodramatic evocation of the future portrays the proletariat as laboring blindly underground to maintain a life of ease and pleasure for the privileged upper class, who live aboveground. Masterman, the dictator of this civilization, is served by a prototypically mad scientist-inventor, Rotwang, who constructs a robot-girl in his laboratory, a living replica of the prophetess, Mary, who is dedicated to leading the workers in their search for a better life. The robot-girl, into whose metal limbs Rotwang infuses life, is equally dedicated to leading the workers to their spiritual destruction. Rudolph Klein-Rogge's interpretation of Rotwang fulfils the popular stereotype of the traditional mad scientist—a role he was later to expand for the equally mad would-be ruler of the world, Dr. Mabuse, in Fritz Lang's film *The Last Will of Dr. Mabuse* (q.v.).

MORGAN: A SUITABLE CASE FOR TREATMENT
(Britain, 1966). Direction: Karel Reisz. Script: David Mercer. Adapted from the play by David Mercer. With David Warner (Morgan), Vanessa Redgrave (Leonie). 8.

Morgan, an artist of working-class origins—who identifies in his private fantasy world with King Kong as well as the principal gorilla in the London zoo—is in the process of being divorced by his rich, upper-class wife, Leonie. Both retain a basic affection for each other, though Leonie is desperate to regain her freedom and marry a man of her own class, a change vigorously backed by her mother. Morgan's own proletarian mother, a doctrinaire communist, is equally against this marriage, which has in her eyes made him a traitor to his class. Morgan, tortured by the loss of Leonie, devises a series of mock-serious and fantastic persecutions of Leonie, her new fiancé, and her pompous, snobbish mother. This eventually lands him in prison.

Released on the very day of Leonie's wedding, Morgan dresses himself up as a gorilla and breaks up her stylish wedding reception on Park Lane. He accidentally sets fire to himself, steals a motorcycle, and crashes into the Thames after a mad dash through central London. Now quite mad, he indulges in a final hallucination, in which all those hostile to him, led by Leonie and her mother on horseback, turn into a reactionary firing squad to execute him as a Marxist martyr. In the last sequence, a pregnant Leonie visits him in the garden of his asylum and nods enigmatically when he asks her if the child she is carrying is his.

Morgan is seen to have been growing increasing insane throughout the film. His mischievous, absurd tricks and half-humorous fantasies gradually deepen into serious hallucinations, spurred on by his jealous desire to hold Leonie. Morgan is a comic loser, for whom everything goes wrong, a fantasist, and a lovable, gangling boy living out of his social element in Leonie's elegant Mayfair townhouse, which symbolizes the impossibility of his social misalliance. David Warner's performance is imaginative and sympathetic.

NATURAL ENEMIES
(USA, 1979). Direction and script: Jeff Kanew. Based on a novel by Julius Horwitz. With Hal Holbrook (Paul Steward), Louise Fletcher (Miriam Steward), Jose Ferrer (Harry Rosenthal), Viveca Lindfors (Dr. Baker). 1a.

Paul Steward is a small-time but successful publisher of a serious and respected journal in Manhattan. He lives in Connecticut with his wife and three children, but his accumulated weariness with life takes the depressive form of contemplating wiping out the whole family as well as himself. He disguises his plan to achieve this domestic holocaust by preparing in his mind the action for a similar event as if for publication. His many "research" conversations result in two notable scenes, first with Harry Rosenthal, an intellectual who was once an inmate in a Nazi concentration camp, and second, with Dr. Baker, an analyst. This is in many ways a remarkable film, sincerely conceived and presented, and made on a low budget. The characters have such unusual lines as, "We know as little about marriage as we do about cancer" and "I've given birth to three children and sometimes think I bought them in a supermarket."

NETWORK
(USA, 1976). Direction: Sidney Lumet. Script: Paddy Chayefsky. With Faye Dunaway (Diana Christenson), William Holden (Max Schumacher), Peter Finch (Howard Beale). 1b, 8.

Veteran television news commentator, Howard Beale, becomes insane when told he is to be dismissed from his network due to falling ratings. He announces in public that he will shoot himself while on the air and takes advantage of a final appearance (offered him to make amends) to denounce in fevered rhetoric the lies told by the media. His ratings immediately rise again, and he is reinstated as a telecaster in a new guise—an insanely fervent apostle of truth who preaches wild sermons, which a young, ruthlessly ambitious executive producer, Diana Christenson, exploits for her *Mao Tse Tung Hour,* a program designed to attract disenchanted youth in the masses. Beale's subsequent denunciations of big business are unexpectedly put in reverse when the all-powerful owner of the network convinces him he should preach the gospel of a "corporate utopia." Once again, the ratings fall, but the network executives contrive to have Beale assassinated while on television to jack up their ratings at all costs. Thus, everyone is satirized in this denunciation of sponsored television—the right, the left, and the center in modern society. The late Peter Finch projects Beale's insanely perjurious accusations with gesticulating fervor, but in hitting out at everything at once the film loses some of its satiric point.

NIGHT PORTER
(*Il Portiere di Notte* Italy, 1973). Direction and script: Liliana Cavani. With Dirk Bogarde (Max), Charlotte Rampling (Lucia). 3.

Max, a former S.S. officer now serving as night porter in a luxury hotel, organizes a so-called therapy club with his Third Reich colleagues, one aspect of which is to discover and destroy evidence of their former sadistic practices. A guest, Lucia, wife of an eminent conductor, arrives and recognizes Max, who had victimized her in a concentration camp and made her his mistress. She is drawn to resume her sadomasochistic relationship with him, only this time he reverses his former role, making himself Lucia's sexual victim. His present-day associates conspire to kill them for fear they will themselves be exposed through the scandal Max and Lucia are causing. Max is shot down, finally, while wearing his former S.S. uniform.

Night Porter has been both praised and condemned,[71] but whatever its artistic qualities its content is significant as one of the films that interrelate sexual sadism with Nazi elitism.

NOW, VOYAGER
(USA, 1942). Direction: Irving Rapper. Adapted from the novel by Olive Higgins Prouty. With Bette Davis (Charlotte Vale), Paul Henreid (Jerry Durrance), Gladys Cooper (Mrs. Vale, Charlotte's mother), Claude Rains (Dr. Jaquith). 1a.

The title of this film comes from Whitman—"Now, Voyager, sail thou forth to seek and find." Charlotte Vale is the bitter and repressed daughter of a dominating mother from one of the old Bostonian Back Bay families. She finally has a nervous breakdown and is sent to a fashionable sanatorium under the direction of the worldly wise and paternal Dr. Jaquith. "I don't believe in scientific terms," he says, "I leave those to the fakers and writers of books." During Charlotte's convalescence on a cruise in the Caribbean and off the Latin American coasts, she is revived by a love affair with an unhappily married man, Jerry Durrance. On her return, Charlotte has recognizably become a far more attractive woman, but her love for Jerry is sufficiently enduring for her to fail to go through with a marriage to a man to whom she becomes for a while engaged in Boston.

After her mother's death, Charlotte suffers a relapse and returns to the sanatorium only to find as a fellow patient one of Jerry's daughters, Tina, a neurotic teenager, whom his wife has rejected as the typical, unwanted waiflike child. Charlotte in a sense adopts her and looks after her, and Tina becomes Charlotte's permanent link with Jerry, the man whom she loves deeply but whom, as things are, she can never hope to marry. The film is well directed in the style of the period and is notable primarily for Bette Davis's realistic study of a nervous breakdown. *Now, Voyager,* however, does not avoid a certain sentimental kitsch quality, which severely dates it.

ONE FLEW OVER THE CUCKOO'S NEST.
(USA, 1975). Direction: Milos Forman. Script: Lawrence Hauben, Bo Goldman. Based on the novel by Ken Kesey. With Jack Nicolson (McMurphy), Louise Fletcher (Nurse Ratched), Will Sampson (Chief Bromden). 1b, 8.

Cuckoo's Nest was the second film (the first was the corrosive comedy *Taking Off*) made in the States by the distinguished expatriate Czechoslovakian film director, Milos Forman. McMurphy is a maverick patient in a state mental hospital, newly arrived for psychiatric observation from a work farm, where he has been serving sentence for assault and statutory rape. McMurphy is resolutely cheerful and insolent in his confrontation with Nurse Ratched, whose authoritarian control of the male ward is inspired by a single objective—to keep the patients as quiet and apathetic as possible. McMurphy's philosophy is the exact opposite—he thinks all the patients should be as fulfilled and active as he is. Although his intransigence is at first mainly facetious, Nurse Ratched sees him as an irresponsible troublemaker.

McMurphy becomes more deeply concerned when he finds out that, although he is quite sane, he is not free to leave the hospital and return to the work farm in the same way the voluntary patients in the hospital can return to normal life. Worse than this, his undisciplined behavior leads him to receive shock treatment against his will. Also receiving this treatment is a massive, silent Indian patient known as Chief Bromden, who is believed to be deaf and dumb, since he passes his time in a nearly catatonic condition. But the Chief is in fact able to speak, and confides in McMurphy that he is using the asylum as a retreat from the society that had done so much to destroy his race and culture. Now feeling desperate, McMurphy determines to escape, though he fails to persuade Bromden (now demonstrably sane, like McMurphy himself) to come away with him. When a young patient in the ward is driven to suicide by the actions of Nurse Ratched, McMurphy attempts to strangle her. He is at once condemned to lobotomy, which renders him virtually catatonic. Heartbroken at the condition of his only friend, the Chief smothers McMurphy with a pillow out of sheer pity, and then takes on himself the fulfillment of McMurphy's mission to escape from this mental prison.

This adaptation of Ken Kesey's novel, which is alleged to have been written under the influence of LSD, and in the original is narrated by the Chief, is a kind of reductio ad absurdum of madness as conceived alike by those who treat it perfunctorily and those who are its representative patients confined together in formalized institutions the discipline of which is designed to give doctors and nurses the minimum work. McMurphy's initially light-hearted desire to burst the repressive system wide open by any means, however crude—such as substituting porno playing cards for the normal deck, organizing an illicit afternoon deep-sea fishing, and introducing liquor and prostitutes into the ward at night— eventually turns sour when the authorities use his quite rationally conceived antics to prove he is insane. His first punishment is shock therapy; his second, the total destruction of his will and personality through lobotomy—the direst of devices, by means of which authority can bring a human being to heel, though one that, we have come to realize in the past few years, is widely used in authoritarian societies. As Tom Milne wrote in a perceptive review:

One Flew over the Cuckoo's Nest has no problems with the problem of enacting madness. Forman has defined his approach by saying, "I can only define 'mental illness' as an incapacity to adjust within normal measure to ever-changing, unspoken rules. If you are incapable of making these constant changes, you are called by your environment crazy." His uniformly brilliant cast (doubtless enormously aided by the fact that the film was shot on location in the Oregon State Hospital with, apparently, a number of real patients as extras contributing to the ambience of tranquil withdrawal) are therefore presented, basically, as entirely normal: one accepts Chief Bromden first as crazy, then as sane, with equal conviction and without having to make any mental or visual adjustment. Their difference lies purely in that inability to adjust to rules—like Martini's destruction of all group games, or Cheswick's need to be an ally no matter what the circumstances—which makes their behaviour both exquisitely funny and infinitely touching. And once, at least, the film takes us right through the looking glass into a world where fact is ruled by fantasy: the scene where Nicolson treats the cheering patients to a baseball commentary in front of a dead TV set whose blank screen, dimly reflecting the excited audience, seems to come alive with the spectacle.[72]

OPEN SEASON
(Spain and Switzerland, 1974). Direction: Peter Collinson. With Peter Fonda (Ken Frazer), John Phillip Law (Greg Anderson), Richard Lynch (Artie Wallace), William Holden (Wolkowski), Cornelia Sharpe (Nancy), Albert Mendoza (Martin). 5, 4.

Open Season begins with a close-up of the American flag and a scene in which a district attorney advises a woman whose daughter, Alicia, has allegedly been raped by three "respectable" young men, not to press charges against them. In spite of this, this strange film is a Spanish-Swiss coproduction and has a British director who initially had a marked taste for subjects with sadistic themes (*The Penthouse,* 1967; *Long Day's Dying,* 1968).

Open Season concerns three young veterans from the Vietnam War, Ken, Greg, and Artie, whose secret sport has become the hunting of people in place of game. On one of their trips they kidnap a couple, Nancy and Martin, who are driving together and cheating on their spouses. They take them to an isolated hunting lodge on a deserted island. After terrorizing them for three days, they let the panic-stricken couple loose for the hunt.

As the three men close in for the kill, Greg is mysteriously shot dead. The marksman proves to be Wolkowski, the father of Alicia. He has planned his vengeance carefully, placing around the island tape recordings, which resound in the ears of the guilty men like the voice of some god. From the tapes we learn that Alicia died after giving birth to a retarded child, Petey, whom we saw briefly near the start of the film being brought by his grandfather to a children's party, which the three young men helped to organize. Wolkowski stalks and kills both Artie and Ken after they kill Nancy and Martin. The film is rather pretentiously sadistic in its deliberate, and somewhat stylized, exploitation of cruelty.

ORDINARY PEOPLE
(USA, 1980). Direction: Robert Redford. With Donald Sutherland (Mr. Jarrett), Mary Tyler Moore (Mrs. Jarrett), Timothy Hutton (Conrad Jarrett), Judd Hirsch (the psychiatrist). 1a.

Ordinary People concerns the Jarrett family (father, mother, and younger son, Conrad), all of whom are deeply affected in very different ways by the recent drowning of the elder son while sailing with his brother. Conrad's intense feeling of guilt in connection with his brother's death drives him to make a suicide attempt, and each member of the family finds that inevitably he or she is forced to set up lines of communication with the others on a level of intimacy that has not existed before. Both parents are at first highly resistant, largely out of fear, and the pace has to be set by Conrad himself, guided by his psychiatrist, who becomes for him through a great part of the film a substitute father figure, owing to the real father's inhibition and shyness. Conrad's mother coldly withdraws, showing a total inability to express any affection for either her husband or her son. The film is sympathetically directed by Robert Redford (his debut as a director); and Donald Sutherland, especially, shows great understanding of the father's psychological dilemma since he is at heart very fond of his son.

OUTRAGEOUS

(Canada, 1977). Direction and script: Richard Benner. Based on the story "Making It," from the collection *The Butterfly Ward*, by Margaret Gibson. With Craig Russell (Robin), Hollis McLaren (Liza). 8.

Outrageous concerns the loving relationship between Robin, a young female impersonator trying to launch himself on a career in show business in back-street clubs for homosexuals, and a schizophrenic girl, Liza, who has spent eight years in a mental institution. As the film begins, Liza escapes from the asylum and takes refuge with her old school friend, Robin, for real care and protection. She is in a perpetually overly excited condition, up and down, and has vague aspirations to become a writer. Her mother, a worn-out, working class woman, is hostile to her and does little but turn up now and then to protest the way of life her daughter has adopted. Officialdom, anxious to get Liza off their hands (they are more concerned about her morals than her welfare) grudgingly lets her have her way, only protesting more forcefully when she becomes pregnant through a casual love affair, which in its way does much to fulfill her need for affection. She is in fact delighted to be pregnant, but when her child is stillborn, she is thrown back into a state of despondency.

The essence of *Outrageous* is the feeling Liza develops for Robin, who is totally dedicated to perfecting his incredibly accurate impressions of film stars and singers—Tallulah Bankhead, Peggy Lee, Bette Davis, Joan Crawford, Mae West, Carol Channing, Ethel Merman, Barbra Streisand, Judy Garland, and Marlene Dietrich among them. The women Robin tends to impersonate are all either overly sexed or overly dominant, or both, in their screen persona. Like Liza, Robin lives in his own world of fantasy—but fantasy that can evidently earn him money and give him a solid career (meanwhile he earns a living as a hairdresser). It is Liza, in fact, who encourages him in his career. "Admit it, Robin, you're different," she says. "Do the clubs . . . for the crazies!" Leaving hairdressing, he turns full-time professional, going to New York from Toronto. Almost immediately he gains success in better-class clubs, becoming in fact as successful as Craig Russell himself in the same profession. He keeps in touch with Liza by telephone, and as soon as she can after the loss of her baby, she rushes to New York to join him. His cheerful commonsense always acts like a tonic, and he manages at the end of the film to convince her that being "mad" together in their different ways is fun. It would seem that her form of insanity has become an acceptable escape from an intolerable life, while Robin, who understands her and fosters all her more positive, "mad" excitements, proves to be her real therapist. All the worthwhile people he knows, he tells her, are "nuts"; after all, New York is a "freak city." In the guise of Peggy Lee he sings, "Can you save me again. . . . It ain't easy in this crazy world. . . . I can never make it in this crazy world without you." The film ends with Liza and Robin dancing together to the song, "Step Out":

You've got to step out into a world you've never seen,
You've got to let the stranger out from inside,

Roll out that stranger that lives inside;
There's a world you've never seen,
Ain't no good living in between,
Step out.

PANDORA'S BOX

(Germany, 1928). Direction: G. W. Pabst. With Louise Brooks (Lulu), Fritz Kortner (Dr. Schoen), Franz Lederer (Alva Schoen), Alice Roberts (Countess Geschwitz), Gustav Diessl (Jack the Ripper). 3.

Wederkind's two plays, *Erdgeist* and *Die Buechse der Pandora*, from which this film was adapted, exposed the bestiality of rich men who were prepared to exploit brutally the helpless prostitutes whom society was pleased to condemn as predators upon men rather than consider as victims of male lust. Pabst made his film a study in abnormal psychology, and followed Wederkind in making Lulu a "personification of primitive sexuality who inspires evil unawares."[73] Louise Brooks played her as wholly innocent. According to her, Pabst met with considerable opposition from his male cast because sexual gratification, not victimization, was to become the emphatic motif of their performances. He met with equal resentment from Alice Roberts, who had to play the lesbian exploiter of Lulu's innocence.[74] Like a child, Lulu satisfies her own sexuality while meeting the needs of her clients, for whom she has no feeling other than her desire to attract them.

Lulu, a prostitute and petty thief, is befriended by a wealthy publisher, Dr. Schoen, who has her educated and trained as a dancer. His sexual need for her is so great that he consents to marry her, although he already has an official fiancée and knows that his own son, Alva, is obsessively in love with her. His wedding reception is broken up through the jealousy of his son, and later Lulu becomes beset by suitors, including the lesbian Countess Geschwitz. Distracted, Schoen tries to persuade her to shoot herself. She resists, and in the struggle she shoots him. After her trial and sentencing for manslaughter, she escapes confinement through a fire at the courthouse and leaves the country with Alva. After many threatening vicissitudes she ends up in the slums of London with Alva, Anna Geschwitz, and the old man she regards as a father. They are all destitute and live on her earnings. Her final encounter is with Jack the Ripper, who kills her. This last sequence is a masterpiece of psychological tension.[75]

PATHS OF GLORY

(USA, 1957). Direction and script: Stanley Kubrick. With Kirk Douglas (Colonel Dax), Adolphe Menjou (General Broulard). 5.

An impossible mission against an impregnable German position is ordered by the French high command in 1916. Colonel Dax, in charge of the raid, is put in a false position when his unit is subsequently court-martialled for cowardice and three men, arbitrarily chosen as scapegoats, are condemned to death. Dax fails to persuade his corrupt superiors, and the three men are paraded for execution before the whole batallion. Dax alone represents a humanitarian attitude and proper sense of justice. One of the victims is reduced to weeping hysteria as he is dragged to the place of execution in full view of the assembled men—an act of the harshest brutality and a convincing portrayal of total breakdown.

PATTON: LUST FOR GLORY
(USA, 1969). Direction: Franklin J. Schaffner. Script: Francis Ford Coppola, Edmund H. North. With George C. Scott (Patton). 5, 7.

The film revolves around George C. Scott's outstanding performance as Patton, which almost seems to amount to full identification. The film, in spite of its well-staged scenes of battle, is basically a psychological study of a man obsessed with his own genius for warfare to the point of believing himself to be a reincarnated general from the historic past. Scornful of others, he reveals a pathological streak when he slaps a soldier who is under medical care for battle fatigue—an action he was to regret when called upon to apologize before a full parade. His greatest rival—and principal individual hate—is the almost equally idiosyncratic British Field Marshal Montgomery—whom Eisenhower was later to favor, owing to political pressure, over Patton, in spite of the latter's spectacular successes when in command of the Third Army in Europe. The film, though revealing Patton's all-but-paranoiac dedication to fulfilling his own destiny in his own way, does not emerge as hostile to him but rather sees him as a professional soldier who drives himself into a position of an extremity that admits of no allowances to diplomacy in the handling of others.

PEEPING TOM
(Britain 1960). Direction: Michael Powell. Script: Leo Marks. With Carl Boehm (Mark Lewis), Michael Powell (Mark's father in childhood sequences), Anna Massey (Helen), Maxime Audley (Helen's mother). 3, 4.

This film was bitterly attacked by the critics for its horrific sexual sadism and perversion at the time of its initial release, and it appears permanently to have damaged Powell's career in Britain. Peeping Tom was, psychologically speaking, made far ahead of its time. Re-released in the US in 1980, the film was reappraised with a far greater enlightenment as to its actual nature. In any event, Powell's general reputation as a leading, if not the leading, British filmmaker of his time—the wartime and postwar period—was reassessed in Britain itself during the 1970s.[76] Nevertheless, Peeping Tom was picketed in places by organized women's groups.

Like the heroes in several of his films, Powell practiced a certain aloofness, the distant manner that conceals the more private, inner urge to create—or in the case of the sociopathic Mark Lewis, the "hero" of Peeping Tom, to murder—as an unavoidable act of destiny. Lewis, by profession a camera technician in a film studio and a would-be director, is obsessed with the need to kill the women with whom he is too withdrawn to associate sexually. It is his destiny to do this because in his childhood he was abused by his psychologist father, who subjected him experimentally to extreme forms of fear and filmed his reactions. Now he murders the women who attract him and who are somehow attracted by him. While pretending to give them film tests—the forward leg of his camera tripod extending phallically upwards with a projecting blade while the camera keeps rolling—the victims back away screaming at the sight of the oncoming knife.[77]

Though the owner of a house, Lewis confines his living quarters to the attic area, where he maintains projection equipment and a laboratory for developing his private films. Here he repeatedly screens his masterpieces of murder. The rest of the house he rents. Among his tenants are a mother and daughter. The mother, though blind, is highly capable of sensing personality. Her daughter begins to fall somewhat in love with Mark and tries throughout the film to overcome his reticence. Eventually, he falls somewhat in love with her and for the first time experiences a certain resistance in himself to the desire to murder a woman. She is perhaps the first woman in his life to offer him real sympathy and some attempt at understanding. She eventually discovers what obsesses him when up in his apartment she accidentally trips the switch of the loaded projector and views one of his studies in murder. Although her life is preserved at the end of the film, it is only at the cost of his death, when the police finally trace him as the murderer.

Peeping Tom is not only an extreme study in voyeurism and male sexual inhibition in the guise of a film noir, it is also, according to David Thomson's perceptive study, "a tribute to the artist as self-destructive terrorist."[78] Commenting on the film's "sexual fantasy," Susan Sontag wrote that it

> is not about a Peeping Tom but about a psychopath who kills women with a weapon concealed in his camera, while photographing them. Not once does he touch his subjects. He doesn't desire their bodies; he wants their presence in the form of filmed images—those showing them experiencing their own death—which he screens at home for his solitary pleasure. The movie assumes connections between impotence and aggression, professionalized looking and cruelty, which point to the central fantasy connected with the camera. The camera as phallus is, at most, a flimsy variant of the inescapable metaphor that everyone unself-consciously employs. However hazy our awareness of this fantasy, it is named without subtlety whenever we talk about "loading" and "aiming" a camera, about "shooting" a film.[79]

PERFORMANCE
(Britain, 1968–70). Direction: Donald Cammell and Nicolas Roeg. Script: Donald Cammell. With James Fox (Chas Devlin), Mick Jagger (Turner). 6, 3.

Chas, a strong-arm man for a gangster organization, is on the run from both the organization and the police after a murder. He eventually poses as an unemployed juggler and friend of a friend of Turner, a retired pop star, with whom he manages to take refuge. Turner and the two girls who live with him, however, are eccentric, drug-addicted, and suspicious that their guest is connected with crime.

Chas himself collapses under the influence of drugs and shoots the sympathetic Turner when finally discovered by agents of the organization, who take him away in what is evidently a ride to his death.

The essence of this baffling film (recut independently of the makers by the Warners editors) is the interchange or duality of personalities, as between Chas and Turner who have, after all, only come together by chance. They are the "performers" suggested in the title, one a supposed juggler, the other a retired singer. Identity switching occurs, one character suddenly substituting for the other, in either what purports to be direct action or in dream. Cammell has admitted taking ideas concerning identity from Borges, Hesse, Artaud, and others. This is the first of Roeg's credits as director, and his past as cinematographer is reflected in the exceptional visual images with which this film is dressed. Turner's house is full of mirror reflections, so that its enclosed, ritualized atmosphere is created in images that are never quite what they seem. The film is in its own special way brilliantly directed and acted, especially by James Fox.

PERSONA

(Sweden, 1966). Direction and script, Ingmar Bergman. With Liv Ullmann (Elizabeth Vogler), Bibi Andersson (Nurse Alma), Margaretha Krook (Psychiatrist), Gunnar Björnstrand (Mr. Vogler), Jörgen Lindström (Elizabeth's son).

Persona[80] is one of the most complex of Bergman's films of psychological maladjustment and indeed one of the most complex films ever made, although it is only some eighty minutes long. Reactions to it have been widely different—from extreme irritation and frustration concerning its significance to affirmations that it is a masterpiece, the intuitive product of a director who possibly ranks highest in achievement of all filmmakers to date. It was, Bergman revealed, born of therapy, conceived in very general terms on paper while he was recovering from a term in the hospital.[81]

A celebrated actress, Elizabeth Vogler stops speaking during a performance of Sophocles' Electra.[82] The play is abandoned, and Elizabeth is found in a psychiatric clinic to have nothing discoverable wrong with her. The total verbal silence she maintains appears to be voluntary, not involuntary. Her woman psychiatrist, in an analysis of the case, stresses the "gulf between what you are with others and what alone," and the fact that "you can refuse to talk so as not to lie." Indeed, she adds, "You can go on playing this part until you tire of it". She admits that reality is diabolical. She also stresses the duality that exists in life. Elizabeth's condition is explained to a young nurse, Alma,[83] whom the psychiatrist assigns to the case as a watchdog, sending the two of them (after Elizabeth has been in the clinic, it would seem, three months) to stay during the summer in a beachhouse on a deserted stretch of coast. It is evident from the start that there is a strong physical resemblance between the two women, though Elizabeth is the elder. Alma, who is only twenty-five, is flattered at first by this assignment and somewhat in awe of her distinguished charge, but she is left to do all the talking and gradually adjusts to the situation by revealing more and more about her own frustrations while seeking to understand those of Elizabeth. It transpires that Elizabeth has a husband from whom (in spite of his affection for her) she feels alienated, and, worse than this, a son whose birth she has resented and whose evident need for her love repels her. (A letter from the husband is read out in part to Elizabeth by Alma, and Elizabeth tears up a photograph of her son, which is enclosed.) Alma, on the other hand, reveals in an outburst of confidences that she has had to undergo an abortion as a result of an early sexual encounter with a boy on the beach, an abortion that was deeply painful because she has always desired motherhood and is looking forward now to having children since she is engaged to be married.

Alma is distressed by what she has revealed about herself, but she is somehow also grateful. "You are the first person ever to listen to me," she says. She seems concerned about her identity. "Can you be two people?" she asks. "I could change myself into you if I tried hard," and she recognizes that they do look alike. Indeed, Alma gradually comes to identify herself with the older woman, while Elizabeth in her turn appears to be studying Alma with great concentration. Their relationship not only deepens but becomes in the latter part of the film profoundly complex, even sadistic, especially when Alma discovers that Elizabeth is writing letters about her to the psychiatrist, one of which she deliberately leaves open for her to read. Increasingly, this mutual identification seems to imply that the two women are really one. In a moment of evident hallucination Elizabeth's husband (Gunnar Björnstrand) appears and addresses Alma as Elizabeth and, watched by Elizabeth, makes the love to Alma that he is not permitted (presumably) to make to his wife. Alma finally tortures Elizabeth with a statement of what she understands to be the true reason for her detestation of her son, and in a climactic moment of identification the faces of the two women merge,[84] and Elizabeth, as if in retaliation, sucks blood from Alma's bared arm, symbolizing at once, it might seem, blood sisterhood and antipathy. (Alma claws at her arm, presses Elizabeth's face to the blood, and then hits out at her venomously.) The period of isolation by the sea ceases when Alma next forces Elizabeth to speak a single word—*Nada* ("Nothing").[85] They pack up to return home—Elizabeth simply disappears on her own; while Alma, after a final incoherent, hysterical outburst to Elizabeth, is left to close the beachhouse and catch a bus back to town. (Since Elizabeth has a car, the more natural thing would have been for her to take Alma back with her.) We have a brief glimpse of Elizabeth under the cameras, which implies a return to her profession.[86]

Such are the principal incidents of the film, by themselves sufficient to establish its psychological mysteries. But many, often small, incidents serve to enrich the film further, and in the end, after many viewings, *Persona* seems increasingly to offer new significances and implications, born of the viewer's individual responses. In order to provoke such active participation, Bergman constantly inserts provocative sequences, individual shots, and momentary incidents, as well as jump cuts and hiatuses of technique in the continuity of the film—which serve to bring the viewer up short and destroy any smoothness in the film, such as the beauty of the visuals, which might lure him into treating the action objectively and dispassionately. Bergman's evident intention is to say that what is happening on the screen is as directly relevant to us as it is to him and to his performers.

This is established by the prologue to *Persona*, which has caused so much discussion. Before this prologue begins, we see two projector carbon rods making contact and igniting, like the fire engendered by the unification of two persons.[87] The prologue itself consists of a succession of seemingly disparate shots of no immediately apparent relevance to the action that follows. These images, many as shocking as those introducing Buñuel's film *Un Chien Andalou*, are:

1. A shot from an early cartoon film—a figure washing, which is followed by a real-life image of washing hands.
2. Shots from an early slapstick film showing a skeleton (standing for death or perhaps Dracula) chasing a man in pantomime.[88]
3. The butchering and evisceration of a lamb.
4. A monk in Vietnam burning himself to death.[89]
5. A hand, palm upwards, into which a huge nail is being hammered in crucifixion.
6. A tarantula spider.[90]

Shots of cold winter exteriors introduce the interior of a morgue, with bodies of men and women lying covered in white sheets. There is the sound of dripping water. Among them is a boy (played by the same child as played the son in *The Silence*). He is alive. A dead woman's eyes open in response to the sudden sound of an alarm clock, a sound that arouses the boy, who begins to read a book.[91] He is next seen reaching up to a screen, wall-sized, on which the huge, blurred faces of Elizabeth and Alma (alternating) are projected. Only after this do the title and credits follow, with flash (subliminal) shots interspersed of the boy, of a seashore, and of the burning priest.

All these expressionist images, with their potential suggestive impact, prompt the viewer not to take the film as a normal form of narrative, and this prompting recurs at various points of the action. At one stage (after Elizabeth has stepped on the broken glass Alma has deliberately placed in her path) an image of the film burning in the projector flares across the screen, and the film has (as it were) to be rethreaded and refocused—again a reminder at a crucial moment that what we are seeing is only a projected image, while the human experience involved is as much our own as that of the characters. On another occasion Alma suddenly turns and takes a snapshot of us (the audience) on the beach. A further, quite different, distancing effect is the sudden instance (the only one in the film) of a male voice-over narration coming at the transition from the hospital to the seashore, where the two women are seen gathering mushrooms (mythical symbol for the other world).

Similarly, images throughout the film suggest withdrawal from facing up to the problems of life. Elizabeth's refusal to speak is itself a crucial act of withdrawal. So is the image of the child in the morgue—symbolic of his enforced isolation from his mother, his search for her, her withdrawal from him. So, in its own way, is Alma's abortion. So are the dark glasses the women wear to hide their eyes from each other, and the blacked-out spectacles that make Elizabeth's husband into a blind man. So is Alma's resumption of her nurse's uniform (her "persona," like Elizabeth's stage makeup) immediately after the crucial pregnancy exposure scene between the two women. When the husband appears and makes love to Alma instead of Elizabeth, both women wear black. Costume is in fact an important factor throughout the film—the women's huge beach hats, which so appeal to Bergman's visual sense but which half conceal their faces, and the alternation of black and white motifs in their clothing.

As the film progresses, the borderline between actuality and hallucination fades. Bergman is quoted as saying, "One is strongly aware that there are no boundaries between dream and reality today."[92] He also declared about the film medium: "I see more and more clearly that the film as an art form is approaching a discovery of its essential self. It should communicate psychic states, not merely project pictures of external actions."[93] This first becomes apparent in *Persona* in the strange, inexplicable night visit, when Elizabeth approaches Alma in her bedroom like a sleepwalker. The images are beautifully realized and mysterious; we see the women with crossed profiles as they face each other, like twin heads on conjoined shoulders. Is it Elizabeth's voice that whispers, "You must go to bed before you fall asleep"? Alma, however, repeats the words as though she had originated them, "I must go to bed before I fall asleep." In the morning, when Alma asks her, "Did you come into my room last night?" Elizabeth merely shakes her head. Does, indeed, Elizabeth actually speak later when the two women fight (slapping each other's faces) and Alma threatens to scald her with boiling water? "No, don't" screams a woman's voice, but it is ambiguous which of them actually utters the words. Elizabeth smiles, almost laughs. Is the scene real, or only a figment of Alma's mind? as indeed must surely be the visitation by Elizabeth's husband, with its strangely formal grouping.[94] It is Alma who says before he appears on the scene, "He is calling again. I'll find out what he wants here in our solitude." Says he, "I do what I can," and Elizabeth uses Alma's hand to touch his face. And Vogler speaks always as if he were addressing both women. The film ends on an enigmatic note—the child is once more seen tracing the opaque lines of the woman's face on the screen-wall, still searching, still wondering. And then the film breaks up once again in the projector and ends in incandescence.

Bergman said that he saw the film as a struggle for dominance between two women, culminating in Alma's taking over of Elizabeth's personality but finally suffering a schizophrenic breakdown, leading literally to this highly vocal woman's losing her capacity to control words.[95] This indeed is the surface action, finely portrayed by Bibi Andersson. But the film as a whole is intended to become a powerful personal reflex for every individual viewer, dealing with issues of identity, of one's own persona, of one's relationships with others.

PLAY MISTY FOR ME

(USA, 1971). Direction: Clint Eastwood. With Clint Eastwood (David), Jessica Walter (Evelyn), Donna Mills (Toby). 3.

Play Misty for Me (the first film to be directed by Clint Eastwood) concerns the appalling experiences of David, who, an attractive disc jockey bachelor in California with a successful late night program, is trying to curb a life of excessive self-indulgence in wild parties and sex and live more austerely for his work. Nevertheless, a woman with a seductive voice on the telephone insists repeatedly that he play "Misty" for her. The woman, a good-looking brunette called Evelyn, tracks him down in the bar he habituates and introduces herself. In a moment of weakness, he consents to drive her home. She immediately proposes he sleep with her. Thereafter, she imposes herself on him at his home by day and by night, arriving always without warning, and the first alarming sign of her mental instability appears when she suddenly pours out abuse at a neighbor who rightly objects to the noise she is making when leaving late into the night.

Although thoroughly alarmed and angered by the manner in which Evelyn claims total possession of his life, David finds her impossible to shake off. Her intense jealousy is aroused by his anxious meetings with Toby, an old flame returned to town, and she makes a violent and abusive scene in a restaurant when she finds him having lunch with a potential sponsor of his program, who happens to be a woman. She even goes so far as to slash her wrists in his bathroom in order to force him to nurse her. Her jealous frenzies lead to outright violence when she steals his keys, has them copied, enters his house in his absence, wrecks the contents, and nearly kills his black woman house cleaner with a carving knife when the latter arrives and interrupts her. Evelyn is then taken away by the police.

The film, mostly well-written and efficiently directed, divides rather awkwardly into two parts bridged by an overly-long, overly-idyllic sequence in which David, relieved of Evelyn's presence, is seen to have become fully involved again with his old love, Toby, in whom he has confided his troubles. Tension returns when suddenly (some months later) he hears the dreaded voice of Evelyn once again on the telephone requesting he play "Misty" for her and saying that she has been released and is at the airport on her way to Hawaii. (There is no mention of the nature of the sentence she received for assault, the treatment she received in the state sanatarium where she was confined, or why so dangerous a patient was released so soon—without any warning, we discover, to either the police or to David.) Her journey to Hawaii proves to be a lie. She enters his house once more that night (he failed to change his locks), and she attempts to kill him with a knife. Meanwhile, Toby, who has had a succession of housemates sharing her isolated cottage by the ocean, has unknowingly let a room to Evelyn, who is using the false name of Annabel (derived from Edgar Allan Poe's poem, from which she once quoted to David on the telephone). We next see Evelyn attack Toby, gag her, and tie her up. She savagely slashes Toby's portrait of David and then uses the knife to start cutting off Toby's hair. She is interrupted by the arrival of a police sergeant, a friend of David since the original case, who, having warned David of Evelyn's release, has gone on to Toby's house to see that she is all right. Evelyn knifes him to death. David then arrives, having closely followed the sergeant in his fast car. Evelyn attacks him too, wounding him with the knife, but in the ensuing desperate, bloody struggle, Evelyn falls over the balustrade of the balcony and is hurled down the cliffside to her death in the ocean far below. David and Toby, thankful for their survival, summon help.

Play Misty for Me is a film of tension rather than a case study of a female sociopath. What distinguishes the film is the intensity and authenticity of Jessica Walter's performance as Evelyn, which not only makes the film grimly alarming but adds a powerful psychological quality to this study of the behavior (though not the treatment) of a demented woman whose possessive jealousy turns her into an insane killer.

PRESSURE POINT

(USA, 1962). Direction: Hubert Cornfield. Based on the novel *The Fifty Minute Hour,* by Dr. Robert Lindner. With Sidney Poitier (psychiatrist), Bobby Darin (Nazi prisoner-patient). 7, 9.

The main action of *Pressure Point* is a story told by a black psychiatrist who once had to deal with a Nazi prisoner-patient. This man's recurrent hallucination was that he and his father were being washed down a sink drain. The Nazi's boyhood was isolated and unhappy because of his father's cruelty, driving the boy to run away from home and exhibit sadistic tendencies of his own. He joined the Nazi party as a result of his rejection by others. The film becomes a kind of textbook demonstration of Nazi psychology.

PSYCHO

(USA, 1960). Direction: Alfred Hitchcock. Script: Joseph Stefano. Based on the novel by Robert Bloch. Music, Bernard Herrmann. With Janet Leigh (Marion Crane), Anthony Perkins (Norman Bates), Vera Miles (Lila Crane), John Gavin (Sam Loomis), Martin Balsam (Milton Arbogast), John McIntire (Sheriff), Simon Oakland (Dr. Richmond). 2, 9.

Psycho is so well known that the barest outline will recall the particular kind of insanity involved in the story.[96] Marion Crane, a trusted secretary employed in Phoenix, Arizona, absconds with a considerable sum of money in order to secure her future life with her impoverished lover. Traveling alone by car in order to put as wide a distance as possible between herself and Phoenix, she stays overnight in a small, almost deserted roadside motel and is mysteriously murdered in the shower. (This killing is carefully calculated to catch the audience napping, since the girl involved is the star of the film, Janet Leigh.) The only people around are Norman Bates—a nervous, seemingly vulnerable, and shy young man who runs the motel—and his mother—who, he says, lives in a house nearby, a gaunt residence built in a style Hitchcock describes as "California Gothic." The vague image of the murderer seen through the opaque shower curtain suggests the figure of a woman, but the young man energetically sets about cleaning up the bathroom to cover all traces of the murder and gets rid of the girl's body by putting it into her car and sinking the vehicle into a deep pond.

Throughout the film Hitchcock uses as far as ever possible the technique of audience identification—first with Marion, and later with Norman—employing the "first-person" camera, which puts the audience visually in their place. This culminates in the dead girl's sister's exploration of the Gothic mansion, with all its revealing imagery of Norman's disturbed mind reaching its climax in the confrontation with Mrs. Bates's stuffed body in the cellar. Gradually the audience becomes involved in the young man's derangement—his obsession with taxidermy (his office at the motel has already been seen to be surrounded by stuffed birds of prey with their static, prying eyes), his anxiety about his unseen mother, a creature of the night associated with the empty, haunted house on the mound behind the motel. This prepares us for the shock of the finale and the scenes involving the young man's incarceration in a police cell, where his absorption into his long-dead mother's identity has become total and her death at his hands and the preservation of her body revealed. He found her with her lover eight years before and murdered them both.

Norman's condition is explained somewhat perfunctorily by a psychologist at the close of the film, which is brilliantly constructed as an exercise in horror rather than as a serious study of an advanced form of mental derangement. Norman's insanity is no more than a story device for Hitchcock. "My main satisfaction," he told Truffaut in the published interviews, "is that the film had an effect on the audiences, and I consider that very important. I don't care about the subject matter; I don't care about the acting; but I do care about the pieces of film and the photography and the sound track and all the technical ingredients that made the audience scream."[97] Nevertheless, the film owes a great deal of its tension to Anthony Perkins's magnificent, sensitive performance as the insane protagonist, with his nervous diffidence, his evasive resistance to any form of curiosity about himself, and his obsessive concentration once he is seen alone.[98]

THE PUMPKIN EATER
(Britain, 1964). Direction: Jack Clayton. Script: Harold Pinter. Based on the novel by Penelope Mortimer. With Anne Bancroft (Jo), Peter Finch (Jake), Eric Porter (Psychiatrist). 1a.

This film traces the nervous breakdown of a woman who, after a series of marriages and seven childbirths, at last finds herself in love and anxious to keep a firm hold over her current husband, a successful scriptwriter with promiscuous tendencies. Discovery of his likely unfaithfulness causes the breakdown, which finally occurs in a store in London, where she has gone merely to distract herself. After some inconclusive sessions with a psychiatrist, the husband's continued unfaithfulness, and her own unsatisfactory skirmishing with compensatory lovers, she lands herself in what may represent emotional security—the arms of her previous husband.

One of the more significant film studies of a woman from the so-called privileged classes who has a nervous breakdown, *The Pumpkin Eater* can be compared with *Red Desert, Summer Wishes, Winter Dreams,* and *Juliet of the Spirits.* For all her earnest efforts, Jo ends up in scarcely better fettle than she was in at the beginning, and this would seem to be the significance of the film, in which so much creative talent has been concentrated, especially that of Anne Bancroft.

REBEL WITHOUT A CAUSE
(USA 1955). Direction and script: Nicholas Ray. With James Dean (Jim), Jim Backus (Jim's father), Ann Doran (Jim's mother), Natalie Wood (Judy), William Hopper (Judy's father), Sal Mineo (Plato), Correy Allen (Buz). 7, 3, 1a.

A cult movie of adolescent rebellion in the mid-1950s, this highly influential film is notable for the varied personal situations and disturbances of the principal characters. It centers on the portrayal of Jim (in jeans and T-shirt), son of a weak father and a domineering mother. Judy is a girl who is unbalanced by the sudden, wholly unexpected withdrawal of her father's affection, which has sexual mistrust and jealousy in it. Plato, whose parents are divorced, is a homosexual who is attracted to Jim. Jim is himself drawn to Judy and quarrels to the point of violence (a knife fight) with her boyfriend, Buzz.

A climax in the film is the endurance test, the "chicken run"—in which cars dash up to the edge of a cliff. Buzz is trapped and killed. Jim and Judy take to each other, but Jim, already in some trouble with the police, is threatened by a gang loyal to Buzz's memory. Jim notably fails to have any understanding with his parents, though his father, the domestic slave of his wife, tries unsuccessfully to approach his son. James Dean's naturalistic study of tongue-tied youth, unable to realize a responsible relationship with anyone except, embryonically, with Judy, was, of course, outstanding, but the supporting players, except for Sal Mineo, tend to give rather obvious performances in order to fulfill their somewhat typed characterizations. Soft and sensitive as Plato, Mineo at the end of the film shoots at Jim's assailants and is in turn shot by the police.

RED DESERT
('Deserto Rosso,' Italy, 1964). Direction and coscript, Michelangelo Antonioni. With Monica Vitti (Giuliana), Carlo Chionetti (Ugo), Richard Harris (Corrado), Valerio Bartoleschi (Valerio). 1a.

Antonioni's film is another in the series of studies by leading contemporary filmmakers of nervous breakdown in women. Having a devoted and successful—but quite insensitive and utterly preoccupied—husband, Ugo, and a small, well-loved son, Valerio, Giuliana has become increasingly estranged from living in the bare, ravaged, industrial environment surrounding her husband's electronics plant in Ravenna (Antonioni's birthplace). The factory stands bright, clear, and smoke-plumed on a stretch of wasteland resembling a desert but including nearby stretches of water accessible to merchant shipping. Giuliana has recently partially recovered from a breakdown and shock following what was purported to have been a car accident, and she is struggling against her absorption back into this dominating world of industry. (At the beginning of the film a strike is in progress and is resolved only at the end.) She has in fact tried to kill herself.

To relieve her tensions, Giuliana has a love affair with a visiting mining engineer, Corrado, a friend of her husband, but it does little for her. Her many dreams and hallucinations turn on the recurrent image of ships, representing movement and escape by sea from the red desert, and they include every kind of craft—from yachts sailing in a sunny, tropical ocean, to the most degraded of merchant vessels. The ships appear on Giuliana's horizon at significant moments in her maladjustment.

In an interview tape-recorded at the Venice Film Festival and conducted by Jean-Luc Godard for the *Cahiers du Cinéma,* Antonioni said of Giuliana's relationship (or lack of it) to her industrial environment:

> It is too easy to say, as some critics have, that I am accusing the world of industry, factories, etc. of turning the people who live there into neurotics. My intention . . . was to point out the beauty in this world, where even the factories have an extraordinary aesthetic beauty. . . . I feel that the neuroses are not a product simply of the environment, but the result of lack of adaptation. . . . The character of Giuliana is like this. Her neurotic state is caused by the gulf she feels between her own sensibility, intelligence, and way of life . . . and the rhythm which is imposed upon her. . . . She is in the position of having to reshape herself entirely as a woman.[99]

Antonioni is also concerned to show how people who have failed to adapt to an environment turn to compensatory forms of escape that are ultimately unsatisfying to them. For Giuliana these are represented by her attempts at being erotic, culminating in her barely consummated love affairs with Corrado and the trivial, dehumanizing orgy with a mixed group of sophisticated friends in a small, isolated hut situated on the waste ground.

The Red Desert was Antonioni's first film in color, and he uses it significantly for psychological implications. The colors and shapes associated with industry are all hard and assured; those with Giuliana are hazy and sometimes distorted—even the grass is gray. He even uses color suffusions for moments of mental aberration, as Hitchcock did in *Marnie.* Similarly, her husband and her small son are well-adjusted to an environment of machinery—this is shown in Valerio's case in his preoccupation with mechanical toys. Sounds, too, are used impressionistically—a woman's voice singing distantly, a woman's scream heard remotely during the orgy sequence, factory sirens whistling at the beginning of the film, and the sudden intrusion of occasional electronic chords.

REFLECTIONS IN A GOLDEN EYE
(USA, 1967). Direction: John Huston. Script: Chapman Mortimer. Adapted from the novel by Carson McCullers. With Marlon Brando (Captain Penderton), Elizabeth Taylor (Leonora Penderton), Robert Forster (Private Williams), Brian Keith (Major Morris Langdon), Julie Harris (Mrs. Alison Langdon). 7, 3.

This film is perhaps most remarkable for its acting, especially by Marlon Brando, who plays Captain Penderton, a homosexual officer tortured by his love for a young man, Private Williams, who is himself obsessed with love for Penderton's sensual wife, Leonora, who in her turn loves a married fellow officer of her husband, Major Morris Langdon. The interrelationships culminate in violence and murder. In his autobiography Huston recorded that he met Carson McCullers and that she "approved on the script."[100] He adds: "I like *Reflections in a Golden Eye*. I think it is one of my best pictures. The entire cast . . . turned in beautiful performances."[101]

Huston had a considerable dispute with his distributors, Warner Brothers, over the use of color. After Huston went to great lengths to make the color motif of the film "a golden effect—a diffuse amber,"[102] Warners permitted only a limited number of prints to be distributed in this form, insisting that the rest be in normal Technicolor.

REPULSION
(Britain, 1965). Direction and coscripting: Roman Polanski. With Catherine Deneuve (Carol), Yvonne Furneaux (Helen), Ian Hendry (Michael), John Fraser (Colin), Patrick Wymark (the landlord), James Villiers (John), Helen Fraser (Bridget). 3.

Roman Polanski's background is of particular interest. Born in 1933 of mixed stock—his father, a Russian Jew; his mother, Polish—Polanski spent his later childhood (ages seven to twelve) in occupied Poland. At the age of eight he escaped with his father's help from the Jewish ghetto in Cracow and survived the period living with a family of peasants. His parents were taken to concentration camps, where his mother died. His father remarried and Polanski at the age of twelve refused to live with him. Polanski (who speaks Russian, Polish, French, Italian, and English) was at first an actor (appearing, for example, in Wajda's film *A Generation*) before becoming a student at the Film School in Lodz in 1954, where he made the celebrated surrealistic short, *Two Men and a Wardrobe* (with the theme, it has been said, of "innocence confronting corruption and losing out").[103] After five years at the school, he spent a further year in Paris before returning to Poland to make at the age of twenty-seven the feature *Knife in the Water* (1962), with script collaboration by Jerzy Skolimowski, who was later to become a distinguished director in his own right. *Knife in the Water* became an award-winning film. Introducing certain Freudian symbols (such as the knife of the title, and a belt), it was a tense study of a relationship between a husband, his wife, and a young male stranger, who becomes a guest on their small yacht. The film had the distinction of being denounced in public by Gomulka, head of the Polish Communist Party, because of its alleged corrupt Western influences in subject and treatment. Polanski left Poland, settling at first in England, where he was to make his next feature, *Repulsion*.

Repulsion is the study of a beautiful young girl, Carol, who, withdrawn since childhood, is totally unable to have any normal relationships with men. Accompanied by ominous drumbeats under the title and credits, the camera moves into a big close-up of Carol's face, especially the eyes. A shot immediately follows of a prone woman, with her face creamed white so that she resembles a corpse, being treated in an upper-class beauty salon. The salon is in South Kensington, London, and it is here that Carol is employed. She lives in a nearby apartment with her sister, Helen, and at times has to put up with the presence of Helen's unpleasantly aggressive boyfriend, Michael, of whom she has developed a jealous dislike, since, among other signs of his intrusive male presence, he leaves his straight-edged razor lying around in the sisters' bathroom.

A crack in the plasterwork of the kitchen wall (later to be of considerable significance) is mentioned but not seen. A point of tension occurs when Helen plans a two-week vacation on the Continent with Michael, leaving Carol alone in the apartment. Carol reacts somewhat like a child in search of a parent, almost as if trying to turn the unwilling Helen into a foster mother. The girls are somewhat isolated by the fact that they are foreigners, though resident and working in London. The tension in the sisters' relationship is stressed by other factors—the constant use of waist-high camera setups; the restless movements of the two women, reflected in camera movement; occasional ceiling-high shots looking down on the sisters; the use now and then of distorted images, such as Carol's face seen reflected in the curved side of an electric kettle. Frequent traveling close-shots give special significance to such objects as the razor. The camera tracks around the apartment, registering details of the drab furniture and ornaments, coming to rest on an old-time family photograph, with the elder Helen, as a child, leaning against her father's knee, while the younger Carol, stands a little aloof, staring away from the family.

Polanski also uses, on the one hand, prolonged periods of silence and, on the other, shock sound effects—especially later in the film, when Carol is suffering hallucinations. Jazz-style music is used, however, to bridge sequences for street montages and the like. Everything points to Carol's increasing isolation, especially as she goes to and from work. In the apartment, in the silence of the night, lying in her room, she has to listen to the noises made by Helen during her lovemaking with Michael. Next door to the apartment block is a convent, down upon which the living-room window looks. There, to the continual sound of a somewhat depressing interval-bell, the white-clad nuns exercise themselves in their open quadrangle. In the house next door there is a child relentlessly practicing scales on a piano.

At work Carol suffers from periods of abstraction and withdrawal, which lead to a reprimand from her employer. She manages to muster some measure of companionship with another girl on the staff and even responds with laughter to her description of Charlie Chaplin—her only naturally outgoing scene in the film. She takes her lunch alone in a small cafe, but her great beauty attracts the attentions of men—from the wolf-whistles of roadworkers to the persistent attempts of an attractive and relatively sympathetic young man, Colin, to date her. She resists these attempts, always withdrawing, her glance directed downward, away from him. Her aloofness only serves to attract him more, indeed to the point of infatuation, and he has to endure unpleasant ribbing by the chauvinistic, upper-class young men he is in the habit of meeting in the pub for drinks.

The first forty-five minutes of the film concerns Carol's gradually increasing withdrawal, both at work and at home with her sister prior to the latter's departure. The rest of the film, some sixty minutes, shows her very rapid decline once she is left alone. The symptoms in the first, wholly naturalistic, section are seen *externally,* as observed behavior—Carol's shock and very rapid retreat when she opens the bathroom door and sees Michael, stripped to the waist and shaving with the razor; her avoidance of stepping on the crooked cracks in the paved sidewalk and her fixation as she stares down at them when sitting on a public seat. The images of this second, longer, and climactic part of the film reflect the *inner* reality of Carol's hallucinated mind. Here the experiences of the audience become subjective, sharing Carol's own mental condition. We experience her hallucinations directly, as she experiences them.

The second part of the film, then, covers Carol's total collapse. The period involved—timeless for her and us alike—appears to be two weeks, while Helen and Michael are in Italy. Carol goes to work, but only spasmodically, as the dialogue indicates when she is reprimanded for her absenteeism and for her personal slovenliness. The emphasis is on the terror her sexual hallucinations visit upon her, mainly at night, and on the violence to which she is finally driven against the two men who manage to intrude upon her guarded privacy—Colin, whose anxiety on her behalf causes him to break into the apartment, and finally the landlord, who enters with a master key in order to collect the rent, which is long overdue. (It is significant that, when speaking to the landlord, Carol utters the word *Brussels,* her childhood home.)

During the two weeks of Helen's absence the apartment becomes a shambles. Polanski emphasizes this by showing repeatedly the increasing disintegration of a skinned rabbit, originally intended for dinner on Helen's last night home and left exposed out of the refrigerator after Michael insisted on taking Helen out to eat in order to get her away from Carol. At one stage in her advanced decline Carol decapitates the decaying body of the rabbit, concealing the head in her purse. It is evident to her employer she is seriously ill, and she is finally sent home in a taxi.

Prior to this, however, she did not resist being taken out by Colin in his sports car but did so violently resist his one attempt to kiss her that she flung open the car door, and, oblivious to surrounding traffic, rushed off, almost causing a street accident. The incident is given its own macabre comment or counterpoint by the presence in the street of three busker musicians, two of them bent, insectlike, playing percussion on spoons attached to their legs. They appear three times in the film, determined to maintain their obsessive rhythms.

As the days draw on, Carol is unable to leave the apartment, which becomes for her a sexual torture-chamber. Day merges with night; the windows remain heavily curtained. The hallucinations build up with shock effect. The walls crack open with sudden, ear-splitting sounds. There are ominous footsteps outside her bedroom. Knocking down a protective wardrobe, a faceless man breaks in and brutally assaults her in bed. Her screams are open-mouthed but silent. The telephone rings with menacing shrillness—an actual event (it is Colin, who is trying to find out if she is all right since she has not appeared at work). The child's piano exercises intensify next door; the convent bell punctuates the action; the street buskers persist in their crazy, rhythmic beat below in the street.

The sounds gather in both suddenness and intensity as the film proceeds, and the images get darker and darker. Finally, the apartment itself changes scale in Carol's distorted perception—the corridors lengthen, the bedroom ceiling descends threateningly as if to crush her, the rooms change shape and increase their perspective—all in the gathering darkness. At one stage the walls themselves become soft, receiving the imprint of Carol's hands as she creeps along them.

Colin eventually breaks in. She spots him beforehand through the spy hole of the apartment door. His face is seen distorted (shot by means of a fish-eye lens). She smashes him to death with a heavy candlestick and drags his blood-stained body into the bathroom, tipping it into the bathtub, which she has previously allowed to overflow so that the floor is awash. She nails up the apartment door with slats of wood, but her efforts are useless—she cannot keep the elderly landlord out. He demands the rent, which Helen in fact left for him. To some extent mollified, he cannot resist making awkward passes at the half-naked girl, sitting in a withdrawn state in her nightdress. She lashes out at him with Michael's discarded razor, cutting him to death. Carol conceals the second body by overturning the sofa on top of it. Then, as if some sexual urge has been satisfied, she slowly carmines her lips. But again the ceilings descend on her, and as she staggers down the apartment corridor, the walls break open with hideous, rending sounds, and powerful male hands reach out to grasp at her breasts and thighs.

When Michael and Helen return, the horrific condition of the apartment is seen once more objectively, as they discover it. Helen becomes hysteric with shock, but Michael's hardened nature enables him to keep his head. Various neighbors meanwhile creep in through the open apartment door and become paralyzed with shock at what they see. They stare down at Carol, who is lying in a catatonic trance under her sister's bed, as if taking her place with her lover. It is indeed Michael who lifts up her prone body in his arms and carries her away from the blood-soaked scene. The camera leaves the staring white faces of the intruders and travels over to the family photograph, zooming slowly in on the isolated image of the child Carol and on her eyes, insanely peering into space.

The critic Colin McArthur pointed out the significance of the film's monosexual scenes[104]—the female chauvinists deriding men in the female sanctum of the beauty parlor; the nuns living apart from men in their convent. The contrast is the general chauvinism of the men gathered in their habitual pub, boasting of their egoistic, predatory pursuit of women for sex. Michael, though not of their group, is the worst chauvinist of all, bullying the complacent Helen. Only Colin shows some actual regard for a member of the opposite sex, Carol, as a person.[105]

In an interview conducted by *Cahiers du Cinéma* Polanski was questioned about *Repulsion:*

CAHIERS: When you wanted to make *Repulsion,* you pushed your goal towards something that interested you.

POLANSKI: Precisely. And the reason why is that I am sexually obsessed.

CAHIERS: You took your ideas from girls you knew?

POLANSKI: A little. I knew a girl who corresponded a little to that one. . . . I would have to see a psychoanalyst. But, after all, I did see some. I showed them my scenario, which they all liked very much, and they said too that I did not need a psychoanalyst because I am perfectly balanced . . . Which grieved me very much, for I always took myself for a madman. . . . That was a blow to me. . . . The more I tell myself unbelievable stories, the more conscious I am that I must render them in a realistic manner. That is what I did in - *Repulsion.* . . . I have made a tour de force. . . . but this tour de force consisted essentially in that: to render the story plausible, realistic. . . . Anyone could tell the story in a grotesque manner. . . . only I told it in a plausible manner, and with a surprising psychological motivation. . . . All the psychiatrists find it true, that film. . . . One enters another landscape. The landscape of the mind.[106]

ROPE

(USA, 1948). Direction: Alfred Hitchcock. Script: Arthur Laurentz. Adaptation: Hume Cronyn. Based on the play by Patrick Hamilton. With James Stewart (Prof. Rupert Cadell), Farley Granger (Philip), John Dall (Shaw Brandon), Joan Chandler (James Walker), Sir Cedric Hardwicke (Kentley), Constance Collier (Mrs. Atwater). 3, 4.

The play takes place during a single summer evening in an apartment in New York from 7:30 to 9:15. Two young homosexuals from well-off families kill a college friend solely for the thrill of it and to prove the superiority of their intelligence to that of anyone else. They hide the body in a chest in the very room where the youth's parents and other friends are soon to join them for a cocktail party. Among the guests is a former professor of theirs who had taught them philosophy, and their combined sense of guilt and bravado lead them to give themselves away in the face of the professor's acute sensibility, knowledge of them, and observation of their behavior.

Hitchcock was bold enough to make this film, his first in color, in continuous, ten-minute takes, the maximum length of film his cameras could take on a single load. The continuity of the action was intended to represent exactly the time the film takes to project. Hitchcock later admitted to Truffaut that he did this as a "stunt."[107] The film, most carefully rehearsed technically, was completed (with retakes) with ten days of rehearsal and eighteen days of shooting. The general effect, however, was scarcely worth all the contrivance since the pace seems slow and the performances muted.

The original play, by Patrick Hamilton, was based on the notorious Leopold-Loeb case in Chicago, in which two youths murdered a third just for the excitement of killing and escaping detection.

THE ROSE

(USA, 1979). Direction: Mark Rydell. With Bette Midler (Rose), Alan Bates (Rudge), Frederick Forrest (Houston Dyer). 6.

This is a remarkable study, in the form of the so-called bio-pic, of the disintegration through alcohol and drug abuse of a talented rock star, Rose, modeled, it would seem, on the late Janis Joplin. The plot complications turn on her up-and-down relationships with her long-suffering manager, Rudge, and on another disintegrating character like herself, Houston Dyer. Dyer is an American army sergeant gone absent-without-leave from Vietnam, whom she picks up, sleeps and quarrels with, and adopts as part of her personal circle during the concert tour she is scarcely fit to undertake. He in turn protects her, abandons her, and rejoins her in the final stages of her last concert tour, at the end of which she collapses, killed by heroin.

THE RULING CLASS
(Britain, 1971). Direction: Peter Medak. Adaptation: Peter Barnes. Adapted from the play by Peter Barnes. With Peter O'Toole (14th Earl of Gurney), Alastair Sim (Bishop Lampton), Arthur Lowe (Tucker), Harry Andrews (13th Earl of Gurney), Coral Browne (Lady Claire Gurney), Michael Bryant (Dr. Herder). 9, 8.

Adapted by Peter Barnes from his own burlesque play, *The Ruling Class* centers upon the delusions of Jack, the 14th Earl of Gurney, after the collapse of the 13th Earl while practicing one of the fetishes he acquired after a lifetime of rigorous service to his country. Believing himself to be Jesus Christ, the new Earl is naturally classified as a paranoid schizophrenic, especially since he preaches the gospel of love. Meanwhile, the family butler, Tucker, reveals his socialistic views because he has been left thirty thousand pounds by his late employer. The family conspire with the butler to induce Jack to marry and produce an heir so that he can be declared insane and confined. He marries his father's mistress, but on the eve of the birth of a prospective heir, the family psychiatrist, Dr. Herder, produces a real schizophrenic, who also believes himself to be God with an energy and conviction that shatters Jack's illusory sense of identity. Jack then switches over to his real identity, that of an extreme right-wing aristocrat with Jack-the-Ripper tendences. After murdering his wife and sister-in-law (crimes for which the socialistic butler is arrested), Jack makes a maiden speech in the House of Lords of insane ferocity, which galvanizes that moribund body into shouts of enthusiasm.

This lengthy film uses satiric burlesque to expose what its makers enjoy feeling to be the baroque archaism of the British hereditary aristocracy, portraying them as macabre and overly privileged decadents, their foibles punctured every so often by the asides made to the audience by the corpulent butler.

SEANCE ON A WET AFTERNOON
(Britain, 1964). Direction and script: Bryan Forbes. With Kim Stanley (Myra Savage), Richard Attenborough (Billy Savage). 3, 2.

Myra Savage, a professional medium who feels that her powers are not properly recognized, conceives the idea of kidnapping a child, with the help of her mild-mannered but sociopathic husband, Billy, and then astonishing the world by "divining" the whereabouts of both the child and the ransom money collected by Billy. The whole plot, though successfully carried out by the subservient Billy, begins to go awry because of Billy's feeling for the child and Myra's giving herself away completely during a seance for the police.

The film is remarkable for the intense, sympathetic playing by Kim Stanley and Richard Attenborough, as the shabby pair of insane contrivers who wade out of their depth in carrying out the kidnapping. In a curious way, they manage to retain our sympathy as Amanda, the abducted child, gradually replaces their own stillborn child in their affections. She is kept in the very room intended for the child who did not survive, redecorated for the purpose of deceiving her to resemble a hospital private ward. Bryan Forbes creates an oppressive atmosphere in his setting of a delapidated, overcrowded Victorian house, in which the couple live and in which they hold their pathetic seances, while the dialogue he has written for Myra and Billy is extraordinarily revealing of the fantasy world in which certain of the insane so completely exist.

THE SEASHELL AND THE CLERGYMAN
('LA COQUILLE ET LE CLERGYMAN' France, 1927). Direction: Germaine Dulac. Script: Antonin Artaud. With Alex Allin.

A silent film of short feature length and an example of the highly individual style of production typical of French avant-garde filmmaking of the 1920s, *The Seashell and the Clergyman*[108] presents a state of mind entirely as a succession of episodes using Freudian imagery to express subjective conflicts. The only real person in the film is the clergyman himself—a man who, having submitted himself to a celibate life, is affected by sexual torment he is unable to resolve. His hallucinations involve the figure of a sensuous but very neutralized and unresponsive woman—a sexual lay figure who excites his desire—and the figure of a uniformed man, who appears as her natural consort—his uniform and saber continually suggesting sexual aggression and effectiveness. Other recurring images include a ploughed field; an anchored ship; phallic breakers of glass, into which the clergyman is constantly and wastefully pouring bloodlike fluid and which he then smashes; a dishlike shell; and a key with which the clergyman unlocks a succession of doors that lead him nowhere.

The film is an interesting attempt to widen the scope of cinema by creating action entirely in terms of dream imagery. It uses an episodic structure, playing out one dream after another without any obvious continuity other than the common theme of sexual repression. It uses the resources of the film—such as slow-motion, superimposition, extreme angle shots, and big close-ups—to emphasize the psychological content. Alex Allin, stepping in as the clergyman for Artaud, who was ill, uses simplistic, exaggerated facial expression to represent the mental-physical suffering that the clergyman is enduring. Artaud disapproved of both how the part was played and how the film was made, and organized a demonstration against the film when it was shown at the Studio des Ursulines. The surrealists among the French avant-garde also rejected the film on the grounds of its deliberate, rationalized, and (they felt) heavy-handed use of dream imagery—text-book Freud in place of the free association that they identified with true surrealism, represented at its best in Buñuel's *Un Chien Andalou* (France, 1928)—made in collaboration with Salvador Dali—and *L'Age d'Or* (France, 1930).

SECRETS OF A SOUL
(Germany, 1926). Direction: G. W. Pabst. With Werner Krauss (Fellman), Pawel Pawlow (Dr. Orth). 3.

G. W. Pabst (1885–1967), born in Vienna, established his career as both actor and director in the theater, entering films early in the 1920s. His first film of consequence was *The Joyless Street* (Germany, 1925), which included Werner Krauss, the protagonist of *The Cabinet of Dr Caligari*, in its cast. *Secrets of a Soul (Geheimnisse einer Seele)* was the first to be made with the intention of illuminating and promoting Freud's theories and with the active collaboration of his close associates, Dr. Hanns Sachs and Dr. Karl Abraham. Pawel Pawlow, a Russian-speaking émigré actor specially chosen by Pabst because he looked the part of an analyst so well, underwent a special course of instruction in Freud's theories and practices before taking on the role of Dr Orth.

The central character, Dr. Fellman, a research chemist who believes himself to be happily married to a wife much younger than himself, becomes alarmed by various inexplicable symptoms in his behavior, the worst of which is a compulsive desire to murder his wife with a knife. At the beginning of the film, he accidentally cuts the nape of her neck while trimming her hair for her. This occurs at the same moment that someone cries, "Murder!" in a neighboring apartment, where a killing has actually just taken place. The symptoms Fellman is experiencing appear to have been triggered by this accidental association and are reinforced by a message he and his wife receive that her cousin, a man of her own age and a somewhat romantic figure in her eyes, is returning home from the Far East and hopes to visit them. In advance of his arrival he sends them a small figurine (an Eastern goddess of fertility with a child in her lap) and an ornamental scimitar. His wife in fact longs to have a child, and it would seem that Fellman is impotent, though he loves children and is seen fussing over a small girl whose mother is visiting his laboratory.

Fellman develops an allergy to using knives at table and even to shaving himself. He becomes subject to nightmares with their own special forms of imagery:

In the first dream . . . he finds himself shut out of his house and at the same time threatened by an image of the cousin, seen wearing a topee. In response to this threat, Fellman levitates. The next image is of model trains running on rails, recalled from the childhood association he had with his wife's cousin. This is followed by the appearance of the statue of the fertility goddess, now of a towering dimension, and of a model city, the chief feature of which is a tall, round tower, surrounded by an outer, spiral staircase which Fellman finds himself unable to climb. His wife's face is seen superimposed on swinging bells in a bell tower, and a phantasmagoria of laughing faces mock him. He believes his wife is betraying him, while he himself is being accused of murder. Fingers are seen pointing at him. Back in his laboratory, he sees an image of his wife sitting in a boat with her lover; she is nursing a child. He tries to slash at the ghost image of his wife with a scimitar.

Fellman wakes up screaming, and his wife rushes into his bedroom to comfort him.

The cousin arrives at the Fellman house while Fellman himself is at work. On his return Fellman greets him with a great demonstration of affection. Nevertheless, he finds himself unable to dine with him at his own table. "I'm afraid I cannot touch a knife. Excuse me," he says. Leaving his wife and her cousin in the house, he goes to dine at a restaurant. After his solitary meal, he departs, leaving his house keys on the restaurant table. At an adjoining table sits a psychiatrist of the Freudian school, Dr. Orth, who picks up the keys and follows Fellman to his home, where he observes him hesitating before the front door. "You do not seem to want to enter your own home," he remarks. He then introduces himself as a psychiatrist and invites Fellman to consult him should he ever feel the need to do so.

Becoming more and more jealous and alienated from his wife since the arrival of the debonair young cousin, Fellman goes to seek consolation at his mother's house. She treats him like a child, cutting his meat for him at table. Finally, he decides to consult the analyst. Orth advises him to leave his domestic environment during a period of treatment. This leads to the second half of the film.

During analysis Fellman reveals the association of the murder in his neighborhood with the cut he made in the nape of his wife's neck. He recalls too a second dream, or flow of images, in which he and his wife were rooting a plant in the earth together and visiting an empty room in which a decorative cradle first appeared and then disappeared the room being finally locked. "We long for children," he says. He claims that he is not *consciously* jealous of his wife's cousin, who still remains his "best friend." Meanwhile, the cousin has thought it best to leave Fellman's home and stay in a hotel.

After a passage of time representing some months of treatment, the second main dream sequence follows, recalled by Fellman for the analyst:

A succession of apparently unrelated images cascade over the screen—Fellman falling through space; a distorted image of the toy train with the cousin's face superimposed; the test tube dropped in the laboratory (Fellman had actually dropped a test tube when told the cousin had just arrived at his house); the enlarged Asiatic goddess; a honeymoon recollection in an Italian setting; the tolling, swinging bells with his wife's face superimposed; the tower with the spiral staircase; the mocking faces of women; the scornful faces of the women assistants in his laboratory when he fusses over a child; a barred-up prison cell; a drum being beaten and accusing fingers being pointed as he cuts the nape of his wife's neck; a dark expanse of moving water (denoting birth); the sight of his wife and her cousin together; his wife carrying a baby doll; a recollection of jealousy in childhood when his wife, as a child, took away a doll he had loved and gave it to her cousin (a younger child than he, though appearing in the dream to be of the same age). The implication of this is that Erich, the cousin, is the father of the child the doll represents, and that his wife is the mother, thus eliminating Fellman's paternity. The finale of the dream is a climax of frantic, frustrated gesticulation by Fellman.

From all this the analyst detects the origins of Fellman's jealousy of Erich developed during childhood. "All other manifestations are secondary," he says. "I have made your subconscious fears known to you."

Eventually Fellman is permitted to return home and face his wife. A coda follows, conceived in the tradition of the happy end, required in popular filmmaking. Fellman is seen on holiday with his wife. He is in the country, fishing. He returns to his wife with his catch. She is holding a baby.

THE SERGEANT
(USA 1968). Direction: John Flynn. With Rod Steiger (the sergeant), John Philip Law (the private). 7, 3.

Filmed on location in France, this film is essentially a psychological study of homosexual obsession. It focuses on the destructive attraction exercised by a handsome young private in the army over a sergeant.

THE SERVANT
(Britain, 1963). Direction: Joseph Losey. Script: Harold Pinter. Adapted from the novel by Robin Maugham. With Dirk Bogarde (Barrett), James Fox (Tony), Sarah Miles (Vera). 3, 2.

Tony, a rich young bachelor engaged to be married, hires a manservant, Barrett, to look after him in the nearly empty house into which he is moving in anticipation of his marriage. Barrett rapidly becomes the dominant force in this partnership, even introducing his corrupt girlfriend, Vera (who poses as Barrett's sister) to seduce the feckless young man and break up his engagement. Tony's attempt to get rid of Barrett and Vera fails, and they are reinstated. Tony's personality becomes totally eroded, and the house becomes a center for drug-induced orgies. The film is a stylistic tour de force on the dual identity theme, or "possession" of one person by another.

SLAUGHTERHOUSE FIVE
(USA, 1972). Direction: George Roy Hill. With Michael Sacks (Billy Pilgrim). Based on a novel by Kurt Vonnegut. 5.

Billy, a prisoner-of-war in World War II and now an optometrist in upstate New York, claims to be "unstuck in time" and to be frequently transported to a distant planet called Tralfamadore. The film moves from Billy's experiences in prison camp (including the destruction of Dresden) to Tralfamadore, and to the circumstances of his life after returning to the States after the war. The hero remains utterly disconnected.

THE SNAKE PIT

(USA, 1948). Direction: Anatole Litvak. Script: Frank Partos and Millen Brand. Based on the novel by Mary Jane Ward. With Olivia de Havilland (Virginia), Leo Genn (the doctor). 1b, 9.

The Snake Pit is another study in some detail of the treatment given an individual who has had a mental collapse. The protagonist, Virginia Cunningham, is fortunate in having a more-than-considerate husband, to whom she was recently married. They have no children. When the film opens, Virginia, confined in a hospital, is responding with some difficulty to the questions put to her in a calm and quiet manner by her doctor, and it is evident she is a very disturbed patient, suffering from depression, fears of persecution, and amnesia. She resents being regimented, as the patients are seen to be after exercise in the grounds, and she is patently unclear quite where she is, believing she may be in some kind of prison, not a hospital. "I have no husband," she says to the doctor, but nevertheless admits she is indeed Mrs. Cunningham.

The doctor interviews Robert Cunningham, and flashbacks establish the extent of his relationship with Virginia and the events leading up to their marriage. She has been responsive to his company but at the same time liable to sudden fits of withdrawal, in one instance hiding away from him for some months when he had to move from Chicago to work in New York. When they meet again—it would seem more by design than by accident on her part—he persistently asks her to marry him; nevertheless, she accuses him of trying to avoid her. They marry, but soon it becomes clear to him there is something radically wrong with her. She cannot sleep; she complains, "There is something wrong with my head." Her final breakdown, leading to hospitalization, comes on 12 May, a date with which she appears to have some distressing association. Crying, "I can't love anybody," she collapses. The doctor asks Cunningham's permission to give her electric shock treatment, and he signs his consent.

Virginia receives a succession of shock treatments, though the actual application of shock is not shown (as it is, for example, in *One Flew over the Cuckoo's Nest*). The successive reports on her response show that the patient is "confused and disoriented," though later showing a "slight improvement." She is taken "out of shock," and she learns, as we do, that she has been confined in the hospital now for as long as five months. She is housed in a large ward, where the nurses seem for the most part unfeeling and autocratic. Her interviews with her doctor (who always appears with a photograph of Freud prominently on display behind his desk) elicit some memories, though she becomes agitated when trying to recollect the period of her family life spent in Chicago; and has to be told her married name—that she is not Virginia Stewart (her maiden name), but Virginia Cunningham. When Robert visits her, she recognizes him, but she is still on her guard, uncertain of relationships, uncertain of time. She does not like to be touched. She feels the cold. But she is starting to recollect times past, before her nervous breakdown.

Under narcotics Virginia recalls the event in Chicago in which, as a young girl, she insisted that her then-fiancé Gordon, drive her back from an important banquet they should have attended together on 12 May—a move that led to his death in a car crash, from which she survived. His death on that date has remained on her conscience. Her sense of guilt has made her feel unfit for marriage. "Robert, you must divorce me," she says when her husband next visits her.

The hospital, grossly overcrowded and understaffed, is anxious to discharge as many patients as possible. Virginia's doctor is criticized by his colleagues because he cares too much for particular patients, such as Virginia. He strongly recommends that she should not be sent away. Nevertheless, she is summoned to attend a staff session, the prelude to possible discharge. She has to face interrogation by other, less concerned doctors than her own, and she breaks down under their bullying (as it appears to her) cross-examination. This experience, built up impressionistically from her point of view, is increased in negativity by a raging storm outside, which rattles the windows, and by the stabbing gestures made by the interrogation doctor, cigar in hand. The scene builds to a climax of renewed breakdown for Virginia—she has an hallucination of a raging sea, into which she is sucked and which is finally cross-cut with the next scene, where she is found immersed in a hot-water tub—another form of treatment. She finds herself in Ward 12, a ward reserved for difficult cases—she apparently felt driven to bite the probing finger of the interrogating doctor during the staff session. Virginia is soon, however, considered fit to be transferred to Ward 1, and her discharge again becomes possible. This, unluckily, is supervised by an autocratic nurse with whom Virginia has had some difficulties before.

A dispute with a fellow patient over possession of a doll leads Virginia to another recollection, which reveals her excessive love as a child for her father and the pain she felt when he once took her mother's side against her over some problem she had with another child about a borrowed doll. She also experienced acute jealousy when her unsympathetic mother had her second child. "I'll run away," she threatened. She also deliberately broke a second doll, a male figure, that her father had given her. After her father's death, her mother remarried and seemed to Virginia always to have little love to spare for her.

Back in the present, Virginia is so troubled by the treatment she receives in Ward 1—where she is, of course, seldom able to enjoy visits from her original doctor—that she attempts to escape, locking herself in the washroom. The nurses persuade her to give herself up by a trick, but when she finally emerges, they take her by force and confine her in a straitjacket. She is transferred again, to Ward 33 this time. Here she is fortunate at least in being allowed visits by her original doctor, but her fellow patients in this ward are more severely disturbed than she has been used to. Many of them are actively insane. Virginia has a vision of herself being sucked into the vortex of a snake pit—an allusion to a treatment used in the far distant past, when snake pits acted as a form of shock therapy for the insane.

Virginia's original doctor is put in charge of her case once again, and, somewhat simplistically, he and Virginia arrive at the solution to her case. In her childhood she felt let down by her beloved father and had felt some childish involvement in his death—she had smashed the doll he gave her as a symbolic slaying of her father. Later, she felt even more directly guilty for Gordon's death and for her rejection of his overbearing assumption that she would naturally want to marry him because he wished it.

The film ends with a dance at the hospital for staff and patients. Virginia, who is about to be discharged, shows significant improvement. There is newfound assurance in her conversation, and she shows care for the less fortunate patients, especially one girl who remains almost wholly withdrawn and resistant to any human contact. This resistance Virginia tries patiently and sympathetically to break down. The girl is allowed to come to the dance, nevertheless. A patient with a good voice sings, "I'm going home"—a moving, if sentimental, moment in the film. Virginia dances with her doctor, and this ends with a somewhat intimate conversation between them as man and woman. He tells her he has neither wife nor children; their place seems, therefore, to have been taken by his patients. He appears also to be the only doctor in this state hospital of the 1940s to be using psychotherapy. "I'm not in love with you any more," she tells him. "You never were really," he replies. Virginia's husband then arrives to take her home. She is seemingly satisfactorily recovered from her prolonged breakdown.

SPELLBOUND
(USA, 1945). Direction: Alfred Hitchcock. Script: Ben Hecht. Adaptation: Angus McPhail. Based on the novel *The House of Dr. Edwardes,* by Francis Beeding. Dream sequences: Salvador Dali. Photography: George Barnes. Music: Miklos Rozsa. With Ingrid Bergman (Dr. Constance Peterson), Gregory Peck (John Ballantine), Leo G. Carroll (Dr. Murchison), Michael Chekhov (the professor). 9.

This comparatively early tour de force in psychological melodrama, with its connecting links to popular concepts in psychoanalysis, was derived initially from a fantasy horror novel *The House of Dr. Edwardes,* which, in Hitchcock's own words: "was about a madman taking over an insane asylum. It was melodramatic and quite weird. In the book even the orderlies were lunatics, and they did some very queer things."[109] But, added Hitchcock: "I wanted to do something more sensible, to turn out the first picture on psychoanalysis. So I worked with Ben Hecht, who was in constant touch with prominent psychoanalysts. I was determined to break with the traditional way of handling dream sequences through a blurred and hazy screen."[110] He obtained Selznick's permission to secure the services of Salvador Dali, the artist who in his youth was associated with the surrealist movement in Paris but disowned by it in the 1930s. (He made the short surrealist film, *Un Chien Andalou* along with Luis Buñuel in 1929.) "The real reason was that I wanted to convey the dreams with great visual sharpness and clarity, sharper than the film itself. I wanted Dali because of the architectural sharpness of his work."[111] The end result was a single dream of sensational visual stylization, divided into four successive parts. Whatever the psychological pretensions of the final screenplay, Hitchcock readily admitted to Truffaut (who does not like the film, considering it "weak in fantasy") that *Spellbound* was "just another manhunt story wrapped up in pseudo-psychoanalysis."[112]

The action concerns the love affair between Dr. Constance Peterson, a psychiatrist employed in a private mental hospital in America, and its new principal, Dr. Edwardes, who has just arrived to take over from the retiring incumbent, Dr. Murchison. It is love at first sight between Edwardes and Constance, but she soon realizes there is something strange about Edwardes, who is suffering from a recurrent nightmare. She recognizes that he is indeed a seriously disturbed amnesiac who has quite inexplicably assumed the identity of the real Dr. Edwardes. Alerted to his mental condition, the imposter reveals he is obsessed with guilt, convinced he must have murdered the man whose identity he has assumed. He disappears from the hospital and is soon wanted by the police. Intuitively convinced of his innocence, Constance tracks him down and takes him to the home of her former professor, where he can receive expert treatment while remaining in hiding. The professor discovers that his new patient feels responsible for the accidental death of his younger brother during their childhood and that his sense of guilt has redoubled since he witnessed the death of the late Dr. Edwardes in a similar manner. The truth, however, is that Dr. Edwardes died by the hand of Murchison, who committed this crime in order to save himself from being retired from his position. When this is finally exposed by Constance in a face-to-face confrontation with Murchison, he threatens her with a revolver (which we see pointed at her retreating figure from Murchison's eyeline). She manages to withdraw safely, and he slowly turns the weapon upon himself (that is, pointing at the audience) and fires. In the original print the whole screen explodes in a flash of red fire, the only moment of color in a solidly black-and-white film. The film ends happily, of course, when the lovers are reunited.

The film enjoyed great success and helped substantially to build Hitchcock's reputation in Hollywood. *Spellbound* cost $1.5 million, but its success with the public resulted in $7 million from the box office. It is generally agreed, however, that it is not one of Hitchcock's better films, and that Gregory Peck, with his very down-to-earth personality, was as unsuitable for the part of the pseudo-Edwardes as Ingrid Bergman was right for Constance, a very vulnerable Hitchcockian blonde. (Both Peck and Bergman were contract players for Selznick, Hitchcock's producer.)

Spellbound was also made at a difficult time in Hitchcock's private life, when he was finally severing his links with England, where he had just worked on propaganda films for liberated France. His mother and his brother William both died before the end of the war. Hitchcock began work on the script while he was still in England with his old scripting associate, Angus McPhail, but disliked the result. Returning to America in the fall of 1944, he entirely reworked the script with Ben Hecht in such a manner that the conception of the original horror novel (with its theme rather like that of *The Cabinet of Dr. Caligari*) was all but totally abandoned. Although Selznick left Hitchcock unimpeded during the actual shooting of the film, he exercised his authority as producer to supervise the final cutting, slicing out some twenty minutes from the finished film. It is known that much of the footage devoted to the Dali dream sequences was never included in the final release print. Indeed, Dali's remarkable draftsmanship, filling the screen with artificial eyes and creating distorted landscapes of luminous clarity with a meticulously exaggerated perspective, is so fantastically schematic that it looks more like a baroque setting for some ballet than the dream imagery of a disturbed mind.

Nevertheless, as the entry of a forty-year-old Hitchcock into the field of dramatized mental disturbance, *Spellbound* is a remarkable, if somewhat absurd, tour de force. He was hardly taking the situation as seriously as he was to do in his later films, *Psycho* and *Marnie*, and the result was that he produced a romantic melodrama far more obviously dated than the best of his work.

THE STORY OF ADELE H.
(France, 1975). Direction: François Truffaut. Script consultation: Frances V. Guille. Based on *Le Journal d'Adèle Hugo*, edited by Frances V. Guille. With Isabelle Adjani (Adèle). 3.

The film, inspired by Professor Guille's biography of Victor Hugo's younger daughter, Adèle, and by the latter's *Journal*, is a psychological study of an extreme case of *idée fixe*. The film opens in 1863 with Adèle's arrival in Halifax, Nova Scotia, in pursuit of the English lieutenant Albert Pinson, with whom she has fallen obsessively in love in Guernsey, where the Hugo family were living in exile from France. Pinson, a man who enjoys numerous affaires with women, is no longer in love with this troublesome girl, if indeed he ever was. He resolutely resists her persistent advances, her threats to disgrace him with the army, her impassioned letters, and her insistence on loaning him money to settle his gambling debts—money she can ill afford out of the allowances sent by her father. Finally she breaks him down, and he lets her sleep with him. This inspires her to write to her father back in Guernsey that she is at last married and also enables her to break up Pinson's engagement to a girl in Halifax by boasting to the girl's father that she is pregnant by Pinson. She then plans to sway Pinson's affections through hypnotism and bribes him by supplying him with a whore. When Pinson's regiment is finally posted at Barbados, she uses the money supplied by her father to pay her fare back to Guernsey to follow Pinson to Barbados, where she lives in destitution in a state of absolute insanity. Madness frees her from her obsession, and she is taken back to her father by a compassionate black woman.

In actuality, the whole prolonged pursuit was to last nine years before Adèle's final collapse into undeniable insanity, a state in which she remained for the rest of her life. The film also stresses the girl's desire to free herself from association with, or dominance by, her famous father, who became a widower during her absence and who had lost his elder daughter, Leopoldine, in a drowning in 1843 at the age of only nineteen. Adèle's recurrent nightmare is that she too is drowning. Though remaining economically dependent on her father's generosity, she resorts constantly to using false identities, and she lies persistently.

Truffaut endeavored to present Adèle's story in the cool, understated, semidocumentary form he had adopted in the case of his other film about a true case, *Le Garçon Sauvage*. He was, he said in his foreword to the published script of his film, "fascinated by the creative process of using real-life events as the basis for a fictional story that would not distort the authenticity of the source material."[113] His technique aims, he added, at giving a "low-key description of strong emotion."[114] He used substantial passages from Adèle's letters and journal,[115] recited by his rather youthful actress, who endeavored to impersonate this woman (who was already thirty-three when she first arrived in Halifax and in her forties by the end of her pursuit of Pinson). A postscript to the film reveals that she did not die until 1915, after having spent forty-three years in asylums.

Truffaut listed the factors that most appealed to him in this story as follows:

1. Her story is the autopsy of a passion.
2. The girl is alone throughout the whole story.
3. She is the daughter of the most famous man in the world.
4. The man is referred to, but never seen.
5. Adèle assumes a number of false identities.
6. Obsessed by her *idée fixe*, she pursues an unattainable goal.
7. Every word she utters and every move she makes is related to her fixation.
8. Though she fights a losing battle, Adèle is continually active and inventive.[116]

Truffaut in fact describes his film as "a musical composition for a solo instrument."[117]

STRANGERS ON A TRAIN
(USA, 1951). Direction: Alfred Hitchcock. Script: Raymond Chandler, Czenzi Ormonde. Based on the novel by Patricia Highsmith. With Farley Granger (Guy), Robert Walker (Bruno), Ruth Roman (Ann), Leo G. Carroll (Senator Morton, Ann's father), Patricia Hitchcock (Barbara Morton), Laura Elliott (Miriam, Bruno's wife). 7, 3.

Guy, a tennis champion, finds himself in conversation on a train journey with Bruno, an admirer and, as Hitchcock said in his interviews with Truffaut, "clearly a psychopath" though "undoubtedly more attractive" than Guy. Indeed, a kind of mutual attraction develops between these two young men, though their relationship is mutually destructive. Bruno soon reveals that he is unusually aware of Guy's personal life and boldly proposes that, since Guy wants to be rid of his wife, Miriam, who will not give him the divorce he seeks, he, Bruno, will murder her if Guy, in fair exchange, murders Bruno's hated father. Both murderers, says Bruno, will be in the clear because of their total absence of any involvement with their intended victims. Astonished and shocked, Guy refuses to have anything to do with the idea, but Bruno nevertheless proceeds with the killing of Miriam and then persecutes Guy to make him complete his side of a bargain. After Miriam's death, Guy, who is under some suspicion by the police—especially because of his engagement to a senator's daughter soon after his wife dies—becomes increasingly troubled because he knows the identity of his wife's killer, while Bruno, paranoiacally angry with Guy, decides to compromise him by placing Guy's identifiable lighter in the very place (a fairground) he murdered Miriam and left her body. The film ends with the macabre death of Bruno, who is crushed beneath a runaway carousel in the fairground, while Guy's innocence is established.

STRAW DOGS

(Britain, 1971). Direction and coscripting: Sam Peckinpah. With Dustin Hoffman (David), Susan George (Amy), David Warner (Henry Miles). 3.

Straw Dogs is concerned with the innate violence in all human beings, which, under stress, can break out from the most seemingly pacific in unexpected fury. David is a young American university graduate student working on his doctoral thesis in Cornwall, England, where he is spending the summer with Amy, his Cornish wife, in an isolated cottage amidst a wild landscape overlooking the ocean. Her partially suppressed sexual resentment of her husband's almost total preoccupation with abstruse calculations builds up. His meek exterior, which provokes the mockery of the local villagers, conceals a marked sense of masculine superiority and drives her to challenge him by re-igniting a passionate relationship she once had with a working-class lad in this small and primitive village. The lad in Amy's past life is now a mature man, a member of a tough and ruthless, peasantlike gang, who are hired to roof the cottage garage. Present also in the village is Henry Niles, a subnormal young man who is being goaded sexually by a village girl, Janice.

Amy flaunts herself in front of her former lover and his mates, hoping to excite her husband's jealousy and rouse him sexually, but the outcome of this smoldering situation is an explosion of extreme violence, culminating in Amy's rape by two members of the gang and in the accidental death of Janice at the hands of Henry. Worked up to a frenzy, a gang of male villagers lay siege to the cottage, where David has decided to harbor the terrified Niles, whose surrender the villagers demand. Tormented by resentment at the mockery to which he has been subjected, David is seized by a demonic fury and slays the lynch mob, one by one, using every device that comes to hand—an old rifle, a steel man-trap, and boiling liquid.

The title of the film derives from a Chinese tradition of setting up sacrificial substitute images, which are treated with temporary deference until they are finally discarded and destroyed. These are straw dogs, like David and Amy in the film. Peckinpah is much influenced by fable and tradition in his more notable films, of which *Straw Dogs* is certainly one, the characters existing in their own right in a realistic Cornish setting and, at the same time, representing archtypical, human antagonisms between man and man, and man and woman.

Along with another British film—Stanley Kubrick's version of Anthony Burgess's novel *A Clockwork Orange*—released at exactly the same time, *Straw Dogs* raised a storm of protest over the seeming permissiveness of the film censorship authorities, who had allowed films that depicted violence so explicitly. Yet both films were in fact highly moral in their basic intention. The sad fact was that the public completely misunderstood the intention of these films and treated them as orgies of display violence. *Straw Dogs* is a film of such extraordinary power that it led Tom Milne, a noted commentator, to remark, "I can think of no other film which screws violence up into so tight a knot of terror that one begins to feel . . . that civilisation is crumbling before one's eyes."[118]

A STREETCAR NAMED DESIRE
(USA, 1952). Direction: Elia Kazan. Adapted from the play by Tennessee Williams. With Vivien Leigh (Blanche), Marlon Brando (Stanley), Kim Hunter (Stella), Karl Malden (Mitch). 1a, 3.

This film followed closely Kazan's stage production of the play in New York, with the same cast of principals except for the introduction of Vivien Leigh as the insane woman, Blanche. Leigh had played the part with great sensitivity in Laurence Olivier's stage production in London. Blanche arrives in New Orleans to stay with her married sister, whom she is shocked to find living with an uncouth husband with whom, nevertheless, her sister is deeply in love. The open hostility that rapidly develops between Blanche and her brother-in-law Stanley is what finally sends her into madness, triggered by his discovery that she has been living a life of prostitution and that her nervous, excessively ladylike manners and constant resort to bathing are a cover for her catastrophic loss of family position and of her youthful husband in the past. (He had proved to be a homosexual and had committed suicide after she had discovered this and repulsed him).

Knowing that Blanche is aiming to break up his marriage to her sister, Stanley rapes her when they are alone in the apartment and, when she becomes insane, forces the issue of having her sent to a lunatic asylum. Vivien Leigh's understanding of Blanche, with her nervous, highly mannered loquacity, her incessant washing of herself and changing clothes, her fear of any bright light that might reveal her aging face, and her brave attempts to explain herself once the truth—or enough of it—is known, offers one of the most sympathetic portrayals of developing mental breakdown in any play or film.

THE STUDENT OF PRAGUE
(Germany, 1913, 1925). Direction: Stellan Rye (1913), Henrik Galeen (1925). With Paul Wegener (Baldwin, 1913), Conrad Veidt (Baldwin, 1925). 2.

Baldwin, a student, gives a sorcerer his image in a mirror in exchange for the gift of wealth and marriage to a beautiful aristocratic woman. The image in the mirror becomes Baldwin's alter ego, which he is eventually driven to destroy. As he shoots down the mirror image, however, he destroys himself. In the second, classic, version[119]—far more sophisticated in technique and more macabre—the mirror image gains in power and stature while the real-life Baldwin diminishes, poisoned by the evil influence that dominates him. The story belongs to the deep-rooted tradition of the *doppelgänger* ("double," or alter ego) as well as to the theme of "possession". The subject was inspired by Poe's story. *William Wilson,* Wilde's *Picture of Dorian Grey,* and the Faust legend, and is paralleled in Stevenson's *Dr. Jekyll and Mr. Hyde.* A further strong influence was that of E. T. A. Hoffman.

SUDDENLY LAST SUMMER
(Britain, 1959). Direction: Joseph Mankiewcz. With Elizabeth Taylor (Catherine Holly), Katharine Hepburn (Mrs. Venables), Montgomery Clift (Dr. Cukrowicz). 3, 9.

Catherine has been insane ever since witnessing the death of her cousin, Sebastian, a poet, while on holiday in Europe. Sebastian's wealthy mother tries to persuade Dr. Cukrowicz, a neurosurgeon, to perform a lobotomy on Catherine, bribing him with promises of a handsome donation to his private hospital. Suspicious of this, the doctor gives Catherine a truth drug, and the hideous facts about what happened emerge: Sebastian was a homosexual whose mother supplied him with the young men he craved; when on holiday, he was killed and his flesh devoured by a band of starving beggars in the ruins of a Spanish pagan temple. As a result of this revelation Catherine is cured but Mrs. Venables becomes insane.

Based on a one-act play by Tennessee Williams and scripted by Gore Vidal, the result is a rather drawn-out, schematized psychological melodrama, drawing on madness to create horror entertainment.

SUMMER WISHES, WINTER DREAMS
(USA, 1973). Direction: Gilbert Cates. With Joanne Woodward (Rita Walden), Martin Balsam (Walden), Sylvia Sydney (Rita's Mother). 5, 1a.

Rita Walden is a middle-aged woman with a well-established marriage to a successful ophthalmologist who is devoted to her. She seems to have all she needs but succumbs to nightmares and hypochondria, though her principal concern seems to be that her son in Amsterdam may be a homosexual and never writes to her. She is somewhat irritated, too, by her young married daughter and her chatterbox mother. When her mother dies suddenly of a heart attack, a family crisis is precipitated over the disposal of her property. Hoping to distract her, her husband takes her with him on a trip to Europe, where he has to attend a conference.

In London Rita has a sudden, unheralded nervous breakdown when she is alone in an Underground station. (This happens in much the same way as it does to the middle-aged wife, played by Anne Bancroft, in Jack Clayton's *Pumpkin Eater* [Britain, 1964] when she collapses in Harrod's store.) Her recovery is effected only when her husband takes her from England to France and she sees how disturbed he becomes when he relives on the site of the Battle of the Bastogne the tensions of the fighting, in which he took part in 1944. Her renewed feeling for her husband and acceptance of her son's homosexuality restores her psychological balance. In spite of sincere and highly professional performances by the stars, so assured in their grasp of every detail of behavior, this film does not escape sentimentality, and the inclusion of clips from Bergman's *Wild Strawberries* does not really illuminate the subject.

SUNDAYS AND CYBELE
(France, 1962). Direction: Serge Bourguignon. With Hardy Kruger (the amnesiac veteran), Nicole Courcel (Gozzi). 2, 8.

This delicately told, superbly acted film concerns the relationship that develops between a young man—who has become troubled and withdrawn following shell shock during war service—and Gozzi—a lonely orphan girl in a boarding school. Pretending to be her long-lost father, the veteran begins to take Gozzi out on Sundays. Gradually, we come to realize the psychotic tendencies of this man, whose relations with the girl, in whom he inspires great love and confidence, take on a certain sexual quality, to which she too responds, leading to a tragic end.

SUNSET BOULEVARD
(USA, 1950). Direction and coscripting: Billy Wilder. With Gloria Swanson (Norma Desmond). 3.

Gloria Swanson plays with fierce intensity Norma, a once-great star of the silent cinema, who now is embalmed in her luxurious mansion and never ceases to relive the past to the point of delusory insanity. It involved considerable courage for Gloria Swanson so readily to parody her own past career and present position in Hollywood twenty-odd years after the coming of sound; it was a brilliant stroke of casting to couple her with Erich von Stroheim, who plays Max, her dedicated former husband-director and now her major housemate and protector in the vast and entirely empty, servantless house. Appearing almost as insane as Norma, Max insistently maintains her illusions, which include the certainty that she will be recalled to the studio to resume her career exactly where it was left off with the coming of sound. Her mental collapse is total when, after being abandoned by the young and unsuccessful scriptwriter she believes to be infatuated, and in love, with her, she attempts suicide. She recovers and, when she realizes she has lost him, shoots him in the back. When her house is invaded by police and newsreel cameramen, she descends the great staircase convinced that Max is directing her once again—lights, camera, action.

SUPERFLY
(USA, 1972). Direction: Gordon Parks, Jr. With Ron O'Neal (Youngblood Priest), Carl Lee (Eddie), Julius W. Harris (Scatter). 6.

Superfly enjoyed phenomenal success in the States partly because of the strident opposition it evoked (in much the same spirit as the opposition raised against *The Warriors,* audiences being bombarded by propaganda to stay away). Superfly (ghetto term for *cocaine*) is being sold very profitably by the black pusher Youngblood Priest and his partner, Eddie, as well as by their supplier, the restaurateur Scatter. The police are also heavily involved in the traffic, and Priest manages to emerge a rich man after violent confrontation with the deputy commissioner, whom he has framed. Priest drives off at the end of the film in a Rolls Royce. For all its reputation or notoriety, the film is routinely made, in comparison with Melvin Van Peeble's film *Sweet Sweetback's Baadasss Song,* which was totally banned by the British censor.

TAXI DRIVER

(USA, 1976). Direction: Martin Scorsese. Script: Paul Schrader. Photography: Michael Chapman. Music: Bernard Herrmann. With Robert De Niro (Travis Bickle), Cybill Shepherd (Betsy), Jodie Foster (Iris), Hervey Keitel (Sport), Martin Scorsese (Passenger watching silhouette). 5, 3.

Travis Bickle, a former marine in Vietnam, has returned to New York in a deeply disturbed state of mind. He is oppressed by the paranoiac nightmare of the mean streets in which he moves and feels an overwhelming sense of defilement from the degenerate society around him. Unable to sleep, he becomes a nightshift cabdriver and escapes into the hallucinatory world of porn film. He also keeps a diary, in which he spells out his hatreds. He tries to date a solitary, cool, rather upper-class girl, Betsy, a campaign worker for a presidential candidate, but loses her when he makes a poor judgment and takes her to a skin flick. His frustrations take the form of setting up an illegal gun collection and undergoing a severe period of training in physical fitness.

His first open action to purge the corruption around him is to shoot in anger a black man he sees stage a holdup in a supermarket. Next, in a campaign to clean up America's urban womanhood, he turns to the rescue of a twelve-year-old girl prostitute, Iris, whom he tries to persuade (in bought time) to amend her life. His final act of social purification is to go on the rampage against Sport—the pimp who controls Iris and her clients—and his underworld associates, mowing them down with ritual fury before attempting to kill himself with a gun that is no longer loaded. Having survived this calamity, he finds himself treated as a national hero by the press, and the film ends in a kind of neutrality over the issues it raises, as if its makers preferred to leave the significance of their film to be resolved by the individual viewer.

Taxi Driver pulsates with rejection of American urban corruption. Travis Bickle, given a compulsive performance by Robert De Niro, shares with Clint Eastwood's enraged cop, Callahan *(Dirty Harry),* a towering inferno of loathing against the shit-society of underworld New York.[120] The expressionist stylization with its extraordinary opening shot of a yellow taxi emerging in slow motion from clouds of white steam, to the foreboding roar of Bernard Herrmann's orchestration,[121] warns us that we are at the gates to hell. De Niro builds up Bickle's misogyny as the driving obsession of a Savonarolla out to reform a corrupt and degraded world and in the process, expressing the reactionary, racist, and other sentiments that make up his closed-in mind. His attempted association with the two contrasting girls to whom he tries to relate—the prim election worker and the flaccid and contented child prostitute—falls apart. He has no capacity in fact to relate to anyone, man or woman, and the ironic happy end thrust upon him at the close of the film in no way leaves him better off as he is absorbed back into the neon-lit hell of New York, New York, the wonderful town. It is American society—not Bickle—that takes the blame for what happened.

Scorsese said that Bickle is "a would-be saint, a Saint Paul [who is] going to help people so much he's going to kill them."[122] The script, says Scorsese, was "succinct, direct, and compact. I only improvised three or four scenes."[123] The diary was brought into the film by Schrader through the influence of the French director Robert Bresson, whose *Diary of a Country Priest* (1950) Schrader so much admired—Bickle's fear that he has cancer apparently derives from similar fears in Bresson's despairing young priest. For Scorsese, however, son of Sicilian immigrant parents living in New York and another film student soaked in movies from childhood, the influences came more from the realistic work of Samuel Fuller, as the authors of *The Movie Brats* point out. *Taxi Driver* is compact with movie-oriented violence, and it is Scorsese himself who plays Bickle's passenger who threatens to blow his wife's vagina apart with a .44 Magnum because he is enraged by the fact that she is having sex with a black man.

THE TENANT
(*Le Locataire,* France, 1976). Direction and coscripting: Roman Polanski. With Roman Polanski (Trelkovsky), Isabelle Adjani (Stella), Shelley Winters (concierge), Melvyn Douglas (Mr. Zy), Jo Van Fleet (Mme Diaz). 3.

Something of a companion piece to Polanski's earlier film, *Repulsion*—with in this case the deranged person a male—*The Tenant* is in fact primarily based on the "possession" of one person (a naturalized Pole living in Paris) by another, a dead woman.

An unassuming clerk, Trelkovsky, has managed to take over an apartment following the death of the previous occupant, Simone Choule, who threw herself from the apartment window. Before she dies, he visits her in the hospital and together with her friend and fellow occupant in the apartment block, Stella, hears the wholly bandaged patient emit a sudden scream when asked if she can recognize her friend. Once he has occupied the apartment, Trelkovsky becomes affected by a feeling of persecution, a conspiracy to get him evicted. He is even convinced that Stella, to whom he is attracted, is part of this plot to be rid of him. Becoming increasingly confined in the apartment (as was Carol, the deranged girl in *Repulsion*), he keeps discovering unnerving items that belonged to Simone. He continues to receive her mail, and when he does emerge to visit the local cafe, he finds himself treated as if he were she. He begins secretly to wear articles of her clothing left in the apartment, and the climax of his terror comes when he loses a tooth, as Simone did, and finds it concealed in the very place where he found her discarded tooth. After twice throwing himself from the same apartment window from which Simone had fallen, he lies bandaged, just as she was bandaged, in the same hospital, and he utters the same cry when Stella tries to induce him to recognize her.

Like *Repulsion* the film is brilliantly realized by Polanski, though the specifically

French atmosphere is to some extent compromised by the appearance of such well-known American stars as Shelley Winters, Melvyn Douglas, and Jo Van Fleet in the otherwise international cast—Polanski playing the leading part himself. The film was released in both English- and French-language versions.

THE TEXAS CHAIN SAW MASSACRE
(USA, 1974). Direction: Tobe Hooper. With Marilyn Burns (Sally). 3, 4.

This somewhat mistitled, low-budget piece of Grand Guignol—it supposedly cost under two hundred thousand dollars but grossed millions—need only be included here because of its considerable reputation, which led to its inclusion even in the 1974 London Film Festival. It exposes far more the maladjustment of those who will pay to see such sickening violence than it does the melodramatic insanity of the characters—three lunatic brothers who massacre all who approach them (on occasion, using a motorized chain saw) and subsequently either mummify their victims or cook them and put their bones on display. The film achieved its success in America through stunt publicity, which included the claim that human bones from India were used as props. The director is quoted as claiming, "It's a film about meat, about people who are gone beyond dealing with animal meat . . . crazy retarded people going beyond the line between animal and human."[124] The film is based on an actual case in Texas during the 1950s—a man who, in addition to grave-robbing, murdered young girls, cannibalized their remains, and displayed their bones as ornaments. Among the bodies found was that of his mother, mummified, the basis for the story which became Hitchcock's *Psycho*.

THREE FACES OF EVE
(USA, 1957). Direction and script: Nunnally Johnson. Based on the case study by Corbett H. Thigpen, M.D., and Hervey M. Cleckley, M.D. Introduction: Alistair Cooke. With Joanne Woodward (Eve White), David Wayne (Ralph White), Lee J. Cobb (Dr. Luther). 2, 9.

This film is derived from the clinical study of Eve White, which eventually became a best seller. Its authors, Drs. Corbett Thigpen and Hervey Cleckley, were involved between 1951 and 1955 in the treatment of a woman with multiple personality. As the principal therapist, Dr. Thigpen (Dr. Luther in the film) was instrumental in achieving the apparent cessation of her symptoms. The case was publicized with the consent of the woman, called Eve in both the book and the film. More recently, in 1977, the patient herself retold the story from her personal standpoint in the book *I Am Eve*, by Chris Costner Sizemore and Elen Sain Pittillo.

The film presents us with three distinct personalities in a single woman. The first is Eve White, who is married and the mother of a five-year old child. The second personality to emerge is Eve Black, the polar opposite of Eve White. The third and final personality to emerge is Jane. Through the help of Dr. Luther

(Dr. Thigpen), she is the personality that comes to dominate and, having resolved her conflicts, remarries. This is similar to Chris Sizemore's actual experiences, as Alistair Cooke's introduction to the film emphasizes. (For her performance as Eve, Joanne Woodward received an Academy Award.)

The film opens with the initial visit of Chris White and her husband, Ralph, to the therapist, Dr. Luther, on the advice of their family physician. Chris is suffering from severe headaches and amnesia, produced by blackouts. The situation appears to cease for a while, until Ralph is astonished one day to find that his wife, who is of an exceptionally quiet, domesticated disposition and homely appearance, has suddenly lavished $218 on fancy clothes and shoes, for which she is unable to account. Moments after he begins to question her, she attempts suddenly to strangle her child and is stopped by her husband just in time. Ralph, a rough and somewhat unimaginative man, is furious as well as alarmed, and they return in great anxiety to Dr. Luther. Eve claims that she is hearing "voices," and then under the doctor's very eyes the personality of Eve Black emerges—brash, youthful, and sex-obsessed—claiming that she never married "that jerk" (Ralph), never had a daughter, is in the process of what she calls "coming out," and hopes to "come out and stay out." She despises Eve White. The astonished therapist (cases of multiple personality were extremely rare and totally outside his experience) feels his way and almost stumbles on the trick of summoning the alternate personality by calling upon her by name.

Eve is admitted as a patient to the hospital for intensive observation and treatment. She appears to be doing quite well when suddenly Eve Black emerges and makes a violent advance to a shocked male attendant. Dr. Luther is called in, and Eve Black comes into ascendency again when he asks Eve White if she is aware of her alter ego, as Eve Black has always been aware of Eve White. Dr. Luther adopts a severer attitude to Eve Black, telling her that if she drives Eve White insane, she too will necessarily find herself confined in a mental institution. Since all Eve Black wants is to get her freedom in order to go out to bars and dance halls and pick up men, the point is well-taken. Luther decides he must tell Eve White about her other personality and also try to explain the situation to her husband, Ralph. At some point in her childhood, he says, her personality divided. Eve is not insane, he says; she has a dual personality. Ralph tries to understand, even be sympathetic, but in the end he fails. The couple are advised to separate for a while. Ralph gets another job in Jacksonville; Eve begins to live alone, and their child goes to live with her grandparents.

Eve Black is released from care, goes out on the town, but reverts to Eve White when a soldier she picks up threatens her with sexual assault. After this unhappy episode, Ralph comes back to take his wife to Jacksonville to prevent further trouble of this kind. His anger is all the worse because he is convinced that the whole dual-identity situation is a hoax. Eve White is unwilling to go to Jacksonville, believing rightly that she is far more disturbed than he thinks her to be. Suddenly Eve White turns into Eve Black before Ralph's astonished gaze and immediately sets about seducing him, demanding that he buy her a fine new dress. Half-fascinated by her sexuality—though she does not permit intimacy—he gives way, and they set off for Jacksonville. After she again goes to town behind his back, Ralph, after hitting her in a fury, leaves for good. Eve Black quits Jacksonville, and divorce follows. It is Eve Black who returns next to Dr. Luther for help. She is deeply upset because the previous night Eve White attempted suicide—she displays her bandaged wrists. Eve Black claims she just took over in time to prevent the attempt from being fatal.

As Eve White again, the woman is put under hypnosis by Luther, who is amazed when she awakes in an entirely new guise—a third Eve. Unaware of her own identity but reasonable and intelligent in her assessment of both the other Eves, she calls herself Jane for want of any other name. In effect she takes over from this moment. Seemingly a balanced, good-looking, and intelligent woman, Jane eventually admits to her would-be fiancé, Earle, that she is the now-celebrated case of multiple personality. She rejects marriage because she feels she is not entirely cured. Indeed, it is Eve White who calls on Dr. Luther the next time, feeling very ill. She is aware of Jane, is prepared to die (that is, disappear for good) in her favor, and hopes that Eve Black too, will disappear. Bonnie, Eve White's young daughter, also prefers her mother to be like Jane.

The multiple personalities are subject to further analysis, and out of this emerges the childhood trauma that is purported to be the starting point for Eve's original split personality. Through a flashback we see her playing as a small child with friends in the tunnel-like cavity beneath her parent's house, which is raised above the ground on blocks. Her mother summons her from this place of concealment and insists that she come and kiss the face of her recently-deceased grandmother—a folk tradition based on the belief that one would miss the dead far less if one gives them a final embrace. Screaming to the point of hysteria, the child draws back in horror. Following this final cathartic revelation, Eve Black emerges to say farewell to Dr. Luther and symbolically present him with her special red dress as a parting gift. With only Jane left, the healthy and fully functioning part of the woman's personality is dominant, and she is ready to marry Earle and reassume the care of her daughter.

Once Chris Costner Sizemore had undergone cure, Drs. Thigpen and Cleckley invited her to demonstrate her three personalities on film under clinical conditions, dressing for the part in each case and answering the questions they put to her. This film has had restricted distribution for classroom use under the title, *A Case of Multiple Personality.*

THROUGH A GLASS DARKLY
(Sweden, 1961). Direction and script: Ingmar Bergman. With Harriet Anderson (Karin), Max von Sydow (husband Martin), Gunnar Björnstrand (father), Lars Passgard (brother Minus). 1a.

The film concerns the interaction between a father, a husband, and a young brother—members of a family living for a while in isolation on an island in the Baltic—and the single woman among them, Karin, a schizophrenic who is temporarily back with them after hospital treatment. Karin's hallucinatory belief in

God is shattered when, instead of seeing God, resplendent in glory, emerging through the wall of the attic room she frequents, all that creeps out is a spider. Her father, however, still manages to maintain the belief that God is love.[125]

TWELVE O'CLOCK HIGH

(USA, 1949). Direction: Henry King. With Gregory Peck (General Savage), Dean Jagger (Major Stovall), Gary Merrill (Colonel Davenport), Hugh Marlowe (Lieutenant Colonel Gately), Paul Stewart ("Doc" Kaiser), Millard Mitchell (General Pritchard). 5.

Made a few years after the Second World War, *Twelve O'Clock High* deals not with insanity as such but with various forms of escape, up to the point of nervous breakdown, that afflict servicemen who are pushed beyond the limits of their endurance in the pursuit of missions assigned them in mechanized warfare. War could be regarded as a form of socially approved and highly organized insanity. It enlists or drafts men into undertakings that under normal conditions would be regarded as intolerable, even criminal. They must murder at sight as many of the enemy as come within their reach; they must bomb indiscriminately from the air the encampments and community areas where the enemy holds out— servicemen, workers, and simple civilians alike, regardless of age or sex; in hand-to-hand combat, they must kill with gladiatorial skill, or be killed. The artificial enragement which bayonet practice involves is in itself an encouragement to adopt savage behavior. The absolute needs of guerilla warfare, resistance action, and sabotage induce men to take skilful delight in the destruction of their fellow creatures, who are themselves equally motivated to destroy human life.

The primitive, traditional view of manhood—that all men worthy of the name are warriors at heart and, only secondarily, peacemakers—still dies hard. In time of war all men are supposed to welcome the opportunity for military enlistment—accepting it as a kind of challenge—and to believe that to die for one's country is the most honorable of deaths, especially in the case of the young, who have the most (in terms of lifespan) to lose. War is normally brought about by the old but conducted by the young. Again, the young, the nation's hope for the future, are the first to be sacrificed.

A division has come to be traditionally accepted between, on the one hand career servicemen and mercenaries (that is, professionals in defense and warfare), and on the other the much larger, civilian wing of the population, who are pressed into active service only in times of emergency. In the past the civil population became directly involved in warfare only through conquest, when they were enslaved or otherwise exploited by their conquerors. With the introduction of mass bombardment from the air and attack by means of powerful, long-range guns and rockets as well as invasion and occupation, war from its inception has potentially involved everyone, servicemen and civilians alike— men, women, and children, from the oldest to the youngest. The stresses and strains of war, battle neuroses, are therefore likely to afflict anyone, and because of the extreme danger of many of the missions demanded of the ordinary serviceman, 20 percent of battle casualties during World War II were—as Huston proclaimed in his long-suppressed documentary, *Let There Be Light*—of a neuropsychiatric nature.[126] Even among men trained in warfare, large numbers suffered severe breakdown.

Twelve O'Clock High concerns breakdown in its severest form among a group of the most highly trained of servicemen—the crews manning a unit in the Eighth Army Air Force, the first U.S. bomber force in 1942 to fly from England to bomb targets in Nazi-occupied Europe and in Germany itself. These raids are all conducted in the daytime. They have to face the stiffest opposition, both from the Luftwaffe's fighters in the air and from anti-aircraft guns on the ground. The film opens with a flight returning from a mission. One craft has to belly-land. The captain emerges, turns aside, and vomits. A severely injured man is taken out raving. It is soon clear that the morale of this particular unit, on which the film centers, is very low. Colonel Davenport, the commander, is too popular with his men and more concerned about their welfare as individuals than with the results they achieve. Discipline is lax; drinking high; officers who should know better (such as Lieutenant Colonel Gately) are avoiding missions on which they should rightly serve.

General Savage, an officer renowned for his impeccable qualities as a leader, is sent in to replace Davenport, who is accused of overidentification with his men. Savage immediately applies shock tactics to shake the unit back to some pride in the war effort, weary and disaffected though they are. In consequence, they come to hate his guts and use every device at their disposal to be assigned elsewhere. Savage sets out to frustrate this and finally succeeds in welding them into a proud, efficient, and, above all, disciplined team. This is done, however, at the cost to himself of a temporary nervous breakdown—even he can become overstressed.

The film realistically portrays the various stages of withdrawal that affect even the most highly trained and disciplined of servicemen, from whom the most is expected in conditions of modern warfare. The first stage of withdrawal is that generated under Davenport. This involves a feeling of disaffection for the war effort. The unit is sorry for itself, considers itself put upon ("We're some kind of guinea pigs"), and becomes less and less efficient in carrying out missions. Concern for individuals is greater than for the unit as a whole. Off-duty drunkenness increases in the officers' club, and even the adjutant general, Major Stovall (who is a First World War veteran), hits the bottle. Those who can avoid duty in the air seem to do so, unobtrusively.

It is this that Savage is called upon to remedy, only to be faced by the almost total opposition of the unit and by the ironic complicity of the unit's doctor, Major Kaiser, who has yet to learn not to let himself be exploited in order that men may avoid a turn of duty. The drift of the film seems to be that in order to restore the morale of the group, Savage is forced to push himself beyond his own, seemingly limitless strength. "Fear is normal," he says to them implacably, "so you'd better forget it. Consider yourselves already dead." He creates a "leper colony," an aircraft to which all the deadbeats are assigned—and it is their job to make their way up and out of it, on their own deserts. Savage insists on "group integrity" at all costs—even abandoning a crippled aircraft if the success of the mission and the safety of the flight as a whole demands it. For him, the group is everything, and its effective performance paramount. That is, until he too cracks.

Before the final, daylight mission, a lengthy raid deep into Germany, for which he has, as usual, assumed command Savage is seized by a sudden tremor so that he cannot lift himself into the aircraft prior to takeoff, and he has to be helped back to his headquarters. The mission departs without him. Throughout the period of its departure from the base, he sits paralyzed in a virtually catatonic state of total withdrawal. Only when the flight returns, reporting total success, does he slowly come to, and then immediately lies down to sleep. It is left open in what condition he will be once he awakens.

VERTIGO
(USA, 1958). Direction: Alfred Hitchcock. With James Stewart (Scottie Ferguson), Kim Novak (Madeleine/Judy). 3.

Scottie Ferguson resigns from the police force because of his sudden affliction with vertigo, which has caused the death of a colleague. He, nevertheless, takes on a private assignment to trace Madeleine, the half-insane wife of a former college friend, Elster, who believes she is the reincarnation of a Spanish ancestor and has attempted suicide. Leaving his own girl friend, Midge, who is trying to cure him of his vertigo, Ferguson, entranced by her air of mystery, falls in love with Madeleine, as she does with him. After their first kiss, however, she runs from him, climbs a bell tower, and falls to her death. (Her death, incidentally, shocks the viewer in a manner similar to that of *Psycho*'s Janet Leigh, which also comes comparatively early in the film.)

After suffering a breakdown, Ferguson, intuitively believing that Madeleine is still alive, meets another girl, Judy, who closely resembles Madeleine (except that she is somehow harder, more vulgar). He at once begins to experience the same love for her. Hitchcock then, daringly, reveals the truth of the matter: Elster in fact pushed the real Madeleine to her death in order to inherit her fortune, and used Judy, his mistress, as an accomplice to impersonate her and deceive Ferguson into believing in Madeleine's suicide. Elster intends Ferguson to act as witness to the seeming suicide. So it is the accomplice, Judy, with whom Ferguson originally fell in love (believing her to be Madeleine, whom he has never actually met). Ferguson, haunted by the likeness between the Madeleine he has known and Judy, induces the girl to wear Madeleine's clothes, and identification is completed when she puts on Madeleine's necklace. Ferguson's vertigo is cured at the moment when, after making her confession to him, Judy, startled by the sudden appearance of a nun, steps backward to her death.

Robin Wood holds this film to be one of Hitchcock's masterpieces, a film both "profound and beautiful."[127] Its incredibility of plot, he states, matters little; it is its theme that matters, as in Shakespeare's plays. But Hitchcock's direct interest in the psychology of his characters is always less than in the development of their overt behavior, and it is left to his interpreters to fathom the nature of Ferguson's malaise.

LA VIE à L'ENVERS
("Life upside Down." France, 1964). Direction and script, Alain Jessua. With Charles Denner (Jacques). 8.

Made by one of France's most interesting and original directors, *La Vie à L'Envers* is about a seemingly very pleasant, conventional young man who realizes suddenly he is happiest when he is alone. He decides to detach himself from his girlfriend, Viviane, from the dull work he has to do at the office, and from association with other people. After his wedding, he walks out from the reception, loses his job, and takes only mild interest when Viviane attempts to gas herself. He sits by himself in his empty apartment until he is persuaded to go to a hospital, where he penetrates further into his private world. The film is made in the spirit of gentle irony, as funny as it is sad. The technique, direct and simple, conveys, through Charles Denner's excellent performance, the perfect calm and happiness Jacques experiences.

VIOLETTE NOZIERE
(France, 1977). Direction: Claude Chabrol. With Isabelle Huppert (Violette Nozière), Jean Garmet (Baptiste Nozière), Stéphane Audran (Germaine Nozière). 1a, 3, 4.

During 1933–34 Violette Nozière of Paris, aged eighteen, began to administer poison to her parents, eventually killing her father. She was arrested, tried, and condemned to death, but later reprieved. During the process her story emerged. Conforming on the surface to her parents' repressive inhibitions, she slipped out of their sordid little apartment at night to live it up. With money stolen from her parents she rented a low-class hotel room in order to entertain students and the like in a pathetic attempt to enjoy what she hoped was a grand passion and achieve some form of luxurious living. She was what Chabrol described as a "pathetic femme fatale by day, reluctant child at night, unhappy child-woman night and day."[128]

Violette's father, a railway engineer, raped her when she was thirteen (or so she alleged) and subjected her to further sexual offenses—the syphilis she contracted came (she insisted) from her parents. The one youth she unreservedly loved, Jean Dabin, was unscrupulous; he sponged on her for money that she stole from her mother's hidden savings. She also blackmailed a certain wealthy "M. Emile," a man never identified but probably her mother's former lover (or so she stated) and whom she believed to be her natural father, who then continually sent her letters and hush money. While Dabin deserted her, she began administering poison to her parents in the guise of medicine, and her father, to whom she gave major doses, died. When she was arrested, she readily confessed her hatred of her father and desire to kill him; although her mother had never given her any sympathy or understanding, the girl did not desire her death.

After her mother brought a civil action against her, Violette stood trial and was condemned to death. The case became a cause célèbre. She was championed by such distinguished people as the poets Aragon and Eluard (who, in a poem dedicated to her, referred to "the terrible serpents' nest of blood relations" that she was driven to destroy), Magritte, and Simone de Beauvoir. Chabrol said, "In trying to bring her to life again, I felt the fascination of her ambiguities: murderer and saint, liar and true heart, childish yet inspired. I had to explore her mind, lay bare her dreams, suffer her daily existence. . . . It is no longer a question of judging, but of understanding."[129]

Chabrol's reconstruction of this extraordinary case emphasizes not only the obsessive sexual fantasies of the girl, so revealingly interpreted by Isabelle Huppert, but the ambivalent nature of her relationship with her mother, which appears to involve strong sexual competition, since Violette believes that her mother was the mistress of the unidentified "M. Emile" and that this rich man was her true father. In style the film combines a suspense-laden, Hitchcock-like treatment (revealing Chabrol's acknowledged devotion to the master) and a documentary-like interpretation, such as Hitchcock himself ventured to try in *The Wrong Man* (1957).

WAR HUNT
(USA, 1961). Direction: Denis Sanders. With John Saxon (Endore), Robert Redford (Loomis). 5.

In 1953, during the Korean campaign, Loomis joins a front-line unit. Here he meets Endore, a man who customarily volunteers to go out at night to kill with ritual fervor whomever of the enemy he can find. Loomis fears for the safety of an eight-year-old orphaned Korean boy, whom Endore keeps closely to himself. When the ceasefire comes, Endore slips away with the child, and it is feared that he will continue with his killing and so start up hostilities again in this sector. When he is discovered by a search party, he turns on them violently with a knife and is shot. The boy takes to his heels and disappears.

Shot on a low budget in only fifteen days, and with Robert Redford's initial appearance in a feature film, this film uncompromisingly shows the insane impulse to kill that is released by war. John Saxon's performance, however, is that of a traditional screen villain rather than an attempt to portray the realities of insanity.

WHATEVER HAPPENED TO BABY JANE?
(USA, 1962). Direction: Robert Aldrich. With Bette Davis (Jane Hudson), Joan Crawford (Blanche Hudson), Victor Buono (Edwin Flagg). 1a, 3.

Blanche, a former film star, suffers injuries when she was supposedly being driven in a car by her alcoholic sister, Jane. Blanche experienced acute jealousy when Jane was a successful child star and later became successful herself as an adult star. Now neither has a career, and they live alone in a great Hollywood mansion—Blanche now confined to her wheelchair. Jane, eccentric and alcoholic to the point of insanity, tries as a middle-aged woman to revive her child performance. Her attempts are aided by the presence of a third member in this insane household, the obese Edwin Flagg, a pathetic eccentric who has been hired by Jane to accompany her child act on the piano.

Meanwhile, Jane starts to torment and starve Blanche, eventually tying her down in bed and leaving her without food. She then murders the home help, who, though previously dismissed, has returned to find Blanche half-dead. Knowing that the police are on their way to the house, Jane moves Blanche away to the beach. It is then revealed that it was Blanche who was driving the car when the accident occurred, and that in a jealous fit she was trying to kill Jane, who was staggering drunkenly along the road ahead of the car. The police finally find Blanche dead and Jane insanely recreating her Baby Jane role.

A Grand Guignol film, *Whatever Happened to Baby Jane?* enjoyed outstanding success in its traditional exploitation of insanity as an element in horrific melodrama. The result is a tour de force performance by Bette Davis, who in a hideous makeup, lurches into mad act after mad act, grotesque in her babylike impersonation.

WHITE HEAT

(USA, 1949). Direction: Raoul Walsh. With James Cagney (Cody Jarrett), Virginia Mayo (Verna Jarrett), Margaret Wycherly (Ma Jarrett). 4.

Cody is a highly professional, sociopathic gangster who has an obsessive love for his mother. A film of considerable violence for its period, with frequent indulgence in killings, it is not deeply concerned with investigating Cody's psychological condition. It shows only his hysteria and violent behavior, associated with recurrent pains in the head. *White Heat,* nevertheless, is one of the earlier films to present the gangster figure (very well played by Cagney) as a person of psychologically abnormal tendencies.

WHO'LL STOP THE RAIN?

(USA, 1978). Direction: Karel Reisz. Script: Judith Rascoe, Robert Stone. Based on the novel by Robert Stone. Camera: Richard H. Kline. With Nick Nolte (Ray Hicks), Tuesday Weld (Marge Converse), Michael Moriarty (John Converse), Anthony Zerbe (Antheil). 5, 6.

Who'll Stop the Rain? (the title is one of the theme songs of the film), or *Dog Soldiers,* is yet another film to act to expunge the insidious and pervasive poison of Vietnam from the bowels of America, though it is handled somewhat obscurely by the English director, Karel Reisz, who exposes in a virtually surrealist narrative the horrors of war-created mental disturbance. John Converse, a war correspondent in Vietnam, arranges with his serviceman buddy, Ray Hicks, to smuggle a sizable package of heroin by ship to his wife, Marge, back home in California, through whom Ray is supposedly to collect his reward. A resourceful man, Ray succeeds in the act of smuggling when he is discharged from the Navy but finds that Marge is totally ignorant about the deal and in any case impaired as a barbiturate addict. Converse, and with him Ray, appears to have been framed by drug-trafficking thugs. Ray, as quick-witted as he is agile, turns the tables on the thugs when they attack him and Marge in the Converses' modest residence, escaping with her to his own hillside shack near Los Angeles. Converse, when he returns to the empty house soon afterward, is seized and tortured by the thugs, who are working for a bent narcotics agent called Antheil. Ray now turns into an obsessive avenger, trying to dispose of the drugs on his own account through a contact he knows, but who fails him. Now victim of harder drugs, he escapes with Converse's wife to a deserted mountainous hideout in New Mexico, formerly a hippie commune. Here they are tracked down by Antheil and his odd array of henchmen, and by Converse. The climax comes as a shoot-out and bomb blast-out, organized by Ray, in which Antheil and his gang perish, while Ray, whose presence has remained undetected, is mortally wounded. Converse and Marge escape, but only after spilling the heroin to waste on the ground when they discover Ray's dead body.

The film suggests a parable along lines more subtle than "He who is led to touch pitch shall find himself, and those he chooses to involve, defiled," and that madness generated among the expatriated communities of soldiers sent overseas becomes contagious in the society that sent them away. Converse, it should be noted, is not a soldier but a commentator, who presumably has some overview of the significance of what is going on; he is a semi-intellectual, disillusioned by the war and the demoralization it has brought about. Ray Hicks, on the other hand, is the ordinary, unthinking guy, dispossessed and underprivileged in times of peace—but the effective man of action during war service—who decides to take vengeance on a society that has advantaged him nothing in the past and has little but naked go-go dancers to offer him on his return from the war. Converse (an unsatisfactorily conceived, and a very secondary, character) seems bent on self-destruction, while Ray, Reisz's evident protagonist, becomes a kind of Sidney Carton, prepared to sacrifice his life in order to reunite Converse and his doped-out wife, though presumably the spilling of the heroin in the dust (a scene reminiscent of the final spilling of the equally corrupting gold dust in *The Treasure of Sierra Madre*) represents some vaguely determined change of heart for the better in both Converse and Marge, who end the film as sole representatives of post-Vietnam American society.

WHO'S AFRAID OF VIRGINIA WOOLF?

(USA, 1966). Direction: Mike Nichols. Script: Ernest Lehman. Adapted from the play by Edward Albee. With Elizabeth Taylor (Martha), Richard Burton (George), George Segal (Nick), Sandy Dennis (Honey). 2a, 3.

Edward Albee's celebrated play is the study of a very special married relationship between two middle-aged people, George and Martha (the names chosen to make the link with George and Martha Washington). He is an undistinguished history professor in an undistinguished college in small-town New England; she, the frustrated and disappointed daughter of the college president. With their common dedication to escaping through alcohol, this childless couple have gradually evolved their own form of sexual combat. While seeming on the surface to split them asunder with their scurrilous, even obscene, abuse of each other, their "games" actually keep them, deep down, closely bound in mutual suffering.

The action of the play, beautifully structured, takes place during the small hours of the morning after a presidential party to welcome new faculty. George and Martha invite a relatively youthful new professor, Nick, and his somewhat brainless wife, Honey, to visit their home to continue the night's drinking. In the period before dawn, they strip both themselves and their guests of all marital illusions in a Walpurgisnacht of needling inquisition, accusation, and wounding self-revelation. Martha even manages to seduce Nick (unsuccessfully, we gather) after a brief excursion to an all-night cafe, and George's revenge is to announce solemnly the death of their only "son," the fondest and deepest illusion of their imaginary world. When the young couple are sent away to recover, however, the first sign of dawn in the sky outside brings George and Martha together once more in the bonds of their unholy matrimony. The dialogue becomes increasingly disconnected and surreal as the effects of the alcohol increase. The play is one of the most revealing of all attempts in the modern theater to express mental sickness and hallucination in a married couple. It is savagely (but also movingly) acted by Elizabeth Taylor and Richard Burton, and Mike Nichols's direction is brilliant.

WISE BLOOD
(USA and West Germany, 1979). Direction: John Huston. Based on a novel by Flannery O'Connor. With Brad Dourif (Hazel Motes), Ned Beatty (Hoover Shoates), Harry Dean Stanton (Asa Hawkes), Amy Wright (Sabbath Lily Hawkes). 2.

Hazel Motes, a young army veteran and grandson of a hell-fire evangelist, adopts dark formal clothing on return to civilian life in Tennessee and sets out in his own way to raise hell with all the mad fervor he inherited from his forebears. In the small town of Taulkinham—the location used is Macon, Georgia, though Flannery O'Connor's town is located in Tennessee—Hazel's disbelief in Jesus and hatred of the concept of sin and its redemption finds expression in the streets in proclaiming a church without Christ. He wins one fervid follower, a youth called Enoch, who steals from the local museum a diminutive mummy, which he declares to be the new Jesus. Taulkinham is in fact riddled with bogus preachers, including Asa Hawkes (a degraded evangelist who poses as being blind) and his unhappy daughter and accomplice, Sabbath, whose aim in life is to seduce Hazel and the phoney huckster, Hoover Shoates, who sells divine insurance and sets up as a rival pavement shouter alongside Hazel. Convinced of his uncleanliness, Hazel finally blinds and tortures himself to the horror of his devotedly maternal landlady, Mrs. Flood, who lovingly undertakes the care of his wasted body when he dies of exposure after fleeing her house.

No summary of this film can do justice to its bizarre, but somehow surrealistically poetic, obsessions. Huston manages to combine burlesque and tragedy in his ruthless exposure of a deeply depressed, not to say insane, man, his religious expression reduced to a fairground barker's sideshow. Hazel's religious promptings finally drive him to a ludicrous form of self-mutilation and a wasting death. His initial attempt at resistance to his "wise blood," lies in his proud possession of a down-and-out car and in a ritualistic visit to the town's seemingly bed-ridden prostitute. The film is at once wildly funny and strangely moving.

A WOMAN UNDER THE INFLUENCE
(USA, 1974). Direction and script: John Cassavetes. With Peter Falk (Nick Longhetti), Gena Rowlands (Mabel Longhetti). 1a.

A Woman under the Influence is the study of an American working-class family, the Longhettis, ironing out their problems in a rough-and-ready, instinctual manner when faced with the mental breakdown of one of its members. Mabel is the wife of a public utilities worker, Nick, and mother of three children. Having packed off the children to spend a night with her mother in anticipation of having her husband to herself for once, she reacts to his sudden message that he has an emergency job to attend to that night by going out and picking up a complete stranger, Garson Cross, with whom she spends the night at home, calling him Nick. The next day Nick brings a gang of his fellow workers to devour Mabel's spaghetti. Mabel tries to dance with one of the guests, and he yells at her. Later, she holds a party of her own for the children and their friends, only to have one father withdraw his child because of what he regards as her strange behavior. Nick, exasperated, hits her. A doctor is called in and, supported by Nick's mother, finally has Mabel committed to a mental institution.

We see nothing of Mabel's experiences under care, but are moved forward six months to the day she is received back into the family. They are nervous about how to treat her, but her one desire is to have the house to herself and be alone with Nick. She climbs up on a settee and sings "Swan Lake," just as she did before being committed. In his anger at this display, Nick threatens to hit her. The outcome is that she attempts suicide, and strangely it is her children who come to her rescue, welcoming her presence without any of the self-conscious complications shown by the adults. She seeks comfort in putting them to bed. Nick, assuaged and overcome by guilt, bandages Mabel's hand and they prepare to go to bed themselves.

In this film Cassavetes uses the techniques of improvisation familiar in his work since *Shadows* (1961), *Too Late Blues* (1962), *Faces* (1968), and *Husbands* (1970). The problems are shown but not resolved; no thesis is attempted, only a record of the behavior of a family muddling through a psychological situation none of them understands either rationally or (except for the children) intuitively.

YOU CAN'T TAKE IT WITH YOU
(USA, 1938). Direction: Frank Capra. Adaptation: Robert Riskin. Adapted from the Pulitzer Prize–winning play by George S. Kaufman and Moss Hart. With Lionel Barrymore (Grandfather Vanderhoff), Jean Arthur (Alice Vanderhoff), Edward Arnold (Anthony P. Kirby), James Stewart (Tony Kirby).

A sentimentally crazy, three-generation family, the Vanderhoffs, own a dilapidated house in New York, which rests on a site coveted by a hard-headed armaments king, Anthony P. Kirby, for building a vast office block. Alice, granddaughter Vanderhoff, complicates the situation by falling in love with Kirby's son, Tony. Grandfather and Grandmother refuse point-blank to sell their beloved establishment and see it torn down for redevelopment. When the impoverished family is finally persuaded to sell, however, Tony deserts his father's business rather than see this happen. This, together with even Kirby's becoming converted to Vanderhoff's view of life, leads to a happy end all around—Kirby relinquishes the property and Alice is left free to marry Tony.

In his warmhearted, meticulous handling of his brilliant cast, Capra ensures that every delightful (if sometimes irritating) eccentricity is fully developed—this is one of the outstanding comedies of the 1930s. The philosophy of the play is: do your own thing, just as you feel like doing it, but with goodwill towards all. In his autobiography, *The Name above the Title* (1971), Capra wrote: "Hidden in *You Can't Take It with You* was a golden opportunity to dramatize Love Thy Neighbour in living drama. . . . The conflict: devour thy neighbour versus love thy neighbour. The weapons: a bankful of money against a houseful of love."[130] Capra and Riskin made changes in the structure of the play to emphasize this, reducing the love story to a form of counterpoint. Capra added, "I elevated the philosophical conflict between the lamb (Grandpa Vanderhoff) and the lion (Kirby, senior) to the 'point' story."[131] The film won the 1938 Oscars for best picture and best direction. It is easy to see its appeal in a world torn by the Munich agreement and Hitler's vicious diplomacy of territorial annexation.

NOTES TO FILMOGRAPHY

1. For longer comments on the film see F. Coppola, program notes issued at the Cannes Film Festival (1979); E. Coppola, *Notes,* passim; M. Dempsey and J. Pym, *"Apocalypse Now," Sight and Sound* (London: British Film Institute, Winter 1979–80, p. 6); J. Tessitore, "The Literary Roots of *Apocalypse Now," New York Times* (21 October 1979).

2. Program Notes issued at the Cannes Film Festival (1979).

3. *Observer* (London) *Sunday Magazine* (2 December 1978).

4. E. Coppola, *Notes,* p. 112.

5. F. Coppola, Program Notes issued at the Cannes Film Festival (1979).

6. Dempsey and Pym, *"Apocalypse Now," Sight and Sound* (Winter 1979–80).

7. T. Milne, *Monthly Film Bulletin,* (London: British Film Institute, March 1980), p. 43.

8. Buñuel, *Belle de Jour,* p. 5.

9. Ibid., p. 6.

10. Aranda, *Luis Buñuel,* p. 226.

11. Ibid., p. 229.

12. Ibid., p. 228.

13. Ibid., p. 229.

14. Buñuel, *Belle de Jour,* p. 7.

15. See Kracauer, *From Caligari to Hitler,* chap. 5.

16. In an interview in 1978, Fassbinder said: "Nabakov is never direct. He handles language as something that reflects, mirrors and re-reflects. If I use glass and reflections in the film, it's derived from Nabakov's linguistic structure. I really tried to transform his language by cinematic means. . . . The significance of glass in this film is that it's transparent and yet it closes in on the characters." From *Boston Phoenix* (24 Oct. 1978).

17. The theme of the double is, of course, constantly recurrent in literature and film. See, for example, O. Rank, *The Double* (New York: New American Library, 1971); A. Artaud, *The Theatre and its Double* (New York: Grove Press, 1958).

18. T. Milne, review of *Despair, Monthly Film Bulletin,* (London: British Film Institute, August 1978).

19. Kracauer, *From Caligari to Hitler,* p. 81.

20. Ibid., p. 83.

21. Ibid., pp. 83–84.

22. In 1960 Fritz Lang made a third film about Mabuse, *The Thousand Eyes of Dr. Mabuse,* in which the destructive identity of the now-dead madman is taken over by a new madman. For Lang's own account of his confrontation with Goebbels, see an interview conducted by Ian Cameron and Mark Shivas in the journal *Movie,* no. 4 (November 1962), reprinted in *Monthly Film Bulletin* (April 1970), p. 80.

23.–25. Fellini quoted in an undated magazine supplement to the *London Daily Telegraph* published at the time of the film's release in London.

26. F. Fellini quoted in Program Notes, *Cinema Texas,* no. 2 (1976), p. 62.

27. The film was much altered by Boorman after its initial release. For details of the film and the changes made, see the review of *The Exorcist* and the subsequent unsigned editorial article in "The Heretic: Speaking in Tongues," in *Monthly Film Bulletin* (October 1977), pp. 210–11; 214. For another film dealing with possession in a religious context, see *The Devils* in this Filmography.

28. For a fuller account of this film, see Manvell, *Ingmar Bergman.* For the script as published, see Bergman, *Face to Face.*

29. See *Sight and Sound* (Winter 1967–68), 14–15, for Christian Braad Thomsen's interview with Bellocchio.

30. R. Hughes, ed., *Film: Book Two: Films of War and Peace* (New York: Grove Press, 1962), pp. 205–33.

31. John Huston, *An Open Book,* chap. 10.

32. Ibid., p. 125.

33. Ibid., chap. 27.

34. S. Kaminsky, *John Huston* (Boston: Houghton Mifflin, 1978), p. 141.

35. See the interview with John Carpenter in *Sight and Sound,* (Spring 1978), 94–98.

36. Quoted in T. Milne's review of the film, *Monthly Film Bulletin* (September 1977), p. 193.

37. Perhaps the best, but still low-key, portrayal of Hitler so far on the screen has been that by Anthony Hopkins in the three-hour film, *The Bunker* (1981), directed by George Schaefer and based on a study by James O'Donnell of Hitler's final days. But this performance appeared in a special production made for CBS-TV, and so lies outside the scope of this book.

38. R. Manvell, *Films and the Second World War,* p. 304.

39.–41. See Truman Capote, *Reality's Reflections,* published in an undated magazine supplement to the *London Daily Telegraph* at the time of the film's release in London. Capote commented on the uncanny physical likeness between the men chosen to play the killers and the original men, whom he had met and known.

42. Monaco, *American Film Now,* p. 290.

43. P. Houston, review of *Klute* in *Monthly Film Bulletin* (November 1971), p. 222.

44. For a very indignant attack, see T. Milne's review of the film, *Monthly Film Bulletin* (May 1973), pp. 99–100.

45. J. Dawson, review of *Last Tango in Paris, Monthly Film Bulletin* (May 1973), p. 100.

46. Ibid., p. 100.

47. T. Milne, review of *Lilith, Monthly Film Bulletin* (December 1966), p. 179.

48. J. Pym, review of *Looking for Mr. Goodbar, Monthly Film Bulletin* (March 1978), p. 49.

49. The action in the film involves this outcome.

50. Review of the film in the *Manchester Guardian,* 12 October 1978.

51.–53. For a detailed account of Syberberg's film see review by Tony Rayns, *Monthly Film Bulletin* (March 1977), pp. 46–47; for that of Visconti's film see review by Geoffrey Noel-Smith, *Monthly Film Bulletin* (October 1978), p. 202.

54. The script for *M* appears in R. Manvell, ed., *Masterpieces of the German* (New York: Harper & Row, 1973).

55. The subject was remade in America in 1951 by Joseph Losey in the form of a new and original work, set in the streets of Los Angeles.

56. Huston, *An Open Book,* p. 79.

57. G. Pratley, *The Cinema of Otto Preminger* (New York: A. S. Barnes, 1971) pp. 112–13.

58. Ibid., p. 113.

59. Ibid., p. 113–14.

60. G. Phelps, *Film Censorship* (London: Gollancz, 1975), p. 54.

61. Gilbert Lély, *The Marquis de Sade* (New York: Grove Press, 1970), pp. 42f.

62. Weiss, who was born in Germany in 1916 and who left Germany an exile in 1934, is also known for such dramatic works as *The Investigation,* a representation of the Auschwitz murder trials in West Germany in 1964–65 in the form of "an oratorio in 11 cantos"; *Trotsky in Exile,* in which he used a magic lantern show technique with filmlike speed; and a play on Vietnam covering some twenty-five hundred years of history. He died in 1982.

63. P. Brook. Introduction to *The Marat-Sade* (New York: Pocket Books, 1966), p. 6.

64. R. Manvell, *Theater and Film* (Rutherford, N.J.: Fairleigh Dickinson University Press, 1979), p. 245.

65. J. R. Taylor, *Hitch* (New York: Berkeley Books, 1980), p. 279.

66. Truffaut, *Hitchcock* (New York: Simon and Schuster, 1967), p. 228.

67. Ibid., pp. 227–28.

68. See R. Wood, *Hitchcock's Films* (New York: Paperback Library, 1970), pp. 163–95.

69. Ibid., pp. 165–66.

70. Ibid., p. 167.

71. For a hostile review, see J. Rosenbaum, *"Night Porter," Monthly Film Bulletin* (November 1974), p. 255.

72. T. Milne, review of *One Flew Over the Cuckoo's Nest, Monthly Film Bulletin* (February 1976), p. 32.

73.–74. See I. Atwell *G. W. Pabst* (Boston: Twayne, 1977), p. 57.

75. In 1980 Walerian Borowczyk produced a new version in German with the title *Lulu.*

76. Michael Powell's many notable films (made in association with the Hungarian, Emeric Pressburger) included the wartime *49th Parallel* (1941) and *The Life and Death of Colonel Blimp* (1943) and the postwar productions, *A Matter of Life and Death* (1946), *The Small Back Room* (1949), and the ballet film, *The Red Shoes* (1948). He also made the little-remembered *Canterbury Tale* (1944), in which the gentleman hero is a sexual pervert. As in most of Powell's films, strong sexual feeling in the characters becomes subject to equally powerful inhibitions.

77. It is perhaps noteworthy that Powell's first contact with filmmaking was working as an assistant with the American director Rex Ingram in the south of France. Ingram was much influenced by the

notorious Aleister Crowley, the model for the protagonist in his film *The Magician* (1926), a film on which Powell, then aged twenty-one, worked.

78. D. Thomson, *Boston Phoenix,* 12 February 1980. At the time Powell, seventy-four, was a colleague of David Thomson at Dartmouth, where he was visiting artist-in-residence.

79. S. Sontag, *On Photography* (London: Penguin Books, 1979), pp. 13–14.

80. The Latin word *persona* means "a mask," especially as worn by actors. As understood by Jung, it signifies the "actor mask" a person assumes for himself or before others.

81. *Bergman on Bergman,* (New York: Simon and Schuster, 1973), p. 196.

82. There is a certain relevance in the choice of *Electra* in this context, since the emphasis in the play is on the attempted silencing of Electra.

83. The names are significant. In Hebrew *Elizabeth* signifies a woman consecrated to God, while *Alma* ("fair" and "kindly" in Latin; "soul" in Spanish) signifies one who is all good. Is Elizabeth's silence linked to the silence of God, as implied in Bergman's previous film, *The Silence?*

84. Alma's cruel analysis of Elizabeth's pregnancy—she *acted* the part of the happy, expectant mother while trying to get rid of the fetus—is told first with the camera continuously on Elizabeth, and then repeated intact with Alma on camera, her face getting nearer and nearer, leading up to a big close-up. Hitherto, each face has been half-lit, half-shadowed. Only when the composite face is shown is the whole lit—once briefly, then again more prolonged, with an asynchronous chord of music.

85. Is there an echo here from Goya's *Disasters of War?*

86. This appears to be a flash shot of Bergman and Nykvist filming the original shot of Elizabeth on the stage in *Electra.* See also Simon, *Ingmar Bergman,* 31.

87. This is suggested in S. Sontag, *Styles of Radical Will.* (New York, Delta, 1781), p. 123.

88. This was in fact a clip used previously by Bergman in an early film, *Prison* or *The Devil's Wanton.*

89. This shot is repeated later on a TV screen in Elizabeth's bedroom at the clinic, together with a Jewish boy photographed in the Warsaw ghetto. Elizabeth recoils at the sight, retreating into the corner of her room.

90. This seems to be linked to Bergman's *Through a Glass Darkly,* in which a spider appears to an insane girl as a symbol of God.

91. Robin Wood in his book on Bergman suggests this might be the same book the child is seen reading at the end of *The Silence: Words in a Foreign Language.* For the imagery of the morgue, Bergman has identified himself with the boy when he was in the hospital. See Wood, *Ingmar Bergman,* 39.

92. Simon, *Ingmar Bergman Directs* (New York: Harcourt Brace, 1972), p. 239.

93. *Bergman on Bergman,* p. 44.

94. In his interview with Bergman John Simon suggested that this, like Elizabeth's visitation to Alma's bedroom earlier in the film, is a dream. It is even suggested that the scene in which Alma forces Elizabeth to speak and she says, "Nada," is another of Alma's dreams. Bergman did not deny this. He regarded Elizabeth as a "monster" who fends off Alma "because she has an emptiness in her." (Simon, *Ingmar Bergman,* 31–32).

95. *Bergman on Bergman,* p. 203.

96. For a full account of the adaptation of the story from a pulp fiction source by Hitchcock and a new writer of quality, Joseph Stefano, see Taylor, *Hitch: The Life and Times of Alfred Hitchcock,* chap. 13. The film was made television-style shortly thereafter, and the budget was a mere $800,000. Shot on the back lot at Universal, the film made $15 million in the USA alone on its first release. For a reconstruction in book form with 1,300 frame blow-ups, see Anobile, *Hitchcock's "Psycho."*

97. Truffaut, *Hitchcock,* p. 211.

98. A great deal is also owed to Bernard Herrmann's extraordinary music score, which dramatizes and underlines the insanity that the action all the time reveals, and with which the audience becomes in large measure identified. Compare the excellent analysis of the film in Wood, *Hitchcock's Films.*

99. Sarris, *Interviews with film directors,* p. 21.

100. Huston, *An Open Book,* p. 361.

101. Ibid., p. 333.

102. Ibid., pp. 332–33.

103. See B. Sulik, Introduction to R. Polanski's *Three Films* (London: Lorrimer, 1975), p. 8.

104. See Colin MacArthur, "Polanski," *Sight and Sound* (Winter 1968–69), 14–17.

105. See also J. A. McCarty, "The Polanski Puzzle," *Take One,* 2, no. 5 (1969), pp. 18–21.

106. *Cahiers du Cinéma in English* (February 1966), no. 3.

107. Truffaut, *Hitchcock,* p. 130.

108. The French usually use the word *clergyman* to signify a Protestant pastor, but since in one sequence the clergyman is seen hearing a confession, albeit in a highly distorted form, there is no

other implication except the use of the word itself in the French title to suggest that he is a celibate Protestant.

109. Truffaut, *Hitchcock*, p. 117.

110. Ibid., pp. 117–18.

111. Ibid., p. 118.

112. Ibid., p. 118.

113. F. Truffaut, *The Story of Adèle H.*, p. 7.

114. Ibid., p. 9.

115. The manuscript of a section of Adèle's diary, written in code, was discovered by Professor Guille in 1955 in the Pierpoint Morgan Library in New York City. Professor Guille published the journal in 1968.

116. Truffaut, *The Story of Adèle H.*, p. 8.

117. Ibid., p. 9.

118. T. Milne, review of *Straw Dogs, Sight and Sound* (Winter 1971–72), p. 50.

119. A further, less satisfactory version was directed by Arthur Robison with sound in 1936.

120. The script was based on Schrader's own experience in the "mean streets" of New York. See Pye and Myles, *Movie Brats*, p. 208, and *Film Comment* (March–April 1976), pp. 6–7. Schrader had a Dutch-Calvinist upbringing, in contrast to Scorsese's Catholic background. Schrader was also the author of an earlier scholarly study, *Transcendental Style in Film: Ozu, Bresson, Dreyer* published in 1972.

121. This was Herrmann's last score for films before he died. His scores for *Citizen Kane* and *Psycho*, among other films, are among the most striking in American cinema.

122. Pye and Myles, *Movie Brats*, p. 208.

123. Ibid., p. 210.

124. John Pym, review of *Texas Chainsaw Massacre, Monthly Film Bulletin* (December, 1976), p. 258.

125. See Manvell, *Ingmar Bergman*, p. 48. The script of *Through a Glass Darkly* is published in *A film trilogy* (London: Calder & Boyars, 1967; New York: Orion, 1968).

126. Statement made in the commentary to the film *Let There Be Light*.

127. Wood, *Hitchcock's Films*, p. 76.

128. See Claude Chabrol, "I Fell in Love with Charlotte Nozière," *Monthly Film Bulletin* (April 1979), p. 88.

129. Ibid., p. 88.

130. F. Capra *The Name Above the Title* (New York: Macmillan, 1971), p. 241.

131. Ibid., p. 241.

Appendix

The Popular Portrayal of Insanity in the Elizabethan-Jacobean Theater
Roger Manvell

Concern with insanity and a marked interest in its dramatic possibilities on the stage preceded the near-obsession with the subject that affected the Elizabethan-Jacobean dramatists in England in the sixteenth century. Characters manifesting various forms of madness appear frequently in Greek classical tragedy.* The concept of madness in Greek culture of the time, the fifth century B.C., was all-inclusive. It embraced the "gift" of prophecy (as in the case of Cassandra in Aeschylus's *Agamemnon* of 458 B.C.), poetic inspiration, excessive sexual lust, and reckless acts of bravery in war. In other words, no attempt was made to differentiate between the various forms of insanity, and, therefore, there was a marked variation in the types of behavior depicted and in audience response. Cassandra's madness, for example, was really a form of prophetic clairvoyance. She appears as the prophetess of doom, blessed by Apollo with the gift of prophecy but also cursed by him (when she denied him intercourse) so that her quite valid prophecies are always disregarded. She foretells the death of her lover Agamemnon, conqueror of Troy, at the hands of his Queen Clytemnestra. Aeschylus seems to be giving her words an almost surreal touch (Louis MacNeice's translation in *Ten Greek Plays,* ed. L. R. Lind [Boston: Houghton Mifflin, 1957]):

CASSANDRA: Ah God, the vision! God, God, the Vision!
A net, is it? Net of Hell!
But herself is the net; shared bed; shared murder.

. . . .

Quick! Be on your guard! The bull—
Keep him clear of the cow.
Caught with a trick, the black horn's point,
She strikes. He falls; lies in the water.
Murder; a trick in the bath. I tell what I see.
CHORUS: You are mad, mad, carried away by the god.

(Lines 1114–16; 1125–29)

She speaks of her "brain on fire" (line 1172) and how "They call me crazy, like a fortune-teller" (line 1273). She laments how the terrible labour of true prophecy,

---

*I am indebted to my friend Professor Carl Ruck, in the Department of Classics at Boston University, for his assistance in the tracing and defining of these examples of insanity in Greek classical tragedy.

327

dizzying prelude, distracts (lines 1115–16). Cassandra's madness is also portrayed in Euripides' *Trojan Women.*

More recognizable forms of madness, as they have come to be understood clinically in modern times, might be said to be represented by Pentheus in Euripides' *Bacchae* (a case perhaps of hysteria); by Pentheus's mother, Agave (an example, one might assume, of schizophrenia); and by Orestes in Aeschylus's *Eumenides* (suffering possibly from paranoid delusions), though madness in this tragedy is expressed not by Orestes himself but by the chorus of the Furies, who pursue him relentlessly at the bidding of the ghost of Clytemnestra, the mother he has slain. The mad Orestes appears also in Euripides' plays *Andromache* and *Iphigenia in Tauris.* Euripides' Medea might be considered at least disturbed, if not actually insane, but she drives Glauke, Jason's new bride, mad with the poisoned robe. Io in Aeschylus's *Prometheus Bound* (Rex Warner's translation) is considered to be mad, wandering as she does and stung constantly by a gadfly through the jealous malice of Hera (Juno):

> wear me away, poor thing, all crazy now in fear of the stinging fly. (lines 580–81)

Sophocles' Philoctetes is driven to despair and nearly to madness, and he may also display symptoms of epilepsy. Afflicted by a painful, festering foot following a snakebite—once again the result of Hera's hatred—he says (Kathleen Freeman's translation in *Ten Greek Plays):*

> Don't be angry with me, if in my madness, buffeted by pain, I speak unreasonably. (lines 1172–3)

Phaedra in Euripides' *Hippolytus* is alleged to be mad by the nurse because she is afflicted by lust and wants to die.

In Sophocles' *Ajax* the protagonist goes mad when he is denied the armor of Achilles, which is rightfully his. His senses are blinded by the jealous goddess Athena when, out of pride, he refuses to accept her aid. In this condition he slaughters cattle instead of his foes and then commits suicide out of shame once he recovers his wits and sees what he has done.

In Sophocles' *Oedipus the King* Oedipus unwittingly slays his father and marries his mother, blinding himself in a paroxysm of guilt once the truth is known. And, finally, Hercules in Euripides' *Hercules Furens,* after his secret return from Hades and his slaying of the usurper, Lycus, is driven mad by his divine persecutor— once more the goddess Hera—and in a blind frenzy murders his wife and children. Thus, in a dozen and more of the surviving plays written by the most renowned of the Greek dramatists within a span of little more than half a century, madness is introduced as an important element, though frequently of a kind caused by divine intervention.

It was, however, Seneca's Roman tragedies, written during the first century A.D., that served as the initial model for the Elizabethans. The mad rages of Hieronimo in Kyd's *Spanish Tragedy* (acted in 1588), of Orlando in Greene's *Orlando Furioso* (1594), and of Titus in Shakespeare's *Titus Andronicus* (1594) were conceived on the Senecan model of sheer, wild rhetoric, leaving the more psychologically oriented characterizations of madness found in the Jacobean drama, starting around 1601, to be directly influenced by the popularization of the psychology of the "humors" and, more particularly, by the melancholic humor associated with insanity.

Madness in the Senecan tradition was occasioned normally by some grave shock, not by an inborn predisposition due to an imbalance in the humorous secretions. The play by Seneca that set the pattern for what might be called the *neoclassical* treatment of madness was *Hercules Furens* (modeled in turn on Euripides), a play effectively written in the high-flown rhetorical style characteristic of the period and with great emphasis on sensationalism.* Seneca's plays were intended for declamation rather than for practical production on a stage. In *Hercules Furens* Juno, queen of heaven, is intent on the destruction of Hercules, son of her husband, Jupiter, by his mistress, Alcmena. Having imposed on him in his infancy twelve seemingly impossible labors, she is furious that he has managed at last to have survived them all. The action of the play begins when he returns from the lower world of Hades to be reunited with his stepfather, Amphitryon, and his faithful wife and children in his royal palace at Thebes, which was, in his absence, seized by a usurper, Lycus. Juno determines to force him to destroy himself by making him go mad. Upon slaying Lycus, Hercules finds his reason suddenly leaving him. His visions are described in highly rhetorical form (from *Seneca's Tragedies*, vol. 1 [Cambridge: Harvard University Press, Loeb Classical Library, 1968]):

> But what is this? Shadows have begirt midday. . . . Who puts the day to flight and drives it back to dawn? . . . See where the lion, my first toil, glows in no small part of heaven, is all hot with rage, and makes ready his fangs. Forthwith he will seize some star; threatening he stands with gaping jaws, and breathes forth fires, and shakes the mane upon his flaming neck. . . . The earth has been subdued, the swollen seas are at rest, the infernal realms have felt my onset; heaven us yet untried. . . . Earth has not room for Hercules. . . . (P. 83).

In his mad fury Hercules slays his children and then his wife, Megara, whom in his hallucination he believes to be Juno herself. After this manic slaughter he collapses, and the chorus prays that he retain his madness and so remain unconscious of his fearful deeds:

> See, prone on the ground, he revolves in his fierce heart his savage dreams; not yet has the baleful power of so great woe been overcome. . . . Not yet has he dispelled all his surging madness. . . . Banish the mad passions of thy soul. . . . Or rather let his mind still be stirred by uncontrolled emotion; madness alone can now make thee innocent. Next best to guiltless hands is ignorance of guilt. (P. 97)

---

*Lucius Annaeus Seneca, the philosopher, like his father Marcus, the rhetorician, was Spanish by birth but educated in Rome. He could study madness firsthand, since he served as senator under the emperors Caligula and Claudius. Agrippina, wife of Claudius, appointed him tutor to her son Domitius, later to become the Emperor Nero, over whom he exercised considerable influence until Nero turned against him, forcing him to commit suicide in the year A.D. 65. The insanity of the Roman emperors is vividly described by Tacitus (see his study of Nero in *The Annals of Imperial Rome, chaps. 12, 14, 15.*) and by Suetonius in *The Twelve Caesars* (Gaius Caligula; Nero).

But when he revives, he is back in his right mind, and confronted by the mangled corpses of his family, he is forced to realize that he himself has slain them. His father, Amphitryon, comments:

> His heart, not yet eased of frenzy's tumult, has shifted its wrath's aim and now, sure sign of madness, he rages against himself. (P. 107)

Prevailed upon not to kill himself, Hercules departs into exile and obscurity.

In Robert Greene's *Orlando Furioso* (1594), the character of Orlando, who likens himself to Hercules, is conceived very crudely as a raving maniac, whose explosive speeches are full of nonsequiturs larded with Latin phrases and classical lore—for example:

> Woods, trees, leaves; leaves, trees, woods; *tria sequuntur tria;* (3.1)

He is later cured by a witch, who sprinkles Latin verses over him. In his astonishment he exclaims,

> Sirrah, how came I thus disguised, Like mad Orestes, quaintly thus attired? (4.2).

The play was not intended to be taken too seriously.

Shakespeare's only Senecan madman, Titus, in the bloody melodrama *Titus Andronicus* (1593–94), is a Roman general. He goes mad finally in the fourth act because of the grievous wrongs done him and his family. He mutilates himself, and his lamentations turn to outright raving in the style of Hieronimo, exploding revenge. In his madness he attires himself as a cook and serves the Roman emperor and the faithless Tamara, his empress and queen of the Goths, with a dish made up from the bodies of her slain children. The play ends in a welter of blood with the violent deaths of Titus, the emperor, and Tamara.

In Kyd's *Spanish Tragedy* (1592; acted 1588) Hieronimo, marshal of Spain becomes insane through shock when his son Horatio is murdered by Lorenzo, the king's nephew. His mad ravings, however, are intermittent; usually, his activities are normal, though he remains afflicted with melancholy. The key maniacal scenes may well be insertions written by another hand, perhaps that of Jonson or Webster. His madness is described by one of his servants:

> Sometimes, as he doth at his table sit,
> He speaks as if Horatio stood beside him;
> Then starting in a rage, falls on the earth,
> Cries out "Horatio, where is my Horatio?"
> So that with extreme grief and cutting sorrow
> There is not left in him one inch of man.
>
> (3.12A.908–13)

His later ravings turn on revenge:

> O no, there is no end: the end is death and madness! As I am never

better than when I am mad: then methinks I am a brave fellow; then I do
wonders: but reason abuseth me, and there's the torment, there's the
hell.

(3.12A.1055–1058)

Hieronimo commits suicide, along with with his wife, Isabella, who has also gone mad.

Elizabethan plays such as these, written prior to 1600, make no mention of madness induced by an imbalance of the humors. Madness either stems from some form of "possession" (as affects Cassandra or Hercules) or from some great shock, such as distracts Hieronimo and his wife.

Theories of mental pathology go back to the classical Greeks. Hippocrates (c. 400 B.C.), whose particular concern was physiology, posited four primary bodily *humors,* which were in theory related to the four primary elements—fire, air, earth, water. The four humors—which ideally maintained a balance in the healthy human body—were melancholy (associated with the spleen), blood, choler (bile), and phlegm. It was Galen (c. A.D. 170) who, much later, associated more specifically the balance of the humors with temperamental behavior, thus establishing the four celebrated temperamental types:

1. Blood, associated with the sanguine temperament
2. Phlegm, associated with the phlegmatic temperament
3. Gall, associated with the choleric temperament
4. Spleen, associated with the melancholic temperament

Galen's association of the bodily humors with the prevailing temperaments was adopted by the medievalists and, duly updated and elaborated in the Elizabethan-Jacobean period in England, received popular expression in the literature and drama of the time. The melancholic temperament, closely associated with depression and insanity, became the subject of both scientific and lay interest. Two widely read treatises, Timothy Bright's *Treatise on Melancholy* (1586) and Robert Burton's *Anatomy of Melancholy* (1621), provide evidence of the deep interest in morbid psychology in Shakespeare's time. Bright's study showed the beginnings of a modern, scientific approach—indeed, the first approach to psychology to be made by an Englishman; Burton's thousand-page book, representing a massive anthology of everything related to the subject, was compiled for the scholarly general reader.

Bright associated unnatural lust with the liver, choler with the gall bladder, and melancholy with the spleen, claiming that excessive secretions led to the emergence of dangerous "fumes": he asserted that foods (especially meat) contained dangerous humors and that melancholy could result from overeating. Actual insanity might come from an "excessive distemper of heat" (see Reed, *Bedlam,* p. 71), caused by a grievous excess in any of the humors, leading to what amounted to a burning out ("adustion") of the humor, expressing itself in excesses of violence and passion. Burton described the humors and their characteristics as follows:

A humour is a liquid or fluent part of the body, comprehended in it, for the preservation of it; and is either innate or born with us, or adventitious and acquisite. . . . Blood is a hot, sweet, temperate, red humour . . . whose office is to nourish the whole body, to give it strength and colour, being dispersed by the veins through every part of it. . . . Pituita, or phlegm, is a cold and moist humour . . . his office is to nourish and moisten the members of the body, which, as the tongue, are moved, that they be not over dry. . . . Choler is hot and dry, bitter . . . gathered to the gall: it helps the natural heat and senses. . . . Melancholy, cold and dry, thick, black and sour . . . purged from the spleen, is a bridle to the other two hot humours, blood and cholera. . . . These four humours have some analogy with the four elements, and to the four ages of man. (*Anatomy*, 128–29)

By the time Burton's *Anatomy* was published, the Elizabethan-Jacobean dramatists were providing a whole genre of plays in which the insane appeared as principal characters, among them, as we have seen, Hieronimo in Kyd's *Spanish Tragedy* and Titus in Shakespeare's *Titus Andronicus* (c. 1593). Later, far subtler studies influenced by the humors psychology include Shakespeare's *Hamlet* (1602) and *King Lear* (c. 1605); Ferdinand in Webster's *Duchess of Malfi* (c. 1614) and Cornelia in his *White Devil* (1612); Sforza in Massinger's *Duke of Milan* (1623); various characters in Middleton's *Changeling* (1623) and Ford's *Lover's Melancholy* (1628); and Penthea in Ford's *Broken Heart* (1633).

Robert R. Reed in *Bedlam on the Jacobean Stage* (1952) and E. A. Peers in *Elizabethan Drama and Its Madfolk* (1914), describe the first attempts to treat the mad scientifically. Bethlehem Hospital in London specialized in the clinical treatment of the insane from the late fourteenth century onward, and opened its doors to the public. Visits to "Bedlam" to watch the curious behavior of the insane became a popular form of amusement, like watching the monkeys in the zoo. In Dekker's *Honest Whore* Friar Anselmo, keeper of the hospital says:

> There are of madmen, as there are of tame,
> All humoured not alike. We have here some
> So apish and fantastic, play with a feather;
> And, though 'twould grieve a soul to see God's image
> So blemished and defaced, yet do they act
> Such antic and such pretty lunacies,
> That spite of sorrow they will make you smile:
> Others again we have like hungry lions,
> Fierce as wild bulls, untameable as flies.
>
> (Part I.5.2)

Parallel with the clinical approach were the treatments associated with religion and superstition, the insane being regarded as suffering from "devil sickness" or "possession" and, according to the tenets of those in charge, treated with either cruelty or humanity. Insanity was commonly believed to be influenced by the phases of the moon or by spells cast by witches, while the rites of exorcism often matched in their violence the violent behavior of the insane. Cures might be attempted by whipping; by immersion in a well; by binding the victim to a cross on which he or she was left extended overnight; by the application of compounds from such herbs as the mandrake root with holy water; or by the so-called darkroom treatment (the treatment Malvolio is given in *Twelfth Night,* though in a comic spirit, when he is considered to have gone mad through excessive vanity), which entailed confinement in a darkened room or cell.

Insanity as understood during the most productive period of the Elizabethan-Jacobean dramatists is represented in the plays themselves. It is a strange and often confusing mixture of accepted superstition, gropings towards a more scientific approach, and (especially in the case of Shakespeare) intuitive penetration that reached towards a more profound psychological realization of the nature of insanity. Shakespeare certainly understood something of the complexity of this aspect of the human psyche. He allows some hesitation even to Polonius in *Hamlet:*

For to define true madness, What is't but to be nothing else but mad? (2.2.93)

Nevertheless, traditional views occur continually in his plays and those of his contemporaries, along with the loose use of the word *mad.* Paralleling common use today, they termed "mad" any odd or extreme action or small aberration, as in Shylock's allusion in *The Merchant of Venice* to people who "are mad if they behold a cat" (4.1.48). There is also the fine "madness" of the poet, the artist, and the lovesick, as in *A Midsummer Night's Dream:*

> The lunatic, the lover, and the poet,
> Are of imagination all compact:
> One sees more devils than vast hell can hold,
> That is, the madman; the lover, all as frantic,
> Sees Helen's beauty in a brow of Egypt;
> The poet's eye, in a fine frenzy rolling,
> Doth glance from heaven to earth, from earth to heaven.
> (5.1.7–13)

In *Romeo and Juliet* Mercutio expects Romeo to "sure run mad" for love (2.4.5); Troilus in *Troilus and Cressida* vows he is "mad in Cressida's love" (1.1.51); and Rosalind in *As You Like It* makes a dark reference in jest to the contemporary treatment of the insane when she suggests:

Love is merely a madness, and, I tell you, deserves as well a dark house and a whip as madmen do. (3.2.426–7)

Also fully recognized was the distinction between congenital imbecility and insanity. There are many characters of poor or slow mentality in Shakespeare's plays. Cloten, for example, in *Cymbeline* is mentally deficient and speaks so. In actuality, imbeciles and the slow-witted, who were quite harmless, were left free in the community, living on charity; those released from mental institutions, such as Bethlehem (Bedlam) Hospital became "Tom-'o-Bedlams," roaming the countryside, the lowest of the low. This is the guise that Edgar adopts in *King Lear.*

The dramatists were no doubt vague as to the real causes of insanity. They cited what appealed to their imagination. "Possession" by evil spirits or the influence of witches, warlocks, and other agents of the devil was commonly accepted. This was the case with Saul in the Old Testament. The Authorized Version of 1611 described his condition: "The spirit of the Lord departed from Saul and an evil spirit troubled him" (1 Sam. 16). Burton wrote:

> The last kind of madness or melancholy is that demoniacal (if I may so call it) obsession or possession of devils. . . . the Devil, spying his opportunity of such humours, drives them many times to despair . . . mingling himself amongst these humours. . . . [Unclean spirits] go in and out of our bodies, as bees do in a hive, and so provoke and tempt us. (*Anatomy,* 124, 174).

Of the possessed Burton added: "Many of them in their extremity think they hear and see visions . . . They think evil against their wills" (Ibid., 948).

The rites of exorcism, practiced to this day, turn on this notion. There is a mock exorcism in *Twelfth Night* of Malvolio the lunatic, who, it is claimed, is possessed by a "hyperbolical fiend" (4.2.26 and 29). Witches might give their charges brews of various kinds to induce hallucinations and destroy a rational balance of mind. The witches in *Macbeth* have an impressive recipe, and Banquo, after the first encounter with them, says:

> Have we eaten on the insane root That takes the reason prisoner? (1.3.84)

The "insane root" in this case was the mandrake (referred to variously as *Solanum somniferum,* deadly nightshade, *Atropa mandragora* and Belladonna), a Eurasian plant with a cleft root alleged to resemble a man and to shriek when uprooted. It was the source of mandragora, a narcotic that caused madness. "Give me to drink mandragora," cries Cleopatra in *Antony and Cleopatra* (1.5.4) when Antony leaves her. In *Othello* Iago laments that neither poppy nor mandragora "nor all the drowsy syrups of the world" (3.3.331–2) will bring him restful sleep, now that jealousy possesses him. Juliet, just before committing suicide, speaks of the "shrieks like mandrakes torn out of the earth, That living mortals, hearing them, run mad." (4.3.47–48)

Other causes of madness were associated with the moon (hence, of course, the term *lunatic*), the disposition of the planets, and the seasons. In Middleton's *Changeling* (c. 1623) Lollio claims it is Luna who has made him mad (3.2.71). Othello is no less positive:

> It is the very error of the moon; She comes more nearer earth than she was wont And makes men mad. (5.2.109)

Other characters, for example Crazy in Brome's *City Wit* claims, "Sure I was planet-struck" (5.1). Thomas Vicary, chief surgeon at St. Bartholomew's Hospital (1548–62) asserts in his *Anatomie of the Body of Man* (1548):

> Also the Brayne hath this propertie that it moveth and followesh the moving of the moone; for in the waxing of the moone the brayne discendeth downwarde and vanisheth in substance of vertue; for then the brayne shrinketh together in itself and is not so fully obedient to the spirit of feeling, and this is proved in men that lunaticke or madde . . . be moste greeved in the beginning

of the newe moone and in the latter quarter of the moone. (Peers, *Elizabethan Drama,* 13)

Seasonal madness is reflected in such phrases, common or less common, as "mad as a March hare" and "midsummer madness". Hares breed in March and so may act wild at this time; "midsummer madness" reflects the common belief that insanity becomes more prevalent then. Another cause of madness was believed to be a worm in the brain. In James Shirley's *Coronation* (1635), the character Arcadius says,

My uncle is something craz'd;/There is a worm in's brain. (3.2.-)

Another cause of madness, confined to men, was thought to be cuckolding. Falstaff says in *The Merry Wives of Windsor:*

If I have horns to make me mad, let the proverb go with me: I'll be horn-mad. (3.5.153)

Madness was also referred to as "ecstasy," and was thought to be brought on sometimes by a quickened action of the pulse and the heart. Leonato in *Much Ado about Nothing* says of Beatrice:

The ecstasy hath so much overborne her, that my daughter is sometimes afeard she will do a desperate outrage to herself. (2.3.166–9)

Under more serious circumstances, Ophelia speaks of Hamlet as "blasted with ecstasy." Indeed, the queen believes it is as a result of "ecstasy" that Hamlet is under the illusion he is seeing his father's ghost:

QUEEN: This is the very coinage of your brain:
           This bodiless creation ecstasy
           Is very cunning in.
HAMLET: Ecstasy!
           My pulse, as yours, doth temperately keep time,
           And makes as healthful music. It is not madness
           That I have utter'd: bring me to the test,
           And I the matter will re-word, which Madness
           Would gambol from.

(3.4.136–144)

Parallel to the Jacobean interest in melancholy and morbid psychology was an obsession with ghosts and other forms of hallucination, and the evil influences of witchcraft. Indeed, madness and witchcraft often coincided. The legal defence put up on behalf of women accused of witchcraft was often that they were insane—that is, possessed by Satan. No less a person that King James I declared that the plea of insanity should no longer be recognized before the law in cases of witchcraft. He maintained that witches should die rather than be exorcized. The protagonists in *Henry VI, Part 1* look on Joan of Arc as a "holy prophetess"

(1.4.102), "devil's Dam" (1.5.5), or "witch" (1.5.6), according to the side they are on. For the English she was an "enchantress" (5.3.42) who relied on "baleful sorcery" (2.1.15) with the "help of hell" (2.1.18). She, however, claims that the visions that inspire her are of divine origin: "God's mother deigned to appear to me", she claims (1.2.78). But to her opponents she is a "vile fiend and shameless courtesan" (3.2.45). She is actually shown by Shakespeare to summon fiends from hell to aid her: "Familiar spirits . . . cull'd / Out of the powerful regions under earth" (5.3.10–11). Finally, the "foul accursed minister of hell" (5.4.93) is burnt alive as a witch.

Although in Shakespeare's plays overtly sane men—such as Brutus in *Julius Caesar*—experience hallucinations others, more obsessive if not actually insane— such as Hamlet and Richard III—experience them more direly. The ghost in *Hamlet* speaks at length and is a prime motivator of the play's action, but this ghost's origin, whether it be genuine or a "goblin damned" (1.4.40), is often put to question. Shakespeare's recognition that ghostly visitations could indeed be hallucinatory, experienced when the mind is overstressed, is never more clearly put than in the dagger speech in *Macbeth:*

> Is this a dagger which I see before me,
> The handle toward my hand? Come, let me clutch thee.
> I have thee not, and yet I see thee still.
> Art thou not, fatal vision, sensible
> To feeling as to sight? or art thou but
> A dagger of the mind, a false creation,
> Proceeding from the heat-oppressed brain?
>
> (2.1.33–39)

Macbeth, a superstitious man deluded throughout the play by the "juggling fiends" (5.7.48), the witches, is obsessed by voices that cry, "Sleep no more" (2.2.42). Both he and his lady experience "terrible dreams" (3.2.18–19) that shake them nightly. He alone sees the ghost of Banquo at the feast, and he declines into a raging maniac by the end of the play, while his wife dies insane, subject to sleepwalking and revealing her guilt in sleep-spoken words. The doctor says that Lady Macbeth is "troubled with thick-coming fancies" (5.3.37–8). Macbeth virtually anticipates Freud in his appeal to his helpless physician:

MACBETH: Cure her of that.
              Canst thou not minister to a mind diseased,
              Pluck from the memory a rooted sorrow,
              Raze out the written troubles of the brain,
              And with some sweet oblivious antidote
              Cleanse the stuff'd bosom of that perilous stuff
              Which weighs upon the heart?
DOCTOR: Therein the patient
              must minister to himself.
MACBETH: Throw physic to the dogs, I'll none of it.

                                            (5.3.39–47)

But the primary cause of insanity was felt increasingly at this time to be some form of excess in the effects of melancholy, the melancholic humor, which became the favorite subject of comment and study by the Jacobeans, referring to every kind of internal imbalance of the humors that led to excessive depression and morbidity.

According to Burton:

> Melancholy . . . is either in disposition or habit. In disposition, is that transitory Melancholy which goes and comes upon every small occasion of sorrow, need, sickness, trouble, fear, grief, passion, or perturbation of the mind, any manner of care, discontent, or thought, which causeth anguish, dulness, heaviness and vexation of spirit, any ways opposite to pleasure, mirth, joy, delight, causing forwardness in us, or a dislike. In which equivocal and improper sense, we call him melancholy; that is dull, sad, sour, lumpish, ill-disposed, solitary, any way moved, or displeased. And from these melancholy dispositions no man living is free, no Stoick, none so wise, none so happy, none so patient, so generous, so godly, so divine, that can vindicate himself; so well-composed, but more or less, some time or other, he feels the smart of it. Melancholy in this sense is the character of mortality. (Burton, *Anatomy*, 125)

Among the melancholics cited by Peers in *Elizabethan Drama* (pages 2, 89) are Aspatia in Beaumont and Fletcher's *Maid's Tragedy* and Euphrasia in their *Philaster*, Mistress Constance in Brome's *Northern Lass*, and Almira in Massinger's *Very Woman*—all studies in deep depression through lost love.

So fashionable was the melancholic mood (like the romantic world-weariness pose of the period of Goethe and Byron and the "aesthetic" pose of the Rossetti period) that Shakespeare repeatedly harped on it in both his lighter and his heavier plays. At the saner end of the melancholic spectrum are such characters as Orsino in *Twelfth Night*, Antonio in *The Merchant of Venice*, and Jaques in *As You Like It*. Orsino's melancholy is caused by lovesickness and inactivity. Antonio is uncertain, however, of the causes of his melancholy. Like Orsino, he opens the play:

> In sooth, I know not why I am so sad:
> It wearies me; you say it wearies you;
> But how I caught it, found it, or came by it,
> What stuff 'tis made of, whereof it is born,
> I am to learn;
> And such a want-wit sadness makes of me,
> That I have much ado to know myself.
>
> (1.1.1–7)

Jaques, on the other hand, is melancholy through too much thought, considered at the time (and perhaps still) the cause of distraction. He is fatalistic, even misanthropic, the typical underemployed intellectual and future existentialist. The well-balanced Duke, in whose rural train he is the self-appointed misfit, has little use for what he regards as Jaques's melancholic pose; Jaques, he alleges to his face, "has been a libertine" (2.7.62). Now that he is a reformed character, he merely wants to indulge himself by chiding the world for the very sins he once enjoyed committing—chiding which the Duke holds to be a "most mischievous foul sin" (2.7.64). Jaques, however, regards his melancholy, expressed philosophically in his celebrated set speech on the seven ages of man (2.7.138–166) with the kind of vainglorious pride characteristic of the egotistic intellectual. This is seen in his interchanges with Rosalind:

ROSALIND: They say you are a melancholy fellow.
JAQUES: I am so; I do love it better than laughing.
ROSALIND: Those who are in an extremity of either are abominable fellows. . . .
JAQUES: I have neither the scholar's melancholy, which is emulation; nor the musician's which is fantastical; nor the courtier's, which is proud; nor the soldier's, which is ambitious; nor the lawyer's, which is politic; nor the lady's, which is nice; nor the lover's, which is all these: but it is a melancholy of mine own, compounded of many simples, extracted from many objects, and indeed the sundry contemplation of my travels, which, by often rumination, wraps me in a most humorous sadness.

(4.1.3–21)

In spite of his frank challenge to the vanity of this egotistical man, the Duke is glad to have him around, for, as he says:

I love to cope with him in these sullen fits, / For then he's full of matter. (2.1.67–8)

Jaques has an ironic sense of humor that appeals to the good-natured and worldly-wise Duke. But, as Burton took pains to point out, melancholy so indulged can readily lead to decline into depression, and even insanity:

It is most pleasant at first, I say, a most charming illusion, a most delightsome humour, to be alone, dwell alone, walk alone, meditate, lie in bed whole days, dreaming awake as it were, and frame a thousand phantastical imaginations unto themselves. . . . He may thus continue peradventure many years . . . but at last a wrecked imagination, his phantasy is crazed, and now habituated to such toys, cannot but work still like a fate; the Scene alters upon a sudden, Fear and Sorrow supplant those pleasing thoughts, suspicion, discontent, and perpetual anxiety succeed in their places. (*Anatomy*, p. 346)

Jaques, therefore, is one of the more complex of the sane melancholics in Elizabethan-Jacobean drama, who thoroughly enjoy their pose of depression and worldly disillusionment and the opportunities it gives them to philosophize in public. The vein runs throughout Shakespeare—in Richard II, in Benedick, and even in such cynics as Iago, Richard III, and Thersites. It is one of Shakespeare's most beautifully conceived and witty parts, a kind of lightweight counterpart to Hamlet, another misfit who assumes actual madness because it suits only too well what is most extreme in his melancholic-depressive temperament. But the melancholic temperament was, as we have seen in Burton, a dangerous one in which to indulge: As a servant says to Christopher Sly in the induction to *The Taming of the Shrew:*

Too much sadness hath congeal'd your blood, / And melancholy is the nurse of frenzy. (Induction, 2.135)

Indeed, Shakespeare refers to the idea that a congealment of the blood, caused by excessive melancholy, is a cause of madness; and Jaques, given to "sullen fits" (2.1.67) and even to "weeping" (2.1.65) is in some danger of mental collapse through his deepening melancholia. However, one had always to judge in Jacobean times between what constituted real depression and what was assumed for some ulterior motive. Referring to the contemporary fashion of posing as being melancholy or even mad, Fletcher in his play *The Mad Lover* (c. 1618) referred to madness as "a gentleman-like humour, and in fashion" (4.1). In *Troilus and Cressida* Ajax refers to the withdrawal of the sulky, homosexual Achilles thus:

Yes, lion-sick, sick of proud heart; you may call it melancholy if you will favour the man, but, by my head, 'tis pride. (2.3.94–96)

Published five years after Shakespeare's death and eight after Burton himself had ceased to write, Burton's *Anatomy* (referred to by its American editors, Floyd Dell and Paul Jordan Smith was "a vast anthology of depression" [p x] as well as "a sort of literary cosmos, an omnium-gatherum" [p. ix] went through no less than five editions in the author's lifetime (that is, between its publication in 1621 and the author's death in 1640). Burton acted as the great compiler of material—knowledge, belief, and superstition—relating to insanity that was current during Shakespeare's productive period, and his work exercised a profound influence on those dramatists—such as Middleton, Massinger, and Ford—who wrote plays concerned with insanity after 1621. The editors said that its title in more modern times would be, "Analysis of Morbid Psychology" (p. xiii), and they regard Burton as "a scholarly and humanistic precursor of Freud" (p. xiii). Burton himself described his book in general when introducing the subject of religious melancholy:

I will set before your eyes in brief a stupend, vast, infinite Ocean of incredible madness and folly: a Sea full of shelves and rocks, sands, gulfs . . . full of fearful monsters, uncouth shapes, rearing waves, tempests, and Siren calms, Halcyonian Seas, unspeakable misery, such Comedies and Tragedies, such absurd and ridiculous, feral and lamentable fits, that I know not whether they are more to be pitied or derided, or may be believed, but that we daily see the same still practised in our days, fresh examples, new news, fresh objects of misery and madness in this kind, that are still represented unto us, abroad, at home, in the midst of us, in our bosoms. (Burton *Anatomy*, 868)

After a lengthy introduction the work was divided into three main parts, the first two dealing with the causes, symptoms, and cures of melancholy, and the last treating specifically the nature of erotic and religious melancholy. Illustrated largely from classical sources with manifold quotations, every nook and cranny in the lore of morbid psychology was expounded. Every potential cause—physical, accidental, or springing from adverse conditions of living was explored. Where internal imbalances were indicated, every kind of remedy to exorcize or counteract them was discussed. The section on lovesickness as a cause of insanity was positively Rabelaisian in its ramifications. The author's enjoyment of his work was evidenced in his good humor (in the modern sense of the word). "Love is madness, a hell, an incurable disease," he wrote. "I shall dilate this subject apart; in the meantime let lovers sigh out the rest" (96). After some two hundred pages of expounding on the problems of love and the most efficacious cures for erotic obsessions, Burton said: "The last refuge and surest remedy . . . when no other means will take effect, is, to let them go together, and enjoy one another. . . . Nature is to be obeyed" (798).

There were many plays dealing with melancholia that appeared during the decade following the publication of *The Anatomy of Melancholy,* including most notably: Fletcher's *Pilgrim* (1621), *Noble Gentleman* (c. 1625), and *The Nice Valour* (date unknown); Middleton's *Changeling* (1623); Massinger's *Duke of Milan* (1623), *New Way to Pay Old Debts* (1626), and *Very Woman* (1634); and Ford's *Lover's Melancholy* (1628) and *Broken Heart* (1633). *The Pilgrim,* written by Fletcher (who had already written *The Mad Lover* [c. 1618], about an elderly general mad with love to the point of violence until he finally wins his lady), contains a scene set in Bedlam (Bethlehem Hospital). It includes a choleric character, Alphonso—said to be "dog-mad"—whom whipping could not cure, and his daughter, Alenda—who suffers from acute love-melancholy. *The Noble Gentleman* has as principal character in a secondary plot Shattellion, a lord who has gone mad through frustrated love for a woman who once refused him, and suffers now from delusions of persecution—his wholly illusory persecutors including the lady he once loved and who now, belatedly, loves him. Finally, when convinced that she does indeed love him and that his fears have been hallucinatory, he falls asleep and wakes fully cured for his insanity. In *The Nice Valour* (a play of uncertain date but probably written in the 1620s) Fletcher used madness for comedy in the character of the Passionate Lord, who seems to assume madness in order to be in the fashion.

Middleton's *Changeling,* a tragedy, involves the theme of counterfeit insanity in its comic subplot. Both Antonio and his friend Franciscus pretend madness—the latter so effectively that he is whipped for his pains. Since he is supposed to have "run mad for love" he at least manages to excite some pity in the lady upon whom he dotes. Both Antonio and Franciscus are confined in a mental hospital, which is presented on stage. Reed, in his book *Bedlam,* claimed that these scenes in *The Changeling* might have represented a satire on Bethlehem Hospital, though the hospital depicted is set elsewhere (pp. 6, 23, 47–48). Alibius, who is in charge, might well have been modeled on the notorious master of Bethlehem at the time the play was written, Dr. Crooke, who, after investigations disclosing his exploitation of his position, was dismissed in 1633.

Massinger's *Duke of Milan* involves a case of insane jealousy and appears to be modeled on Burton's explanation of the disorder. Sforza, the duke, is obsessed with possessive love for his wife, Marcella, to the extent that he commands her death if he himself should die when forced to go abroad. He returns and, convinced of his innocent wife's adultery, succumbs to his jealous impulses—the outcome of immoderate love as Burton interpreted it. As a result, he kills his wife but succumbs to doting over her preserved body in the belief that she is still alive. He dies anticipating she is about to wake, and in dying he cries out, "My whole life was a frenzy" (5.ii). As Burton said:

> Of all passions . . . Love is most violent, and of those bitter potions which this Love Melancholy affords, this bastard Jealousy is the greatest. . . . Tis a more vehement passion, a more furious perturbation, a bitter pain, a fire. . . . a gall corrupting the honey of our life, madness, vertigo, plague, hell. (*Anatomy*, 840)

Indeed, Burton might have been describing Othello when he said of the jealous man:

> He will sometimes sigh, weep, sob for anger . . . slander any man, curse, threaten, brawl, scold, fight; and sometimes again flatter, and speak fair, ask forgiveness, kiss and coll, condemn his rashness and folly. . . . then eftsoons . . . rave, roar, and lay about him like a madman, thump her sides, drag her about perchance. . . . she is a whore, etc., by and by with all submiss compliment intreat her fair. (Ibid., 841)

Massinger's *New Way to Pay Old Debts*, a comedy, portrays the climactic madness of the unscrupulous usurer, Sir Giles Overeach, whose "brain turns" (5.1) in the final act, when he becomes maniacal because his daughter has married her lover against her father's will. He is overcome and carried "to some dark room" (5.1) for treatment. In *The Very Woman* the daughter of the viceroy of Sicily, Almira—a study in the choleric form of love-melancholy—suffers hallucinations and raves for revenge when her rejected suitor, Antonio, wounds the obnoxious Cardenes, the man she loves, in justifiable self-defence. Later in the play, Almira is cured of her choler and accepts the love of Antonio.

Ford, perhaps more than any other dramatist of the later period, drew his case studies of madness from Burton. *The Lover's Melancholy* involves not only the melancholy of Palador, prince of Cyprus, who believes for a while that he has lost his love, but the outright madness of his near-senile father, Meleander, caused by the apparent loss of his daughter. He suffers "close-gripping grief" (4.2.12) and he "sleeps like a hare, with his eyes open" (2.2.2). His case is a curious mixture of choler and melancholy. He is attended by a physician, Corax, who has evidently read Burton in his various strange attempts to cure his patient, who is finally brought back to some semblance of health when his daughter is restored to him. Penthea, in *The Broken Heart*, suffers from love-melancholy because she has been forced into marriage with the elderly and jealous Bassanes, a man she hates. A conventional woman, she feels that she cannot resort to her lover; so she goes mad and dies of self-imposed starvation. "So down she drew her veil, so died" (4.4.19). Bassanes's outrageous jealousy of his bride, enhanced by his seeming impotence, seems directly derived from Burton, like the case of Sforza, described above. Bassanes is conceived as a pathetic character as a result of his intense suffering.

If the publication of *The Anatomy of Melancholy* in 1621 was something of a watershed, there can be little doubt that the two greatest writers on the subject of insanity, Shakespeare and Webster, drew on the same points of interest that inspired Burton in the direst concepts of insanity. This was revealed in two of Webster's great plays—*The White Devil* (1612) and *The Duchess of Malfi* (c. 1614)—and in Shakespeare's preeminent studies of madness—King Lear, Lear's Fool, Ophelia, and Hamlet. Webster's Cornelia in *The White Devil* is an entirely non-melodramatic study of melancholia. Cornelia is a good and virtuous woman caught up in the basest of Machiavellian court intrigues, which involve the unscrupulous and bloody actions of her son Flamineo, and of her daughter Vittoria. Her helplessness in the face of murderous evil finally drives her insane when Flamineo murders her other son, Marcello—the shock that turns melancholy into full madness. In *The Duchess of Malfi* a formalized and macabre parade of madness attends the final dissolution of the doomed duchess—a prey, along with her small children, to the machinations of the psychopathic Ferdinand (a victim of *Lycanthropia,* or imagined transformation into a wolf that mutilates the dead), of his Machiavellian brother, the cardinal, and of their agent, Bosola, who finally turns against them. The duchess manages to retain her sanity to the bitter end of her persecution. The sheer imaginative force of Webster, the nearest to an Edgar Allen Poe in the Jacobean theater, is remarkable for his capacity to lend poetry to the intensity of his dire tragedies.

It is with Shakespeare that we reach the highest level of intuitive understanding of insanity, in *Hamlet* and *King Lear. Hamlet* belongs to the group of Jacobean characters who, for one reason or another, find it necessary (as it seems to them) to assume madness. The greatness of Shakespeare's characterization emerges when we see that this assumed madness, the celebrated "antic disposition" (2.1.172), merges with the excesses of melancholy in his own nature. Nevertheless, he claims:

> I am but mad north-north-west; when the wind is southerly I know a hawk from a handsaw. (2.2.405)

Thus he conforms to the Elizabethan-Jacobean conception of mad behavior—for example, in his visit to Ophelia, which Polonius, a stickler for sound interpretations, immediately accepts as signs of

> the very ecstasy of love,
> Whose violent property fordoes itself
> And leads the will to desperate undertakings
> As oft as any passion under heaven
> That does afflict our natures.
>
> (2.1.102–6)

Shakespeare in *Hamlet* faces us with the ultimate ambiguity of madness because the part was conceived intuitively and not by the textbooks of the time. Hamlet merely conforms to textbook behavior when he is performing for others—the sharp inconsequence of his insulting interchanges with Polonius, with their obscene undermeanings; his bitter melancholia in his dialogue with his mother; his withdrawal from court society; and his savagery with Claudius's secret agents, the spies Rosencrantz and Guildenstern. He is sane enough with those he loves and trusts; acute in his critical remarks on acting, addressed to the players; profound to the end in his observations on life, made to his friend, Horatio. But his behavior to Ophelia borders always on insane melancholia in his bitter disillusion with her weakness of character, and in the soliloquies his melancholy often gives rise to near-insane outbursts of violent vituperation. When finally fraught enough to take action, he kills Polonius like a rat in the wainscot and slays Claudius in a hysterical fit of excitement. It is a direct result of this rich ambiguity that more has been written about Hamlet in the way of interpretation than of any other character in dramatic literature, and success in playing the part on the stage has been the ambition of all great actors from Shakespeare's time to the present.

Ophelia, victim of the machinations of her father and Claudius, succumbs to her own weakness. Taken conventionally in the spirit of the time, she is the evident victim of love-melancholy, and the shock of her father's violent death at the hands of her lost love thrusts her over the border into insanity. Though her mad scenes with the king, queen, and her brother, Laertes, are written with such pathos (and again with an undercurrent of obscene double entendre) as to constitute a magnificent theatrical tour de force, Shakespeare is content to let her form of madness remain conventional; and her death offstage by drowning, as described so pictorially by the queen, conforms to this.

It is with *King Lear* that Shakespeare reaches his highest level in the understanding and presentation of madness in theatrical form. The king's near-senile blindness and vanity lead him to dismiss those most devoted and faithful to him (his daughter Cordelia; his aide Kent) and put himself in the hands of his venal daughters. He only retains as companion his fool, whose caustic sharpness of wit seems "all licensed" (1.4.223) in the bitter home truths he utters to his master's face. In other words, because he is accepted as partially insane, the fool's remarks are either overlooked, indulgently forgiven, or, if resented too immediately, lead to the traditional punishment for the mad—a sound whipping.

The court fools held a special place in privileged society. The lowest class of fool was no doubt little more than a man of poor mentality but with a clownlike capacity to "play the fool." But a more fully accredited fool in court circles was no doubt a man of wit who assumed the guise of madness in order to be allowed licence to express his witticisms at the expense of his betters. The profession, like a branch of acting, even appeals to an "intellectual" like Jaques in *As You Like It*, who, as we have seen, is highly entertained by his encounters with that sharp-witted professional, Touchstone, whose brain he finds to be "as dry as the remainder biscuit / After a voyage," (2.7.39–40) and whose remarks are "cramm'd with observation" (2.7.40–41). "I am ambitious for a motley coat," says Jaques to the Duke (2.7.43). When the Duke agrees he should have one, Jaques adds:

> I must have liberty
> Withal, as large a charter as the wind,
> To blow on whom I please, for so fools have:
> And they that are most galled with my folly,
> They most must laugh.

$$(2.7.47–51)$$

The fool in *King Lear* is of such a kind, but he is so close to Lear, a kind of alter ego at the other end of the social spectrum, that his wits appear to turn in tune with his master's, and he disappears wholly from the play once Lear's balance of mind is restored. It is out of his very insanity, his lack of reason, that his reproachful wisdom flows. He is the most surreal of Shakespeare's characters, his mind flowing rationally-irrationally from point to point but somehow always appositely. His very disappearance is somehow in keeping with his character. All we hear about him is that he has "much pined away" (1.4.80) in the absence of his favorite among Lear's daughters, Cordelia.

As for Lear himself, he is not mad in any Elizabethan-Jacobean sense of the word, nor even in modern terms, at the beginning of the play. He merely wants, at the age of eighty, to hand over power to his successors and indulge his final years. The tragic flaw in his nature is that, when it comes to the carefully planned ceremony of divestment or abdication, neither Cordelia—his favorite daughter, with whom he plans to end his days—nor Kent—his most trusted and honest aide—will play up to his egotistical demands. He is indeed, as he himself admits late in the play, "a very foolish, fond old man" (4.7.60), and, as Goneril shrewdly adds, likely to show an "unruly waywardness that infirm and choleric years bring with them" (1.1.302–3) once he comes to stay with her along with his train of unruly knights. For he expects to remain a king in name and status without any of kingship's responsibilities. Once faced with barefaced opposition to his will and dignity, frustration and choleric rage encourage the seeds of madness to grow in him, as he is the first to realize:

> O let me not be mad, not mad, sweet heaven!
> Keep me in temper, I would not be mad
>
> (1.5.51–52)

And:

> O how this mother* swells up toward my heart!
> Hysterica passio, down, thou climbing sorrow,
> Thy element's below.
>
> (2.2.56–58)

Faced finally with utter deprivation, he is forced to shelter with the lowest of the low among his former subjects—the poor, naked Tom o'Bedlams. His wits leave him, as they leave the Fool. They are both stark mad, subject to hallucination, and Lear remains totally insane until he is rescued by Cordelia, who brings

---

Mother signifies here the old meaning of "womb" or "belly." Hysteria was held to be an upward swelling of the womb or belly, or of vapors emanating from it—the word *vapors* surviving into common use in the eighteenth century, when ladies were constantly suffering from them. The very interesting introduction by Shakespeare of the medical term *hysterica passio,* current at his time, at a highly emotional moment in the play implies that members of the audience would understand its significance. Lear is referring to pain caused by the vapors rising from the belly and affecting the heart; he is trying, he says, to suppress them. The term is used in medical literature of the period, for example, in Harsnett's *Declaration.*

forces from France to wrest him and his former kingdom from the rapacious grasp of her sisters. Lear awakens to sanity, roused from his bed to the curative strains of music.

There has been no single body of literature, dramatic or otherwise, more consistently dedicated, during the span of some fifty years or so, to the nature of insanity, than the work of the Elizabethan-Jacobean dramatists. The only parallel is the modern film, which—stretching back over a similar period of time (the fifty years since the 1920s)—with the backing of contemporary psychology, depicts every form of insanity recognizable to the lay minds of the filmmakers and their audiences. The greatness of the achievements of the Elizabethan-Jacobean dramatists lay in the intuitive artistry they brought to the subject, which constantly overcame the limitations of contemporary clinical knowledge of the mind and its functions. That Shakespeare rose above all others, more especially in *Hamlet* and *King Lear,* was only to be expected, but his transcendence should not be allowed to overshadow what many other dramatists of his time managed to illuminate out of the subject of insanity.

Bibliography

General Psychological Works

From the many works in the first part of the book, the following are those to which most frequent reference was made.

Bacon, S. D. "Current notes: A Student of the Problems of Alcoholism Views *The Lost Weekend.*" *Quarterly Journal of Studies on Alcoholism* (December 1948), 402–5.

Bedrosian, R. C. and S. A. Kagel. "A Woman under the Influence: An Example of Multiple Victimization Within a Family." *American Journal of Family Therapy* 7, no. 3 (1979): 51–59.

Bockoven, J. S. *Moral Treatment in American Psychiatry.* New York: Springer Publishing Co., 1963.

Boyers, R., and R. Orrill, eds. *R. D. Laing and Antipsychiatry.* New York: Harper & Row, 1971.

Bozzuto, J. "Cinematic Neurosis Following *The Exorcist.*" *Journal of Nervous and Mental Disease* 161(1974): 43–48.

Bromberg, W. *Crime and the Mind: An Outline of Psychiatric Criminology.* New York: Greenwood, 1948.

———. *The Mold of Murder: A Psychiatric Study of Homocide,* New York: Grune, 1963.

Brower, D. "An Opinion Poll on Reactions to *The Lost Weekend.*" *Quarterly Journal of Studies on Alcoholism* 7 (1946): 596–98.

Brown, N. O. *Life Against Death: The Psychoanalytic Meaning of History.* Wesleyan, Conn.: Wesleyan University Press, 1959.

———. *Love's Body.* New York: Random House, 1968.

Burton, R. *The Anatomy of Melancholy.* Edited by F. Dell and P. Jordan. New York: Tudor Press, 1941.

Cason, H. "The Concept of the Psychopath." *American Journal of Orthopsychiatry* 18 (1948).

Chodorkoff, B., and S. Baxter. "Secrets of a Soul: An Early Psychoanalytic Film Venture." *American Image* 30 (1973): 221–47.

Deutsch. A. *Shame of the States.* New York: Harcourt, 1948.

Ellenberger, H. *The Discovery of the Unconscious.* New York: Basic Books, 1970.

Erikson, E. *Childhood and Society.* New York. W. W. Norton, 1963.

Fanon, R. *The Wretched of the Earth.* New York: Grove Press, 1966.

Ferber, A., ed. *The Book of Family Therapy.* Boston: Houghton Mifflin, 1973.

Flanagan, J. C. *USAAI, Aviation Psychology Research Report, No. 1.* Washington, D.C.: U.S. Government Printing Office, 1948.

Foucault, M. *Madness and Civilization: A History of Insanity in the Age of Reason.* New York: Random House, 1973.

346

Frankl, V. E. *Man's Search for Meaning.* Translated by Ilse Lasch. Boston: Beacon Press, 1962.

Frazier, S. H. "Violence and Social Impact." In *Research and the Psychiatric Patient,* edited by J. C. Schoolar and C. Gaitz. New York: Brunner-Mazel, 1975.

Freud, S. *New Introductory Lectures on Psychoanalysis.* Translated by J. Strachey. New York: W. W. Norton, 1964.

Fromm, E. *The Anatomy of Human Destructiveness.* New York: Holt, Reinhart and Winston, 1973.

Goffman, E., ed. *Asylums.* New York: Doubleday, 1961.

———. *The Presentation of Self in Everyday Life.* New York: The Overlook Press, 1973.

Grinker, R. *The Borderline Syndrome.* New York: Basic Books, 1968.

Grinker, R., and J. Spiegal. *Men Under Stress,* Philadelphia: Blakiston Press, 1945.

Guerin, J. P., ed. *Family Therapy: Theory and Practice.* New York: Wiley & Son, 1976.

Hagenauer, F., and J. W. Hamilton. "*Straw Dogs:* Aggression and Violence." *American Imago* 30 (1973): 221–45.

Hale, G. N. *Freud and the Americans.* New York: Oxford University Press, 1971.

Haskell, M. *From Reverence to Rape: The Treatment of Women in the Movies.* New York: Penguin Books, 1973.

Hesler, H. "The Effects of Vicariously Experiencing Supernatural Violent Events: A Case Study of *The Exorcist*'s impact. *Journal of Individual Psychology* 31 (Nov. 1975): 158–70.

Kardiner, A. *The Traumatic Neuroses of War.* New York: Hoeber, 1941.

Jarvie, I. C. *Toward A Sociology of Cinema.* London: Routledge, 1970.

Jones, M. *The Therapeutic Community.* New York: Basic Books, 1953.

Kesey, K. *One Flew Over the Cuckoo's Nest.* New York: Viking Press, 1962.

Kuhn, T. *The Structure of Scientific Revolutions.* Chicago: University of Chicago Press, 1970.

Laing, R. D. *The Divided Self.* New York: Penguin Books, 1965.

Lemert, E. "Paranoia and the Dynamics of Exclusion." *Sociometry* 25, no. 1 (1962).

Lester, D. "Murder: A Review." *Corrective and Social Psychiatry* 19, no. 4 (1973): 40–50.

Lief, A. *The Commonsense Psychiatry of Adolf Meyer.* New York: McGraw-Hill, 1948.

Lifton, R. J. *Thought Reform and the Psychology of Totalism: A Study of Brainwashing in China.* New York: W. W. Norton, 1961.

Lunde, D. *Murder and Madness.* Stanford, Calif.; San Francisco Book Company, 1976.

Mahler, M. "A Study of the Separation-Individuation Process and Its Possible Application to Borderline Phenomena in the Psychoanalytic Situation." *Psychoanalytic Study of the Child* 26 (1971).

Marcuse, H. *Counterrevolution and Revolt.* Boston: Beacon Press, 1972.

———. *Essays on Liberation.* Boston: Beacon Press, 1969.

Mayer, J. P. *Sociology of Film: Studies and Documents.* Revised ed. New York: Arno, 1971.

Megargee, I. "Undercontrolled and Overcontrolled Personality Types in Extreme Antisocial Aggression." *Psychological Monographs* 80 (1966).

Miller, M. "Prognosis in Periodic and Daily Inebriates." no. 6 *Quarterly Journal of Studies on Alcoholism* 5 (1944): 430–34.

Munsterberg, H. *The Photoplay: A Psychological Study.* New York: Dover Publications, 1970.

Murray, H. *Explorations in Personality: A Clinical Experimental Study of 50 Men of College Age.* New York: Wiley, 1938.

Ovesey, L. "Pseudohomosexuality, The Paranoid Mechanism and Paranoia." *Psychiatry* 18 (1955): 163–73.

Perrucci, R. *Circle of Madness: On Being Insane and Institutionalized in America.* Englewood Cliffs, N.J., Prentice-Hall Inc., 1979.

Perry, J. W. *The Self in Psychotic Process.* Berkeley and Los Angeles, University of California Press, 1953.

Quen, J. "Anglo-American Criminal Insanity: An Historical Perspective. *Journal of the History of the Behavioral Sciences* 10 (July, 1974): 313–23.

Rabkin, L. "The Celluloid Couch: Psychiatrists in American Films." Presented at the annual meeting of the American Psychological Association, Division 10 (September 1977).

Reichman, F. F. *Principles of Intensive Psychotherapy.* Chicago: University of Chicago Press, 1950.

Reiff, P. *The Mind of the Moralist.* New York: Doubleday, 1961.

Renner, J. A. "The Changing Patterns of Psychiatric Problems in Vietnam," *Comprehensive Psychiatry* 14, no. 2 (1973): 169–81.

Rosen, G. *Madness in Society.* New York: Harper & Row, 1969.

Satten, J., K. Menninger, and I. Rosen. "Murder Without Apparent Motive: A Study in Personality Disorganization." *American Journal of Psychiatry* 117 (1960): 48–53.

Scheff, T. *Being Mentally Ill: A Sociological Theory.* Chicago: Aldine Publishing Co., 1966.

Works about Films and Allied Subjects

Adair, G. *Vietnam on Film.* New York: Proteus, 1981.

Artaud, A. *The Theatre and its Double.* New York: Grove Press, 1958.

Butler, I. *The War Film.* New York: A. S. Barnes, 1973.

Cook, J., and M. Lewington. *Images of Alcoholism.* New York: Zoetrope, 1979.

Eisner, Lotte. *The Haunted Screen: Expressionism in the German Cinema.* Berkeley and Los Angeles, University of California, 1969.

Geduld, M. *Filmmakers on Filmmaking.* Bloomington: Indiana University Press, 1967. (Statements by Buñuel, Bergman, Fellini, Antonioni, etc.)

Gelmis, J. *The Film Director as Superstar.* New York: Penguin Books, 1974. (Statements by Cassavetes, Bertolucci, Forman, Polanski, Coppola, Penn, Nichols, Kubrick, etc.)

Glucksman, A. *Violence on the Screen: a Report on Research into the Effects on Young People of Scenes of Violence in Films and Television.* London: BFI Publications, 1971.

Greenberg, H. R. *The Movies on your Mind: Film Classics on the Couch from Fellini to Frankenstein.* New York: Saturday Review Press, 1975.

Harcourt, P. *Six European Directors.* Baltimore: Penguin Books, 1974.

Huaco, G. A. *The Sociology of Film Art.* New York: Basic Books, 1965.

Jones, M. D. and F. McClure. *Hollywood at War.* New York: A. S. Barnes, 1975.

Kawin, B. F. *Mindscreen: Bergman, Godard, and First Person Film.* Princeton: Princeton University Press, 1978.

Kracauer, S. *From Caligari to Hitler: a Psychological History of the German Film.* Princeton: Princeton University Press, 1947.

Kolker, R. P. *A Cinema of Loneliness: Penn, Kubrick, Coppola, Scorsese, Altman.* New York: Oxford University Press, 1980.

Manvell, R. *Films and the Second World War.* New York: A. S. Barnes, 1974.

Manvell, R., and H. Fraenkel. *The German Cinema.* New York: Praeger, 1971.

Mason, J. L. *The Identity Crisis Theme in American Feature Film: 1960–69.* New York: Arno, 1977.

Mellen, J. *Women and their Sexuality in the New Film.* New York: Horizon, 1973.

Monaco, J. *American Film Now: the People, the Power, the Money, the Movies.* New York: Oxford University Press, 1979.

Movie Lot to Beachhead: the Motion Picture Goes to War and Prepares for the Future. Editors of *Look Magazine.* New York: Arno, 1980.

Powdermaker, H. *Hollywood, the Dream Factory.* New ed. New York: Arno, 1979.

Pye, M., and L. Myles. *The Movie Brats.* New York: Holt, Rinehart and Winston, 1979.

Reed, R. R., Jr. *Bedlam on the Jacobean Stage.* Cambridge: Harvard University Press, 1952.

Rosten, L. C. *Hollywood: the Movie Colony, the Movie Makers.* New ed. New York: Arno, 1970.

Sandford, John. *The New German Cinema.* New York: Da Capo, 1980.

Sarris, A. *The American Cinema: Directors and Directions, 1929–1968.* New York: E. P. Dutton, 1968.

————. *Interviews with Film Directors.* New York: Avon, 1969. (Interviews with Antonioni, Bergman, Buñuel, Chabrol, Dreyer, Fellini, Hitchcock, Huston, Lang, Peckinpah, Welles, etc.)

Shain, R. *An Analysis of Motion Pictures about War Released by the American Film Industry 1939–1970.* New York: Arno, 1976.

Shindler, C. *Hollywood Goes to War: Films and American Society, 1939–1952.* London: Routledge and Kegan Paul, 1979.

Simon, B. *Mind and Madness in Ancient Greece: the Classical Roots of Modern Psychiatry.* Ithaca: Cornell University Press, 1979.

Taylor, J. R. *Cinema Eye, Cinema Ear.* New York: Hill and Wang, 1964. (Includes studies of Bergman, Buñuel, Fellini, and Hitchcock.)

Tuska, J. *Close-Up: the Contemporary Director.* Metuchen, N.J.: Scarecrow Press, 1981. (Includes critical essays on Peckinpah, Altman, Scorsese, and Polanski.)

Tyler, P. *The Hollywood Hallucination.* New ed. New York: Simon and Schuster, 1970.

————. *Magic and Myth in the Movies.* New York: Holt, 1947.

Wahl, O. "Six TV Myths about Mental Illness." *TV Guide* (13 March 1976).

White, D. M. and R. Averson. *The Celluloid Weapon: Social Comment and the American Film.* Boston: Beacon Press, 1972.

Works about Individual Directors

Allen, Woody
Lax, E. *On Being Funny: Woody Allen and Comedy.* New York: Woodhill, 1979.

Palmer, M. *Woody Allen.* New York: Proteus, 1980.

Yacowar, M. *Loser Take All: the Comic Art of Woody Allen.* New York: Ungar, 1979.

Script. Allen, W. *Interiors.* In *Four Films of Woody Allen.* New York: Random House, 1983.

Altman, Robert
Feineman, N. *Persistence of Vision: the Films of Robert Altman.* New York: Arno, 1978.

Kass, J. *Robert Altman.* New York: Popular Library, 1978.

Antonioni, Michaelangelo

Armes, R. *The Ambiguous Image.* Bloomington: Indiana University Press, 1976.

Cameron, I., and Robin Wood, *Antonioni.* New York: Praeger, 1969.

Cowie, P. *Antonioni, Bergman, Resnais.* New York: A. S. Barnes, 1968.

Hass, R., ed. *Focus on Blow-Up.* Englewood Cliffs, N.J.: Prentice-Hall, 1971.

Leprohon, P. *Michaelangelo Antonioni.* New York: Simon and Schuster, 1968.

Lyons, R. J. *Michaelangelo Antonioni's Neo-Realism.* New York, Arno, 1973.

Scripts. Michaelangelo Antonioni: *Blow Up,* London: Lorrimer, 1971; *The Passenger,* New York: Grove Press, 1975.

Bergman, Ingmar

Bergman, I. *Bergman on Bergman.* New York: Simon and Schuster, 1973.

Cowie, P. *Sweden.* 2 vols. New York: A. S. Barnes, 1970.

Donner, J. *The Personal Vision of Ingmar Bergman.* New York: Arno, 1964.

Kaminsky, S. M., ed. *Ingmar Bergman: Essays in Criticism.* New York: Oxford University Press, 1975.

Manvell, R. *Ingmar Bergman: an Appreciation.* New York: Arno, 1980.

Simon, J. *Ingmar Bergman Directs.* New York: Harcourt Brace, 1972.

Sontag, S. *Styles of Radical Will.* New York: Farrar Straus and Giroux, 1969.

Ullmann, Liv. *Changing. New York: Knopf, 1976; Bantam, 1978.*

Wood, R. Ingmar Bergman. New York: Praeger, 1959.

Young, V. *Cinema Borealis: Ingmar Bergman and the Swedish Ethos.* New York: Avon, 1971.

Scripts. Bergman, I.: *Face to Face,* New York: Pantheon, 1976; *Through a Glass Darkly,* in *Three Films by Ingmar Bergman,* New York: Grove Press, 1970; *Persona,* New York: Grossman, 1972.

Buñuel, Luis

Aranda, F. *Luis Buñuel: A Critical Biography.* New York: Da Capo, 1976.

Buache, F. *The Cinema of Luis Buñuel.* New York: A. S. Barnes, 1973.

Durgnat, R. *Luis Buñuel.* Berkeley and Los Angeles, University of California Press, 1970.

Kyrou, A. *Luis Buñuel: an Introduction.* New York: Simon and Schuster, 1963.

Mellen, J., ed. *The World of Luis Buñuel.* New York: Oxford University Press, 1978.

Script. Buñuel, L. *Belle de Jour.* New York: Simon and Schuster, 1971.

Capra, Frank

Capra, F. *The Name above the Title.* New York: Bantam, 1971.

Maland, C. J. *Frank Capra.* Boston: Twayne, 1980.

Chabrol, Claude

Armes, R. *The French Cinema since 1946.* Vol. 2: *The Personal Style.* New York: A. S. Barnes, 1966.

Wood, R., and M. Walker. *Claude Chabrol.* New York: Praeger, 1970.

Coppola, Francis Ford

Coppola, E. *Notes: a Record of the Day-to-Day Events . . . During the Making of Apocalypse Now.* New York: Pocket Books, 1979.

Johnson, R. K. *Francis Ford Coppola.* Boston: Twayne, 1980.

Pye, M., and L. Myles. *The Movie Brats.* New York: Holt, Rinehart and Winston, 1979.

Dreyer, Carl Theodor
Bordwell, D. *Filmguide to The Passion of Joan of Arc.* Bloomington: Indiana University Press, 1973.
Dreyer, C. T. *Dreyer in Double Reflection.* New York: E. P. Dutton, 1973. (Translation of *Om Filmen,* his writings about the film, edited by D. Skoller.)
Milne, T. *The Cinema of Carl Dreyer.* New York: A. S. Barnes, 1971.

Fassbinder, Rainer Werner
Rayns, T. *Fassbinder.* 2d revised edition. New York: Zoetrope, 1980.

Fellini, Federico
Bachman, G. *Fellini: an Interview.* Bk. 1 of *Film.* New York: Grove Press, 1959.
Bondaneila, P. *Essays in Criticism: Federico Fellini.* New York: Oxford University Press, 1978.
Budgen, S. *Fellini.* London: British Film Institute, 1966.
Fellini, F. *Fellini on Fellini.* New York: Delacorte, 1974.
Murray, E. *Fellini, the Artist.* New York: Ungar, 1976.
Perry, T. *Filmguide to 8½.* Bloomington: Indiana University Press, 1975.
Rhode, E. *Fellini's Double City.* In *The Emergence of Film Art,* edited by L. Jacobs. 2d ed., New York: W. W. Norton, 1979.
Rosenthal, S. *Cinema of Federico Fellini.* New York: A. S. Barnes, 1974.
Ross, L. "Fellini." *New Yorker* (30 October 1965).
Salachas, G. *Federico Fellini.* New York: Crown, 1969.
Solmi, A. *Fellini.* New York: Humanities Press, 1967.
Script. Fellini, F. *Juliet of the Spirits.* New York: Ballantine, 1966.

Frankenheimer, John
Pratley, G. *The Cinema of John Frankenheimer.* New York: A. S. Barnes, 1969.

Herzog, Werner
Goodwin, M. "Herzog: the God of Wrath." In *American Film* (June 1982), 36–73.
O'Toole, L. "The Great Ecstasy of Filmmaker Herzog." In *Film Comment* (November–December 1979), 33–48.

Hitchcock, Alfred
Anobile, R. J. *Alfred Hitchcock's Psycho.* New York: Avon, 1974.
Durgnat, R. *The Strange Case of Alfred Hitchcock.* Boston: MIT Press, 1975.
LaValley, A. J., ed. *Focus on Hitchcock.* Englewood Cliffs, N.J.: Prentice-Hall, 1972.
Naremore, J. *Filmguide to Psycho.* Bloomington: Indiana University Press, 1973.
Spoto, D. *The Art of Alfred Hitchcock.* New York: Hopkinson, 1976.
Taylor, J. R. *Hitch: The Life and Times of Alfred Hitchcock.* New York: Berkley, 1978.
Truffaut, F. *Hitchcock.* (interviews). New York: Simon and Schuster, 1967.
Wood, R. *Hitchcock's Films.* New York: A. S. Barnes, 1965.

Huston, John
Huston, J. *An Open Book.* New York: Knopf, 1980.
Kaminsky, S. *John Huston.* Boston: Houghton Mifflin, 1978.
Pratley, G. *The Cinema of John Huston.* New York: A. S. Barnes, 1976.

Ross, L. *Picture*. New York: Avon, 1952.

Script. Huston, J. *Let There Be Light*. In Book 2 of *Film*, edited by Robery Hughes. New York: Grove Press, 1962.

Kazan, Elia
Kazan, E. *Kazan on Kazan*. Edited by M. Ciment. New York: Viking Press, 1972.

Kubrick, Stanley
Kagan, N. *The Cinema of Stanley Kubrick*. New York: Grove Press, 1975.

Walker, A. *Stanley Kubrick Directs*. New York: Harcourt Brace, 1971.

Lang, Fritz
Eisner, L. *Fritz Lang*. Edited by D. Robinson. London: Secker and Warburg, 1977.

Jensen, M. *The Cinema of Fritz Lang*. New York: A. S. Barnes, 1969.

Script. *M.* In *Masterworks of the German Cinema*, edited by R. Manvell. New York: Harper & Row, 1973.

Mamoulian, Rouben
Milne, T. *Rouben Mamoulian*. Bloomington: Indiana University Press, 1970.

Nichols, Mike
Schuth, H. W. *Mike Nichols*. Boston: Twayne, 1978.

Pabst, G. W.
Atwell, L. *G. W. Pabst*. Boston: Twayne, 1977.

Peckinpah, S
McKinney, D. *Sam Peckinpah*. Boston: Twayne, 1980.

Penn, Arthur
Cawelti, J. G. *Focus on Bonnie and Clyde*. Englewood Cliffs, N.J.: Prentice-Hall, 1973.

Wood, R. *Arthur Penn*. New York: Praeger, 1969.

Polanski, Roman
Butler, I. *The Cinema of Roman Polanski*. New York: A. S. Barnes, 1970.

Kiernan, T. *Repulsion: Life and Times of Roman Polanski*. New York: Grove, 1980.

Leaming, B. *Polanski*. New York: Simon and Schuster, 1981.

Script. Polanski, R. *Repulsion*. In R. Polanski, *Three Films*. London: Lorrimer, 1975.

Preminger, Otto
Pratley, G. *The Cinema of Otto Preminger*. New York: A. S. Barnes, 1971.

Preminger, O. *Preminger: an Autobiography*. New York: Doubleday, 1977.

Ray, Nicholas
Kreidl, J. F. *Nicholas Ray*. Boston: Twayne, 1977.

Roeg, Nicholas
Feineman, N. *Nicholas Roeg*. Boston: Twayne, 1978.

Resnais, Alain
Armes, R. *The Cinema of Alain Resnais*. New York: A. S. Barnes, 1968.

Monaco, James. *Alain Resnais*. New York: Oxford University Press, 1979.

Ward, John. *Alain Resnais, or the Theme of Time*. New York: Doubleday, 1968.

Russell, Ken
Atkins, T. R. *Ken Russell.* New York: Simon and Schuster, 1976.

Baxter, J. *An Appalling Talent: Ken Russell.* London: Michael Joseph, 1973.

Wilson, C. *Ken Russell: a Director in Search of a Hero.* London: Intergroup Publishing, 1974.

Truffaut, François
Insdorf, Annette. *François Truffaut.* Boston: Twayne, 1980.

Script. Truffaut, F. *The Story of Adèle H.* New York: Grove Press, 1976.

Scorsese, Martin
Monaco, J. *American Film Now: the People, the Power, the Money, the Movies.* New York: Oxford University Press, 1979.

Pye, M., and L. Myles. *The Movie Brats.* New York: Holt, Rinehart and Winston, 1979.

Welles, Orson
Bazin, A. *Orson Welles.* New York: Harper & Row, 1978.

Cowie, P. *The Cinema of Orson Welles.* New York: A. S. Barnes, 1972.

Gottesman, R. *Focus on Citizen Kane.* Englewood Cliffs, N.J.: Prentice-Hall, 1971.

———. *Focus on Orson Welles.* Englewood Cliffs, N.J.: Prentice-Hall, 1976.

Higham, C. *The Films of Orson Welles.* Berkeley and Los Angeles, University of California, 1970.

McBride, J. *Orson Welles.* New York: Viking, 1972.

Script. *Citizen Kane.* In P. Kael, *The Citizen Kane Book.* Boston: Little, Brown, 1971.

Wilder, Billy
Dick, B. F. *Billy Wilder.* Boston: Twayne, 1980.

Madsen, A. *Billy Wilder.* London: Secker and Warburg, 1968.

Seidman, S. *The Film Career of Billy Wilder.* Boston: G. K. Hall, 1980.

General Index

Abolitionist view, 52
Abraham, Karl, 72, 115
Adam, Brooke, 154
Adler, A., 34
Aesculapius, 25
Aggression, 102
Aggression-frustration theory, 101
Aherne, Brian, 176
Albee, Edward, 319
Alcoholics Anonymous, 135, 136
Alcoholism: as a medical model, 135
Aldrich, Robert, 317–18
Allen, Woody, 19, 252
Allin, Alex, 294
Alpert, Richard, 168
Altman, Robert, 19, 246–48
American Journal of Family Therapy, 41
American Psychiatric Association, 153, 179
American Psychoanalytical Association, 75
Anatomy of Melancholy (Burton), 23
Andersson, Bibi, 282
Anti-establishment movement, 50
Antipsychiatry, 45, 49, 50, 52, 168, 169, 178
Antonioni, Michelangelo, 155, 286–87
Anxiety reactions, 118
Aranda, Francisco, 195
Ardrey, R., 85
Army Medical Corps, 177
Arnold, Edward, 161
Arthur, Jean, 161
Ashby, Hal, 205, 243
Astaire, Fred, 71
Attenborough, Richard, 207, 264, 295
Ayres, Lew, 176

Bacon, S. D., 138
Bancroft, Anne, 286, 306
Bartlett, Hall, 203
Bates, Alan, 165
Bateson, G., 40
Beach Boys, 139
Beatty, Warren, 198
Beauchamp, Christine, 63, 65

Bedrosian, Richard, 41, 42, 43
Beers, Clifford, 24
Behavioral discontrol, 105
Being Mentally Ill (Scheff), 51
Bellochio, Marco, 234
Bellow, Saul, 157
Benner, Richard, 275
Bergman, Andrew, 160
Bergman, Ingmar, 19, 43, 180, 218, 228–29, 252, 279–82, 312–13, 325
Bergman, Ingrid, 175, 301
Berliner Tageblatt, 81
Bernheim, H., 61
Bertolucci, Bernardo, 257–58
Bible, the: and madness, 22
Blake, William, 18
Blatty, William Peter, 66, 226–28
Bogarde, Dirk, 209, 212
Bogart, Humphrey, 150, 152
Boorman, John, 227–28
Borderline personality, 20, 78–80, 88, 124, 131, 142–44
Born criminal, 98
Bottome, Phyllis, 174
Bourguignon, Serge, 307
Boyer, Charles, 174
Bozzuto, J., 67
Brainwashing, 113, 121
Brando, Marlon, 21, 258, 287–88
Bresson, Robert, 212, 309
Breuer, Josef, 236
Brill, A. A., 149–50
Bromberg, Walter, 91, 98
Brooks, Dr., 179
Brooks, Peter, 266–68
Brooks, Richard, 248–51, 259–60
Brower, Daniel, 138–39
Brown, Norman O., 50, 167
Brunswick, Ruth Mack, 35
Buñuel, Luis, 19, 194–96, 221–24
Burton, Richard, 180, 225, 320
Burton, Robert, 23
Byington, Spring, 161

Cagney, James, 99, 318
Caine, Michael, 93, 182
Calley, Lieutenant, 126
Cambridge University, 163
Cammell, Donald, 278
Capote, Truman, 104
Capra, Frank, 160–64, 174, 322
Carroll, Leo G., 175
Cartwright, Veronica, 155
Case study movies, 177
Cassavetes, John, 40, 41, 43, 321
Cates, Gilbert, 306
Cavalcanti, Alberto, 207
Cavani, Liliana, 271
"Celluloid Couch: Psychiatrists in American Films," (Rabkin), 172
Chabrol, Claude, 199, 204, 316–17
Chapman, Mark, 109
Character disorder, 123, 124, 131
Charcot, Jean Martin, 59–61
Child murder, 81
Chodoff, Paul, 52
Cimino, Michael, 131, 207
Class conflicts, 159
Clayton, Jack, 251, 285–86, 306
Cleaver, Eldridge, 85
Cleckley, Harvey, 66, 98, 100, 310–12
Clifford, Graeme, 234–35
Clift, Montgomery, 177, 238
Clutter family, 104
Cobb, Lee J., 176
Cobbs, P. M., 154
Coconscious personality dissociation, 65
Colbert, Claudette, 172
Collinson, Peter, 274
Combat fatigue, 113, 114, 117, 118, 120, 122
Common-sense theory, 33, 35
Communication, family, 39
Community Mental Health Center, 51, 52
Concini, Ennio de, 244
Conrad, Joseph, 189, 224
Conspiracy, 153
Conspiratorial model, 26, 40, 156
Cook, Elisha, Jr., 150
Cooke, Alistair, 66, 311
Cooper, Gary, 160, 174
Cooper, James Fenimore, 131
Coppola, Eleanor, 192
Coppola, Francis, 189–92
Corman, Roger, 196–97
Cornfeld, Hubert, 284
Counter-culture, drug-oriented, 53
Cult films, 164
Curtis, Jamie Lee, 92

Curtis, Tony, 92
Custer, General George, 83

Dali, Salvador, 301
Dass, Baba Ram, 50, 168
Davis, Bette, 34, 272, 318
Dawson, Jan, 258
Dean, James, 106, 107, 108, 141, 151, 286
Death instinct, 70,
De Broca, Philippe, 254–55
De Havilland, Olivia, 47
De-institutionalization, 45, 49, 51, 52, 109
Delirium tremens, 134, 135, 138
Demonic possession, 18, 57
Deneuve, Catherine, 196
De Niro, Robert, 21, 109, 208, 308
De Palma, Brian, 155, 181, 182, 183, 216
Deutsch, Albert, 46
Deutsch, Helene, 35
Dickinson, Angie, 93, 182
Dieterle, William, 118, 246
Dietrich, Marlene, 197
Diller, Phyllis, 144
Disciplinary-administrative problems, 123
Dishonorable discharge, 123
Dix, Dorothea, 24, 45
Dmytryk, Edward, 201
Dollard, J., 101, 103
Donner, Clive, 202
Dostoevsky, Fyodor, 211
Douglas, Kirk, 52
Dreyer, Carl, 212
Drug abuse, 134, 140, 145
Drug culture, 139, 140
Dulac, Germaine, 294–95
Dunaway, Faye, 198
Dürer, Albrecht, 18
Durham Rule, 97

Earp, Wyatt, 83
Eastwood, Clint, 213, 283–84, 308
Ebbinghaus, H., 162
Ecological approach, 38
Edison, Thomas, 18
Edwards, Blake, 207
Effective activity, 118
Ellenberger, H., 58, 63
Ellis, Havelock, 91
Esalen Institute, 169
Ethology, 85
Exorcism, 57, 58
Experimental learning theory, 65
Explorations in Personality: A Clinical Experimental Study of 50 Men of College Age (Murray), 163

Failed ego identity, 142
Fairbanks, Douglas, 173
Falk, Peter, 41
Family model, 26, 39
Family therapy, 38, 39, 156
Fanon, Franz, 84, 85, 88, 154
Farmer, Frances, 234–35
Fassbinder, Rainer Werner, 209–12, 323
FBI, 155
Fear of death, 115
Fechner, G. T., 162
Fellini, Federico, 19, 217–21
Feraing, F., 176
Ferenczi, Sandor, 115
Fields, W. C., 160
Film noir, 176
Finch, Peter, 271
Flanagan, J. C., 118
Flynn, John, 297
Fonda, Jane, 126, 178
Fonda, Peter, 217
Forbes, Bryan, 293–94
Forman, Milos, 53, 272–73
Fowles, John, 204
Frankenheimer, John, 114, 245–46, 265–66
Franklin, Benjamin, 24, 59
Frazier, Shervert, 105, 106, 108
Freedman, Lawrence, 109
French Revolution, 44
French Royal Commission, 59
Freud, Sigmund, 24, 25, 31–36, 39, 47, 57, 60, 61, 63, 65, 67, 70, 72–76, 81, 89, 91, 99, 115, 116, 126, 148, 149, 151, 156, 162, 163, 173, 236–42
Friedkin, Michael, 67, 68, 205, 225–28
From Caligari to Hitler (Kracauer), 60
Fromm-Reichmann, Freida, 35
From Reverence to Rape (Haskell), 34
Furie, Sydney J., 256–57

Gable, Clark, 46
Galeen, Henrik, 305
Gance, Abel, 113, 253–54
Garfield, S., 162
Garfunkel, Art, 77
Garland, Judy, 140
Garrit, Pat, 83
Gavin, John, 66
Genn, Leo, 47
Germ theory, 25
Godard, Jean-Luc, 287
Goebbels, Joseph, 173
Goffman, E., 49, 157
Goldblum, Jeff, 155
Goldman, Bo, 53
Goldman, Eric, 99

Goldwyn, Samuel, 72, 173
Good life, the, 38
Goodman, Paul, 167
Gottlieb, T., 59
Goya, Francisco, 18
Grable, Betty, 46
Granger, Farley, 150
Great Depression, 159–60, 162
Green, Guy, 268
Green, Hannah, 35
Greenstreet, Sydney, 150
Grier, W. H., 154
Griffith, D. W., 113
Group bonding, 121
Guille, Frances V., 302
Guinness, Sir Alec, 244

Hagenauer, Fedor, 86, 88, 89
Hall, E. T., 86
Hamilton, James W., 86, 88, 89
Hammett, Dashiell, 150
Haskell, Molly, 34
Hart, Moss, 161
Harvey, Laurence, 65
Harvey, William, 23
Hauben, Lawrence, 53
Hebb, D. O., 121, 122
Hecht, Ben, 176
Heisler, H., 67
Helplessness, 117, 120
Hendrix, Jimi, 141
Herr, Michael, 190
Herzog, Werner, 156, 188, 191, 243–44
Hickock, Dick, 248–51
Hidden Dimension, The (Hall), 86
Hill, George Roy, 297
Hinckley, John, Jr., 109
Hippocrates, 22, 23, 25
Hirsch, Judd, 183
Hitchcock, Alfred, 66, 89, 90, 150, 175, 176, 182, 205, 227, 235–36, 246, 268–69, 284–85, 287, 292, 300–302, 303, 315, 317, 325
Hitler, Adolph, 162, 173, 174, 244
Hoffman, Dustin, 86
Holden, William, 176
Holiday, Billie, 77, 256
Homeopathic medicine, 23
Hooke's Law of Elasticity, 121
Hooper, Tobe, 310
Hopkins, Anthony, 264, 324
Hopkins, Miriam, 214
Hopper, Dennis, 192, 217
Horney, Karen, 34, 36, 37
Hospital general, 23
Houston, Penelope, 256

Hugo, Adèle, 302
Human potential movement, 169
Humours theory of illness, 22
Huston, John, 177, 236–42, 264, 287–88, 320–21
Huxley, Aldous, 212
Hydrotherapy, 48
Hypnosis, 59, 60
Hysteria, 57, 59, 60, 63, 65

Id, 25
"Images of the Mind: Psychiatry in the Commercial Film," (Schneider), 172
Impaired model, 26
Implosive therapy, 67
Impotence, 72, 73, 74
In Cold Blood (Capote), 20
I Never Promised You A Rose Garden (Green), 35
Information explosion, 37
Inner archetypal mediators, 168
Instinctual life, 54
Institute of Analytical Psychology (Zurich), 163
Interaction: mother/child, 40; mother/daughter, 35, 36
Interdependence, 77
Interdisciplinary approach, 162
International Congress of Psychology, 162
Interpretation of Dreams, The (Freud), 73
Inter-rater reliability, 21

Jackson, Glenda, 267
Janet, Pierre, 59, 61
Jannings, Emil, 197
Janov, Arthur, 178
Janowitz, Hans, 200
Jessua, Alaim, 316
Johnson, Nunnally, 310–12
Jones, Brian, 141
Jones, Ernest, 115
Jones, Maxwell, 45
Joplin, Janis, 139–41
Jukes family, 98
Jung, Carl, 34, 163

Kael, Pauline, 53, 92, 157
Kanew, Jeff, 270
Kastle, Leonard, 245
Kaufmann, George S., 161
Kazan, Elia, 305
Keaton, Diane, 260
Kennedy, John F. (U.S. President), 83, 103, 153
Kennedy, Robert, F., 83, 84
Kent State massacre, 84
Kernberg, O., 79
Kerr, Deborah, 251
Kesey, Ken, 50, 52, 53, 179, 273

Kessel, Joseph, 195
King, Henry, 313–14
King, Martin Luther, Jr., 84, 103
Kingsley Hall, 51
Kinski, Klaus, 188
Kirk, Michael, 52
Kiss, The (Klimt), 78
Klimt, Gustave, 78
Kohut, H., 88, 89
Koster, Henry, 243
Kracauer, Siegfried, 61, 200, 214
Kraepelin, Emil, 98
Krafft-Ebing, Richard, 91
Kramer, Stanley, 175, 253
Krauss, Werner, 200
Kubrick, Stanley, 84, 113, 215–16, 276, 304
Kurtin, Peter, 81, 82, 83

Labeling theory, 51
Laing, R. D., 43, 50, 51, 167, 168
Lambroso, Cesare, 98
Lang, Fritz, 20, 80, 81, 82, 173, 214–15, 262–63, 269, 323
Lange, Jessica, 235
Lansbury, Angela, 53
Lasch, Christopher, 89
Lavi, Deliah, 227
Leary, Timothy, 50, 167, 169
Leigh, Janet, 66, 90, 92, 315
Leigh, Vivien, 305
Leites, N., 172
Lemert, Edwin, 156
Lemmon, Jack, 207
Lennon, John, 109
Lifton, Robert, 125
Lindner, Robert, 98
Litvak, Anatole, 46, 47, 298–300
Loach, Ken, 229–34
Loeb, Leopold, 150
London blitz, 116
London Daily Sketch, 137
Lorenz, Konrad, 85
Lorre, Peter, 82, 150, 263, 264
Losey, Joseph, 297
Luftwaffe, 117
Lumet, Sydney, 224–25, 259, 271
Lumière Brothers, 18

McArthur, Colin, 291
McCarthy, Joseph, 154
McCullers, Carson, 288
McDougall, James, 115
MacLean, P. D., 105
McNaughten, Daniel, 97
McNaughten Rules, 81, 97

Mafia, 110
Magnetism, 24
Maharaji, 50
Mahler, M., 79
Malick, Terrence, 106, 194
Mamoulian, Reuben, 61, 63, 213
Mankiewicz, Joseph L., 306
Mansfield, Jayne, 141
March, Fredric, 61, 214, 245
Marcus, Samuel Dr., 174, 175
Marcuse, Herbert, 50, 167
Marx Brothers, 160
Mask of Sanity (Cleckley), 98
Masochism, 72, 74
"Masochism and Ego Identity in Borderline States," 142
Massachusetts Mental Health Center, 157
Massina, Giulietta, 21, 221
Mate, Rudolph, 206
Mayer, Carl, 200
Mazursky, Paul, 197
Medak, Peter, 293
Medical model, 25, 120
Megalomania, 151, 156
Megargee, I., 102, 103, 105
Menninger, Karl, 45
Menninger Psychiatric Clinic, 104
Mental hospital, 44
Mercer, David, 233
Mesmer, Friedrich Anton, 24, 58, 59
Mesmerism, 57, 59
Metacommunicating, 40, 41, 43
Metropolitan Museum of Art, 90
Metz, Ulrich, 173
Meyer, Adolph, 33, 34, 35
Midler, Bette, 20, 140, 142, 143
Miles, Vera, 66
Milieu therapy, 24
Milius, John, 190
Milland, Ray, 21
Miller, Arthur, 212
Miller, David, 201–2
Miller, N., 101, 103
Milne, Tom, 211, 259, 273, 304
Mineo, Sal, 152
Monaco, James, 256
Moral insanity, 98
Moral model, 26
Moral treatment, 44
Morrison, Jim, 141
Movies: A Psychological Study (Wolfenstein and Leites), 172
Mr. Sammler's Planet (Bellow), 157
Multiple drug abuse, 20, 139, 140, 142
Multiple personality, 63, 65, 66, 68
Mumford, Lewis, 167

Munch, Edvard, 18
Murphy, Dudley, 224
Murray, Henry, 163, 164
My Lai massacre, 126
Myth of Mental Illness (Szasz), 49

Nabokov, Vladimir, 209–11
Narcissistic rage, 48
National Institute of Mental Health, 169, 179, 183
Neumann, Hanns, 72
Neuropsychiatric casualties of war, 175
New Statesman, 137
New York Star, 46
New York Times, 82, 137
New York University, 138
Nichols, Mike, 203, 319–20
Nicholson, Jack, 53, 179
Nicole, J. E., 47
Nietzsche, Friedrich, 89
Nimoy, Leonard, 154

Oates, Warren, 106
Oberon, Merle, 176
Object constancy, 79
Object relations theory, 78, 79
Obsessive/compulsive neurosis, 74
O'Connor, Flannery, 320
Oedipal conflict, 36
O'Neill, Eugene, 224, 259
"On the Characteristics of Total Institutions," (Goffman), 49
Oregon State Hospital, 179
Osmond, H., 25
O'Toole, Peter, 157
Overcontrolled murder, 102, 103, 105

Pabst, G. W., 71, 72, 113, 254, 276, 295–97
Pacino, Al, 152
Page, Anthony, 245
Pakula, Alan J., 256
Paranoia, 20, 147, 148, 149, 151, 152
Paranoia culture, 154
Paranoid schizophrenia, 147
Pardes, Herman Dr., 183
Parks, Gordon, 307
Peck, Gregory, 175, 301
Peckinpah, Sam, 83, 304
Peebles, Melvin van, 308
Peel, Robert, 97
Penis envy, 35
Penn, Arthur, 103, 104, 198
Pentagon, 116
Perkins, Anthony, 66
Perls, Fritz, 169
Perruci, Robert, 51

Perry, Frank, 206–7
Perry, John Weir, 168, 169
Personal space, 85
Personality and Psychotherapy (Dollard and Miller), 101
Phallic mother, 35
Pinel, Phillipe, 24, 44, 98
Pinter, Harold, 202
pleasure principle, 70
Polanski, Roman, 288–92, 304–10
Politics of Experience, The (Laing), 50
Pommer, Erich, 200–201
Possession, 21, 22, 66, 67, 68; demonic, 57, 58; lucid, 58; psychiatric interpretation, 57; somnambulistic, 58
Post-traumatic stress disorder, 113, 126, 131
Powell, Michael, 90, 277–78, 324
Power, 148, 152, 154, 155
Powerlessness, 152
Preminger, Otto, 265
Pritchard, J. C., 98
Presidential Commission on Obscenity and Pornography, 93
Prince, Morton, 63, 65
Private war, concept of, 124
Protestant Reformation, 23
Pseudohomosexuality, 152
Psychedelic model, 26
Psychiatric Interview, The (Sullivan), 35
Psychiatrist: portrayal of, in movies, 172–83
Psychoanalytical model, 26
Psychohistory, 83
Psychological moratorium, 141
Psychopath, 98, 100, 102, 124
Psychopathic inferiority, 98
Psychosexual theory, 60
Psychotics, 32, 33
Psychotic hero, 99
Psychotic's world, 168
Pusegur, Marquis de, 59
Pym, John, 260

Quarterly Journal of Studies on Alcohol, 134, 135
Quinlan, Kathleen, 245

Rabkin, Leslie, 172, 175
Rapper, Irving, 272
Ray, Nicholas, 286
Redford, Robert, 274
Redgrave, Sir Michael, 207, 264
Reisz, Karel, 270, 318–19
Remick, Lee, 207
Riefenstahl, Leni, 244
Rites of Passage, 141
Robeson, Paul, 224
Rockland State Hospital, 46

Roeg, Nicolas, 77, 192–95, 278
Rogers, Ginger, 71
Rolf, Ida, 169
Romantic Period, 33
Romanticism, 24
Rorschach ink blot test, 176
Rosenberg, Ethel and Julius, 154
Rosenthal, Robert, 169
Ross, Colin, 72
Rossellini, Roberto, 218
Rossen, Robert, 258–59
Rowlands, Gena, 21, 41
Rush, Benjamin, 24
Russell, Bertrand, 168
Russell, Craig, 275
Russell, Ken, 212–13
Rydell, Mark, 292–93
Rye, Stellan, 305

Sachs, Hans, 72, 76
Sade, Marquis de, 89, 266–68
Sadism, 72, 74, 89, 91, 92, 93
Sanders, Denis, 317
Sartre, J. P., 85, 212, 237
Satten, Joseph, 104
Scapegoating, 157
Schaffner, Franklin, 277
Scheff, Thomas, 51, 157
Schlesinger, Arthur, Jr., 18
Schneider, Irving, 172
Schrader, Paul, 309, 326
Scientific method, 23
Scorsese, Martin, 125, 308–9
Scott, George C., 112, 277
Scream, The (Munch), 18
Screwball comedies, 160
Self-destruction, 142
Self-fulfilling prophecy, 51
Sexual brutality, 89
Seyle, Hans, 122
Shadoian, J., 99
Shakespeare, William, 213
Shapiro, E. R., 79
Sheen, Martin, 106, 190
Shelley, Mary, 213
Shell shock, 113, 115, 116, 175
Shepard, Sam, 235
Siege of Trencher's Farm, The (Williams), 86
Siegel, Don, 213
Siegler, M., 25
Sinatra, Frank, 151
Sizemore, Chris Costner, 310–12
Smith, Perry, 248–51
Social bonding, 118, 120
Social model, 26, 120
Social psychiatry, 51, 83

Social role of mental illness, 51
Sociopath, 131
Somnambulism, 59
Son of Sam, 167
Sontag, Susan, 278
Sorbonne, 167
Spacek, Sissy, 106
Spanos, N. P., 59
Spinoza, Benedict, 23
Soul on Ice (Cleaver), 85
Sound-on-film, 18
Stamp, Terrence, 204
Stampfl, L. T. and Lewis, D., 67
Stanley, Kim, 294
Starkweather, Charles, 106, 108
State hospitals, 46
Stein, Gertrude, 31
Sternberg, Josef von, 197
Stevenson, Robert Louis, 61, 213, 305
Stewart, Jimmy, 161, 162
Stirner, Max, 89
Stoppard, Tom, 209
Strachey, J., 156
Strauss, R., 136
Stress, as conceptual model, 121
Studies on hysteria, 75
Study of the person, 163
Substance-induced disorders, 134
Substance-use disorders, 134
Sullivan, Harry Stack, 32, 33, 34, 35, 36
Sutherland, Donald, 154, 274
Swanson, Gloria, 307
Syberberg, Hans-Jurgen, 261–62
Syphilis bacillus, 25
Systems perspective, 169
Szasz, Thomas, 49, 97

Taylor, Elizabeth, 320
Taylor, John Russell, 268
Teachings of Don Juan, The: A Yaqui Indian Way of
    Knowledge (Castenada), 168
Territoriality, 85
Thanatos, 70
Thigpen, Corbett, 65, 66, 310–12
Third World, 84
Thomson, David, 278
Thought reform, 114
Time, 109
Tone, Franchot, 176
Torrey, E. Fuller, 179
Totalism, psychology of, 114
Transsexual, 183
Traumatic neurotic reactions, 113
Traumatic war neurosis, 114, 117
Trephination, 22

Trigger for emotional problems, 67
Truffaut, François, 268, 285, 302–3
Tuke, William, 44, 45

Ullmann, Liv, 229
Unconscious, 60
Undercontrolled murder, 102, 103, 105
University of Texas, 103
Universum Film Aktiengesellschaft, 72

Valli, Frankie, 126
Vampire of Dusseldorf, 81
Veidt, Conrad, 200
Vietnamization, 123
Vietnam syndrome, 113
Vietnam War, 83, 84
Visconti, Luchino, 261–62
Voight, Jon, 126
Von Harbou, Thea, 81
Vonnegut, Kurt, 50

Walken, Christopher, 21
Walker, Gerald, 206
Walker, Robert, 150
Walsh, Raoul, 318
Ward, Mary Jane, 46
Watergate conspiracy, 155
Watts, Alan, 167
Wederkind, Frank, 276
Weil, Kurt, 177
Weimar Republic, 162
Weiss, Peter, 324
Welles, Orson, 21, 204
West, Mae, 140
White, Eve, 65, 66
Wiene, Robert, 199–201
Wilde, Oscar, 305
Wilder, Billy, 260–61, 307
Winters, Shelley, 197
Withdrawal, defensive, 115
Wolfenstein, M., 172
Women: brutalization of, 80
Wood, Robin, 269, 315
Woodward, Joanne, 311
Worcester State Hospital, 45
World War I, 71
World War II, 46, 110
Wundt, W., 162
Wyler, William, 118, 204

Xerxes (king of Persia), 148

Zanuck, Darryl, 46

Index of Film Titles

Advise and Consent, 152
Aguirre, Wrath of God, 148, 156, 188, 191
All Quiet on the Western Front, 113
All the President's Men, 154
Apocalypse Now, 21, 124, 126, 131, 189–92
Awful Truth, The, 160

Badlands, 28, 29, 96, 105, 106, 108, 109, 194
Bad Timing, 70, 76, 77, 79, 181, 192–94
Belle de Jour, 19, 194–96
Best Years of Our Lives, 118
Big Parade, The, 113
Billy Jack, 125
Blind Alley, 175, 176
Bloody Mama, 196–97
Bloody Noses, 92
Bloody Valentine, 92
Blow Out, 155, 156
Blow-Up, 155, 156
Blue Angel, The, 197
Blue Collar, 154
Blume in Love, 178
Bob and Carol and Ted and Alice, 169, 197
Bonnie and Clyde, 103, 194, 198
Boomerang, The, 173
Boston Strangler, The, 198–99
Boucher, Le, 199, 204
Boys in the Band, 152
Breathless, 108
Brewster McLoud, 18

Cabinet of Dr. Caligari, The, 57, 60, 66, 173, 199–201, 295, 301
Caine Mutiny, The, 148, 152, 201
Captain Newman, M.D., 118, 201–2
Carefree, 173
Caretaker, The, 202
Caretakers, The, 203
Catch-22, 203
China Syndrome, The, 154, 156
Citizen Kane, 21, 148, 204, 249
Clockwork Orange, A, 84
Cobweb, The, 177

Collector, The, 204
Coming Apart, 178
Coming Home, 126, 131, 205
Compulsion, 205
Conversation, The, 156
Coogan's Bluff, 177
Cruising, 152, 205–6

Dark Mirror, The, 176
Dark Past, The, 176, 206
Dark Waters, 176
David and Lisa, 177, 206–7
Dawn, 113
Days of Wine and Roses, 207
Dead of Night, 207
Deer Hunter, The, 21, 124, 126, 131, 207–9
Despair, 66, 209–12
Detective, The, 151, 152, 177
Devils, The, 212–13
Dirty Harry, 213, 249, 308
Dr. Dippy's Sanatorium, 172
Dr. I'm Coming, 178
Dr. Jekyll and Mr. Hyde, 57, 61, 63, 68, 213–14
Dr. Mabuse, the Gambler, 148, 173, 214–15
Dr. Sex, 178
Dr. Shrink, 178
Dr. Strangelove, or How I Stopped Worrying and Learned to Love the Bomb, 153, 215–16
Domino Killings, The, 154
Don't Look Now, 77
Double Bind, 40
Dressed to Kill, 66, 93, 181, 216
Duck Soup, 160

Easy Living, 160
Easy Rider, 217
8½, 19, 217–18
El, 76, 195, 221–24
Emperor Jones, 148, 224
Equus, 169, 180, 224–25
Evil Speak, 92
Exorcist, The, 20, 57, 66, 67, 68, 179, 225–28, 251
Exorcist II: The Heretic, 225–28

Eye for an Eye, An, 92
Eyes of Laura Mars, 66, 109

Face to Face, 180, 228–29
Fame, 180
Family Life, 229–34
Fear Strikes Out, 177
Fine Madness, A, 178
Fists in the Pocket, 234
Flame Within, The, 173, 174
Four Horsemen of the Apocalypse, The, 113
Frances, 37, 234–35
Frenzy, 90, 235–36
Freud: The Secret Passion, 177, 236–42
Friday the Thirteenth, 92, 109
Frozen Scream, 92

Gaslight, 76
Godfather I, 110
Godfather II, 110
Grapes of Wrath, The, 159
Gun Crazy, 242

Halloween, 92, 93, 109, 183, 242
Happy Birthday to Me, 92
Harold and Maude, 169, 243
Harvey, 18, 243
Hearts of the World, 113
Herz Aus Glas, 243
Hitler: The Last Ten Days, 148, 244–45
Home of the Brave, 175, 177
Honeymoon Killers, The, 108, 245
Howling, The, 109

Iceman Cometh, The, 245–46
I'll Be Seeing You, 118, 246
Images, 19, 246–48
In Cold Blood, 103, 104, 248–51
I Never Promised You a Rose Garden, 180, 245
Innocents, The, 251
Interiors, 19, 43, 252
Invasion of the Body Snatchers, 154
Isn't Life Wonderful?, 113
It Happened One Night, 160
It's a Mad, Mad, Mad, Mad World, 169, 253
It's My Turn, 181

J'Accuse, 113, 253–54
Jud, 125
Juliet of the Spirits, 19, 21, 76, 217–20, 254, 286

Kameradschaft, 113
King of Hearts, 18, 159, 164–70, 254–55
Klute, 178, 256

Laddie, 175
Lady in the Dark, 177
Lady Sings the Blues, 256
Last Tango in Paris, 77, 257–58
Let There Be Light, 177, 237, 258
Lilith, 258–59
Locket, The, 176
Long Day's Journey Into Night, 259
Looking for Mr. Goodbar, 77, 259–60
Losers, The, 125
Lost Weekend, The, 20, 134, 135, 138, 139, 145, 260–61
Ludwig, 261–62
Ludwig: Requiem for a Virgin King, 261–62
Lunatics, The; or Dr. Goudron's System, 172

M, 20, 70, 80, 81, 82, 150, 262–63
Macabra, 92
Magic, 66, 207, 264
Magic Christian, The, 169
Maltese Falcon, The, 150, 264
Manchurian Candidate, The, 65, 114
Maniac, 92
Man Who Fell to Earth, The, 77
Man with the Golden Arm, The, 265
Marathon Man, 154
Marat-Sade, The, 169, 266–68
Mark, The, 177, 268
Marnie, 268–69
Metropolis, 269
Mr. Deeds Goes to Town, 18, 160, 174, 175
Mr. Smith Goes to Washington, 160, 174
Morgan: A Suitable Case for Treatment, 169, 233, 270
My Man Godfrey, 160

Natural Enemies, 43, 270–71
Network, 154, 271
Nightmare Alley, 176
Nightmares, 92
Night Porter, 126, 271
Nothing Sacred, 160
Now, Voyager, 28, 30, 31, 34–37, 38, 43–44, 272

Oh, God, Book II, 180
Old Man's Place, The, 125
One Flew Over the Cuckoo's Nest, 20, 30, 45, 49, 52–54, 156, 178–79, 272–73
Open Season, 125, 274
Ordinary People, 40, 183, 274
Outrageous, 169, 275

Pandora's Box, 76, 276
Parallax View, 154–56

Passion of Joan of Arc, The, 212
Paths of Glory, 113, 276–77
Patton, 112, 148, 277
Peeping Tom, 90, 177
Performance, 77, 278–79
Persona, 19, 279–82
Plastered in Paris, 173
Play Misty for Me, 283–84
President's Analyst, 177
Pressure Point, 177, 284
Private Benjamin, 181
Private Worlds, 174, 175
Prom Night, 92, 109
Psycho, 66, 89, 90, 92, 93, 177, 182, 227, 242, 246, 248, 284–85, 315
Pumpkin Eater, The, 285–86, 306

Rebel without A Cause, 38, 84, 151, 286
Red Desert, 286–87
Reflections in a Golden Eye, 152, 287–88
Repulsion, 246, 288–92
Reveille, 113
Rope, 150, 205, 292
Rose, The, 20, 134, 139, 140, 141, 145, 292–93
Ruling Class, The, 169, 293

Scenes from a Marriage, 43
Schizoid, 92
Scream for Revenge, 92
Seance on a Wet Afternoon, 293–94
Seashell and the Clergyman, The, 294–95
Secret Passion, The. See *Freud: The Secret Passion*
Secrets of a Soul, 19, 31, 70, 71–76, 173
Sergeant, The, 152, 297
Serial, 180
Servant, The, 297
Shadow on the Wall, 177
Shame of the States, 46
Silent Scream, 92
Simon, 181
Slaughter, 125
Slaughterhouse Five, 297
Snake Pit, The, 20, 30, 45–49, 53, 177, 180, 203, 298–300
Snuff, 92
Soylent Green, 154
Spellbound, 175–76, 300–302
Splitting, 79
Stardust Memories, 181
Starting Over, 180
Story of Adèle H., The, 76, 302–3
Strangers on a Train, 150, 303
Straw Dogs, 70, 80, 83–89, 304
Streetcar Named Desire, A, 305

Student of Prague, The, 305
Stunt Man, The, 157
Suddenly Last Summer, 306
Sugarland Express, 108
Summer Wishes, Winter Dreams, 286, 306
Sundays and Cybele, 169, 307
Sunset Boulevard, 76, 307
Superfly, 307–8
Sweet Sweetback's Baadasss Song, 308
Sybil, 66

Taking Off, 178
Taxi Driver, 109, 124, 125, 131, 249, 308–9
Tell England, 113
Ten, 180
Tenant, The, 66, 309–10
Terror Train, 92
Testament of Dr. Mabuse, The, 173
Texas Chainsaw Massacre, The, 90, 92, 310
They Live by Night, 108
Thieves Like Us, 108
Three Days of the Condor, 154, 156
Three Faces of Eve, The, 154, 156, 177, 310–12
Through a Glass Darkly, 312–13
Twelve O'Clock High, 28, 117, 118–21, 175, 313–15
Twilight's Last Gleaming, 154

Unmarried Woman, An, 20, 178

Vertigo, 315
Vie en L'Envers, La, 316
Violette Nozière, 316–17
Visitors, The, 125

Walkabout, 77
War Hunt, 317
Welcome Home Soldier Boys, 125
Westfront, 113
Whatever Happened to Baby Jane?, 317–18
What's New Pussycat?, 177
When the Clouds Roll By, 173
White Heat, 20, 29, 96, 99, 106, 318
Who'll Stop the Rain?, 124, 318–19
Who's Afraid of Virginia Woolf?, 42, 43, 77, 319–20
Wise Blood, 310–21
Woman in the Window, 176
Woman under the Influence, A, 20, 30, 31, 37–44, 77, 321
Women in Love, 77

You Can't Take It with You, 18, 159, 160, 161–64, 174, 322
You Only Live Once, 108

Index to Appendix

Aeschylus, 327, 328
Agamemnon (Aeschylus), 327
Ajax (Sophocles), 328
Anatomie of the Body of Man, The (Vicary), 334
Anatomy of Melancholy, The (Burton), 332, 334, 339, 340, 341
Andromache (Euripides), 328
Antony and Cleopatra (Shakespeare), 334

Bacchae, The (Euripides), 328
Beaumont, Francis, 337
Bedlam on the Jacobean Stage (Reed), 331–32, 340
Bible, The (Authorized Version), 334
Bright, Timothy, 331
Broken Heart, The (Ford), 332, 340, 341
Brome, Richard, 334, 337
Burton, Robert, 331–32, 333, 334, 337, 339–40, 341

Changeling, The (Middleton), 332, 334, 340
City Wit, The (Brome), 334
Coronation, The (Shirley), 335
Cymbeline (Shakespeare), 333

Dekker, Thomas, 332
Duchess of Malfi, The (Webster), 332, 342
Duke of Milan, The (Massinger), 332, 340

Elizabethan Drama and its Madfolk (Peers), 332, 335, 337
Eumenides, The (Aeschylus), 328
Euripides, 328

Fletcher, John, 337, 339, 340
Ford, John, 332, 339, 340, 341

Galen, 331
Greene, Robert, 328, 330

Hamlet (Shakespeare), 332, 333, 335, 336, 342–43, 345
Henry VI, Part I (Shakespeare), 335–36
Hercules Furens (Euripides), 328–29

Hippocrates, 331
Hippolytus (Euripides), 328
Honest Whore, The (Dekker), 332

Iphigenia in Tauris (Euripides), 328

Jonson, Ben, 330
Julius Caesar (Shakespeare), 336

King Lear (Shakespeare), 332, 333, 342–45
Kyd, Thomas, 328, 330–31, 332

Lover's Melancholy (Ford), 332, 340, 341

Macbeth (Shakespeare), 334, 336, 345
Mad Lover, The (Fletcher), 339, 340
Maid's Tragedy, The (Beaumont and Fletcher), 337
Massinger, Philip, 332, 339, 340
Merchant of Venice, The (Shakespeare), 333, 337
Merry Wives of Windsor, The (Shakespeare), 335
Middleton, Thomas, 332, 334, 339, 340
Midsummer Night's Dream, A (Shakespeare), 333
Much Ado about Nothing (Shakespeare), 335

New Way to Pay Old Debts, A (Massinger), 340, 341
Nice Valour, The (Fletcher), 340
Noble Gentleman, The (Fletcher), 340
Northern Lass, The (Brome), 337

Oedipus (Sophocles), 328
Orlando Furioso (Greene), 328, 330
Othello (Shakespeare), 334

Peers, E. A., 332, 335, 337
Philaster (Beaumont and Fletcher), 337
Pilgrim, The (Fletcher), 340
Prometheus Bound (Aeschylus), 328

Reed, Robert R., 331–32, 340
Romeo and Juliet (Shakespeare), 333

Seneca, 328–29
Shakespeare, William, 328, 330, 332–39, 342–45

Shirley, James, 335
Sophocles, 328
Spanish Tragedy, The (Kyd), 328, 330–32

Taming of the Shrew, The (Shakespeare), 338–39
Titus Andronicus (Shakespeare), 328, 330–32
Treatise on Melancholy (Bright), 331–32
Troilus and Cressida (Shakespeare), 333, 339

Trojan Women, The (Euripides), 328
Twelfth Night (Shakespeare), 333, 334, 337

Very Woman, The (Massinger), 337, 340, 341
Vicary, Thomas, 334

Webster, John, 330, 332, 342
White Devil, The (Webster), 332, 242

Images of Madness

The Depiction of Insanity in the Feature Film

MICHAEL FLEMING and ROGER MANVELL

This book presents the first fully researched assessment of the American and European cinema's portrayal of insanity in key feature films over half a century. In addition, it relates the very varied interpretations of madness in these films to the clinical theory and practice of their period. The more notable films have been the subject of technical discussion by psychologists, psychiatrists, and clinicians in their specialist journals, and this body of critical evaluation, virtually unknown to film critics and historians, has been drawn upon to give additional valuable insight to the discussion of the films involved.

People with disturbed minds have featured as central characters in Greek classical tragedy, the Elizabethan-Jacobean theater, and the Gothic horror novel of the eighteenth and nineteenth centuries. The modern twentieth-century cinema has continued this tradition. Several hundred feature films have turned on insanity since *The Cabinet of Dr. Caligari* first appeared in post-World War I Germany some 65 years ago, and raised critical controversy concerning its treatment of madness on screen. Major directors as varied as Lang, Pabst, Hitchcock, Huston, Truffaut, Altman, Lumet, Kubrick, Chabrol, Fellini, Buñuel, Bergman, Polanski, Fassbinder, Roeg, and Herzog have made films about characters whose minds were in one way or another severely disturbed. Among these have been such notable films of the past and the present as *Aquirre, Belle de Jour,*